D0883188

Out of Sight

Lynn Abbott

and

Doug Seroff

University Press of Mississippi / *Jackson*

781.773
A132o

Out of Sight

The Rise of African American Popular Music

1889–1895

American Made Music Series
Advisory Board

David Evans, General Editor
Barry Jean Ancelet
Edward A. Berlin
Joyce J. Bolden
Rob Bowman
Susan C. Cook
Curtis Ellison
William Ferris
Michael Harris
John Edward Hasse
Kip Lornell
Frank McArthur
W. K. McNeil
Bill Malone
Eddie S. Meadows
Manuel H. Peña
David Sanjek
Wayne D. Shirley
Robert Walser
Charles Wolfe

www.upress.state.ms.us

Copyright © 2002 by University Press of Mississippi
All rights reserved
Manufactured in the United States of America

10 09 08 07 06 05 04   4 3 2
♾

Library of Congress Cataloging-in-Publication Data

Abbott, Lynn, 1946–
Out of Sight: the rise of African American popular music, 1889–1895 / Lynn Abbott and Doug Seroff.
p. cm. — (American made music series)
Includes bibliographical references (p.) and index.
ISBN 1-57806-499-6 (cloth: alk. paper)
1. African Americans—Music—Hisory and criticism. 2. Popular music—United States—To 1901—History and criticism.
I. Seroff, Doug. II. Title. III. Series
ML3479 .A2 2003
781.64′089′96073—dc21   2002007819

British Library Cataloging-in-Publication Data available

Contents

Chapter 2. 1890

Chapter 3. 1891

Chapter 4. 1892

Chapter 5. 1893

Chapter 6. 1894

Chapter 7. 1895

Acknowledgments

In the early 1980s, when we began our survey of African American newspapers on microfilm, we were motivated by a common interest in the early evolution of black vocal harmony singing. We gradually began to appreciate the broader context. In 1989 we inaugurated a series of five essays which appeared in *78 Quarterly* under the title "100 Years from Today." Our intent was to bring to light and comment on the music-related citations we were discovering in 1890s newspapers. Those essays represent the rough beginnings of the book at hand.

Special thanks to *78 Quarterly* editor Pete Whelan for his early support and continued cooperation; and to Ray Funk, who was in on our early black newspaper research and who remains a valued friend and colleague.

Thanks to Dr. David Evans for friendship, advice, and a critical reading of the manuscript which inspired many significant improvements.

Thanks to Wayne D. Shirley for an equally illuminating review of the manuscript and for responding to our many requests for copies of sheet music and copyright deposits held by the Library of Congress.

Thanks to Chris Ware for the book jacket art and for his enthusiastic support of our work.

We are grateful to the Fisk University Library in Nashville for the use of resources and facilities, most notably their extraordinary collection of African American newspapers on microfilm and their incredible body of materials relating to the Fisk Jubilee Singers. Thanks particularly to Special Collections Librarian Beth Madison Howse for many years of assistance and kindness.

The Hogan Jazz Archive at Tulane University in New Orleans also threw open its doors to us. We are grateful for our long-term working relationship with curator Dr. Bruce Boyd Raeburn and his staff, especially Mrs. Alma Freeman, who negotiated an endless river of requests on our behalf. Thanks as well to the staff of Tulane's Howard Tilton Memorial Library, especially in the Music, Microforms, and Interlibrary Loan divisions; and to the Amistad Research Center, which is also located on the Tulane campus.

We thank the staff of the Center for Popular Music at Middle Tennessee State University in Murfreesboro, especially Bruce Nemerov, for assistance and encouragement. The staff of the Country Music Foundation Library in Nashville, specifically Bob Pinson, Ronnie Pugh, and Alan Stoker, were also helpful over many years. Thanks as well to the Nashville Public Library; the New Orleans Public Library, especially the staff of the Louisiana Division; the Earl K. Long Library of the University of New Orleans, especially Interlibrary Loan librarian Evelyn Chandler; and the Virginia State Library in Richmond, Virginia.

Thanks are due to the Portage County Historical Society Museum in Ohio, which houses many personal effects of Frederick and Harriet Loudin; the Detroit Public Library, which houses the E. Azalia Hackley Collection, which contains the invaluable Leota Henson Turner scrapbooks; Deborah W. Walk at the John & Mable Ringling Museum of Art in Sarasota, Florida; the Alabama A&M University Library, and the Scarritt-Bennett Library in Nashville.

Thanks to Rob Bird for sharing the results of his research on the 1870s *New York Clipper*; Lucius Edwards at Virginia State College in Petersburg, Virginia, for sharing information from his collected oral history of Petersburg's African American churches; Toni Passmore Anderson for making available her research on the original Fisk Jubilee Singers; Robert Cogswell for photographic services and encouragement; Pen Bogert for sharing his research on African American musical activity in Louisville, Kentucky; Ray Buckberry for sharing his research on Ernest Hogan; Tim Brooks for sharing his research on pioneer-era recordings and Michael Montgomery for sharing sheet music from his collection.

Many of the documents examined for this book are housed in libraries outside of the United States. We were heavily dependent on research assistance from friends and colleagues abroad, especially in pursuing the extensive nineteenth-century history of African American minstrels and jubilee singers in Australia and New Zealand.

In Australia, help came from Gary LeGallant, who freely shared the prodigious results of many years of research. Gary unfailingly responded to our requests and inquiries.

In New Zealand, Tony Hale devoted many hours to library research on our behalf, with assistance from Stuart R. Strachan at the Hocken Library, University of Otago, Dunedin, and Ms. Fay Hutt at the Alexander Turnbull Library in Wellington.

Dr. Ross Clark of the University of Auckland kindly responded to our questions about Maori singing, and we were further aided by the Early Settlers Museum in Dunedin; the National Library of Australia, Canberra, ACT; the Mitchell Library (State Library of NSW), Sydney; and the Latrobe Library (State Library of Victoria). Thanks also to Tony Backhouse in Sydney for friendship and facilitation; also to Chris Bourke in New Zealand and Rick Milne in Melbourne.

Dr. Viet Erlmann shared products of his research into the tours of Orpheus McAdoo's Virginia Jubilee Singers in South Africa. Thanks as well to Rob Allingham in South Africa, especially for shared recordings. Rainer E. Lotz shared his research on African American musicians in Europe. We acknowledge assistance from the Royal Library of Stockholm, Sweden. Thanks also to Tommy Lofgren of the Scandinavian Blues Association, as well as Claes Hedman and Lars Dahlgren.

Musician-friends James Bryan, Betty C. Carter, Les Muscutt, and Duck Baker were kind enough to demonstrate various pieces of 1890s sheet music for us on the fiddle, piano, banjo, and guitar, respectively, and we thank them as well for enlightening us on various matters of pure musicology.

Linda Abbott assisted in processing the manuscript. Others who have given valuable support, encouragement, and assistance over the years include Allan Jaffe and family, Bill Russell, and Richard B. Allen.

We further acknowledge the uncommon generosity of Johnny Parth, architect of the indispensable Document 5000 series of cd reissues, which has made available to researchers and fans the total body of early African American recorded music. Finally, we acknowledge Robert M. W. Dixon, John Godrich, and Howard W. Rye, the compilers of *Blues and Gospel Records 1890–1943*, whose painstaking discographical research is so often taken for granted as common knowledge.

–Lynn Abbott and Doug Seroff, June 2001

Introduction

Between January 1889 and December 1895, at least one thousand lynchings of African Americans were perpetrated in the United States.[1] This was a terrible period in the history of American race relations, yet it witnessed the emergence of ragtime and the birth of an African American popular entertainment industry. *Out of Sight* traces the events and developments, the contradictions and redemptive energies that characterized the rise of black popular music in the midst of an American racial cataclysm.

Professional jubilee singing companies experienced wrenching changes. During 1889 and 1890 heroic jubilee troupes headed by Fred Loudin, Orpheus McAdoo, and Sissieretta Jones carried the slave spiritual choruses to the public stages of every inhabited continent. But during the course of the 1890s, jubilee singing faded into the background, while the popularity of "authentic" minstrelsy soared. For the most part, the public no longer cared to differentiate between a minstrel and a jubilee singer.

Just prior to the commercialization of ragtime, a new style of "vaudevillized minstrelsy" expanded professional opportunities for a broad range of African American performers and musicians. Black show-business trailblazers such as Ernest Hogan, Billy McClain, and Irving Jones began to redefine minstrelsy by updating its black vernacular elements. Moreover, African American women finally gained the minstrel, vaudeville, and burlesque stage and exerted an immediate influence as dancers, singers, and comedians. On the other hand, ragtime minstrelsy became a sinkhole for the era's great black prima donnas, whose best efforts had failed to secure a place on the mainstream operatic stage, on account of racial prejudice.

Within the black communities, vocal quartets, string bands, mandolin clubs, and brass bands were supplying music for all occasions, from funerals to serenading parties and "rag" dances. The black community music of this momentous period was as eclectic as could be, and contained the seeds of almost every American music style that would subsequently emerge. Dedicated black music educators directed the up-and-coming generation of singers and musicians to new high levels of proficiency and professionalism. Antonin Dvorák's famous pronouncement of 1893, that "the future music of this country must be founded upon what are called the Negro melodies," excited the process. The 1893 World's Columbian Exposition was an unprecedented cultural marketplace that helped define the terms underlying the impending commodification of black popular music.

The 1889–1895 era in African American music has not been previously subjected to much scholarly consideration. By the time we began our study, it was too late to gather oral history; there were no living informants. The raw materials that we needed to reconstruct the circumstances of the period were buried in contemporaneous newspapers, journals, and magazines. *Out of Sight* is built on thousands of references to black music and entertainment, which we mined from a variety of period sources, concentrating particularly on African American community newspapers.

Black community newspapers of the 1890s were, for the most part, weekly publications of generally less than ten pages. Their primary motive was to agitate for civil rights and equal protection under the law, but they also publicized and commented on the social, religious, and cultural life of their respective communities, and in so doing, managed to preserve a vivid representation of the dynamics of black folk and popular music.

The history of African American newspapers can be traced to 1827, when *Freedom's Journal* was inaugurated in New York City. By 1891 there was at least one book devoted to the subject, I. Garland Penn's *The Afro-American Press and Its Editors.*[2] By Penn's count, there were ten race papers active in 1870; thirty in 1880; and by 1890 one hundred fifty-four. However, more than a few of these papers suffered painfully short life-spans, and for many there are no known surviving copies.[3]

For this study, we have focused primarily on surviving runs of 1889–1895 editions of eleven exemplary race weeklies: the *Indianapolis Freeman*, the *New York Age*, the *Cleveland Gazette*, the *Detroit Plaindealer*, the *New Orleans Weekly Pelican*, the *Richmond Planet*, the *Topeka Weekly Call*, the *Kansas State Ledger*, the *Kansas City American Citizen*, the *Parsons Weekly Blade*, and the *Leavenworth Herald*.

The *Indianapolis Freeman* was an especially generous supplier of music and entertainment news. Commencing publication on July 14, 1888, it was one of the most widely distributed race papers of the 1890s, and it was eventually adopted as a "central headquarters" for news and gossip from black professional musicians and entertainers on the road. As early as 1891, black showmen were touting the *Freeman* as "the Colored *New York Clipper*," the African American alternative to the most popular weekly mainstream entertainment trade paper of the period.

The *Freeman* was founded by Edward Elder Cooper, a refugee from Southern slavery who settled in Indianapolis in 1882.[4] Cooper ran the *Freeman* from 1888 until 1892, when he sold out to George L. Knox, a fellow Indianapolis "businessman of the most progressive ideas." Like Cooper, Knox was born in slavery, near Statesville, Tennessee, in 1841. In 1863 he stole away with the Union Army. Reaching Indiana in 1864, he found work as a hostler, yardman, porter, and, finally, a barber. From 1866 until 1884 he ran a one-chair shop in the village of Greenfield. Moving to Indianapolis in 1884, he worked his way up from "country barber" to proprietor of the fashionable Bates House and Grand Hotel barbershops, catering exclusively to whites.[5] Knox ran the *Freeman* from 1892 until it folded in the early-1920s.

From its inception, the *Freeman* was intended to be a "National Illustrated Colored Newspaper," offering "a complete review of the doings of the colored people everywhere." To reach "colored people everywhere," points of distribution were established at barbershops, pool rooms, and other "safety zones" throughout black America. The edition of May 4, 1889, informed that, in Memphis: "Copies of the Freeman may be bought of the agent Mr. John N. Daniel, No. 4 Dupree street or at Mr. F. B. Davis' barber shop, 160 Poplar street or at Mrs. Woods confectionery store, 162 Poplar street, at barber shop 139 Beale street, or barber shop next door to Alabama Snack house Beale and Mulberry street or Miss Maria Williams 150 Desoto street on sale every Saturday afternoon."

An early variation of the illustrious Freeman *masthead: "And Ethiopia Shall Stretch Forth Her Hand."*

In order to fulfill its promise of national news coverage, the *Freeman* assembled a vast network of community correspondents. In this way it was able to broadcast news from places which would have otherwise had no public voice, especially in the South, where the dominant society viewed black newspapers as agents of conspiracy and rebellion. The *Freeman* published reports not only from major southern cities like Memphis, Houston, and Dallas, but from little country "burgs" like Normal, Alabama; Yazoo City, Mississippi; and Villa Rica, Georgia, where a *Freeman* agent was "ordered to get out of the town" after "a very narrow escape from Judge Lynch's court. . . . The charge against me was not rape, but it was for trying to get subscribers for a 'nigger paper.' That I had a narrow escape is proven by a rope being drawn."[6]

For a variety of reasons, including "the rope being drawn," black newspaper ventures in the South suffered an uncommonly high mortality rate. It was disappointing to see the surviving run of the *New Orleans Weekly Pelican* come to an end on November 23, 1889, just eleven months into the period under study. Fortunately, an alternative source came to light with the *Southwestern Christian Advocate*, which got its start in New Orleans in 1873 as "The Organ of Northern Methodism in the South."

The rallying cry of Northern Methodism in the South was "Negro redemption."[7] In 1884 the *Southwestern Christian Advocate* was placed under a black editor, Rev. Marshall W. Taylor, and when Rev. Taylor died in 1887, the editorship fell to Rev. Aristides E. P. Albert, a "Creole of Color" who had arrived in New Orleans with the first wave of freedmen from the sugar plantations of St. Charles Parish.[8] Rev. Albert ran the *Southwestern Christian Advocate* throughout the 1889–1895 period.

Among the few southern race weeklies for which there is a substantial surviving run from the 1889-1895 period, the *Richmond Planet* was launched in Richmond, Virginia, in 1884. Editor John Mitchell Jr. was born in adjacent Henrico County on July 11, 1863. In 1881 he graduated from "the Richmond Normal and High School with high honors," and in December 1884, at age twenty-one, Mitchell "took the editorial charge" of the *Planet*: "He was forward in denouncing outrages upon colored people and made a specialty of condemning the lynch law."[9]

We excavated some particularly compelling music-related news from the cluster of fiercely independent papers that operated in eastern Kansas. The *Leavenworth Herald* first hit the streets on February 17, 1894. Its owner and editor, B. K. Bruce Jr. was born to slave parents on a farm near Brunswick, Missouri, and was named after his uncle Blanche Kelso Bruce, the black Reconstruction-era Senator from Mississippi.[10] After graduating from Kansas State University "with highest honors," Bruce Jr. settled in Leavenworth to serve as the principal of a junior high school.[11] In 1892 he made a near-successful attempt to gain the office of Kansas State Auditor.

Sarcasm was a favorite device of 1890s African American newspaper editors, and B. K. Bruce Jr. may well have been the most sarcastic of all. On March 10, 1894, he took aim at a group of "Back to Africa" advocates: "Have Gone to See Pa and Ma—After juggling coacoanuts [*sic*] with African apes awhile, they will sing 'America'—30 Negroes of Atlanta, Ga., started to the 'Dark Continent' this week to cheer up Mamma Lo Bengula—Papa's body has been preserved in gin and the Ephriams and Susans will get to see it—'Well, ef heah ain't de chilluns.' "

B. K. Bruce Jr.'s editorial explorations are noteworthy because they are the context for the earliest known printed references to piano "rags." In later years, Bruce Jr. may have written off his adventures in race journalism as a potential liability. His biographical sketch in the 1927 edition of *Who's Who in Colored America* says nothing about his newspaper work, concentrating instead on his subsequent career as "the only colored man in the United States or elsewhere that teaches young white men for Commissions in the United States Army and Navy, and also prepares young men for entrance into the Naval Academy at Annapolis and the Army Academy at West Point."

Although black minstrel companies made many important breakthroughs during the 1889–1895 period, they weren't entirely accepted in the "Stage" columns of the African American press until after 1895, when ragtime confirmed their "legitimacy" in the marketplace. We found a very different source of news about black minstrel companies in the columns of "America's Oldest Sporting and Theatrical Journal," the *New York Clipper*. The main concern of the *New York Clipper* was entertainment business. Its weekly "Minstrel and Variety" column incorporated reports from correspondents representing all sorts of traveling companies, including "authentic" African American minstrels. The *Clipper* also yielded a substantial amount of information about black musical activities in dime museums and circus sideshows.

Additional sources for this study include foreign press commentaries generated by the international tours of various jubilee singing troupes, black prima donnas, and "authentic" minstrels of the era. These include clippings from Australia, New Zealand, South Africa, India, Japan, and various places in the West Indies, originally collected in scrapbooks by some of the artists involved. Finally, we spot-checked various mainstream American dailies for relevant coverage of some of the major black music-related events of the period.

Our study rejects all preconceptions of what constitutes "authentic" African American music. It casts a wide net, from the street fiddler to the concert diva. This allows the full scope of the story to unfold, and the themes to reveal themselves organically. The pictures which emerge don't always conform to previous assumptions.

THE SOUTHERN OUTRAGES.
The trees of Georgia Still bearing evil fruit.

Freeman, *January 18, 1890.*

With so much hard evidence at hand, we felt little need to engage in speculation. Admittedly, portions of this history remain incomplete; nevertheless, *Out of Sight* provides fact-based concepts which should be useful to any future studies.

Our documentation establishes the essential connection among all categories of African American music of the period under study: folk and school-trained, sacred and secular, recreational and professional, etc. The strict divisions sometimes imagined by modern scholars simply did not exist. There were many avenues of intersection, and racial crossroads as well. By the 1890s, appreciation of African American music was widespread across race lines. White Kansans had ample opportunity to see rags performed by black piano professors years before Ben Harney put ragtime piano playing on the map in New York City, in 1896.

On May 18, 1896, the United States Supreme Court, in its *Plessy vs. Ferguson* decision, elevated Jim Crow discrimination to the law of the land. Three months later the words "rag time" first appeared on sheet music.[12] With the popularization of ragtime, black music suddenly became a medium of cultural and commercial exchange, and previously submerged musical practices became a "tool kit" for modern popular music. Despite serious resistance, black performers made real inroads in the popular entertainment arena, but only by means of an iniquitous Jim Crow bargain, which had consequences for one hundred years or more.

Much of what took place during the 1889–1895 period has remained out of sight, but not outside the pale of modern experience. Our research exposes many unsuspected late-nineteenth-century sources of modern American cultural practices and expressions. The slang term "out of sight," for example, is popularly associated with the 1960s, and more particularly with the "soul music" classics "Out of Sight" by James Brown (1964) and "Uptight" by Stevie Wonder (1965). Modern slang dictionaries trace its origin to 1950s jazz musicians.[13]

In 1890, sheet music publisher Will Rossiter introduced his latest hit, "It's 'Way Out of Sight." In 1891 the "Out O' Sight Musee and Theatre" opened in Evansville, Indiana. In 1892 a mainstream newspaper reviewed a concert appearance by the Fisk Jubilee Singers: "In an artistic sense it was the acme of success and in the language of the galleries 'out of sight.' " In 1893 a black community reporter in Richmond, Virginia, described a local production of *Uncle Tom's Cabin* with a portrayal of Topsy that, "using common parlance, was 'out of sight' "; and another black reporter in Kansas City, Missouri, characterized a local performance by itinerant pianist Blind Boone as, "(excuse expression) clear out of sight."

This vernacular phrase must have existed somewhere, over the intervening generations, until it came into vogue again in the 1960s, without any appreciable change in its heavily nuanced meaning. By extension, "out of sight" becomes a metaphor for the vast, hidden pools of contemporaneous literature which document the African American musical practices and developments of 1889–1895.

Freeman, *January 18, 1890.*

Taken as a whole, the collected music-related references of 1889–1895 give the effect of a diary, bent on everyday concerns, slowly building an overview. Trends and phenomena are revealed through a preponderance of specific details accumulated in weekly installments of news, gossip, and critical commentary. These accounts provide glimpses into intricate, hidden paths of continuity from the black music of the years just prior to the inauguration of ragtime to twentieth-century blues, jazz, and gospel.

Out of Sight

Chapter One

1889

Frederick J. Loudin's Fisk Jubilee Singers and Their Australasian Auditors, 1886–1889

The years 1889 and 1890 bore witness to a unique moment in the history of spiritual, or "jubilee," singing, a zenith which was unfortunately short-lived. In 1889, through the dauntless agency of Loudin's Fisk Jubilee Singers, the spiritual light from the slave cabins of the American Southland shone in a wild New Zealand gorge. The following year Loudin's troupe gave a concert in the Taj Mahal. At the same time, McAdoo's Virginia Jubilee Singers sang spirituals in the native schools and mission stations of Zululand, South Africa, and the Tennessee Jubilee Singers gathered golden encomiums throughout the Caribbean.

The driving force behind this apogean movement was Frederick J. Loudin, a bass singer of "phenomenal profundity and volume" and a jubilee entrepreneur extraordinaire. Loudin was born in the free state of Ohio on June 27, 1842.[1] He grew up in Ravenna and first experienced racial inequality there. After the Civil War Loudin relocated to Memphis, and he was singing in a church choir there in January 1875 when he was recruited into the Original Fisk Jubilee Singers.

Loudin quickly became one of the Fisk Jubilee Singers' most important soloists and added his exceptionally deep bass voice to the concerted harmony of the jubilee choruses. He also could have made a legitimate claim to the title "orator." Throughout his career Loudin used the jubilee platform to make public statements on the issue of civil rights. He was, in retrospect, the most politically outspoken black entertainer of the nineteenth century.

In May 1875, just four months after Loudin had joined, the Fisk Jubilee Singers sailed for Europe on a three-year fund-raising tour in the interests of Fisk University. In February 1877 they were presented to the Queen of Holland in an elaborate reception at the Hague, where many Dutch people had never before seen a black person. The highlight of the Fisk Jubilee Singers' second tour of Europe was the November 4, 1877, command performance before Emperor Wilhelm I and the German royal family. When Berlin's world-renowned music critics added their emphatic endorsement of the Fisk Jubilee Singers' performances, it betokened the European validation of African American musical culture.

Nevertheless, when the Fisk Jubilee Singers returned to Nashville in 1878, the administrators of Fisk University concluded that the jubilee fund-raising idea had run its course, and they unceremoniously disbanded the troupe. George L. White, the troupe's director, knew the American public was still eager to hear the internationally celebrated Fisk Jubilee Singers; in September 1879 White reorganized the Jubilee Singers, entirely independent of Fisk University, but still carrying the name and still featuring Frederick J. Loudin.

As the primary singing attraction and public spokesman for the new, independent troupe of Fisk Jubilee Singers, Loudin became the motivating force behind their 1879–1882 "civil rights tours" in support of the ill-fated Civil Rights Bill of 1875.[2] This civil rights campaign brought Loudin into a personal relationship

Frederick J. Loudin, basso and proprietor of Loudin's Fisk Jubilee Singers. (courtesy Fisk University Library, Special Collections)

with President James A. Garfield. After Garfield's assassination and the Supreme Court's ruling that the Civil Rights Bill of 1875 was "unconstitutional," Loudin's life seems to have changed. In late 1882 he seized the leadership of the Fisk Jubilee Singers from George L. White and began his incredible odyssey as a globe-trotting jubilee singer-manager.

In April 1884 Loudin's Fisk Jubilee Singers set out on a six-year-long world tour. They spent the first two years in England.[3] On May 14, 1886, at the end of a forty-day ocean voyage from Liverpool, Loudin and his troupe landed at Williamstown, the port of Melbourne, Australia. Touring Australia and New Zealand for the next three years, they netted a sum equal to nearly half a million contemporary U.S. dollars. Responsibility, credit, and proceeds all belonged to Frederick J. Loudin.

The roster of Loudin's Fisk Jubilee Singers comprised sopranos Mattie Lawrence (prima donna soloist), Belle Gibbons, Maggie Carnes, and Patti Malone; contraltos Georgie Gibbons and Maggie E. Wilson; tenors R. B. Williams and John T. Lane; and bassos Loudin and Orpheus M. McAdoo; plus Loudin's niece Leota Henson (nee Turner), who served as accompanist on the harmonium for the jubilee choruses and on pianoforte for secular solos. To a great extent, the reputation that Loudin's Fisk Jubilee Singers had earned in Europe assured them a warm reception in Australia. On May 31, 1886, they were formally introduced to Melbourne by means of a private recital for about 150 leading citizens. According to accompanist Leota Henson, "Printed invitations were sent to the most prominent people in the city. The newspapermen were also there . . . The next day the newspaper came with a fine account of the program and after that our concert dates came in thick and fast."[4]

• ***June 1, 1886:*** "Private Concert," "Yesterday afternoon a private concert by the Fisk Jubilee Singers was given in the Grand hotel, under the auspices of a committee specially formed to welcome and introduce them to Australia . . .

The Dean [i.e., Melbourne's chief clergyman], in introducing the Jubilee Singers to the audience, expressed his belief that the abolition of slavery was the great outstanding characteristic of the nineteenth century. The American slaves, on their emancipation, did not turn their minds to ambition or revenge, but the first thing they cried for was education. The services rendered by the Jubilee Singers to the cause of education were well known, and he had great pleasure in welcoming them to Australia.

Mr. F. J. Loudin, the musical director of the Jubilee Singers, then made a few introductory remarks. He said that if it were not for the fact that this was the first time they had been in Australia, he would not have thought it necessary to make any speech. Had he been in Britain or Germany, or their own native America, he would have been sure a large part of the audience was familiar with the origin and character of the music they were about to sing. The music was not the production of Handel or Haydn, or any of the great masters, but it was the music of nature, of a people oppressed long and sore through a night of bondage. The songs they sang were principally songs sung by the slaves during the time of their enslavement . . .

[Following the short concert, which included renditions of 'Turn Back Pharoah's Army,' 'Rolling through an Unfriendly World,' 'I've Been Redeemed,' and 'Swing Low, Sweet Chariot,'] Mr. Loudin tendered the thanks of the Jubilee Singers to the audience for their presence, and for the cordiality with which they had been welcomed in Melbourne. It was of no little importance to them coming fresh to Australia to know the kind of reception they would get. They had received letters from the colonies of the most cordial character, and they expected to receive a cordial welcome. They had not been disappointed. He thanked the committee especially, and last but not least, the venerable dean, from whom he had received a long letter, nearly a year ago, encouraging the singers to visit Australia. The dean had been among the first to welcome them. (Applause).

Sir James MacBain moved a vote of thanks to Mr. Loudin and the singers, expressing at the same time the high appreciation in which their services were held, and bidding them hearty welcome to Australia . . . He felt it impossible to give adequate expression to the feelings with which he had listened to the singers. Their music was the music of nature—of nature, after having triumphed over tyranny and oppression. It appealed more to the heart and the feelings than any classical music. Similarly in Scotland, and indeed in every country, the songs which were identified with the struggles and the patriotism of the people were the most effective. Mr. Loudin and his party were the representatives of a ransomed race. Their sacred melodies and hymns could not but produce an excellent effect. The effect of a beautiful hymn, with beautiful music, must be good even upon the most hardened nature. They welcomed Mr. Loudin and his party, and gave them the right hand of fellowship. They might well call them their sisters and brothers. They wished them God-speed, believing they could not fail to do an immense amount of good. He believed their entertainment would be highly successful. (Applause)" (*[Melbourne] Daily Telegraph*).

Loudin's Fisk Jubilee Singers gave their first public concert in Melbourne on June 7, 1886, at the town hall. Local critics were enthusiastic.

• ***June 8, 1886:*** "Anyone who wishes to have a splendid and almost perfect illustration of what 'expression' means in music should not fail to hear the Fisk Jubilee Singers. The singers, individually considered, have voices of excellent quality, and they sing together with the most even and balanced effect, with thorough sympathy, with accuracy of intonation, with an attentive regard to light and shade, with dynamic power accenting each phrase and each word in accord with the meaning thereof; and, in short, they warble with all their souls" (*[Melbourne] Daily Telegraph*).

• ***June 11, 1886:*** "The Opening Night of the Fisk Jubilee Singers," "The Fisk Jubilee Singers struck the Melbourne public at once. The audience on the first night (Monday, June 7th) was immense. Large numbers paid the 5s. for the reserved seats, and money for the 3s. and lower-priced seats was refused. But what was more, the audience was delighted. His Excellency Sir H. B. Loch and Lady Loch were present, together with a good many other prominent citizens. The Hon. James Balfour, M. L. C., occupied the chair. He opened the meeting with a cordial little speech, in which he sketched the history of the singers through their various campaigns. As the sweet strains of 'Steal Away to Jesus' stole upon our ears it was quickly manifest that the singers had stolen upon the affections of their hearers. The piece closed with their impressive chanting of the Lord's Prayer. After this opening number their success was assured; the evening was simply a succession of triumphs. As to time, they sang with the precision of musical machines; as to sweetness and gravity of voice, it is safe to say that the Melbourne public have not for a long time, if ever, heard eleven voices together so good in themselves and so harmoniously blended. As to purity of intonation and distinctness of articulation, it would be difficult to their being excelled in these respects. And then the earnestness with which they one and all sing is perhaps the most captivating thing of all about their performance. To me it was quite a revelation . . . I came away after spending the most enjoyable musical evening that has ever fallen to my lot" (*Christian World*).

• ***June 12, 1886:*** "These singers, through constant practice, have arrived at perfection of style in their rendering of part-songs, so that their manner may be studied with advantage by all those who are actually engaged in Melbourne in contributing to concerted harmonies of the human voice" (*Argus*).

The furore that the Fisk Jubilee Singers created in Melbourne continued undiminished for weeks. This account appeared after their ninth performance at Melbourne Town Hall:

• ***June 17, 1886:*** "There was some grumbling as to the arrangements at the doors, but the manager explains that it was due to the fact of the public crushing in so long before the time announced for opening, and, further, that they never anticipated having so large an audience" (*[Melbourne] Daily Telegraph*).

On June 19 the same newspaper wrote: "The success of the Fisk Jubilee Singers now appearing at the Melbourne's Town-hall is something unprecedented in the annals of the colony. The audiences are phenomenally large, and the enthusiasm created by the singers is extraordinary." Incredibly, the Jubilee Singers gave twenty-one successful concerts at Melbourne Town Hall in twenty-three days and were able to attract packed houses in and around Melbourne for fully ten weeks. Finally, it was reported:

• ***August 13, 1886:*** "There was an immense audience at the last concert of the Melbourne series of the Jubilee Singers . . . The audience extended over the area, balcony and south gallery, and even the orchestra behind the singers found occupants . . . The last night of the Jubilees in Melbourne may be said to have fitly crowned a series of triumphs" (*Christian World*).

Lord H. B. Loch, governor of Victoria, and his wife, Lady Loch, were powerful friends who were very helpful to Loudin and his troupe during their thirty-nine month sojourn in Australasia. On July 20 Loudin's Fisk Jubilee Singers gave a "Grand Charity Concert" under the patronage of Lady Loch, in aid of the Convalescent Home for Women, the Salvation Army Prison Gate Brigade, and other local charities. According to the *Advertiser* of August 6, 1886, the Jubilee Singers "visited the Benevolent Asylum and sang to the inmates a number of well-known sweet melodies . . . The aged people listened with a pleasure and interest which made their faces a study to the onlooker and many were the grateful expressions at the close of the service . . . One aged inmate was overheard saying that he had not expected to have listened to such music until he had reached heaven." Throughout their Australasian tour, Loudin's Fisk Jubilee Singers honored their public service responsibilities with benefit concerts, complimentary tickets for orphanages, and such.

Frederick J. Loudin was also scrupulously attentive to his business responsibilities. While in Melbourne, he ordered a reprinting of J. B. T. Marsh's *The Story of the Jubilee Singers* and sold many copies at four shillings each. The frontispiece of the 1886 Melbourne edition notes the completion of 125,000 copies printed. It also claims that each of the approximately 110 jubilee songs included in the volume "is copyright in the Australasian Colonies (including New Zealand and Tasmania)." The sale of the books added significantly to concert revenues, and Loudin's enthusiastic salesmanship during the intermission was a subject of press notice:

• ***June 8, 1886:*** "The interval was occupied by the sale of the book containing the story of the organization and the words and music of the principal songs, and those who wished to 'adjourn' outside were politely told that they would have to repay on re-entering" (*[Melbourne] Herald*).

• ***August 6, 1887:*** "'An eye for the beautiful.' That is the last touch with which Jubilee Loudin gives to his speech when introducing the jubilee memorial book. It 'takes' amazingly; nobody dares to refuse to buy after that" (*[Brisbane] Telegraph*).

Leaving Melbourne on August 11, 1886, the Jubilee Singers embarked on what Loudin called "our country trip";[5] the newspapers referred to it as their "colonial tour."[6] It was during this time that the Jubilee Singers visited the Maloga Mission Station. Loudin's first meeting with the aboriginal people of Australia was very memorable. He described it in a letter to the *Detroit Plaindealer*:

• ***July 20, 1888:*** "From the Antipodes," a letter from F. J. Loudin, dated June 11, 1888, from Brisbane, Queensland: "At Malaga [*sic*] we visited the mission station. We drove out for the purpose of singing to them. They were very shy at first and were very uncommunicative. We were shown through their little houses, many of which they had built themselves. Quite a number of them speak English very well. But after we had sung to them it seemed to be the key to their hearts, for it regularly opened their sympathies. It was strange to witness the effect the old slave songs born in the Southern plantations of America made upon these people at the Antipodes. Many of them wept as they listened to the weird plaintive melodies. While they seldom sing themselves, they seem to be exceedingly fond of music, more touched in fact by it than it has ever been our privilege to witness in any other people. After the singing was over they grasped us by the hand, many of them with the tears streaming from their eyes, thanking us again and again for what to them had been a great treat. When we were to leave the settlement they all came out to bid us good bye, and as we drove away so long as we could see the settlement, handkerchiefs, hats and hands were being waved from the treetops or from wherever a native could hold on long enough to wave his hat or hand" (*Detroit Plaindealer*).

Loudin's Fisk Jubilee Singers traveled to New South Wales, beginning their first season in Sydney at the YMCA hall on October 4, 1886, where they gave daily concerts through the month of October. The first half of November was also spent singing in and around Sydney. The concerts were well attended and the press was generally favorable.

• ***October 6, 1886:*** "All the poetry, passion, exuberant fancy, and deep religious feeling of the coloured races is embodied in their songs. Their music is different to the melodies of any other race, and the wild thrilling plantation ditties have a fascination entirely their own . . . The Fisk Jubilee Singers have undoubtedly brought part singing to a very high pitch of perfection, and in addition to this the quaintness of their plantation ballads is striking and original. We have seldom seen an audience so unanimous in its applause, and the Jubilee Singers should do well in Sydney if plaudits are a fair criterion of success" (*Sydney Morning Herald*).

The racially biased, sarcastically inclined Sydney *Bulletin* expressed a different opinion:

• ***October 12, 1886:*** "The Fisk Jubilee Singers are still jubilating at the Sydney YMCA Hall. The gate money looks well, and Lord Carrington has promised to be present on Friday, the 15th. It might be well, however, if there was a little less hymn book—and second-rate hymn book at that—in the entertainment, for a dash of profane cussedness goes well with a Sydney audience" (*[Sydney] Bulletin*).

Racial prejudice found a more palpable expression while the troupe was in Sydney.

• ***October 8, 1886:*** "Hotel Snobbery in Sydney," "The cultured and talented and world-renowned 'Fisk Jubilee Singers'. . . have, metaphorically, had the doors of the leading hotels in Sydney slammed in their faces, because of the colour of their skins . . . We could laugh, if it were not for the humiliation of knowing that it will go forth to England and Europe that Sydney publicans have been able to offer such insult to persons of culture and refinement . . . We confess to being almost bewildered. We had thought that the battle of 'civil rights' for men of all colour had been fought out and settled in America, and little expected to see such an exhibition of caste prejudice here" (*[Sydney] Christian Monitor*).

Loudin's Fisk Jubilee Singers opened in Auckland, New Zealand, on November 26, 1886. Press reports make it clear they enjoyed a very lucrative engagement at the city hall, with extra concerts being scheduled. December 4, 1886, the Singers gave a Saturday matinee at which children from Auckland's orphanages were admitted free and all other children were admitted for one shilling.

Leaving Auckland after two weeks, they traveled overland to Napier, and then headed north along the east coast for concerts in Gisborne at the beginning of 1887. Turning back south along the coast, they stopped at Napier and Hastings, then continued to Waipawa, Waipukurau, and Woodville. The trip is described in the personal diary of tenor singer R. B. Williams, quoted in a 1991 article in a New Zealand journal:

> The Fisk Jubilee Singers travelled around New Zealand by boat, train and horse drawn carriages, performing in just about every town, small or large . . . But the tour was slow going. On January 13, 1887, the troupe left Waipukurau: "We have a ride of three hours by train to Dannevirke, then by coach 17 miles to Woodville . . . Coaching is so hard. Conversation on the way very lively and instructive. We are in the heart of the famous 70 miles bush. Nice hall to sing in—Woodville is only 15 years old.
>
> "January 14: Today we start for Palmerston [North] through the beautiful Manawatu gorge. Oh, such scenery: rugged grandeur, steep cliffs, narrow and dangerous roads. All of us in high glee. We pick ferns on the way. Arrived at Palmerston sick and hot. Sing in good concert to full house."[7]

The Jubilee Singers' tour of New Zealand reached a high note at Wellington early in February 1887, when a series of ten concerts at the Opera House reportedly took in an astounding fifteen hundred pounds. The Australian magazine *L'Entre Act* commented, "The people who are really making the money in New Zealand are the Fisk Jubilee Singers."[8]

Loudin's Fisk Jubilee Singers crossed over to the South Island, beginning their tour at Picton, then proceeded to Blenheim and Nelson, and

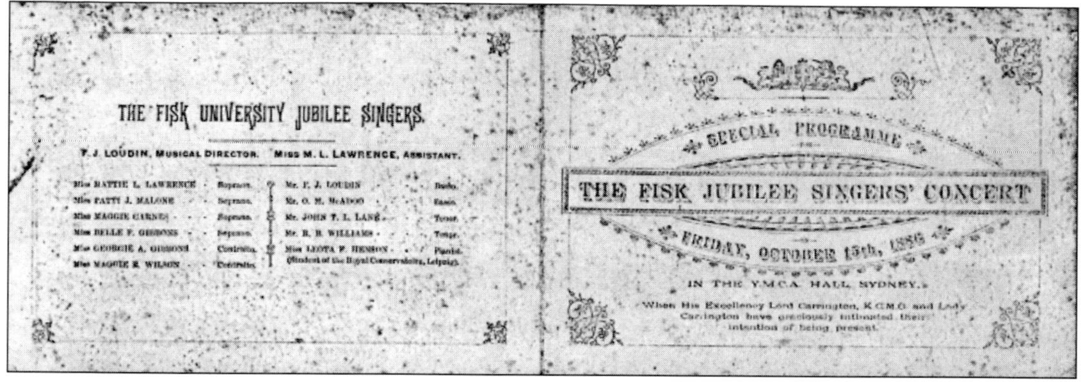

THE FISK UNIVERSITY JUBILEE SINGERS.

F. J. LOUDIN, MUSICAL DIRECTOR. MISS M. L. LAWRENCE, ASSISTANT.

Miss HATTIE L. LAWRENCE	Soprano.	Mr. F. J. LOUDIN	Basso.
Miss PATTI J. MALONE	Soprano.	Mr. O. M. McADOO	Basso.
Miss MAGGIE CARNES	Soprano.	Mr. JOHN T. L. LANE	Tenor.
Miss BELLE F. GIBBONS	Soprano.	Mr. B. B. WILLIAMS	Tenor.
Miss GEORGIE A. GIBBONS	Contralto.	Miss LEOTA F. HENSON (Student of the Royal Conservatoire, Leipzig.)	Pianist.
Miss MAGGIE E. WILSON	Contralto.		

SPECIAL PROGRAMME

THE FISK JUBILEE SINGERS' CONCERT

FRIDAY, OCTOBER 15th, 1886

IN THE Y.M.C.A. HALL, SYDNEY.

When His Excellency Lord Carrington, K.C.M.G. and Lady Carrington have graciously intimated their intention of being present.

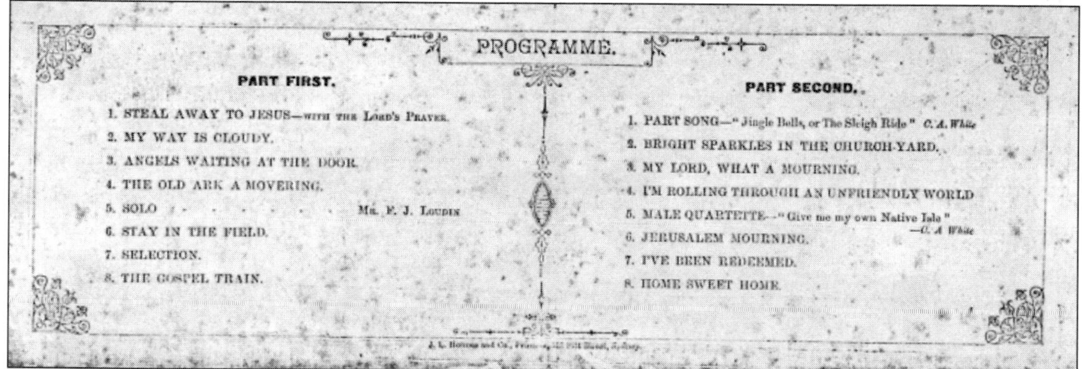

PROGRAMME.

PART FIRST.

1. STEAL AWAY TO JESUS—WITH THE LORD'S PRAYER.
2. MY WAY IS CLOUDY.
3. ANGELS WAITING AT THE DOOR.
4. THE OLD ARK A MOVERING.
5. SOLO . . . . MR. F. J. LOUDIN
6. STAY IN THE FIELD.
7. SELECTION.
8. THE GOSPEL TRAIN.

PART SECOND.

1. PART SONG—"Jingle Bells, or The Sleigh Ride" C. A. White
2. BRIGHT SPARKLES IN THE CHURCH-YARD.
3. MY LORD, WHAT A MOURNING.
4. I'M ROLLING THROUGH AN UNFRIENDLY WORLD
5. MALE QUARTETTE—"Give me my own Native Isle" —C. A. White
6. JERUSALEM MOURNING.
7. I'VE BEEN REDEEMED.
8. HOME SWEET HOME.

Program, Loudin's Fisk Jubilee Singers at YMCA Hall, Sydney, Australia, October 15, 1886. (courtesy Fisk University Library, Special Collections)

reached Christchurch on March 14, 1887. On March 25 the local *New Zealand Referee* described their splendid reception: "Fisk's Jubilee Singers can probably claim to have received the best all round patronage accorded to any kind of travelling company that has visited Christchurch for many months . . . our residents—from the aristocrat to the humble 'working man'—have flocked to the Theatre Royal in large numbers, and paid their four, three and two shillings for admission willingly, and bought the book, giving the history of the Singers, at four shillings apiece, too!"

The Jubilee Singers opened a two weeks' engagement in Dunedin on April 2, 1887.

• ***April 6, 1887:*** "The Fisk Jubilee Singers, who have been gathering an extraordinary amount of current coin during their tour of New Zealand, appeared for the first time in Dunedin at the Garrison Hall on (2nd), and were accorded a very enthusiastic reception" (*Otago Witness*).

The Singers made their way to the southernmost part of the South Island, to Invercargill, where they gave four concerts at the Theatre Royal in late May, concluding their tour of New Zealand. Returning to Australia, Loudin's Fisk Jubilee Singers gave their first concert in Adelaide, at the YMCA Hall, on June 20, 1887.

Two years later, when the Jubilee Singers arrived in New Zealand for a second tour, Fred Loudin related some details of the intervening period to a reporter from the Wellington *Evening Press*:

• ***February 14, 1889 (Wellington, New Zealand):*** "A Chat With Mr. Loudin," "In the course of a conversation yesterday with Mr. Loudin, manager and musical director of the Fisk Jubilee Singers company, now performing at the Opera House here, a representative of the *Evening Press* gleaned the following interesting particulars of the company's movements and experiences since their last visit to this city two years ago:

From Invercargill, said Mr. Loudin, we went to Adelaide for the opening of the exhibition there, and made a stay of a month, and then found things so dull in South Australia that we went round to Brisbane, where we met with wonderful success. We were unable to get a public hall large enough there to sing in, but the proprietors of the *Courier* newspaper had put up a big building, divided into two or three flats, and we endeavored to hire one of these. At first they would not let the building for our purposes, but finally gave way, and that was the means of converting the particular flat in question into a public hall, now called after us, I believe, 'Jubilee Hall.' We had a most pleasant time in Brisbane, the people being very hospitable. Lady Musgrove was also very kind to us. From there we came overland to Newcastle, but I omitted to say that while at Brisbane Sir Samuel Griffiths and the then Colonial Secretary took us in the yacht 'Lucinda' to St. Helena, where the prisoners are, a trip we thoroughly enjoyed. At Newcastle we met with a new experience for us in the colonies, and one that reminded us of our treatment in certain parts of America. The hotels would not take us in. The proprietors gave no reasons, but just refused to have us. This was all the better for us in the end, as the leading citizens of the place opened their houses to us, and we were far better off than if we had gone to an hotel. We thence went to Melbourne for some time, doing excellent business, and also visited South-west Victoria, and next went to Tasmania (Hobart), where I was taken really very ill indeed, and had to give up singing with the company, who had to go on without me to Sydney. This was the first time, with the exception of one night at Fielding in this colony, that I had missed a performance with the company since we started 15 years ago. Our season in Sydney, a most successful one, commenced just after Easter, and lasted four weeks. We also performed with like success at Bathurst and out Orange way, and then we worked along across through New South Wales and Victoria to Adelaide again, and through South Australia, and went to Port Augusta and Port Perry. At one of the small towns there we had an experience of an amusing character. We arrived on a Saturday, on the evening of which trade is generally in full swing. Having occasion to go out to purchase some small article before our concert commenced I found all the shops were closed because of our being in the place. At Port Augusta we visited the ostrich farms, where now there are some 500 birds . . . From there we went to Broken Hill, the journey being of a most interesting character. Having heard of the bad water there we took along with us 15 gallons of our own supply, because there was a typhoid fever scare on there. How the people at Broken Hill drink the water there and live I don't know. It is got from a mudhole five miles from the town, and if you let a glass of it stand for a few moments there will be a sediment at the bottom an inch thick. On the journey there, for over 180 miles we did not cross or see a single stream of water. There is so much dust at Broken Hill that it nearly buries you up as you stand. There are no defined streets, and the houses stand anyhow, with no fences around them. There are two very good hotels, and about every other house is a grog shanty. The 'pubs' are never closed on Sundays or any other time. The people were very hospitable, however, although peculiar. I went down the big mine 215 feet right into the lode, which is twice as wide as Cuba-street. The mine manager, Mr. Patterson, took me round and showed me the smelting process, &c. It was a marvelous sight . . . Thence we went to Melbourne for the Exhibition, and took a month's holiday, and then came on to New Zealand" (*Wellington Evening Press*).

The Jubilee Singers carried the spirituals to remote outposts on this adventurous tour. Their audiences crossed lines of class and even nationality, attracting everyone from "clergymen and ministers of various denominations, and leading citizens seldom seen inside a theatre" to the disruptive "larrikin element."[9]

• ***September 10, 1887:*** "The most unique, original, pleasing, elevating, and amusing entertainment which has been ever given in Tamworth was started in the Oddfellow's Hall, last Wednesday . . . the hall crowded from ceiling to floor with an audience reaching from top to bottom of the social ladder . . . Only a few members of the larrikin element were heard to express outside the hall disparaging and vulgar remarks about the entertainment and entertainers; but, on the principle that it is unfair to expect more from a pig than a grunt, the opinion of this 'push' may be fairly discarded . . .

. . . [T]he expressions of surprise uttered by some members of the audience plainly evinced the Arcadian simplicity in which quite a number of our community live with regard to the world's entertainments. 'Why, that's a black man?' and 'Oh! my! they're all blacks?' were amongst the remarks heard. Verily, many of the folk who 'steal away to Jesus' in the solitude of their own homes, are to be envied for their simplicity of soul" (*Tamworth Observer*).

• ***September 21, 1888:*** "It is not a performance which appeals merely to the musical amateur or the educated ear (though it delights both) but it takes captive and holds entranced from start to finish auditors of every class, age and stamp. The central Australian nigger, the street Arab, the bucolic youth from the far interior, the Afghan camel wallah, and the rudest forecastle hand, though they may not perceive and intelligently appreciate the musical effects of the songs, all submit to the spell which the Jubilee Singers throw over both cultured and uncultured auditors . . . such a musical treat is seldom indeed vouchsafed to up-country residents, and we should imagine that few who were present last night can refrain from attending again" (*Port Augusta Dispatch*).

The Jubilee Singers' Australasian tour took them to many small towns that lacked a hall of sufficient size to accommodate the crowds. As a result, concerts were sometimes held in unlikely facilities. The following report came from Kiama, down the coast from Sydney:

• ***June 2, 1888:*** "In the evening the Agricultural Pavilion, which, notwithstanding some palpable inconveniences attending the use of it, was the only available building that could have accommodated them, was filled with not merely the largest audience it ever contained—which is saying nothing—but with the largest crowd of people, or very nearly so, that it was capable of containing, or, as nearly as can be ascertained, about 600 persons. These came from every part of the south coast that was within a day's drive; and the appearance of the buggy lamps (especially at the time the visitors were leaving the ground) extending in an unbroken line almost from that spot to Terralong-street was in itself quite phenomenal" (*Reporter and Illawarra Journal*).

In mid-April 1889, Loudin's company completed their second lengthy tour of New Zealand, where the jubilee songs made a lasting impression. In 1942 a Wellington reporter observed: "What is interesting musically to recall is that the [Fisk] singers were the first to introduce to New Zealand that type of evangelical song known as the negro spiritual, and after they departed it was common to hear such numbers as 'Steal Away,' 'Good News,' 'In That Morning,' 'Swing Low Sweet Chariot,' sung in some of the non conformist churches."[10]

"Same"—The Maori and the Fisk Jubilee Singers

More than one account of their tours of New Zealand dwells on the rapport between Loudin's Fisk Jubilee Singers and the Maoris, New Zealand's aboriginal people.

• ***February 21, 1887:*** "The Jubilee Singers Among the Maoris," "Notwithstanding all that the Jubilee [Singers] have seen during years of travel, it was reserved for the Maoris of Greytown to show them something new and give them something to remember. On Saturday afternoon the Singers went to the Papawai pah by invitation of the natives and were received with a feeling akin to joy. It was evident that a strong sympathetic feeling exists between these people of color. The welcome was such a glad one that the Singers soon felt at ease and scattered among the native women and children, chatting in a most friendly way. After inspecting some carved slabs, which are to be used for the erection of a meeting house, the Singers were entertained at dinner in the large building close by. In the evening about twenty Maoris dressed in striking costumes gave a dance of welcome; this was followed by other dances of various significance, and concluded with a song of farewell and dance combined. The Jubilee Singers had never seen anything of the kind before, and they were much interested in watching the grotesque attitudes and listening to the peculiar shouts of the dancers. A presentation of a mat to each of the Singers concluded the exercises. The Singers expressed their warm thanks to the natives and Mr. C. Jury, in return thanked the singers for their kindly visit. Then the Singers gathered in a group and sang 'Swing Low, Sweet Chariot,' the rich harmony telling upon natives and Europeans with good effect. Again they sang and then concluded with a beautiful parting song addressed more particularly to the Maoris. The Singers returned to Greytown well pleased with the events of the day" (*Wairarapa [New Zealand] Standard*).

• ***December 1887:*** Loudin reports: "It was a little awkward at times, I must tell you, for when I met a Maori on the street I was compelled to rub noses with him, and that is a form of salutation to which I am not accustomed . . . The hearts of the people were touched. They came again and again, and when we asked them the reason, they indicated that they recognized a kinship . . . they were quite clear that Maoris were 'same,' pointing to our faces. We were present at a war dance in New Zealand, and were much interested in the proceedings. I had many interesting conversations with the Maoris about the lives and hopes of colored people. I spoke to them in the most forceable language at my command of the terrible dangers of 'fire water' " (*Fisk Herald*).

• ***January 15, 1887:*** "An Interview with Mr. Loudin," "And whilst in New Zealand [Loudin] made good use of his opportunities both to become acquainted with Maori character and to express his views on the manner in which he considered they should be treated in regard to education . . .

Mr. Loudon [*sic*] is a little weak on the subject of the natives of New Zealand. He candidly stated that he and his party looked upon the Maoris with the greatest interest and affection, for he regarded them as brothers and sisters, as members of the great race of colored people of which he and his friends were themselves members. This was well enough; but Mr. Loudon forgets the very marked difference between the Maoris and the American negroes. The latter are clever, and above all they are not lazy or indolent . . . What a contrast to the natives of New Zealand! These poor creatures are still in the last stage of savagery. . . They will not work; they live in lazy luxury. . . In natural attainments, they are equally behind their American cousins. What colonial can imagine a band of Maoris singing the lovely melodies and part songs which the Jubilee singers render. . .

It is all very well to talk of educating the Maori. Surely the whites are placing no restrictions on the advancement of the native race in that direction. . .

At any rate it is always well when an intelligent foreigner visits a country. . . The views which they express at different times, before educated audiences are sure to have some beneficial effect. And as the leader of the band of Jubilee singers is undoubtedly in earnest in his regard for the natives of New Zealand, he may rest assured that his casual references to their condition and probable future must have a great and lasting effect, both on the natives themselves, and on the people who are now their betters, but who treat them as equals" (*Waipawa Mail*).

• ***February 25, 1889:*** "A large number of the Papawai natives, with a vivid recollection of the pleasant times spent with the company on a previous occasion, assembled at the Club Hotel, where they [the Jubilee Singers] were staying and paid their respects to them in a royal manner" (*South Wairaraga Advocate*).

• ***April 13, 1889:*** "The Maoris appear to be greatly interested in the Fisk Jubilee Singers, and lose no opportunity of accosting and speaking to them. One old tattooed warrior, when asked his opinion of them, gravely replied: 'Oh! all the same the Maori.' They say they are all their brothers from over the water" (*Wanganni Chronicle*).

• ***December 3, 1892:*** "Among [Loudin's] collection of Australasian curios may be mentioned the 'Meri-meri' stone from New Zealand—this stone is of a dark green color and is shaped something like the head of an ax, only thinned down to a cutting edge on each side. It is the emblem of tribal authority among the Maoris . . . It was given to Mr. Loudin by the widow of a Maori chief as the highest testimonial of her regard" (*Cleveland Gazette*).

In January 1887 a *Waipawa Mail* reporter questioned, "What colonial can imagine a band of Maoris singing the lovely melodies and part songs which the Jubilee singers render?" Yet, in fact, Westernized four-part harmony singing seems to have been a standard part of Maori culture through the better part of the twentieth century. Maori music history has not been well documented; however, commercial recordings of the Rotorua Maori Choir were made as early as 1929.[11] These close-harmony recordings, as well as others of more recent vintage, raise questions as to whether the early appearance of the great Fisk Jubilee Singers may account, in some manner, for the enduring affinity for Western close-harmony singing among the Maori.

Australasian Music Appreciation

The first thing a good singer has to learn when he joins the company is that his voice has to blend with the others, and the harmony has to be perfect; and the singers become extremely sensitive to the least absence of harmony. The object aimed at is to make the voices blend into one grand whole—one beautiful volume.

—Frederick J. Loudin, 1886

There are no sound recordings of Loudin's Fisk Jubilee Singers. Nevertheless, solid, credible conclusions can be drawn about their music from literally thousands of published descriptions of their singing. Existing evidence supports the assertion that the troupe that made the 1884–1890 world tour was the finest company of spiritual singers ever assembled.

The Australasian daily newspapers all had music critics; some were remarkably astute. Along with describing the merits of the singing, their comments sometimes identified singularities of African American spiritual harmony singing which Australasians found "so vitally different from anything ever heard on the local boards." The most perceptive and far-seeing commentators noted a momentous, new approach to arranging and performing choral music. A few saw much more than this. For at least one critic, Loudin's Fisk Jubilee spirituals beckoned lost memory, "a sort of 'childhood days (very far back indeed) now flit before me' feeling, it seems to be."

The June 5, 1886, edition of the *Melbourne Daily Telegraph* offered what Loudin found to be an intelligent analysis of the "Fisk songs":

A musical phrase has occurred to some rapt enthusiast at a camp meeting, he has poured it out unconsciously (like Goëthe's harper "Singing as the birds sing"), one after another of the congregation has caught the tune; after two or three repetitions they have harmonised it in a ready but not rough way; like wavelets in a pool the people have joined in the widening flood of sound till the simple notes have grown to a mighty strain sung in perfect accord by hundreds or thousands of rich mellow voices. Such is the "genesis" of most of the tunes in the Fisk singers' repertoire. This music is, as it has been perfectly defined, "the music of nature." At the same time a connoisseur recognizes that it is a standard to which musical art should in a large degree approximate itself. It is astonishing to notice that these untutored minstrels have unconsciously adopted methods which some of our greatest recent composers have been struggling to introduce. Take the case of rhythm. The music of their songs exactly follows the words. Not only are short syllables distinguished from long by the accent put in them, but by the value and length of the notes themselves—short notes to short syllables, and longer notes for long ones. Now this system is exactly what a modern influential school of Italian composers has been fighting for. As might be imagined, it makes closer that subtle, but still powerful, connection between the sound of the music and the sense of the words, which results often in effects startling in their impressiveness. Many hearers may not be able to analyse the effect of the Jubilee singing, but much of it springs from this cause. When we come to speak of the harmonising of the songs, we are simply astonished at the effects produced by simple means. That we should be shows the valuable artistic mission which these singers perform in bringing us back to see the value of unadorned purity in music. Here again we find a counterpart of the Fisk songs in the efforts of great living composers. One of the most swing effects [*sic*] in the whole of modern dramatic music is the famous "Ave," opening the prologue in heaven of Boito's opera "Mefistofele," where the hushed voices of the choir repeat the prayer on one drawn-out common chord. Exactly the same device is found in most of the songs under notice. Take the one, "I've Been Redeemed"; in twelve bars, with one exception, the only harmonic changes are from a tonic to a dominant bass; and yet, with exquisite singing, this does not become monotonous. In another song we find a "rising scale on a pedal bass," to speak technically. This is a form which sent half the critics of Europe mad with delight when Mozart employed it in "Don Giovanni." And yet American slaves would hardly get many chances of going to the opera to hear "Don Giovanni." Just as Giotto and the great early painters used only two or three simple colours to paint frescoes unsurpassed since for directness of pure feeling, so these slave singers, with the best musical means they could employ, expressed their feelings of exultation or grief in a fervour which is touching, chiefly because it is so unaffected. Their efforts may be employed on musical ideas which are common to many peoples, but they are never commonplace. Their simplicity is not childish, but childlike. It will astonish many readers to learn what is really the closest analogue to this jubilee music. Not Christy minstrel songs or modern ballads, but the most ancient Gregorian music of the liturgy of the Romish Church. Both have been the artless, unaided production of musically uncultivated people; both have been found especially well adapted for ready comprehension and easy performance by large masses of people. At the time when slave songs were sung by slaves it would have been hard for a traveller who shut his eyes and listened to their musical structure alone to know whether he was listening to the negroes in the sugar-brake or to the chant of monks in the Lateran Basilica at Rome. This likeness to the Roman music is especially noticed in the song "Go down Moses." Here alternate unison and harmonised passages suggest very much the singing of the Romish choir... Some few of their songs are much wilder in character and stranger in rhythm than the great majority of which the above remarks are true. Such are "The Love Feast," in which most extraordinary intervals of a seventh appear unexpectedly; or "Daniel," in which the time has a certain uncouthness imparted to it by the constant avoidance of the interval of the fourth. Space forbids us mentioning other peculiarities of this most interesting music. No critic can afford, however, to disregard them, and they will be interesting if watched for by the ordinary listener, for whom they have been here pointed out. As a German critic has observed, it is quite possible that some great musician may yet do for these melodies what Liszt and Brahms have done for those of Hungary... Even here, in our own City, we may take a lesson, from one of those Fisk singers' melodies, "They led my Lord away." Here the story is told in a recitative on one note... The flow and ebb of the volume of sound gives a wonderful, undulating undercurrent to the harmony. The soft pianissimo effect is almost indescribable. We do not exaggerate in saying that it is more like the echo of distant music borne towards the hearer by the wind, or like the sound which comes from a vox angelica stop placed far at the back of some great organ. With a full recollection of the three finest choirs in Europe, Mr. Leslie's late choir, the Dom choir at Berlin, and the Papal at the Sistine Chapel, we assert that, in the matter of absolute accuracy of intonation and finished graduation of tone, the Fisk singers may take their place beside them. By earnest application and self-sacrificing zeal bestowed on simple musical materials, they produce an almost magical result. To the critic, the more he knows of music the more he will find their music luminously suggestive; the non-critical hearer will be carried away with delight at hearing melodies prompted by nature untaught transformed into examples (in their way) of highest art. Perfection of performance, casting a halo of irresistable charm around the simplest and purest material—this is the musical lesson of the Fisk Jubilee Singers.

Loudin referred to this article in an interview which appeared in the *Daily Telegraph* on October 3, 1887: "Questioned as to the quaint melodies of the Jubilee Singers, Mr. Loudin declined to attempt a scientific analysis of the differences between their music and any other. Only in Melbourne and in Berlin has he seen that attempted with success. In the columns of 'The Daily Telegraph' a critical notice appeared of the music of the singers, which he felt to be most philosophically correct. 'But for myself, I would not attempt it. All I know is the effect.' "

• ***August 19, 1886:*** "The singing of this company defies description—words are but of little service—it must be heard that any idea of its excellence may be formed. Long and systematic training has made the singers mechanically perfect, and the fact that they lose themselves in the spirit and the sentiment of what they sing, together with the great natural ability, leave nothing to be obtained. No such concerted singing has been heard before, and the pleasure of hearing them is intensified by the clear enunciation of every word" (*Kyneton Observer*).

• ***August 25, 1886 (Sandhurst):*** "The majority of items on the programme were sacred negro melodies, and they were sung with an unsurpassed unity of voices, individual prominence being subordinated by the effort to accomplish this. At times the listeners would be borne away with the soft murmurs of the vocalists, when suddenly a wild continuous shout would intersperse it. The selections were rendered with a thrilling earnestness, and they seemed to put their heart and soul into their execution. We finally say that those who have neglected the opportunity of hearing what might be properly termed 'the best united singers in the world,' have missed a rare treat" (*Bendigo Evening News*).

• ***December 4, 1886 (Auckland):*** "The crowded houses that greet the performance of the Jubilee Singers every night, are an illustration of the fact that one touch of nature shows the whole world kin. It is a triumph of nature and common sense over conceit and conventionalism, and there is more genuine and real appreciation of the delightsomeness of sweet sounds in a single night at the City Hall than in a hundred assemblies listening to classical music" (*Observer*).

• ***December 29, 1886 (Hawke's Bay):*** "[W]hatever may be said, or suggested by nose-in-air or lip-in-curl, by a few, a very few, fast wedded to the European style of music—the audience were more than satisfied, were delighted with the entertainment. The strange wailing choruses, rising and falling, told with remarkable effectiveness. Do they recall in us a neglected transmitted memory of primeval days, when our savage progenitors sang in some such wise? Surely this is the only explanation of the thrilling effect . . . a sort of 'childhood days (very far back indeed) now flit before me' feeling, it seems to be . . . We are still savages enough, the most civilized of us, to enjoy savage music, when we get it good, as the Jubilee Singers serve it out to us. We cannot understand, but we feel its power over us . . . The passages characterised by a strange and wild weirdness can be easily distinguished, and these are they that affect the hearer most deeply . . . one of the principal features of their special music is the neglect of all the rules of time. Our notation marks are quite worthless for indicating the *time* of any passage, and any person who undertakes to sing the Jubilee hymns from the printed score will make a dreadful bosh of it" (*Evening News*).

• ***March 15, 1887:*** "Fisk Jubilee Singers," "Generally, the theme as it were, is enunciated and carried on either by soprano or bass . . . and the refrain is then taken up by the other voices joining the background of the harmony. The effect of this novel style of singing it is impossible to describe; but it is exceedingly pretty" (*Telegraph*).

• ***March 17, 1887:*** "A Chat with a Jubilee Singer," an interview with Frederick J. Loudin contained the following: "Were the harmonies you use specially written for you?"

"Oh, no; the harmonies that we have are not written at all. The melodies and harmonies are such as existed among the slaves in America. The slaves themselves made them, as the necessities of the time inspired them. Our people are very emotional, and especially so in religious matters. Not being able to read, nor allowed to learn to read, they put everything into music and hymns, as they called them" (*Lyttelton [New Zealand] Times*).

• ***April 26, 1887 (Timaru):*** "The effect upon the audience was remarkable. The applause that followed the first number was the involuntary acclamation of people whom novelty and surprise have for a moment dazed; but as the *repertoire* was opened and re-opened, and gem after gem was brought forth, the audience first grew deeply attentive, then became entranced, and finally entered into a state of sympathetic enthusiastic delight. From first to last the performance was a triumph" (*South Canterbury Times*).

• ***April 27, 1887:*** "Is music more admirable as the vehicle of emotion, or as the handmaiden of cultivated taste? This is a question which we have debated with ourselves for any number of years past, and we had almost arrived at a state of equilibrium when the Fisk singers came along and threw their weight into the scale. The melodies of the heart leave the harmonies of culture far in the background . . . These visitors have spoiled us for hereafter, how shall we listen with appreciation to the offerings of ordinary musicians?" (*South Canterbury Times*).

• ***August 30, 1887 (Toowoomba):*** "The music they sing in the part-singing is not so difficult as some of the easiest glees and madrigals, but no hearer can help recognising that their singing has attained a standard of perfection. The effects produced by the rendition of the melodies are astonishing. There is an absolute perfection of vocalisation; a perfectly even balance of voice; and such a correct blending of each part whether in passages of whispering pianissimo or in the declamatory forte that the ear revels in sweet sounds. In the Jubilee Singers part singing, by natural ability and by long training has reached absolute perfection... Listening one grows almost intoxicated with the pleasure" (*Chronicle*).

• ***December 2, 1887 (Melbourne):*** "These singers have given us a grand lesson if we will only acknowledge the fact and profit by it, for they have taught us what true music is in such a way which we have never before experienced in Melbourne. They have taught us also another and a nobler lesson, to consecrate our several gifts and talents to the service of the Master who gave them and to the good of those around us" (*Spectator*).

• ***February 8, 1888 (Marlborough):*** "We have been gravely assured by various musical people that 'there is nothing in the Jubilee Songs,' that 'it isn't music at all,' and so on and so on. The question then arises—what is it that draws vast audiences, that holds them spell-bound, that thrills them, and carries them away in their own despite, that makes part singing pall upon one for a year afterwards? It is not for us to answer. We leave those who last night crammed Ewart's Hall to its utmost capacity, and rewarded every effort of the accomplished troupe with appreciative applause—to answer that. Those who heard the Fisk Singers on their former tour of the Colony had not forgotten them. From up-country solitudes and the backwoods, as well as from every home in the country, the people have been flocking everywhere to hear their 'wondrous melodies.' Wherein lies their charm one cannot tell, but more captivating minstrelsy was never heard. Rude, barbaric, and quaint is their music, but it is more; it is pregnant with thoughts, emotions, aspirations; it has the 'one touch of nature' which the Master assures us 'makes the whole world kin.' It is a music eminently 'understanded of the people.' These airs have a history. Sung as they are now by a group of gifted singers, each one and all trained as well as gifted, they are the perfected version of the original. The originals were the outpourings of overladen hearts, of irrepressible humour, of devotion, of despair; the rude utterances of slaves bending under the yoke and smarting under the driver's whip. The songs of a nation tell its history most eloquently, somebody says, and the songs of slavery fulfill this. One hears the rude prayer, the momentary joyousness, the firm faith of the slave; one sees as in a panorama the daily toil, the nightly rest, and the occasional camp meeting and the abandonment of the soul that used to come in the intervals of labor. That is why they are welcome, that is why, though they do not please the fastidious, they please the people.

Last night's concert was an eminent success, the house was literally packed, and scores (they would have been hundreds in a city) stood without and listened enthralled. The programme was varied somewhat. Mr. Loudin came forward and said that they had decided as it was a short season, to give their favourite songs and they would therefore vary the items. It is, in this case, needless to go through the programme *seriatim*. Only one variation we will chronicle, 'Bright sparkles in the churchyard,' one of the most exquisite melodies ever listened to. It is quite impossible to do the singers justice. The leading soprano, Miss Johnston, sang 'The song that touched my heart,' exquisitely; that adverb only will describe it. The voice of the principal contralto singer is one of the richest and truest voices ever heard. Of the bass of Mr. F. J. Loudin and Mr. McAdoo we can say nothing. They were simply perfect. Of the choruses, when all the voices blended like the pipes of one magnificent organ, no more can be said than that they were the grandest exhibitions of harmony that could be heard. Miss L. F. Henson's manipulation of the organ was splendid, hers was a true accompaniment and on each side of her stood two delightful singers, one with a flute-like voice. The blending of voices was wonderfully sweet, and was like a collection of reeds. This evening the company give their last concert, unless providence and the Union Company enable them to stay here over Saturday. It has been generally hoped that Mr. Loudin would to-night introduce into the programme 'I'm a rollin through an unfriendly world,' and sing his masterpiece, 'Rocked in the cradle of the deep' " (*Marlborough Express*).

• ***April 10, 1888:*** "The music is of such a class as to overturn all preconceived notions of what constitutes 'popular' music . . . The originalities are such as can hardly fail to interest any musician who has a mind susceptible of influence outside his own groove" (*Sydney Morning Herald*).

• ***June 7, 1888:*** "[W]e were struck in 'Bright Sparkles' and in 'We Shall Walk Through The Valley,' with a peculiar effect, reminding us of Palestrina. We wonder if the negroes of Louisiana ever listened to strains of the 'Lamentation of Jeremiah.' It is not impossible that they may have caught the tones from some Cathedral in Baton Rouge or New Orleans" (*Bathhurst Free Press*).

• ***July 20, 1888:*** " 'My Lord is writing all the time,' then a medley, and the song, 'I'm rolling through an unfriendly world.' Each of these showed that music had possibilities of expression above and beyond that commonly accepted by ordinary critics and musicians" (*Shepparton News*).

• ***September 21, 1888 (Newcastle):*** "Their effects lie all on the surface; no analytical search for *motif* is required; they are *natural;* and all one has to do is listen without effort and be charmed. The music is as unforced as the laughter of children—and the negro has been very aptly described as the ever juvenile race of humanity. The rolling sound waves are provocative of contagious excitement, and dramatic effect and point are lent by distinct interjectional chords now and then, as if in individual cases excitement has risen to a pitch beyond control while variety is added to effect by plaintive and pleasing minors" (*Port Augusta Dispatch*).

• ***March 5, 1889 (Napier):*** "The voices blend perfectly, the harmony is delightful, and the spirit of the words is expressed. There is a resonant quality of tone in their voices, especially the soprani and contralti, which gives them a character altogether distinct from the voices of Europeans" (*Evening News*).

• ***April 24, 1889:*** "The extraordinary sudden changes in the choruses were never heard before, but in the manner they are rendered, pleases, whilst it surprises. The richness of tone resembles nothing so much as the rolling of an organ in the interior of a cathedral" (*Manawatu Herald*).

• ***May 22, 1889:*** "The startling novelty of the strains, the abrupt bars, the quaint periods, especially of Mr. Loudin in the 'rolling' song, all combined to make the concert so vitally different from anything ever heard on the local boards, that the audience sat enraptured for two hours" (*Cootamundra Liberal*).

• ***June 14, 1889:*** "Points—The Fisk lights and shades of harmony are nearly as exquisite as the lovely tints of the sky at concert last evening" (*Telegraph*).

• ***July 9, 1889:*** "One hardly knows which to admire the most: the musical perfection at which they have arrived, or the undercurrent of religious fervor which seems to inspire each chorus. Every now and again there is a deep ring almost of sublimity and pathos in both the words and music, and then there comes, in striking contrast, some humorous incident of modulation or expression which shows in a marked degree from when both had their origin" (*[Rockhampton] Morning Herald*).

Minstrelsy and Loudin's Fisk Jubilee Singers

Loudin's Fisk Jubilee Singers were the first company of jubilee singers to appear in Australia and New Zealand, but not the first troupe of African American entertainers to appear there. Apparently, the first to arrive were Corbyn's Georgia Minstrels, who landed in Sydney on December 6, 1876. In June 1877 they presented *The Octoroon* at the Bijou Theater in Melbourne, featuring "slave songs, champion tambourinist, . . . negro choruses, real plantation walkround," etc.[12] Corbyn's Minstrels were followed almost immediately by Charles B. Hicks's Georgia Minstrels, who had made their first big impression in Indianapolis and Chicago in 1865. As Hicks related:

> In Chicago it was a big thing, and on the return of the western armies from the wars, under Sherman and Sheridan, we did an immense business. In August, 1866, we went to Boston; then to Halifax Nova Scotia, St. Johns, New Brunswick, arriving in New York in 1868, in which year we sailed in the steamer "Etna," for Liverpool, where we played under the management of Sam Hague. Afterwards visited the provinces: Ireland, Scotland, and Wales, Hamburg, Dresden, Vienna, Berlin, &c . . .
>
> After a prosperous tour extending over three years, we returned to America in 1872. We then worked all the States and visited Canada; then got back to California, and after a long stay in that State, started off for a New Zealand and Australian tour.[13]

• ***July 14, 1877:*** "The Georgia Minstrels," "Mr. Hicks' singing of that plaintive melody, 'Massa's in the cold, cold ground,' has been received with very hearty applause, and the baritone of the company, Mr. Matlock, evokes very enthusiastic plaudits by his genuine minstrelsy. Mr. Bowman has also a very pleasing voice. Judge Caruso with his side-splitting stump speech, elicits roars of laughter nightly,[14] and the other members of the Company contribute their share to the general excellence of the entertainments. The dancing and tumbling must be seen to be thoroughly appreciated" (*Wellington [New Zealand] Advertiser*).

Charles B. Hicks's Original Georgia Minstrels had a long, successful run at Queen's Theater in Sydney in 1878, presenting a dramatization of *Uncle Tom's Cabin*. The troupe consisted of fifteen black male performers, including Hicks, "Judge" Crusoe, John R. Matlock, Andrew Jackson, Hosie Easton, R. B. Lewis, Taylor Brown, Billy Saunders, John Morton, Jimmy Mills, Billy Wilson, D. A. Bowman, Keenan, Thomas, and Harris. In 1888, while Loudin's Fisk Jubilee Singers were still in the country, Charles B. Hicks returned to the Antipodes with the Hicks-Sawyer Minstrels.

Many Australasian commentators could only conceive of the Fisk Jubilee Singers' entertainment as a different kind of minstrelsy. There wasn't always malicious intent in such commentaries, but when the spirituals were associated with the spirit of minstrelsy, racist rhetoric and behavior inevitably followed. Even some of the most sympathetic auditors couldn't stop themselves from noting that "authentic negroes of course they are, with all that sense of the ludicrous." It seems no matter their intent, no amount of talent could ameliorate their dark complexions; Loudin's Fisk Jubilee Singers were "minstrels" if the public chose to conceive of them that way.

ACADEMY OF MUSIC.

BIJOU THEATRE.

Lessee, Mr. G. B. W. Lewis. Directress, Mrs. G. B. W. Lewis.

—:o:—

TREMENDOUS ATTRACTION

RE-ENGAGEMENT FOR TWO NIGHTS ONLY OF

CORBYN'S ORIGINAL GEORGIA MINSTRELS

REAL NEGROES FROM THE SLAVE STATES,

In conjunction with MR. G. B. W. LEWIS'S

FIRST-CLASS DRAMATIC COMPANY.

—:o:—

This evening, June 19,

Greatest and most successful production of modern times, Dion Boucicault's Sensational Drama, in five acts,

THE OCTOROON

In conjunction with the latest novelty,

Corbyn's Original Georgia Minstrels.

The splendid New Scenery by Mr. H. Grist.
Prompter, Mr. Walter Carle. Mechanical Effects by Mr. H. Pitt.
Properties by Mr. J. Adamson.
Incidental Music arranged by Mr. J. Wright.
The whole produced under the sole direction of Mrs. G. B. W. LEWIS.
SLAVE SONGS, CHORUSES, PLANTATION WALK-ROUND, &c.,
Introduced into this splendid Drama, for this occasion only, by

Corbyn's Original Georgia Minstrels.

CAST OF CHARACTERS.

George Peyton	Mr. Hans Phillips	Jules Thibodeaux	Mr. Tasman
Jacob M'Closky	Mr. A. Boothman	Jackson	Mr. Forbes
Salem Scudder	Mr. Fred. Thorne	Solon	Mr. Young
Pete	Mr. J. P. Hydes	Wah-no-tee	Mr. Henry E. Walton
Sunnyside	Mr. H. Saville	Mrs. Peyton	Mrs. W. Ryan
Lafouche	Mr. Flexmore	Zoe	Mrs. G. B. W. Lewis
Paul	Miss Lizzie Dixon	Dora Sunnyside	Miss Flora Anstead
Ratts	Mr. H. Daniels	Grace	Miss Jessie Dixon
Colonel Poindexter	Mr. W. H. Wallace	Dido	Miss Jessie Grey

Yellow Girls, Slaves, Deck Hands, &c.

The scene is laid in the Delta of the Mississippi River, on the Plantation of Terrebone.

PROGRAMME OF SCENERY, &c.

ACT I.—Plantation of Terrebone.

SONG AND CHORUS—"My old Kentucky home"...GEORGIA MINSTRELS
DOUBLE SONG AND DANCE ... MESSRS. COPELAND AND YOUNG
PLANTATION WALK-ROUND ... ... GEORGIA MINSTRELS

ACT II.—The Landing of the Atchafalaya. The Lumber Shed.

ACT III.—Parlour and Hall of Terrebone. The Slave Sale.

Songs, &c., introduced during the Act:

BIG BLACK FOUR (new) ... ... Only done by the GEORGIAS
BANJO SOLO ... ... By G. H. CARTER, Champion Banjoist
SONG AND CHORUS—"Massa's in the cold, cold ground" ... GEORGIAS

ACT IV.—Boiler Deck of the Magnolia. Landing of the Wood Pile.

SLAVE CHORUS—"Row, Molly, row" ... ... GEORGIA MINSTRELS

The Lynch Trial. The Ship on Fire. Destruction of the steamer.

ACT V.—SCENE 1—The Red Cedar Swamp. Wah-no-tee tracking M'Closky. SCENE 2—The Negro Quarters. SCENE 3—The Cane Brake. SCENE 4—Parlour and Hall of Terrebone.

SONG AND CHORUS—"Nellie was a lady" ... GEORGIA MINSTRELS

Mournful death of Zoe, the Octoroon.
Exciting Finale and Imposing Tableaux.

WEDNESDAY, JUNE 20,

FIRST PERFORMANCE OF PUPILS OF MR. SIMMON'S DRAMATIC ACADEMY.

Prices of Admission—Dress Circle, 5s.; Stalls, 3s.; Family Circle, 2s.; Upper Circle, ONE SHILLING.

Doors open at a Quarter past Seven; commence at Quarter to Eight sharp.

Box plan at W. H. Glen's, Collins street, where seats may be secured for Dress Circle, Stalls, and Family Circle.

Program, Corbyn's Georgia Minstrels in Australia, Lorgnette, *June 19, 1877.*

• ***September 3, 1886:*** "[T]hey gave as an encore the old plantation melody, so often burlesqued by the minstrel troupes, 'Children follow me.'... [Loudin] showed in his encore song, 'The laziest man in town,' that he could appreciate and give effect to humor, and with bones or tambo would make a good corner man" (*Castlemaine Leader*).

• ***September 8, 1886:*** "One enthusiastic individual at the Fisk Jubilee Singers' entertainment of Monday night was loud in the praises of the singers, somewhat to the discomfort of a few sitting around. During one of the songs he was expatiating on their merits, and when one of the sudden transitions from *forte* to *pianissimo* was made he was heard to exclaim, 'No more burnt cork for me'" (*Ballarat Star*).

• ***March 1, 1887 (Blenheim, New Zealand):*** "The Fisk Jubilee Singers", "Some of us have heard the Georgia Minstrels, a coloured band of niggers, who drew crowded houses throughout the Colony some years ago, but as the music that was to be provided for us was to be of a far different character to that associated with the 'chair business' [i.e., minstrelsy]... there was a great deal of speculation as to the impression the visitors would make upon our minds" (*Marlborough Express*).

• ***June 22, 1887 (Adelaide):*** "The Fisk Jubilee Singers," "As a concert troupe, pure and simple, they occupy a unique position. They sing negro melodies which we have heard travestied by professors of 'nigger minstrelsy'; they give plantation songs, but not 'plantation breakdowns'; they appear with colored faces... not the burlesque tint taken in their dressing rooms by the aid of burnt cork" (*Express and Telegraph*).

• ***June 30, 1887:*** "The Jubilee Singers," "The reputation of the Jubilee Singers is as unique as it is universal. When first told of their performances, but before hearing them, one is apt to form the precipitate conclusion that they are but another band of those vulgar negro minstrels, so many 'troupes' of which have of late years stumped the countries inhabited by English-speaking peoples. Nothing could be further from the truth. Authentic negroes of course they are, with all that sense of the ludicrous, that ingenuousness and naivete, and that capacity of facial expression for which their race get credit with the populace. But they are more" ("Melpomene," *Advertiser*).

• ***December 2, 1887 (Melbourne):*** "[It] is a matter of regret, when grown-up people appear unable to distinguish hymns from comic songs, as was the case at one concert given during the company's present stay, when 'I'm rolling through an unfriendly world,' 'Didn't My Lord Deliver Daniel?' and 'The Gospel Train' were received with laughter and applause, as though they had been Christy minstrel selections" (*Spectator*).

• ***April 14, 1888 (Sydney):*** "A good deal of the performance of last Monday struck me as approaching very near to the confines of both blasphemy and burlesque—as savoring, in fact, very much of the Salvation Army, plus considerable vocal skill and frequent pathos and refinement... such numbers as 'The Band of Gideon' and 'Walk into Jerusalem, just like John' seemed only to need burnt cork and shirt-collars, with bones and banjo, to become the genuine minstrelsy of the almost defunct 'Ethiopian Serenader' " (*Society*).

• ***August 9, 1888:*** " 'My way is cloudy,' 'Nobody knows the trouble I see, Lord,' and 'I'm rolling through an unfriendly world,' followed in due order, and the latter song, being of a less serious tone than its predecessor, excited the applause of the audience, many of whom had evidently expected to hear 'nigger' songs of a very different description" (*Inglewood Advertiser*).

The Slippery Slope of Variety and Comedy

The truth of the matter is, Australasian audiences often didn't know what to make of the entertainment offered by Loudin's Fisk Jubilee Singers. This description appeared in the *Mount Barker Courier* (South Australia) of October 26, 1888:

> A cabinet organ covered with a crimson cloth beautifully worked with lilies gave a pulpit-like air to the platform, and the weird solemnity of the opening number 'Steal Away to Jesus' added to the feeling of church. The Lord's Prayer does not call for hand clapping and feet-stamping, and doubtless the incongruity of the situation had much to do with the restraining applause at its conclusion. The hearty vigorousness of 'Good News, the Chariot's A-coming,' seemed to reassure the audience, who, however, did not gain courage to encore until the rollicking gaiety of the chorus 'The Old Ark's A-Movering' dissipated the latent feeling of conventicle and gave patent proof that after all it was a concert and not a purely religious service that was being listened to.

Loudin's Fisk Jubilee Singers had only been in Australia two months when a newspaper critic suggested they add a bit more "variety" to their concerts, by way of more "secular music." The Australian public demanded a little comedic relief to leaven a program of sacred songs. Thousands of miles from home, Loudin's Fisk Jubilee Singers couldn't ignore their obligation to entertain. But any overt attention to variety in the Jubilee Singers' program, especially any suggestion of comedic intent that might be associated with the spirituals, set F. J. Loudin's Fisk Jubilee Singers on a "slippery slope" in Australasia.

Australian audiences were still very unfamiliar with the peculiarities and conventions of African American musical culture. When Frederick J. Loudin employed certain physical gestures in his vocalizing, or brought in a bit of vocal improvisation, eccentrically drawing out the word "rolling" in the spiritual "I'm Rolling through an Unfriendly World," the startlingly original effect was mistakenly interpreted as comedic. Several spirituals, including "The Old

Ark's a Moverin'," were taken for comic minstrelsy simply because troupes like Hicks's Georgia Minstrels had earlier performed them in Australasia as parodies, subtly sabotaging them.

The traditional African American sacred repertoire consists of hymns of unmitigated earnestness, solemnity, and pathos, and also narrative songs of a much more informal nature, songs that employ folk homilies and a kind of romantic levity which has no parallel in the austere hymnody of nineteenth-century Protestantism. It was the latter sort of folk spiritual that largely inspired derisive minstrel parodies and sometimes created confusion among otherwise sympathetic white audiences.

In America, minstrelsy as an institution habitually made a mean joke of the incongruities evident in the process of assimilation. Australasian audiences had a somewhat different appreciation of the "race joke." What Australasian audiences found strange and unfamiliar—the folk-poetry of the spirituals, the many peculiarities of traditional African American music culture—they often perceived as ludicrous, ridiculous, and humorous.

Several Australian reviews raised an issue that hadn't received much attention from either American or European critics. According to the *Hamilton Spectator* of January 13, 1888, "The whole question is, whether the singing of the slave hymns, etc., to afford entertainment and enable the singers to make money . . . is legitimate and proper, or does it not amount to a burlesque of what should be regarded as sacred." While some criticisms of this type were apparently made in good faith, at their root they seem to be saying that spiritual singing on the public stage necessarily constituted a burlesque of itself.

It should be pointed out that the difficult matter of singing the Lord's song in a strange land was a very serious issue within *insular* African American culture, back to the first public exposure of the traditional racial hymns by the Original Fisk Jubilee Singers in 1871. Maggie Porter Cole, the soprano soloist of the original Fisk troupe, once explained that "the boys and girls could remember how their parents had sung the songs when they huddled together by river banks and on hillsides to worship, and the children felt that those things were sacred. They were for God and for their parent's talks with God, and they were not for white men's ears."[15]

There was wisdom in this reluctance. White Australian audiences put Frederick J. Loudin and his Fisk Jubilee Singers in an impossible position. How could they negotiate this complex web with grace as well as profit? In Australia, as in America, white folks were rejecting not the singing itself, but the *principles that underlied jubilee singing.*

• ***October 9, 1886 (Sydney):*** "This mixture of religious and ridiculous themes is slightly incongruous to English ears, but quite in keeping with the fervid, volatile nature of the dark-skinned races of the sun" (*Echo*).

• ***January 20, 1887:*** "The Jubilee Singers," "Sometimes the audience are quite unable to resist a laugh at the un-hymnlike words, or the ludicrous turns in the melody. (We are compelled to use the word 'ludicrous' again, because we can think of no other that nearly expresses the effect)" (*Wauganni Herald*).

• ***March 26, 1887:*** "In spite of its title, 'I'm Rolling through an Unfriendly World' turns out to be, as rendered by the Jubilee Singers, a humorous ditty of the most infectious kind. To listen to the catchy chorus, 'I'm ro-a-ll-ing,' would upset the gravity of anybody whose midriff is not made of cast-iron" (*New Zealand Methodist*).

• ***May 5, 1887 (Dunedin):*** "Although the rendering of these melodies may be to some degree a representation of the music of the Christian

Negroes in slavery, it must be plain to everyone who hears the present company, that there is a strong attempt made after effect; and parts, which in a negro meeting would be natural enough to the spirit of the gathering, are so exaggerated by the power and art of the singers as to produce the effect of a burlesque. Of course the company is travelling, as all companies do, for the sake of raising money, and the temptation to produce mirth is exceedingly strong, and in the music they sing there are many opportunities for introducing ludicrous passages, and this appeared conspicuously in 'I'm Rolling through an Unfriendly World,' 'The Gospel Train,' and 'Daniel.' The most serious words are brought out in too comical a fashion to be natural to the heart of any devout man, be he Negro or European . . . the remarks are written in all charity, but with a strong sense of duty to speak" (*Protestant Ensign*).

• ***JANUARY 3, 1888:*** "The whole question is, whether the singing of the slave hymns, etc., to afford entertainment and enable the singers to make money . . . is legitimate and proper, or does it not amount to a burlesque of what should be regarded as sacred . . . For ourselves, we . . . regret that the Fisk Singers did not illustrate their undoubted musical capacity without parodying the devotional exercises of their forefathers" (*Hamilton Spectator*).

• ***JANUARY 14, 1888:*** "The 'slave' melodies, whilst musical and rhythmical, jarred somewhat on one's ear, the familiar indulgence in the use of sacred names and the apparent flippancy with which spiritual subjects were alluded to, provoking the risible faculties of those present instead of inclining them toward praise for the people who had been delivered from 'the house of bondage' " (*Geelong Times*).

• ***APRIL 10, 1888 (SYDNEY):*** " 'Away Over Jordan' was another of those peculiar negro compositions which are so difficult to understand without a knowledge of the people represented by the Jubilee Singers. When Mr. Loudin broke in with, 'You say you are sailing for the skies, why don't you stop your telling lies,' he brought down the house. There was nothing in the song intended to excite laughter, however. Those who composed that song intended it as a religious exhortation of a most practical nature, but the words, and the manner in which they were introduced proved irresistible to the audience" (*Echo*).

• ***AUGUST 9, 1888:*** "In the number, 'I am rolling through an unfriendly world,' the voice of Mr. Loudin was heard on the word rolling in sustained rumbling tones that had a comical effect" (*Mount Alexander Mail*).

• ***SEPTEMBER 21, 1888:*** "[M]any of the compositions on Bible themes, sung to the quick and catchy melodies of the old plantations, are such as to disagree somewhat with preconceived notions as to the fitness of things" (*Port Pirie Advocate*).

• ***JANUARY 4, 1889:*** "The incongruous jumble of temporal with spiritual matters is clearly portrayed in such items as 'The Gospel Train,' the 'Old Ark's a Moverin,' 'Peter, go ring dem bells,' and so forth, and serves to show the simplicity of the negro character . . . while the singing of 'I'm a rolling,' and 'Didn't my Lord deliver Daniel from the Lion's Den, and Jonah from the belly of the wh-h-ale' are irresistibly mirth-provoking" (*Timaru Evening Mail*).

• ***JANUARY 19, 1889:*** "There is apparent, moreover, a growing tendency to introduce 'selections,' by which are meant secular pieces. This of course was a feature of their previous concerts, and many of the solos, quartettes, and glees then rendered live among our pleasantest recollections. For popular effect such a feature unmistakably tells and it is now made more prominent than before. We have introduced medleys, snatches of popular songs, with abrupt transitions from one to the other. It is very funny no doubt, but we cannot help asking, is it quite worthy of singers of the talent and reputation of the Fisk Jubilee Company? We expect something superior to the run of a Christy Minstrel entertainment from such gifted musicians, and a feeling of regret is experienced" (*New Zealand Methodist*).

• ***February 9, 1889:*** " 'The old ark a moverin,' and 'I'm rollin' through an unfriendly world' of course caught the attention of the audience at once, and evoked the greatest laughter and applause, as they always do" (*Marlborough Express*).

• ***July 23, 1889:*** "An Australian audience, doubtless, finds some little difficulty at first, on deciding whether to maintain a sanctimonious silence from respect to the *libretto,* to laugh heartily at the oddity of the performance, or to applaud the excellence of the harmony. Laughter and applause, however, are soon selected as appropriate to the occasion" (*Bulletin*).

The "oddities" that distinguished "The Old Ark's A-Movering" and "Rolling through an Unfriendly World" would no doubt have elicited chuckles from black audiences back home in the States. While there was no precedent for humor in European religious performance, there had always been a lighter side to the black folk religious repertoire. It entailed deliberate effects that were honestly enjoyed in context. To cultural outsiders, however, the humorous aspects of jubilee singing tended to confirm the notion that they were listening to the delightful outpourings of an inferior race of people.

Mean Judge Williams

Frederick J. Loudin's growing financial success in Australasia made him vulnerable to jealous criticism and nefarious schemes. All hell broke loose in May 1889 when a civil litigation was brought against Loudin by the Jubilee Singers' Australian advance agent, Edward Price, who claimed that he was not merely an agent, but a partner with Loudin in the management of the company. Price's suit was frivolous, and it was ultimately dismissed, but not before Judge Williams expressed his personal animosity toward Loudin's Fisk Jubilee Singers and the "goodie goodies" who supported them with their attendance.

• ***May 2, 1889:*** "The principal was Mr. Loudin, the conductor of the Fisk Jubilee Singers, and the claim made by his agent [Price] was so unreasonable that it is a wonder anyone ever presumed to bring it forward, or that a clever lawyer should have been misled into taking it up.

The jury most righteously refused to admit it, and under the direction of the judge, which was clearly and strongly in favor of the defendant [Loudin], judgement was entered for the defendant, with costs.

We say the judge's direction was in favor of the defendant, and in his remarks he showed that he felt that a wrong had been attempted to be done.

This makes it all the more remarkable that his Honour should have apparently gone out of his way to indulge in wholly undeserved strictures on the conduct of the defendant, and on the 'goodie-goodies,' as he called them, who have given the Fisk Singers their patronage . . .

But what grounds had His Honour for making the remarks which he did respecting the defendant in this case. He said 'the plaintiff and defendant were six of one and half-a-dozen of the other: there was not much to choose between; Loudin managed to gull the public,' and so on.

Now, as a matter of fact, Mr. Loudin did not gull the public . . . If everybody did not know this, it was at the fault of those who were not at the pains to pay ordinary attention . . . Besides, the singing of the Minstrels was no 'gull,' as the crowded audiences everywhere over the Australasian colonies testified . . . A stranger in a strange land appealed to him for a simple right; and, to the praise of Mr. Justice Williams be it said, he obtained it amply; but His Honour should not have marred the grace of his decision by indulging irreverently what seems to be a prejudice; even though the suppliant of justice was but 'a showman with a travelling troupe of coloured singers' " (*Evening Standard*).

Not only Judge Williams, but predictably, the gleefully racist Sydney *Bulletin* couldn't resist taking a cheap shot at Loudin.

• ***May 11, 1889:*** "The sacred bottom is at last knocked out of that sorrowful nigger entertainment known as the Fisk Jubilee Singers, which Mr. F. J. Loudin has been running round Australia in the name of Heaven. At Melbourne Supreme Court recently Mr. Loudin and his late manager came to legal blows in connection with the division of the spoil, and now a multitude of parsons and other professional pietists are dimly conscious that they have snuffled and wept tears of joy over a show which is no different to Hicks' Black Minstrels in the sight of the gods. It was stated by Purves, Q.C. [Queen's Council], that he and Sassiety at large believed the Fisk Jubilee Singers to be engaged in Keeping the Old Ark a-movering on philanthropic lines. What with those little books at 4s. each, the harmonium and other tricky accessories, it is probable that a guileless public did regard Loudin as a kind of Uncle Tom, until last week's proceedings burst up the joke. That most of the nigs must have been born after Emancipation Day was overlooked when they were warbling their tommy-rot about Stealing away, &c. Now they stand revealed as a secular crowd of more or less cullud pussons who never were the slaves of anybody except showmen, and the long-headed Loudin is Rolling On with a net profit of L8500. Hallelujah!" (*Bulletin*).

• ***June 17, 1889:*** "A few weeks since, in Melbourne, Mr. Price, late agent for the Fisk Jubilee Singers, sued Mr. Loudin, manager of the company, for money alleged to be due on a partnership in the company. The question for the court first to decide was whether Price was a partner or an agent. The evidence of the former amounted to nothing; for the latter it was so conclusive that the court will not be called upon to consider the money claim at all. But in declaring the judgement of the court Mr. Justice Williams, following suit of Price's counsel, went out of his way to make an attack upon the company. His words were to the effect that the Jubilee Singers have been going through Australasia pretending to sing for a charitable object, whereas they were all the time singing for themselves. The report of his words has gone through Australasia, and strange to say some persons, including several in Brisbane, now say that they understood the case as Judge Williams misunderstood it; that they thought the Jubilee Singers were singing for the Fisk University. . . . We have before us a copy of a pamphlet issued by the company in tens of thousands of copies. The paragraph referring to the Fisk University begins with these words: 'Although we are not now engaged in singing for Fisk University, that institution is as dear to us as when we were labouring for its establishment.' The *Sydney Daily Telegraph*, under date October 4, 1886, and therefore prior to the first visit of the singers to Brisbane, distinctly stated in an appreciative article that the singers were travelling on their own account, and 'that, like any other purely commercial speculation of the kind, it relies on its own inherent good qualities to attract an audience.' We have before us a copy of a New Zealand journal, bearing date June 1, 1889. Referring to Judge Williams's remarks, it says: 'Speaking of New Zealand, which has been twice visited by this talented troop of singers, we venture to say that no one need be under the slightest misapprehension with regard to the object for which the concerts were given. Mr. Loudin was careful to explain that while the troupe as originally constituted had travelled through America and Europe to raise funds for the Fisk University, the company of which he was manager were now singing for their own personal benefit.' The *Evening Standard*, of Melbourne, has a leading article strongly condemnatory of Judge Williams's censure. We are authorised by his Honour the Chief Justice, Sir Charles Lilley, to say that having been deeply interested in the Fisk University, and in the efforts made to raise money for its establishment, he specially noticed the work of the company which came here two years ago, and that at all times coming under his observation Mr. Loudin, the manager, was careful to explain that the company was travelling entirely on its own account. We are further authorised by Mr. Loudin to say that he will give £100 to the Brisbane hospital, if anyone can bring forward any statement made by him, calculated even to create the impression on the most careless hearer, that the company was singing for the Fisk University" (*Telegraph*).

Loudin had earned a small fortune for his labors in Australasia, and the *Bulletin* was not alone in expressing its resentment that an American Negro was about to carry away so much good Australian currency. A reporter from the *Herald* conducted a telephone interview with Loudin following the disposition of his court case. The reporter's questions contained veiled accusations based on Judge Williams's contention that Loudin had deceived the Australian public. Loudin made his feelings clear: "I don't like it to be said that I am deluding, or gulling, the people, something that has been entirely foreign to my mind." After a few more tactless questions, Loudin grew tired of the imputations:

> We made our name while singing for [Fisk] University; and, of course, we desire to keep up the identity, that is all—not at all to impose on the people. The thing is common enough in business firms; and even to come to troupes—see how the Christy's Minstrels, in London, at James' Hall, insist upon being "The Original Christy Minstrels"...
>
> Suppose now, that instead of continuing to give concerts when the troupe had got all the funds they wanted for the University in Nashville, they had disbanded, what would have been the result? Would not, and I ask the question fairly and honestly—would not the public have been deprived of the many delightful evenings and much good music?
>
> But even so—I do not think any single individual who has come to hear us, or has given us his or her patronage, regrets it in the least or begrudges it; and in spite of the hard things attempted to be said of me, I believe I have been the means of furnishing the people with many pleasant hours, and no one blames me for it. If some white man had run the troupe instead of me he would have been eulogized and flattered. I am not wronging the troupe at all. They are satisfied perfectly. They are seeing the world instead of settling down at home. It is their own free choice and desire. I take the risks and ensure them their salaries. If they are satisfied, who should object?[16]

• ***May 4, 1889:*** "The Fisk Jubilee Singers In Court—[Loudin] had written agreements with some of the singers. The agreement with [bass singer Orpheus M.] McAdoo was for two years, from August 1885, made in London, at about L10 or L12 a month, all board and expenses paid, and a return passage to Virginia... He increased his salary and those of the others... He had received L32,000 up till August 1888. He had paid out about L24,000, which would leave a profit of about L8,000. He was worth about L14,000 or L15,000" (*Adelaide Observer*).

An October 1886 clipping from the *Fisk Herald* indicates that L10 Australian equaled $50 U.S. Therefore, if the above figures are accurate, Loudin's profit, after expenses, from the three-year Australasian tour was $40,000, or about $400,000 today.

• ***June 8, 1889 (Brisbane):*** "The Fisk Jubilee Singers opened at the Centennial Hall on Wednesday night and got their usually big reception. In view of recent proceedings down South, Loudin explained that the company was not, nor had been since '78, warbling for the Fisk University. Loudin reckons they are doing a tour for their own benefit and the benefit of the audiences that roll up to plank the dollars. And the audiences reckon they get enough for their money, and that's all there is in it" (*Boomerang*).

In the summer of 1889, Loudin's Fisk Jubilee Singers completed their three-year mission in Australasia. The next year would find them on the last leg of their unprecedented world tour, heading home by way of the Orient.

A "Black Patti" for the Ages: The Tennessee Jubilee Singers and Matilda Sissieretta Jones, 1889–1891

In February 1889, J. R. Smith's Tennessee Jubilee Singers concluded a groundbreaking six-month tour of the West Indies, a defining event in late-nineteenth-century African American entertainment. This tour marked the successful debut of professional jubilee singing in the Caribbean, and it launched the international career of the brilliant young soprano soloist Matilda Sissieretta Jones, the "Black Patti."

Jones was a product of the fertile African American church-based vocal music culture that emanated from Providence, Rhode Island. At the close of the 1880s, the reigning queen of Providence's prodigious black musical community was Flora Batson, principal star of the Bergen Star Concert Company, which was owned and managed by her white husband, James G. Bergen.[17] According to the October 27, 1888, edition of the *New York Age*, "Manager Bergen has probably 'brought out' more first class colored talent than any other man living."

It was Manager Bergen who "brought out" Matilda Sissieretta Jones. On April 5, 1888, she made her New York debut in a "Bergen Star Concert" at Steinway Hall. Also on the bill was basso Lewis (or Louis) L. Brown, of Philadelphia. Three months later the Tennessee Jubilee Singers Company was assembled in New York, expressly for a West Indies tour, with featured soloists Matilda S. Jones, Lewis L. Brown, and Will H. Pierce, another product of Providence, Rhode Island's "high-class" black musical community. Other members of the company included Jones's husband, Richard; chorus members Kate Johnson, Hattie Brown, John Woolford, and James G. Stevens; piano accompanist Annie M. Smith; and a white musical director, Prof. A. K. La Rue. Their departure from New York was noted in the August 4, 1888, edition of the *Age*: "Mrs. Matilda Jones, a young lady of 20 years, and Mr. W. H. Pierce of Providence will be stars of the affair. Mrs. Jones is called the 'Black Patti.'"

The African American press had little to say about the Tennessee Jubilee Singers until they returned to the States in February 1889. A detailed account of their West Indies tour is preserved in an interview with Will H. Pierce; it appeared later that year in consecutive issues of the *Indianapolis Freeman*:

> June 15, 1889:
> "We left New York on August 2d [1888] on the steamer *Athos*, we arrived at Kingston, Jamaica on the 10th [and] we opened at the Royal Theatre on Monday evening the 12th to overcrowded house. We had the patronage of his excellency, Hon. J. C. Robinson, Governor and Lady Robinson."
> "How long did you remain in Jamaica?"

"We gave sixty performances in Jamaica altogether then we traveled through the Windward Islands playing to packed houses, after which we crossed the Isthmus of Panama, stopping at Aspinwall, where we played a week at the celebrated Sarah Bernhardt Theatre which was the handsomest theatre I have ever seen and I have visited the finest in America. Then we played in Panama where we had the most cultured audiences of our tour, we played here for two weeks, this is also the place where Madame Jones was first styled the Black Patti. We were entertained here by Signior Lucia Famori. Mr. Louis L. Brown the Baritone of the troup and vocal director (who allow me to remark right here) is undoubtedly the finest baritone singer who ever left the American shores. In Panama he was styled as an artist of the Italian school. By the critics he was called the Black Mario, Folio, Dragmia, and several others of the Italian school. One of the papers went so far as to say that he was a greater artist than Santely, England's great bouffe baritone. Everywhere he was received as one of the favorites of the company. Mme Jones was a success such as never been achieved by a colored soprano in this section. Nightly the stage was perfectly covered with floral tributes presented by the ladies, she also received seven solid gold medals during the tour."

"I noticed that Miss Anna Smith left shortly after you had been abroad, what was the cause?"

"She was engaged as an accompanist and not being able to handle our music she was of course dismissed to our sad regret."

June 29, 1889:

"After leaving Panama, where did you next go?"

"We then went to Colon for the second engagement, then we went to Trinidad. Here we were tendered a reception in the Princess Building. There were about 1,200 people at this reception and 500 couples took part in the grand march. We next went to Barbadoes, where we were tendered a reception at the hands of Hon. Sir Conrad Reeves. From here we went up in the Dutch land, or what is better known as Dutch Guiana, playing a week to people who could not understand us."

"From here we went to Demarara [*sic*, Demerara, i.e., British Guiana]. This is where we first met with the green eyed monster of this country, prejudice."

"In what way did these people show prejudice?"

"The night we opened we had eighty people in the house. When our manager went upon the stage and told the audience that he would not permit his company to be insulted, that the company had a good backing and money enough to pay our way, that we would give another concert on Monday evening and if we don't have a good audience, we would not give any more concerts here. On Monday evening the house was packed."

"From here we went to St. Kitts. We were now enroute for our native country, America. Here we played two nights to overflowing houses and would have remained longer but our steamer sailed for America on the third day."

"How do you think your company compared with those that have been abroad before?"

"I do not think there was ever a company that went from America doing the same line of work that could be compared with us."

"You see we had a chorus that sang Jubilee selections, a quartette that sang operatic selections besides a high class of solos."

"How long were you abroad?"

"Six months."

"Giving a rough estimate, how much do you think the manager cleared?"

"I should say $4,000 in American money, besides our expenses were high, we traveling everywhere first-class."

"How do the people there compare with the American Negroes intellectually?"

"As a mass there is no comparison, but they are greatly mixed. There is what they call the Creole Spaniards and the Collies [*sic*].

"The Creole Spaniards like a noise. Chorus singing seems to be their favorite, but the Colliers like the solos, and secular music."

"Mr. Louis L. Brown was a great favorite among this class. The low class are called niggers there, the same as the high class here. They are particularly fond of the humorist, and a man does not have to be much of a comedian to set them wild. High tragedy would go there for they like something excitable."

July 13, 1889:

"Who was in your choruses?"

"Miss Hattie Brown, Baltimore; Miss Kate Johnson, New York; Mr. Joseph G. Stevens, Detroit; Mr. John H. Woolford, Philadelphia, and the solo singers used to sing with them on certain selections. The chorus was very nicely trained by Prof. A. K. LaRue, who was accompanist and musical director."

"I suppose you had a great deal of fun?"

"No end of it; it would have amused you to see us riding from Kingston to New Castle on small mules. Well you would have burst your sides had you noticed 'Lew' Brown and myself hitching our mules together and then trying to drag Miss Jones' and Miss Brown's behind us. But the funny thing was at St. Anns Bay, our manager had a guarantee for a packed house to play at court house."

"He sent Mr. Jones in advance with the advertising, the distance was fifteen miles, and Mr. Jones had often boasted of his superb horsemanship. He started on a two year old filly, which had not been broken to the saddle. He had been gone about two hours when we discovered him coming back leading the horse, covered with mud from head to foot. The horse had evidently been trying to ride Mr. Jones."

"Our experience as sailors we found had been sadly neglected. After leaving port generally the only food that was consumed by most of the party was soup, but our party seemed to take great delight in feeding the fishes."

"Mr. Jones seemed to have a particular fancy for it."

"We all learned to play lawn tennis while aboard. Mr. Woolford became such an expert at the game that he won a prize at the Queen's Park races in Demorara."

"The ladies, too, desired to eat up all the sugar cane on the island. Miss Jones appeared to have a special contract."

"I never will forget the day that I went to the Jewish synagogue and was thrown out by one of the Rabbis, at the same time being reminded by him that you can never enter with shoes on. Not being desirous of exposing my dogs, I, of course, stayed out, and I might tell you a hundred such instances, but time will not permit me."

"I heard a little something about your manager misrepresenting his company, claiming that they were traveling in the interest of a school in the South. Is this true?"

"Yes, we were represented as one of the original Tennessee Singers Co., and I, myself, have never been to Tennessee as yet. I reside in Bedford, Mass., when at home, and that is quite a distance from Tennessee.

"Smith was one of the toughest managers that I have ever had any dealings with. Our contract was signed to sing three nights a week, and we sang every night in the week and Sunday nights for a change, and now and then a matinee was thrown in. It was also inserted in contracts that we would receive full pay at all times except when at quarantine, or in case of fire. At Barbadoes on the 8th of last November, we lay at quarantine one hour, and he deducted one week's salary."

"From the time we left St. Kitts, his motive was to send us home on the Commonwealth and he meet us in New York, but that did not work. He then made us work our way home, giving three concerts at Trinidad, two at St. Kitts to big business, for which we received nothing but our boat fares. He would frequently give benefits for different members of the company, but he always took the money and we got the benefit of his spending it."

"I will say for the people of the West Indies they are the most hospitable that I have had the pleasure of meeting. You are always welcome to their homes, their carriages are at your disposal, in fact their hearts are open to you."

"We at last arrived in New York, last February, and shortly after, our company disbanded."

"I expect to visit West Indies and Central America again, but if I ever go with Jim Smith I hope to be under the influence of chloroform."

In closing, the interviewer thanked Will H. Pierce "for giving readers of the *Freeman* a sketch of The Tennessee Concert Company's trip abroad, and for exposing the rascality of

James R. Smith. This man took advantage of a class of poor people in one country by using a poor people in another country as an inducement. These kind of men should be exposed, for the white man has been robbing his colored brother all his days and it is time it ended."

Reviews in various West Indian newspapers confirm that J. R. Smith had been handing out a completely bogus story, incorporating historical details of the original Fisk Jubilee Singers' tours to lend verisimilitude to his false claim that the Tennessee Jubilee Singers had sung "before all the Crowned Heads of Europe" and were in their "Fifteenth Annual Season" as a spin-off from the original Fisk troupe. In a lofty speech before each concert, Smith would explain how, in 1873, the Fisk Jubilee Singers had split into three factions, "one of which, containing three members of the original Jubilee Band of singers, is now in our midst."[18]

The name "Tennessee Jubilee Singers" helped cinch Smith's deceit. "Rhode Island Jubilee Singers" would have been more appropriate. The troupe's principal vocalists were all from the Northeast, and they reflected the high quality of vocal training that could be obtained in that region. Indeed, they were fully capable of succeeding on their own merits. West Indian newspapers gave rhapsodic reviews of their performances, declaring the Tennessee Jubilee Singers the finest group of vocalists that had ever visited the Caribbean. Their jubilee choruses made a distinct impression on West Indian audiences. In Jamaica, the *Colonial Standard* wrote: "The Camp Meeting songs, though to the unaccustomed ear they seem at first somewhat grotesque and incongruous, had a quaint charm of tender sentiment and melodious expression, which in the end captivated the hearts of the audience . . . there was an exquisite blending of sweet harmony and clear, effective enunciation."[19]

The Port-of-Spain Gazette was particularly struck by the body movements which accompanied the jubilee choruses:

> [T]heir Choruses have come upon us as a revelation and a surprise. When heard for the first time their performances produce what is so great a desideratum in modern existence a new sensation, and we must add, one of the most piquant and delicious kind. In the Choruses, particularly, the exhilarating and pleasing effect is quite unexpected, of the happy expression of quaint, vigorous, original African feeling controlled, harmonised and refined under the powerful influence of civilized musical science . . . The two lady-singers in the Choruses are good musicians; their movements whilst singing are quite a novelty and very amusing. They are a civilized edition of the more demonstrative and coarse gesticulations of old negro camp-meetings, in their ecstatic fervor. With the ladies the movements are a lively and graceful combination of what might otherwise be a jerk or a sway, and the effect is one of quite taking surprise. In listening to and seeing the movements of the singers we find the spicy originality of negro-minstrelsy, made fit for the educated eyes and ears of the refined occupants of the drawing room.[20]

The Georgetown, Demerara *Daily Chronicle* confirmed, "The bodies of the singers sway in time with the music and . . . they put their whole heart and soul into it . . . They are a living protest against modern namby-pambyism."[21] A review in Kingston, Jamaica's *Daily Gleaner* observed, "Of the choruses, all were given with perfect time and harmony, carefully studied inflection and precision which characterise the vocalization of this excellent company of singers. The most noticeable was perhaps Roll, Jordan, Roll, though much applause followed the amusing Mary Had A Little Lamb, with a chromatic scale of 'bleats.' "[22]

The company's featured soloists also captivated their West Indian audiences. The December 15, 1888, edition of the Georgetown *Daily*

Chronicle expressed the opinion that the Tennessee Jubilee Singers' reputation in the West Indies "largely rests with the two principal vocalists, Mme. Mathilda S. Jones and Mr. Louis L. Brown." The reviewer went on to note, "[T]he former is described as 'The Black Patti.' But the designation does injustice to the lady. Possessed of few of the airs and graces of a petted prima donna, she is pre-eminently a platform singer; and though her voice is not distinguished by the inherent sweetness of Adelina Patti's, it has much of the bravura . . . and it is withal well-trained, of extensive register, and remarkable for clear enunciation."

Following the Tennessee Jubilee Singers' return to New York, the first substantial notice of Matilda S. Jones in the African American press was an article by Florence Williams in the February 16, 1889, edition of the *New York Age.* Florence Williams was a black newspaper critic and musical entrepreneur. Under the headline, "A Singer's Triumph—Laurels Won by Madame Matilda S. Jones in the West Indies and Central America," she reported:

> Mme. Matilda S. Jones has returned from the West Indies and Central America, where she went under the managing Bureau of Abbey and Grau of this city last August. She brings home a large number of testimonials of her success in the German, Spanish and English languages. She sang in over 26 towns and cities, ranging from 2 to 42 nights in succession in one place. This is doing remarkably well. I cannot cite an instance where a colored singer has had such a run of success and still left behind the enthusiasm that was instilled upon presentation. It was at Kingston, Jamaica, that her triumph was established. For 42 nights she held her audience spellbound, and on leaving the hall was compelled to go between two files of officers in order to reach her hotel. So great was the enthusiasm of the people, that they would have raised her from the ground and carried her on their broad shoulders to her destination. At one time it required the efforts of 60 policemen to quiet the applause, which lasted for 30 minutes. On another occasion the company was unable to carry on the concert and was compelled to break it up so deafening were the shouts for the "Black Patti," as they called her.
>
> Mme. Jones was well decorated. She received eight medals and three necklaces made from native gold and of native workmanship. She also received from the coolies two bracelets of solid silver of fine workmanship and eight sovereigns from Colon to be converted into a medal, she leaving too soon for the work to be done. The medals and necklaces were presented to her by the highest officials of the different places, such as His Excellency Sir William Robinson, K. C. M. C.; Lady Robinson and His Worship, the Mayor of Port of Spain. The Generals, Counselors, Governors and Majors of the different islands seemed to take great delight in presenting to Mme. Jones the many tokens of appreciation in the name of the citizens. That Mme. Jones has established a reputation that cannot be gainsaid is readily seen by the hundred press notices that the Tennessee Jubilee Singers' Company have in their possession. To attempt to describe in print the excellency of this prima donna would be a failure.

Apparently, the New York managing bureau of Abbey and Grau had contracted J. R. Smith to manage the West Indian tour. Henry Abbey, the Abbey of Abbey and Grau, also managed Adelina Patti, i.e., "the white Patti," during her American tours.

On March 11, 1889, J. R. Smith promoted a concert at Steinway Hall in New York "for the benefit of the Kennesaw Educational Fund of Georgia." L. L. Brown appeared on the bill, and local soloist Cora Lee Watson assumed the mantle of "Colored Patti."[23] She "attempted the flower song from 'Faust.'"[24] In addition, "Mr. James Jackson played the guitar with all the ease and skill borne of years of practice. Mr. Owens King gave his usual bill of funny imitations. The De Wolfe sisters came bouncing, tripping, charming and full of chic." Finally, there was the Kennesaw Quartet, "a creditable combination that mingles the sentimental with plantation melodies."[25]

It came out in the next week's *Age* that J. R. Smith had neglected to pay the artists who took part in the Kennesaw Educational Fund concert. While L. L. Brown "expressed himself disgusted and disappointed with those concerned," Florence Williams chalked it up to "The Ways Of The World."[26] In the meantime, J. R. Smith had arranged for the Tennessee Jubilee Singers to reconvene in New York City on April 3, 1889, for a "Welcome Home" concert at Mount Olivet Baptist Church. The concert came off as advertised, and it was positively reviewed in the April 6, 1889, edition of the *Age:*

> Mt. Olivet Baptist Church was well filled on Wednesday night when the Tennessee Concert Company made their collective debut before a Metropolitan audience. The program varied between ballads, love ditties and plantation melodies. The jubilee songs were rendered by a sextet and met with more favor than the classical selections. Mme. Matilda S. Jones received an ovation. Her voice is of good volume, excellently managed, and her trills well done. Mr. L. L. Brown, as a polished baritone, stands among our foremost artists. His shading and articulation showed to good advantage. Mr. Pierce's tenor is of that delicate order that ranks as a jewel in parlors.

The Mount Olivet concert concluded J. R. Smith's festering relationship with the Tennessee Jubilee Singers. Florence Williams broke the news in the *New York Age* of April 13, 1889:

> Mr. Smith claims that the singers have become swell-headed and did not wish to accord him any credit whatever for his share in bringing them before the world. The company having gained recognition as singers under his management, then rebelled against him and thus broke their contract. In talking with two of the disbanded artists I find there is another version of the story. Mr. Brown, the tenor, and Miss Kate Johnson, the alto, are the only members of the company now in the city. They both claim that the company had been duped by the wiley ways of the manager. The contract was not

MOUNT OLIVET
BAPTIST CHURCH,
53rd Street, near Seventh Avenue,
(REV. D. W. WISHER, PASTOR).
Wednesday Evening, April 3d,
JAS. R. SMITH, Manager.

GRAND CONCERT
For the purpose of extending a welcome home to the
Tennessee Concert Company
After a most successful South American and West Indian tour, where they swept the "Carribeans," and illustrated the wonderful strides and progress which is being made by the Colored Race of America.
The only Company which has shown the World the
TRUE ART OF HARMONY.
THE COMPANY:
MME. MATILDA S. JONES
(The Black Patti).
Miss India R. Bell,
Miss Kate Johnson,
Miss Abbie Jerley,
Mr. Lewis L. Brown,
Mr. W. Pierce.
Mr. W. J. Strathmore,
Mr. G. H. Johnson,
Mr. D. R. Jones,
Mr. J. H. Woolford.
Prof. A. K. LA RUE, Pianist.
The TENNESSEANS on this occasion will be augmented by extra selected talent.
The Proceeds from the above Concert to be applied to
The Current Expense Fund of Mt. Olivet Baptist Church.
Board of Trustees:
T. H. Woody, President; J. Arthur Barrett, Sec. J. A. Comey, Treas.; H. L. Jones, Lewis Bird, C. H. Smith, J. C. Mosely, J. O. Overhizer, W. H Isaacs.
ADMISSION, - 50 CENTS.
CHILDREN, - 25 CENTS.
No Reserved Seats.
Tickets to be obtained from members of the above church, also at the doors on the evening of the concert.
mh23 2t

New York Age, *March 23, 1889.*

broken by any action of company, but by the manager. It appears that according to the agreement, traveling expenses including board were to be paid from the receipts of the concerts by the manager, but up to the rupture the boarding house proprietors have failed to receive the moneys as promised. When Miss Johnson called upon Mr. Smith for the necessary money to pay her board, she was told by that gentleman to go and hustle. At this remark Miss Johnson took umbrage and told the manager that it was undignified and not in keeping with the proprieties. Mr. Brown was the next applicant for money and they had it out in the style of "nip and tuck." This so astounded Mr. Smith that he thought it was wise to sell out his rights in the concert to be held at Mt. Olivet Church to a Col. Dusenbery. When the company heard of this traction they grew suspicious and vowed that not one of them would go upon the platform until their just claims were settled. After much contention the matter was settled by paying the artists.

When Mr. Smith found out upon the turning over of the receipts by Dusenbery that he had been outwitted he denounced the company as ingrates and surrendered them their right to act for themselves. The company will go forth to win upon their own merits without their white manager, the same as the Stewart Concert Company and the Loudin Fisk Jubilee Singers. A persimmon is not a plum, although it looks like one. And things are indeed not what they seem.

After breaking with J. R. Smith, Matilda S. Jones, L. L. Brown and Will H. Pierce appeared with the Excelsior Quartette, one of the most successful black professional vocal harmony groups of the era, and other popular stars at Dockstader's Theater on Broadway, where they were billed as "The Georgia Minstrels."

• ***April 13, 1889:*** "The Georgia Minstrels have drawn good houses at Dockstader's all this week, commencing with a sacred concert on Sunday evening. Mr. L. L. Brown, the phenomenal baritone, the charming DeWolff sisters, Mr. W. H. Pierce, tenor; the popular Excelsior Quartet; Wesley B. Morris, Billy Wilson, H. [Horace] Weston in banjo selections; Mr. Jones, vocalist; Mr. Lee Allen, tenor; W. Owens King, mimic; and Mrs. Matilda S. Jones comprised the company. Each selection was well given and appreciated. J. H. Booker was stage manager and Wm. Coleman, interlocutor" (*New York Age*).

• ***April 13, 1889:*** "Dockstader's Theatre was opened for a week April 8 by a Georgia Minstrels troupe, whose inaugural performance was fairly attended. They give a melange of jubilee and minstrel business combined, and the genuineness of the colored coterie makes the entertainment interesting" (*New York Age*).

• ***April 20, 1889:*** "It may be surprising to note the names of some of the artists who appeared in the Georgia Minstrels in New York last week. An actor's lot is not a happy one; up today and down tomorrow" (*Indianapolis Freeman*).

Despite the *Freeman's* sensitivity to the "Georgia Minstrels" rubric, there is nothing to indicate that Matilda S. Jones and her fellow Tennessee Jubilee Singers were "down," or that they compromised their repertoire or performance style in any way while performing at Dockstader's Theater.

In hometown Providence, Rhode Island, after the Georgia Minstrels date, Matilda S. Jones received another medal, "this time from the Irish patriots of the Parnell Association of Providence . . . Her sweet strains of Irish songs touched their patriotic spirit."[27] Florence Williams began to handle Matilda S. Jones's bookings during this time, and she reported on May 11, 1889, that her client had just completed a week of engagements in Philadelphia. Shortly thereafter, Matilda S. Jones, L. L. Brown, and Will H. Pierce agreed to make a "short Southern tour" under the management of B. F. Lightfoot, a black dramatic actor and elocutionist, also from Providence, Rhode Island.[28]

• ***May 18, 1889:*** "The first of the Southern series of concerts given under the management of Mr. B. F. Lightfoot, took place at the Soldier's

Home Theatre, Hampton, Va., May 13th. The artists were Mme. M. S. Jones, prima donna soprano; Mr. Louis L. Brown, baritone; and Mr. B. F. Lightfoot, elocutionist. The Hampton Normal School Quartette, Miss M. Hamlin, accompanist, [also participated] . . . The house was well filled . . . The Normal School Quartette sang with good harmony and their plantation melodies pleased very well. Mr. Louis L. Brown appeared for the first time here and made a decided hit. He opened with 'Hybria Cretan' which was rendered in a finished manner. His tones were pure, clear and deep. Mme Jones appeared here about ten days before and had won a place in the hearts of the audience, so she had no trouble in holding them with her sweet voice . . . [The following day the] same company gave a successful concert at the Court House" (*Indianapolis Freeman*).

• ***June 15, 1889:*** "The Lightfoot Concert party with Mme Jones and Mr. Pierce in the company, gave three successful concerts last week, two in Hampton and one in Norfolk. This week they appear in Portsmouth and Chesapeake City [all in the Tidewater section of Virginia]" (*Indianapolis Freeman*).

• ***June 22, 1889:*** "Mme Jones, Mr. Will Pierce, Mr. B. F. Lightfoot and Mr. D. R. Jones are at present in Baltimore where they will give two concerts for the benefit of Asbury M. E. Church on the 26th and 27th inst. Mr. Louis L. Brown, baritone, joins the company here" (*Indianapolis Freeman*).

• ***July 13, 1889:*** "Two Star concerts were given at the Asbury M. E. church, Baltimore, under the management of Mr. D. R. Jones. The artists were Mme. M. S. Jones, soprano, Mr. Will H. Pierce, tenor, Mr. B. F. Lightfoot, elocutionist. The Phoenetic Quartette of Baltimore, composed of Messrs. Dungee, Hawkins, Nichols and Lee, Mr. Charles Dungee, accompanist. The audience was small both evenings yet the artists gave an exceedingly fine concert. Mme. Jones was in excellent voice and made a decided hit, as did Mr. Will H. Pierce, his topical and humorous songs kept the audience in a roar of laughter. Mr. B. F. Lightfoot was a success. The Quartette had the good taste to select glees that were pleasing to the audience . . . They are to give another concert at the Centennial A.M.E. Church on the 4th and then close their spring season" (*Indianapolis Freeman*).

• ***July 27, 1889 (New York City):*** "Musical and Dramatic," "Mr. W. H. Pierce is doing so well in Baltimore that he has not returned to the city . . . Mr. and Mrs. Jones passed through the city on their way home from Baltimore, where they have been giving a series of concerts. Mme Jones was tendered a fine reception . . . at the residence of Mr. and Mrs. Elijah Johnson . . . one of the wealthiest colored men in Baltimore . . . Mme Jones gave her farewell concert at North Street Baptist Church to a large and enthusiastic audience. After the concert a committee requested her to delay her departure, as the church people wished to tender her a reception. But being pressed for time, she was compelled to decline and hasten to this city to attend to business relating to her trip to the West Indies" (*New York Age*).

Matilda S. Jones had been recruited by Florence Williams to head up a new venture, the New York Star Concert Company, through which Williams hoped to duplicate the Tennessee Jubilee Singers' original triumphs in the West Indies. On October 15, 1889, the New York Star Concert Company gave a "Farewell Concert" at Zion A.M.E. Church in Greenwich Village; it fetched a brief review in the October 19, 1889, edition of the *Age*: "The concert . . . was one of the finest ever given in this city. The ease and grace of Mme. Jones' execution was something wonderful. It is to be regretted that there were not more present to hear her, but when it is remembered that there was a rally at the church Sunday, lecture of Monday night and the short notice, it is easily accounted for."

The October 26, 1889, edition of the *New York Age* confirmed that Florence Williams and her New York Star Company were "Off for the West Indies," but without their star attraction:

> On Sunday last, at 8 A.M., the New York Star Concert Company sailed by the Atlas steamship *Athos* for Kingston Jamaica. The party consisted of eight persons, five gentlemen and three ladies, including Miss Florence Williams, the manager of the company.
>
> Miss Williams was quite unfortunate on the day the steamship was advertised to sail in losing three important members of her troupe—Mme. Matilda S. Jones of Providence and Mr. and Mrs. Randolph of New York, who waited until the last hours before sailing to inform Miss Williams that they would not fulfill the conditions of their contracts. Mme. Jones had been extensively advertised in the West Indies as the star of the combination and her defection at the last moment put the manager at great disadvantage and expense. Mme. Allen of New York was secured to fill Mme. Jones' place. She has a splendid soprano voice, of high register, sweet tone and thorough culture. Mr. Randolph was the pianist of the troupe, and by refusing to fill his engagement Miss Williams was compelled to sail without having secured any one to fulfill his important place.

The same news was given a more negative slant in the November 9, 1889, edition of the *Freeman*:

> On Sunday A.M. Oct. 20th a concert company under the management of Miss Florence Williams of the *New York Age,* known as the New York Star Concert Company sailed by steamship *Athos* for Kingston, Jamaica, they intend to visit West Indies, South and Central America. Mme. M. S. Jones, one of the finest Prima Donna's of the race styled "Black Patti" was to have gone as star. But we are informed owning to a refusal on the part of the manager of the company to sign some certain contract the Mme. would not leave her home at Providence, R. I. So Mme. Allen of New York a singer of very little Providence was engaged to fill her place. Mr. and Mrs. Randolph who was also to [go] with the party accepted an engagement to travel in Canada; however, a party of eight was made up; those we know of are Miss India Bell of Providence, Messrs. Jerry Lightfoot, and W. Watts, New Bedford, Mass. Success to them.

The subsequent struggles of Florence Williams and her New York Star Concert Company were duly recorded in the *Freeman* and the *Age*.

• ***November 23, 1889:*** "A letter from a citizen of Kingston, Jamaica says that the New York Star Company is having a very poor season, and that the citizens are by no means pleased with the company, with the exception of Miss Allen and Mr. Watts" (*Indianapolis Freeman*).

• ***December 7, 1889:*** "The Kingston, Jamaica *Post* of Nov. 2, in referring to the two performances of the New York Concert Company, of which Miss Florence Williams of [New York] is manager, and who left New York for the West Indies on October 20, speak in the very highest praise of Mme Allen, the star of the troupe, of Mr. Brown, the bone soloist, and of Miss India Bell, the mezzo soprano. From the general tenor of the *Post*'s review of the first two performances . . . the company promises to have a reasonably successful tour in the West Indies" (*New York Age*).

Earlier reports in the *Age* shed some light on "Mr. Brown, the bone soloist." It was noted on May 11, 1889, that, "Mr. George W. Brown of Providence, R.I., is the only bone soloist imitator that the race has. He is adept in this role." And on September 28, 1889, it was reiterated: "The only bone soloist who imitates the washer woman, horse-cars, cow-bells and rain drops with any exactness and precision is George Brown. It is indeed a treat to hear him."

In spite of the positive press reports, the New York Concert Company was foundering. Before the end of 1889, Florence Williams was compelled to leave troupe members to fend for themselves in Kingston while she returned to New York to recruit new talent.

• ***December 14, 1889:*** "Miss Florence Williams, manager of the New York Concert Company, which sailed for the West Indies on October 20th, is expected to arrive in New York on Wednesday in search of some new talent for her company, which does not seem to be giving entire satisfaction" (*Indianapolis Freeman*).

• ***December 14, 1989:*** "Mr. Louis L. Brown, of Green's minstrels, who is considered by many musical critics as being the finest colored baritone singer in America, is negotiating for a trip to the West Indies. Mr. Brown proved a success in that country on his previous tour, which ended last February" (*Indianapolis Freeman*).

• ***December 21, 1889:*** "There are two parties negotiating with Mme Mathilda S. Jones, prima donna, for a trip to the West Indies & South America and if terms can be agreed upon she will sail in a few days with her own company" (*Indianapolis Freeman*).

• ***February 1, 1890:*** "Miss Williams' Troupe," "A Kingston Merchant Tells of the Misconduct of the Men in Jamaica": To the Editor of the *New York Age:* "In justice to Miss Florence Williams, I have been forced to forward to you these lines with the hope that you will give them a place in your most valuable paper. Some four months ago I became acquainted by letters with Miss Williams. I learned that it was her intention to bring a troupe of singers out to Jamaica. I advised her that if she brought a first class company down she would be almost certain of success. She then appointed me as one of her agents and as such I advanced the passage money for the company out to Jamaica. To my surprise and utter dissatisfaction, nearly all of them, with the exception of Madame Allen, Miss Bell and Mr. Brown, turned out a complete failure. Two or three performances were given, but failed on account of the inefficiency of the men. Mr. Watts instantly became the leader of the men, who followed him and took to giving entertainment in rum shops and bar-rooms, which lowered the company to such an extent that Miss Williams became entirely helpless. I assure you that I have never witnessed such unmanly conduct as that displayed by Watts towards the women who had traveled from so far with him . . . But this is not all. He managed by begging and by the aid of the Odd Fellows, to get some £20, but he simply cleared out and left his friends in the lurch. Miss Williams found out her mistake when it was too late and had to start by the aid of a friend, whom I will not name, to get the right people to augment the number of those she has left behind her, and where the friends she made during her short stay are anxiously waiting to see her reap the reward she deserves, for no mistake about it she is a brave little woman."

"A. E. Lunan, Kingston, Jamaica, Jan. 6" (*New York Age*).

• ***February 8, 1890:*** "A Successful Singer," "Some Facts Concerning Mme. Matilda S. Jones," "Mme. Matilda S. Jones has had a more extended experience, considering her short career as a singer, than any of the present lyric stars who have graced the boards since the time of the Black Swan [Elizabeth Taylor Greenfield] . . . Since her return from abroad, being of a progressive mind as well as one of those who believe that you can't learn too much, she placed herself under the tuition of an Italian and French singer of some renown, Senora Adeil Byround de Combries. She will no doubt add these new acquirements to her program on her second trip abroad" ("Fay," *New York Age*).

• ***February 22, 1890:*** "J. R. Smith, who managed the Tennessee Jubilee Singers during their West Indian tour, and of whom it is said, did not use the troupe well, is trying to negotiate with some of the same people for a trip to England,

Germany and the West Indies. A burnt child dreads the fire, and yet there are those who will jump at the idea, simply because Smith is a white man" (*Indianapolis Freeman*).

Finally, Florence Williams was able to secure what she had been after all along—the services of Matilda Sissieretta Jones, the Black Patti.

• ***March 22, 1890:*** "Off For The West Indies," "After many exasperating delays, Miss Florence Williams left New York for the second time last week with the New York Concert Company. Those of the troupe were Mr. David R. Jones [*sic*], Mme Mathilda Jones, leading soprano, and Mr. Jackson, the pianist, all of Providence. Mr. Louis L. Brown, baritone; Mr. Boswick, basso; and Miss Katie Johnson, alto soloist and jubilee singer... It took some very lively work to get off upon such short notice, but it was accomplished, with the exception of getting Mr. W. H. Pierce, tenor of Baltimore, in readiness. Three members of the company originally taken to the West Indies by Miss Williams are in Kingston. They are Mme Allen, Miss India Bell and Mr. Brown. It is not known when the company will return to New York" (*New York Age*).

By the time they reached Kingston, the New York Concert Company had reverted to the name associated with Matilda S. Jones's initial West Indian triumphs, the Tennessee Jubilee Singers.

• ***April 11, 1890:*** "Some of Our Professionals," "The Tennessee Jubilee Star Singers, Miss Florence Williams, manager, reached Kingston, Jamaica, West Indies, March 20, and were enthusiastically received" (*Detroit Plaindealer*).

• ***May 3, 1890:*** "Miss Williams' Company Sings Before Jamaicans," "Condensed from the *Jamaica Post* (April 1)," "Saturday night's concert was perfect in every respect. It opened with a piano solo by Mr. Jackson, the pianist of the company... After his piano solo the company appeared in force and sang the Lord's Prayer. Miss Katie Johnson who is a favorite was received with applause when she stepped forward to sing 'Till the Snow-flakes come again.' She is an alto of great range and power and is especially rich in the lower notes... Next followed the jubilee song entitled 'Judgement will find you so,' by the company...

A burst of applause announced the appearance of Madame Jones who was prettily dressed in blue velvet faced with a swansdown. She had chosen 'When the blue birds build again,' a song which showed her phenomenal range of voice... Naturally rich and full, it is cultivated to the highest pitch and her compass, her mastery over every note, her expression, her trills and shakes, tell at once why she has been termed, and rightfully termed, the Patti of her race. As an encore she gave 'No sir,' and it fairly brought down the house... Next came Mr. L. L. Brown, a first class baritone, with the pathetic song, 'Only to see her face.'... Miss India Bell sang alone in 'Mottoes that are framed upon the wall.'...

Several other songs and duets were given and then the long evening came to a close by the entire company giving a finished rendition of 'God save the Queen' " (*New York Age*).

• ***May 24, 1890 (Kingston, Jamaica, West Indies):*** "Miss Williams Writes About the Tour of the Tennessee Jubilee Singers in Jamaica—Their Concerts in Kingston and Neighboring Towns": "May 1—The Star Tennessee Jubilee Singers are still holding their own in Kingston, where they have been giving concerts since the 22nd of March, to good houses. They have only sung out of Kingston twice since they opened here... The first place played at out of town was Old Harbor, a town made famous by the constant coming of visitors to view the spot where Christopher Columbus first landed... Mr. L. L. Brown has many admirers, and the names of both Brown and Mme Jones are constantly upon the lips of the people. Mme Allen has also won many friends, who delight to hear her sing. Miss Katie Johnson, who is one of the best in her line, receives a favorable comment from the press at every performance. We sang the following day at Port Royal, having his Honor, Rodney M. Lloyd and staff among the audience" (Florence Williams, *New York Age*).

• ***June 14, 1890 (New York City):*** "Mr. R. D. Jones, one of the managers of the Tennessee Jubilee Singers, arrived here on Tuesday of last week and left on Thursday . . . taking some new talent, among them W. H. Pierce and Miss Brown of Baltimore, and Miss Alice M. Franklin, elocutionist and dramatic specialist. Mr. Jones brought particulars of the death of Mr. L. L. Brown at Kingston" (*New York Age*).

• ***September 13, 1890:*** "The citizens of Kingston, Jamaica, W.I. propose the erection of a memorial tablet to the late Louis L. Brown, Esq., late of Philadelphia, who in his lifetime, was one of the greatest baritone singers the race had produced. His recent death was a sad blow to his many friends in this country and abroad, where he had achieved a great reputation and won golden encomiums" (*Indianapolis Freeman*).

• ***November 1, 1890:*** "A letter from R. D. Jones, one of the managers of the Tennessee Jubilee troupe, of which his wife is star, tells of the success of the company in Haiti. He reports all of the company are well, with the exception of Miss India Bell, of Providence, R.I., who is not expected to live. George W. Brown and Will H. Pierce are also members of this company. They will probably visit England and Cuba before returning" (*Indianapolis Freeman*).

The mysterious death of L. L. Brown and the report of India Bell's life-threatening illness are sober reminders that the 1890s foreign tours of African American jubilee troupes were not made on flowery beds of ease.

• ***December 27, 1890:*** "The Tennessee Jubilee Singers, Mme Mathilda S. Jones, leading soprano, sang at the President's Palace in Port-au-Prince, Hayti, November 27th" (*Cleveland Gazette*).

• ***January 31, 1891:*** "*Lightbourn's Mail Notes* of St. Thomas, W.I., in its issue of January 8, contains the following: The Allemania from Haiti brought to our shores yesterday Mme Mathilda S. Jones and her talented company of Jubilee Singers. On repeated occasions we have had the pleasure of mentioning the great success which this new celebrated prima donna has attained in the West Indies, in fact each island has been but a fresh field in which to gather laurels. It has now been two or three years since Madame Jones made her debut before a West Indian audience at Jamaica and starred. In Haiti she and her company have just met with great success and we hope that a portion is in store for them here" (*Indianapolis Freeman*).

• ***February 14, 1891:*** "J. B. Healy, of Healy & Bigelow, has returned from a ten weeks' trip to the West Indies, where he had the satisfaction of witnessing the triumph of two of his medicine companies. Mr. Healy . . . left one troupe at Kingston and a second touring the interior of the island . . . A third company is now in Bermuda, at Hamilton. Mr. Healy is to organize new troupes for Barbadoes, Trinidad and Demerara . . . While at Hayti he met Donovan & Lowanda's Circus, which, he says, has been quite prosperous . . . Mr. Healy adds that Americans will learn with interest of the remarkable success achieved in the West Indies during the past two or three years by Jones' Tennessee Jubilee Singers, headed by Mme. M. Sissieretta Jones, the colored prima donna, and her husband Dick Jones, formerly of the Narragansett Hotel, Providence, R.I. W. H. Pierce is also in the troupe. They have made big money, and Mme. Jones has been the recipient of numerous gold and jeweled medals, decorations, etc." (*New York Clipper*).

• ***May 1, 1891 (Port of Spain, Trinidad):*** "[The Tennessee Jubilee Singers] gave their first concert at the Prince's Building last night to a fairly well attended house . . . The Prima Donna, Madame Jones sung as sweetly as a nightingale and as the liquid melody rolled from her lips the audience sat spellbound only at the conclusion to break into deafening cheers and encores. She was literally covered with medals and on her head was the golden tiara studded with diamonds which had recently been presented to her in Demarara" (*Port of Spain Gazette*).

• ***July 17, 1891:*** "Another Colored Patti," "From the *New York Recorder,* July 7—The steamship *Muriel,* from St. Kitt's, which arrived in port yesterday, brought Mme. Mathilde Jones, the colored Patti, who has been known as the 'Sweet Singer of Tennessee,' and her opera company of twenty-eight, all colored. The Madame is quite dark and very handsome. She has just completed a tour of the West Indies, surprising the people with the sweetness of her Tennessee voice. Her husband is her agent. His duties are so numerous that he forgot to declare all of the company's baggage . . . Two express wagons were in waiting for the precious baggage, but not withstanding the sulphurous language of the drivers, two hours were consumed before matters were finally straightened out" (*Detroit Plaindealer*).

While revisiting the Black Patti's West Indian triumphs, an article in the August 29, 1891, edition of the *Freeman* also provided some more-or-less accurate background information, under the triple headline, "The Black Patti," "The Race's Most Brilliant Song Bird, Madame M. Sissieretta Jones," "From The Village Maid To The Proud Rank Of A Queen Of The Lyric Stage":

> This charming and celebrated singer was born Jan. 5th, 1868 [*sic*] at Portsmouth, Virginia. When very young Madame Jones displayed a great love for music . . . She commenced her instrumental education at the age of 15 at the Academy of Music, Providence, R.I., under the tutelage of Baroness Lacombe, an eminent Italian preceptor, and Mr. Monros, also eminent in the world of music.
>
> At 18 she commenced vocal training at the Conservatorium at Boston, where she made such rapid progress that she was at once pronounced America's future Afro-American Queen of Song.
>
> In 1887 being asked to sing at a grand entertainment for the benefit of the Parnell Fund before an audience of five thousand she carried the great gathering by storm, and had them, metaphorically speaking, at her feet, by her daring bewildering flights of matchless melody. She repeated her triumph shortly afterwards at the Boston Musical Hall at a grand Star concert directed by J. G. Burgen [*sic*] . . . She so distinguished herself that she was induced to make a tour of the chief cities of New England.
>
> She commenced her professional career in 1888 at Wallack's Theatre, New York City, where no other Afro-American artist had ever appeared, and from that day to this her career has been one chain of unbroken triumphs and vocal achievements. About this time William Piesen, musical director of the Little Tycoon Opera Company, having heard of the madame's fame, improved the first opportunity to hear her sing . . . He telegraphed Henry Abbey, the great manager of Patti . . . which resulted in her being secured for the great West Indian tour . . .
>
> Before entering upon her West Indian Trip she sang before all the newspaper critics of New York City. The *Times* spoke of her as a phenomenal singer without an equal in her race . . . The *New York Clipper* gave a glowing account of her, and gave her the name of the "Black Patti." On the 28th of July, 1888, she started on her West Indian trip, appearing first for two months in Kingstown [*sic*], Jamaica, where her success was very great. The trip lasted eight months, during which time she appeared in all the different colonies of the West Indies. Upon her return home to Providence she was received and feted in a manner due her exhalted triumphs . . .
>
> After needed recreation and rest she made a starring tour throughout the largest cities of the Union with unequivocal success. While on this trip she met Mr. Mikado, of Australia [*sic,* Orpheus McAdoo], who offered her a great consideration to visit the Indian Continent on a professional trip which, owing to a promise to return to the West Indies, she was compelled to decline. The story of her triumph, measured by years is a short one, but within the same time, we know of no Afro-American songstress who has so filled the measure of brilliant achievements upon the lyric stage.

During the fall of 1891 a decidedly less accurate Black Patti biography crept into the

Greatest Musical Attraction for the Season.
"BLACK PATTI!"
The Queen of Song.
Recalled again, and again. She sang "The Cow are in the Clover," very effectually, her upper notes being especially sweet. at the end received a grand ovation. N. Y. Herald,
She sings like Patti, without the slightest effort, her voice is well cultivated, her high notes enable her to effectually render the most difficult compositions.--N. Y. World.
Mme. Sissiereta Jones

Freeman, *June 17, 1893.*

columns of the African American press. Perhaps traceable to a mainstream paper, it seems to take up where J. R. Smith's mischievous pseudo-history of the Tennessee Jubilee Singers left off:

• ***November 22, 1891 (Baltimore, Maryland):*** "The Colored Patti," "November 6—Mme. Sissieretta Jones, called by her colored admirers, 'the colored Patti,' made her first appearance in a concert in Baltimore at the Trinity African Methodist Episcopal church, Linden avenue and Biddle street, last night. Mme. Jones possesses $3,000 worth of diamonds, and has received presents of various kinds. Last night she wore more than a dozen medals conferred by distinguished personages. She says she received medals as testimonials for her rare musical abilities from Queen Victoria, and King of Denmark, Dom Pedro, Charles Stewart Parnell and the President of Hayti. She was born in Cape Town, Africa, of full-blooded Africans, twenty-two years ago, and received her musical education in London. She has been a professional singer for five years, and has visited nearly every country on the globe. She possesses a rich soprano voice. The audience last night was large" (*Topeka Weekly Call*).

Sissieretta Jones was an unprecedented success in her first years as a professional African American prima donna. She was the first black female vocalist to gain international stardom. Her travels of the late 1880s and early 1890s opened the West Indies as a touring venue for other African American touring companies.

Other "Colored Pattis" and "Queens of Song," 1889

While Matilda S. Jones was making waves in the West Indies, Providence, Rhode Island's other, more established black prima donna, Flora Batson was also expanding her horizons. In the fall of 1888, Flora Batson launched a coast-to-coast tour of the United States. She spent the spring of 1889 traversing the Deep South, and by fall she was out in San Francisco. Madame Marie Selika, the third great black prima donna of the era, also made a sweeping tour of the southern states during 1889.[29]

• ***February 2, 1889:*** "Miss Flora Batson, The Colored Jenny Lind," "The greatest singer from the eight million of colored people in America will sing for Tulane Avenue Baptist Church Feb. 4;

Central Church, Feb. 5; Old Baptist Church, Feb. 6; Union Bethel Church, Feb. 7; Austerlitz Street Baptist Church, Feb. 8; Tulane Avenue Baptist Church, Feb. 11; Sixth Baptist Church, Felicity street, Feb. 12; St. Mark's Fourth Baptist Church, Feb. 13; St. James A.M.E. Church, Feb. 14. Tickets 25 cents" (*New Orleans Weekly Pelican*).

• ***February 23, 1889 (New Orleans, Louisiana):*** "After singing four nights this week in Mobile, Ala., to large houses, Miss Batson returns to our city and will sing at Zion Traveler's Church, Carrollton, this evening, Feb. 23; Winan's Chapel, Feb. 26; St. James, Feb. 27; Geddes' Hall, for benefit of Louisiana Orphan Asylum, Feb. 28; Sixth Baptist Church, Felicity street, Mar. 2; Town Hall, Gretna, March 10 or 12 . . . When the above dates are filled Miss Batson will have sung seventeen nights in New Orleans, and, as the interest increases, the number is likely to run up to twenty or thirty nights before the great 'Song Bird' is permitted to leave. It is the general verdict that her singing here has fully justified the magnificent notices of the eastern press" (*New Orleans Weekly Pelican*).

Note: Almost all of the Flora Batson appearances listed in the above two citations were in black neighborhood churches and social halls.

• ***March 2, 1889:*** "The Stage," "The Selika combination composed of Madame Selika, her husband Sampson W. Williams and Miss Hallie Q. Brown, have taken Savannah, Ga., by storm" (*Indianapolis Freeman*).

• ***March 2, 1889 (New Orleans, Louisiana):*** "Madame Marie Selika, prima donna soprano, supported by Miss H. Q. Brown, the renowned elocutionist; Mr. S. W. Williams, the baritone, and Mr. F. K. Burch, solo pianist, will arrive in the city in a few weeks—just prior to Mardi Gras, and will give several concerts, etc., before departure" (*New Orleans Weekly Pelican*).

• ***March 23, 1889:*** "The Crusade says Madame Selika is a Cherokee. We have heard she was a Creole. After all, she may be just 'plain common everyday colored people'" (*Indianapolis Freeman*).

• ***April 6, 1889:*** "It was reported and 'went the rounds of the press' that Madame Selika refused to sing in an Opera House, South, because the managers refused to sell first-class seats to colored people. At the same time she was being billed and heralded as a Cherokee. Now, the same thing is being said of Miss Flora Batson. The fact of the matter is they will all sing when the receipts justify it. Neither do they draw the color line on those who wish to hear them" (*Indianapolis Freeman*).

• ***April 20, 1889:*** "Manager and Mrs. Flora Batson Bergen, after a successful tour of all the leading cities of the South, left Nashville, Tenn., last week for Chicago, where they sang April 19 . . . The press of the South has praised Miss Batson's singing in very strong terms. As an old gentleman said in Memphis, 'She sings the devil right out of the white folks, and when you get the devil out of the white people they are just as good as colored people'" (*New York Age*).

• ***June 1, 1889:*** "The Stage," "Mme. Selika is still in the South. Last week she appeared to good houses in Alabama" (*Indianapolis Freeman*).

• ***July 13, 1889:*** "Mrs. Flora Batson-Bergen" "Her Great Success in Denver, Colorado," "Since Manager and Mrs. Bergen left New York last October they have traveled over 5000 miles, singing in all the leading cities of the South and West with unparalleled success. Mr. W. I. Powell of Philadelphia, the popular baritone and 'King of Fun,' joined the Bergen party at Chicago in April and he is making a great hit in the West. For the past five weeks 'The Queen of Song' and 'The King of Fun' have sung to good houses in Denver, in white and colored churches, Catholic and Protestant. Thrice they have been greeted by immense audiences in the Tabor Grand Opera House, and last week, after singing two nights for St. Mary's Cathedral, a church having over 4,000 members, so infatuated were the Catholics with Miss Bergen's singing, she was engaged to sing three solos at the Sunday evening service at the great Cathedral . . . The Rocky Mountain *Daily News* says 'her progress through the country has been one of continued triumph.' She will next be heard at Manitou Springs at the foot of Pike's Peak; then at Leadville and next at Salt Lake in the great Mormon Temple . . . After leaving Salt Lake the leading cities of California will be visited until San Francisco and the Golden Gate are reached and the name of Flora Batson shall have become a household word from the Atlantic to the Pacific" (*New York Age*).

• ***October 5, 1889 (San Francisco, California):*** "Miss Flora Batson made her first appearance before a California audience on Monday evening, Sept. 9, at the Third Baptist Church. A crowded house gave her a most hearty welcome. She also sang at Oakland and at Bethel A.M.E. and Zion A.M.E. Churches in this city . . . Her audiences were composed of the best people in the city, fully one-half being white. The Baptist Church is one of the finest in the city. It was handsomely decorated and the repeated encores and magnificent floral testimonials were but a slight indication of the hold she has upon the hearts of the people" (T. B. Morton, *New York Age*).

• ***December 27, 1889 (Topeka, Kansas):*** "Madame Selika, the world renowned prima donna, supported by Mr. L. W. Williams [*sic*], the colored baritone, gave two entertainments at the Metropolitan this week, Wednesday and Friday evenings, under the auspices of the Dispatch Band association. Mr. [*sic*] Selika is one of the finest singers it was ever our pleasure to hear, and the association did itself great credit in bringing such musical talent to our city, and our people did themselves and the association injustice and discredit by failing to crowd the house both evenings" (*Kansas City American Citizen*).

Other Jubilee Singers, 1889

The artistic and financial achievements of Loudin's Fisk Jubilee Singers and the Tennessee Jubilee Singers evinced a heightened international interest in the slave spirituals and the racially distinctive style of choral singing associated with them. In 1889, university-sponsored jubilee singers and privately financed jubilee companies were active in the United States, touring widely with varying degrees of success. Black press reports of 1889 describe how jubilee singing was also being perpetuated at the community level, through churches and civic groups.

• ***March 2, 1889:*** "The Stage," "The [Mumford's] Fish [*sic*] Jubilee Singers appeared in Jacksonville, Ill., last week. There are eight vocalists in the company, four ladies and four gentlemen, and a lady accompanist" (*Indianapolis Freeman*).

Note: In 1884 the original Fisk Jubilee Singers split into two factions, one under Frederick J. Loudin, and the other under soprano Maggie Porter Cole and her husband, Daniel Cole, a tenor. The Cole faction soon came under the management of Charles Mumford, a white man, said to be from Red Bank, New Jersey. Mumford's Fisk Jubilee Singers included (at different times) several former members of the famous group that had toured under the auspices of Fisk University during the 1870s; along with Maggie Porter Cole, these included Jennie Jackson DeHart, Georgia Gordon Taylor, and B. W. Thomas. Mumford's Fisk Jubilee Singers continued making successful U.S. tours through the turn of the century and beyond. In 1895 and into 1896 they toured in Europe, visiting Sweden, Russia, Finland, Lapland, and perhaps other Scandinavian countries.

• ***March 9, 1889:*** "Miss Mathilda S. Jones formerly of New Orleans, has been singing in the West Indies and Central America. She received magnificent presents from her hearers. She was

Mumford's Fisk Jubilee Singers, 1895. Standing, left to right: Charles Lewis, Charles Johnstone, C. W. Payne, J. N. Caldwell. Seated, left to right: Tilly Williams, Charles Mumford, Maggie Porter Cole, Cora Cole, Charles Sumner Byron. (courtesy Royal Library of Stockholm, Sweden)

formerly a member of St. James Church Choir in New Orleans" (*Indianapolis Freeman*).

Note: This report confuses the Tennessee Jubilee Singers' emerging "Black Patti," Matilda S. Jones, with Mathilda (Tillie) Jones, the similarly named prima donna soprano of the New Orleans University Singers. The New Orleans University Singers were an independent, professional spin-off from a jubilee troupe that had originally been dispatched from New Orleans' Methodist-sponsored Freedmen's school in 1877 to help raise funds to save a faltering Colored Orphan's Home on Bayou Teche. Tillie Jones was a founding member of the troupe, which remained active until her death in 1897.[30]

• ***March 23, 1889:*** "The Stage," "Every college now-a-days has its jubilee singers. The latest entry are the Tuskegee Jubilee Singers who are 'doing' Georgia" (*Indianapolis Freeman*).

Note: This is the earliest-known reference to a troupe of Jubilee singers touring in the interest of Tuskegee Institute. Traveling choirs and quartets from Tuskegee became a formidable power in the field of spiritual singing.

• ***March 30, 1889 (Topeka, Kansas):*** "The Jubilee Singers," "The closing entertainment of the Library hall course occurred last evening, when the [Mumford's] Fisk Jubilee Singers made their debut before a Kansas audience. It seems strange that this famous musical organization, which has sung almost all over the world, should never until now have visited Kansas, a state toward whom they and all their race must feel most kindly... The... Jubilee singers will always find a warm welcome waiting them when they visit Topeka again" (*Topeka Capital Commonwealth*, reprinted in *Indianapolis Freeman*).

• ***March 30, 1889:*** "The Stage," "The Tennessee Warblers, composed of the Pugsley Brothers, of Nashville, Tenn., are singing in St. Louis to crowded houses" (*Indianapolis Freeman*).

Note: Through the resounding influence of the Fisk Jubilee Singers, the city of Nashville and the state of Tennessee became synonymous with "authentic" jubilee singing. Unlike many contemporaneous independent, professional troupes who took the names "Nashville" or "Tennessee," but were in fact from Brooklyn or Peoria, the Tennessee Warblers were actually organized in Nashville by brothers L. E. and R. C. Puggsley. By 1889 they were well established, singing "the best class of Jubilee music."[31] During the early 1890s, their program became more varied. Their roster for 1892 included ragtime piano pioneer Ruby Shelton. In 1895 they took out soon-to-be-famous comedian-producer Salem Tutt Whitney, and by 1897 they were also carrying Whitney's future brother-in-law, "trick and descriptive pianist" W. A. Baynard.[32] R. C. Puggsley, the troupe's original "lion basso," appears to have remained active, both as a performer and manager, into the late 1920s.[33]

• ***July 13, 1889 (Boston, Massachusetts):*** "Mr. Hamilton, with four young men from Tuskegee Normal School in Alabama, is here raising money for the school by giving concerts. They sang for the Sunday school of the 12th Baptist Church to the great delight of the children" (*New York Age*).

• ***August 17, 1889 (New York City):*** "Mrs. Rosetta Smith of 228 Sullivan Street is still traveling with the Norfolk Jubilee Singers, of which she is the leading soprano singer. The troupe is having great success. Mrs. Smith is one of the leading singers of Bethel Choir" (*New York Age*).

Note: The group mentioned here had no connection with the Norfolk Jubilee Quartet, which was organized in Norfolk, Virginia, shortly after World War I and began recording for Okeh in 1921.

• ***October 5, 1889 (New York City):*** "Mr. George E. Barrett left town on Tuesday to join [Mumford's] Fisk Jubilee Singers at Cincinnati, enroute to San Francisco. This is Mr. Barrett's 12th season" (*New York Age*).

• ***October 11, 1889 (Detroit, Michigan):*** "The New Orleans University Glee Club," "One of the most enjoyable entertainments of the season was the one at fraternity hall last evening given by the New Orleans University Glee Club, for the benefit of the Second Baptist Church. The company, composed of seven members under the management of Mr. F. S. Thomas, is well organized and is on the road for the purpose of raising funds for the completion of an Industrial School, which they are erecting in the South. Last week they entertained large audiences with their melodies at Wonderland" (*Detroit Plaindealer*).

Note: This report refers to the New Orleans University Singers with star soprano Tillie Jones, nee Mrs. F. S. Thomas. Their claim to be still operating as charitable fund-raisers proved fraudulent.

• ***November 22, 1889 (Detroit, Michigan):*** "The Rev. Thomas Johnson of the Providence Baptist church of Chicago has organized a corps of Jubilee Singers who are giving concerts in this city to raise funds for repairs of their church" (*Detroit Plaindealer*).

• ***November 29, 1889 (Detroit, Michigan):*** "Hampton Visitors," "Gen. S. C. Armstrong of the Hampton Normal and Industrial Institute of Hampton, Va., accompanied by four Afro-American singers and two Indians from Dakota, spent Monday in [Detroit]. In the evening an interesting exposition of his work was given at the Woodward Ave. Baptist Church, and addresses were made by the Indian students and two of the Afro-American young men. The exercises were made more interesting by the excellent singing of the Quartet, and a fine impression was made by the practical evidence of the noble work being accomplished at Hampton. The Singers left Tuesday afternoon for Ann Arbor, where they will give an entertainment at University Hall. The gentlemen composing the Quartet are Messrs. Boykin, Daggs, Wainwright and Clayton" (*Detroit Plaindealer*).

Note: The Hampton Institute Jubilee Quartet was a front-runner in the transition from mixed choral groups to male quartets as the preferred vehicle for jubilee singing. In 1887 a male quartet of students and alumni supplanted Hampton's student choir on fund-raising tours. This trend-setting group was perhaps the first male quartet to achieve wide recognition as spiritual singers. The famous Hampton Quartet was known for its unembellished traditional arrangements of plantation melodies. Basso J. N. Wainwright joined the Hampton Institute Quartette in 1889, and the article above may be describing his first tour with the group. Wainwright continued his remarkable career with the Hampton Institute Quartette until his retirement in 1937!

• ***December 21, 1889 (Springfield, Massachusetts):*** "The Maryland Jubilee Singers went to Holyoke. . . These jubilee singers are led by Mr. Howard J. Williams and wife. They offered to give their church a sacred concert last Sunday night, and, because the pastor objected to charging an admission of 15 cents for the paying of the singers, they would not sing" (*New York Age*).

• ***December 28, 1889 (Troy, New York):*** "The Eastern Star Troupe of jubilee singers gave an old fashioned jubilee concert for the benefit of A.M.E. Zion Baptist Church. Their rendition of old time plantation songs were excellent" (*New York Age*).

Rev. Marshall W. Taylor

One thing African American newspaper editors did to promote black pride was to let flow a river of laudatory biographical sketches of "Race Men of Note"—doctors, lawyers, politicians, preachers, teachers, businessmen. Among those who came up for recognition in the *Indianapolis Freeman* in 1889 was the late Rev. Marshall William Taylor, former editor of the *Southwestern Christian Advocate* and compiler of a historic book, *Collection of Revival Hymns and Plantation Melodies.*

• ***March 9, 1889:*** "Rev. Marshall W. Taylor, D.D.," "The late Doctor Taylor. . . was one of the most gifted. . . men the race has yet produced. He was born in Lexington, Ky., July 1, 1846, of poor, uneducated, but respectable parents. He was of Scotch, Irish and Indian descent on his father's side, and African–Arabian stock on his mother's side. His education was picked up from such private schools and teachers as could be obtained in those days. His family moved to Louisville later on, and he entered the law firm of Kirkland and Barr, after which he opened a Freedmen's school at Harrisonburg, in the same State. In 1869 he was licensed to preach as an M.E. minister, and began his upward career. In his peregrinations as a minister he held charges and preached in the States of Arkansas, Texas, Missouri, Indiana, Kentucky, Ohio, Louisiana and the Indian Territory. He had conferred upon him the title of Doctor of Divinity by the Central Tennessee College in 1879, and was elected editor of the *Southwestern Christian Advocate* in 1880.[34]... He died in this city [Indianapolis] in June, 1888.[35] He wrote several volumes, among which are 'Universal Reign of Jesus,' 'Life of Downey, the Negro Evangelist,' 'Plantation Melodies,' and 'Life of Mrs. Amanda Smith, the Missionary.' (These books can be ordered through *The Freeman.*) His widow and three children still reside in this city" (*Indianapolis Freeman*).

Less than two years after his passing, the details of Rev. Taylor's biography were already getting muddled. However, his *Collection of Revival Hymns and Plantation Melodies* survived to ensure him a certain immortality. First published in 1882, it remained in print throughout the 1889–1895 period, and it was still being advertised for sale in the *Southwestern Christian Advocate* in 1897.

A legacy of scholarly interest in Rev. Taylor's *Collection of Revival Hymns and Plantation Melodies* began in 1928 when Newman I. White complained that Taylor had neglected to note which of the included songs were black plantation melodies and which were white revival hymns. To White, these two song types were "indistinguishable in the book, without the aid of dialect, because without dialect they were so in actual fact."[36] In 1943 George Pullen Jackson, the most zealous apostle of the now generally discredited theory that Negro spirituals have white origins, concluded that Rev. Taylor's book was "the worst" of all the early published sources of black religious folksongs, because "its tunes are uniformly the most bafflingly illiterate strings of notes on record."[37] This seems to be the usual reaction of musicians who try to negotiate the scores as notated. Nevertheless, Jackson included twelve examples from Rev. Taylor's collection in his "Tune Comparative List" of "Melodies of White People Paired with... Negro-Sung Variants."[38] In 1976 Irene V. Jackson-Brown postulated that *Revival Hymns and Plantation Melodies* was an early "Afro-American denominational hymnal," in the tradition of A.M.E. Church founder Richard Allen's compilation from 1801, and was "thus of great significance."[39] Robin Hough added in 1988, "What Taylor accomplished in publishing his hymnal was the production of a text that is as interesting for its political and religious agenda as it is for its musical content."[40]

During Rev. Taylor's tenure as editor of the *Southwestern Christian Advocate* (1884–1887), the paper recorded at least four practical applications of *Revival Hymns and Plantation Melodies.* These brief but specific, contemporaneous documents explain something that has evaded all previous studies of Taylor's song collection—how it was actually put to use:

1. At Sixth Street M.E. Church, New Orleans, on the night of Sunday, October 12, 1884, "the editor of the SOUTHWESTERN preached, and his inimitable choir rendered the 'Song of the Hills' from Taylor's Plantation Melodies as a post lude."[41]
2. In the spring of 1885, Rev. Taylor attended a morning "chapel service" with the students of Straight University, the Congregational Church–sponsored freedmen's school in New Orleans. The service began with a "Scripture lesson," followed by "singing," then a prayer and several speeches: "Then came more of the Delicious singing, concluded by two selections from the 'Plantation Melodies, of the South;' by the Negroes, viz: 'Rock my soul in the bosom of Abraham' and 'Go thou and prophesy.' Just think of three hundred children, with a keen religious nature, and the Spirit of the Fathers upon them, singing idyls of the race; to the motion of head and foot; and the swelling of the chest with the struggling emotions, and the power of the Spirit with in them, and you have it. Was it a play? No, it was the germ of a powerful on coming people bearing to their higher sphere the poetic feeling of their sires."[42]

3. Later that same year a Texas-based correspondent to the Southwestern Christian Advocate, Rev. W. H. Jackson, described a revival meeting in Pattison, Texas, which featured "Sister Fanny Tibbs, who is a member of W. Tabernacle M.E. Church, Galveston. She is the greatest rivalist [*sic*] of a lady as ever seen. She carries Dr. Taylor's 'Plantation Melodies' as her music, and can beat anyone using them."

   "She has memorized a great number of them, and is a great help to a preacher in a protracted meeting. She is a member of a singing band at the above named church, and they adopt Dr. Taylor's 'Plantation Melodies.' "

   "Sister Tibbs is the wife of Bro. Solomon Tibbs, a local preacher of Mt. Vernon Church, of Houston, Texas. He has a wood yard on the W.N.G.R.R. We heard Bro. Tibbs preach a sermon which was well done, and should he go out as a pastor, he has the help in the person of his wife . . ."

   "The people gather from far and near to hear her sing. I fully believe that she can beat the author [i.e., Rev. Taylor], suiting the tunes to songs of said book."

   "I advised her to get a hundred copies, and enter upon the sales and teachings of the book, for great success awaits her."[43]
4. On January 22, 1886, Rev. Taylor "preached and lectured" at a Methodist Episcopal Church in Meridian, Mississippi: "The Dr. was introduced to the audience by Rev. J. Campbell; after reading from the scriptures, we were led in prayer by Rev. Ramby of the first Baptist Church."

   "We had the pleasure after this of joining in with the Dr. in singing one of his 'Plantation Melodies,' which was as manna falling from the heavens, and served as precious oil upon the head of each, and thence into the heart. From this every one was made so that pen, ink, or time couldn't tell."[44]

Rev. Taylor's musical legacy is further ensured by his grandson, jazz saxophonist and composer Sam Rivers, who is best known for his participation in the avant-garde movement of the 1960s.[45]

It would appear that Sol Tibbs and Fanny Tibbs, the "great lady revivalist" who could beat Rev. Taylor at "suiting the tunes to the songs" in his book, also had a musical heir. Early-1900s' editions of the *Indianapolis Freeman* identify a young black minstrel singer–song writer from Texas or Louisiana named Sol Tibbs. Tibbs is known to have had at least one of his songs published, a 1901 version of "Mama, Mama Make Cinda 'Haive Herself.' "[46] On the road with Rusco and Holland's Minstrels in the fall of 1902, Tibbs was "singing with success a funny original parody on [John Queen's hit song of 1900,] 'Goo-Goo Eyes.' It deals with Booker T. Washington's reception by President Roosevelt."[47] Tibbs was touring with A. G. Allen's New Orleans Minstrels in the fall of 1905 when he fell sick and died in Sumter, South Carolina.[48]

Selected, Annotated Chronology of Music-Related Citations, 1889

• ***January 19, 1889 (Rochester, New York):*** "Blind Tom Concerts," "Blind Tom gave a concert at the new Opera House last Sunday evening . . . Blind Tom has grown decidedly corpulent, and is much more dignified than in the past. There are none of the antics which used to characterize his performance. He made a few introductory remarks and throughout the concert gave a running description of his past life and of his old habits. The selections given were by Thalberg, Liszt, Wellenhaupt and other well-known composers, as well as several by himself. He is much more intelligent in a general way than is popularly believed" (*Cleveland Gazette*).

Note: Thomas Wiggins Bethune—"Blind Tom"—was born a slave in Georgia in 1849 and was placed on exhibit before the age of ten as a blind slave boy piano prodigy.[49] He was perhaps most famous for his ability to reproduce instantaneously, after just one hearing, any passage played for him on the piano; and it was customary for someone to come forth from the audience during his concerts and challenge him to do so. Due to a history of unscrupulous management, Blind Tom was, in the eyes of the African American press, "still a slave" in the 1890s.

Blind Tom. (courtesy 78 Quarterly*)*

• ***February 2, 1889 (New York City):*** "There is nothing that so charms the soul and sets the heart strings of a colored individual vibrating to their highest tension as music. Notwithstanding the cold winds of Monday afternoon a number of small and half grown children dived from back yards, alley ways, front houses, and in fact from every conceivable outlet in an uptown street, to enjoy the sweet strains of music set forth from a band of colored brethren consisting of a violin, banjo, guitar and clappers with an occasional chorus . . . They seemed to feel the electric darts as the music wafted on, and at last their pent up spirits found an outlet; away they went flying around and around on the sidewalk, feet keeping a patter with the music. Pennies and five cent pieces came jingling down upon the side walk, which kept a little fellow at work. By some chance he happened to look up and espied a little midget of six or seven summers looking out of a window. 'Come down Jennie, come down,' he yelled . . . Jennie dashed down the stoop with saque wide open, hat in hand, shoes untied, stockings, one brown and the other black, tied with white strings, which had lost their hold. On she speeded, threw down her hat and entered the space. 'Give us "shortening bread," mister,' she said, as she took up the sides of her dress with the grace of a duchess and set in. You should have seen the way that baby danced the shuffle, double and single, the curving and twisting of the body, the running on the heels, the side step, the back step; in fact all kinds of steps, that would have done credit to a minstrel performer. The crowd just went wild and yelled. Just then some one cried out, 'Cheese it! the cop!' and the crowd dispersed in a hurry" (Florence Williams, *New York Age*).

• ***February 2, 1889 (Cleveland, Ohio):*** "The entertainment given by Light of the West Lodge, F.A.A.M., at Weisgerber's Hall Thursday evening, the 24th, was . . . largely attended . . . The quartettes by the Star Quartette, accompanied by Miss Geneva Lucas, were well rendered . . . Miss Birdie Green, by her pleasing singing of the waltz song, 'Irene, Good Night,' was encored. . . . Dancing to the music of Boston's orchestra filled the time until an early hour" (*Cleveland Gazette*).

Note: The "waltz song, 'Irene, Good Night,'" was an 1886 sheet-music effort by Cincinnati-born African American composer Gussie L. Davis. In addition to parlor renditions by the likes of Birdie Green, "Irene" was widely circulated on the minstrel show routes.[50] Its waltz time and similar lyric passage, "good night, Irene, good night," suggest that it informed the popular folksong "Good Night, Irene," which is commonly associated with Huddie Ledbetter.

• ***February 9, 1889 (Cleveland, Ohio):*** "By some oversight . . . mention was not made of the entertainment by the choir of St. Johns church which occurred on the evening of the 17th ult . . . Several numbers were well rendered by the choir . . . The Star Quartette delighted the audience with two spirited and tuneful numbers . . . [and] Miss Eva Green and E. Osborn sang White's comic duet 'Aunt Peggy and Uncle Dan' in costume, which captured the audience" (*Cleveland Gazette*).

• ***February 9, 1889 (Rochester, New York):*** "Blind Tom . . . blackened his manager's eye at an entertainment held at Elmira recently. The manager did not retaliate. Tom cannot see at all, but he knows where a man's head is at by instinct" (*New York Age*).

• ***February 23, 1889 (Bridgeport, Connecticut):*** "Peck & Fursman's 'U.T.C.,' with the Hyers Sisters in the cast, did a fair business [February] 16. A driving rain interfered with business at night" (*New York Clipper*).

Note: Twenty-seven years after Harriet Beecher Stowe's illustrious novel first took hold on American readers, it was being subjected to every possible stage interpretation, from high-minded morality play to slap-stick minstrel farce. So prevalent were the professional minstrel troupes and musical comedy companies that specialized in presentations of *Uncle Tom's Cabin* that by 1889 they were commonly referred to in the profession as "U.T.C.'s" or " 'Tom' shows."

• ***March 2, 1889 (Middleton, Connecticut):*** "The old, yet ever new play of 'Uncle Tom's Cabin' will be presented here . . . with the well known Hyers Sisters as the two Topsys. Only a few years ago, the best of classic was rendered by the Hyer Sisters in a satisfactory manner, before critical and cultured audiences" (*New York Age*).

Note: The popularity of the Hyers Sisters, Anna Madah and Emma Louise, predated even that of the original Fisk Jubilee Singers, alongside whom they had appeared at the historic second World's Peace Jubilee in Boston in June 1872. The Hyers Sisters are best remembered for their stellar roles in the original late-1870s productions of "Out of Bondage." The precise spelling of their last name can still be called to question.

• ***March 2, 1889 (New Orleans, Louisiana):*** "Notes About Town," "The Pelican Brass Band was organized on the 23d of January, 1889, with Mr. J. Dresch as leader and Messrs. S. S. Decker, J. B. Humphrey, E. J. Palao, J. O. Hogart, J. T. Hall, Samuel Kincey, William Crawford, A. W. Clark, J. Bates, Jas. Bernard, Jas. Taylor, the members" (*New Orleans Weekly Pelican*).

Note: James B. "Jim" Humphrey is cited in the popular history of jazz as a highly influential New Orleans–based itinerant brass band instructor of the 1890s and the progenitor of one of New Orleans' most distinguished jazz families.

• ***March 9, 1889:*** "C. P. Stinson, of Pittsburgh, has accepted an offer from Hague's Minstrels, of London, and will go there in June to play an engagement of four months. He is to be introduced there as the leading mandolin player of the world. He will also appear in Edinburg and Liverpool. Mr. Stinson is well known in Pittsburgh as a teacher of guitar and mandolin lessons. Some of his pupils come a distance of 100 miles to take lessons" (*Cleveland Gazette*).

• ***March 16, 1889 (Washington, D.C.):*** "The evening of the 2nd was of peculiar interest to home folks. The fact that Miss Julia C. Wormley, a general favorite by birth and every alliance a Washingtonian, was to make her debut as a dramatic reader before critics gathered from the four corners of this broad land, brought together a large and distinguished gathering in spite of the rain storm. The Berean Baptist Church was filled to its utmost capacity... Miss Wormley... read with marked intelligence and made her gestures with an ease and grace not usually seen in a debutante... While her reading of 'Lasca' and 'Cambyses and the Macrabian Bow' immediately established her success for the evening, her exceptionally charming rendition of 'Aunt Sophrina Tabor at the Opera,' won for her a double encore" (*New York Age*).

Note: Abundant references to "elocutionists" (dramatic readers, recitationists) such as Julia C. Wormley, Hallie Q. Brown, Ednorah Nahar, Henrietta Vinton Davis, B. F. Lightfoot, Charles Winter Wood, etc. indicate the popularity of this nearly forgotten art during the 1890s. Generally speaking, African American elocutionists withdrew from the professional stage about the same time that commercial sound recording technology was being perfected. Still, there are a few examples preserved on "pioneer era" 78s. Most notable and commonly encountered are the four fine Paul Laurence Dunbar recitations recorded for Victor in 1909 and 1911 by James A. Myers of the Fisk Jubilee Quartet. More obscure examples include Edward Sterling Wright's 1914 Edison cylinders and Charles Winter Wood's 1923 selections for Paramount.

• ***March 16, 1889 (Palatka, Florida):*** "The Putnam Quartet (of Putnam House), consisting of Messrs. Sighter, McMullen, Carter and Davis, E. F. Codett, manager, gave a concert in the parlors of the hotel which was well received by the guests" (*New York Age*).

• ***March 23, 1889:*** "Race Gleanings," "Sam Williams is the colored giant of Georgia. He lives near Albany, is six feet six and wears a number 16 shoe. He performs a few tricks and is a song and dance artist, when not working in the field" (*Indianapolis Freeman*).

• ***March 23, 1889:*** "Three Colored Artists Of New York: Mme. V. A. Montgomery, Miss Blanche D. Washington, and Mrs. Albert Wilson," "They were all born of poor, hard working parents; their studies began in a day when prejudice was deeply felt, when they appeared before the public which was not ready to appreciate them. Our people had so long been accustomed to the weird, wildly enlivening strains, of stringed instruments that to many well-meaning persons the piano required so much attention and particularly, delicate supple hands, (so, forming a striking contrast to the requirements of a fiddle, banjo, or guitar) the music roll and piano suggested 'school-bred worthlessness' this and dishearting showers of comments, criticisms, and from persons whose knowledge of music was pitifully lacking in every essential was brought to bear upon any who appeared before our audiences with notes. Undaunted, these women struggled...

Miss Blanche D. Washington... At the age of thirteen she commenced the study of the piano under some of the most prominent professors of New York City... At the age of fifteen she began teaching some little friends of hers, and from that time on her life has been passed chiefly in teaching music... With justifiable pride she may refer to many of her former pupils... chief of whom are Mrs. Albert Wilson, accompanist to Flora Batson; Miss V. Hunt, organist of Mt. Olivet Church... and others...

Mrs. V. A. [Virginia] Montgomery was born in New York City. Her education in music is due mainly to the indefatigable efforts of her mother, Madame Magnan... When she was but eight years old she first appeared as accompanist to her mother in Cooper Union, the affair being a concert given for the benefit of Shiloh Presbyterian Church, Henry Highland Garnet, D.D., pastor... For twelve years she has held the position of organist in Bethel A.M.E. Church, the largest A.M.E. Church in the city at the present, and for a number of years she has officiated as organist of St. Philips, the only colored Episcopal church in the city . . .

"Mrs. Albert Wilson, better known as Mme. Gassaway, was born and educated in New York City. She began the study of music at the tender age of seven years under the direction of Miss Blanche D. Washington . . . In looking over the annals of music she saw no field so uncultivated as the true art of accompanying well. Henceforth this became her specialty . . . In 1881–2, as Miss Georgia Miller (her maiden name), she was connected with the New Orleans University singers, meeting with splendid success always. With them she traveled extensively East, West and South . . . Among the many artists she has accompanied can be mentioned 'Selika,' the peerless queen of classical arrangement; Mme. Nellie Brown Mitchell, Mme. Stewart, Cora Lee Watson, and Flora Batson, with whom she traveled considerably" (Victoria Earle, *Indianapolis Freeman*).

• ***March 30, 1889:*** "Race Gleanings," "A 'cake walk' took place, Wednesday night, at the 'Cotton Palace,' New Orleans, La., at which a number of fashionable white ladies paced for a pound cake" (*Indianapolis Freeman*).

• ***April 6, 1889:*** "Savannah Negroes refuse to work in gangs with Italian laborers. The line must be drawn somewhere. It has also been noticed that in New Orleans that Negroes have almost entirely monopolized the business of making hand organ street music, once peculiar to the Italian" (*Indianapolis Freeman*).

• ***April 13, 1889 (New York City):*** Advertisement: "A Grand Musical Feast at the First A.M.E. Zion Church . . . Ye Old Folks' Concert—singing tunes that our forefathers sung 100 years ago and wearing their Sunday meeting clothes" (*New York Age*).

Note: The "old folks concert" was a standard form of American entertainment in the late nineteenth century.[51]

• ***April 27, 1889:*** "Church Music," "We notice with some emotion that Bishop B. T. Tanner has lifted up his voice in the *Christian Recorder* against the modern solo and soloist in the church service.

Dr. Tanner's objections are as unique as the Egyptian mummy, if not so antique. He thinks the soloist usually sings for fame and not for God; that the solo is too generally devoid of Christian spirit; that it distracts attention from the sermon and from true worship; that it, in effect, destroys the short, long and common metre singing of the congregation, which we opine is an undisguised blessing; in short, we gather from Bishop Tanner's article that if he were the controlling influence he would remove the organs, bounce the choirs and jump down on the soloists in all the churches of the African Methodist Episcopal denomination.

Before Bishop Tanner was elevated to the Bench of Bishops a few months since he was regarded as one of the most cultured and progressive men in his connection. It looks as though his translation had twisted his head toward the dead past" (*New York Age*).

• ***May 11, 1889:*** "The Excelsior Quartette was very successful at Worth's Museum, New York City, last week. This quartette has more steady engagements than any other colored quartette in the country" (*Indianapolis Freeman*).

• ***May 11, 1889 (New York City):*** "Prof. Banks' prize cane and cake walk caught the crowd that was looking for fun 'off the Bristol.' The walkers were numerous and the din was equal to an indoor cyclone. The lucky walkers were carried off their feet, so great was the enthusiasm" (*New York Age*).

• ***June 1, 1889:*** "The Stage," "Miss Mary E. Harper, elocutionist, heads the William Jay Jubilee Literary Musical Troupe, who are travelling in the interest of the Rankin-Richards Institute at Windsor, N.C. The New England

Press speaks in glowing terms of the troupe" (*Indianapolis Freeman*).

• ***June 1, 1889 (New York City):*** "The Young People's Association connected with Abyssinia Baptist Church gave a highly interesting entertainment. The choruses were rendered with great effect. The male quartet acquitted themselves with usual honors in their rendition of 'The Huntsman's Horn'" (*New York Age*).

• ***June 8, 1889 (New Bedford, Massachusetts):*** "The Salem Baptist Church opened their annual May festival last Wednesday evening with a war concert. A chorus of twenty-five voices, under the direction of Sergeant William Carney, sang very well, and Prof. T. W. Jackson rendered several comic songs he used to sing in war times on his autoharp" (*New York Age*).

• ***June 15, 1889:*** "Sin Killer Griffin is organizing a Gospel army of colored Baptists at Denison, Texas for the invasion of Africa" (*New York Age*, reprinted from *Waterbury American*).

Freeman, *April 13, 1889.*

Note: It seems likely that this is the same Sin Killer Griffin who was recorded at a state prison farm in Texas in 1934 for the Library of Congress.

• ***June 22, 1889 (Pittsburgh and Allegheny, Pennsylvania):*** "The cantata of Esther was presented at the Bijou theater last Tuesday evening to a large house, under the auspices of the Cantata Musical Association. The costumes were rich and the staging was all that could be desired. Miss Kate Kelley, the acknowledged Nightingale of the West, assumed the role of Queen Esther, and in her usual way, sang with such sweetness as to completely capture the audience. Mrs. Susie Lee, as Zerish, sustained her reputation as a first-class actress and singer. Miss Florence Stevenson, as the Prophetess, sang in her usual sweet style and won a deserved encore. Chas. Mahoney, as the Jew, both sang and acted well. C. Waters, as King, and Chas. Waters, as Haman, sang fairly well, but in the duet, 'A song of Joy,' it was difficult to hear them in the rear of the house. The chorus was good. Taking everything into consideration it was one of the best entertainments ever given in the city" (*Cleveland Gazette*).

Note: "The Cantata of Esther, the Beautiful Queen," a costumed musical drama based on the Old Testament story, was published in 1856 by William Batchelder Bradbury, who also wrote such songs as "Sweet Hour of Prayer" and "Rally Round the Flag." "Queen Esther" became a popular and ambitious vehicle for nineteenth-century African American school programs as well as church and community entertainments among the "aspiring" strata of black society. The successful presentation of "Queen Esther" early in 1871 by a group of Fisk University students under music instructor George L. White inspired the organization and initial tour of the Fisk Jubilee Singers. Music historian Wayne D. Shirley has noted that "Queen Esther" was still being presented by black community church groups in Washington, D.C., in the 1960s.[52]

"Programme," Fisk University presentation of "Esther, The Beautiful Queen," 1871. (courtesy Fisk University Library, Special Collections)

• ***June 29, 1889:*** "Wanted for Stetson's Mammoth Spectacular Double 'Uncle Tom's Cabin' Company, Full Cast of A No. 1 'Tom' People, must be Good Dressers on and off the Stage, A No. 1 Leader for Band and Orchestra, White and Colored Musicians, Colored Quartet, those playing Brass preferred. White and Colored Drum Majors. No Mashers, Kickers or Drunkards Wanted . . . This monster organization opens early in August, with the most complete and best equipped outfit of any 'Tom' Show on the road. The uniforms worn by the two distinct bands will the finest money can procure . . . We will also introduce on the stage a pack of genuine Siberian and Cuban Bloodhounds and the Smallest Pony and Donkey in the World" (*New York Clipper*).

• ***June 29, 1889:*** At a reception for the Cuban Giants baseball team in New York City, "The vocal selections by Messrs. Allen, Booker, Coleman and Dixon were highly appreciated" (*New York Age*).

Note: This is the famous Excelsior Quartette.

• ***July 6, 1889 (Orange, New Jersey):*** "At Music Hall on last Friday night, the performance by the Theodore Drury Operatic Concert Company was excellently rendered. The costumes were exquisite, and there was no occasion for criticism. Everyone seemed to enjoy the evening's entertainment. The only drawback was the conduct of a number of white lads in the hall,

Advertising placard, Stetson's "Uncle Tom's Cabin" Company. (courtesy Charles Horner)

who would, in case of applause, stamp their feet, yell and whistle. The statement of several New York papers and the *Sunday Call* of Newark, that the scenery and plays of the company were in some way defective, or disgusting, were utterly without foundation" (*New York Age*).

Note: Behind the color bar, Theodore Drury's Colored Opera Company provided a much-needed stage for African American operatics. Theodore Drury's ongoing career spanned half a century.

• ***July 13, 1889 (New Orleans, Louisiana):*** "The Sunflower Quartette will give an entertainment at Tulane Avenue Baptist church on Monday evening, the 22d. A feature of the evening's pleasure will be the auction of a number of old maids. A . . . cake will also be given to the winner. Admission 10 cents" (*New Orleans Weekly Pelican*).

• ***July 27, 1889 (New Orleans, Louisiana):*** "The Climax Colored Minstrel Company, managed by L. Therence and E. J. Devizin, have just closed an engagement in the lot at Canal and Villere streets. They will take the road soon" (*New Orleans Weekly Pelican*).

• ***July 27, 1889 (New Orleans, Louisiana):*** "Notes About Town," "The Pelican Brass Band, whose headquarters are at 227 Gravier street, and, of which Profs. J. B. Humphreys [*sic*] and Jas. T. Bate are the managers, goes to Shell Beach tomorrow" (*New Orleans Weekly Pelican*).

• ***July 27, 1889 (Providence, Rhode Island):*** "The Twilight Banjo and Guitar Quartette of Providence will soon add mandolins to their other string instruments" (*Indianapolis Freeman*).

• ***August 3, 1889 (Providence, Rhode Island):*** "The Twilight Banjo and Guitar Quartette will assist B. F. Lightfoot in a recital to be given in Town Hall, Jamestown, R.I. next Monday. This quartette is composed of J. S. Brown, J. H. Barnett, banjoists; W. J. Brown, J. H. Easton, guitarists (of Providence, R.I.)" (*Indianapolis Freeman*).

• ***August 3, 1889 (New Orleans, Louisiana):*** "On the evening of the 29th ult., a grand concert was given at Laharpe M.E. Church by the Invincible Jubilee Quartette. A large crowd was present and were well pleased with the entertainment" (*New Orleans Weekly Pelican*).

• ***August 3, 1889 (Providence, Rhode Island):*** "A quartette has lately been organized in Providence, R.I. known as the East India Quartette. The following are members: Alex B. Parker, tenor; D. B. Parker, soprano; F. S. Brown, baritone; W. R. Brown, basso. They will take to the road in the fall" (*Indianapolis Freeman*).

• ***August 10, 1889:*** "[An] enterprising Negro named Sam Anderson . . . is a native of South Carolina, who went to Europe some years ago with a minstrel troupe. The company got stranded and brought up in France. In the course of his wanderings he has learned to speak two or three foreign languages, and in Nantes, he married a French woman who owned a restaurant and a concert hall and is now her business manager. He is a shrewd, enterprising man in his way, and his black skin does not go against him at all in France" (*New York Age*).

• ***August 10, 1889 (Oneida, New York):*** "A regular praise meeting was held last Sunday evening at the A.M.E. Zion Church. The exercises consisted of prayers and exhortations, singing of plantation melodies, jubilee and gospel songs" (*New York Age*).

• ***August 10, 1889 (Kaaterskill, New York):*** "The first musical of the season was given by Mrs. Martha Weems. Guitar duet, A. Bohler and A. L. Morton; trio, Mrs. M. Weems, Miss Sadie Turpin, and Mrs. Victoria Miller; original selections, Dudley B. Clark; selection, Kaaterskill Quartet; Whistling solo, Miss Nellie May; the closing piece was sung by Miss Mary Brown, assisted by the quartet" (*New York Age*).

• ***August 17, 1889 (Saratoga Springs, New York):*** "There will be a harmonica contest between J. Hawkins and L. Jackson... Mr. Richard Marks the colored basso, and Luke Pulley of N.Y.C. are reaping harvests around the hotels here with their excellent pianist, and Mr. Marks is a drawing card wherever he goes" (*New York Age*).

Note: Luke Pulley blossomed during the mid-1890s as the pianist and orchestra leader of two major "plantation shows," "The Old South" and "The South Before the War." During the late 1890s Pulley was seen in big-time vaudeville as "the 'Black Pader Whiskey.' "[53] He offered a racial perspective on the character "Padewhiskie," originated by white "comedian-pianist" Will H. Fox[54] as a parody of world-famous Polish concert pianist Ignace Paderewski. In 1901 Pulley was selected to manage "the 200 colored cake walkers and dancers" on tour with "Wm. A Brady's 'Uncle Tom's Cabin.' "[55]

• ***August 31, 1889:*** "Mr. Loudin and his companions of the Fisk Jubilee Singers, so long and favorably known at Chautauqua, are at present in New South Wales and have sent to the sufferers of the Johnstown calamity the proceeds of a benefit concert amounting to $800. The troupe will soon go to India, and thence home via China, Japan, and the Sandwich Islands, and spend several months on the Pacific coast" (*New York Age*, reproduced from *Chautauqua Assembly Herald*).

Note: The fatal "calamity" at Johnstown, Pennsylvania, occurred on May 31, 1889, when several thousand people were drowned in a flash flood.

• ***September 7, 1889 (Jamaica, New York):*** During a local Emancipation Day celebration, "A band of vocalists with guitars and banjos, sang through the village in the afternoon, to the great delight of all who heard them. Their voices harmonized finely and the effect was excellent" (*New York Age*).

• ***September 7, 1889 (Poughkeepsie, New York):*** "The grove meeting at Wiley's Grove on August 11, was one of the largest and most successful ever held. There must have been 5,000 or more on the ground and the best of order was observed during the services. The meeting was under the direction of Rev. Adam Jackson. The singing by an excellent jubilee troupe from New York City was a feature of the meeting" (*New York Age*).

• ***September 21, 1889:*** "Willie Cook, the young violinist, returns to Washington, D.C., from Berlin in a few days. Because of straining his fingers he will be unable to practice for two or three months" (*Cleveland Gazette*).

Note: This is Will Marion Cook, who came to prominence as musical director of the famous Williams and Walker Company productions of the early 1900s.

• ***September 21, 1889 (New Orleans, Louisiana):*** "A grand vocal quartette contest concert will be given by the 'Careful Builders Circle,' for the benefit of Mount Zion's Church, on Monday Oct. 14...Admission fifteen cents" (*New Orleans Weekly Pelican*).

• ***September 28, 1889 (Saratoga Springs, New York):*** "Within ten days Saratoga will be blessed with two companies performing 'Uncle Tom's Cabin' " (*New York Age*).

• ***September 28, 1889:*** "The roster of the Boston Pavillion 'U.T.C.' Co. is as follows: Irad L. Garside, manager;...James Blocker, boss canvassman, with nine assistants; Prof. H.A. Lutrell, leader; ...Sam Lucas, Mrs. Lucas, Fanny Hooker, M. G. Johnson, Claude Lucas and the Old Dominion Quartet" (*New York Clipper*).

• ***October 4, 1889:*** "The [office of the Charleston, South Carolina,] *World* was serenaded this morning by three colored youths, who are called the Twin Brothers' Band. They play on two guitars, a fiddle, a mouth organ, and a call bell, and really made delightful music. The 'Twin' who played the guitar, mouth organ and call bell, the last named with his foot, had but one arm. He manipulated the guitar by a stick tied up to his stump. The violinist imitated the mocking bird to perfection. After rendering a number of arias, they departed begging the *World* to say, however, that they can be engaged for balls, dancing schools, etc" (*Detroit Plaindealer*, reproduced from *Charleston World*).

• ***OCTOBER 5, 1889 (NEW YORK CITY):*** "Theodore Drury Opera Company, under the management of G. H. Barnett, will give a Concert at Clarendon Hall, 13th St. bet. 3rd and 4th Aves., N.Y., Thursday and Friday evenings, Oct. 10 and 11, 1889. Mme. Albert Wilson, Pianist. Prof. Sol Thompson, Musical Director. A scene from 'Il Trovatore' will be sung with Mr. J. Stanton as Manrico and Miss Maggie Scott as Leonora...Admission, 25 cents. Reserved seats, 35 cents. The Decorations, Costumes and Scenery used in this Concert are the property of the Theodore Drury Opera Company" (*New York Age*).

• ***OCTOBER 12, 1889 (NEW BEDFORD, CONNECTICUT):*** "The Whaling City Quartet will give a concert in the Zion Church" (*New York Age*).

• ***OCTOBER 12, 1889 (CLEVELAND, OHIO):*** "Our Man about Town," "The Man About Town ran across the veteran cornetist, Mr. John Wilson, of Detroit, the first of the week and was told by him that Manager Drew, of the Star Theater, refused to allow his orchestra to play in his theater. It had been engaged by Mr. Draper, of the Uncle Tom's Cabin Company, to furnish music during the company's week's stay at the Star. Drew claimed that he was not drawing a 'color line' but desired the theater orchestra to play because he believed it was larger and would make better music. He also said that he was confident that he could make more money with a 'white' than a colored orchestra. In this last assertion he betrayed his true feelings in the matter and evidenced prejudice. Colored people should give his cheap theatre and museum a wide berth until he becomes better acquainted with Cleveland and steps into the ranks of the progressive population of the city" (*Cleveland Gazette*).

• ***OCTOBER 12, 1889 (CLEVELAND, OHIO):*** "Our Man About Town," "Have you seen them?: I mean the 'pompadours' some of the young men are sporting. Mirth provoking! Why Billy Kersands' mouth in its palmiest days, couldn't equal the average kinky-haired 'pompadour.' I saw one Sunday evening in church that attracted more attention for a time than those 'cake walkers' who came in just as services *were over,* and walked way in down front to seats, making as much noise as five persons...The fellow's hair was cut short with the exception of a great large bunch just over his forehead. It made him look like something trying to *fly*. Make a study of the pompadours you see and there will be no necessity for attending theaters for amusement for the next six months" (*Cleveland Gazette*).

• ***OCTOBER 12, 1889 (MEMPHIS, TENNESSEE):*** "Wiley Stuart's Colored Minstrels failed to put in an appearance at the Natatorium Sept. 26–28, and are reported to have stranded in Nashville" (*New York Clipper*).

• ***OCTOBER 19, 1989 (BOSTON, MASSACHUSETTS):*** "The concert given by Miss Ednorah Nahar at the Charles Street Church was unfortunate in occurring in a very stormy and disagreeable evening, and the audience was lessened thereby. The program was a bright and attractive one, with such names as Miss Nahar, Mrs. Fenderson, and Dr. Shuebruk well known to Boston audiences, assisted by such promising young musicians as Miss Cora Lee Watson, Mr. Moses Hodges, Mr. Joseph Douglass and Miss Gertrude Thompson, the whistler" (*New York Age*).

Note: The latter-named artists lived up to expectations. Cora Lee Watson later sang with Thearle's Original Nashville Students, a well-known professional touring troupe. Baritone Moses Hamilton Hodges became a member of Orpheus M. McAdoo's Virginia Jubilee Singers, and he sang with that company in South Africa, Australia, and New Zealand during the 1890s. Joseph Douglass, grandson of Frederick Douglass, was one of the most celebrated black violinists of the ensuing decade.

• ***October 19, 1889 (New Orleans, Louisiana):*** "Notes About Town," "The Excelsior Brass Band, still the pride of this city, is ready to furnish music for occasions at moderate prices . . .

Don't fail to attend the grand ball to be given by the Pelican Brass Band, at Longshoremen's hall, Monday Oct. 21st. Admission 25 cents" (*New Orleans Weekly Pelican*).

• ***October 26, 1889 (New Orleans, Louisiana):*** "Notes About Town," "The Alliance Brass Band, under the leadership of Victor Lacorbiere, gives another of their notable balls on the 4th proximo, at the Globe's hall. Admission, 15 cents" (*New Orleans Weekly Pelican*).

• ***October 26, 1889 (New Orleans, Louisiana):*** "Notes About Town," "Tonight at the Veterans' hall a dancing festival will be given for the benefit of the Ladies Veterans' Red Circle. The Tio and Doublet string band will be on hand with their popular music" (*New Orleans Weekly Pelican*).

Note: Al Rose and Edmond Souchon's oral history–driven book *New Orleans Jazz: A Family Album* (1967) refers to the "Tio-Doublet String Band (1889), dance quartet. A. L. Tio, Anthony Doublet, v; Prof. William J. Nickerson, viola; Paul Dominguez, Sr., sb"; and the "Tio-Doublet Orchestra (1888–1890), dance orchestra. Charles Doublet, c; Anthony Doublet, v; Anthony Page, tb; Lorenzo Tio, Sr., Luis Tio, cl; Dee Dee Chandler, d."

• ***October 26, 1889:*** "Green's Colored Minstrels are made up of the following people: Bobby Green (proprietor and manager) Chas. A. Crusoe (business manager), Geo. A. Skillings, Philip H. Boyer, Burt Hawkins, Jos. Augustus, Lewis L. Brown, Billy Jackson, Bunch Stanton, Charles Bloom, Harry Jones, George W. Brown, Alfred Holbery, William Moon, Joseph Dabney, D. C. Moore and Robert Douge" (*New York Clipper*).

• ***November 2, 1889 (New Orleans, Louisiana):*** "Notes About Town," At a "subscription soiree last Saturday at the Amis Sinceres' Hall . . . Prof. Wm. Nickerson's (Excelsior) string band furnished some choice music" (*New Orleans Weekly Pelican*).

Note: Popularly remembered for having given Jelly Roll Morton his first piano lessons, Prof. William Nickerson was New Orleans' most eminent black music professor of the 1890s.

• ***November 2, 1889 (New Orleans, Louisiana):*** "Notes About Town," "The Co-Operators' Fancy dress and characteristic ball, which is to be given on the 2d of December, at the Globe Hall, is still the principal topic of conversation among the elites of the 2d and 3d Districts. So far there are three young ladies contesting for the gold-headed silk umbrella. The Alliance Brass Band will furnish music for the occasion. General admission, 25 cents" (*New Orleans Weekly Pelican*).

• ***November 2, 1889 (New Orleans, Louisiana):*** "Notes About Town," "The Golden Leaf Quartette won the medals in the contest at Mt. Zion's church" (*New Orleans Daily Pelican*).

• ***November 2, 1889 (New Orleans, Louisiana):*** "Last Sunday at the residence of Mr. O. Piron, 463 N. Claibourne st. the Lyre Musical Society was organized with the following officers: O. D. Pavageaux, president; August Pageau, vice president; V. P. Thornhill, correspondending secretary; G. V. Watts, financial secretary;

C. Guyber, assistant secretary; O. Piron, treasurer; R. St. Cyr, first warden; Lino de la Rose, second warden; Mr. Lucien Augustin, musical director. The object of the society is to encourage and perpetuate the art of music among its members. Among the prominent musicians present were Profs. Louis and Lorenzo Tio, Caque, Messrs. R. Tournade, A. Page and F. Leclerc. After the meeting several classic pieces was skillfully executed" (*New Orleans Daily Pelican*).

• ***November 8, 1889 (Kansas City, Kansas):*** At a "Musical and Literary concert given at the First Baptist church," the "Quartette, 'Johnstown's Flood,' words and music by P. C. Thomas, sung by Misses D. Matthews, Consavella Smith, G. B. Williams and R. A. Bradford, was the grand quartette of the occasion" (*Kansas City American Citizen*).

• ***November 9, 1889:*** "The Griswold U.T.C. Co. which was organized at Chicago last week has among its members the Imperial Colored Quartette. They are booked for 21 weeks and will visit California and British Columbia" (*Indianapolis Freeman*).

• ***November 23, 1889 (New Haven, Connecticut):*** At Zion A.M.E. Church in New Haven, "The Olio Quartet was noted for its fine harmony and excellent time . . . Mme. M. O. Bell, Miss Mamie Ricks, Messrs. John Q. Anthony and William T. Blount" (*New York Age*).

• ***December 6, 1889 (Detroit, Michigan):*** A Thanksgiving entertainment sponsored by the Meylkli and Minuet Social Clubs included mixed quartets, orchestral pieces, tableaux, readings, and a "grand chorus" under the direction of "Miss Azalia Smith" (*Detroit Plaindealer*).

Note: Miss Azalia Smith, later Madame E. Azalia Hackley, was born in Murfreesboro, Tennessee, on June 29, 1867, and moved to Detroit with her family three years later. Her name appears in reports of the musical activities of Detroit's "black society" throughout the 1890s. During the early 1900s she established herself as one of the premier race women in American music; after earning an international reputation as a concert soloist, she championed a very effective crusade for the perpetuation of black folk music, holding festivals, contests, and lectures in many cities across the United States.

• ***December 7, 1889 (Washington, D.C.):*** "A violin recital was given at the chapel of All Souls', on Fourteenth and L streets, last evening, by Mr. William Cook [Will Marion Cook], which was largely attended. Mr. Cook is the son of the late John H. Cook, who was a successful practitioner at the District bar. The young colored violinist is very popular in this city. He has just finished his studies at the Berlin Conservatory of Music, where he has been under the tutelage of Prof. Joachim, being one of sixteen pupils selected by that great musician, on account of his talent, to be especially trained by him. The programme was a carefully selected one, the rendition of the mazurka of Wieniawski and the ballad of Vieuxtemps by Mr. Cook were brilliant . . . Mr. Cook will visit several of the leading cities and give recitals before returning again to Germany, which will be in about three months, to finally perfect himself in his chosen profession. The talented young artist was ably assisted by Mr. R. W. Thompkins, Mrs. S. C. Waring and Mrs. Alice Davis. The latter lady proved herself a discreet and careful accompanist" (*Cleveland Gazette*).

• ***December 21, 1889:*** "A tear for the old, old fashions. Scene: Crowded ball room. Lights burning green and blue, hold nectarine decoctions. Sway over particular organisms. Twenty-five 'sets' waiting 'que vie' for word of command. Two fiddles rasp, one guitar strums, and the command, 'honahs all,' starts the impatient throng in motion. No 'engagement cards,' no 'select' sets pre-empted the livelong evening by the ultra 'fashionable,' but a complete absence of the 'lines' and conventionalities, with but one desire, 'fun' " (*Indianapolis Freeman*).

The Minstrel Profession

"Ethiopian minstrelsy," the original American entertainment phenomenon, consisted of comic interpretations of musical and cultural expressions of plantation slavery—the characteristic singing, banjo-playing, fiddling, dancing, and story-telling—by white stage performers in blackface makeup. Early white troupes such as Christy's, Bryant's, and the Virginia Minstrels were the commercial outriders who introduced most of the world-at-large to the peculiarities of African American folk culture. In the process, the popular image of black culture and identity came into the de facto possession of white minstrel "delineators," and the first white minstrel stars to mimic authentic nineteenth-century black folk arts on stage—Joel Sweeney, Dan Emmett, etc.—became improperly identified with their creation.

Even sympathetic abolitionists succumbed to the allure of comic stereotyping and the comfortable feelings of superiority that seem to have gone along with it. On assignment at Hilton Head, South Carolina, in the fall of 1861, when slaves from surrounding plantations were gathering under the protection of Union forces as "contrabands of war," a New York–based Civil War field correspondent for the *National Anti-Slavery Standard* confessed: "I believed that the appearance and intelligence of Southern field hands were greatly libelled by the delineators of negro character at the concert saloons. Now I cannot but acknowledge that instead of gross exaggeration the 'minstrels' gave representations which are faithful to nature. There were the same grotesque dresses, awkward figures, and immense brogans which are to be seen every night at Bryant's and Christy's."[56]

While striving for a certain level of straightforward, artful imitation, white minstrel comedians invariably focused on aspects of slave culture which heightened the contradictions of the acculturative process. "Grotesque dresses, awkward figures, and immense brogans" were screaming targets. Symbols of acculturation under duress, they became active ingredients in minstrel humor.

Ethiopian minstrelsy set the ground rules for the appearance, in the late 1850s, of "genuine" African American minstrels.[57] African American minstrels were inescapable heirs to the theatrical conventions of their white forebears. Working through excruciating contradictions, they began the long process of reestablishing the rights to their own creative identity.

Charles B. Hicks Abroad, 1889–1895

African American minstrelsy has a father figure in Charles B. Hicks, who helped launch the Original Georgia Minstrels in 1865. He was reportedly born into slavery in Baltimore, Maryland.[58] Hicks was said to be "a very fine specimen of an Octoroon; is almost white; has a Caucasian head and face; and is possessed of great intelligence."[59] But in 1907 a foul-mouthed commentator for the Australian *Illustrated Sports and Dramatic News* recalled it differently: "When the Hicks-Sawyer Minstrel Co. came to Australia about 18 years ago, the coons were bound to the managers by contracts which practically allowed them nothing save board and lodging. Colonel B. Hicks, a monstrous wooly-headed person, was a regular nigger driver and a furious gambler as well. His performers groaned under his Tyranny."

Charles B. Hicks, 1877. (courtesy Tasmanian State Library)

A historical account of Hicks's Original Georgia Minstrels is contained in a lengthy, four-part newspaper interview with founding member J. R. Matlock, conducted while the troupe was touring New Zealand in 1877. Matlock was born in 1839, one of 350 slaves on a cotton plantation in Franklin County, Tennessee. Mixing vivid recollections of the whip and the auction block with accounts of various slave customs, he described some of the musical experiences that he brought from slavery to minstrelsy:

> On the Saturday evenings, after the work is done, [the slaves] assemble in crowds round the out-door fires, and . . . hold a weekly concert, if the overseer don't interfere. Two or three of them have fiddles, others have tin cans, clappers and banjos, while the jawbone music is a very strong element at these entertainments . . . a mule's jaw, with the teeth very loose and rattling, so that when you shake it, it makes first-class music. Then we have jubilee songs and plantation walk-rounds . . . The great holidays that slaves have are, or at all events were, at Christmas time. Shortly before then, they finish up the year's work with a grand "corn shucking," and on these occasions the slaves from two or three plantations combine together to make the work lighter. "Shucking" means piling up the corn, and this is done with a good deal of system, the "drover," who sits at the top of the stack, gives out the air, for it is done with singing accompaniments, like the sailors' "Yo, heave ho!" when pulling on a rope; and then in the evenings after the work, there are grand "to-do's." There is the fiddler and other instrumentalists who keep the game alive. The principal instruments are the mule's jawbones, combs (with paper wrapped around them), [and] banjos, the strings of which are made of strong horse-hair, while cheese boxes do for the frame-work.[60]

In 1848 Matlock was sold to a man who operated a livery stable in Tuscumbia, Alabama. When the Civil War broke out, his new master was "appointed quarter-master to the Alabama Brigade," and Matlock "went with him as his body servant." In this capacity, Matlock was present at the Battle of Shiloh. In 1862 he managed to defect to "a regiment of Illinois soldiers (Northerners)" and make his way North; and in the spring of 1864, after obtaining an education, Matlock got a job as a waiter at the Sherman House Hotel in Chicago:

> Being now very proud of my military knowledge, I resolved to form a zouave company of blacks, and I was helped by a young drummer [Taylor Brown] who had first come from Missouri, and who had been all through the war. So we set to work and soon got together a very respectable company of blacks. We had uniforms made for us, and got a good lot of musical instruments, and used to meet and drill at night in one of the city halls. Bye and bye, when our band got on, we gave a "show" and cleared over 20 dollars the first night. We then used to show regularly once or twice a month . . . We used to give the old plantation scenes which were new to the Chicago people, and they patronized us liberally . . . We have now got along to the summer of 1864.
> Mr. Hicks first arrived in Chicago this year,

> in search of black talent to form a minstrel troupe . . . and I promised I would go with him. With the money I had made in the Zouave Company I was now able to go to a singing school, where I worked hard and tried to learn music . . . Mr. Hicks then went along to Georgia . . . When Mr. Hicks returned in 1865 we made a start—and that before the close of the war . . . Our new troupe gave its first performance, so far as I was concerned, in Chicago.[61]

Over the next twenty years, Charles B. Hicks piloted "genuine" African American minstrel troupes through most of the United States and Canada, England and Ireland, Austria and Germany. He made the name "Georgia Minstrels" famous in Australia and New Zealand when he first brought his company there in 1877. In 1888 Hicks embarked on a second tour of Australasia, this time at the head of the Hicks-Sawyer Minstrels.[62] Remaining abroad until his death in 1902, Hicks occasionally relayed news to the *New York Clipper*:

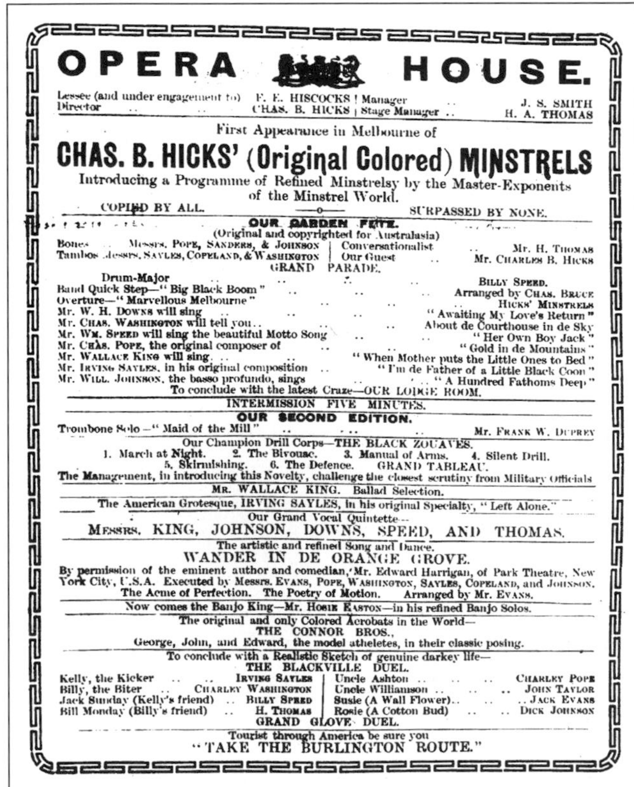

OPERA HOUSE.

Lessee (and under engagement to) F. E. HISCOCKS | Manager .. J. S. SMITH
Director .. .. CHAS. B. HICKS | Stage Manager .. H. A. THOMAS

First Appearance in Melbourne of

CHAS. B. HICKS' (Original Colored) MINSTRELS

Introducing a Programme of Refined Minstrelsy by the Master-Exponents of the Minstrel World.

COPIED BY ALL. —o— SURPASSED BY NONE.

OUR GARDEN FETE.

(Original and copyrighted for Australasia)

Bones .. Messrs. POPE, SANDERS, & JOHNSON | Conversationalist .. Mr. H. THOMAS
Tambos Messrs. SAYLES, COPELAND, & WASHINGTON | Our Guest .. Mr. CHARLES B. HICKS

GRAND PARADE.

Drum-Major .. .. .. BILLY SPEED.
Band Quick Step—"Big Black Boom" .. .. .. Arranged by CHAS. BRUCE
Overture—"Marvellous Melbourne" .. .. .. HICKS' MINSTRELS
Mr. W. H. DOWNS will sing .. .. .. "Awaiting My Love's Return"
Mr. CHAS. WASHINGTON will tell you .. .. .. About de Courthouse in de Sky
Mr. WM. SPEED will sing the beautiful Motto Song .. .. "Her Own Boy Jack"
Mr. CHAS. POPE, the original composer of .. .. "Gold in de Mountains"
Mr. WALLACE KING will sing .. .. "When Mother puts the Little Ones to Bed"
Mr. IRVING SAYLES, in his original composition .. "I'm de Father of a Little Black Coon"
Mr. WILL. JOHNSON, the basso profundo, sings .. .. "A Hundred Fathoms Deep"

To conclude with the latest Craze—OUR LODGE ROOM.

INTERMISSION FIVE MINUTES.

OUR SECOND EDITION.

Trombone Solo—"Maid of the Mill" .. .. .. Mr. FRANK W. DUPREY

Our Champion Drill Corps—THE BLACK ZOUAVES.
1. March at Night. 2. The Bivouac. 3. Manual of Arms. 4. Silent Drill.
5. Skirmishing. 6. The Defence. GRAND TABLEAU.
The Management, in introducing this Novelty, challenge the closest scrutiny from Military Officials

MR. WALLACE KING. Ballad Selection.

The American Grotesque, IRVING SAYLES, in his original Specialty, "Left Alone."

Our Grand Vocal Quintette—
MESSRS. KING, JOHNSON, DOWNS, SPEED, AND THOMAS.

The artistic and refined Song and Dance.
WANDER IN DE ORANGE GROVE.
By permission of the eminent author and comedian, Mr. Edward Harrigan, of Park Theatre, New York City, U.S.A. Executed by Messrs. EVANS, POPE, WASHINGTON, SAYLES, COPELAND, and JOHNSON.
The Acme of Perfection. The Poetry of Motion. Arranged by Mr. EVANS.

Now comes the Banjo King—Mr. HOSIE EASTON—in his refined Banjo Solos.

The original and only Colored Acrobats in the World—
THE CONNOR BROS.,
George, John, and Edward, the model atheletes, in their classic posing.

To conclude with a Realistic Sketch of genuine darkey life—
THE BLACKVILLE DUEL.

Kelly, the Kicker .. .. IRVING SAYLES | Uncle Ashton .. .. .. CHARLEY POPE
Billy, the Biter .. CHARLEY WASHINGTON | Uncle Williamson .. .. .. JOHN TAYLOR
Jack Sunday (Kelly's friend) .. BILLY SPEED | Susie (A Wall Flower) .. .. .. JACK EVANS
Bill Monday (Billy's friend) .. H. THOMAS | Rosie (A Cotton Bud) .. .. DICK JOHNSON

GRAND GLOVE DUEL.

Tourist through America be sure you
"TAKE THE BURLINGTON ROUTE."

Lorgnette, *February 1889.*

• ***January 19, 1889:*** "New Zealand Echoes from the Hicks-Sawyer Minstrels," "The 'Big Black Boom' has struck 'Maiori Land' (Aukland), and what is more, with much success. The troupe arrived at Wellington from Queensland after a very rough sea voyage . . . The fame of our baseball team seemed to have proceeded us, and the two clubs there met us on the wharf, and welcomed us . . . Our march to the hotel was a perfect ovation. Sig. Agrati, our business agent (formerly of the Cooper & Bailey Circus) had done the town in circus style, and our band gave the natives a big surprise as we marched along, playing the old Tammany Quickstep, 'Solid Men to the Front.' . . . New Zealand has the [base]ball fever . . . We defeated the Wellington Club easily, but it is only fair to say that it was the first game many of them had ever seen played by any team acquainted with the many fine points of the game. Among the first to greet us after our opening, were Geo. Turner and Harry Crawford, who arrived here ten days ahead of us, to join Clark's All Star Co. . . . Hosea Easton joined us in Sydney . . . Irving Sayles in his 'Silence and Fun' has hit them hard, while our vocal quintet has been a very strong card. The weather here is beautiful and Summery. Strawberries, large as hen's eggs, are plentiful . . . From here we go to Dunedin, Tasmania, Hobart and Lancaster, and expect to reach Melbourne early in February" (*New York Clipper*).

• ***April 27, 1889:*** "The roster of Chas. H. Hicks' Minstrels on their present tour of Australia includes Wallace King, Chas. Pope, John Taylor, Hosie Eaton [*sic*], Connor Bros. (George, Edward and John), Irving Sayles, J. R. Matlock, Chas. Washington, Billy Saunders, H. Copeland, Chas. Bruce, J. J. Cameron (business manager), C. B. Hicks (manager)" (*New York Clipper*).

• ***September 14, 1889:*** "Notes from the Antipodes," "Hicks' Minstrels and Frank Clark's Co., consolidated, are drawing crowded houses at Victoria Hall, Melbourne . . . Hiscock's New London Pavillion Co. opened Aug. 17. Among them are several American favorites, Tom Sadler, John Morton and F. West, negro comedians" (*New York Clipper*).

• ***November 9, 1889:*** "The Hicks-Sawyer Minstrels closed their season at Sydney, Aus., Sept. 1. The quartet—King, Downs, Thomas and Johnson—three Connor Brothers and Jack Evans are engaged at the Alhambra Music Hall for six months. Chas. Bruce and Frank Duprez join Gaylord's Wild West, Mr. Bruce as band leader. They are present playing with Murray & Marion's Minstrels, Haymarket Theatre. Chas. B. Hicks joins the Wild West staff. The minstrels will be reorganized after the Wild West tour, and return to America via New Zealand for next season, with many new features. Show business is very dull in Australia. There are many American professionals at the Antipodes" (*New York Clipper*).

While Hicks continued to supply the *Clipper* with upbeat reports on the progress of the Hicks-Sawyer Minstrels, the February 22, 1890, edition of the *Indianapolis Freeman* informed that "C. H. [*sic*] Hicks' Minstrels, which started out to Australia in search of their fortune, has disbanded and that some of the company are in pretty embarrassing circumstances." By Hicks's account, the Hicks-Sawyer Minstrels were still doing "a fine business" in the colonies when he departed for India with Harmston's Circus in 1891. Other correspondents suggest a less rosy scenario.

• ***March 1, 1890:*** "Charles B. Hicks' American Colored Minstrels were at Auckland, N.Z., as late as Jan. 24, and were quite the rage there. W. H. Speed, W. Wesley, Billy Saunders, Irving Sayles, Eva Tremaine, Frank Duprey, Connor Bros., Copeland, Washington, Johnson and others are in the party" (*New York Clipper*).

• ***March 29, 1890:*** "Notes from the Antipodes," "Manager Chas. B. Hicks, of the Hicks-Sawyer Minstrels, writes from Wellington, N.Z., as follows: 'We have been doing a fine business on our farewell tour through Maori land, and the boys are all well. New Zealand is full of shows . . . Harmston's Circus arrived on the Alameda from 'Frisco, and are doing well at Auckland. We play at Christ Church, Canterbury, March 17, three weeks, thence to Dunedin, opening there Easter Monday . . . I leave for America by the April steamer" (*New York Clipper*).

• ***May 17, 1890:*** "Hicks & Sawyers Minstrels, who have been in Australia for the past two seasons, were due in Portland, Oregon last month" (*Cleveland Gazette*).

• ***May 24, 1890:*** "New Zealand Notes from Chas. B. Hicks' Minstrels," "From beneath the Southern Cross we greet old friends. Our present tour through New Zealand has been a success, and for the first time we have made a tour of the West Coast, playing to splendid houses. Our trip had to be shortened on account of the band being previously engaged. We have had to close two nights, as 'La Grippe' caught us, leaving only seven people fit for work . . . We will shortly close our New Zealand tour . . . and sail for Tasmania, and from there go on to Melbourne and Sydney, and then to the Sandwich Islands, stopping at Honolulu on our way to 'Frisco. The boys are all well, and keeping things lively with bat and ball, having played forty-seven games in Australia. We have several novelties for next season, including a tenor singer and two native Hindoos, who do a startling act" (*New York Clipper*).

• ***May 24, 1890:*** "Homeward Bound, Returning in Triumph, the Monarchs of All, Chas. B. Hicks' (Original Colored) Minstrels, Season 1890–91,"

"After two years' absence in Australia, New South Wales, Queensland, Tasmania, South Australia and New Zealand, specially engaged for the Jubilee Festivities at Auckland, and the only company allowed to appear in the Grand Exhibition Concert Hall in the Great South Sea Exhibition, under the patronage of His Excellency the Earl of Onslow, Governor of New Zealand, and Lord Carrington, Governor of New South Wales, and... presented by Manager Joubert, Chairman of Exhibition Committees, with the Royal Exhibition Banner, raised over the Governor's Court during the opening ceremonies, for the Excellent Music discoursed by our Grand Parade Band—Charles Bruce, Leader; Frank Duprez, Trombone Soloist.

We fear no rivals... Chas. B. Hicks, Sole Proprietor and Manager (the man that never failed)" (*New York Clipper*).

• ***June 21, 1890:*** "Notes from the Antipodes," "Chas. B. Hicks, of the Hicks-Sawyer Minstrels, writes as follows from Hobart, Tasmania, May 7: 'We close our tour of Tasmania tonight, and it has been the most successful we have made... Irving Sayles is the hit of the trip... His song, "Father of a Little Black Coon," gets three and four encores nightly. Today we lost our mascot. After traveling over the entire route with us, "Jumbo" succumbed to "La Grippe." He... was the ugliest cur that ever walked, but faithful... We sail for Melbourne [May] 8, and are looking forward to soon meet old friends again. We will open at Ballarat [May] 14, and will present our new first part, "The Valley of Ferns," arranged by W. H. Speed' " (*New York Clipper*).

• ***February 14, 1891:*** "C. B. Hicks is still in the Australian colonies, making money with good old 'U.T.C.,' 'The Octoroon' and a minstrel show, all in one" (*New York Clipper*).

• ***June 6, 1891:*** "Charles B. Hicks, of colored minstrel fame, has gone to India with Harmston's Circus. Other members of his former company, Wallace King, R. Downes, W. Johnson and Connor Bros., are at Sydney Aus., at the Alhambra" (*New York Clipper*).

• ***August 1, 1891:*** "Interesting Notes from the Antipodes," "Chas. B. Hicks writes as follows from Cooktown under date of May 10: 'I have joined Harmston & Sons' Circus and Wild West for a tour of Java and India as general manager, sailing from here in the British India mail steamer May 11... I have sold all interest in Australian shows... At Theis I met Wallace King, W. H. Donns, Will Johnson, Harry Thomas and Little Dixey, and the Connor Brothers. They are still at the Alhambra Music Hall doing well, and are engaged for another year. Met Geo. Fortescue and the "Evangeline" Co. *en route* to Melbourne. Charley Pope and Irving Sayles are both located at Frank Clark's, Melbourne. Billy Speed and his dusky braves are battling in South Australia' " (*New York Clipper*).

• ***June 18, 1892:*** "All the way from Shanghai, China, comes the news from the veteran Chas. B. Hicks that Harmston & Sons' Great London Olympic and American Wild West is reaping a rich harvest in that city... Mr. Hicks is the manager of the troupe, and Robert Love is general agent" (*New York Clipper*).

Hicks's departure from Australia with Harmston's Circus marked the end of his historic, long-standing connection with African American minstrelsy. When he finally did make a brief journey home in 1894, it was to assemble a company of white performers to take back to China. He landed in San Francisco on August 25 and made his way to New York City; on November 15, 1894, "Col. Hick's Oriole Troupe of Vaudeville Performers" left New York bound for Shanghai,[63] and Hicks never returned to the States again. On June 8, 1895, he reported, "I have resumed my old position as general manager of Harmston's Circus." When he died at the end of 1902, the father figure of "genuine" African American minstrelsy was in Surabaya, Java, entirely divorced from his roots.[64]

Like Loudin's Fisk Jubilee Singers, Charles B. Hicks's Minstrels left a living legacy of African American entertainers in Australasia. On December 12, 1912, a reporter for the *(Broken Hill) Barrier Daily Truth* reminisced: "Nearly 24 years ago the Hicks-Sawyer minstrels appeared in the Theatre Royal, and the company was one of the strongest of its kind seen in Australia—in fact, no minstrel show has approached it since. The company included such artists as the late Wallace King (the silver-toned tenor of 'Sally Horner' fame)... the one and only Irving Sayles, and Charley Pope. Of the crowd Sayles is still a favorite with metropolitan vaudeville patrons, and the majority of the others have been gathered to their forefathers, but their capabilities as singers and entertainers still live fresh in the memories of those who have heard and seen them." Irving Sayles remained a popular performer on Rickard's Tivoli theater circuit until his death at Christchurch, New Zealand, in 1914. Charley Pope was still appearing on the Australasian professional stage in 1924.[65]

McCabe and Young's Minstrels, 1889–1892

The 1889–1895 period witnessed a great expansion of African American minstrelsy. Black minstrel companies continued to work within the old-line conventions, but from a new perspective. They weren't simply "delineating" black character and culture, they were manifesting black talent and creativity, and they stretched out, almost subconsciously, with innovations. They represented African American interests in ways that white minstrels in blackface never could.

The presentations of the "classic" black professional minstrel companies of the 1890s conformed to a certain pattern. When the minstrels hit town it was an all-day affair. Upon arrival, they launched a street parade featuring a brass band, some top-hatted, eccentric "walking gents," perhaps a few exotic animals, a "joy wagon," and a "rube" or "pickaninny" band. The parade was often followed by a challenge baseball game, with members of the troupe squaring off against the local community's best. In the evening there would be an outdoor orchestral concert, followed by the actual show.

The show was cast in three time-honored parts: first, the old-fashioned minstrel semicircle—Tambo and Bones, Mister Interlocutor, etc.—with singing and joke-telling, to the accompaniment of a small "orchestra"; second, the olio, a quick-paced variety presentation of singers, dancers, vocal quartets, acrobats, slack wire artists, male and female impersonators, contortionists, ventriloquists, magicians, etc.; and finally, a musical farce-comedy production, or afterpiece, often with a plantation setting. This format accommodated an enormous range of talent. No act was too high-toned, and none too bizarre.

Most African American minstrel companies of the 1889–1895 period were owned and controlled by white men. McCabe and Young's Minstrels, like Charles B. Hicks's Original Georgia Minstrels, was an African American minstrel company under African American proprietors. D. W. McCabe was from Boston; and Billy Young was from Cincinnati, perhaps by way of Kentucky.[66] Their partnership dated from the late 1870s. By 1889 McCabe and Young's Minstrels were well entrenched on the national scene, including the southern states, and were making annual forays to Cuba.

• ***February 16, 1889:*** "McKabe [*sic*] and Young's combination played to appreciative audiences at St. Augustine, Fla., Jan. 28 and 29. The troupe is first class in every particular. Messrs. McKabe and Young deserve great credit for refusing to yield to the urgent request of some of the white citizens who urged them not to reserve any of the parquette seats for colored people, as it would hurt them financially, for the white people would not patronize them. The committee making the request was plainly told: 'We will take the risk of financial loss, as we value our principle. Any colored lady or gentleman will have the equal right of any white lady or gentleman at our performances in this or any other city.' These are the kind of managers needed in a number of squeamish northern cities" (*Indianapolis Freeman*).

• ***April 13, 1889:*** "The following people have signed with McCabe & Young's Minstrels for next season: William Wisdom, Thomas Brown, Charley Wab, Jos. Dupree, Henry Hutchison, S. S. McKinnery, Walter Dickson, Henry Carson, Al. Thomas, Eugene Hillman, Thomas Price, Bob Vernon, Ed. Campbell, Brewer Bros., William Johnson, Wm. Young, Tom McIntosh, Will Gause [*sic*], Slone Edward, and the Cuban Sextet, of Havana, Cuba" (*New York Clipper*).

Among those listed as having signed with McCabe and Young's Minstrels for the 1889–1890 season, William "Billy" Wisdom (a.k.a. William H. Windom) was a fledgling singer-songwriter who went on to coauthor hit songs with Gussie L. Davis and garner recognition as "the most famous idolized minstrel ballad singer of his time."[67] Comedian Tom McIntosh, on the other hand, had most of his illustrious career behind him. He had toured with Charles B. Hicks and Billy Kersands in the 1870s and 1880s editions of the Original Georgia Minstrels, and he was still plowing the minstrel routes when he died in 1904.[68] McIntosh's stage partner for the 1889–1890 season with McCabe and Young was quintessential African American female impersonator William (or Willis) Gauze. "The Great Gauze" remained a prominent performer for several decades. He toured Australia with McAdoo's Minstrels at the turn of the century, and in 1924 he returned to Australia as a member of W. C. Buckner's Dixie Jubilee Singers.[69]

• ***April 27, 1889:*** "McCabe & Young's Minstrels close their season May 6 at Kansas City, Mo." (*New York Clipper*).

• ***June 22, 1889:*** "Billy Young, of McCabe and Young's Minstrels, is spending his vacation at Kansas City. D. W. McCabe and Alf. White are busy at work at Des Moines, Ia., writing and arranging an entire new show for the coming season. The first part will be called 'The Return to Africa.' The company will carry their own scenery for this production. Alf. White, Carter Gumpkins, James Randolph, Dick Weston and Henderson Smith have lately signed, making a company of thirty people. McCoy and Mahara drive over to the Capitol daily with their little yellow horse to see what new ideas Mr. McCabe has for the coming season" (*New York Clipper*).

E. H. McCoy and W. A. Mahara had a financial interest in McCabe and Young's Minstrels. In the fall of 1889 these two white men also put out McCoy and Mahara's "Silver King" Company. W. A. Mahara's continued association with McCabe and Young culminated in the formation of Mahara's Colored Minstrels in 1892.

• ***August 10, 1889:*** "McCabe & Young's Minstrels opened their season at St. Joseph, Mo. Their first part is something new to the minstrel business. They do not use the bones and tamborine, but open with brass. They carry three sets of costumes for the street parade . . . McCoy & McHarahn [*sic*] will organize a No. 2 party, which will open at Pittsburg, Pa., Oct. 3 . . . Mr. McCabe will leave the No. 1 Co. for Pittsburg, Aug. 26 to begin writing up for the No. 2 Co., and arranging a different show" (*New York Clipper*).

• ***November 23, 1889:*** "The McCabe and Young band escorted Macoy & Mahara's 'Silver King' Co. from the depot to the hotel at Cedar Falls, Ia., and there they celebrated the one hundredth nights' performance of the two shows the present season" (*New York Clipper*).

At the beginning of 1890, McCabe and Young's Minstrels were completing a string of one-night stands in central Illinois. From there they dropped into Kentucky and set a southerly course. The following show stops are noted in the "Routes" columns of the *Clipper:*

> Frankfort, Kentucky, January 20–21, 1890; Lexington, January 24; Danville, January 25; Bowling Green, January 27; Memphis, Tennessee, January 30–February 1; Birmingham, Alabama, February 3–4; Pensacola, Florida, February 6–7; Mobile, Alabama, February 8; New Orleans, Louisiana, February 10–12; Brunswick, Georgia, February 13; Jacksonville, Florida, February 14–15; St. Augustine, February 17–18; Key West, February 24-March 1.

• ***January 11, 1890:*** "It has been reported that some members of our company found a pocketbook that a man claimed to have lost on the train near Pittsfield, Ill., where the company were detained all day Dec. 27 by a search warrant. The true facts are that this man lost at gambling a considerable amount of money belonging to the house he represented, and in order to 'square' himself pretended it was stolen. At the hearing the Judge at once released the members of the company, who reciprocated by singing 'The Court House in the Skies,' at the request of the Court" (*New York Clipper*).

• ***February 1, 1890:*** "W. A. Mahara is now doing the advance for the McCabe & Young's Minstrels" (*New York Clipper*).

• ***February 22, 1890:*** "McCabe & Young's Minstrels played at St. Augustine, Fla. on Monday and Tuesday to big business. This company is doing the largest business of any coloured troupe on the road" (*Indianapolis Freeman*).

• ***March 8, 1890:*** "Havana Happenings of McCabe & Young's Minstrels," "We opened to 8,000 people at Theo La Ticca, playing two nights, and turning away hundreds. We hold first honors of American successes in Havana and have created a big sensation. Russell Harrison and party sailed on the same steamer with us from Tampa, Fla., and we gave him a grand concert out at mid sea. His party and the Governor of Havana and his consort filled ten boxes both nights. Master Prince McCabe was presented with $30 in gold by the Governor. The Cubans have beat us two games of baseball. D. W. McCabe is organizing a Cuban band of thirty people to play the States on our return" (*New York Clipper*).

• ***March 15, 1890:*** "Notes from McCabe & Young's Minstrels," "Our trip to Cuba was a success. All the boys laid in a full supply of fine clothes and diamonds . . . The company attended three receptions given in our honor by Cuban friends. McCabe & Young's band will be principally made up of Cubans next season, as Manager McCabe has contracted with six of the best Havana musicians" (*New York Clipper*).

McCabe and Young's Minstrels were on the cutting edge of African American minstrelsy. Their business was reportedly thriving, and their Cuban sojourns appeared to be touching off significant cross-cultural reverberations. Following their Cuban engagement, McCabe and Young's Minstrels bobbed up in Mississippi, headed North. The *Clipper*'s "Routes" column preserves these dates:

> Jackson, Mississippi, March 20; Natchez, March 21; Port Gibson, March 22; Greenville, March 24; Pine Bluff, Arkansas, March 28; Texarkana, March 29; Hope, March 31; Arkadelphia, April 1; Hot Springs, April 2; Little Rock, April 3; Rogers, April 10; Eureka Springs, April 11; Carthage, Missouri, April 12; Joplin, April 14; Webb City, April 15; Fort Scott, Kansas, April 18; Nevada, Missouri, April 19; Rich Hill, April 21; Garden City, Kansas, April 25; Dodge City, April 29; Topeka, May 1; Lawrence, May 2; Leavenworth, May 3.

• ***May 3, 1890:*** "The following people have signed with McCabe & Young's Minstrels for next season: Billy Young, George Jackson, Brewer Bros., Walter Dickson, Tom Brown, Henry Hutchison, George Bayley *[sic]*, Eugene

Hillman, Prof. S. S. McKinney, Lewis Hunter, Princie McCabe, Jules Johnson, Slone Edwards, Walter Mitchell, Daniel Sanders, Lozeze, Marta Martine Joncamena, Zama Harreatine, Joseph Dupree, Robert Vernon and Docker Jaspine. The company expect to receive their stage wardrobe from Havana about the first of July. A Summer tour of a month or so is contemplated" (*New York Clipper*).

• ***May 17, 1890:*** "The famous McCabe & Young's Operatic Minstrels close a successful season of 47 weeks, at Omaha, May 19 . . . Address all communications to D. W. McCabe, Ninth Street Theatre, Kansas City, Mo." (*New York Clipper*).

• ***May 31, 1890:*** "McCabe & Young have received twenty-five old gold silk half plug hats, twenty-five assorted colors chair covers and twenty-five high-collared coats from Havana, Cuba. Mr. McCabe is now ordering all new printing. Our time is filled, our people all engaged, and we will open next August in fine shape" (*New York Clipper*).

• ***September 6, 1890:*** "The new Congressional first part, written by McCabe and Young and Billy Wisdom, was produced for the first time at San Francisco last week . . . Master Princie McCabe in his new song, 'Sweet Little Black Sport,' took the Westerners by storm. The 'Frisco Glee Club gave the boys a wine party after the show Aug. 25" (*New York Clipper*).

• ***December 27, 1890:*** "McCabe & Young's Minstrels report business to be continually large . . . A reception was tendered them by the Cuban Band, at Key West, Fla. The company will tour the Bahama Islands. Billy Wisdom was the recipient of a valuable diamond ring upon his twenty-fourth birthday anniversary recently" (*New York Clipper*).

• ***January 24, 1891 (Richmond, Virginia):*** "McCabe and Young's Colored Minstrels performed three nights last week, Jan. 15th, 16th and 17th 1891, at Barton's Opera House Cor. 8th and Broad streets. Their rich and rare jokes produced continuous applause. Their different specialties are very fine and were highly enjoyed by the audience. It was an all around good play" (*Richmond Planet*).

• ***February 7, 1891:*** "Business continues good. Richards & Pringle's Georgia Minstrels met us at Danville, Va. The boys gave us a grand serenade at the depot, and presented us with a dozen boxes of fine cigars and a case of beer. We spent a very pleasant half hour" (*New York Clipper*).

• ***February 28, 1891:*** "Big business is still the rule. The Excelsior Quartet joined at Philadelphia. The company now consists of thirty-eight people, and a different parade is given daily. During the next month the company will play nothing but return dates. Mr. McCabe will give up the management of the troupe at Boston. A tour of Europe will probably be made this Summer. McCabe and Wisdom have finished their new burlesque, and it will be presented in New York City before too long" (*New York Clipper*).

• ***March 28, 1891:*** "McCabe & Young's Minstrels are doing well on all their return engagements through Maryland and Pennsylvania. None of the company were seriously hurt in the recent accident on the Cumberland Valley Railroad" (*New York Clipper*).

• ***May 2, 1891:*** "McCabe & Young's Minstrels closed their long and successful season April 18 at Brooklyn. The company will open their next season early in August at Boston" (*New York Clipper*).

The June 6, 1891, edition of the *Clipper* included a request from Billy Young to "tell his friends that, notwithstanding any contrary reports, there is not one particle of enmity existing between Mr. Young and his late partner, Mr. McCabe." No explanation was offered for the seemingly sudden dissolution of McCabe and Young's longstanding partnership. Young did not return for the 1891–1892 season, nor did Billy Wisdom.

• ***June 6, 1891:*** "Manager D. W. McCabe is making big preparations for the coming season. There will be . . . a new afterpiece, called 'The Brooklyn Handicap.' George Jackson and Frank Broom will return from England in July, to join the company . . . The season will open on or about Aug. 15. D. W. McCabe is spending his vacation at Nowin, S.C., with his wife" (*New York Clipper*).
• ***June 20, 1891:*** "Billy Wisdom, stage manager of McCabe & Young's Minstrels for five years, has just closed a six weeks' engagement at the Ninth Street Museum, Philadelphia, and will go on the steamer *Republic* for the Summer to do end and general work with Speck's Phonographic Comedy Co. Mr. Wisdom is giving the finishing touch to a number of new acts for colored minstrel performers" (*New York Clipper*).

Continuing as sole proprietor and manager, Dan McCabe retained the name McCabe and Young's Minstrels for the sake of continuity.
• ***July 25, 1891:*** "McCabe & Young's Minstrels will begin rehearsals at Philadelphia July 28. The roster: D. W. McCabe, E. L. Roy, B. C. Pukson, M. A. Colla, G. A. Watson, H. G. Hutchison, S. S. McKinny, Lewis Hunter, Walter Dickson, Eugene Hillman, Geo. Jackson, Bob Vernon, Billy Johnson, Harry Eaton, W. H. Pierce, Joseph Dupree, John Eason, Prince McCabe, Geo. C. Young, C. Rosenfelt, Jalvin and Pamplin, D. W. Saunders, George Bailey and the Brewer Family—six in number" (*New York Clipper*).

Route listings in the *Clipper* for McCabe and Young's Minstrels during the last five months of 1891 show the following:

> Nashville, Tennessee, August 20–22; Galveston, Texas, September 28–29; Victoria, Texas, September 30; Columbia, Texas, October 1; Houston, October 2; Dallas, October 3; Fort Worth, October 5; Hot Springs, Arkansas, October 20; Rolling Fork, Mississippi, October 27; New Orleans, Louisiana, October 28–31; Nashville, Tennessee, November 19–21; Wilmington, North Carolina, December 4; Durham, December 7; Lynchburg, Virginia, December 9; Richmond, December 10.

• ***September 26, 1891:*** "A large crowd of people witnessed the grand moonlight parade at Memphis, Tenn., Aug. 26, when sixty-five people in line, ten mounted buglers and thirty mouth pieces in the band, all dressed in Zouave costumes. Buglers as Turks, fifteen in drum corps, in Mexican costumes, and walking gents, all in long white cape coats. There were forty boys with torches and red fire, making one of the grandest sights ever witnessed at Memphis. The city was taken by storm, and opening night people were turned away. The members are all in high spirits, and the Zouave Gun Drill has added a big feature" (*New York Clipper*).
• ***October 31, 1891:*** "We have put in eight successful weeks in Texas, opening all of Mr. Greenwall's circuit, and playing to the capacity of nearly all the houses. The company is the best that Mr. McCabe has ever put together. It comprises twenty-six people, all of whom are hard workers" (*New York Clipper*).

McCabe and Young's Minstrels closed out the year with a tour through Mississippi, Arkansas, and Georgia. At the beginning of 1892, they were preparing to embark for Havana.
• ***January 2, 1892:*** "Notes from McCabe's Minstrels—Business is larger than ever. The illuminated parade has been a success. Edward G. Roy has been called back to the company to take charge. D. W. McCabe has sailed for Hayti in advance. The company [will] put in a two weeks' tour in the West Indies, opening at Havana Jan. 4" (*New York Clipper*).
• ***January 9, 1892:*** "D. W. McCabe has arrived at Havana, Cuba, and was royally entertained by the numerous friends he met there two years ago . . . The company will tour Hayti, Jamaica and Central America. They will put on a big company at Havana, as there will be excursions

run from every point of the island. The party will arrive from Key West Jan. 4, and go to Cenfurgoes for a run of ten days; then return to begin rehearsing for Havana" (*New York Clipper*).

• ***January 16, 1892:*** "Notes from McCabe's Minstrels—at Cuba," "The boys are highly amused at the odd ways that business is done in Cuba. First, the railroad rate is fourteen cents per mile, third class. You pay fifty cents for each trunk, every 100 miles or less, and get a nice hotel rate of four dollars a day, and eat two meals only. The beds are one sheet on an iron spring. The theatres are very large, pretty, and seat lots of people. The weather has been very pleasant, and we have attended many social parties and have had a fine trip. Santiago Pubillones has made everything very pleasant for us. We were met by his entire No. 1 Circus at Cardenas, and they gave us a fine time. All the boys are laying in a full supply of diamonds . . . McCabe, in his Spanish comedies, was more than a hit. The company opens at the Theatro Payret, Havana, on Jan. 15, then go to Hayti for a season" (*New York Clipper*).

• ***February 6, 1892:*** "Notes from D. W. McCabe's Minstrels in Cuba," "McCabe's Big Minstrel Exposition opened at Theatro Payret, Havana, Cuba, and report large business. The show consists of sixty people. Mme. Sereveti made her debut with the company Jan. 24. McCabe produced the opera 'Africana' [January] 25, 26, 27. The Charleston Quartet joined [January] 24 . . . We had the opportunity to see a bull fight, which was novelty to us . . . The company will sail for Mexico Feb. 15 to fill a two weeks' engagement at Theatre National" (*New York Clipper*).

• ***February 20, 1892:*** "We are now playing the interior towns . . . Sig. Enero Seymong, flutist, joined us at Cardenas . . . The company includes: D. W. McCabe, manager; E. L. Roy, advance; R. G. Phippins, interpreter; Gordon Collins, John Brewer, Walter Dixon, S. S. McKinnie, Billy Johnson, Geo. Catlin, J. Jalvan, J. Pamplin, W. S. Jefferson, Bob Vernon, H. G. Hutchinson, Ned Johnson, John Eason, John Vigal, Master Hillar Brewer, Master Perl Brewer, Master Prince McCabe, Banao Pamproni, Arthur M. Howe, Ed. A. Denton and Chas. Lamps" (*New York Clipper*).

• ***February 27, 1892:*** A letter from McCabe and Young's Operatic Minstrels, posted from Havana, reported: "We have been on the island of Cuba nearly one month, and shall remain at least two weeks longer. The boys are enjoying excellent health, and business is good. The 'great and only' Jalvan was presented with a handsome diamond pin on the night of Jan. 22 by members of the company. He has been the principal 'hit' of the show this season; as a juggler he is unsurpassed. We gave a grand moonlight parade on January 16th., leaving the Theatre Payset with over 300 people in line . . . We are the second colored show that ever showed on this island, but I am of the opinion that it will be only a matter of time when they will visit here every season" ("Bano," *Indianapolis Freeman*).

• ***March 12, 1892:*** "We sailed from Havana. Cuba, Feb. 11, arriving at Progressor, Yucatan, 13, and opened the same night. The only notification the natives had of what we were going to do was our street parade . . . John Brewer and family put on his spectacular burlesque, 'The Bull Fight,' and the natives simply went wild over it . . . Billy Johnson's old man specialty continues to receive many encores. Gordon Collier and Geo. Catlin, in the Chinese burlesque, simply have to hide themselves every night . . . We run four nights at Progressor, and Manager D. W. McCabe has everything in readiness to open at Merida [March] 18" (*New York Clipper*).

• ***March 26, 1892:*** "D. W. McCabe's minstrels are making a highly successful tour in Yucatan and Mexico; they will return to America soon and close the season" (*Indianapolis Freeman*).

• ***March 26, 1892:*** "McCabe's Minstrels . . . arrived at Vera Cruz March 3, after five day's sail on board the Ward Line Steamer, *Yucatan*... Capt. Allan informed us that he would be obliged to remain overnight at Tampico, Mexico, and assisted us in getting our baggage ashore, and we gave a performance and turned 'em away before 7 o'clock. The passengers all attended, with the officers of the steamer, after which the boys furnished the music, while everyone danced until 3 A.M. There is going to be an amateur bull fight tomorrow ([March] 6) in which Gordon Collins and John Brewer are to assume the leading roles... Billy Johnson and Walter Dixon are to be the judges... We will remain here two days longer, and open at the City of Mexico March 9 at the large Theatre Orrin, for a two weeks' run... We are happy to think there is no more water between us and the Land of the Free" (*New York Clipper*).

• ***April 2, 1892:*** "Notes from D. W. McCabe's Minstrels in Mexico," "After a long spell of sickness Manager McCabe has recovered. No medicine seemed to do him any good, and he finally got to drinking Mexican native 'polkie,' which cured him at once" (*New York Clipper*).

• ***April 30, 1892:*** "Notes from D. W. McCabe's Minstrels in the City of Mexico," "We opened at the Teatro Circo Orrin... The grand illuminated parade, headed by D. W. McCabe's dancing horse, set the public wild. The Teatro Ciro Orrin... seats about 4,500 people, and was packed from pit to dome. The Orrin Bros. did us many favors, and they are without a doubt the Barnum-Bailey firm of Mexico. D. W. McCabe's dancing stallion, which he bought at Pachia for $500, was sold for $750 in this city at sight after the second parade. Ed. L. Roy has gone in advance to Central America, where the company will make a short visit" (*New York Clipper*).

• ***May 7, 1892:*** "McCabe's Concert Co. have returned from a short tour through Central America, joining the big show at Auguwas, Calientes. The season will close at San Antonio May 15. The next tour will open at Philadelphia Aug. 20... A big festival and reception will be given at San Antonio on the closing night" (*New York Clipper*).

Despite the optimistic reports, this seemingly successful tour came to a sudden and disastrous conclusion:

• ***May 21, 1892:*** "McCabe's Minstrels Stranded and McCabe's Whereabouts Unknown," A letter from "S. S. McKinney, Leader of Band and Orchestra," mailed from Laredo, Texas, revealed, "McCabe's Minstrels stranded at Monterrey, Mexico. Manager Dan McCabe leaving the show very suddenly on the night of May 7th, leaving behind unpaid bills and salaries, and the people nearly penniless. The show has had a very prosperous season financially, and it is not for the want of capital that it went to pieces, but purely through the dishonesty of McCabe and Roy, whose whereabouts are unknown at present. The people, through the kindness of friends, have gotten as far as this place, where the Opera House was kindly donated by Manager Solon and two performances were given" (*Indianapolis Freeman*).

Note: This news was similarly reported in the May 28, 1892, edition of the *New York Clipper*.

After stranding his company in Mexico, D. W. McCabe was not much heard from until the summer of 1894, when he surfaced in Chicago at the head of a new company. McCabe continued to work in minstrelsy until his death on October 20, 1907.[70] Billy Young lived to boast on the occasion of his fifty-first birthday, October 31, 1911, that he felt "like a youth in his teens—voice clear as a bell and reaching the same notes as I did when McCabe and I used to sing the 'upper tens' and the 'lower fives' twenty-five years ago."[71] In the fall of 1913, Young was forced off the road by "lung trouble," and he died before the end of that year.[72]

Chapter Two

1890

Loudin's Fisk Jubilee Singers Come Home

In 1890 the foreign adventures of professional jubilee singers acquired mythic characteristics, as if a holy mission was reaching its culmination. The most farseeing jubilee pilgrim of the era was undoubtedly Frederick J. Loudin. Completing his three-year tour of Australia, New Zealand, and Tasmania in late 1889, Loudin directed his Fisk Jubilee Singers into even more exotic fields—Ceylon, India, Burma, Malaysia, China, and Japan. In these previously uncharted waters, Loudin's Fisk Jubilee Singers rounded out their six-year-long world tour.

Before they could begin the final leg of their odyssey, it was necessary to replace two singers who had resigned at the end of the Australasian tour. Tenor R. B. Williams decided to remain in Wellington, New Zealand, with his Australian wife, to settle down, raise a family, and establish a law practice;[1] and basso Orpheus McAdoo elected to return straightaway to America, to organize a jubilee company of his own. The roster of Loudin's "homeward bound" troupe included Patti Malone, Maggie Carnes and Addie Johnson, sopranos; Maggie Wilson and Georgie Gibbons, contraltos; John T. L. Lane and G. F. Simpson, tenors; F. J. Loudin and C. Nelson, bassos; and Leota Henson, pianist.[2]

Foreign press clippings in a scrapbook kept by Leota Henson[3] and a retrospective account that Loudin gave in the 1892 edition of *The Story of the Jubilee Singers* preserve a composite picture of their travels in the Orient. As Loudin recalled, they had a disappointing start at Colombo, Ceylon (Sri Lanka): "On the 25th of October [1889], we embarked on the magnificent ship 'Orizaba,' of the Orient line, homeward bound via Ceylon . . . We landed in Columbo, after seventeen days' sail. Unfortunately, we found that our agent, who had preceded us by a month, was unable to fix a date for us which would suit the date of our arrival and departure, as the only available hall in Columbo had been previously engaged; so, after three days spent in Ceylon, during which time some of us visited Kandy, about forty miles from Columbo, we left for Calcutta . . . A number of Europeans at Columbo were greatly disappointed because we did not give a concert."[4]

By Loudin's account, the voyage from Colombo to Calcutta "was a very rough one, as during two days we were on the edge of a cyclonic storm." At Calcutta, there was some initial confusion about what the Jubilee Singers' name represented: "The popular idea runs on the Jubilee of Her Majesty's [Queen Victoria's] reign, which was celebrated with more or less pomp and ceremony a short time ago. The Jubilee Singers have no connection with that event."[5] During their two-week stay in Calcutta, Loudin's Fisk Jubilee Singers received the patronage of Lieutenant Governor Lord Landsdowne, who had first met the Jubilee Singers when he was Viceroy of Canada. Concerts were divided between the Calcutta Opera House and Bishop Thorburn's Dhurrumtolla Street Methodist Episcopal Church.

• ***December 2, 1889:*** "A fair house assembled at the Opera House on Saturday night [to see the Jubilee Singers]. Among the audience were several of our best musicians, who listened with critical ears, and at the conclusion of the concert pronounced it a rare musical treat. There is something quite out of the ordinary run in their singing. The rhythm and phrasing of their own 'Slave Songs' and 'Spirituals' exercises a species of fascination on the hearers, while the charming way in which their voices blend cannot fail to please even the non-musical ear... The reception accorded to the Jubilee Singers in Calcutta has not been characterized by the enthusiasm which they have evoked in Europe, America and the Colonies, and must be a novel experience to people who for 18 years have been singing to vast audiences. But the same set of conditions they have hitherto met with does not exist in India" (*Indian Daily News*).

• ***December 3, 1889:*** "The Fisk Jubilee Singers gave their first performance on Monday last at the Opera House and a curious performance it was. No one seemed to be able to make up their minds as to the merits of the items. Quaint it certainly was, and in fact so novel that it took one's breath away and left one still wondering" (*Indian Planters' Gazette*).

• ***December 12, 1889:*** "With the sacred concert in the Methodist Episcopal Church last evening, the visit of the 'Fisk Jubilee Singers' to Calcutta has come to an end. Their advent has been an event in the annals of the metropolis, which should not be allowed to pass unnoticed. It cannot be denied that their reception here was not what was anticipated, notwithstanding that negro minstrelsy has ever proved a great attraction to the people of the city... That [the Jubilee Singers] were not received with more enthusiasm in Calcutta is not greatly to our credit, we think... If their visit to India tends to but awaken in us an interest in the Negro race, it will not be in vain that they have come to these shores" (*Statesman*).

Loudin admitted, "[O]ur audiences were... almost exclusively European and Eurasians, as the natives were but little attracted by us."[6] The Jubilee Singers were more warmly received in other parts of India. From Calcutta they traveled inland to Asansol, Allahabad, and as far north as Ambala. They also sang at Delhi and Agra, the scene of a "jubilee experience" without parallel, as described by Loudin: "At Agra is built that wonderful tomb, the Taj-Mahal, acknowledged by the whole world to be the most beautiful monument the earth had yet possessed... It goes without saying that we, like others who have made pilgrimages to this tomb, built by Shah Jehan for his devoted wife Banos Begum, were overpowered by its indescribable beauty, but we were destined to have an experience of which we had not dreamed."[7]

The following morning, with the permission of the custodian, Loudin's Fisk Jubilee Singers gave a performance in the Islamic shrine: "We gather around the sarcophagi and soon the great lofty dome echoes the first Christian song it has ever caught up... As the tones of that great song, 'Steal Away to Jesus,' which we had sung before emperors, presidents, kings and queens, awoke the stillness of that most wonderful of temples, we were so much overcome by the unique circumstances that it was with the utmost difficulty we could sing at all. 'I've Been Redeemed' and 'We Shall Walk Through The Valley' were sung, and thus closed one of the most remarkable events in the history of the Fisk Jubilee Singers."[8]

Among those who witnessed this remarkable performance was a reporter for the *Delhi Gazette*: "When we say that it takes twenty seconds by the watch for the last faint echoes of a note to die away, musicians who have not seen the Taj, can estimate the difficulties attending any vocal performance in it... Yet these difficulties were successfully overcome by the Fisk Jubilee Singers, and the treat afforded to the few who were privileged to attend, is not likely to be forgotten for the rest of their lives. Henceforth the

Taj and the Singers from the Far West will ever be connected in our memory."[9]

An article in the *Delhi Gazette* of December 20, 1889, drew far-reaching conclusions from the advent of the Jubilee Singers:

> Within the last half century a cave of harmony has been opened which was previously unknown to civilised ears, and there is probably not a home throughout the world boasting of any refinement where nigger melodies are not familiar. The most down-trodden race on earth has presented a gift to mankind that is appreciated in proportion to the refinement of the listeners, for none but those who have studied music seriously, can realise at its full significance the fact that the melody of the negro has, as it were, sprung up spontaneously. Like the tea-plant in Assam the precious gift was there growing wild, and only required cultivation to make it excel in richness and flavour all that had been done elsewhere by the most elaborate training. For there can be little doubt that the negro population, as a mass, is more musical than any race in Europe.

From a business standpoint, the Jubilee Singers' sojourn in Bombay was more outstanding, as Loudin described: "In Bombay we sang with even greater success, as the Parsees came in large numbers to hear us, and our hall was nightly crowded to its utmost capacity, many persons sitting on the stage behind us."[10] Reviews in the local English-language dailies confirm their success in Bombay.

• ***January 8, 1890:*** "This company were again most successful in their concert on Monday evening, on which occasion his Excellency Lord Reay was present. The hall was literally packed, even to the spiral staircase, which offered seats for a few who could not reach the gallery. Every item on the programme, and many additions, owing to encores, were rendered in a perfectly artistic and finished manner. . . One feels assured whenever those sweet, perfectly trained voices blend together, that a mistake, a false note or tone, is out of the question. . . The whole company seem to be beyond criticism, one feels inclined to combine the sublime with the ridiculous and compare their singing to a sound good 'kick,' something which can be felt and not described" (*Times of India*).

• ***January 10, 1890:*** "Everything on that evening must have appeared strange to the spectators. . . The company rose and sang 'Steal Away to Jesus.' It is a wild, thrilling melody wrung from the hearts of slaves who had only their God to look to, for in this world they had but misery and woe. It is a wild wail, pathetic and weird, sung by perfect part singers and electrified all who heard it. Some could not sustain the sudden thrill, and left the room. On the conclusion of the melody there was a dead silence for some moments, and then there was such applause as has seldom greeted a public performer in this city. . .

On Tuesday they gave their 'Farewell' performance to a crowded house—not a space being available, either in front or even at the back of the singers, which in itself goes to prove how successful they have been during their short stay. The singing throughout was, as before, perfect, and many of the pieces again and again applauded, leaving no alternative but double encores at times" (*Bombay Gazette*).

From Bombay, Loudin's Jubilee Singers took a train to Madras, where they opened on January 11, 1890.

• ***January 13, 1890:*** "The first concert given by this troupe. . . attracted but a poor audience. Perhaps this was in part due to the unfortunate disappointment which many incurred the previous day. Fresh to India and its ways, the Company had relied on the statement of a railway official in Bombay, had missed the M.R. Co.'s train at Raichore on Thursday and had been compelled to put in some 22 hours at the above delightful junction" (*Madras Times*).

• ***January 14, 1890:*** "Vocal music of the same character has never yet been performed in this

City and, in our opinion, never will be again" (*Madras Times*).

Loudin described the continuing journey:

> We sailed from Madras along the east coast of India, calling at the various ports until Coconada [Kakinada] was reached; then, crossing the Bay of Bengal, our next stop was at Rangoon in Lower Burma. For a stay of one week our work here was very profitable, most of our concerts being given in the Methodist Church. Here also we had the opportunity of coming in contact with the native population. The Baptist have a strong hold here, especially among the Karens.
>
> We were asked to sing to their schools, and one beautiful morning we drove out . . . They were gentlemanly and ladylike and greeted us most heartily. We sang a number of pieces for them, which they seemed most thoroughly to enjoy, many of them being moved to tears. They, in turn, sang for us a number of the Moody and Sankey hymns, which they did very well, indeed.[11]

Leaving Rangoon, Loudin's Fisk Jubilee Singers sailed down the coast of the Malay Peninsula to Pinang, and on through the Strait of Malacca. On February 9, 1890, they began a successful series of five concerts in Singapore.

• ***February 15, 1890:*** "There was a very well-filled house last night on the occasion of the farewell performance of the Jubilee Singers, who leave to-day per S.S. Sachsen for Hongkong on their way home to America" (*Singapore Free Press*).

Loudin's Fisk Jubilee Singers arrived in Hong Kong during the annual "race week" festivities (horse races), which diminished concert attendance. The Hong Kong *Daily Press* reported, "The Company have, rather unfortunately, happened on a bad time for entertainments here, or otherwise their concerts would have received the liberal support they undoubtedly deserve."[12] From Hong Kong, they sailed to Shanghai to begin two weeks of concerts, only to discover that "many of the leading Europeans . . . had gone to the races at Hong Kong."[13]

Loudin had hoped to make an extended visit to Japan, but steamship schedules prevented it. Their first concert in Japan was at Nagasaki: "Having arranged with the Steamship Company to delay the sailing of our steamer for about twelve hours, we were enabled to give a concert which was very successful indeed."[14] Moving on to Kobe, Loudin noted, "[W]e spent about a week, singing to crowded houses nightly, our audiences here consisting, as in other Oriental cities, chiefly of Europeans; still a much larger percentage of the Japanese attended our concerts than any of the other Oriental races."[15] Reviews in the *Kobe Herald* were sympathetic.

• ***March 28, 1890:*** "They come from no musical cultivation whatever, but are the simple, ecstatic utterances of wholly untutored minds. From so unpromising a source we could reasonably expect only such a mass of crudities as would be unendurable to the cultivated ear. On the contrary, however, the cultivated listener confesses to a new charm, and to a power never felt before, at least in its kind. A technical analysis of these melodies shows some interesting facts. The first peculiarity that strikes the attention is in the rhythm. This is complicated, and sometimes strikingly original. But although so new and strange, it is most remarkable that these effects are so extremely satisfactory" (*Kobe Herald*).

• ***March 29, 1890:*** "[Just] as the weather was storming outside, so did the audience inside the Theatre storm the house with rapturous applause . . . Next came a selection in which Mr. Loudin sang 'A Hundred Fathoms Deep' to the accompaniment of Miss Henson on the piano. In this Mr. Loudin's basso was heard to great advantage, and if we are not mistaken we have never heard a lower note rendered by an amateur or professional in either China or Japan" (*Kobe Herald*).

On March 31, 1890, Loudin's Fisk Jubilee Singers opened in Yokohama, the final show stop on their "homeward bound" tour, and Loudin assured, "Our hall was crowded nightly with eager listeners, many of whom were Japanese."[16] Loudin gave a wistful account of their departure for the States: "It is now Thursday, the 3rd of April . . . and we are on board the 'Rio de Janeiro.' The ship weighs anchor and we are on our way home again, it being just six years to the very day of the week, day of the month, and hour of the day, since we had sailed from New York. The morning is rough. Hours after our ship had started, Fujiyama was still in plain view, and we looked with longing eyes back to this beautiful land where our stay had been much too short, either for profit or pleasure."[17]

Landing in San Francisco on April 20, 1890, Loudin's Fisk Jubilee Singers became the first African American musical company to complete an around-the-world tour. This was accomplished under a black manager and with resounding financial success. From San Francisco, the company traveled back east to their respective homes, giving concerts along the way. Loudin recounted a distressing incident of their homecoming: "We sang at Pueblo [Colorado]. Our next point eastward was Colorado Springs, forty-two miles distant, but we were compelled to return to Pueblo after our concert to get a place to sleep, as no hotel in Colorado Springs would keep us. Our next appointment was still east of Colorado Springs, so I was compelled to pay the passage of twelve people eighty-four miles to get a place to sleep. Surely this is the 'land of the free and the home of the brave.' "[18]

During the course of their six-year voyage around the world, incidents of outright racial discrimination had been few and far between. Back in "the land of the free," however, racial discrimination would haunt them everywhere they went.

With plans to reconvene in the fall for a "domestic" tour, Loudin's Fisk Jubilee Singers disbanded for the summer. Loudin had returned to America a wealthy man. In hometown Ravenna, Ohio, he and his wife, Harriet, were able to build a lavish home on the corner of Walnut and Riddle Streets, which they called "Otira," after a famous gorge in New Zealand:

> The hall of the dwelling has a paneled wainscoting of a combination of all the different kinds of wood he brought with him . . . The sliding doors separating the drawing room from the library are of Australian kauri, while the panels are of mottled kauri and honeysuckle. The dining room is wainscoted with Australian cedar.
>
> Facing one as they enter the beautiful stained glass doors of the house, stands a clock similar in size and form to the grandfather's clock of ye olden time, which is made of teak wood and was brought by Mr. Loudin from Burma. It was made in Rangoon at the government prison . . . by a Burma convict. The wood is almost as heavy as iron, and resembles the polished face of dark granite. A year and a half was required to make it . . . The clock stands eight feet in height and is one mass of bas-relief, gods, dragons and various monsters . . .
>
> Among his collection of Australian curios may be mentioned the "Meri-meri" stone from New Zealand . . .
>
> Japanese swords and armour, beautiful specimens of inlaid lacquered work, specimens of Japanese art and native drawings occupy prominent places about the house . . . The house is a maze of beautiful, rare and costly things, which only serve to bewilder the observer who makes but a casual inspection.[19]

Loudin's summer hiatus was eventful. In late June, he and Patti Malone visited Fisk University and participated in the Commencement Day exercises. Loudin was a speaker, and he rendered a bass solo. Patti Malone took time to provide musical instruction to the Jubilee Club, and she led the choir in singing the jubilee song "In Bright Mansions Above."[20] On a business trip to Cleveland a couple weeks later, Loudin was refused accommodations at the American House hotel.

"*Otira,*" [Ravenna, Ohio] Record-Courier, *March 10, 1971. (courtesy Portage County Historical Society Museum)*

Back in Cleveland at the end of July, Loudin and his family were guests of honor at a reception hosted by black Ohio state representative John P. Green and his wife.

• ***August 2, 1890:*** "Last week Friday [July 26] Mr. and Mrs. John P. Green . . . tendered Mr. and Mrs. F. J. Loudin, Mrs. A. F. Henson and Miss L. Henson, sister and niece of Mr. Loudin, a reception . . . All who read know the grand success of Loudin's Fisk Jubilee Singers . . . During the evening [Leota Henson] rendered such piano solos as 'The Storm at Sea' by Sidney Smith; a 'Nocturne,' and 'Allegro Cassique' by Ravina . . . Her rendition of the celebrated selection 'The Last Hope' by Gottshalk stamps her as much more than an ordinary artist. Mr. Loudin sang 'Thy Sentinel Am I,' by Watson; Pinsuti's 'Bedouin Love Song,' and 'A Hundred Fathoms Deep.' But it is in such selections as 'Nazareth' by Gounod, and 'Calvary' by Rodney, that his grand basso voice is heard at its best. So much feeling and power are evidences as to thrill one from head to foot" (*Cleveland Gazette*).

Troupe member Addie Johnson was also active during her summer break in hometown Richmond, Virginia. As "eminent Prima Donna" of the Addie Johnson Concert Company, she appeared in at least one local concert, which was advertised and reviewed in the *Richmond Planet*.

A HUMILIATING FACT.

One of the most extensively traveled men in this State is Mr. F. J. Lowden, of Ravenna. He is besides a gentleman of fine education and courtly manners, and is widely known as the manager of a company of "jubilee singers." It is necessary to an understanding of what follows to explain that he is a colored man. In the course of his travels abroad Mr. Lowden dined by special invitation with the Right Honorable William E. Gladstone, then premier of the British Government, Hon. John Bright, and other very distinguished men of Great Britain. He sat at table one evening with the late Emperor William of Germany, the Crown Prince, and Prince Charles, in the imperial palace at Potsdam. In nearly every European capital he has been received as an honored guest by the men who shape the destinies of empires. The rulers of India, China and Australasia have taken him by the hand as a man and a brother. He has met on equal terms the best statesmen of his native land. After fifteen years of traveling and of mingling freely with the mighty ones of earth, Mr. Lowden came to Cleveland on a little matter of business on Tuesday and was denied a room and temporary board at one of the hotels on the ground of his color! In justice to this city it must be said that there is probably not another place of public entertainment in it with any claims to respectability where any discrimination is made on that ground. It is humiliating to think there is even one such place.—Sunday's Leader.

Yes, it is "humiliating" in the extreme, and none can appreciate the fact more than our people.

However, the Leader is not sufficiently "humiliated" to cause it to publish the *name* of the hotel in which Mr. *Loudin* was insulted. Why didn't it say that it was that second-class hotel, the American House? Was it afraid of losing the hotel's advertising patronage and was it loth to injure the business of a place which permits such American citizens as Mr. Loudin to be so grievously insulted in its office? It certainly looks like it.

The American House is not alone—there are other second and third-class places of business here that do the very same thing whenever they dare to. And it only remains for the other local newspapers to treat such affairs as Mr. Loudin's, in the "Covert" way the Sunday Leader has the one in question, to cause not only those in the second and third class but many in the first class to discriminate against our people. They would do it now but for fear of a public sentiment which frowns down such disgraceful proceedings in this city, and causes injury to come to the business of the discriminators when the press properly sets forth facts, and awakens it.

The Sunday Leader editorial given above does not impress the careful Afro-American reader as coming from a *true* friend—one who feels the strength of a correct position and dare hold all parts of it if need be aggressively.

Cleveland Gazette, *July 12, 1890.*

• ***August 30, 1890:*** "The Addie M. Johnson Concert," "She Carries the House by Storm," "The Addie M. Johnson concert was given last Monday night at the 5th St. Baptist Church . . . 'With her faults I love her still' was splendidly sung by Mr. M. Sydney Mayo . . .

Upon the appearance of Miss Addie M. Johnson, she was greeted with applause, and sang with charming sweetness, 'Waiting.'

The selection from H.M.S. Pinafore was very fine. Edward Clay cut a handsome figure in the attractive captain's uniform of H.M.S. Pinafore . . . while J. M. Jasper as Dick Deadeye was a decided success, the pipe, the blackened eye, the hump on the back, the limp made realistic the rendition . . . Miss Addie M. Johnson . . . sang with exquisite expression 'Down on the Suanee River.' . . . Her travel in foreign countries has added to the charming excellence of her voice. It is elastic and capable of accomplishing the most difficult evolutions in music. Everyone should hear her" (*Richmond Planet*).

On October 13, 1890, in Prof. Frederick J. Loudin's home town, Loudin's Fisk Jubilee Singers began their first American tour since 1884.

• ***October 18, 1890 (Ravenna, Ohio):*** "Loudin's Fisk Jubilee Singers opened the season here the 13th, 14th and 15th, to crowded houses" (*Cleveland Gazette*).

Race relations in the United States had profoundly deteriorated during Loudin's six-year absence abroad. One newspaper source asserted that Loudin had only returned to his native country "from a sense of duty." In retrospect, Frederick J. Loudin can be seen as the most politically outspoken African American entertainer of the nineteenth century. During the Fisk Jubilee Singers' North American tours of 1879–1882, Loudin had used his high visibility as the troupe's spokesman to press the case for civil rights. Whenever they had encountered discrimination, Loudin had made a public protest from the stage the following day, and his complaints had often drawn the attention of the press. During his 1890s North American tours, Loudin again refused to bow to Jim Crow.

• ***November 1, 1890 (Cleveland, Ohio):*** "Loudin's Fisk Jubilee Singers," "This excellent company made its first appearance in this city since its return from its famous tour around the world at the Music Hall last week. On the first night nearly 5,000 people were present and nearly as many attended the second evening. Mr. Loudin's and Miss Johnson's solo work, as well as the company's singing, brought forth storms of applause, and deserved every bit of it. Perhaps as interesting as any part of the programme was Mr. Loudin's talk of their trip around the world, and his scoring of the American House of this city for refusing him accommodation when on a visit to Cleveland this summer, met the hearty approval of every person present" (*Cleveland Gazette*).

• ***November 25, 1890:*** "Drew the Color Line," "Several members of the 'She' theatrical company put up at the American House on Sunday, but left this morning saying that they would not stay in the house where there are 'niggers.' This referred to the Fisk Jubilee Singers, who left the city at noon to-day. The 'She' people kicked about eating in the same dining room with them. The clerk says that the colored people occupied a table by themselves and behaved themselves as ladies and gentlemen. He told the members of the 'She' company they could leave if they wanted to. The Jubilee Singers felt bad over the matter this morning, but admire the stand of the hotel clerk" (*Columbus Dispatch*).

• ***March 11, 1892:*** "Mr. F. J. Loudin, the well-known manager of the Fisk Jubilee singers, comes back from his last trip abroad bereft of all his patriotism and love for the American flag. He has had more indignities heaped upon him in one day in the land of his birth than in all the six years that he has spent abroad. He declares in all earnestness that the Afro-American cannot appreciate or measure the feelings of true manhood until he leaves his native land and journeys among people who recognize worth under a black skin without effort . . . His travels have extended all through Europe, parts of Asia and all Australia, and he has been brought into contact with all classes of society, and nowhere save in this country does an Afro-American have to stop and consider where he may get a meal without insult, where he may go to church without reproof.

Mr. Loudin met many Afro-Americans who are engaged in successful businesses, some of whom fought manfully for the Union cause, but who have foresworn all allegiance to their inhuman mother country; and while he himself returns to the United States from a sense of duty, he does not blame them in the least" (*Detroit Plaindealer*).

• ***May 6, 1892 (Milwaukee, Wisconsin):*** "May 2 . . . The Nashville jubilee singers gave one of their pleasant concerts at Lincoln hall on Friday evening, the entertainment was highly praised by the daily press. During the progress of the concert one of the singers took occasion to speak of the prejudice against Afro-Americans in this city. He said his company and himself had been refused accommodation in several hotels of the city simply because of their color, he contrasted the cities of Europe where it is generally supposed every man is not born equal, to the cities in this country of the 'brave and the free' in the former cities they were treated as the equal of any, it remained for them to come to this free (?) country to be insulted and oppressed, because of the color of their skins, we are very glad the gentleman had the courage to speak of the matter where he did. Those citizens of Milwaukee who were present could not help but feel a little ashamed of their city, wherein such a state of affairs existed, yet there are a few of our Afro-American citizens who should know better who claim we need no civil rights bill in this state" (*Detroit Plaindealer*).

• ***May 24, 1892 (Fort Wayne, Indiana):*** "F. J. Loudin, the manager and director, gave a short address between the first and second parts of the program. He said he thought his company sang in Fort Wayne in 1879 or 1880, and while here they met the Wilberforce company from Ohio . . . Since the Fisk Jubilee Singers were here before they have made a tour around the world, singing their way.

Not until they arrived in this country on their return was the color line drawn. Nowhere around the world were they barred from public accommodations until they reached the home of the brave and the land of the free.

In Fort Wayne yesterday afternoon the proprietor of the hotel at which the company arrived came to the speaker and informed him that his waiter girls threatened to go on a strike if the colored company remained at the house. The hotel keeper said: 'I will keep you, and take the consequences.' The speaker said he did not want to put the hotel man in an embarrassing position and so the company left the hotel" (*[Fort Wayne] Daily Gazette*).

Loudin's Fisk Jubilee Singers made seasonal tours throughout the 1890–1895 period. They covered the northern states from Iowa to the Atlantic Coast and into Canada, and they managed to penetrate as far south as Richmond, Virginia. Their concerts were often held in churches, including many African American churches.

• ***December 2, 1890 (Steubenville, Ohio):*** "The Fisk Jubilee Singers gave a most excellent concert in the Opera House last night under the auspices of the Epworth League of Hamlin Church. The singing was beautiful, artistic and highly enjoyed. The house was large and gave the Fisk people $160 and the League $100, the latter to go into the church building fund.

Prof. Loudin of the Nashville Students [*sic*] gave the audience last night a well merited rebuke when he stopped the singers to allow those were in a hurry to get out a chance to go, remarking that those who kept their seats paid to see the show out, and did not propose that they be annoyed in this way. When will Steubenville audiences learn manners?" (*Daily Gazette*).

• ***December 13, 1890 (Pittsburgh, Pennsylvania):*** "Frederick Loudin's Fisk Jubilee Singers were at the old City Hall (Dec. 5th) . . . Between the first and second parts, Mr. Loudin gave a description of the countries he has passed through since he last faced a Pittsburgh audience . . . He also addressed the Presbyterian Sunday School (Dec. 7) on the same subject . . . The Fisk Jubilee Singers are to appear at Wylie Ave. A.M.E. Church on Dec. 18" (*Indianapolis Freeman*).

• ***February 7, 1891 (Washington, D.C.):*** "Loudin's Jubilee Singers met with a crowning success while here; they sang in all of the principal colored churches in the city" (*Indianapolis Freeman*).

• ***March 11, 1891 (Fulton, New York):*** "The singers have a peculiar style of their own. It is not exactly the colored people's dialect or style. It is about the medium between the negro melodies and regular concert singing. They are interesting and gave good satisfaction" (*Fulton Times*).

• ***March 12, 1891 (Rochester, New York):*** "Seven years ago this troupe was heard at the Brick church and since that time it has made a six years tour of the world. Those who heard them on the occasion of their previous visit heard again the clear soprano of Miss Patti J. Malone, recognized once more the splendid basso of F. J. Loudin and listened again to the sweet, weird chorus melodies rendered by the entire company, sung with a rhythm and thrilling effectiveness peculiar to and only attained by these singers.

The concert was given under the auspices of the Epworth league of the First Methodist Episcopal Church" (*Rochester Morning Herald*).

Note: The Epworth League was for many years the official young people's organization of the Methodist Episcopal Church. It was established in 1889, from previously existing young people's societies in the Methodist Episcopal Church.[21]

• ***March 25, 1891 (Geneva, New York):*** In a review of Loudin's Fisk Jubilee Singers' appearance in Geneva: "In a strict sense, these melodies are classical. They have a distinct and separate rank in the world of music. They have taken their form not solely from the circumstances of the negroes of the South; but through the contact of at least four elements: 1. the African character, as it is in the home of the race; 2. the modification that occurred through the transfer to this country, and the condition of slavery; 3. the admixture of strains caught up, from the works of the world's composers, and interwoven with the songs of the Africans, natural or acquired; and 4. last, not least, the special adaptation of the negro to musical conception, and expression, by the quality of his voice, and the remarkable sense of harmony and of the language of music which belongs to his race . . .

It is only requisite to add, for understanding, that intelligent amateurs, and cultivated musicians, heard the concert, on Wednesday evening, carrying in their minds some or all of these considerations; they heard, as critics, learners or observers; and we hazard nothing in saying, in that view, that this concert was one of the most instructive and enjoyed musical entertainments ever given in Geneva.

For there was more in the entertainment than music—there was a race-study as well; not a comparison of physical characteristics, so much as mental; and not so much the mental, as of the spiritual; inasmuch as nearly all the songs sung were of a religious, or semi-religious character.

". . . [M]uch of what was presented, was as new to the younger colored people, reared in the north, as to any of the audience. Likewise there were some Genevans who not understanding fully nor appreciating the circumstances under which the plantation melodies grew up—melodies that no one knows accurately the origin of—were inclined to regard them as travesties and burlesques of sacred things" (*Geneva Courier*).

• ***June 26, 1891:*** "The simple announcement of the marriage . . . of Miss Addie W. Johnson of Richmond, Va., to a Mr. Sharpe, of England, last week may have received only a glance by the thousands, but there is something behind. The Englishman crosses the main to marry the woman of his choice, an Afro-American . . . Miss Johnson was a member of the far famed Fisk Jubilee Troupe, of which Mr. Loudin is manager. She is the second of this organization to fall into the meshes of Venus, and reliable report has it that Patti Malone has a beau in New Zealand, while our own Maggie Wilson refused many very flattering offers in the Orient" (*Detroit Plaindealer*).

Note: Addie Johnson's British husband, Lauchlan G. Sharpe, had served as an advance agent for Loudin's Fisk Jubilee Singers in Australia and the Orient, and he had accompanied them on the trip back to America.

• ***September 26, 1891:*** "Mr. Harry T. Burleigh of Erie, passed through the city this week for Ravenna, where he joins Loudin's Jubilee Singers for the coming season" (*Cleveland Gazette*).

• ***October 10, 1891 (Cleveland, Ohio):*** "Loudin's Jubilee Company drew a large crowd to Music Hall Tuesday evening (6th), and sang, as it always does—exceedingly well. Mt. Zion church received the proceeds, having engaged the company for that evening. Next Monday evening (12th) the company concerts again. Shiloh church will receive a percentage of the receipts" (*Cleveland Gazette*).

• ***October 17, 1891:*** "Harry T. Burleigh of Cleveland expected to join the Fisk Jubilee Singers, but the First Presbyterian church in whose choir he sang refused to let him go and raised his salary as a retainer" (*Indianapolis Freeman*).

• ***January 21, 1892 (Uxbridge, North Ontario, Canada):*** "It was a large and appreciative audience that listened to Loudin's Jubilee Singers in the Methodist Church last Friday evening. They are without a doubt the best company of colored singers that ever visited Uxbridge. We will not attempt to describe their performance of Friday evening. Suffice it to say that the large audience sat spellbound under the influence of their sweet voices. Each member was almost perfect in its rendition. Loudin, the great basso, has a voice of remarkable power. During the intermission the manager gave an interesting account of their trip around the world. There is no singing so sweet as that of the colored people, and a good company will always be well received in Uxbridge" (*North Ontario Times*).

• ***March 7, 1892 (Battle Creek, Michigan):*** In a review of Loudin's Jubilee Singers' appearance in Battle Creek: "Mr. F. J. Loudin has a wonderful bass voice and has made an equally wonderful record in singing. He commenced his solo work in 1874, and since that date has with three or four exceptions, given a solo at each concert given by the troupe. During that time the troupe has given over three thousand entertainments. Probably no other singer in America has a record equal to this" (*Battle Creek Daily Moon*).

• ***March 16, 1892 (Rockford, Illinois):*** "Court Street A.M.E. Church was packed to the doors last evening to hear the Fisk Jubilee Singers. People went there expecting to enjoy an evening of more than ordinary pleasure and yet those who did not experience an agreeable surprise in the entertainment were without power of appreciating rare music.

The troupe consists of nine people under the management of Mr. F. J. Loudin who is not alone a successful manager and concert director, but is one of the finest bassos in the world. He is the life and soul of the troupe, and sings as if life possessed no other happiness for him than to use that magnificent voice of his to charm and please the world. He also demonstrated in the fifteen minute interval between parts that he is a graceful and entertaining speaker as well" (*Republican*).

• ***March 29, 1892 (Grinell, Iowa):*** In a review of Loudin's Fisk Jubilee Singers' appearance in Grinell: "While the old abolition spirit which cast a glamour around the melodies of slave days is fast dying out, yet the sweet beauty and melody of many of these familiar songs will find a responsive feeling in human hearts for generations yet to be" (*Grinell Herald*).

• ***April 6, 1892 (Muscatine, Iowa):*** In a review of Loudin's Fisk Jubilee Singers' appearance in Muscatine: "There were fifteen numbers in the program, and almost as many encores and voluntaries—solos, trios, male and female quartets, and choruses, and who that listened to this succession of splendid song, with the grand waves of those choruses sweeping over one at intervals, can begin to say which was best, or can say anything except that it was one great festival of music? How they sang! Each singer was a host. The volume of voice from those ten vocalists was like the massing of a hundred ordinary singers. It recalled the song,

Glory, glory, how the wildwoods rang.
Glory, glory, how the freedmen sang!

With what clearness the different parts rang out, but with what beauty every part contributed to the harmony of all! One expects to hear some such singing in the land of Beulah" (*Daily News-Tribune*).

• ***April 30, 1892 (Evanston, Illinois):*** "Loudin's Original Fisk Jubilee Singers gave one of their unexcelled concerts to a crowded house at the First M.E. Church, on Tuesday evening, the 19th. Every number save two, on the programme were encored. While all the singing was good, it would be almost folly to particularize, but I cannot help mentioning the excellent number in which the female quartet, composed of Misses Malone, Callaway, Wilson and Gibbons rendered the beautiful song 'Greeting To Spring,' to the music of Strauss, and divine 'Beautiful Blue Danube Waltz.' Mr. Loudin has just cause to feel proud of his band of sweet singers. They are all ladies and gentlemen and modest in their demeanor, and altogether different to the many so-called jubilee singers picked up in the cities and palmed off as belonging to some colored college in the South . . . It is to be regretted that so few colored people were there to hear them. Mr. Loudin's description of their travels around the world since 1884 was very interesting" (*Indianapolis Freeman*).

Updates on the whereabouts of Loudin's Fisk Jubilee Singers during the 1892–1893 touring season were interspersed with reports on Loudin's new investments. For a time in 1892 and 1893, Frederick J. Loudin was one of the most visible black capitalists in America. On November 17, 1892, a three-story brick factory building, the home of the F. J. Loudin Boot and Shoe Manufacturing Company, was dedicated in Ravenna, Ohio. Within six months this new factory was reportedly employing "nearly seventy hands, among whom are a number of Afro-Americans, and is turning out about three-hundred pairs of shoes a day."[22]

In April 1893 the *Cleveland Gazette* announced: "Mr. F. J. Loudin . . . has been made president of the F. J. Loudin Shoe Manufactory Co. of Ravenna. He is the first Afro-American to be so honored by a joint-stock manufacturing company, all the other members of which are white. Mr. Loudin is patentee of 'The Loudin Key Locker' and 'The Loudin Window Locker,' which he is also pushing. Nothing slow about him."[23] Loudin's namesake shoe factory was hailed by the African American press as a source of race pride.

• ***December 2, 1892:*** "The New Enterprise," "The F. J. Loudin Shoe Manufacturing Company is the most creditable enterprise that has sprung into existence since the freedom of the American Negro . . . This enterprise of Mr. F. J. Loudin should stimulate and kindle the ambition of every colored man" (*Detroit Plaindealer*).

• ***July 1, 1893:*** "Our people in the various communities should see to it that one or more of their retail shoe dealers have in stock the Loudin shoe. When they are in stock purchase them. We must help one another more than we do, if any are ever to be successful in business" (*Cleveland Gazette*).

Despite such optimistic predictions and calls for support, Loudin's shoe manufacturing business was short-lived. The *Ravenna Republican* reported on December 27, 1893, that the "Loudin Shoe Company shut off steam Saturday night, after a month run, during which time many thousand pairs of shoes were manufactured." The same paper later informed that all the stock had been attached by creditors. Failure was attributed to a lack of sufficient working capital. Another probable factor was that Loudin simply wasn't able to devote enough time to this enterprise. At any rate, the ill-fated venture in shoe manufacturing had no visible effect on the progress of Loudin's Fisk Jubilee Singers.

• ***October 1, 1892 (Ravenna, Ohio):*** "Mr. and Mrs. F. J. Loudin left Tuesday (27th) with their famous Fiske Jubilee Singers for their annual tour. There are in all 12 members of the company, which opened in Youngstown, Tuesday evening" (*Cleveland Gazette*).

• ***October 21, 1892 (Springfield, Ohio):*** "Loudin's famous jubilee singers, gave a grand concert at North street church, Friday evening, the 14th. There was quite a large number out to hear these famous singers. But there was not enough to justify them to visit this city again, however, they rendered one of the finest programs ever witnessed by the people of this city. The company consist of the following well known talent: Mr. and Mrs. Loudin, Miss Pattie Malone, Miss Mamie P. Calanary [*sic,* Calloway], Miss Gant, Mr. W. E. Geary, Miss Maggie Wilson, Miss Georgie Gibbons, Miss Leola P. Henson, Mr. John T. Lane, Mr. J. H. Brooks" (*Detroit Plaindealer*).

• ***December 27, 1892 (Kokomo, Indiana):*** "The concert given at the Main street Christian church last night by the Fisk Jubileeans was 'out of sight' in more senses than one. In an artistic sense it was the acme of success and in the language of the galleries 'out of sight.' In a corporeal sense it was 'out of sight' to the five hundred people who might have seen and enjoyed it but who did not. The church in which the concert was given seats upwards of six hundred persons" (*Kokomo Dispatch*).

• ***May 2, 1893 (Warren, Pennsylvania):*** "Having heard the Fisk Singers a number of times . . . To those who have never heard them, I would say go, as their renditions of Southern plantation secular and religious music are bewitching, and the naturalness with which they present it, a feature. A characteristic of this class of music are the ever present syncope, which is evidently of Spanish origin and possibly grew out of the exchange of slaves with Cuba, where national song and dance is in unrestful measure" (William H. Dana, *Chronicle*).

• ***December 30, 1893:*** "The Fisk Jubilee Singers in Richmond," "The Fisk Jubilee Singers appeared before Richmond audiences twice this week for the first time.

The entertainment was given at the True Reformers' Hall last Tuesday and Wednesday nights and was under the auspices of the YMCA, R. T. Hill, Esq., president.

The audiences were not as large as was desired, but was very appreciative and so pleased were the management with the excellence of the programme rendered, that they are not at all [disappointed] over the failure to realize a financial success.

The singers were Miss Patti J. Malone, Soprano; Miss Mayme P. Calloway, Soprano; Miss G.A. Mackell, Soprano; Miss Maggie E. Wilson, Contralto; Miss Georgie A. Gibbons, Contralto; Mr. John T. A. Lane, Tenor; Mr. J. H. Brooks, Tenor; Mr. F. J. Loudin, Basso; Mr. W. E. Geary, Basso; Miss Leota F. Henson, Pianist, and the programme was:

Part First—Steal Away to Jesus, The Lord's Prayer, O, Brethren, Rise and Shine, The Crucifixion, The Old Ark's a Movering, Selection, Mary and Martha, Selection, Robert, Idol of My Heart, My Lord Delivered Daniel? [*sic*]

Part Second—Glee, Jingle, Jingle, Bells, Bright Sparkles in the Churchyard, Selection, Over the Hill at Break of Day, Sometime, Hard Trials, Selection, The Angels Waiting Door, Swing Low, The Benediction, or Good Night.

The singers were repeatedly encored and they responded with surprising good nature, rendering what appeared to be an inexhaustible number of plantation melodies which stirred the very souls of those who listened to them.

One of the special features is the elimination of the Negro dialect and yet the retention of the Negro melody. . .

Mr. F. J. Loudin has a wonderful voice, possessing a richness and mellowness which is charming and being reinforced by an articulation that is superb.

It is not difficult to see that he is the life of the company, and that his personality affords inspiration to those by whom he is surrounded . . . Miss Henson, the pianist, is very fine" (*Richmond Planet*).

• ***November 9, 1895 (Pittsburgh and Allegheny, Pennsylvania):*** "Jubilee Singers," "Mr. F. J. Loudin's Fine Company Receives Splendid Notices in the West," "The following is from the Muscatine (Iowa) *Daily News and Tribune*, and is of general interest to music lovers: 'Loudin's Original Fisk Jubilee Singers were with us again last night at the First Congregational church, where they delighted a large and enthusiastic audience. Like good wine, they improve with age. There is a freshness, sweetness and blending of voices in their singing which none of the other so-called jubilee singers can even imitate, and one gets but a faint idea of the charm and pathos of those old plantation melodies by listening to any other company of singers who attempt to sing them. No organ could blend in more perfect harmony than did the voices of those singers last night. Their shading is perfection itself—now soft as the aeolian harp under the touch of a master hand; now swelling into a fortissimo which thrills you through and through. When the company was here three years ago it seemed as if no improvement was possible, but the general verdict of those who heard them last evening was that they are even better now than ever before. It is truly remarkable how this organization has been maintained with so high a standard of excellence, both as to the personnel of the company and the excellence of their music. Scores of imitators have arisen and after a little time have ceased to exist as an organization, while Loudin's Fisk's have gone steadily on achieving new triumphs and adding fresh laurels to their crown; no matter whether in Europe, Australia, India, Japan, or their own native America, their march has been one of triumph, and the critics of all nations have sung their praises in loftiest tones. Of the programme last night we have no space to speak at length. Encores were frequent and were goodnaturedly responded to, many of their songs were new to our people. Of the voices all are exceptionally fine and in this connection the tenors may be especially mentioned. The altos also are pure, rich and full. Miss Calaway has a high pure soprano voice and in her solo, The Enchantress, she showed remarkable sweetness, power and flexibility of voice. A new soprano voice since the singers were last here, Miss Sagwar, has a rich smooth metzo soprano voice and her rendering of Old Folks at Home was highly enjoyable. Of the lion basso, Mr. Loudin, no more can be said than that his voice is, if possible, more powerful and richer than ever. His solo captured the audience last night and he was compelled to respond to a very enthusiastic encore. Miss Malon's [*sic*] rich soprano voice was heard to fine advantage in the choruses, while the artistic execution of the accompanist, Miss Henson, was beyond criticism. Loudin's Fisk's will always be welcome to Muscatine' " (*Cleveland Gazette*).

Jubilee Singers on the Home Front, 1890

Loudin's Fisk Jubilee Singers were not alone on the home front. Formidable competitors included the "other" Fisk troupe, Mumford's Fisk Jubilee Singers, featuring Maggie Porter-Cole; the New Orleans University Singers; and others whose efforts were noted in the African American press of 1890.

• ***February 8, 1890 (New York City):*** "Morrison's Jubilee Troupe from Tennessee filled their engagement . . . and moderately gratified an assemblage composed mostly of the race sustaining that class of amusements [i.e., white people], but recalling nothing of the Fisk University students or their contemporaries" (*New York Age*).

• ***March 8, 1890:*** "The exercises at Bethel Lyceum last Friday drew out a large and appreciative audience . . . [The program included] a tenor solo by Mr. S. T. Mosely of the Tennessee Star Singers. To an encore he responded with the duet 'The Old Oaken Bucket,' with Mrs. Thorpe. The celebrated Thorpe Family captivated the audience with their fine selections, assisted by Messrs. Mosely and Wm. Dean. The kindness of Mr. Wm. H. Morrison, the manager of the Thorpe Family and Tennessee Star Singers" (*New York Age*).

• ***April 19, 1890:*** "The Tuskegee Industrial School has a troupe of Jubilee Singers on the road" (*Indianapolis Freeman*).

• ***April 26, 1890 (Pittsburgh, Pennsylvania):*** "The New Orleans Jubilee Singers rendered a fine programme in Odd Fellows Hall (April 18)" (*Cleveland Gazette*).

• ***May 16, 1890:*** At the "State Afro-American Convention" in Detroit, Michigan, "Mrs. Maggie Porter Cole's exquisite rendition of 'Nearer My God To Thee'. . . touched the hearts of every member of the convention" (*Detroit Plaindealer*).

• ***May 23, 1890:*** "The Jubilee Singers of New Orleans will treat the 900 boys and girls at the New York Juvenile Asylum at 176th St. and 10th Avenue, at one of their characteristic concerts in the asylum chapel at 11 a.m. today" (*Detroit Plaindealer*).

• ***May 30, 1890:*** "Her Sweet Voice," "Mrs. M. L. Cole, whose sweet voice has charmed the members of many legislatures on many occasions, leaves Lansing, June 4 for Fargo, N.D., where she joins [Mumford's] Fisk Jubilee Singers for a two months' tour of the Northwest. Mrs. Cole was an original member of the troupe [i.e., the original 1871 edition of the Fisk Jubilee Singers]. The season will close at Bay View in August" (*Detroit Plaindealer*, reprinted from *Detroit Tribune*).

• ***June 7, 1890:*** "The Stage," "Mrs. M. Porter-Cole . . . will rejoin the Fisk Singers under the management of Mr. Mumford next month. She takes the place of the leading soprano, formerly held by Mrs. J. Jackson-DeHart of Cincinnati, whose poor health necessitated a vacation" (*Indianapolis Freeman*).

• ***June 14, 1890:*** "The New Orleans Jubilee Troop and a large number of prominent ministers will be in attendance . . . [at] a campmeeting at Boston, Pa., for four days" (*Cleveland Gazette*).

• ***June 28, 1890:*** "The Tennessee Warblers have reorganized and have now a first class company on the road. They are now on tour through the oil regions of Pennsylvania, and they will play New York State and Canada before returning South. Mr. L. E. Puggsley, the energetic manager" (*Indianapolis Freeman*).

• ***July 5, 1890:*** "Nova Scotia has just afforded an extraordinary exhibition of color-line prejudice. When [Mumford's] Fisk Jubilee Singers appeared in Halifax recently they were guests at a leading hotel. They went to Bridgewater and were there refused accommodations at any hotel or private house, and had to drive twelve miles to Lunenberg to obtain supper and beds" (*Cleveland Gazette*).

• ***July 5, 1890 (Jackson, Tennessee):*** "'The Fiskites In The Lead,' "We have a very commodious and neat school building erected in 1889 . . . Mrs. L. E. Robinson, nee Miss Ewin [one of the teachers at the school], is a graduate of Fisk University . . . She was at a time connected with the Fisk Jubilee Singers prior to her calling here. Her stay at this place speaks louder than words . . . It is well to note one of her many qualifications and that is, she is an excellent vocal and instrumental teacher. Her instrumental and vocal culture is not surpassed by any in town, colored or white" (*Indianapolis Freeman*).

• ***July 12, 1890:*** A letter from Lizzie Ewing Robbins responded to the statement above that she was a Fiskite: "I am represented as being a graduate of Fisk University and also of having been connected with the Fisk Jubilee Singers. I never was a student of Fisk University, but received my education at Central Tennessee College, located at Nashville, Tenn. I was never at any time connected with the Fisk Jubilee Singers, but am one of the Original Tennesseans from Central Tennessee College" (*Indianapolis Freeman*).

Note: The Tennesseans were one of the truly legendary jubilee companies of the Reconstruction era. Formed in the immediate wake of the Fisk Jubilee Singers, the Tennesseans' tours of 1872 and 1873 raised funds enough for the construction of a dormitory at Central Tennessee College, now known as Meharry Medical College. The troupe later toured independently, under the proprietorship of their organizer, Prof. J. W. Donovin. They remained professionally active until at least 1884.

• ***July 25, 1890:*** "Patrons of Music," "Mrs. Maggie L. Porter Cole, Lansing's sweet singer, was born in slavery in Lebanon, Tenn. At the age of 13 she was one of 300 scholars that gathered in the old hospital barracks the first week the Fisk school was opened. After two years in this institution she enlisted as a teacher and taught her first school at Bellevue, a few miles from Nashville. While at home during the Christmas vacation her school was burned by the Ku klux; but she re-engaged to another district and followed the profession until 1871, when she joined the famous jubilee singers.

During the years that Mrs. Cole was a member of this organization she visited Europe three times, where the company gave concerts throughout England, Scotland and Germany. During these trips she sang before Queen Victoria, Emperor William, Crown Prince Frederick and others of the crowned head.

Mrs. Cole has resided in Lansing for the past four years, where she conducts classes in voice culture and participates in concerts . . . Recently

Maggie Porter-Cole, circa 1872. (courtesy Fisk University Library, Special Collections)

she went to the northwest to take the place, for the rest of the season, of one of the jubilee singers, who was compelled to retire because of sickness" (*Detroit Plaindealer*).

• ***September 6, 1890:*** "The Lewis Brothers, jubilee singers and orchestral performers, will be engaged for the Democratic celebration, Boyles Grove, Ill., September 4th" (*Indianapolis Freeman*).

• ***October 11, 1890:*** "The Stage," "Singleton's Jubilee Singers are touring in Illinois and Indiana" (*Indianapolis Freeman*).

• ***October 31, 1890:*** "On The Road," "There will be this season three companies of Fisk singers on the road, one of which has been trained by Mrs. Ella Shepherd Moore, the pianist of the 'Original Fisk Singers,' and makes its debut this season. The second under the management of Mr. Loudin and contains some of the singers who have recently returned from the Old World and such others as he found desirable to secure since. The third, that of which Mrs. Maggie Porter Cole is leading soprano. Since the retirement of Mrs. Jackson-DeHart, Mrs. Cole is probably the only one of the 'original' eleven singers who started out in '71 on the stage, Mr. Loudin not joining the troupe until '74" (*Detroit Plaindealer*).

Note: This citation is notable for its uncommon accuracy, but it should also be noted that only the troupe under Ella Shepherd Moore's direction was authorized by Fisk University, or was engaged in institutional fund-raising. This was the first university-affiliated company of Fisk Jubilee Singers in twelve years, and it only remained in the field for one season. One member of this company, Thomas W. Talley, went on to distinguish himself as an educator, research chemist, and folklorist. He compiled the seminal book *Negro Folk Rhymes*, first published in 1922.

• ***November 8, 1890:*** "Mrs. Ella Shepard Moore, of Washington, D.C., has been in Nashville, Tenn., training the new company for Fisk University. Mrs. Moore was with the original troupe of Jubilee Singers, sharing in their struggles and triumphs" (*Indianapolis Freeman*).

• ***November 8, 1890 (Cincinnati, Ohio):*** "Mrs. Jennie Jackson DeHart, well-known as the leading soprano singer of the Fisk Jubilee Singers, of Nashville, Tenn., after many solicitations on the part of friends, has decided to teach a class in vocal culture at her home on Chapel street, Walnut Hills. Those desiring to enter should do so at once and thus secure the full course of lessons" (*Indianapolis Freeman*).

• ***December 20, 1890 (Newburyport, Massachusetts):*** "Jubilee Singers," "The Fisk Jubilee Singers sang in the North Congregationalist Church. These earnest workers are trying to raise money to build a Bible School to be connected with Fisk University. One feature was the refined and cultured manner of their singing, the absence of all 'acting,' which some jubilee singers seem to think a necessity" ("Virginia," *Indianapolis Freeman*).

"A Woman with a Mission": Madame Marie Selika, 1890

By 1890, Madame Marie Selika was an internationally traveled concert singer with more than a decade of professional stage experience to her credit. Working her way from Kansas City to New York City during the spring of 1890, Madame Selika paused to reflect on her mission as a singer.

• ***January 10, 1890 (Kansas City, Kansas):*** "The Selika concert at the Tabernacle was not a great success, financially. . . The programme rendered was: 'If Thou Could'st Know,'—Arditti—S. W. Williams; "Lacca La Notti [*sic*],"—Verdi—Madame Selika; 'White Squall,'—Mr. S. W. Williams; 'Flowers of the Alps,'—Madame Selika; 'The Grand Duet,' I'll Troubadour [*sic*]—Madame Selika and Mr. Williams. . . Master Charles Sumner Bryan [*sic*], the boy pianist, is certainly a wonder. . . His soul creeps out to the tips of his fingers" (*Kansas City American Citizen*).

Note: Charles Sumner Byron went on to accompany Mumford's Fisk Jubilee Singers during their 1895 tour of Europe. He remained there performing with an African American quartet called the Black Troubadours.[24]

• ***February 8, 1890:*** "The Stage," "Mme Selika, undoubtedly the greatest living prima donna of her race, sang to a crowded house at Allen's Chapel, Kansas City, Mo., on Monday evening the 29th ult" ("Trage," *Indianapolis Freeman*).

• ***March 21, 1890:*** "Mme Selika and S. W. Williams are working their way East from Kansas and Nebraska" (*Detroit Plaindealer*).

• ***May 3, 1890:*** "Mme Selika has announced herself a woman with a mission. She is willing to make a sacrifice of her life that the colored race of America may learn of higher music than that with which they have heretofore been acquainted. Her work so far, however, has been somewhat disappointing. But her efforts to elevate her race, she says, will only end with her death" (*Indianapolis Freeman*).

• ***October 4, 1890 (New York City):*** "A Grand Jubilee and Prize Concert," "There will be a grand musical and literary jubilee and prize concert at A.M.E. Zion Church, corner West 10th and Bleeker streets, Rev. A. Walters, pastor, commencing Monday, Oct. 20, 1890, and continuing five nights until Friday, Oct. 25. Proceeds for the benefit of renovating the church. The following talent has been secured: Mme. Marie Selika, Mme. Nellie Brown Mitchell, Miss Edna Brown, Mme. Annie Smith, Miss Maggie Scott, Mme. Bertie Toney Davis, Miss E. Belden, Mr. C. T. Mosley, Mr. Theo. Drury, Miss Blanche Wendell, Miss Sarah Chase, Prof. W. F. Craig and orchestra, and a chorus of thirty voices, under the management of Prof. S. P. Thompson. Mme. Albert Wilson, accompanist" (*New York Age*).

LEWIS ENG CO BOSTON
MADAME SELIKA,
To Appear in Grand Concert, Monday night, at Second Baptist Church.

Freeman, *April 14, 1894.*

• ***October 25, 1890 (New York City):*** "The series of musical and literary entertainments conducted for five nights during the week at A.M.E. Zion Church . . . have resulted in deserved success . . . Monday night opened with an address by T. Thomas Fortune . . . Tuesday night the star singer was Mme. Marie Selika, who was billed as 'Boston's Creole Patti,' but nevertheless maintained her reputation as an artist" (*New York Age*).

• ***December 20, 1890:*** "Mme. Selika in Brooklyn," "The music loving public turned out in large numbers to listen to Mme. Selika and Mr. Veloska at Association Hall Monday evening . . . The appearance of Mme. Selika fairly carried the audience by storm and her selection from 'Il Travatore' was rendered with marvelous ease and grace . . . The musical director announced a recitation, 'A Romance by the Seaside' by Mr. Williams, which did not appear on the program. Mr. Williams lost the attention of the audience by not reading sufficiently loud at the beginning and the romance proved to be so long that it was to be regretted that he was not forgotten entirely. Much credit, however, is due Mr. Williams for his staying qualities while constantly being interrupted by hisses. The home talent was all that could be expected. Mme. E. Savalle-Jones appeared to have regained the sweetness in her voice of years ago" (*New York Age*).

Selected, Annotated Chronology of Music-Related Citations, 1890

• ***January 4, 1890 (Indianapolis, Indiana):*** "Christmas was celebrated throughout the city by numerous literary entertainments, parties and general good times . . . The quartette concert at Quinn's Chapel for $50 was won by the Gunard. It was a close contest between them and the Colfax Quartette, who desire to meet the Gunards again in the near future" (*Indianapolis Freeman*).

• ***January 17, 1890:*** "Ida Mae Yeocum, the wife of Rev. William H. Yeocum pastor of the Allen A.M.E. Church on Lombard Street in Philadelphia, has been refused admission to the Philadelphia Musical Academy on account of her color, and a suit in equity against the institution will follow" (*Detroit Plaindealer*).

Note: Ida Mae Yeocum is one of the earliest African American woman composers known to have had her work commercially published. Her piece entitled "The Song of the Women" dates from 1900.[25]

• ***January 18, 1890:*** "The San Lonei Quartette of New York has the fever of most all traveling colored specialty people and are playing the West. Success seems to attend them" (*Indianapolis Freeman*).

• ***January 18, 1890:*** "A banjo quartette of youths has been lately started in Providence [Rhode Island], known as the Peerless Banjo Quartette" (*Indianapolis Freeman*).

• ***January 25, 1890:*** "The Stage," "Mr. and Mrs. Sam Lucas have at last reached Boston, where they are so popular. They have spent about seventeen months in the west, where they were very successful. Mr. Lucas being engaged as stage manager at one of the theatres in Denver for 9 months. They spent the past week in Providence, the guest of Mrs. Louisa Mars, Mrs. Lucas' sister. They opened in Boston Monday, at Austin's Nickelodeon for a two week's engagement, after which they will give a concert in Providence" ("Trage," *Indianapolis Freeman*).

• ***January 25, 1890:*** "The Stage," "In 1882, while B. F. Lightfoot was employed as a hallman at the Narragansett Hotel, Providence, R.I., Mme. Modjeska and her husband, Count Charles

Freeman, *January 25, 1890.*

Bozenta, came there to stop for a week. Lightfoot, by waiting on them from time to time, became acquainted, and both took quite a liking to him, and when they visited Providence in '84 Lightfoot had acquired considerable dramatic knowledge; and when he called upon them the madame expressed her hope that she never came to the city but what he (Lightfoot) should call and see them. On Tuesday of last week, while Mr. Edwin Booth and Mme. Modjeska were playing in Providence, Lightfoot called upon them at the Narragansett Hotel, where he was well received and entertained for nearly two hours. Before leaving he was requested to give a short recital for the madame and a few of her company, on Thursday afternoon at 3. The request was responded to and there were present, besides Madame Modjeska and husband, Messrs. Otis Skinner, Beaumont Smith, Robert M. Oberle. The first recitation rendered by Mr. Lightfoot was 'Othello's Apology' and the second 'The Modern Cymra.' The latter selection embraces the lunatic, the lover and poet, and when he came to the part where the lover goes mad he portrayed it so naturally that he caused Mme. Modjeska to scream outright" ("Trage," *Indianapolis Freeman*).

• ***February 8, 1890:*** "The Stage," "Blind Tom, the musical phenomenon whose name has been familiar in thousands of households for years, appeared last Saturday evening at the Grand Opera House, Davenport, Ia., to a large and fashionable audience" (*Indianapolis Freeman*).

• ***February 8, 1890:*** "The Stage," "Prof. J. S. Bonner will give a consolidated Jubilee concert at the Gosling's Hall, Shelbyville, Tennessee . . . A street parade will take place at one o'clock by the troupe. This bids fair to be the best concert ever given by colored people in that city" (*Indianapolis Freeman*).

• ***February 8, 1890:*** "The Stage," "News reaches us that Walker's Refined Colored Minstrels are meeting with good success. At Selma, Ala., the 22nd ult., they played to a packed house. Haynes & Fisher, neat song and dance team, scores a hit. Willie Cheatham is said to be the youngest comedian on the road and is doing good work. Britt Craig, the tenor, is singing his favorite song, 'Dimpled Hands,' and receiving many encores night after night. Prof. J. Sander's orchestra is acknowledged to be one of the best on the road. George Y. Stevens, the basso, left on the 23rd ult., for Birmingham, Ala." (*Indianapolis Freeman*).

Note: This citation appears to harbor an early reference to William Cheatham of "the famous Cheatham Brothers," forgotten legends of African American minstrelsy. At St. Louis, Missouri, in 1898, William and Lawrence Cheatham formed the Cheatham Brothers' Black Diamond Minstrels, including Thomas Turpin, musical director, "truly phenomenal in his piano solos and rag-time playing"—and "Master Louis Chavan [*sic*, i.e., Tom Turpin's ragtime piano protege Louis Chauvin], of St. Louis, Mo., who, as a boy vocalist and dancer has no equal."[26] It was reported in the *Freeman* of January 20, 1906 that "Larry Cheatham, of the Cheatham Bros., died at the St. Vincent's Hospital, January 6, at Birmingham, Ala. Interment at Montgomery, Alabama, his late home, January 8."

• ***February 22, 1890:*** "The Stage," "Miss Ednorah Nahar, elocutionist, of Boston, has been making a successful Southern tour, being highly complimented everywhere she appeared. On Monday evening, the 24th, she will appear at Steinway hall, New York. Miss Nahar made her debut as an elocutionist about three years ago and since that time has been the most successful financially, of the race" ("Trage," *Indianapolis Freeman*).

• ***February 22, 1890:*** "The Stage," "On Monday evening the Hyer Sisters had a packed house at Los Angeles, Cal." (*Indianapolis Freeman*).

• ***February 22, 1890 (Louisville, Kentucky):*** "The Choir Contest," "The choir contest was held the 14th inst. The hall was filled to overflowing . . . At eight P.M. Rev. William J. Simmons addressed the audience, after which the following programme was rendered: Song, by Sunlight Glee Club; prayer, Rev. William J. Simmons; song, Sunlight Glee Club. Then came the contest. The following choirs sang choruses twice: Fifth Street, Green Street and Lampton Street church choirs. The judges retired. Song, University League Club; song, Sunlight Glee Club. Judges decided as follows: First prize, $25, Fifth Street Choir; second prize, $15, Green Street choir, and third prize, $6, Lampson Street choir, Judges: Messrs. H. Burch, B. Wilson and C. Alpiger" (*Cleveland Gazette*).

• ***March 8, 1890:*** "Doc Sayles, Harry S. Eaton, Cicero Reed, B. Miner, Chas. Davis and Alex. Macy are the comedians with Rusco & Swift's Minstrels. Tom Williams joined the show at Waterloo, Ia., and has taken hands again with his old partner, Harry S. Eaton." (*New York Clipper*).

• ***March 8, 1890:*** "The Hub Quartette of Boston played the Keith's Bijou Theatre, Philadelphia last week" (*Indianapolis Freeman*).

• ***March 21, 1890:*** "Prof. J. B. Scott, of Pontiac [Michigan], teacher of Banjo, will be pleased to give lessons to those who desire" (*Detroit Plaindealer*).

• ***March 22, 1890:*** "Mr. Harry A. Williams has been traveling with the Frazier Quintette (English ladies) through England since Feb. 6th as tenor soloist, and is meeting with great success" (*Cleveland Gazette*).

• ***March 22, 1890:*** "The Excelsior Quartette which has delighted so many people in the East by their imitation of Barnum's Steam Organ are at present in Nebraska" (*Indianapolis Freeman*).

Note: The "imitation of Barnum's Steam Organ" was a popular vocal quartet device of the 1890s, and it finds several parallels on later commercial recordings. In 1924 "Barnum's Steam Calliope" was recorded by a well-seasoned vaudeville quartet called the Sunset Four. In the same year a similar effort, titled "Calliope Song," was waxed by the Seven Musical Magpies of Cleveland, Ohio, and in 1927 the Birmingham Jubilee Singers added their rendition in a medley of onomatopoeic effects entitled "The Steamboat."[27]

• ***March 29, 1890 (Richmond, Virginia):*** "The Moore St. Baptist Church Choir has, by consent of the Church, determined to purchase an organ at a cost of fifteen hundred dollars, making themselves responsible for the payment thereof. The act in itself is unprecedented in the history of the Baptist church of this city, and deserves the commendation and support of the church-loving community of Richmond and vicinity" (*Richmond Planet*).

• ***March 29, 1890:*** "Has the [mainstream daily] *Cleveland Leader* stopped using the word Negro (spelled with a capital 'N') and begun the use of the word 'darky?' Read the following from the Sunday issue: 'George Washington, a *darky*, who has been employed for some time at the Carleton Hotel, Memphis, Tenn., has a fortune in his mouth. Yesterday he attracted a large crowd by whistling a very beautiful *darky* melody, making perfect harmony in first and second at the same time' " (*Cleveland Gazette*).

• ***April 4, 1890 (Topeka, Kansas):*** "Topeka is blessed with plenty of musical talent and much good music. Aside from several brass bands, string bands and mandolin clubs, there are two harmonica bands, Reniz's [*sic*, Renix Brothers?] and Dennie's, composed of fine young men each. These harmonica bands were out last week serenading their friends, among whom were the families of Mr. G. W. Cable, S. G. Watkins and W. J. Johnson" (*Kansas City American Citizen*).

• ***April 11, 1890:*** "Some of Our Professionals," "The Hyers combination is playing to good business through the Canadian cities" (*Detroit Plaindealer*).

• ***April 11, 1890 (Jackson, Michigan):*** "A Jubilee Concert—the members of the A.M.E. Church gave a genuine jubilee concert at the K. of P. Hall . . . which was well attended and highly appreciated. After delighting the audience with vocal and instrumental music there was a cake walk for the young folks which was indulged in by about 12 or 15 couples...Miss Ella Leatherman presided at the organ during the concert. The proceeds of the above concern was $33.35" (*Detroit Plaindealer*).

• ***April 18, 1890 (Detroit, Michigan):*** "The 'Song Recital' under the direction of Misses E. Azalia Smith and Mabel Hill took place at the Second Baptist Church...before a fair audience. The participants were all very cordially greeted and rendered a program of twelve excellent numbers, consisting of songs, readings, duets, trios, quartettes and instrumental solos. It must be said however, that the singing was not up to the usual standard and the instrumentalists carried off the honors for the evening. The entertainment was for the benefit of the improvement fund of the church and about $45 was netted. Members of the Meylkdi, Minuet and Silver Leaf Clubs were in attendance to represent their organizations" (*Detroit Plaindealer*).

• ***April 19, 1890:*** "Lee Allen, John H. Booker, Wm. Coleman and Wm. Dixon, of Denver, under the name of the 'Excelsior Quartette' are filling engagements in Colorado, Nevada and California. They are said to be excellent singers" (*Indianapolis Freeman*).

• ***April 19, 1890:*** "S. B. Hyers, proprietor of the Hyers Colored Comedy Co., writes that his business manager, Miles Berry, suddenly left the company at Brompton, Ont. Manager Hyers is confined to his bed with a broken leg, but the company continue their travels" (*New York Clipper*).

• ***May 2, 1890 (Pontiac, Michigan):*** "Prof. A. R. Binga, teacher of guitar, is doing a nice business, and has a large class" (*Detroit Plaindealer*).

• ***May 2, 1890:*** "Church News," "A choir contest was given in the Fleet Street A.M.E. Zion Church, New York recently, between the Concord Baptist, Union Bethel, Bethany Baptist and the home choir. The scoring points were time, harmony and volume, and the prize, a silver center table was awarded the Fleet Street Choir" (*Detroit Plaindealer*).

• ***May 10, 1890 (Baltimore, Maryland):*** "By far the most popular and interesting entertainmant of the season was given at Dashane Post hall on Monday evening, May 5th, by the Kingston Club. The occasion was a phonographic entertainment, and that most wonderful of modern inventions did its part in amusing and entertaining the very large audience which had assembled to hear it. Its speeches were grand, its songs sweet, its jokes good and its laughter very hearty. The very interesting performance of the phonograph was followed by an informal soiree, and with the very excellent music furnished by the Noetick Orchestra [*sic*], this part of the program was as much enjoyed as the former part" (*Indianapolis Freeman*).

• ***May 24, 1890:*** "Mr. Harry T. Burleigh, Erie, Pa.'s most promising baritone, has been engaged for Y.P.S. meetings" (*Cleveland Gazette*).

PROF. N. H. PIUS.
Musical Director, Hearne Academy.

Freeman, *May 10, 1890.*

PROF. N. H. PIUS.
Musical Director, Hearne Academy

Prof. Pius is a resident of the state of Texas and was born at Mobile, Ala., Sept. 27, 1868.

Very soon after his birth the family moved to Galveston Texas where they have remained and become real estate owners.

When very young he was sent to public school where he was kept in constant attendance for seven years. He was shrewd from the beginning and in the autumn of '84 he entered Leland University, at New Orleans, La., and graduated in the spring of '89 with good honors. He taught public school in summer each year at Shiloh, Georgia. While attending school he became a deciple of the Lord and has proven a Christian worker in the Baptist denomination. Since his graduation he has had employment as a teacher in the public schools at Galveston.

In January of the present year he accepted the position which he now fills, as director of the musical department at Hearne Academy, an institution founded by the Baptist denomination.

As a Sabbath school worker, he shows exceptional ability. He seems to be especially talented for music. At the instrument or as a vocalist his proficiency is not wanting. The characterizing feature was excellently displayed when he was manager of the Sidney Woodward Concert Company during the summer of 1889, when Galveston was held spell-bound for twelve nights in succession by the company under his management. His record as a manager of musical entertainments is well known and he is making the musical department of the Academy a success. The culture shown by the singing clubs of the institution since they have been under his direction add new lustre to his to his crown as a musician.

Freeman, *May 10, 1890.*

• ***May 31, 1890:*** "New York City News," "On Sunday last, there was buried from 194 Bleeker street, a man whose name once was the synonym for skill upon the banjo, Horace Weston. His career is a striking example of the rise and fall of natural genius in the fickle field of fancy. Years ago he stood without a peer, and in clever measure, thumbed his melodies of the day before the crowned heads and rulers of the world. From troupe to troupe he drifted and through loose and careless habits gradually fell from grace, and saw the championship drift away from him" (*New York Age*).

• ***June 7, 1890 (New York City):*** "Deaths in the Profession," "Horace Weston—Too late for even brief notice in our last issue came the news that at 6:30 o'clock Friday evening, May 23, Horace Weston, the noted banjo player, died at his residence, No. 195 Bleeker Street, this city, after an illness of about two weeks. Only a short time before his death Mr. Weston was contemplating a visit to the West. He intended visiting Montana, and had arranged for engagements through J. C. Hennessy, of Butte City. He was, however, delayed from making the start on account of a severe attack of rheumatism, which finally culminated in dropsy, causing his death. Horace Weston was born at Derby, Ct., in 1825. It has been erroneously stated that he was at one time a slave, which is utterly false, as he was a free born Yankee. His father, Jube Weston, was a musician—performer and teacher—and likewise a teacher of dancing. Horace, at seven years of age, learned to play upon the accordeon, at Waterbury, Ct. He progressed to second violin at ten years of age, and also the violincello and double bass, slide trombone, guitar and dancing, in all of which he was an adept. From this he began teaching dancing. In 1855 he first began playing a banjo. He was at that period in New York State, and having broken his guitar, he borrowed a 'tub banjo' and sat up all night practicing, in which time he learned a couple of tunes and an accompaniment to sing to. He then struck Hartford, and secured a situation to drive a hack for Mr. Litchfield. He made himself a banjo out of a peck measure, and, in the course of a month's time, he gave his employer notice, left his employ and began playing banjo in the streets. At the breaking out of the war, in 1861, he went to Philadelphia, and thence to Harrisburg, in company with others, for the purpose of enlisting in the United States Army. They were refused, as no colored volunteers were received at that time. He next went to Boston and shipped in the United States Navy, taking his banjo along and practicing off watch hours, and received fifty cents per month from each sailor of the crew for playing for their amusement. He afterwards entered the army, and was wounded several times in battle. He went back in the navy, and, again being wounded, he threw his banjo overboard and afterwards enlisted in the Fifty-fourth Massachusetts Volunteers. He was discharged in July, 1863, and then began playing the banjo with Buckley's Minstrels. Later he traveled through Maine with the same company, and left them to join the Georgia Colored Minstrels about 1867. He then came to New York, played in the old Palace Garden, Mercer Street, for a year, and then took an engagement in the old Bowery Theatre, where he played two months. He then again joined the Georgia Minstrels and traveled through the British Provinces, after which he returned to New York and engaged at Harry Hill's, where he played six months. He then returned to Boston and opened a place during the Boston Jubilee, after which he went with Barnum's Show for the season. In January, 1872, he engaged with John Casey, on Sixth Avenue, this city, next to the Masonic Temple, and played there for two years. He then changed to No. 33 Bowery, at Paul Baur's saloon, and played three months, and from there to Carroll's, at Twenty-second Street and Sixth Avenue, where he performed two years. He next went to Robinson Hall to play, and during all these years he also taught the banjo and had a great number of pupils. During 1876, 1877 and 1878 he played on the boat Plymouth Rock, under Jarrett & Palmer, and in 1878 he was transferred to their 'Uncle Tom's Cabin' Co., and with that company sailed for Europe in August, 1878. The company opened in London, at the Princess' Theatre, on Oxford Street, and played three months. Here he made the great hit of his career, and performed nightly with the company, and at the same time played at the Royal Aquarium Theatre, meeting with the same success. He then visited Berlin, meeting with immense success there also, and opened at the Italia Theatre, in Breslau, Ger., where he played six weeks, receiving a large salary. He then opened at Strauss Theatre, Vienna, and from there went to Hamburg, and thence to France, and returned to America after one year. In England he won a very peculiar seven string banjo, in a banjo contest with an English player, which he carried home to America and presented to the late James W. Clarke. On his return home, in 1880, he came to New York City again and engaged with Mr. Carroll on Sixth Avenue. It was in this year that the artist first formed the acquaintance of S. S. Stewart, who was then becoming known as a banjo manufacturer. After playing awhile in New York City, he joined the 'Uncle Tom's Cabin' Co. again, and after leaving them joined Haverly's Georgia Minstrels, playing in Boston and New York. He then went to Coney Island for the summer. Afterwards he joined Callender's Minstrels for a tour, playing in all the cities and towns from New York to Oregon. After leaving this party on their return trip, at Chicago, he went to Philadelphia and opened at the Broadway Gardens, under F. Thorn's management, where he remained several weeks. Since that time he had traveled with various organizations, among which are Smith's 'Uncle Tom's' Co. and 'Arkansas Traveler' Co., all the time meeting with his usual success. He was a large and powerful man, sociable to an extreme degree. His superiority as a banjoist is attested by the fact that he possessed fourteen medals won by him in Europe and this country. Even royalty had applauded and generously awarded his skill. His wife, Alice Weston, is also a very good banjoist. The reason that Mr. Weston had ceased to travel with minstrel companies was because of his physical condition. He was a sufferer from chronic rheumatism, and at times was able to walk only with the assistance of crutches. Besides this he suffered from the effects of a wound received in the late war, which had troubled him more or less for several years. The funeral occurred from deceased's late residence afternoon of [May] 25, and was attended by a number of colored relatives and friends. The body lay in a black walnut casket, decked with wreaths of flowers. Rev. W. H. Wise delivered a touching eulogy, and the remains were carried to Evergreens Cemetery" (*New York Clipper*).

• ***June 7, 1890 (Cleveland, Ohio):*** At an entertainment given in St. John's A.M.E. Church, "Mr. Harry T. Burleigh, of Erie, Pa., was the only solo vocalist of the evening. He fully sustained his reputation as Erie's most promising baritone, by the fresh and natural, yet artistic rendition of his numbers. His voice is strong and expressive, and of excellent quality and range. His recalls were as many as his numbers" (*Cleveland Gazette*).

• ***June 7, 1890 (Richmond, Virginia):*** "The Second Baptist Church . . . by a unanimous vote decided that no more festivals shall be held in the church. They in no uncertain tones declared that they would no longer make God's house a house of merchandise" (*Richmond Planet*).

• ***June 28, 1890:*** "The Bluff City Quartette, consisting of Miss Mattie Cooper, soprano; Miss F. J. Thompson, alto; C. J. Williamson, basso; I. N. Dunlap, baritone; and Mrs. J. A. [Julia] Hooks, pianist and manager, went from Memphis, Tenn., to Kansas City, Mo., last week to give a series of concerts" (*Indianapolis Freeman*).

• ***July 11, 1890:*** "The Lyceum of the Second Baptist church was closed for the season last Wednesday evening, with a musical and literary entertainment. The program [included] Piano solo, Miss Azalia Smith . . .; Spider and the fly—Cows in the clover, Mr. William Gauze . . . the 'female impersonator,' was very clever in his impersonations, and during his performance every face in the audience was covered with smiles" (*Detroit Plaindealer*).

• ***July 12, 1890:*** "C. G. Phillips' No. 1 Colossal 'Uncle Tom's Cabin' Acrobatic and Specialty Show [includes] forty horses and forty people; twenty bloodhounds, darkeys and ponies" (*New York Clipper*).

• ***July 19, 1890:*** "Mrs. A. S. Steel, matron of the Colored Orphans Home at Chattanooga, Tenn., is traveling with six little orphans whose songs and recitations are everywhere favorably received" (*Cleveland Gazette*).

• ***July 25, 1890 (Ft. Wayne, Michigan):*** "Miss Ollie Brown has a large class of white scholars in music, some 15 in number, this speaks well for the teacher, showing that the color line is broken as there are so many white teachers in the city" (*Detroit Plaindealer*).

• ***August 1, 1890 (Detroit, Michigan):*** "Miss Nahar and Mr. Winter Wood," "During the past week Detroit audiences have been favored by the presence of Miss Ednorah Nahar and Mr. Winter Wood both promising aspirants for histrionic honors . . .

Mr. Charles Winter Wood whose first appearance here three years ago will be remembered by many shows the improvement made

A GLORIOUS INNOVATION. NOTHING SUCCEEDS LIKE SUCCESS.

PROF. WILLIAMS & CO'S. MAMMOTH RAILROAD SHOWS, EQUINE WONDERS AND WORLD'S FAIR CARNIVAL.

EVERY ACT A FEATURE.

Praised by the Press and the Public. WATCH FOR NEW AND STARTLING ANNOUNCEMENTS. Amazing and Rapturous Revelations in the Realm of Entertainment. Look out for our great tour of the East next season.

PROF. WILLIAMS & CO.

New York Clipper, *August 2, 1890. Black pioneer circus impresario Eph Williams was described in an 1897 edition of* Freeman *as "the only Negro circus owner in America." In 1909 he emerged as the sole proprietor of Eph Williams' Troubadours, which became better known by the title of its signature musical farce-comedy production, "Silas Green from New Orleans."*

in the years spent in study and his selection from the 'Bells' was especially good. Miss E. Azalia Smith shared with him the honors of the evening, her solo 'Meditation' deservedly winning an encore . . . Mr. Smallwood's clarionet solo and the selections by Mr. Finney's Orchestra closed a concert of unusual merit" (*Detroit Plaindealer*).

Note: Theodore Finney, whose orchestra closed this concert, was a fixture on the Detroit music scene. "Born in Columbus, Ohio September 1, 1837, Finney came to Detroit . . . at the age of 20. With his friend and fellow violinist, John Bailey, he organized the Bailey and Finney Orchestra, a popular ensemble that performed on excursion boats and for private parties and special events up until Bailey's death in 1871. Reorganizing the group in 1872, Finney spent the next 28 years establishing high musical standards via his well disciplined ensembles."[28]

• ***August 8, 1890 (Kalamazoo, Michigan):*** "The Long Lake camp meeting closed last Sunday . . . It did succeed in representing the colored people before the community in a creditable manner . . . The choir rendered choice music from the latest collection of revival songs and church anthems, which was a decided improvement on the old random way of singing" (*Detroit Plaindealer*).

• ***August 9, 1890 (St. Louis, Missouri):*** "The lawn fete given at Paragon Elevated Garden by the Young Men's Commercial Club . . . was the finest specialty show ever presented by the colored people of St. Louis . . . The club was especially fortunate in securing the services of Sig. Moletamo, the colored Cuban . . . He is a prestidigateur of the first order. His first act was called 'Aerial Suspension' and consisted in elevating a female several feet above his head . . . and moving her about in mid-air at his will . . . He walked barefooted up and down a ladder whose steps were razor-edged swords . . . [H]e . . . set fire to water; ate fiery pitch, and blew tongues of flame a foot in length from his mouth and nostrils. He changed water to wine, and performed many other tricks of legerdemain that baffled any natural solution. Especial praise is due Miss Alice Williams, St. Louis' favorite pianist, who, with Moletamo, bore the honors of the evening. Dan E. Washington (late of Harrison's Minstrels) gave sound representations on the 'bone' which tended to redeem the reputation of those degraded instruments . . . After the rendition of the program, dancing and other social festivities were indulged in" (*Indianapolis Freeman*).

Note: According to Tom Fletcher, in *100 Years of the Negro in Show Business*, "Daniel Washington . . . and his tall beautiful wife, Minnie, comprised a team that won all of the *Cake Walk* prizes in St. Louis and the neighboring towns. Finally they joined the Harrison Brothers' Company . . . Dan . . . was one of the principal end-men. He was an expert at rattling the bones, and . . . besides the regular specialty featuring the *Cake Walk*, Dan would do a *'bone solo'* on the program . . . He did imitations of drum corps, tap dancing and of a barber clipping hair."

• ***August 15, 1890:*** "A Band In Himself—How A Two Fingered Young Man Makes A Living," "The accompanying clipping is now going the rounds of the press:

A remarkable young colored man is Benjamin Franklin Dixon of St. Louis. He has but two fingers, yet with the aid of mechanical arrangements he can play on eight musical instruments at will—the harp, horn, harmonica, brass and snare drums, triangles, bells and pipes. A brass and leather contrivance around his neck holds the wind instruments, so that by stooping forward slightly he can reach them with his mouth. An electric button under one foot connects with the snare drum and bells. The bass drum and the cymbals he plays by means of a cord fastened to his elbow. The other elbow operates the triangle. On his head is fastened a frame with bells in it, and while arms, head and feet are busy he carries the air he is playing on a harp.

Dixon lost the greater part of his hands two years ago. He and another Negro were rivals for the favor of the same girl. Dixon won, and the jealous suitor put a dynamite rocket in his bedroom. When it went off it took with it eight of Benjamin's fingers" (*Detroit Plaindealer*).

• ***August 15, 1890:*** "Among those present at a grove meeting conducted by Miss Gabriele Greely, daughter of Horace Greely in a pine grove on their farm at Chappaqua, New York Sunday afternoon, Aug. 3 was O. C. Gilbert, an old personal friend of Mr. Greely. He was invited to assist in the services and in company with a quartette composed of Afro-American talent sang several numbers from a collection of jubilee songs" (*Detroit Plaindealer*).

• ***August 16, 1890:*** "Scintillations," "Our colored folks should stir themselves and get up a lively campmeeting—*Shelbyville* (Ind.) *Republican.*

"Should 'get up a lively campmeeting,' hey? That word 'lively' evidently is very expansive. Let's be etymological for a nonce. Lively (when applied to a colored campmeeting) means, in a monkeyish manner; plenty of shouting; wide-mouthed singing; ten-mile-reaching 'Yes, lordy.' We see; business is dull in Shelbyville and the weather is warm. 'Presto.' We can kill dull time at a 'Nigger Campmeeting.' Ah, ye unregenerated man!" (*Indianapolis Freeman*).

• ***August 29, 1890 (Detroit, Michigan):*** "Music And Dancing," "The Diversions Offered By Mr. And Mrs. Finney," "Preeminent among the many courtesies extended to this season's visitors will be cherished the memory of the Musical given by Mr. and Mrs. Finney Monday August 25. . . . The following program was excellently given:

Overture—From Dawn to Twilight, C. W. Bennet, Finney Orchestra; Passing out of the shadow—John Hoskins, Miss L. F. Preston; Solo—Sthoner, Praum op. 95, H. Lichner, Amanda Luckett; When the Leaves Begin to Fall, Mascotte, Mrs. Thos. H. Cole; Waltz de Concert, Earnest, Finney Orchestra; Die Ervarting, Melnotte, E. Azalia Smith; Selection—Tricotrin, C. W. Bennett, Finney Orchestra. Then a social hour spent around the tables on which delicious viands were served, and the feature of the evening to the merry young people began. Dancing to the music of Finney's orchestra is a delight of which they never tire, and the early hours of the morning were far spent when the tired revelers bade goodbye to their hosts and repaired to their homes" (*Detroit Plaindealer*).

• ***August 30, 1890 (Cincinnati, Ohio):*** "No decent self respecting man or woman in this city will be sorry to learn of the death of Pat Harris, lessee of Robinson's Opera House, who died by his own hand the past week in Baltimore. Coming here a few years ago as proprietor of the Dime Museum on Vine street, he was only too glad then to receive the patronage of our people who flocked there in great numbers to see the many 'fakes and frauds' exhibited. In a few years, having accumulated a fortune, he leased the old Robinson Opera House, where the race first established a 'Negro Row' in the balcony, and culminating in debarring them altogether save in the 'pigeon roost' among a lot of white bums. All honor is due our people here when it can be said that no respectable person attended the performances after his last edict against the race . . . Probably it was remorse for our people that caused him to end his life by shooting himself through the head. Let us hope so at any rate" (*Indianapolis Freeman*).

• ***September 20, 1890:*** "Eddie Moore, the wonderful little Negro boy piano prodigy, gave concerts at the St. Charles street Theatre, New Orleans, on Sept. 12th and 13th, '90" (*Indianapolis Freeman*).

Note: Eddie Moore went on to study in Europe. However, sad news was reported in the *Freeman* of May 2, 1896: "Eddie Moore, the musical prodigy, of New Orleans, who has been studying music in Stuttgart, Germany, is dead."

• ***September 20, 1890:*** "Charles Winter Wood and Miss Okey Lucas delighted the Afro-Americans of Omaha, Neb., Thursday of last week. They are now in Denver" (*Indianapolis Freeman*).

• ***September 20, 1890 (Cincinnati, Ohio):*** "Miss Hallie Q. Brown, the queen of elocution, in tragic, pathetic and humorous reading at Allen Temple A.M.E. Church, will give one of the best entertainments that has been given in this city" (*Indianapolis Freeman*).

• ***September 20, 1890:*** "W. Oscar Abbott, typewriter and stenographer at THE FREEMAN office, is quite a mandolin and violin player" (*Indianapolis Freeman*).

• ***September 20, 1890 (Cincinnati, Ohio):*** "The Band Contest," "The musicians of different cities held their convention last Thursday at the Lookout House, and paraded the streets in full uniform in the afternoon, after which the different bands competed with each other. The following bands were present: The Hotel Brotherhood Band of Indianapolis, the Stockland Cornet Band, the Georgetown, Ky., Band, which won the prize, and the Cincinnati Cornet Band" (*Indianapolis Freeman*).

• ***September 20, 1890:*** "Indianapolis is proud of her brass bands, and none is more deserving of praise than our Brotherhood Military Band. Last Thursday, the 11th, this band won the prize at the Cincinnati Band Contest . . .

Dave Gee, the cornet virtuoso, is meeting with success as instructor of the Brotherhood Band" (*Indianapolis Freeman*).

• ***September 20, 1890:*** "Prof. Fred Wiche, Bloomington, Ill., has organized a brass band consisting of sixteen mouth pieces" (*Indianapolis Freeman*).

• ***September 20, 1890:*** "William Duker, trick musician, has contracted with Sackett's Musee Circuit. Mr. Duker can play twelve instruments" (*Indianapolis Freeman*).

• ***September 27, 1890:*** "The Hygeia Colored Club of Old Point Comfort, Virginia gave a concert in the parlor of the hotel at that place Tuesday evening. It was one of the finest of the finest" (*Indianapolis Freeman*).

• ***October 2, 1890:*** "On Sunday, August 31, the white firemen of New Iberia gave an excursion from New Iberia to Thibodaux, and employed the colored string band of New Iberia, of which

Mr. Joe Adams was leader. Joe Adams had been run away from Thibodaux during the strike of 1887. The whites of Thibodaux objected to the colored bands playing because they don't allow the Negroes privileges. Plots were made to kill Mr. Adams. They struck him and attempted to knock him off the train, and they shot at him three times. Two white gentlemen saved his life, after having been beaten over the head with pistols, and one shot in the leg. Mr. Riggins, of the ice factory of Thibodaux, and Mr. Pattin, city marshal of New Iberia, saved his life. His brother, Geo. W. Adams, who was a member of the band, attempted to go to his rescue, when three pistols were pointed at his breast" (*Southwestern Christian Advocate*).

Note: During the "strike of 1887," 10,000 sugar plantation workers, 9,000 of them black, quit the cane fields of Lafourche Parish in a bid for decent wages. This resulted in the "Thibodaux Massacre," in which "300 armed white vigilantes murdered over 50 black people. The Thibodaux Massacre ended the strike, fatally wounded the labor movement, and initiated a racist reign of terror in the Louisiana sugar region."[29]

• ***October 3, 1890:*** "The *Baptist Pioneer* . . . cites the fact of minstrel troupes coming South and advertising themselves as 'all white' to cater to bourbon prejudices. The theatres have a little pen for 'colored people only.' Into this, the *Pioneer* complains, numbers of Afro-Americans go to hear those minstrel troupes belittle them in the most degrading and obscene manner" (*Detroit Plaindealer*).

• ***October 18, 1890 (New Orleans, Louisiana):*** "Land of Sunshine," "This is a southern metropolis, regardless of the boast of our sister cities . . . Our people have in the musical line the Excelsior and Onward Brass Bands and the Trio [*sic*, Tio] and Doublet Orchestra . . . We have the following literary and musical organizations: the Marchale Niel Literary Circle; this circle has one of the largest circulating libraries for its members and friends, in the city; the Emmerson Cotetie [*sic*], with library; the Calanthe Circle, the Electra Circle, Knights of Mirth, Chess Club, the Jopenica and Heliotheope [*sic*] Circles. The vocal talent [is] of no mean order here. Prominent among them are Mesdames A. J. Yarrington, Abbie Write Lyons[30], Nellie Williams and A. J. Dyer; Miss M. Cayoux; and Messrs T. L. Gaste, J. H. Beaurpear, J. W. Joublance and A. Popeliench; as a pianist Mrs. C. McCarthy has the field to herself. There are numerous other fine performers here of almost every line" (J. M. K., *Indianapolis Freeman*).

• ***October 25, 1890:*** "Lew Johnson's Famous Magnet Minstrels and Uniformed Electric Band, three years en route through the West and Northwest with a standard reputation. We do not have to carry a regiment of small salary people with this old reliable organization to draw houses . . . Now en route, date after date, behind the so called Colored Colossal Minstrels, and the general verdict of Press and Public is, Lew Johnson's company excel all Colored Minstrels that have appeared prior to them in their cities. Permanent address, 'Music and Drama,' San Francisco, Cal. Lew Johnson, Manager" (*New York Clipper*).

• ***October 25, 1890 (Washington, D.C.):*** "On Friday night the Cook orchestra gave a recital at the Berean Baptist Church, with the assistance of Misses Julia and Eunice Wormley. Miss Eunice Wormley's solo and Miss Julia Wormley's reading were creditable pieces of work. The Cook orchestra has an excellent reputation for its ability to interpret and render well the better class of music. This reputation was admirably sustained by its playing on this occasion. Mr. Wm. Cook after whom the orchestra is named, is the leading violinist. Mr. Cook plays so well and throws so much spirit in his work that the rest of the orchestra cannot but partake largely of his enthusiasm and strive to do good work. There are over twenty men in the orchestra under the direction and management of Maj. C. A. Fleetwood of the War Department and Mr. R. W. Thompkins of the Treasury. The organization is headed by Hon. Frederick Douglass as president" (*New York Age*).

• ***October 25, 1890 (Richmond, Virginia):*** "Miss Ednorah Nahar gave one of her grand renditions Monday night, 20th inst., at 3rd St. A.M.E. Church to an enthusiastic audience.

Mrs. Rosa K. Jones, the accomplished pianist rendered an instrumental solo.

'Steal Away' was well rendered by the Hartshorn Memorial College students.

'The Black Regiment' was rendered by Miss Nahar. . . It was surprising to note the fire manifested in her every motion while reciting this magnificent production. 'Who Did Swallow Jonah?' an amusing musical selection was sung by the Hartschorn Memorial young ladies.

'O Restless Sea' was sung by Mrs. Henrietta Jones . . .

'The Smack in School' and 'Kentucky Philosophy' were splendidly rendered by Miss Nahar. She was encored and returned to give another amusing selection.

'Safe in My Father's Home,' by the sweet-toned Miss Mildred Cross, gave entire satisfaction. She was encored, and sang 'Sweet Heart.'

'My Way is Clouded,' by the Hartschorn students, was next rendered.

'Three Dialects—Irish, Negro and Yankee' was admirably rendered by Miss Nahar. . .

Mr. Conway Reide gracefully sang 'Marguerite.' He was encored, and returned to sing 'Slavery Days.'

'Nobody Knows the Trouble I See' was sung by the Hartschorn students. They returned and sang 'You Shall Gain the Victory'" (*Richmond Planet*).

• ***November 1, 1890:*** "The Stage," "The Parker House Quartette composed of King Beasley, William Dansby, John Smith and Edward Taylor, is an organization of Anniston, Alabama" (*Indianapolis Freeman*).

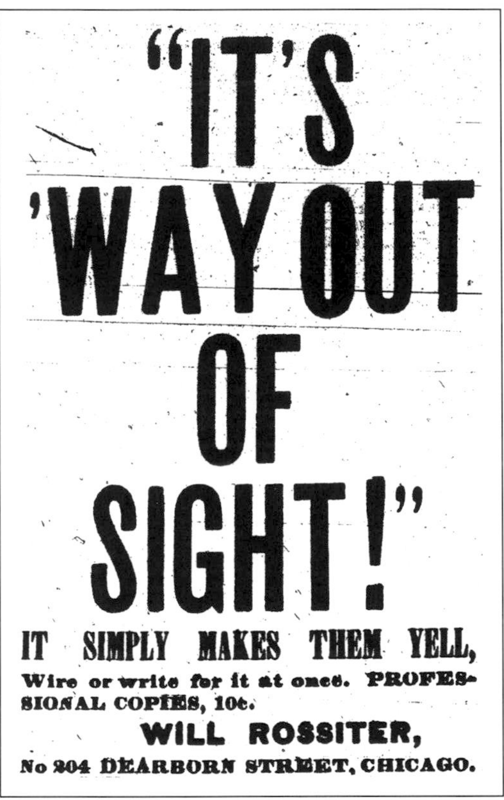

New York Clipper, *November 8, 1890. This ad announces the latest sheet music title from mainstream Chicago-based publisher Will Rossiter.*

• ***November 8, 1890 (Staunton, Virginia):*** "There was a young man before the Mayor for dancing the Mobile-buck on the platform. He was fined $2 for the Mobile and then the chief-of-police put on a dollar and a half for the Buck" (*Richmond Planet*).

• ***November 14, 1890:*** "Mr. Hans Shadd, Mrs. Elizabeth Armstrong, Mrs. Henry Jones and Mrs. Elizabeth Clark sang in the choir when the old Bethel Church of Philadelphia was dedicated and sang at the dedication of the new Bethel two weeks ago" (*Detroit Plaindealer*).

Note: In his "Pencil Pusher Points" column in the October 18, 1913, edition of *Philadelphia Tribune*, black historian William Carl Bolivar noted, "The first break away from lined out singing in Bethel Church was in 1840, when a quartette was organized consisting of Mrs. Margaret Jones, Miss Elizabeth Clark and Messrs. Hans Shadd and John Johnson."

• ***November 15, 1890 (Boston):*** "New England Conservatory," "Nov. 10—For the past week or more discord has prevailed at the New England Conservatory of Music and indignation reigns among the residents of this city. Some two or three months ago the Conservatory received applications for the admission of two colored young ladies, Miss Maude Cuney, daughter of the Collector of Customs at Galveston, Texas and Miss Florida DesVerney, whose father is a wealthy cotton dealer of Savannah, Ga. Both are prepossessing in appearance, intelligent and cultured. The application stated that the young ladies were colored and asked if there was any objection, to which the management replied it would be all right; that the young ladies would be received and treated as well as any of the students there. Miss Cuney, accompanied by her mother, called in person upon the directors, thereby rendering any misunderstanding regarding complexion utterly impossible. The young ladies arrived and for a while all was well. It appears, however, that there are pupils at the institution, several Southern white young ladies (?) who claimed to have been insulted by being compelled to more or less associate with those in question. Their prejudices gradually waxed stronger until, influenced by threats to withdraw from the institution, the vice-president sanctioned the idea of sending to the parents of the two pupils, letters informing them of the disagreeable feeling that existed, and suggested that they board outside the building, but continue in their studies. To this the father of Miss Des Verney readily consented, while Mr. Cuney emphatically refused; and at the same time instructed his daughter to remain. But she needed no urging for, at the beginning, she made up her mind to stay" (*New York Age*).

Note: Maud Cuney-Hare is probably best remembered for her 1936 book, *Negro Musicians and Their Music.*

• ***November 21, 1890 (Detroit, Michigan):*** "Glee Club Entertainment," "The Wayne Glee Club will give a grand vocal, instrumental and promenade concert, Thursday evening, Dec. 11, at Fraternity Hall. The club will be assisted by Mr. E. H. Hagen, basso, Peoria, Ill., Mr. Frank Liner, tenor, Cincinnati, and Mr. W. M. Lewis, guitarist, of Chicago. One of the interesting features of the program will be a drill by twelve members of the club under the direction of Mr. E. H. Hagen. Prof. Finney's orchestra will render music for the concert and promenade. General admission 25c, reserved seats, 25c" (*Detroit Plaindealer*).

• ***November 28, 1890 (Detroit, Michigan):*** At a gathering in a private home, in honor of a local pastor, "About half-past the o'clock as everyone was having a good time they were startled by the sound of music which on investigation proved to be the Jeffrie Cornet Band. They were invited in and rendered a few of their choice pieces. The party broke up with a taffy pulling" (*Detroit Plaindealer*).

• ***November 29, 1890:*** "Whistling for the Wind," "George H. [*sic*] Johnson, the whistling Negro in the Battery scene of 'The Inspector,' is a familiar figure on the North River ferryboats, where he whistles for pennies. Eighteen years ago he went with the Georgia Minstrels on a tour of the Old World. In Vienna they stayed two months. While there he fell in love with a white woman. She had no objection to his color, and they were married. Soon afterward they came to this country, and have lived happily together ever since. A daughter was born to them, and she has inherited the whistling abilities of her father. When Dramatist Wilson approached Johnson on the subject of joining his company the whistler stuck out for a fair salary. He said that he could pick up over $15 on the boats, and get a regular salary from a phonograph company for whistling in their machines. Wilson had to pay him $25 a week. Since his engagement he has had an offer from Mrs. William K. Vanderbilt, who wishes him to whistle for her one night after the theater performance. Mrs. Vanderbilt will not go to a variety theatre, but she is anxious to see all the best performers" (*New York Sun*, quoted in *New York Age*).

Note: Between 1890 and 1909, George Washington Johnson waxed versions of his two "Great Specialties," "The Laughing Song" and "The Whistling Coon" on numerous occasions for several different companies. In 1894 an Edison Records catalogue noted, "Up to date, over 25,000 of these two songs have been made by this artist, and orders for them seem to increase instead of diminish."[31]

• ***December 5, 1890:*** "At a dance held in Gilliands opera house of Van Wert, O., Thanksgiving evening William Stewart, a musician and plasterer, shot Ham Proost fatally and seriously wounded Oliver Ramsey because they objected to his going into the hall" (*Detroit Plaindealer*).

• ***December 5, 1890 (Amherstburg, Ontario, Canada):*** "On Sunday the 23rd of last month the A.M.E. church made a grand rally for the church debt . . . At the evening service a male quartet from the 'Sunny South' rendered a few of their selections" (*Detroit Plaindealer*).

• ***December 6, 1890 (Camden, New Jersey):*** "The celebrated Miller Quartette Concert Company of Philadelphia is composed of William A. Miller, director and accompanist; Miss M. Campbell, soprano; L. W. Parker, tenor; Miss C. B. Webb, contralto; W. F. Miller, basso; Henri Strange, elocutionist" (*Indianapolis Freeman*).

• ***December 6, 1890 (Terre Haute, Indiana):*** "The Olive Leaf Quartette, of South 14th St., challenges any quartette in the state, Magnolia Quartette preferred" (*Indianapolis Freeman*).

• ***December 20, 1890:*** "The Stage," "The Cyclone Quartette consisting of Messrs. G. L. Green, S. L. Barbour, W. A. Reid and well-known bass singer Alf H. Lindsay, formerly of San Francisco, has just closed two weeks engagement at the New State Opera House, Spokane, Washington" (*Indianapolis Freeman*).

• ***December 20, 1890 (Maysville, Kentucky):*** "The Maysville Glee Club will go to Flemingsburg on the 26th to participate in the entertainment with the Cooking Club of that place. They will be accompanied by Prof. Venie's string band" (*Indianapolis Freeman*).

• ***December 20, 1890:*** "The Stage," "Mrs. Hattie Hays, the vocal and guittarist [*sic*] will soon move to Dallas, Texas." (*Indianapolis Freeman*).

• ***December 20, 1890 (Baltimore, Maryland):*** "For some weeks the colored people in different sections of the city have been delighted with the singing of two soloists hailing from Raleigh, N.C. They are Prof. Simmons and Mr. Henry Tate. Prof. Simmons has a finely developed and musical bass voice . . . Mr. Tate has a fine, sweet and melodious soprano voice . . . Mr. Tate impersonates, by dress and action, a lady singer in several pieces, much to the amusement and pleasure of his auditors" (*Indianapolis Freeman*).

• ***December 20, 1890:*** "J. H. Harris of Xenia, Ohio, is . . . a professor of music, he was the pipe organist at Quinn Chapel under Rev. T. W. Henderson; he once played a difficult piece six parts for Blind Tom to imitate; he is in his 23rd year" (*Indianapolis Freeman*).

• ***December 20, 1890 (Chicago, Illinois):*** "If you wish to acquire the art of dancing, visit the Ideal Academy every Friday evening, Arlington Hall" (*Indianapolis Freeman*).

• ***December 20, 1890:*** "The Stage," "Allen's Brass Band, of Beaufort, S.C., has just returned home from filling an engagement at Augusta, Ga." (*Indianapolis Freeman*).

• ***December 20, 1890:*** "The Stage," "Professor M. S. Simmons, colored, of North Carolina, and late of Baltimore, gave a musical concert in the Bethel church, Philadelphia last Tuesday and the affair netted him $55 . . . After the entertainment he escorted Mrs. Ella Banks to her home, on Fifteenth below Lombard. The woman testified before Magistrate Diamond yesterday that the 'Professor' had attempted to assault her. The accused denied the charge. He was placed under $500 bail" (*Indianapolis Freeman*).

• ***December 20, 1890 (Chicago, Illinois):*** "Robt Mott and F. I. Edwards' immense Turkish bath rooms at 462 State Street . . . This enterprise fills a long felt want of the race, owing to its unusual magnetic cures and is recommended by the profession as [a] sure cure for rheumatism, stiffness and hundreds of human complaints. The attendants are the experienced Messrs Edwards and James Warren, who were several years attendants at the Palmer House barber shop rooms" (*Indianapolis Freeman*).

Note: Robert T. Motts filled a greater "long felt want of the race" in 1905 when he opened the Pekin Theater on State Street—"the only first-class and properly equipped theatre in the United States, owned, managed and controled by colored promoters." [32]

• ***December 27, 1890 (Philadelphia, Pennsylvania):*** "R. Henri Strange, the colored tragedian, will appear as Shylock at the Academy, Jan. 12, in aid of a fund for the erection of a theatre for colored actors in the city. The cast will include P. French, W. H. Bennett, C. B. Yancey, W. H. Cole, L. W. Parker, J. L. Jenkins, A. H. Jackson, G. Solomon, Flora Pedro and Ada Rolen" (*New York Clipper*).

African American Minstrel Companies in the South

By 1890 African American minstrel companies had successfully invaded at least one frontier that remained out of bounds to professional jubilee singing troupes—the American Southland. The accessibility of southern venues to African American minstrels was due in part to the fact that, unlike jubilee singing, minstrelsy didn't challenge white people's presumptions of racial superiority or ask to be taken seriously. Another important factor in African American minstrelsy's southern invasion was the method of transportation. Large, successful black minstrel troupes insulated themselves from the Jim Crow pitfalls of public conveyance and lodging by traveling in and living out of privately owned railroad cars which they arranged to have shuttled from town to town. The performers kept out of danger by avoiding unnecessary personal contact with local whites.

At the same time, fraternization with local black community organizations was common. Nationally prominent African American minstrel troupes captured the imagination of black southerners in a special way. Not only did the "colored population" come out strong for their shows; representative social clubs, fraternal orders, and musical groups lavished them with suppers, receptions, and dinner parties. The support that black southerners demonstrated for African American minstrel companies during the 1890s demonstrated the commercial viability of black minstrel entertainment for black audiences, paving the way for "modern" troupes like the Rabbit Foot Minstrels and "Silas Green from New Orleans," who traversed the American Southland from the earliest years of the twentieth century until minstrelsy finally wore itself out in the 1950s.

Richards and Pringle's Original Georgia Minstrels and Billy Kersands, 1889–1895

The African American minstrel troupe that captured the largest and most loyal black southern following during the 1890s was Richards and Pringle's Georgia Minstrels. When they played the Avenue Theater in New Orleans in 1887, the *Daily Picayune* noted, "Colored people are turned away nightly. There would be millions in it if the manager could give up the biggest part of his house to the colored people instead of the smallest, when the genuine Georgia Minstrels play their engagements."[33] At Memphis in the fall of 1896 the *Freeman* noted, "Richards & Pringle's Georgia Minstrels succeeded in drawing. . . in the neighborhood of 5,000 people—4,000 Negroes and 1,000 whites, the largest indoor paid audience ever known in that city."[34] By the turn of the century Richards and Pringle's *Freeman* correspondent could claim with certain conviction, "The Georgias reign supreme in the South."

Black turn-of-the-century community musical organizations treated members of Richards and Pringle's Georgia Minstrels like visiting royalty. While playing New Orleans in 1898, the "Georgias" were feted by Prof. W. J. Nickerson and his Student Orchestra, which included Nickerson's daughter Camille, piano; T. V. Baquet, cornet; and Baquet's son George, clarinet.[35] At Sedalia, Missouri, on March 25, 1899, they were banqueted by "Messrs. Williams and McCallahan, managers of the '400' club."[36] Later that year at Pensacola, Florida, they were "entertained most royally by the celebrated Utopia Club" with its "Pensacola orchestra of color. . . Prof. Ed Wyer, clarionet, Wm. Wyer double bass, Wm. Pontz cornet, Miss Flo Wyer piano and Ed Wyer Jr. 1st violin."[37]

The troupe's white proprietors, O. E. Richards and C. W. Pringle, attached themselves to an agglomerated history that claimed direct descent from the Georgia Minstrels of the 1860s. The credibility of this claim was largely fastened to their perennial star comedian, Billy Kersands, who first toured with a troupe of "Georgias" in 1871, under Charles B. Hicks's management. Kersands's unflagging charisma was an essential factor in Richards and Pringle's southern triumphs. When they showed at Houston, Texas, on January 8, 1901, representatives of the black community in Galveston arranged to "run a special excursion from Galveston to Houston, over the S.P.R.R., and carried nearly 400 people to see Billy Kersands and the big show. Long live Billy. He will ever be appreciated in this section of the country."[38]

Widely heralded during the 1890s and thereafter as an "unconscious," "nature-gifted" performer, Billy Kersands was one of the original architects of African American minstrelsy's "ancient oddities." According to a retrospective sketch in the *Freeman*, he was born in 1842 in Baton Rouge, Louisiana, then "went to New York and engaged in the boot black trade."[39] However, a later sketch in the same paper insists he was actually born on Hester Street in New York City.[40]

Charles B. Hicks recalled having first seen Kersands perform in 1870 "at Jake Berry's Cellar Music Hall, Broadway and Prince street, New York, billed as 'Cudjoe the Wonder,' admission ten cents, doing the 'essence of old Virginny'. . . I was then enroute to England with the 'Georgias,' but it had a lasting impression on me, so much so, that, upon my return in 1871, I hunted him up. . . Then it was that he commenced a career that placed him in the front ranks of minstrelsy. His 'Old Aunt Jemima' became a household word."[41]

Kersands's "Essence of Virginny" was a vernacular dance that required a nimble "combination of knee work and head buttoning to keep time with the music."[42] His song "Old Aunt Jemima" was, in effect, a vehicle for stringing together traditional floating verses. The connecting rod was a repeatedly chanted vocal refrain—"Old Aunt Jemima, oh, oh, oh." A different group of verses is given for "Old Aunt Jemima" in each of three different Georgia Minstrels songbooks.[43] The version in *Willie E. Lyle's Great Georgia Minstrels Song Book* (1875) includes these two:

My old missus promised me,
Old Aunt Jemima, oh, oh, oh,
When she died she'd set me free,
Old Aunt Jemima, oh, oh, oh,
She lived so long her head got bald,
Old Aunt Jemima, oh, oh, oh,
She swore she would not die at all,
Old Aunt Jemima, oh, oh, oh.

I went to the hen-house on my knees,
Old Aunt Jemima, oh, oh, oh,
I thought I heard a chicken sneeze,
Old Aunt Jemima, oh, oh, oh,
'Twas nothing but a rooster saying his prayers,
Old Aunt Jemima, oh, oh, oh,
He gave out the hymn, "Such a gittin' up stairs,"
Old Aunt Jemima, oh, oh, oh.

"Old Aunt Jemima" was commercially recorded at least one time, in 1947, by an excellent white male quartet known as the Singing Sentinels.[44] The "my old missus" verse was in the air by 1845, when this variation was cited in a mainstream magazine:

Massa and Misse promised me
When they died they'd set me free;
Massa and Misse dead an' gone,
Here's old Sambo hillin'-up corn![45]

Highly suggestive of "authentic slave humor," the "my old missus" verse turned up during the 1920s in published collections of Negro folksongs[46] and on early "Race" and "Hillbilly" recordings by black vocal quartets and white southern string bands.[47]

The ubiquitous "hen house" verse takes off on "Down in the valley on my knees, asked my Lord, 'Have mercy, please,' " from the jubilee song "Every Time I Feel the Spirit." It is preserved, in subtle variations, on early race recordings, including the 1931 recording of "Who Stole the Lock (from the Henhouse Door)" by one of Birmingham, Alabama's greatest black community quartets, the Dunham Jubilee Singers.[48]

In 1880 Billy Kersands introduced "Mary's Gone Wid a Coon," a forerunner of the "coon song" phenomenon that soon came to dominate the repertoire of black and white minstrels. While keeping pace with trends in minstrel song and humor during the 1889–1895 period, Kersands was not expected to be an innovator; Billy Kersands made his way into the twentieth century as a living treasure of African American minstrelsy, "the old wagon that never broke down."[49]

Some particular accounts of the 1889–1895 activities of Richards and Pringle's Georgia Minstrels and their star comedian are preserved in the *New York Clipper* and various African American weeklies.

• ***June 1, 1889:*** "The Stage," "Richards and Pringles, colored Georgia Minstrels, headed by the famous Billy Kersands closed their season last Saturday night, in Chicago. Colored talent in all lines of the business are wanted for next season" (*Indianapolis Freeman*).

• ***October 21, 1889:*** "The following from McComb, Miss., dated Oct. 5, comes from Richards & Pringle's Minstrels: 'Billy Kersand and Miss J. A. Watts, and Billy Farrell and Miss W. Gauze were married here today. They received many presents from the company, and have the best wishes of their many friends" (*New York Clipper*).

Note: This was obviously intended as a joke, since Gauze and Watts were both female impersonators. That it originated from McComb, Mississippi, in the fall of the year suggests that Richards and Pringle were already coordinating their troupe's southern tours to follow the harvest season. During the 1890s and early 1900s, autumns in the Mississippi Delta were increasingly congested with African American minstrel shows.

• ***April 12, 1890:*** "The old reliable Richards & Pringle's Famous Georgia Minstrels, Silver Cornet Band and Classic orchestra, just closed a successful season of 37 weeks. The man in white perambulated every Sunday. Now reorganizing for the season of 1890–1891 . . . and will be headed by the only and original Billy Kersands, the man with many imitators, but no equals. Wanted, Colored talent in all branches . . . Richards & Pringle, care National Printing Co., 119 Monroe Street, Chicago, Ill." (*New York Clipper*).

Note: Such phrases as "The man in white perambulated," or "The ghost makes his usual weekly visits" are variations of the popular show-business expression, "The ghost walks," which signified that paydays were being regularly met.[50]

• ***December 27, 1890:*** "Notes from Richard & Pringle's Georgia Minstrels," "We are now in the twentieth week of our present season, and everything is sailing smoothly with O. E. Richards as captain and C. W. Pringle as our pilot. There has not been any dissention in the ranks since we started out. Charles Walker is at present on the sick list. Chas. Wallace, Will Eldridge, Tom Brown and Frank Mallory have of late been investing in precious stones. W. O. Terry was presented lately with a beautiful diamond pin by Will Gauze. The presentation took place on the stage . . . Afterwards there was a popping of corks. Jim Gilliam is at present leader of the band, this being his fifth season as the occupant of that position. The Vestibule Car Porters and Continental Guards' Drill emanated from the Mallory Bros. (Frank and Ed), and is under the personal supervision of Frank Mallory. Billy Johnson joined us some time ago, and as an aged negro delineator he is 'way up.' Dennis B. Rice has purchased a home at Clarksville, Tenn. The ghost makes his usual weekly visits" (*New York Clipper*).

• ***May 22, 1891 (Detroit, Michigan):*** "Mr. Wm. Gauze, the famous male soprano of Detroit has just closed a season of 40 weeks with the Richard and Pringle minstrels and can be seen shaking hands with his many friends" (*Detroit Plaindealer*).

• ***May 23, 1891:*** "Since our arrival at Chicago most of the company have departed for other climes. Billy Kersands has gone to Louisville. Thomas Brown opened at the Buckingham Theatre May 18. Wm. Johnson is visiting his parents at Charleston, S.C. Wm. Eldridge is with his mother at St. Louis. Prof. Charles Johnson, leader of orchestra, is traveling with Thearle's 'U.T.C.' Co. W. O. Terry is at his home, Charleston, W. Va., and Dennis B. Rice is located at Clarksville, Tenn., with his wife and little daughter. John H. Grant is doing the swell at New Orleans. James Lacey has the leadership of an orchestra at Kansas City. Chas. Wallace is kept quite busy arranging music for several Chicago firms. Frank Mallory is on his way to his home at Jacksonville, Ill. . . . His brother, Ed., is spending his vacation with his parents, his wife and child having joined him, from Galveston, Tex. Ed. is having a brand new cornet manufactured for his express use . . . James Gilliam remains in the Windy City. Will Gauze will play several weeks through the West, after a brief visit to his home, Windsor, Ont. Managers Richards & Pringle are at Chicago, making big preparations for next season" (*New York Clipper*).

• ***June 27, 1891:*** "Manager O. E. Richards has returned to Chicago, from his recent trip to the Hawkeye State, where he visited his relatives and numerous friends . . . C. W. Pringle remains at his post of duty . . . Jno. H. Grant has returned to Chicago from New Orleans, the climate of the latter place having proved disasterous to his health . . . Chas. Walker . . . with the others of his quartet will commence an engagement at the Olympic June 29. Chas. Johnson, leader of orchestra, has completed his Summer engagement with Thearle's 'U.T.C.,' and is now on his way to his home at Lawrence, Kas." (*New York Clipper*).

• ***October 18, 1891:*** "Stage Notes," "Richard and Pringle's minstrels report a good success through the South with old time favorite Billy Kersands" (*Topeka Weekly Call*).

• ***October 24, 1891:*** "Ed. Mallory, of the Mallory Bros., with Richards & Pringle's Minstrels, was presented by his wife with a handsome cluster diamond pin, at Galveston, Tex., on Oct. 2. The Venetian Mandolin Drill, as produced by them, is said to be a pleasing success" (*New York Clipper*).

• ***October 31, 1891:*** "Our Musical People," "Richard's & Sprigle's [*sic*] Minstrels are now doing the Southern States. They appeared in Columbus, Miss. last week" (*Indianapolis Freeman*).

• ***January 3, 1892 (Topeka, Kansas):*** "The grand minstrel performance at Crawford's opera house on the 22nd, headed by Billy Kersands, the emperor of comedians, was one of the finest we have had for years" (*Topeka Weekly Call*).

• ***March 12, 1892:*** "Stage," "The original Georgia Minstrels with Billy Kersands are in California" (*Indianapolis Freeman*).

• ***August 5, 1893:*** "Richards & Pringle's Georgia Minstrels open their seventeenth regular season at Valparaiso, Ind., Aug. 12, with the following roster: Billy Kersands, Tom Brown, Ganzer [*sic*], Jas. White, Hillman and Vernon, C. A. Walker, J. A. Howard, Hi Wooten, J. A. Watts, Prof. C. F. Alexander, Jas. Y. Gilliam, Jas. Lacey, Jas. Moore, D. B. Rice, W. O. Terry, Walter Mitchell, H. Woodley, Sargeant Reims and his twelve Dohamy [*sic*] cadets. O. E. Richards is the sole owner and manager; R. A. Rusco, agent, and Geo. Gurgen, assistant agent" (*New York Clipper*).

• ***November 11, 1893:*** "Tom Brown's original production of 'A Game of Craps' and his 'Old Fashion Cake Walk' are meeting with success through the Southern States" (*New York Clipper*).

• ***October 20, 1894:*** "Notes from Richards & Pringle's Minstrels," "We played in Charleston, W. Va., Oct. 8, and as it is the home of W. O. Terry, who is connected with the company, a large audience assembled. There are ten Knights of Pythias with the show, and after the performance Capital City Lodge, Knights of Pythias, gave them an enjoyable reception. Sir Knight Jones delivered an address of welcome to the visiting Knights and was responded to by W. O. Terry. Then all sat down to a bounteous feast. During the evening the minstrel orchestra discoursed delightful music. Billy Kersands, James White and James Moore did their share toward making the occasion lively" (*New York Clipper*).

• ***January 18, 1895:*** "At Donaldsonville, La., on the 6th inst Billy Kersands, the noted colored minstrel at the head of Richards & Pringle's Georgia Minstrels, was married to Widow Armstrong [*sic*], one of the best known colored residents of Donaldsonville and who is reputed to be quite wealthy. The ceremony was to have taken place on the stage of Phoenix Opera House during the performance of the Georgians, but owing to the opposition of the Strong family who are devout Catholics, the project was abandoned and the couple were united by the parochial priest, Very Rev. Father Dubernard" ("Brotherhood", *Kansas City American Citizen*).

Note: Kersands's new wife, Louise, also became his regular stage partner. Her maiden name may have been Fernandez. An article in the December 23, 1905, edition of the *Freeman* identified her as "the Widow Strong . . . a Louisiana girl, born and reared in the town of Donaldsonville, sixty-four miles west of New Orleans, on the Texas and Pacific Railroad, where she is recognized by both races as one of the most estimable women in the community. Until her marriage to Mr. Kersands, she was proprietress of the best kept restaurant in the town of Donaldsonville."

• ***May 18, 1895:*** "Notes from Richards & Pringle's Minstrels," "We closed May 11, at Fargo, N.D., our twenty-fourth season on the road . . . A number of the old folks have signed for next season, including Billy Kersands, which makes his eleventh year with the show. We will open about Aug. 1" (*New York Clipper*).

• ***July 13, 1895:*** "The following have signed with Richards & Pringle's for next season: Billy Kersands, Eugene Hillman, Robt. Vernon, Neil Moore, Bobby Kemp, Marsh Craig, Jalvan, Pickaninny Quartet, Reese Bros., Brown and Thomas, Jas. Lacy, W. O. Terry, D. B. Rice, John Easson, S. B. Foster, Wm. Lacy, Jas. F. Leitch, Crescent City Quartet (Watts, Collins, Becker and Wooten), W. C. Tiede, John Terry, Oscar Hodge . . . O. E. Richards, sole proprietor. Their season opens at the Alhambra, Chicago, Aug. 11. They travel in their private car, Georgia" (*New York Clipper*).

In 1903 the Georgia Minstrels and Billy Kersands finally parted ways, and Kersands went out under his own name. In Texas during the fall of 1906, his ancient powers were reconfirmed: "At Texarkana we were compelled to deputize thirty police to keep order, so large were the crowds eager to pay homage to the exalted ruler of Negro minstrelsy, the one man who, through wind and tide, has proved himself a minstrel king, true and noble, pure and simple—a singer natural as the changes of nature . . . Billy Kersands—a man whose gestures and every character of stage deportment has been copied and imitated for many years, but never equalled, the real beacon light of genuine minstrelsy."[51]

Billy Kersands "took his final curtain call" on June 30, 1915, at a theater in Artesia, New Mexico, where he suffered a fatal heart attack after his second performance of the evening. He was seventy-three.[52] *Freeman* columnist and fellow performer Salem Tutt Whitney eulogized him as the "best known and best beloved minstrel America has known, regardless of color. Billy's name was a byword for minstrelsy the country over."[53] Another eulogist spoke of "OUR BILLY . . . Possessed with no college education, but owner of the greatest asset 'Mother Wit,' he vied with the best in educating mankind."[54]

Cleveland's Colored Minstrels, Season of 1890–1891

The front page of the November 30, 1889, edition of the *Clipper* carried a biographical sketch of white minstrel entrepreneur W. S. Cleveland: "William S. Cleveland, the youngest and most daring of this day's managers of minstrelsy . . . was born at Chillicothe, O., twenty-eight years ago, and, as a youth, worked in his native place as a printer. His love of the show business began early, with his connection, in a subordinate capacity, with the Opera House at Chillicothe. He was afterwards a circus billposter and programmer... His first minstrel experience was gained in the Thatcher, Primrose & West Co., and later he was with M. B. Leavitt's and other enterprises... Next year... Mr. Cleveland promises to send out four distinct companies, one of them a genuine blackface party."

The "genuine blackface party" that W. S. Cleveland assembled for the 1890–1891 season was billed as a "Colossal Colored Minstrel Carnival" incorporating "nearly all the best colored artists in the universe." Conspicuous on the roster of the 1890–1891 edition of Cleveland's Colored Minstrels was Tom McIntosh, one of the very few old-time minstrel comedians considered to rank with Billy Kersands, along with the legendary composer James Bland, plus Doc Sayles, Henderson Smith, and others of note.

• ***May 17, 1890:*** "The following people have been engaged for Cleveland's Colored Carnival Minstrels for next season: Tom McIntosh, James Bland, Billy Farrell, Harry S. Eaton, Cicero Reed, Master Reed, the Twilight Quartet, Grant and Williams, Jalvan, James Wilson, Billy Jackson and Pete De Rose, the San Souci Quartet, Tom Lewis, Billy Johnson, Doc Sales, Master McIntosh and Alf. White" (*New York Clipper*).

• ***July 5, 1890:*** "For several years past the country has been flooded with small bands of colored minstrels, each band comprising from fourteen to twenty people, who have traveled under the titles of Georgias, Alabamas, Black Boys and Colored Minstrels, giving performances that were painful to behold, not alone to the audiences, but to the performers themselves. Manager W. S. Cleveland, who is ever on the alert to give his patrons something new, therefore concluded to have the leading genuine colored minstrel company, as well as the two largest white minstrel companies in the world, and... he has succeeded in getting under contract nearly all the best colored artists in the universe, and will have a company comprising sixty genuine performers, prominent among whom are Tom McIntosh, James Bland, Will Eldridge, Doc Sayles, George Tichner, Four Brewer Bros., Eaton and Williams, the San Souci Quartet, the Twilight Quartet, Billy Farrell, Smart and Taylor, the Great Jalvan, Prof. James Wilson, W. C. Harris, Henderson Smith, Mons. Le Vard, Frank Warner and Tom Jones, together with acrobats, comedians, singers, dancers and musicians, who will present a unique entertainment with many novelties original with

GENUINE BLACK PERFORMERS.
200 WANTED! 200
FOR THE SEASON OF 1890-91, FOR
CLEVELAND'S
COLOSSAL COLORED CARNIVAL.
Who do not require cork and wear natures wigs. COMEDIANS, VOCALISTS AND MUSICIANS, WOMEN AND CHILDREN, who have previously faced the footlights, will please address as below, giving previous experience, salary expected, and enclosing House bills as an evidence of capacity.
I WANT ALL THE GREAT COMEDIANS EXCEPT GEORGE WILSON (THE CHINESE).
400 THREE GIGANTIC TROUPES, 400
EACH KNOWN AS
W. S. CLEVELAND'S MAGNIFICENT MINSTRELS.
Will monopolize the UNITED STATES, CANADAS and AUSTRALIA, SEASON '90, '91, the enlistments for which are going on, and for which FOUR HUNDRED of the best men that black their faces are wanted in addition to the most
AMAZING AND EXPENSIVE SPECIALTIES,
For which I will GIVE UP MORE MONEY than any manager living, and I want to hear from all the world's celebrities. ADDRESS AT ALL TIMES, THE YEAR 'ROUND,
W. S. CLEVELAND, care Courier Lithographing Co., Buffalo, N. Y.

New York Clipper, *October 12, 1889.*

Manager Cleveland. This company is already booked in most of the leading theatres of this country, from Maine to California, and New York to New Orleans" (*New York Clipper*).

• ***August 2, 1890 (Joliet, Illinois):*** "July 29—The biggest link in the chain forming Minstrel Magnate Cleveland's gigantic burnt cork trust reached here early Saturday morning, and at noon made the inaugural parade . . . The performance was greeted by an audience that packed the house to the walls. Standing room was sold, and hundreds were turned away. When the curtain went up on the Toreador first part, a setting was revealed that has never been approached in magnificence by anything ever seen here . . . The orchestra wore green silk plush, trimmed with lilac satin and gold. The singers were in blue plush, pearl satin and silver, and the ten end men wore red plush and gold. The principal comedians, Tom McIntosh, James Bland, Doc Sayles and Billy Farrell, were attired in the finest satins, in varied colors . . . It is composed of the following artists: Tom McIntosh, F. McIntosh, Billy Farrell, Four Brewer Bros., Harry Eaton, Tom Williams, Grant Williams, Smart Taylor, Palmer McClain, Louis Rector, W. Pickett, Jas. Jalvan, Jas. Wilson, Will Levard, George Litchner [*sic*], W. Henderson, Henderson Smith, R. Dougern, J. Robinson, F. Warner, Carter Lumpkins, Alf. White, Elmer Farrell, Henry Thomas, Ollie Hall, Darivis Cain, Sam Burrus, Doc Sayles, T. H. Moxley, L. Preston, L. Hunster, San Souci Quartet, Australian Quartet, Bluson Dodson, Hume, Johnson, Bowman, Price, Sam Henry, J. Wilson, G. Hill, Dave Johnson, Peter Jackson, Jim Wright, Sam Terry, Arthur Fallon, Jas. Tyler, Malvin Perry, Collins Bolton, Sam Griffin, P. G. Scott, Wm. Redmond, G. Hill, Chas. Smith, Sam Butler, J. Powell, Alex. Chasman, Tom Russell, T. Jones, Sam Morris, a military band of twenty-eight, under the leadership of Prof. Henderson Smith; an orchestra of eighteen, under the direction of [William] Henderson" (*New York Clipper*).

• ***September 20, 1890:*** "Notes from Cleveland's Colored Minstrels," "At last we are once more upon our native heath, arriving at Stillwater, Minn., Sept. 8, from Winnepeg, Man. The boys exchanged several simoleans with the 'Canucks' for new clothes . . . 'The Feast of the Voudoos,' a new and unique act, created by manager Harry Semon, will be produced this week . . . James Bland is making a tremendous impression with his refined and easy style on the tambo end, and Tom McIntosh has 'em going his way on the bones end . . . The Toreador Quartet—Kennedy, Clark, Thompson and Griffin—get a double encore every night . . . Tom Williams is doing captivating work with his banjo. The Egyptian jugglers are doing well" (*New York Clipper*).

• ***September 27, 1890:*** "Tom McIntosh, of Cleveland's Colored Minstrels, was married to Hattie Booker, Sept. 17, on the stage of the Academy of Music, Milwaukee, Wisc., just after the evening performance and in the presence of the entire audience" (*New York Clipper*).

• ***October 11, 1890:*** " 'The Voudoos' Feast' . . . has proved a decided go . . . Lon Lewis, our robust tenor, . . . sings Banks Winter's 'Neona.' James Bland has purchased the largest diamond ever worn, probably, by a colored performer . . . Levard, sword walker, is very indignant at yet another sword walker at the Grand Museum, New York City, for being advertised as Le Vard . . . Harry Eaton, our popular stage manager, celebrated his thirty-ninth birthday last week" (*New York Clipper*).

• ***November 15, 1890:*** "Harry W. Semon, manager of W. S. Cleveland's Colored Minstrels, is proving himself a strict disciplinarian. The other day he censured one of the ebony performers in language severe. The object of the remarks exhibited great amazement and exclaimed: 'Mr. Semon, I'se 'stonished! 'Deed I am. Who'd 'spect that sich remarks would eber be 'dressed to me. Do you s'pose, sah, dat Mr. Clebeland wud talk like dat to [white blackface minstrel star] Mr. Billy Emerson?" (*New York Clipper*).

• ***January 10, 1891:*** "Billy McClain, of Cleveland's Colored Minstrels, while performing on the stage in San Francisco Thanksgiving Matinee fell from his trapeze and had three teeth knocked out but is getting along all right. George Taylor of the Eclipse Quartette fell dead in his dressing room at Lincoln Neb., of heart disease. Cleveland's boys have a traveling organization of Knights of Pythias" (*Indianapolis Freeman*).

• ***January 16, 1891:*** "A number of the members of the Cleveland Colored Minstrel Company got into a fight with trainmen on the Missouri Pacific between St. Joseph, Mo. and Atchison, Ks. last week. Tom McIntosh the principal comedian was badly hurt" (*Detroit Plaindealer*).

• ***February 21, 1891 (Erie, Pennsylvania):*** "Cleveland's Colored Minstrels gave a first class performance at the Opera House... Mr. Ollie Hall of the Challenge Quartette gave a very pleasing rendition of the hymn 'Jesus, Lover Of My Soul' to the tune of 'In The Gloaming'" (*Cleveland Gazette*).

• ***February 28, 1891:*** "John Brevier [*sic*], of the Cleveland Colored Minstrels during his recent engagement in San Francisco, Cal., was presented with a gold badge inlaid with diamonds from King Kalakaua for his excellent handling of the drum major baton. Joseph Jalvin and James Wilson, Egyptian jugglers, received flattering press notices everywhere for their clever work. Billy McClain, slide trombone and comedian, is traveling correspondent and agent for THE FREEMAN" (*Indianapolis Freeman*).

• ***March 7, 1891 (New York City):*** "H. R. Jacob's Theatre—Cleveland's Colored Minstrels began a weeks' engagement at this house night of March 2, making their first New York appearance. This aggregation of colored members is strong in point of numbers, but is a trifle disappointing in singing, dancing, dialogue and repartee. An acrobatic song and dance, styled 'The Four Models of Grace,' was one of the most artistic bits of the bill... 'The March of the Mozambique Guards' was one of the best things of the evening. Tom McIntosh is still funny in spots, though his efforts to amuse are nowadays labored, rather than spontaneous or natural. Much was expected of the first part singing, in which this race are known to produce great harmony, but the major part of their vocal numbers consist of end songs, by comedians who rely on facial distortions and 'mouthings,' which are neither funny nor pleasing... James Wilson did a neat juggling and necromancer act, and Billy Farrell contributed an original specialty with amusing effect... The large audience included a goodly number of colored people, who seemed to vastly enjoy the ludicrous portion of the program. The bill ends with a short sketch, 'Stealing Chickens,' in which the Four Brewer Bros. create quite a deal of amusement. Following is a full roster of the performers: End men—Tom McIntosh, James A. Bland, Billy Farrell, Doc Sayles; interlocutor, G. W. Pickett; vocalists—Billy McClain, Dan Palmer, John Brewer, P. Brewer, George Williams, Tom Williams, John Taylor, Walter Smart, Coley McGowen, Frank Kennedy, Ollie Hall, Charles Carey, Al. Porter, Gus Davis, J. Wilson, W. F. Fields, Hilliard Brewer, Pearlie Brewer; orchestra—W. H. Henderson, H. Smith, T. O. Moxley, R. I. Dogue, C. B. Lumpkins, S. R. Burns, Will Preston, Harry S. Stafford, Len. Fields, L. S. Hunter and Walter Berry" (*New York Clipper*).

• ***March 7, 1891:*** "Sixteen members of W. S. Cleveland's Colored Minstrels have organized a Knights of Pythias Lodge, styled Tousaint Lodge No. 1" (*New York Clipper*).

• ***March 28, 1891:*** "In The Line Of Minstrelsy," "During the New York engagement of the

Cleveland Minstrels Richard K. Fox, of the Police Gazette, presented Billy McClain with a $15 set of six ounce gloves and a $22 training bag, which he uses in his act. McCabe and Young and the Cleveland boys met in New York and a general good time was had. Eugene Hillman, of the McCabe and Young Company, joined Cleveland's Minstrels in New York on the 9th of March. Miles Terry, of the old Callender Company, the solo slide trombonist, also joined the Cleveland Company. He and Billy McClain make a team . . . Billy Farrell joins the Bohee Brothers' Minstrels in England, June 12th for the season of '92 and '93. James Bland of Cleveland Minstrels, took New York by storm . . . The Clevelands call *The Freeman* the *New York Clipper* for colored professionals since Billy McClain has been our correspondent. Webster Sykes died in London, England, February 3rd, '91. He was a member of the old Callendar troupe and of the team of Woodson and Sykes, formerly a Memphis team" (Billy McClain, *Indianapolis Freeman*).

Note: Over the next several years, the image of the *Freeman* as "the black *New York Clipper*," the African American alternative to the most popular mainstream entertainment trade paper of the era, was consciously nurtured and developed.

• ***May 8, 1891 (Paterson, New Jersey):*** "The Cleveland Minstrels," "Our troupe has just parted with a fellow companion whom we were sorry to lose. Our worthy brother Carter Simpkins left us on the evening of the 30th at Frankfort, Pa., the company going to New York immediately after the show. Before we said good bye, the quartette consisting of Messrs Frank Kennedy, James Tyler, Ollie Hall and Ed. Thompson sang the 'Knight's Farewell,' which was followed by that ever popular song, 'Should old acquaintance be forgot,' by Prof. Henderson Smith, with band accompaniment and Tom McIntosh, the great comedian, with Messrs Billy Farrell and Dock Taylor rendered the song in a way which will never be forgotten. Then, after shaking hands, Mr. Simpkins left for his home in Chicago, carrying the well wishes of the entire company, and the regrets of the Toussaint lodge, No. 1, traveling Knights of Pythias, of which he is . . . commander.

Billy Farrell has received an offer to star in a piece called 'Hands across the Sea,' written by Ed. Thompson, our king and basso.

James Bland, the comedian and popular songwriter, and Jalvin, the juggler, left us at Washington, D.C., on the 26th of last month, Mr. Bland going to England and Jalvin to Australia.

Henderson Smith, our band leader, is all smiles at the prospect of an early visit from his wife.

Mr. Dan Louden, late of the McCabe and Young minstrels, joined our company at Frankfort, Pa.

Tom McIntosh, our comedian, was presented with a Knights of Pythias charm by his many friends at Charlottesville, Va. It is a beauty, being set with diamonds, and Tom is singing [James Bland's] 'Carry me back to old Virginia,' but not to live or die.

Speaking of talent among the race, the Cleveland minstrels can boast of some of the smartest young men in the country. There is Mr. Dan Palmer, who has a fine baritone voice, and composed the baritone solo, 'Queen of my heart.' It is a very pretty song and is being used by all the Cleveland companies. Next comes Mr. George Williams, of the late team of Grant and Williams. He is the composer of the acrobatic song and dance that the New York papers praised so highly entitled 'Four models of grace.' Then there are the two wonders of the 19th century, Smart and Taylor, being only 19 and 20 years old. They composed the words and music of the song and dance entitled 'Invitation.' This song is being used by the New Orleans, Geo. Wilson, and Richard and Pringles Georgia minstrels. Kansas City, Mo., is the home of these two little wonders. They are both fine vocalists, dancers and comedians.

We are coming North, en route to Maine . . . Our route this week is, Paterson, N.J., May 3–4; Bridgeport, Conn., 6; New Haven, Conn., 6; Danbury, Conn., 7; Meriden, Conn., 8; Hartford, Conn., 9; and Worcester, Mass., 11" ("Ollie," *Detroit Plaindealer*).

• ***May 9, 1891:*** "The boys have organized two baseball clubs, and are getting into condition to give the ballplayers a rub the coming season, as the company does not close . . . Tom Wilson is receiving three and four encores nightly with his new banjo . . . Prof. W. H. Henderson, the leader of our orchestra, has been receiving press notices for his fine violin playing" (*New York Clipper*).

• ***May 16, 1891:*** "James Bland, the comedian, has left Cleveland's (colored) minstrels, and gone back to England. Henderson Smith, the cornetist, leads the minstrel band" (*Cleveland Gazette*).

• ***May 16, 1891: (New Haven, Connecticut):*** "The Boys Look Well," "The boys of the Cleveland show are doing well, they have their spring suits and overcoats and look as bright as a silver dollar . . . Prof. W. Henderson, our [orchestra] leader, receives flattering press notices every where for his wonderful execution on the violin and his superb orchestra. Leo Baily, of McCabe & Young's show, joined us as trombone soloist but they all know that McClain is in the street with his slide along with the best . . . The Cleveland show does not close this season" ("B.M." [Billy McClain], *Indianapolis Freeman*).

• ***June 13, 1891:*** "Jalvan, the juggler, late of Cleveland's Colored Minstrels, and Pamplin, the contortionist and Zouave drillist, late of McCabe & Young's Minstrels, have joined hands and will do a novelty act next season" (*New York Clipper*).

• ***October 17, 1891:*** "Oliver Cromwell Hall, vocal leader of the late Cleveland Colored Minstrels, now of Chicago, was married at Lockport, N.Y., Oct. 8, to Lavina Morgan, of that city" (*New York Clipper*).

• ***November 14, 1891:*** "Doc Sayles, formerly of Cleveland's Colored Minstrels, has retired from the profession, and is now the proprietor of a cafe at Chicago, called 'The Showman's Rest'" (*New York Clipper*).

• ***December 12, 1891:*** "Ollie C. Hall, vocal director of the W. S. Cleveland late Colored Minstrels, has organized a quartet, and it will be known as the Original Alabama Merry Makers. The quartet: Ollie Hall, Robt. Tasker, Chas. Saulton and John Hawkins. They are *en route* to the Pacific Coast" (*New York Clipper*).

Mahara's Minstrels, 1892–1895

After McCabe and Young's Minstrels stranded in Mexico in May 1892, former advance agent W. A. Mahara stepped into the breech and assembled a troupe to enter the 1892–1893 season as "Mahara's McCabe & Young's Minstrels." When friction developed over Mahara's right to exploit the original McCabe and Young label, the name was shortened to Mahara's Colored Minstrels. In 1894 "the cards were shuffled most interestingly" when D. W. McCabe introduced a new troupe of "McCabe & Young's" Minstrels, while his old partner Billy Young "went to work for Mahara." These doings inspired W. C. Handy to reflect, "Show business has always been the same in some of its respects. The dog-eat-dog equation goes back even further than I can remember."[55]

Taking up McCabe and Young's old route of travel, with its southern sweeps and forays to Cuba, Mahara's Colored Minstrels remained a powerful force in African American minstrelsy until W. A. Mahara's death in 1909.[56] Today, Mahara's Colored Minstrels is probably best remembered for having served as a launching pad for W. C. Handy, who first joined them in 1896.[57] During the 1892–1895 period, W. A. Mahara's great band featured brass specialists Fred Simpson and Moses McQuitty, whose long, illustrious careers would span the decades from the appearance of ragtime to the rise of jazz.

• ***October 1, 1892:*** "McCabe & Young's Minstrels, under the management of W. A. Mahara, opened their season at Elgin, Ill., last week. The opera house was crowded. The first part is elaborately arranged with silks, satins and plushes. The orchestra are attired in outing costumes, and the ballad singers are dressed in blue plush coats and vests and white satin pants. The end men represent sailors on their arrival in port, the senior end men appearing as visitors in evening dress. The company: Billy Farrell, Gil Gay, Christian, the Brewer Family, Gordon Collins, Daniel Palmer, Fisher and Preston, Williams, Moxley and Scott, Prof. C. B. Lumpkins' orchestra and Prof. J. W. Campbell's band. The executive staff: James McCabe and Harry Young, proprietors [!]; W. A. Mahara, manager; Jack Mahara, advance agent" (*New York Clipper*).

• ***December 17, 1892:*** "Notes from Mahara's Minstrels," "Business, so far this season has been remarkable . . . Gill Gary, our serpentine dancer, was presented with a diamond pin, by the members of the company . . . Alf. White, musical director" (*New York Clipper*).

• ***February 25, 1893:*** "From Mahara's, McCabe & Young Minstrels," "We have been doing good business through Northern Iowa and Dakota, though we struck snowbanks and blizzards. At times our trains have been delayed so as to prevent us from reaching our destination until long after dark. Late arrivals are the Mallory Bros., Al. Watts, Harry Fiddler, George Jackson and Pearl Brice. The show will tour Northern Michigan and Canada during the spring" (*New York Clipper*).

• ***March 18, 1893:*** "The Mallory Bros., of Mahara's, McCabe & Young's Minstrels, are said to be doing well with their double mandolin song and dance, entitled 'The Mandoliers' " (*New York Clipper*).

• ***September 9, 1893:*** "Mahara's Minstrel Items," "Geo. L. Moxley is doing full justice to Chas. K. Harris' song, 'Fallen By the Way Side.' Harry Fiddler and Al. Watts continue to make them laugh. Master Eugene, the eight year old comedian, is meeting with great success. The new drill, by Al. Watts, introducing Gil Garay in a serpentine dance, and Master Hilliard Brewer, the contortionist, is doing much credit to the show" (*New York Clipper*).

• ***November 18, 1893:*** "Notes from W. A. Mahara's Mammoth Colored Minstrels," "For the last two weeks our business has picked up remarkable, almost reaching our last season's receipts. Our company now numbers twenty-six people. New arrivals are Henry Henderson, comedian and acrobat; Paul Jones, whistling specialist. Little Sam Young is now doing his laughing coon song in the first part" (*New York Clipper*).

• ***January 27, 1894:*** "Notes from Mahara's Colored Minstrels," "Business since the holidays has been improving. The company now numbers thirty-two people. Recent arrivals: Joseph Holcomb, Tom Nash, John Logan, George James, Harry Williams, George Clark and Ed. Bagley. Jack Mahara, business manager" (*New York Clipper*).

• ***March 10, 1894:*** "Mahara's Minstrel Notes," "We are now touring Texas, and have been very successful in gaining a good reputation, also financially. The show is now coming north. Harry Fiddler and Gordon Collins are successful in their new burlesque act on the Corbett and Mitchell fight. Moxley and Brewer are singing

Charles K. Harris and Mr. Graham's latest song creations . . . Master Eugene, the child prodigy, is the hit of the show" (*New York Clipper*).

• ***August 4, 1894:*** "Notes from Mahara's Mammoth Minstrels," "Roster of No. 1 Co.: W. A. Mahara, manager; Jack Mahara, agent . . . Prof. Henderson Smith, leader of band, with sixteen pieces; George Armstrong, leader of orchestra, with nine pieces; George Moxley, stage manager, making his third season with this company; Gordon Collins, Al. Watts, Billy Young, Jack Harris, Dave Smith, the Three Romains Bros., acrobats and grotesque dancers; Billy Hughes, Albert King, Frank Jackson, Harry Hunt, H. Lewis, Fred Sampson, W. Pearl, H. C. McVoy, Jas. Hart, Earnest McCoy, Mathews Shealey, C. Haskell, Connors Bros., Master Eugene, the Long Family, acrobats, five in number, just from Cuba; Georgan, West, Peasley and Thompson, buglers, and the Pickaninny Band of twelve. Our spectacular street parade will far surpass all previous attempts for novelty. The season is solidly booked, in week stands mostly. No. 1 opens Aug. 10; No. 2 Co. opens Sept. 1" (*New York Clipper*).

• ***August 18, 1894:*** "Notes of Mahara's Mammoth Colored Minstrels," "Frank Patrick, Jiles Jordan, Joe Holcomb, Johnny Green, Hilliard and Eugene Brewer, Willie Farrell, E. M. Roberts, F. Burk, R. N. Thompson, Chas. A. Hunter, M. McQuitty, D. C. Scott, Clifford Bell and Boy Jack are the latest additions . . . Boy Jack's flying trapeze will be featured with the show" (*New York Clipper*).

• ***September 8, 1894:*** "Notes from W. A. Mahara's Colored Minstrels," "Business is good with us. Charles Webster and Harry Fiddler are new arrivals. Henderson Smith has left, and Frank King has taken his place and is leading our band of sixteen in good shape" (*New York Clipper*).

• ***October 20, 1894:*** "Notes from W. A. Mahara's Colored Minstrels," "We are once more in Texas, having finished our Mississippi tour at Jackson. The show is, without a doubt, the best Manager Mahara has ever brought South, carrying forty people in all, and using two special cars to transport the people and scenery. Our Winter parade uniforms arrived at Waco, and are handsome, being made up of silk plush cloth, in variegated colors, Newmarket style. Our parade is catching the people in great shape, being a decided novelty. It is headed with four carriages, with Manager Mahara in carriage No. 1. Eight jockey uniformed drum majors follow after the carriages. Then comes the feature, Prof. Jackson's Solo Band of twenty pieces. At Pilot Point, Texas, Oct. 8, we opened Gee's New Opera House, the entire house being sold before our arrival in town, this making the sixth new house we have opened this season. Our California tour will start after a few stands in Arkansas, Tennessee, Alabama and Florida. We are booked solid for eight months" (*New York Clipper*).

• ***November 3, 1894:*** "Notes from Mahara's Minstrels," "Jack Mahara, who was shot Oct. 20, by train robbers, near Wagoner, I.T. [i.e., Indian Territory], while doing advance work for his company, is under the care of two physicians, and is doing very well . . . Mahara's Minstrels, when playing Wagoner, called on him in a body, and the band played several selections at his request . . . Harry Fiddler and Gordon Collins, comedians of Mahara's Minstrels, were banquetted by the local colored club, of Coffeyville, Kan" (*New York Clipper*).

• ***February 16, 1895:*** "Notes from Mahara's Colored Minstrels," "We are now touring the Pacific Slope . . . and the 'ghost' walks every Sunday. Fred W. Simpson, the trombone soloist, has purchased a new seventy-five dollar trombone" (*New York Clipper*).

Note: Self-taught virtuoso slide trombonist Frederick Ward Simpson was "born and reared in Indianapolis,"[58] and by 1890 he was a leading member of Indianapolis' Brotherhood Band.[59]

His 1892–1895 tenure with Mahara's Minstrels marked the beginning of Simpson's brilliant career as a minstrel bandsman.

• ***June 1, 1895:*** "Harry Fiddler has returned home from the Pacific Coast and Alaska, after a successful season with Mahara's Minstrels" (*New York Clipper*).

• ***June 8, 1895:*** "The show has closed a very successful season of forty-two weeks . . . [and] will open in September, at Chicago" (*New York Clipper*).

• ***July 20, 1895:*** "Notes from the Mahara Minstrels," "The latest addition to the company is the original Nashville Students, eight in number. Mr. Mahara intends making [them] a strong feature in the free concert given daily by his company. A portable stage will be erected each day in the most prominent street of the cities that they visit, and a performance of pleasing plantation and old time melodies will be rendered" (*New York Clipper*).

• ***July 27, 1895:*** "Marie Simpson, cornet soloist, has signed, and will be featured in the street concerts . . . Jas. R. Johnson and the Nashville Quartet, George L. Moxley, tenor singer, and Lewis Jones' pickaninny band of twelve, have also signed" (*New York Clipper*).

Note: George L. Moxley, though "white in appearance," was "by birth and at heart a Kentucky Negro."[60] A note in the February 7, 1903, edition of the *Freeman* informed that "the veteran minstrel middle man, tenor solo singer and stage manager, was . . . in the barber business . . . at present." An update later that fall said Moxley was "still barbering in Martinsburg, W. Va. He is tenor singer for the First Methodist Church and his wife is organist."[61] Looking back in 1907, Moxley reminded *Freeman* readers that when he had "started in the business . . . 27 years ago, there was no avenue for the colored entertainer but Uncle Tom's Cabin, the minstrels and the jubilee companies."[62]

W. C. Handy recalled in *Father of the Blues* that, during his tenure with Mahara's Colored Minstrels (1896–1903), Moxley had been the troupe's interlocutor. In response to a letter from Handy, pursuant to the publication of *Father of the Blues*, Moxley recalled: "I began singing to the public in my 13th year at the Philadelphia Centennial of 1876 . . . In 1894 I joined W. A. Mahara . . . and was with him 12 or 14 years . . . I worked with several ofay [white] outfits in my time without any trouble. W. A. Mahara was the only Minstrel Company I traveled with, but I put on an Elks' Minstrel once in Shreveport and one in Dayton, both ofays. They would have hung me in Shreveport had they known that I was colored . . . I was 70 years old December 17, 1935."[63]

• ***September 7, 1895:*** "Notes from Mahara's Minstrels," "We opened Aug. 24, at Manitowoc, Wis. The curtain went up at 8:15 and the 'S.R.O.' sign was displayed at 8 o'clock. We opened with the original flower garden first part, written by Billy Young, especially for this company. The natural flowers perfumed the whole house. Our wardrobe for the first part consists of blue, black and orange satin suits. The orchestra is dressed in white satin full dress suits. Billy Young arrived for rehearsal direct from New York City, with a trunk packed full of new songs, new gags, recitations, etc. As Billy is a great favorite from the Missouri River to the coast of California, we have a treasure in him. Geo. L. Moxley, who has made himself well known for the use of his counter tenor voice and who is also stage manager, is taking from two to four encores nightly singing 'Annie Laurie' in the first part. Bob Webster, whom the people call the Black Emerson, keeps the people on his side of the house highly interested at each performance. Jas. Johnson, our basso soloist, is doing himself great credit. We have twenty-six people, all told. Our street parade is very attractive; we have ten beautiful silk and satin banners with inscriptions. Our band is under the leadership of Bob Thompson, with fourteen people, supported by a strong drum corps, under the leadership of Bob Webster. Our special [railroad sleeper] car, the Maharajah, is newly painted in attractive colors . . . We carry a cook, waiter and porter" (*New York Clipper*).

The Legend of Orpheus McAdoo, 1890–1900

Legions of African American jubilee singing companies sprang up in the early 1870s, hoping to capitalize on the public interest aroused by the Original Fisk Jubilee Singers. Through the 1870s and 1880s, there were probably more African American entertainers gainfully employed as jubilee singers than in any other branch of professional entertainment.[64] Times changed and so did public taste. In the early 1890s a powerful surge of enthusiasm for a "new style" of authentic African American minstrelsy began to register in the marketplace, anticipating the explosive popularization of ragtime. Under this new regime, a much broader spectrum of black musical and theatrical talent found a place on the professional platform, but the *tone* of these entertainments often pandered to popular racist sentiment. Coon songs, cake walks, racially deprecating jokes, blackface makeup, etc., were all part of the ascent of secular black professional entertainment. These profound changes are reflected in the career of Orpheus McAdoo. The compromises that McAdoo made in his musical enterprise over the course of the turbulent 1890s are representative of changes in black popular music and entertainment generally.

Orpheus McAdoo Jr. was born in slavery in Greensboro, North Carolina, January 4, 1858, the eldest son of Orpheus and Margaret McAdoo. He had two brothers, Eugene and Fletcher, and one sister, Bessie. All four children attended Hampton Institute, in the Tidewater section of Virginia.

Orpheus Myron McAdoo, circa 1899. McAdoo's young son is inset at upper left. (courtesy National Library of Australia)

It was written that, following Emancipation, Margaret McAdoo "gathered the children of her neighborhood in Greensboro, N.C. and taught them the art of reading, which she had managed to acquire herself while still a slave. Both she and her husband were examples of the sturdy character and ability to improve small opportunities, which many of the older freed people brought with them out of the hard school of slavery."[65] Similar qualities of resourcefulness and ambition are evident in the professional life and international adventures of their son Orpheus McAdoo Jr., an intrepid entrepreneur-performer, a spiritual grandparent of modern popular "world music."

While a student at Hampton Institute, Orpheus McAdoo sang bass with what seems to have been the first officially sanctioned Hampton Student Quartette.[66] After graduation, he taught school in rural Virginia for three years, then returned to Hampton to head the institute's preparatory school. In August 1885, McAdoo joined Frederick Loudin's Fisk Jubilee Singers on tour in London, and he sailed to Australia with them the following year. Despite his membership in Loudin's Fisk Jubilee Singers, McAdoo remained devoted to Hampton Institute. McAdoo wrote to his mentor General S. C. Armstrong, founder and president of Hampton Institute, from Australia: "What I wish now is that you send me a half dozen of the 'Hampton Song Books.' I mean of the plantation melodies. I have several friends to whom I would like to present them . . . The 'Fisk Singers' use quite a number of the 'Hampton Students' songs and in many cases they are the general favorites. Please charge them to me and oblige by sending them as early as possible. I am quite well and greatly enjoying my stay in this, the 'Land of golden fleece.' "[67]

At the close of their three-year tour of Australasia, toward the end of 1889, Orpheus McAdoo quit Loudin's Fisk Jubilee Singers and returned to the States to organize a company of his own. The *Indianapolis Freeman* informed, through its "Stage" column of February 22, 1890, that "Orpheus M. McAdoo, for the past five years leading baritone of the Loudin Fisk Jubilee Singers . . . is now in this country, forming a troupe to carry abroad; first playing through Great Britain . . . [H]e seems quite sanguine over his prospects."

In organizing his company of jubilee singers, McAdoo first secured Miss Belle F. Gibbons, who, like McAdoo, had toured Australia with Loudin's Fisk Jubilee Singers. McAdoo visited Hampton and enlisted his younger brother, Eugene, into his new singing company. Eugene M. McAdoo was twenty-one years old, a fine bass singer, recently graduated from Hampton Institute. In Washington, D.C., McAdoo recruited soprano soloist Madame J. Stewart Ball, and she introduced him to a charming young contralto, Mattie E. Allen, who also joined the new company.

Continuing up the East Coast, McAdoo made stops in Baltimore and New York City. It was during this time that McAdoo approached Sissieretta Jones, and it was later recalled in the *Freeman* that he "offered her a great consideration to visit [the] Indian Continent on a professional trip which, owing to a promise to return to the West Indies, she was compelled to decline."[68] In Boston McAdoo booked Moses Hamilton Hodges, a bass-baritone who had distinguished himself as a member of the Lew Male Quartette.[69]

By early March of 1890 McAdoo had filled his roster. No doubt in honor of his roots at Hampton Institute, he named his troupe the Virginia Concert Company and Jubilee Singers. The March 15, 1890, edition of the *New York Age* assured, "Mr. McAdoo is a gentleman of pleasing manners and of great business tact, and will doubtless win success for both himself and his company wherever he may go. The company leaves for Glasgow on April 19."

McAdoo's Virginia Concert Company and Jubilee Singers got off to a shaky start in the British Isles, as McAdoo confided in a letter to General Armstrong: "Since reaching Great Britain I have found many unexpected difficulties to surmount. Upon our arrival in Glasgow I found that a company of dissipated people calling themselves 'The Jubilee Singers,' and in some instances 'The Virginia Jubilee Singers' have most thoroughly disgusted the better class of people and it was almost impossible to get a hearing . . . with such a set of people to proceed me it was impossible to succeed. We sang in

Glasgow and vicinity but lost money every night. I lost the first ten days $500. I came down to London, where I have had some better chances. I shall, I hope leave here soon for South Africa and Australia. I feel quite sure of success and I am not at all discouraged."[70]

A short time later McAdoo's Virginia Jubilee Singers sailed for South Africa, and on June 30, 1890, they opened at Vaudeville Hall in Cape Town. Among those who attended the Virginia Jubilee Singers' debut concert in South Africa were Lord and Lady Loch, old acquaintances of McAdoo's from his visits to Melbourne, Australia, with Loudin's Fisk Jubilee Singers. Lord Loch had since become the governor of Cape Colony. Just as it had for Loudin's Fisk Jubilee Singers in Australia, the endorsement of Lord and Lady Loch helped set the tone for McAdoo's enormous success in South Africa, where the local dailies generally concurred, "singing such as given by the Virginia Concert Company has never before been heard."[71]

McAdoo's Virginia Jubilee Singers, talented, cultivated representatives of the race, immediately challenged presumptions held by most of South Africa's white colonists, much to the delight of the educated portion of the native population. John T. Jabavu, editor of the newspaper *Imvo Zabantsundu*, explained:

> As African[s] we are, of course, proud of the achievements of those of our race. Their visit will do their countrymen here no end of good. Already it has been suggested to many who, without such a demonstration, would have remained skeptical as to the possibility, not to say probability, of the Natives of this country being raised to anything above perpetual hewers of wood and drawers of water. The recognition of the latent abilities of the Natives, and of the fact that they may yet play a part peculiar to themselves in the human brotherhood, cannot fail to exert an influence for the mutual good of all the inhabitants of this country. The visit of our friends, besides, will lead to the awakening in their countrymen here of an interest in the history of the civilization of the Negro race in America, and a knowledge of their history is sure to result beneficial to our people generally.[72]

In subsequent letters to General Armstrong at Hampton, McAdoo described the social conditions he encountered in South Africa: "There is no country in the world where prejudice is so strong as here. The native today is treated as badly as ever the slave was treated in Georgia. Here in Africa the native laws are most unjust; such as any Christian people would be ashamed of. Do you credit a law in a civilized community compelling every man of dark skin, even though he is a citizen of another country, to be in his house by 9 o'clock at night, or he is arrested? . . . Indeed, it is so strict that natives have to get passes for day travel."[73]

Those in McAdoo's Concert Company were able to travel as freely as they did in South Africa under the curious governmental dispensation of "status as an 'honorary white,' which the English colonies and the Boer republics were prepared to grant to all bona fide black American citizens."[74] McAdoo's troupe appeared in all the larger cities and made adventurous forays into the most remote regions of South Africa. They visited the diamond mines and gold fields, the mission stations and native schools, the houses of Parliament, the kraals of Zululand. Troupe member Eugene McAdoo wrote to *Southern Workman*, the monthly journal of Hampton Institute, describing a trek from Grahamstown, South Africa, into the bush, to visit the campus of Lovedale Institute, "this African Hampton":

> Our company was in Grahamstown, when there came a letter from the officers of the Lovedale Institute to my brother, begging that we pay them a visit and sing our songs for them. The school is about sixty miles from Grahamstown, and there is no railroad. The regular mail coach was too small to carry our large party—so a long, covered "Dutch Wagon" was chartered. This was drawn by eighteen huge oxen, in charge of the owner and a native boy.

> We had to leave Grahamstown on Sunday night in order to get to Lovedale in season to sing on Wednesday. We arranged ourselves as comfortably as possible in our close quarters, and for the first few miles enjoyed it, but in a little while the constant jolting began to make us ache all over and we were indeed glad to welcome the sun . . . the heat was so intense that it was next to impossible to travel in the middle part of the day. After two days and three nights our sixty miles were accomplished, and we were in the beautiful little town of Alice, and just across the river, surrounded by the most beautiful tropical trees, and the ground enclosed by a splendid cactus hedge, was the school . . .
>
> We were soon shown to the Assembly Room where we were to sing [for the students] . . . There were nearly five hundred of them, and their faces were a picture of interest and anticipation. We sang for them for nearly a couple of hours, and then they favored us with some of their songs, which we thoroughly enjoyed, for their voices were indeed good. In passing out, many of them shook our hands and bade us good-by after thanking us for our singing.[75]

McAdoo's Virginia Concert Company and Jubilee Singers had a profound effect on South African audiences of both races. According to the *Kaffrarian Watchman and Government Gazette:* "Our natives who attended the concerts were simply enraptured with the singing, and some of them, I believe, would have pawned even their hat for the wherewithal to go to them. Their admiration of their American cousins must really have been very great, for on the day the troupe left the town one of the classic crowd was heard to say in the deep drawling style—'We shall never again hear such splendid singing until we go to Heaven.' "[76]

Similar testimony was given in the October 1, 1890, edition of a native-oriented mission newspaper, *Leselinyana:*

> They held their concerts in every town (possible) to get to. They always began by singing "The Lord's Prayer" (Matthew 6:9–13), a verse saying "But deliver us from the evil one." They started it with high voices, still repeating it, their voices began to go down, slowly-slowly, till only the breath finished or stopped . . .
>
> Sirs, I have got no words to explain the way in which these people sang. If not mistaken, I can say that they sang like the angels singing hosanna in Heaven . . . They are great musicians in singing; they are civilized in education, thus, why they are so famous. At their last concert, on the 16th of August, [1890] Mr. McCadoo [*sic*], the head of the American Great Singers, stood, told the people that: the blacks of America are very civilized; they have surprised the whites, and the whites once decided to send them back to Africa. People laughed a little, and said: "Come back! Come back to Africa, your grandfather's country."[77]

This refreshing report was authored by "J. Semouse." Not long after it was published, Josiah Semouse joined a "Native South African Choir" that toured Great Britain and the United States. This mixed chorus, also known as the "African Jubilee Singers," was an African by-product of the Virginia Jubilee Singers' tour.[78] McAdoo's tour was a pivotal event in the development of South African choral music. Christian missionaries and white minstrel companies had already been at work in South Africa for many years, and they no doubt introduced the native population to Methodist hymns and the principles of Western four-part harmony. However, McAdoo's company was first to bring the slave spirituals; and their coming touched off an outbreak of native four-part harmony singing that continues to this day. Into the twenty-first century, there are still native quartets and choral groups in South Africa performing and recording African American spirituals in English, sometimes preserving classic nineteenth-century harmony "arrangements."[79]

Among black South Africans, the spiritual songs of slavery gained a new life and function. A hybrid adaptation of four-part vocal music known as "mbube," "cothoza mfana," or "isicathamiya" remains a popular musical expression in black South Africa, particularly among migrant workers. Isicathamiya is a distinctively South African choral form, combining elements of Western harmony and African musical culture. After more than a hundred years of absorption and characteristic development, this music is popularly identified as "traditional Zulu choral," yet its similarities and connections in repertoire to black American spiritual singing are striking and unmistakable.

Group chant is another characteristic practice that links black vocal groups in South Africa and America. Chant is an age-old, widespread tradition in Africa. Modern South African vocal groups make liberal use of chanted refrains; that is, a harmonized word, phrase, or speech sound rhythmically repeated as background for the lead voice. The creative employment of idiosyncratic, chanted "group refrains" such as "clanka-lanka," "hum, hum, bah," "doo-wop," etc., is also a signature element of twentieth-century African American a cappella quartet singing. It is the background chant that propels the music. The lead voice may drop out altogether, but the chant invariably continues unaffected.

The *Cleveland Gazette* served as a conduit for news from McAdoo's Virginia Concert Company and Jubilee Singers during their historic 1890–1892 tour of South Africa. The *Gazette* had a particular interest in native Ohioan Mattie Allen and tended to spotlight her role in the company's success:

> To hear her sing, and not seeing the singer, one would judge at once it was a male tenor. Miss Allen is a native of Columbus, O., where she was born about twenty-three years ago, and there she enjoyed the advantage of a good education, being educated along with white pupils in the mixed schools of that city. She is tall and stately looking, very fair, and could easily pass for white, did she desire . . .
>
> After graduating from the Columbus, O., high school, she taught school for several terms, at Circleville and Cadiz, O., but becoming tired of teaching she signed a contract as soloist with the McAdoo Concert Co., and sailed with them a year ago for a three years' tour of the old world . . .
>
> To many a young woman, the idea of such a trip, so far from home, amidst strangers, would have caused them to recoil, but Miss Allen is quite masculine in her will, and nothing ever daunts her.
>
> The circumscribed limits of the school room was always an undesirable restraint to her. She was restless, and like a caged bird, longed for freedom, for the possibilities and probabilities of the great world. As she often said: "I want to do something and be something, I want to make a name!" [80]

On January 10, 1891, the *Cleveland Gazette* brought news of a "Wedding in the Transvaal": "Exceptionally fine invitations announcing the marriage, January 27th [1891] at Port Elizabeth, Cape Colony, South Africa, of Miss Mattie E. Allen of Columbus, Ohio, and Orpheus Myron McAdoo have reached many of their friends in this country."

Under the headline "The McAdoo Jubilee Singers in South Africa," the *Cleveland Gazette* of

Mattie Allen McAdoo. (courtesy Gary LeGallant)

April 11, 1891, carried a lengthy, flattering and detail-filled review from the *Transvaal Advertiser*:

> Mr. Orpheus M. McAdoo must be congratulated on drawing his honor, President Kruger, out of his shell, and inducing him to attend a public entertainment on Friday at noon. His honor, punctual to his engagement, attended at the theater, just as the gun boomed forth the hour of twelve noon . . . His honor was received by Mr. McAdoo and conducted to a seat in front. The "Volkslied" was then sung in English by the jubilee singers, the whole of the vast audience standing. The translation was made by Mr. Leo Weinthal, and reflected the greatest credit on his ability. The anthem would have been sung in Dutch but for the risk the singers ran in failing to learn the words correctly. His honor was evidently greatly pleased with the cordial reception accorded to him, and greatly enjoyed the entertainment. The opening items, "Steal Away to Jesus," "The Lord's Prayer" and "Get You Ready," were exceptionally well rendered and secured loud applause. In place of item No. 3 an old slave song, "Nobody Knows The Trouble I Have Seen," was substituted, and so plaintive was the melody that tears could be seen stealing down the rugged features of the president. After the singing of "Good News" Mr. Orpheus McAdoo's powerful basso voice was heard to great advantage in the rendition of "Poor Black Joe," whilst the hidden chorus gave Pretoria a sample of pure harmony. "Peter, Ring Them Bells" was another acceptable item, and the "Jingle, Jingle, Sleigh Bell" chorus with bell accompaniment created a perfect furore.
>
> Mr. McAdoo at this stage announced that in consequence of the hour there would be no interval, and in a short speech thanked his honor for his presence, remarking that when back in America they would be proud to boast of having performed before the president of the great South Africa republic.
>
> The second half of the programme was opened by a medley consisting of selections from airs of all nations, followed by the singing of "The Old Ark's a 'Movering." At this stage his honor left. Madame Bell then sang "The Old Folks at Home" in a splendid manner, securing an encore. After the song of "Wrestling with Jacob," in which Miss Belle Gibbons' rich contralto voice was heard to great advantage, the troupe gave an imitation of the Pretoria band. The greatest praise we can bestow on the effort is to say that all the bands in Pretoria rolled into one could not produce such rich volume of sound or harmony as the jubilee singers. "Hard Trials," "Bingo Was His Name," and "Sweet Chariot," concluded one of the pleasantest afternoons ever spent by Pretorians.

In an article titled "A Colored Opera Company—The Success of the Virginia Jubilee Singers in Africa," the *Cleveland Gazette* of October 31, 1891, revealed the full extent of Orpheus McAdoo's professional ambitions: "The Virginia Concert Company . . . is warmly commended by 'The Burlesque,' a weekly newspaper, and 'The Star,' a daily, both published in Johannesburg, South Africa . . . In his 'Star' interview, Mr. McAdoo said: 'I have met with financial success far and away beyond my wildest dreams and anticipations. In all my travels I have met with the most flattering receptions, and the press, generally, have been unanimous in their kind expressions of praise. When I have finished with my present line of business, my crowning ambition is to open a first class opera company in Great Britain, return to South Africa, and my ultima Thule is Australia, and home again to Virginia.' "

McAdoo was definitely on his way to Australia, but his "crowning ambition . . . to open a first class opera company" was never realized. In fact, as his stay overseas drew on, McAdoo found it advantageous to leaven his jubilee entertainments with more and more variety and eccentric novelty. After a quarter-century of popular currency, "serious" jubilee singing had begun to lose the prevailing taste. McAdoo was attentive to these trends.

In late January 1892, McAdoo's Virginia Concert Company and Jubilee Singers concluded their first South African tour and set sail for Australia, to pick up where Frederick J. Loudin had left off. Indeed, they were readily accepted there as direct descendants of Loudin's Fisk Jubilee Singers. News of McAdoo's continued success in Australia and New Zealand reached the States through both the *Cleveland Gazette* and the *Indianapolis Freeman*. The *Gazette* reported on July 30, 1892: "The world renowned McAdoo Jubilee Singers are now in New Zealand. In speaking of the concert given in Kyabram, the *Free Press* said: 'The performers show unmistakably the excellence of their attainments. But perhaps in no department do they shine with such undimmed lustre as in the rendering of the celebrated Jubilee Choruses. Here they stand alone, their peculiar style of producing the weird concord of sweet sounds being apparently inimitable.'" Several weeks later, the *Freeman* reproduced a lengthy review from Bourke, Australia, dated September 17, 1892:

> On Wednesday evening the Virginia Concert Company, or the Jubilee Singers—the name by which they are more familiarly known—made their first appearance in Bourke . . . , and Albert hall was well filled. There is very little pretension about the company, all of whom are American natives, an organ, a piano and several chairs being the only furniture required by them on the stage. But all the effect of stage scenery so necessary to other performers would not make the soul-stirring melodies of the Jubilee Singers one whit more beautiful. Each and every one has a magnificent voice of its own peculiar class and range. The programme was a mixed one, containing both sacred and secular selections. The opening chorus was followed by the singing of "The Lord's Prayer." "Get you ready, there's a meeting here tonight," was sung most vociferously, and was very descriptive of the calling of a meeting of slaves. Mr. O. McAdoo then sang the bass solo, "A hundred fathoms deep." He has really a wonderful voice, and one would imagine that his lowest note, the four-barred G, which is fully and fairly taken, comes from the soles of his boots. An encore could only be expected, when Mr. McAdoo sang "Old Black Joe," the rest of the singers, who had retired to the back of the stage behind a screen, joined in the chorus. The effect was astonishing . . . The chorus, "The Band of Gideon" was well given, and then Miss Laura A. Carr won an encore for her soprano solo, "When the swallows come again." This singer is as black as the ace of spades, but when you hear her sing, a lover of music feels that she must have a soul as white as the driven snow. The chorus "Ring Those Chiming Bells," was followed by a quartette, "Josephus and Bohuncas," by Messrs. Collins, Hodges, and J. and O. McAdoo. This was very funny, and "The bulldog on the bank, and bullfrog in the pool" was given as an encore. This caused considerable merriment. The first part of the program was concluded by the chorus, "Good News, The Chariot's Coming." After an intermission of ten minutes for the manipulation of "ice water," as suggested by Mr. McAdoo, the second part was commenced by the rendition of a sweet pretty medley of English, Irish, Scotch and American songs. Unfortunately, Miss Mattie Allen was indisposed, and had to be excused from singing "Mona," and Miss Belle Gibbons filled the vacancy by singing "The song that reached my heart." . . . Miss Julia C. Wormley gave a recitation, which told a beautiful story about an old choir singer, the effect being considerably added to by the company softly singing "Rock of Ages." Miss Wormley, in reply to vociferous applause, gave "The Hindoo's Paradise," the funniest item of the evening. The song and chorus "Mother, is Massa Going to Sell me Tomorrow," was nicely sung by R. H. Collins and the company . . . M. Hamilton Hodges then charmed the audience with a fine baritone song, entitled "Only the sound of a voice." . . . A duet, "Good-night beyond," was given by Messrs. Collins and Julius [*sic*] McAdoo. The glee, "Good-night, gentle folks," brought the concert to a close.

Miss Julia C. Wormley, elocutionist of Washington, D.C., had joined McAdoo's Virginia Concert Company in South Africa in July 1891. Subsequent press reports confirm her remarkable powers as a dramatic reader, and her contribution to the popularity of McAdoo's troupe.

The male quartet was a favorite element of McAdoo's Virginia Jubilee Singers and Concert Company, as it had also been with Loudin's Fisk Jubilee Singers. Selections performed by these two famous quartets reverberate in the recorded repertoire of African American vocal groups of the 1920s. Loudin's Fisk quartet had scored a particular hit with "The Buzzing Bumblebee." The following contrary appraisals provide a good description of this "depictive novelty":

• ***October 5, 1886:*** "A part song, 'Give me my native isle,' by the four male singers, was well done, but in the encore, 'The Three Bumble Bees,' or as called here, 'The Three Jolly Chafers,' the buzzing 'zumzum' was not so good" (*Sydney Morning Herald*).

• ***May 3, 1887:*** "The Whip poor-will was sung as quartette by four male voices and was very well received, the audience imperatively demanding an encore, to which the vocalists responded by singing an extremely funny selection entitled 'The bumble bee,' in the chorus of which an imitation was given of the noise made by that insect" (*Otago Daily Times*).

These descriptions are redolent of a recording titled "Mosquito," made by the (African American) Livingstone College Male Quartet in 1927, which also features an insect-imitating, harmonized "zumzum" chorus.[81]

McAdoo's male quartet had similar success with two humorous selections, "The Bulldog and the Bullfrog" and "Josephus and Bohuncus," which was recorded by two different African American vocal groups in the 1920s, the Birmingham Jubilee Singers and the Old South Quartet:

There was a farmer who had two sons
And these two boys were brothers.
Bohunkus was the name of one,
Josephus was the other.
For these two boys he bought two suits
For them to wear on Sundays.
Bohunkus wore his every day,
Josephus wore his Monday. . . .[82]

McAdoo's Virginia Concert Company and Jubilee Singers had a varied program and a large repertoire.[83] They sometimes put aside their standard mix of jubilee and high-class secular tunes for a special children's concert, or a "request concert," in which all the selections were taken from audience requests. The company also gave "Scotch concerts" which consisted in large part of songs they'd learned during their 1890 sojourn in Scotland. McAdoo very deliberately evaluated and accommodated the musical appetites of his audiences.

Many of the same jubilee choruses performed by Loudin's Fisk Jubilee Singers during their Australasian tour of 1886–1889 were reproduced by McAdoo's Virginia Jubilee Singers. By 1893, Australian audiences had been listening to jubilee singing for almost a decade and were attuned to subtle variations in song arrangements employed by the McAdoo troupe, as opposed to the earlier Loudin company. One Sydney review noted: "In their previous visit to Australia the chorus 'Steal away to Jesus' was received everywhere as one of the prettiest hymns ever sung and as it formed the opening piece at last night's concert it was well received. The time in which it was given was, however, different from that which marked its rendering some four years ago." The same reviewer drew particular attention to the jubilee song "Didn't My Lord Deliver Daniel": "sung as sung at the negro camp meetings. To describe the shouting, the intense enthusiasm, is impossible; Salvation Army fire is tame in comparison."[84] Jubilee songs remained at the heart of the McAdoo troupe's repertoire, which, however, was increasingly infiltrated by novelty effects.

The spring of 1893 brought special tidings from the McAdoos.

• ***May 27, 1893:*** "The GAZETTE acknowledges the receipt of a card from Mr. and Mrs. Orpheus McAdoo, who are now in Hobart, Tasmania, with their jubilee company, announcing the birth of their 'jubilee baby' Thursday afternoon, February 9, at 4:20 o'clock. . . Master Myron Holder McAdoo and mother are quite well, thank you, and at home every afternoon from 4:30 to 6 o'clock—in Hobart, Tasmania" (*Cleveland Gazette*).

McAdoo's company never toured North America, nor did Orpheus McAdoo ever resettle in the United States after joining Loudin's Jubilee Singers abroad in 1885. During the summer of 1895, McAdoo and his party returned to South Africa for a second extended tour. At this critical juncture, McAdoo transformed his troupe from the Virginia Concert Company and Jubilee Singers to McAdoo's Minstrel and Vaudeville Company. According to one Cape Town newspaper, McAdoo intended to introduce the South African public to "the genuine American negro as a comedian, singer, dancer, banjoist and general mirth maker."[85] To that end he brought several variety artists from America, most notably, Joe Jalvan and Jerry Mills. Mills was an acrobatic singing comedian whose long, successful career later included a term as stage manager of the Pekin Theater in Chicago. Jalvan was a juggler extraordinaire. In Cuba with McCabe and Young's Minstrels in 1892 he was proclaimed "the principal 'hit' of the show."[86] Jalvan was still in show business in August 1929, when the *Chicago Defender* reported that he was "filling an engagement with J. B. Boston's carnival at Witman, Mass.," and incidentally informed that Jalvan's real name was Joseph O'Brien and that he was originally from Williamsport, Pennsylvania.[87]

McAdoo's revamped minstrel presentation was well received. The highly varied program was described in detail in the April 29, 1898, edition of the Kimberly, South Africa *Diamond Fields Advertiser:*

> The proceedings commenced with the minstrel entertainment, the grouping of the troupe being especially picturesque. Jalvan and Mills kept the house in a continued roar, the latter received a triple encore for his song, "Fly, Fly Fly." Another popular item was "I'se gwine back to Dixie," by Mr. McAdoo, the chorus being effectively rendered by the company in modulated tones. Mr. Hodges showed his fine baritone to advantage in a hunting song, and again demonstrated his ability as interlocutor. Mr. Collins rendered "Ma Onliest One" tastefully. Misses Gibbons and Webb contributed a couple of well-sung ballads. In the Olio, Jerry Mills in "Silence and Fun" went through a remarkable performance, every method of perambulation being adopted, except the correct one. His finale consisted in an exposition of high kicking. Jalvan introduced an entirely new juggling performance . . . His effective trick with the lighted lamp, which is a marvel of dexterity, was greeted with loud applause. Madame McAdoo, Miss Robinson, Mr. Hodges and Miss Anderson gave examples of their vocal abilities. Miss Anderson received a triple encore for the old favourite "The Cows are in the Clover." The performance concluded with "The Cake Walk," in which the members of the Company advanced by pairs in a most graceful manner to a large cake placed on a table, the audience selecting the winners by acclamation. After considerable competition the prize was awarded to Jalvan and Miss Gibbons.[88]

During this apparently successful tour, members of McAdoo's company expressed dissatisfaction with their wages. In Durban in April 1898, four members of the company refused to perform unless their salaries were raised, and tenor Will Thompson left McAdoo's troupe and joined the Buffalo Glee and Concert Company in Cape Town.[89]

In the summer of 1898, with the Boer War pressing, McAdoo and company said their last goodbyes to South Africa and headed back to Australia, where their familiar program of jubilee choruses and "high-class" secular solos, "humorous" quartets and dramatic recitations was augmented by "Ten Minutes [of] Fun with Mr. Jerry Mills" and "Ten Minutes Entertain[ment]—'The King of Jugglers'—The Only Jalvan."[90]

It became Orpheus McAdoo's late ambition to assemble and import to Australia a full-scale "modern" African American minstrel troupe. Leaving his Jubilee Singers to continue their work, McAdoo sailed for America on a talent-scouting expedition that rocked the black show business world. Announcements in the *Freeman* and other race weeklies began to appear several weeks before his arrival in March 1899: "Mr. Orpheus McAdoo, (Sole Lessee, Palace Theatre, Sydney Australia)... Seeking Musical, Minstrel and Vaudeville attractions... Engagements for 6 to 12 months. Good salaries and return fares. Only Colored Artists Engaged. None but Best need Apply. Also Sopranos, contraltos, tenors and bassos required for Jubilee Singers and Concert Company."[91]

At Indianapolis, McAdoo visited the offices of the *Freeman*, and the edition of April 1, 1899, noted:

> Mr. McAdoo has seen the better part of the world. He is prosperous, and an Australian by adoption. He was a classmate of Booker T. Washington [at Hampton Institute]. In his accent he is decidedly English. He dresses well; in the style of the English upper class—high tile hat, band of black approaching the top, Prince Albert coat, unusually long from the waist down. He wears a few diamonds within the bounds of propriety... He talks fluently, easy conversant with African stories. Mr. McAdoo will sail from Vancouver for Australia about the 17th of May, with a company of about twenty-five performers. From all indications he is a thorough gentleman from tip to tip, and if Queen Victoria should knight her very worthy subject, his elegant physique, noble bearing and charming manners would reflect some credit to the Queen, as well as honor to McAdoo.

At St. Louis in April 1899, McAdoo contracted Prof. Henderson Smith to assemble a band to take to Australia. This was a tremendous coup for McAdoo; Smith was one of America's most highly respected bandmasters, popularly acclaimed as "the black Sousa." The band assembled for the trip included "Prof. Henderson Smith, solo B cornet; Jessie E. Smith, solo B cornet; James P. Jones, solo clarinet; Oscar Lindsey, solo alto; John Brower [*sic*, Brewer], 1st alto; James Harris, 1st trombone; Alonzo Edwards, 2d trombone; Pete Woods, baritone;

PROF. HENDERSON SMITH.

Prof. Henderson Smith, bandmaster of John W. Vogel's "Darkest America" band, stands without a peer in his particular line. He is the acknowledged colored bandmaster of America; and enjoys the honor and distinction of being the only colored cornetist ever connected with the late P. S. Gilmore's Famous Cornet Band. Prof. Smith spared no pains or expense in securing for his present band the best and costliest musical talent in the profession and wherever they have appeared this season the press and public have unanimously proclaimed it to be by far the greatest colored band they have ever had the pleasure of listening to. Such selections as "William Tell," "The Poet and Peasant," and "Ernani" are among the numbers rendered by Prof. Smith and his associates, and is in itself a guarantee of the high standard of music rendered by this famous band.

Freeman, *November 20, 1897.*

Edward Tolliver, tuba; Turner Jones, bass drum; F. Poole, snare drum; J. H. Herd, cymbals; George Henry, drum major; John Pramplin, lightning gun driller."[92]

Henderson Smith became the McAdoo Minstrels' faithful correspondent to the *Freeman*. His vast professional experience and considerable candor yielded a uniquely revealing body of correspondence.

McAdoo also recruited diva Flora Batson and her current stage partner, respected bass-baritone soloist Gerard Miller. In addition, he signed the spectacular contortionist William Ferry, known as Ferry the Frog; the well-known vaudeville song-and-dance team of Hen Wise and Kate Milton; and the prince of "male mezzo sopranos," female impersonator Willis Gauze. In all, McAdoo engaged thirty-two performers.

McAdoo named his new troupe the Georgia Minstrels and Alabama Cakewalkers. On Saturday, May 13, 1899, members of the newly formed company assembled in Chicago and boarded a train for San Francisco. Shortly thereafter, the first of Henderson Smith's correspondences appeared in the *Freeman*:

> The railroad officials said that this companies' manager Mr. O. M. McAdoo, purchased more tickets and laid down more money than any other company who ever traveled over their road . . . Each and every member of the company received from $75 to $150 before leaving Chicago . . . Prof. Smith broke the monotony of this long ride by having band rehearsals, and with the exception of a piccolo player, he says he will have a first-class band by the time we land in Australia in June. We are sorry to have to inform your readers of Mr. Chas. Walker having his hand caught in the door and took off one of his fingers on the left hand, but the Santa Fe officials done all in their power to make him comfortable, and to-day he is resting easy; his dog jumped out of the car window, so now his finger and dog are both gone.[93]

McAdoo's Georgia Minstrels, Sydney Mail, *July 15, 1899.*
(courtesy State Library of N. S. W. and Gary LeGallant)

On May 24, 1899, the company reached Honolulu. A letter to the *Freeman* from Smith was published July 29, 1899:

On board Steamship Moana, June 2nd. [1899]—Since my last letter to your valuable paper, and thinking our American friends would like to know of our long journey, I will tell you of a few incidents since our arrival at Honolulu. After our arriving there the Manager of the Opera House prevailed upon our genial proprietor, Mr. O. M. McAdoo to give a matinee and all hands consented. Prof. Henderson Smith made a parade with his band and although we only had two hours notice we played to over $800 . . .

Aukland, New Zeland [*sic*], June 6th—This is one of the most lovely spots on earth and we had the pleasure of meeting Jalvin [*sic*] our American juggler who is playing dates and a splendid time was spent with him; also Mrs. O. M. McAdoo met her husband here and spent the day with him. Miss Ganey went with Mrs. McAdoo to strengthen the Jubilee company . . .

Sydney, June 10—We arrived safe after a stormy night coming into Sydney and found the most beautiful harbor and city with the most genial people to meet and from our reception and courteous treatment a man is a man here. There is no color line to fight. You are known for what you are . . . I have had the pleasure of meeting our own Wallace King, who spent a pleasant evening with me last evening. His voice has improved wonderfully and he don't look a day older. I also met Manuel Sontang, contortionist. Col. Chas. B. Hicks is still manager of Harmston's circus and cabled Prof. Smith at Aukland welcoming him and his band into the country. We will open on Sunday night the 17th and rehearsals are now progressing fine with all well . . . Henderson Smith. Permanent address, 338 George st., Sydney, Australia.

Smith's letter also noted: "Since our arrival we have learned that a man named Curtis has gone to America after another colored show and my advice to performers is not to come here at present as the country is too small for 3 colored companies. Besides this man Curtis' reputation here is not the best. It is only done to help monopolize this country and it is too far for our performers to come and fight with one another."

The advent of M. B. Curtis's Afro-American Minstrels and Vaudeville Company in Sydney was an ominous development for Orpheus McAdoo and his company. M. B. Curtis was a famous white stage actor with a notorious personal history. In September 1891, he was accused of murdering a policeman in San Francisco. The *Clipper* followed the long saga of his three trials, one ending in a hung jury, another in a mistrial. It wasn't until August 1893 that Curtis was finally acquitted.[94] Two months later he was arrested in Taunton, Massachusetts, "on a writ of attachment for $800 in favor of . . . his late manager."[95] Then, on December 29, 1894, the *Clipper* reported that Curtis had "sailed for Europe . . . accompanied by a physician, and that he is going to a sanitarium in Germany."

Back in the United States in 1899, M. B. Curtis must have sensed the potential for quick profit in Orpheus McAdoo's idea. Following close on McAdoo's heels, Curtis organized an even larger and more outstanding troupe, including two of African American minstrelsy's most brilliant stars of the day, Ernest Hogan and Billy McClain. He also signed the venerable Madah Heyers and the fascinating N. Clark Smith Pickaninny Band of Kansas City, which was described in the May 26, 1899, edition of the mainstream daily *Kansas City Star* under the headline "A Big Trip For Black Boys": "The Pickaninny band is well known in Kansas City. It was organized three years ago by M. C. Smith [*sic*], a negro composer. It is made up of twenty-five negro boys, all under 18 years of age. They play all the popular band music."[96]

When M. B. Curtis's Afro-American Minstrels and Vaudeville Company opened at the Criterion Theater in Sydney, Australia, on July 2,

1899, they touched off what Henderson Smith described as a "managers war" between Curtis and McAdoo: "Upon their arrival in this country our genial manager opened the doors of his theatre and gave them all private boxes and showed them all the courtesy of a gentleman. But upon their opening Mr. Curtis shut his doors in our faces and would not admit one of us. So Mr. McAdoo changed our day of matinee from Wednesday to Tuesday and Mr. Curtis learning of this changed his to the same date, "a most unprofessional trick," and while his stars and magnates made their boasts they came here to run us out. I will say that we are still here, with no complaints to make against our manager."[97]

From the day they arrived in Sydney, the mighty M. B. Curtis Company seemed to have things their way. The Sydney *Referee* noted in its issue of July 12, 1899:

> Mr. Curtis' Afro-American Minstrel Company entered upon its second week . . . there was a splendid house . . . The duel scene which concluded the first part, between Mr. "Billy" McClain and Mr. Earnest [*sic*] Hogan, aroused great merriment. The same couple of artists also kept the house in splendid humor by their antics in the Rag Time opera, while the former [McClain], who is practically the life of the show, contributed several coon songs and gags in his own inimitable fashion. Miss Madah A. Heyer, "the Bronze Patti" was heard to great advantage in a couple of operatic selections; the Kentucky Four did some exceedingly clever buck and wing dancing; and Siren [Navarro], the liliputian creole contortion dansuese, twisted and twirled in a risque and an alarming fashion. The performance concluded with the laughable Cake Walk in which the competition between the various couples was very keen.[98]

It became clear to McAdoo that his troupe could not compete successfully, and he decided to make a retreat. On July 12, 1899, McAdoo's Georgia Minstrels and Alabama Cakewalkers departed from Sydney to make a tour of the colonies, and shortly thereafter, Henderson Smith wrote: "[A]s I told you, we are now in a theatrical fight. It remains to be seen which one will win, but as we were here first and Mr. McAdoo's reputation is so good it looks like 100 to 1 in our favor. So far we have shut them out of this section and perhaps they will claim they run us out of Sydney and we will give them the benefit of the doubt . . . We are all in good spirits and good health and no one wishes to be home as yet."[99]

No sooner did McAdoo's company leave Sydney than Curtis's company began to crumble. In correspondence dated July 27, 1899, Henderson Smith declared victory for McAdoo in the "managers war." According to Smith, "many disagreeable incidents" arose between Curtis and "his people," and when Billie McClain and others attempted to "quit Mr. Curtis over non-payment of salaries," Curtis "went so far as to draw his revolver":

> [O]ur manager Mr. McAdoo went back 500 miles to protect them if necessary, in case they were without means. But after Mr. Curtis heard of it he made apologies and induced them to return to work. But I received a letter from McClain saying he wanted to join [the McAdoo company] . . . I told you there was a managers fight on I am proud to tell you that the colored manager has won. We have completely shut Mr. Curtis out of all Australia and he leaves with his company for New Leland [*sic*], a distance of 1200 miles. They were to play Sydney for 5 weeks, but their business fell to nothing and he was compelled to leave . . . I will say that we are still here with no complaints to make against our manager . . . Our salaries have been paid far in advance, and no one wishes to return.[100]

Two weeks later the *Freeman* reported "the information that owing to bad business and worse management the M. B. Curtis Afro-American Minstrels and Vaudeville Company has stranded. Curtis skips the country owing salaries and fifty of America's leading vaudeville and minstrel stars thousands of miles from their homes in a bad financial way, not a few in the party being almost penniless."[101]

Billy McClain managed to defect from Curtis to McAdoo as soon as the salary trouble started. McClain wrote from Melbourne, on August 14, 1899, that he'd opened with McAdoo's Minstrels, with an increase in salary.[102] Professor Henderson Smith confirmed: "We now have with us Billy McClain who has charge of our stage, and since his arrival we have seen many changes for the best."[103] McClain was a dynamic, independent-minded, and sometimes volatile genius, one of the premier producers of the new African American minstrelsy. His stature in the profession is confirmed by this short commentary from the *Freeman* of June 6, 1900: "It is said that Billy Kersands is the greatest colored performer, followed closely by Billy McClain and Ernest Hogan."

M. B. Curtis's Afro-American Minstrels weren't the first black American minstrel troupe to founder in Australia. The Hicks-Sawyer Minstrels had arrived in 1888, when F. J. Loudin's Fisk Jubilee Singers were still there, and, according to reports in the African American press, they were forced to disband in 1890, leaving some of the performers "in pretty embarrassing circumstances."[104] Several members of the Hicks-Sawyer Minstrels never made it back to America; some were still professionally active in Australia, and Professor Smith often mentioned them in his letters to the *Freeman*:

> Perhaps a word about some of the oldtimers that came out here with the Hicks & Sawyers' Minstrels years ago will interest some of our old performers at home—Billy Speed and Andrew Jackson are in Freemantle, W. A., doing quite well, bill posting and running a booking shop. Wallace King, Chas. Pope and Irving Sayles are with Harry Rickards in Sydney.[105] Poor Bill Johnson, the bass singer is dead, also is Hosie Easton; they are both buried at Sydney. John Matlock is in Melbourne, playing at different times with home talent. Bowman is in India. Chas. B. Hicks was in Java when I last heard from him, Chas. Bruce is also with him. Brown & Mills are both dead; and I fear poor Horace Copeland will be left here to die after our departure, but at present James P. Jones of Columbus, O., and myself are looking after him, as he is paralyzed and cannot help himself.[106]

Horace Copeland had been a member of what was perhaps the first African American minstrel company to appear in Australia. Copeland recalled:

> I was one of the first colored clog dancers in America and a member of many of the leading minstrel companies. I was founder and principal comedian and dancer of Corbyn's Georgia Minstrels that left San Francisco, Nov. 8, 1876, and arrived in Sydney, Australia the 6th of December; then came Chas. B. Hicks' Georgia Minstrels, both companies playing Melbourne the same time. So Hicks put on "Uncle Tom's Cabin" and it had a run of one hundred and two nights; he hired two of our ballad singers, and of course that stopped us from leaving town for a while . . . [After replacement singers were brought from America] we put on the "Cabin" in Sydney. Both companies were playing to big business for about five weeks. So our manager blocked Hicks, and he could not get a theatre, only at Adelaide, so it was only a matter of time and he went broke, and we got him with our show.[107]

Returning to Australia with the Hicks-Sawyer Minstrels in 1888, Copeland suffered a paralytic stroke in Albany, West Australia, and the company left him stranded there, without funds. Copeland's experience is symptomatic of the desperate, cut-throat business practices that proliferated among African American entertainers in Australasia during the late nineteenth century. Orpheus McAdoo remained aloof from such practices. He and other professional entertainers in Australia helped rescue Horace Copeland and finally get him back to his home in Cincinnati, Ohio.

According to Prof. Henderson Smith, Orpheus McAdoo contributed $125 toward the welfare of the abandoned members of Curtis's

Afro-American Minstrels, and members of McAdoo's troupe raised another $100. Then the American Consul in Sydney decided to "come to their rescue" by sending the Curtis minstrels to Auckland, New Zealand, under the protection of the American Consul there.[108] This enabled the company to remove themselves from Sydney, where their business had failed famously.

On August 27, 1899, as the McAdoo Company prepared to sail from Sydney for a tour of Western Australia, Henderson Smith sent a letter to the *Freeman* in which he expressed his feelings about the fate of the M. B. Curtis troupe, perhaps a bit too pointedly: "The Curtis Company got to New Zealand and we were glad of it for we had many friends among them and it was too bad they followed such a low man to fight a gentleman because he was colored. No man ever stood better than O. M. McAdoo. Both as a gentleman and a financier."[109]

In New Zealand the Curtis troupe "formed themselves into a commonwealth, under the Management of Mr. Ernest Hogan."[110] They quickly resumed their successful tour: "The Afro-American Negro minstrel combination (not now known as the 'ill-fated Americans') with Ernest Hogan at their head . . . have been playing to splendid business."[111]

A printed program, dated 1899, delineates the complete presentation given by the troupe at the Opera House in Wellington, New Zealand; it began with a "Grand First Part. Showing the Interior of the Palace of the Emperors of Minstrelsy and gathering of the Mastodon Senate. Grand Opening Overture by N. Clark Smith's Pickaninny Band."[112] There is also this local newspaper review of their performance:

> Opening with a lively vocal and instrumental overture . . . The setting of the stage for the first part was effective, the orchestra being terraced behind the half-circle of 25 singers, flanked by a strong compliment of "bones" and "tambos."
> The soloists included some good singers, notably Messrs. L. H. Saulsbury (tenor) and R. Logan (bass). Mr. Ernest Hogan's imitation of a negro preacher's speech sent the house into uproarious laughter, and the various appearances of the "Unbleached" fun-maker were signals for more laughter. The audience could not get too much Hogan last night. The chorus singing and orchestral work were bright features, and the witticisms of the end men were original, wholesome, and laughter-raising . . . The second part displayed the dancing talent of the company, and in the Kentucky Four (Misses K. [Katie] Carter and M. [Muriel] Ringold and Messrs. A. [Amon] Davis and Livers) . . . quite new effects in dancing being presented. Miss Madah Hyer was heard in operatic selections, and proved herself a capable singer . . . Mr. Saulsbury, her companion, singing his part from the end of the dress circle balcony. A "turn" by Siren [Navarro] introduced that young lady as a fair skirt dancer and clever contortionist. "The Unbleached American" kept the house highly amused with song and story, and then the "Black Dante" held a seance . . . A one-act musical melange entitled "Rag Time Opera," in which the whole company took part, afforded yet another vehicle for good singing and much laughter, and the whole concluded with a feature new to Wellington—a cake walk.[113]

Hogan's Minstrels also offered "Uncle Eph's Return," a plantation story in one act, by Ernest Hogan, and, of course, they presented a dramatization of *Uncle Tom's Cabin.* Young Muriel Ringgold, dancer with the Kentucky Four, and later a foremother of black vaudeville, made a hit with her "Topsy."

When McAdoo's Georgia Minstrels and Alabama Cakewalkers opened in Sydney, Easter weekend 1900, with concerts at the Palace Theater, McAdoo staged *his* interpretation of *Uncle Tom's Cabin.* The *Referee* of April 25, 1900, reported the following cast of characters:

> Uncle Tom—Billy McClain, Simon Legree—Gerald Miller, Marks—Ferry, Van Tomp—Charlie Walker, Phineas—Leon P. Rooks, Mr. Shelby—Hen Wise, Little George—Miss A. Young, George Harris—S. A. Fitzgerald, Mr. Sims—Henderson Smith, St. Clair—Louis Clifton, Sambo—Turner Jones, Quimbo—Frank Poole, Skiggs—E. Tolliver,

Rastus—J. Taylor, Solomon Jude—John Pamplin, a fugitive slave—Pete Woods, Adolph—J. Small, Eliza Harris—Gauze, Mrs. Shelby—Flora Batson, Miss Ophelia—Ida May, Mrs. Solomon Jude—Grace Jones, Lucy—Miss A. Florence, Cassy—Madame Cordelia, Aunt Chloe—Jerry Mills, Topsy—Kate Milton, Little Eva—Little "Daisy Bell," Harry—Baby Willie . . . Incidental to the piece the following artists will take part in a specialty programme: Gauze, Miss Flora Batson, Chas. Walker, Jerry Mills, Katie Milton, Hen Wise, & Ferry ("The World's Greatest Contortion Wonder"), & McAdoo's popular Georgia Quartette.

A review in the *Truth* judged: "They gave a remarkably vivid, at times gruesome picture of what slave life meant. The audience was held enthralled, and loud and sustained outbursts of applause greeted their efforts. Mr. Billy McClain as Uncle Tom scored an immense success, and Miss Katie Milton, who played Topsy, the sinner, the 'Imp wot growed,' shared with him the honors of the evening. But all did well."

Muriel Ringgold and Kate Milton, the two "Topsys," helped to pave the road for a generation of female vaudeville "coon shouters" and comediennes. The makeup and persona of the fictional character "Topsy" had great resonance in early-twentieth-century black vaudeville entertainment.

Between Hogan's Minstrels and McAdoo's Minstrels, Australians got a full dose of the new African American minstrelsy. Along with street parades, incredibly diverse vocal and instrumental music, comedy, dance, magic, juggling, contortion, and male and female impersonation, there were demonstrations of the new invention that would soon revolutionize the entertainment industry, Edison's Talking Machine, plus a "reproduction by means of Cinematograph (moving) pictures of some of the leading scenes from the Passion Play of Ober-Ammergau."[114] McAdoo's company featured a one-act comic opera, *Off to the Transvaal,* starring Flora Batson, and a play by Billy McClain titled *Boer Justice,* which capitalized on emotions aroused by the bloody war in progress between the British and the Boers, and which probably drew on McAdoo's familiarity with the South African situation.

These two stellar African American minstrel companies introduced Australasia to ragtime. In America, ragtime was already affecting cataclysmic changes in popular entertainment. Ernest Hogan was a conspicuous player in ragtime's initial commercial ascendancy. His 1895 sheet music hit, "La Pas Ma La," was one of the songs that prefigured the appearance of ragtime,[115] and his infamous 1896 hit, "All Coons Look Alike to Me," is routinely credited with touching off the worldwide ragtime craze. In 1899, while Hogan's Minstrels dished out their "Rag Time Opera" for the people of Australia and New Zealand, McAdoo's Minstrels put on a "Georgia Camp Meeting—Introducing the American Rag-Ma-La-Dance by the Company."[116]

By some reports, the Australian public was not so well prepared to absorb the impact of modern, ragtime minstrelsy. According to Henderson Smith, "It is hard for the public to catch on to the rag time music which is so popular in America. Still you can hear little boys trying to whistle certain strains."[117]

Another member of McAdoo's troupe explained that Australian audiences were "very peculiar, a comedian must be careful with his gags, many jokes that would bring down the house in America, are considered very indecent in the colonies. Many times I have watched the audience while a comedian was working, and when he had finished the audience would sit as though they were glued to their seats, they could see nothing funny in it. It took us but a short time to learn, that in order to make good with the audience we would have to find out what they wanted."[118]

Judging from a lengthy review which appeared in the *Brisbane Evening Observer* of January 18, 1900, McAdoo's Minstrels understood well what Australian audiences wanted:

> The one feeling of regret which pervaded the thoughts of those who left the Opera House last night after the first performance of Orpheus McAdoo's Georgia Minstrels was that they did not live over in the United States, where shows like that were, presumably, the rule and not the exception, and their visits were not, like angels, remarkable for their rarity. Here in Australia the European imitation of a "nigger minstrels" performance is well known . . . But the best of them here lack the freshness and originality of the real thing that Mr. M'Adoo set before the large and enthusiastic audience last night . . . [T]he absolutely "new" way of conducting the first part has everything to recommend it . . . The company jumped into the good graces of their hearers as soon as the curtain rose, the overture "The Honolulu Dance," by the full stage, being given with a dash and go which captivated senses . . . The "southern" accents of the performers blended well with their quaint actions. After the overture Mr. [Hen] Wise sang with all the necessary action, and with excellent effect, a descriptive ballad, "What you are to-day," in which he acquitted himself most creditably, there being an insistent demand for a repetition, which was good-naturedly complied with . . . Third on the list was one of the successes of the evening—a "telephonic interrogation" entitled "Hello, My Baby," sung by Misses Jones, Ida May, Kate Milton and Willis Gauze. The . . . clever dancing which followed the last verse quite decided the audience that they wanted more, and . . . they had it again. The two low comedians of the company—Billy M'Clain and C. W. Walker—had their hearers in fits of laughter throughout the evening, their reappearance on the stage after their turns in the first part being always the signal for fresh outbursts of mirth. Before the interval ballads were well rendered by Mdme. Cordelia, who sang "She was bred in old Kentucky" most acceptably, her voice being remarkable in its evenness of tone; and by Messrs. Gerard Miller and Jones. The latter gave a tasteful rendering of "Because," the last chorus being taken by a quartette consisting of Messrs. Millar, Poole, Rooks and Jones, in which a sotto voce part was given with really fine artistic feeling. The first part closed with a Cake Walk, in which four couples, led by Mr. C. W. Walker and Miss Ida May, competed for the favor of the audience. The Cake Walk is new in Brisbane, and must be seen to be appreciated. No amount of description could give any idea of its oddity or charm. But it caught on, the spectators quite entering into the spirit of the thing, and loudly announcing their choice at the termination.
>
> The second part opened with the farce which commonly ends the performance. A clever knock-about act by Jerry Mills was the chief thing to be noticed in it. The "Human Frog"—Ferry—is . . . the best contortionist Brisbane has ever seen . . . It is a pleasure to watch him. A Female impersonator—Willis Gauze—so deceived his hearers that he was allowed to go off the stage after his first song without any suspicion of his sex, and it was not until he dropped his voice to a deep bass in his second contribution that his identity was revealed. Miss Susie Anderson, who is described as the black Melba, showed herself the possessor of a sweet, true soprano in her two songs, "Blackberries" and "The Cows are in the Clover" (evidently an American variant of the old English ballad). John Pamplin did some neat juggling and sleight of hand, while Mr. Collins wound up the specialties with "The Absent-minded Beggar," the spirited air eliciting a perfect shower of coins from all parts of the house. The programme was brought to an end with "Off to the Transvaal," a comic opera in one act, which served to introduce a new soprano—Miss Flora Batson, the possessor of a voice of a large range. It would be difficult to particularise all the good points of the performance.

Orpheus McAdoo's exemplary variety show traveled up the West Australian coast as far as Perth, where Professor Smith complained that the troupe hadn't received the *Freeman* for a month: "[W]e seem to be shut out from the world for news of our brother professionals at home."[119] Early in January 1900, the *Freeman* published another letter from Henderson Smith, now enroute to exotic Tasmania:

> Since writing you last we have learned of the death of our greatest song-writer—Gussie L. Davis,

McAdoo's Minstrels in cake walk pose. (courtesy Gary LeGallant)

who we all loved as a gentleman and author; and we, as members of the McAdoo Company extend our deepest sympathy to the bereaved wife of Mr. Davis . . . There was many wet eyes when I read the news from my wife, who learned of it upon her arrival in San Francisco and immediately notified us, and that night the show went with a lull . . . We are on our way to Tasmania to spend the hot months of summer. We are all well . . . Billy McClain auctions off all the cast-off clothing to the aboriginals . . . Pete Woods, our baritone player has proven himself quite a rag-time writer. He has composed a rag march and dedicated it to a Melbourne belle (Neitta) . . . After spending six weeks or more in Tasmania we go to Queensland for a tour . . . Our business has been something marvelous turning people away nightly and we are pleased to see our genial manager do the business as he deserves it.[120]

In Brisbane, at the turn of the century, the McAdoo company again crossed paths with Hogan's Minstrels, and it appears that Henderson Smith got an earful from Hogan. Smith's letter of January 27, 1900, was a public apology of sorts:

Dear sir, since last letter . . . we have had the pleasure of meeting the now famous Ernest Hogan company. And while we had some differences through the Australian papers, who wished to form a bad feeling through their columns, I have learned through Mr. Hogan . . . that the articles I forwarded to you were without foundation, and also that my letters to you, while I meant no personal harm to a member of the company, it has caused considerable comment and pain to some of them, and not wish to mislead my American friends or do any injustice to a member of the said company . . . I hope you will publish same in justice to them . . . and both companies have met here in Brisbane, and we are both doing a big business. A huge banquet was given by the members of the Hogan show and all differences are amicably settled.[121]

Following this report, Professor Smith's letters to the *Freeman* became less frequent and less candid.

More than one hundred black American entertainers witnessed the dawn of the twentieth century under Australasian skies, and among them were the cream of the vaudeville and minstrel stage. There were nearly as many first-rate black acts in Australia at this time as there were back in the States, a ludicrous situation which ultimately bred quite a lot of unhappiness. Other members of both the Hogan and McAdoo companies also wrote to the *Freeman*. Their reports of triumphs on the stage are spotted with numerous incidents of fighting, dismissal "for misconduct,"[122] and general malaise. Professor Smith's letter in the *Freeman* of February 17, 1900, conveyed a warning from minstrel veteran Tom Logan: "I am requested by Tom Logan to advise all colored performers that if they know which side their bread is buttered they will stay as far from Australia as possible. Don't let those who are here 'jolly' you to come. Over 99 per cent of those now here wish to God they'd never left the United States! . . . Some through pride may write or come back and say 'It's great' but Logan's advice is to do all your 'two stepping' in America and leave this country to those who call it 'great' (no joke)."

Eight months after their arrival in Sydney with M. B. Curtis, Ernest Hogan and thirty-one members of his company quit Australasia and sailed for Honolulu, arriving on March 14, 1900, to begin an extended engagement at the Orpheum Theater. From there they returned to America. Before the year was out Hogan was given the opportunity to return to the Antipodes with his own company, but he sent a press release, published in the Australian press, which stated: "Ernest Hogan's Western summer tour is cancelled. One year's continuous work in Australia and Honolulu—overworked. My physician recommends rest."[123]

Having fulfilled their one-year contracts, Prof. Henderson Smith and other members of McAdoo's Minstrels sailed from Sydney on May 9, 1900, aboard the steamer *Mariposa.* The ship reached San Francisco on June 1, but wasn't permitted to dock until the following day, "on account of the bubonic plague which was raging furiously when they left Sydney."[124] Henderson Smith made his way home to Chicago, where he opened a saloon, the Buffalo Buffet, at Twenty-Ninth Street between State and Dearborn, which became a favorite watering hole of black show people. It would be three years before Smith, seemingly exhausted and disillusioned, resumed his professional travels with another road show.

Billy McClain's wife, acclaimed soprano soloist Madame Cordelia, had arrived in Australia in late March of 1900, apparently to join McAdoo's company. But by early May, Billy McClain and Madame Cordelia were appearing under Harry Rickard's management, beginning a long engagement at the Tivoli Theater in Sydney. Their original sketch titled "The Darkie's Serenade" found an "enthusiastic reception."[125]

In August 1900, McAdoo Company veterans Charles W. Walker and his partner Ida May, known as "America's Gold Medal Cake Walkers," appeared at the Tivoli Theater in Sydney with Billy and Cordelia McClain, African American tenor Wallace King, Ferry the Frog, and white talent. After long runs at the Tivoli, Billy and Cordelia McClain, Walker, and May appeared at the Bijou Theater in Melbourne, where: "Their plantation ditties, serio-comic songs, laughable farce and diverting 'cake-walk' were among the most generously applauded items of a first-class programme."[126] In November this foursome was seen at Rickard's Theater in Melbourne and the Tivoli Theater in Adelaide with the Pope and Sayles Minstrels. In May 1902 Charles Walker and Ida May began a two- month tour of New Zealand heading one of Harry Rickard's vaudeville road companies. Later that year they were back at the Tivoli in Sydney.[127]

On March 2, 1908, the *Freeman* published a letter from Charles Walker, "late of the Colts & Walker song and dance team, previously with Billy McClain & Walker, and present time in England under the name of Walker & May. I would love to hear from my old friends who would care to write to me . . . I am also sending you a clipping to show you I am still doing well." Several weeks later the *Freeman* published an article from an unidentified British journal, probably the clipping Walker alluded to, under the headline "Blind Comedian's Success":

> Every night at Collins's Music Hall, Islington, London, and the Empress Theatre, Brixton, the twinkling feet of Walker and May, colored comedians and dancers, win thunders of applause.
>
> The woman comes forward to bow and smile. The man's bold, intelligent eyes roam over the house as though he appreciated the flicker of every clapping hand. But he can see nothing for he is blind . . .
>
> Behind this dancing in darkness there is hidden a story of amazing pluck and stoicism. Walker always danced. Even in the days when he was a pickaninny there was laughter in his feet. He danced as one who loves dancing. He had a genius for dancing. He made a reputation for dancing in two hemispheres.
>
> Then suddenly, when he was in Australia, in the heyday of his prosperity, all the light and, as it seemed to him, all the dancing, of his life were suddenly shut out. Atrophy of the optic nerve blinded him almost instantly . . .
>
> It seemed to him that his profession was gone, and that starvation could be his only end . . . But in the darkness that encompassed him so suddenly he wrestled with himself and in spite of his blindness he had the courage, the audacity to determine to go on being "funny."
>
> He had engagements at several music halls in London, but, thinking that no manager would engage him if he knew the secret of his blindness, he made up his mind not to give it away . . .
>
> Soon after his arrival in England he went to the Brixton Music Hall, and without any practice gave his usual turn. He walked quite naturally to the stage by the side of his wife and danced elaborate coon dances and cake walks without a mistake. The second part of the turn was with his wife, and here again he accomplished the feat by dancing and singing and talking humorous dialogue without any one in the audience knowing he was blind.
>
> His wife helped him by saying occasionally under her breath, "one step this way," or "Not so far back," and also by lightly touching him to show him where she was . . .
>
> For eighteen months he earned a living in this way, and no one until then knew that he was blind. He was able to do it by knowing the position of every musical instrument in the orchestra. While the orchestra was playing he felt safe, as he knew from the sounds of the musical instruments exactly where he was. When the orchestra was silent he moved about as little as possible.
>
> As he got on the stage he tapped the drop curtain with his hand, and then boldly walked forward into darkness—smiling. And for nearly a quarter of an hour he danced about the stage, and walked backward and forward and laughed and sang—in darkness.
>
> It was only at the end of eighteen months that he told the manager of a music hall he was blind.[128]

Billy and Cordelia McClain remained in Australia through 1901. McClain took advantage of his popularity to indulge his special interest in prizefighting. For a period in 1900, it appears that he managed the Australian heavyweight champion Peter Felix. Returning to America in 1902, McClain reunited with Ernest Hogan to pioneer the original "Smart Set" Company.

Ferry the Frog scored an immense hit in Australasia, and he was in no hurry to return home. After a very lengthy run at the Tivoli Theater in Sydney and engagements in Melbourne and Adelaide, he began an extended, conspicuously successful tour of New Zealand, first with P. R. Dix's Minstrels and later with a company under his own management. At the Alhambra Theater in Dunedin a reporter noted:

> The attraction of the evening was, however, the appearance of a contortionist, Ferry known as the "Human Frog." The curtain rises on a scene representing a pool surrounded by ferns, moss and appropriate greenery. An enormous green frog gravely hops out of the pond, stares solemnly round

at the audience and jumps about in front of the water. A more realistic scene can hardly be conceived and the naturalness of everything is a little short of marvelous. Froggy—or rather Ferry—after hopping about for a minute or two climbs up on a stump about 5 ft. high, and then proceeds to execute some of the most extraordinary contortionist feats imaginable. A description of these would be deemed almost incredible, and Ferry's performance must, as handbill announces, "be seen to be believed." For 15 minutes this remarkable man continues to force his anatomy into positions and attitudes such as baffle description and the audience sits in silent amazement, wondering what he will do next.[129]

The *Sydney Morning Herald* of April 28, 1900, carried ominous news: "During the week Mr. McAdoo has suffered from a somewhat serious attack of illness." On May 12 the *Otago Witness* reported: "Mr McAdoo . . . is ill in Sydney, where Mrs. McAdoo is watching over his recovery." On the morning of Tuesday, July 17, 1900, less than six weeks after his minstrel company had departed for America, Orpheus Myron McAdoo died at a private hospital in Moore Park, Sydney. His death doesn't appear to have been related to a reported outbreak of bubonic plague. An obituary in the *Sydney Morning Herald* disclosed: "Some sixteen months ago Mr. M'Adoo contracted a serious illness which necessitated his undergoing an operation.[130] He subsequently visited America and returned to the colonies in apparently improved health. However, seven weeks ago he was again taken ill in Sydney . . . From the first his symptoms were serious, and despite the efforts of medical advisers he gradually sank. He became unconscious on Monday morning (16th) and died yesterday morning."[131]

Another obituary appeared in Sydney's *Sunday Times* of July 22, 1900:

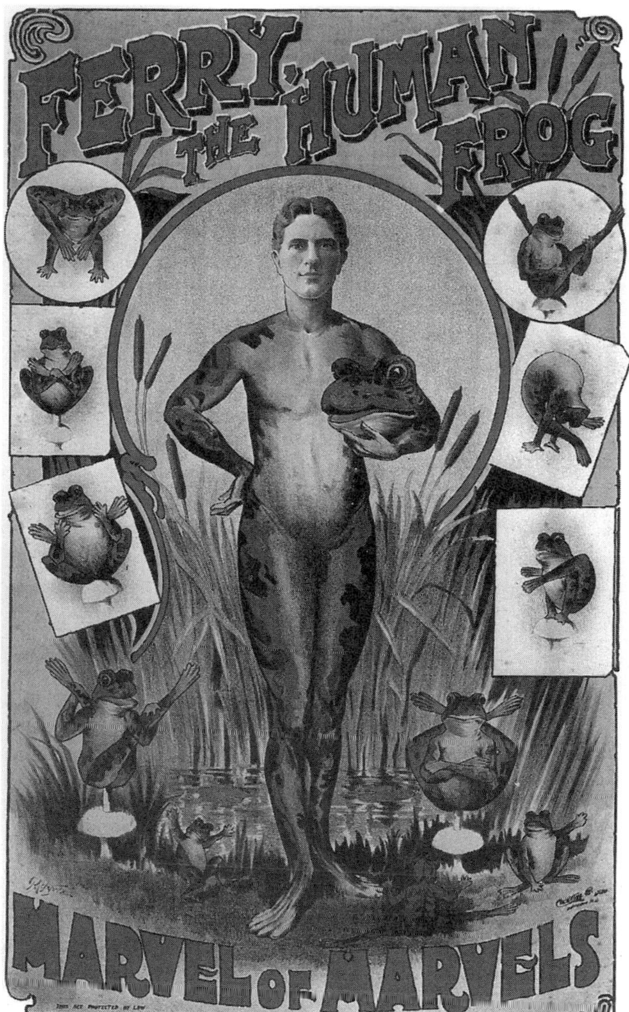

Advertising placard for William Ferry, "The Human Frog." (courtesy Otago Early Settlers' Association, Dunedin, New Zealand)

Mr. Orpheus M. McAdoo, proprietor of the Jubilee Singers, whose death occurred during the week, was one of the most popular managers who has ever visited Australia and his loss will be universally regretted. For some considerable time past his health was anything but satisfactory but notwithstanding this, few of his friends considered, when he announced some six weeks ago that he would "Lay up for a few days," that the end was so near at hand. Day by day, however, he became worse, and about five weeks ago he was removed from his hotel to a private hospital. No one was allowed to see him, not even his wife, or little son, until finally it was realised that his case was completely hopeless. The funeral took place on Thursday afternoon and was largely attended.

At age forty-two, Orpheus Myron McAdoo was laid to rest in Waverly Cemetery, Sydney, in his "adopted country." McAdoo's death certificate states the cause of death as "Pernicious anemia; Dilation of the heart; Cerebral anaemia syncope."[132] In a letter posted from Toowoomba, Queensland, Australia, on July 23, 1900, and published in the October 6, 1900, edition of the *Freeman*, the famous performer Willis Gauze provided a more personal explanation of McAdoo's death: "I wish to inform you of our beloved manager, Mr. O. M. McAdoo's death, and we mourn for him as manager and gentleman—for a better man never lived—and his treatment of us was so very nice that we say, may his soul rest in peace. The minstrel company he brought out was the cause of his death. I never traveled with such people before. You need not believe any base reports you hear about our deceased manager for they are untrue. I, myself, was never treated better in all my life by a manager. The company that Mr. McAdoo brought over here was not all a very clever set, and he treated them too good, and they are trying to vilify him in lowest terms, but God is just, and Mrs. McAdoo is a fine lady."[133]

Orpheus McAdoo's final resting place, Sydney, Australia (photo by Gary LeGallant).

Shortly after her husband's funeral, Mattie Allen McAdoo and their son Myron returned to America.

McAdoo's Jubilee Company was well established in Australasia and survived the death of its director. Tenor R. H. Collins became manager of the troupe known as McAdoo's Fisk Jubilee Singers, Prof. C. A. White served as accompanist and musical director, and Orpheus McAdoo's brother Eugene was basso and treasurer. Soprano Dazalia Underwood was a featured soloist, as was Belle F. Gibbons, "who may be described as a tenor or high baritone . . . heard in the old plantation song 'She Was Bred In Old Kentucky.'"[134] Willis Gauze was also with the troupe when they began a long tour of New Zealand in the late fall of 1900. One reviewer was moved to comment: "He looks a comely woman in a low-cut dress, strange to say."[135]

In February 1901 R. H. Collins wrote to the *Referee* from Christchurch, New Zealand: "Some time has elapsed since I have written to your paper. Since then the Jubilee Singers have been reorganised, and Mr. Eugene McAdoo and myself are proprietors, and therefore, responsible persons for the above-named organisation. The form of entertainment has changed, inasmuch as we have omitted from the programme 'The Passion Play' and the phonograph, and reverted to the old style of the Jubilee Singers, which has made the performance more acceptable with the public . . . Our season in Christchurch has been most successful . . . We go to the West Coast on Friday next . . . We have a considerable lot to do in New Zealand yet before leaving it."

Before the end of 1903 Eugene McAdoo and soprano Euna Mocara broke with the troupe and began to concertize as a trio, possibly with Belle Gibbons as the third member. In 1904

McAdoo and Mocara left Australia for England, where they formed another trio with Laura A. Carr, who had been a member of Orpheus McAdoo's jubilee troupe during the early 1890s. Known as the Fisk Jubilee Trio, they were active in Great Britain for years. A promotional booklet for their 1910–1911 season describes a full touring itinerary and a very familiar repertoire of spirituals, as well as such McAdoo Company chestnuts as "The Bull Dog on the Bank" and "Maggie, the Cows Are in the Clover."

Meanwhile, R. H. Collins brought replacement singers to Australia, reportedly negotiating through "musical agents" in the United States. In October 1904 an Australian observer noted: "The Fisk Jubilee Singers have a lien upon Australia . . . They have been touring the Victorian Provinces, and are reported to have done good business all along the line. The company has now been considerably strengthened by new talent, and comprises ten members, all of whom are said to possess excellent voices. The new tenor . . . Clarence Tisdale, is a vocalist of high repute and culture. His voice resembles very much that of the late Wallace King."[136] This combination of Fisk Jubilee Singers toured Australia through 1906. They supplemented their vocal music program with a moving-picture display, an innovation that Orpheus McAdoo had inaugurated in 1899. After 1906, the troupe slipped into an inactive phase, though individual members still appeared occasionally with local talent.

By 1916 the Australasian branch of Fisk Jubilee Singers, still featuring Prof. C. A. White and Belle F. Gibbons, was back on tour, but business was "only fair" until the spring of 1917,[137] when white native Australian and "well-known descriptive vocalist" Marshall Palmer joined as business manager: "Since then they may be said to have taken quite a new lease of life . . . The company still specializes in old-time numbers, beloved by audiences for their pathos and melody. Among these are 'Steal Away,' 'The Lord's Prayer,' and 'Who Built the Ark?' "[138]

The Australasian Fisk company started taking white Australians into its ranks as early as 1905. By the time Marshall Palmer came, the troupe was thoroughly integrated; there was even an aboriginal voice in the mix, contralto Claire

Cover of Fisk Jubilee Trio promotional booklet. Left to right: Laura Carr, Eugene McAdoo, Euna Mocara. (courtesy Gwendolyn Belcher Eichelberger)

Solly, from Western Australia. Belle Gibbons, the last remaining holdover from Loudin's Fisk Jubilee Singers, became increasingly important as a symbol of continuity and authenticity. When she first arrived in Australia with Loudin in 1886, Gibbons was a soprano, but with McAdoo's Jubilee Singers she switched to a contralto, and with the latter-day Australasian Fisk Jubilee Singers she became a "Lady Baritone."

On March 9, 1918, these Fisk Jubilee Singers began a long tour of New Zealand at Dunedin. Four months later Marshall Palmer reported "tremendous business in this country. . . a clear profit of 2000 pounds. We are extending our tour for a further four months."[139] New Zealanders obviously embraced this somewhat "removed" company as if they were "the old Fisks." The apparent consensus of local critics was that their programs were "quite up to the standard of the old original company."[140] A reporter in Auckland disclosed, "The Fisks seem to have friends in all the most out-of-the-way places as well as in the big centres. They were treated like royalty by the Maoris in Gisborne, and entertained and made the recipients of valuable gifts by Sir James & Lady Carrol, the Maori member and his wife."[141]

The Australian Fisk Jubilee faction continued touring for many more years. Contralto Violet McAdoo, reportedly the daughter of Orpheus McAdoo by a common-law marriage to an Australian woman,[142] joined these Antipodean Fisks in 1920. Prof. C. A. White stayed on as musical director until his death in Sydney on February 6, 1922. Belle Gibbons was present as late as 1925. The *New Zealand Herald* of April 13, 1925, acknowledged her in an article headed "Fisk Jubilee Singers": "It was gratifying to note that the services of Miss Belle F. Gibbons, a prominent lady baritone touring with a company of Jubilee Singers in New Zealand something like a quarter of a century ago, has been enlisted in the present coterie. Though her work was

Shades of the Original Fisks!

A BRISBANE correspondent forwards us an extract from the "Courier" of that city, protesting against the use of the title of "Fisk Jubilee Singers" by the combination of artists now touring the North, under the management of Marshall Palmer.

There can be doubt of the justification of "A.T.N.'s" remarks, for, as he says, the title is a misnomer. However, Mr. Marshall Palmer has, for several years, managed a company of singers known as the Fisks, but he makes no claim as to their being identified with the original Jubilee Singers, who made vocal history in this country over a quarter of a century ago.

However, in view of the fact that the article in question provides some of the old-timers with something to reminise upon, we reprint it herewith:—

Sir,—I was indeed pleased with Mr. Arthur Poole's letter (which was in Thursday's "Courier"), in which he protests against the beautiful "Jubilee' songs being introduced in the Brisbane theatres by "so-called Fisk Singers." I had, in the distant past, the wondrous privilege of hearing, many times, the "original Fisk Jubilee Singers," and never before, or since, have I heard such soul-stirring music. Since then I have heard many companies calling themselves "Jubilee Singers," and it was like—well, as though one of our leather-jacket birds was trying to imitate a nightingale, only worse, much worse. Even now, when I recall Louden's "Roll, Jordan, Roll," I ache to hear it again, and their wonderful "Steal Away to Jesus,," "Swing low, Sweet Chariot," "John Brown's Body," I realise that never again in this world, shall I hear such music. When "John Brown's Body" was sung in London— I think it was in 1872— the dense mass of people rose and cheered until the "Singers" answered "God Save the Queen." They also sang it in Boston to an audience of 40,000. The scene was indescribable. The thousands of people were on their feet, ladies waved their handkerchiefs, men threw their hats in the air, and the Coliseum rang with cheers and shouts of "The Jubilees! The Jubilees for ever!" My advice to the present-day "Jubilees" is to stick to comic and jazz, and I am sure the public will be thankful. As far as true "music" is concerned, "we're rolling through an unfriendly world."—I remain, sir, &c.,

A.T.N.

May 23.

"Shades of the Original Fisks," Everyones Magazine, *November 6, 1924. (courtesy Gary LeGallant)*

naturally not equal to her former standards in the solo number, 'The Vale of Yesterday,' her assistance in the many Jubilee Choruses was invaluable, and it was clear also that her methods permeated the company's interpretations."

Documentation establishes that African American tenor Huntley Spencer, who came to Australia with the Hugo Minstrels and joined Marshall Palmer's Fisk Jubilee Singers in 1918, took a touring company of Fisk Jubilee Singers to New Zealand as late as 1936,[143] fully fifty years after Loudin's Fisk Jubilee Singers arrived in Melbourne and introduced themselves to the Australasian public.

Chapter Three

1891

New Departures in African American Minstrelsy

The year 1891 witnessed a "new departure" on the professional stage, a more representative and progressive style of black entertainment which scored increasingly big with the public. Shrewd, progressive performers and open-minded producers set a course away from the traditional minstrel show format toward a variety program that was more like vaudeville. This new departure, though inexorably tied to minstrelsy, provided a platform for a much fuller expression and development of African American stage arts.

The leaders of this new departure were William Foote's Afro-American Specialty Company and Sam T. Jack's Creole Burlesque Company. It could be said that neither of these companies were actually minstrel troupes. The Creole Company was developed in response to the increasing public demand for burlesque entertainment, while the Afro-American Specialty Company was more in the nature of a musical drama company: "the intention is to show every phase of negro character." However, both of these companies retained certain structural and referential elements of minstrelsy. The public-at-large was unprepared to see the creative products of African Americans in any other light.

The distinguishing element of Sam T. Jack's Creole Burlesque Company was its flashy chorus of beautiful African American women, the first of its kind on the American stage. The old-line African American minstrel companies—McCabe and Young's, Richards and Pringle's, W. S. Cleveland's, etc.—were all fraternities of men, even to their magnificently gowned operatic divas. The success of the Creole Burlesque Company "was looked upon as the acceptance of Negro women on the stage."[1] Opening the door to a sparkling legion of women singers, dancers, comediennes, and actresses, this massive innovation signified a new level of authenticity in African American minstrelsy.

Foote's Afro-American Specialty Company also featured women, but not in burlesque; the male and female performers of Foote's Afro-American Specialty Company were the embodiment of a panoramic "Negro evolution" theme, representing the cultural progress of the race since slavery. Their efforts can be seen as a metaphor for the new era in African American entertainment that was in the process of unfolding.

The progress of these two "new departure" companies was duly noted in the mainstream *New York Clipper*. A few of the African American weeklies took notice as well, but with a dash of well-founded skepticism. The *Cleveland Gazette* expressed its particular disappointment when Madame Marie Selika, one of the most highly trained of the aspiring black operatics, took the "downward step" of joining William Foote's Afro-American Specialty Company. *New York Age* editor T. Thomas Fortune expressed hopes that there would soon be space for African Americans on the operatic stage, but it wasn't until the 1950s that the New York Metropolitan Opera Company accepted its first African American member.

As it turned out, minstrelsy was just beginning to tighten its grip on African American popular entertainment in 1891. Before the end of the 1890s, all three of the reigning "Black

Queens of Song," Marie Selika, Flora Batson, and Sissieretta Jones, would have to compromise their ambitions and resign themselves to singing occasional operatic excerpts in expansive "vaudevillized minstrel" road shows. They would not be alone in this regard, as W. C. Handy observed in his autobiography, *Father of the Blues*: "[A]ll the best talent of that generation came down the same drain. The composers, the singers, the musicians, the speakers, the stage performers—the minstrel shows got them all."[2]

William Foote's Afro-American Specialty Company

William Foote's Afro-American Specialty Company was a fresh endeavor in African American stage entertainment. Its theme of "Negro evolution" introduced a new perspective that was judged too progressive for mainstream America. The Afro-American Specialty Company was designed for export, and for that, it lasted less than a year.

The white man behind the Afro-American Specialty Company, William Foote, had been active in the minstrel profession since before the Civil War. An advertisement in the November 24, 1888, edition of the *Clipper* celebrated his thirty-year milestone.

• ***February 28, 1891:*** "The Decline of Minstrelsy," "After Thirty-five Years Experience as an Amusement Caterer, Mr. William Foote Decides on a New Departure with Afro-American Talent," "A man who has been identified with negro minstrelsy for thirty-five years, must have a most interesting story to tell; and if he has devoted much of his spare time from practical affairs to study and research along this line, more interesting will be his conversation in consequence. On the Santa Fe train from Denver one evening recently, a [newspaper reporter] fell into conversation with Mr. William Foote . . .

Mr. Foote . . . has been identified with Negro minstrel troupes from the days of George Christy. He was for many years manager of Haverly's Mastodon minstrels . . . For three years,

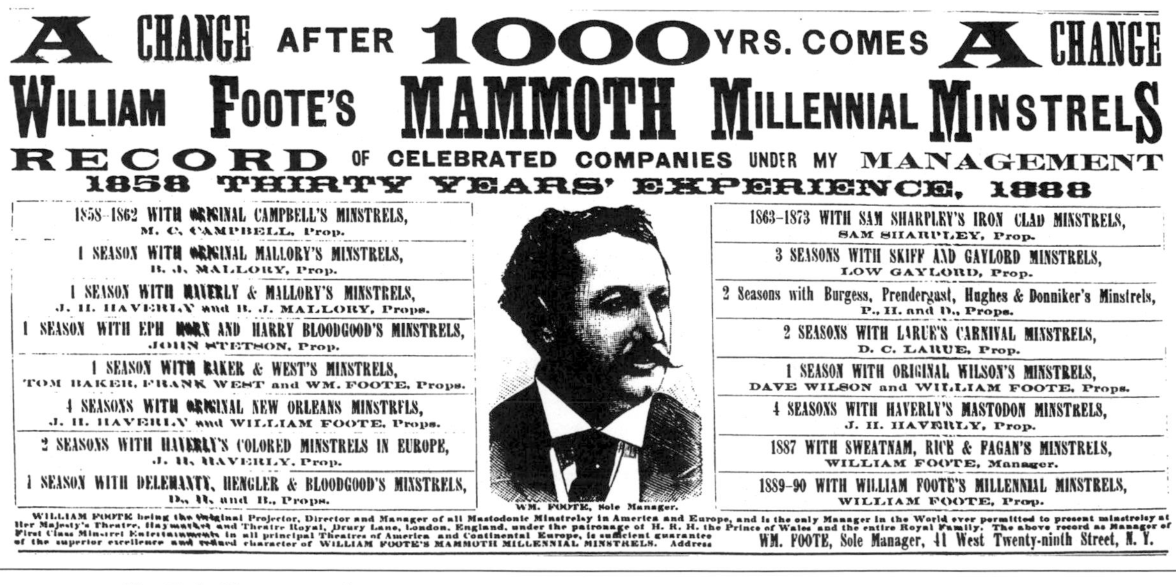

New York Clipper, *November 24, 1888.*

Mr. Foote, in London, successfully controlled the Mastodons. While in London Mr. Foote spent many an hour in the British Museum, turning over numberless volumes treating of Africa and its people. He made copious notes of the humorous side of the Negro character, as described by African travellers from the days of Mungo Park to the time of Livingstone.

His study at that time was made for the purpose of getting new material, new business for his company; but the growing popularity of rival companies, which under the guise of burnt cork, were introducing variety business into minstrel show, led him to lay aside certain cherished ideas for a more convenient opportunity. The degeneration of minstrel companies was rapid. Instead of portraying the comicalities of the Negro character, business from variety shows and the gradual growth of the burlesque and the farce comedy, developed a new field for comedians and no more study of the Negro was made. The public became tired of he who, as Mr. Foote said, 'blackened their faces to hide their gall.'...

Through all these years Mr. Foote has been studying the problem of how to rescue Negro minstrelsy and bring it again to its former popularity... He has nosed through the Astor Library and the Cooper Institute; he has wandered about the haunts of the Negro in town and country; he has talked with them, attended their churches and schools, observing and noting many a bright action and funny gesture, until of the humorous side of the Negro he has become an authority.

From a mass of material thus gathered, Mr. Foote hopes to evolve an evening's entertainment that will be edifying, interesting and highly amusing. It is his aim to portray the progress of the Negro from savagery, through slavery to the fullness of his powers as citizen, making the comical side of the Negro's character prominent throughout" (*New York Age*, reprinted from the white daily *Pueblo [Colorado] Opinion*).

• ***February 28, 1891:*** "The African and the Foot Lights," "The rise and fall of Negro Minstrelsy will occupy a not unimportant chapter in the dramatic history of the future. From the very beginning the whole fabric was reared upon a foundation of the wildest extravagance, grotesqueness and caricature, and as the years rolled along it became worse in these respects, so that now few attempts are made to pawn off such spurious wares upon the amusement public. In the present presentation of the drama the Afro-American has a very small, if any, part, either as an impersonator or as a character in the play. Is the time ripe for him to take his place upon the boards and become embodied in the framework of the drama? We think so. So, also does Mr. William Foote...

Mr. Foote...has many big ideas about his pet project to give the Afro-American his legitimate place in the drama and upon the stage. He has a magnificent field upon which to draw. There is as much humor and wit and pathos in the African nature as in the Irish, and given a proper opportunity to display these we believe he would take with the amusement public" (*New York Age*).

• ***February 28, 1891:*** "Wanted: High Class Colored Artists, of unmistakable Negro Origin, possessing superior talent in any branch of amusements and desiring engagements in Europe 1891–1892 and returning to World's Fair in Chicago, 1893. Only the best representatives of Afro-American talent in the world can secure equitable and liberal pay, by addressing, William Foote, Manager, 106 West 28th Street, New York City" (*New York Age*).

• ***March 28, 1891:*** "Wm. Foote is traveling through the South in search of colored people for a company that he is preparing for a two years' tour of Europe. The new venture will be

GENUINE NEGRO TALENT WANTED,

MUST BE UNMISTAKABLE AFRICAN DESCENT,

For two years' tour of Europe, with all expenses from New York and salaries guaranteed. Male and Female Colored Artists with extraordinary ability, not depending on knowledge of English language, can secure permanent and immediate engagement. WANTED—20 Colored Acrobatic Song and Dance Men; 20 Colored Wing and Song and Dance Ladies; 20 High Class Specialists, Soloists, Male and Female Instrumental and Vocalists; 20 one Soloists and Banjo Experts; 20 Drum Majors. All must be useful, all must be (genuine) Negroes and Sensational Specialists. Apply immediately to WILLIAM FOOTE, late Manager Haverly's in Europe and Her Majesty's Theatre, London. Permanent address, No. 106 W. TWENTY-EIGHTH STREET, New York City.

WANTED,

COLORED TALENT.

Must be Unmistakeably of Negro Origin.

Any amount of money will be paid for

A BLACK PHENOMENAL FEATURE.

Must be a "NONE SUCH," and not "FREAK" or "MONSTROSITY." Must be HIGH CLASS, and not depending on English language for success. Must be a SOLITAIRE to grace as "Centre Stone" the Cluster of Colored Character Celebrities that tour Europe for two years, and return to World's Fair in Chicago in 1893. Apply to WILLIAM FOOTE (Late Manager Haverly's in Europe, and Her Majesty's Theatre, London), 106 WEST TWENTY-EIGHTH STREET. N. Y. CITY.

New York Clipper, *March 28, 1891.* New York Clipper, *April 4, 1891.*

known as Wm. Foote's Colored Character Concerts, and the intention is to show every phase of negro character as it exists in the several sections of this country. Mr. Foote says he has already secured some excellent colored talent, and is considering many offers" (*New York Clipper*).

• ***April 4, 1891:*** "Manager William Foote . . . reports rapid progress in the formation of his new colored minstrel and concert troupe, with which he hopes to astonish England. His advance agent, R. A. Cunningham, who has had wide experience, will sail for London this week to arrange the final details, and Mr. Foote and the company of forty people will leave late this month, opening at London. Manager Foote contemplates a two years' tour, after which he will return to this country for an extensive trip here. He has planned his entertainment, he says, so as to truthfully depict the course of the African, from the jungle to the parlor, and his colored performers will represent the negro's progress as a savage, a slave, a soldier, a citizen and a lawmaker. It ought to be a novel show" (*New York Clipper*).

• ***April 25, 1891:*** "Manager William Foote, of whose big scheme we have already written, has recently accomplished a *coup d'etat* in the engagement for a term of three years of Marie Selika, the 'Black Patti,' and a singer whose reputation is very firmly established. Mme. Selika and husband, M. Velonski, the tenor [*sic*, i.e., Selika's husband, Sampson T. Williams, a bass-baritone singer whose stage name was Signor Velosko], will be the stars in Foote & Co.'s enterprise, which has rapidly assumed formidable shape. About April 26 the steamship *Vandam,* which has been specially chartered for the purpose, will sail with the entire party of forty or more people for Hamburg, Ger., where the European tour will open. Charles R. Dockstader goes as stage manager, James Sullivan in charge of the dancing. John B. Donniker will probably be the musical director. The costumes, which are said to be very elaborate, nearly all being of silk and satin, are by Paul Vernon . . . All the performers are colored" (*New York Clipper*).

• ***May 9, 1891:*** "Madame Selika is said to get $7000 a year and has a contract for three years with Foote's Afro-American Specialty Company, that left for Europe a few weeks ago. Song and dance and other acts, as well as solos, will be given. Selika surprises all her friends and admirers in taking this downward step" (*Cleveland Gazette*).

• ***May 23, 1891 (Hamburg, Germany):*** "Turned 'Em Away," "May 18—The African-American Character Concert Co. arrived here in good shape and opened last night to a packed house. Hundreds were turned away. The performance moved smoothly and the forty odd genuine negro vocalists, dancers and specialists acquitted themselves very creditably. Mme. Selika (the 'Black Patti') was encored to the echo, and received floral tributes in abundance. Mintz Mason and Carrie Brown scored distinct hits, and the male quartet went like wild fire . . . The management have hit the bull's eye squarely in their aim of illustrating every phase of American negro character from the cradle to old age and from slavery to citizenship" (Wm. Foote, *New York Clipper*).[3]

• ***June 6, 1891:*** "Gossip Of The Stage," "Probably the most refined and elevated Afro-American amusement company ever organized was brought together recently by Mr. William Foote for a tour of Europe. All of his stars are new in this line, and instead of making plantation melodies and peculiar dialect their forte, they have a sort of historical bearing in portraying the different evolutions from 1860 to 1891. With such stars as Mme. Marie Selika, leader of the burlesque opera, and her husband Mr. Veloska, baritone; Mme. Mamie Flowers, a noted soprano as leader of the choruses and Mr. H. E. Jones, as banjoist and guitarist, one can see the organizer's intention was to elevate the character of the minstrel show and possibly draw a new interest" (W. L. M. Chaise, *New York Age*).

• ***June 13, 1891:*** "Wm. Foote's African American Concert Co. are reported to be meeting with much success at the Flora Concert Hall, Hamburg, Ger., where they will remain a month and perhaps longer. Managers from various European cities have expressed their thorough satisfaction with the performance" (*New York Clipper*).

• ***June 20, 1891:*** "Wm. Foote's African-American Character Concert Co. have closed their month's engagement at Altoona, Ger., where their performances gave great satisfaction. Manager Foote has under way a plan for the organization of a 'U.T.C.' Co., to appear at the Concordia Theatre, Berlin, next Winter, with Germans in the white roles and real negroes as the other characters. He will not close his concert company, but will have two distinct organizations . . . On June 16 the company began a fortnight's engagement at the Stadt Theatre, Hanover" (*New York Clipper*).

• ***July 18, 1891:*** "William Foote, writing from Hanover, Ger., under date of June 28, states: 'Our Hanover engagement closed with tonight's performance. From here we go to Magdeburg, where we play at the Flora Concert Haus until July 10, when we open at Cologne for two weeks. Berlin will probably not be reached until September' " (*New York Clipper*).

• ***August 1, 1891:*** "Wm. Foote's African-American Concert Co. opened at the Kaiser Garden, Cologne, Ger., July 12, to splendid success" (*New York Clipper*).

• ***August 8, 1891:*** "The Sweet Singer," "The lyric stage to-day possesses no soprano the equal of Madame Selika, our own peerless singer. When I say this, I do not mean when measured by the standard of Negro excellence, but I mean this as a broad sweeping assertion . . . Her maiden name was Price, and she was born in Natchez, Miss. Her mother died when she was quite small, and her father, H. Price, with several other daughters came to Cincinnati to live. Selika was raised by an elder sister, Mrs. Holloway. Her voice was first remarked upon in the Allen Temple Sunday-school where she sang; afterwards she took part in nearly all the Sunday-school and church entertainments in Cincinnati. From Cincinnati she went to Chicago, where her voice was tested, and here she was married to her husband, who is now traveling with her, Mr. Sampson W. Williams. After their marriage he put her under the musical training of Farina. From Chicago she went to California and remained under a teacher there for three years, after which she returned east, and she now claims Columbus, Ohio as her home, having purchased property in that city. She is at present on a three years' tour of Europe, having signed a contract calling for $21,000" (*Cleveland Gazette*).

• ***September 5, 1891:*** "William Foote, the minstrel manager, with his company of jubilee singers, are at present at Strasburg, Ger., and will shortly go to Wanheim. Mr. Foote reports that business has been good throughout Germany" (*New York Clipper*).

• ***October 3, 1891:*** "Wm. Foote has disposed of his interests in the African-American Character Concert Co. to Col. James Todd, who had previously been managing director of the company. After Nov. 1, the title of the company will be changed, and a tour of Norway, Denmark and Sweden is contemplated. Later the company will appear in France. Mr. Foote is at present in France, but will shortly visit London, from whence he will sail for New York early in October. Upon his arrival Mr. Foote will at once begin the organization of a colored jubilee festival for the World's fair at Chicago in 1893" (*New York Clipper*).

• ***October 23, 1891 (New York City):*** "Personal," "Mr. William Foote writes me from Germany that he has met with tremendous success with his combination, 'The African in Slavery and Freedom,' and that the best musicians of the Fatherland have been captivated and captured by the splendid voice of Madame Marie Selika. He talks of producing 'Uncle Tom's Cabin.' He expects to remain in Europe until the World's Fair opens, when he will descend upon the Windy City and rob it of some of its conceit" (T. Thomas Fortune, *New York Age*).

• ***November 14, 1891:*** "Manager William Foote, who has returned from his German tour with the colored minstrel troupe . . . has sold out his interest in the minstrels, he says, and left them in the midst of a successful engagement in Berlin. Mr. Foote will be in the ring again before long. His next venture, he states, will be a novel one, but it will be minstrelsy, for he will not desert that form of entertainment" (*New York Clipper*).

• ***January 23, 1892:*** "Among the steerage passengers landed at Locust Point, Baltimore, Md., Jan. 11, from Bremen, were Mr. and Mrs. Charles R. Dockstader and ten colored male and female members of Dodd's Black Comic Opera Co. Mr. Dockstader . . . said that with forty colored men and women, all good vocalists and musicians, he left New York last May. Wm. Foote had organized the venture in this city [New York]. The whole of the saloon accommodations on the steamship *Zaandam* had been chartered by the backers of the combination. The company opened at Hamburg, at the Flora Gardens, which have a capacity for 10,000 persons. For four weeks the attendance was immense. Then, in turn, Hanover, Magdeburg, Zerbt, Dessau, Cologne, Mont Gladbach, Aschen, Mainz, Coblentz, Strasburg, Frankfort-on-the-Main, Hamburg, Ems, Berlin and other cities in Northern Europe were visited. Afterward, many were revisited by request. During the tour dissatisfaction broke out or sickness compelled the return of members to the States. On December 21, 1891, at Copenhagen, the enterprise collapsed, but not, Mr. Dockstader said, without every member having been paid to date. The originators of the project lost 60,000 marks. Twelve of the company remained at Copenhagen . . . Mmes. Zelika and Valeska, two colored prima donnas [*sic*, Madame Selika and her husband], were in the company when it left New York" (*New York Clipper*).

At least one faction of Foote's Afro-American Specialty Company remained in Europe and continued touring under the management of Foote's original advance agent, R. A. Cunningham. As Cunningham's Negro Singers, they were still playing dates in Scandinavia in 1895. William Foote returned to the domestic scene.

• ***May 28, 1892:*** "Haverly's Mastadon Minstrels will begin operation May 30, at Chicago. Their tour will extend to the Pacific Coast, and will be under the personal direction of J. H. Haverly, assisted by Wm. Foote" (*New York Clipper*).

• ***June 24, 1893:*** "Wm. Foote, manager of Haverly's Cri-Garten Theatre, Chicago, while in this city [New York] last week, made an engagement with Sergeant Sims and his Columbian Cadets to appear at that house. The cadets are twelve negro boys from the Bahamas, who appear in a sketch called 'La Bivouac,' in which they present all the exercises of a soldier on the tented field. Each boy is . . . armed with a carbine and bayonet. The act is said to be clever, but . . . permission to exhibit in this city was refused because of the intervention of the children's society" (*New York Clipper*).

"Cuninghams Negor-Sangkor," 1895. (courtesy Swedish Royal Library, Stockholm)

Foote's Afro-American Specialty Company was short-lived, but its "Negro evolution" theme reverberated not only in professional minstrelsy but in church, school and other black community entertainments, well into the twentieth century.

Sam T. Jack's Creole Burlesque Company

Press reports in the *New York Clipper* during the spring of 1891 document a powerful trend toward burlesque and farce comedy on the American popular stage.

• ***March 14, 1891:*** "At present it looks as though the main attraction for the vaudeville theatres for 1891–92 would be burlesque. Already many organizations are projected, and on many stages the female form, in gorgeous costumes, surrounded by magnificent scenery, will be on view, where heretofore straight variety has been the rule" (*New York Clipper*).

• ***March 28, 1891:*** "The Future of the Vaudeville Stage," "The straight variety companies of today are unquestionably partaking more and more of the farce comedy order, and are gradually booking in the better class of houses, while burlesque *per se* is gradually coming to the front in the vaudeville theatres and minstrel organizations. In the last named class of attraction the old time semi-circle of burnt cork performers is no longer seen. The Southern darkey of ten years ago is a thing of the past. It is common nowadays for a minstrel soloist to sing an Irish ballad, while the genuine colored man's dialect is very seldom heard. A careful perusal of the past few years' records of minstrelsy will show that class of entertainment is changing. Today thousands of dollars are spent on gorgeous stage settings and costumes. The performers appear in spangles and tights, court wigs and gowns. Will a few years change all this, and place shapely women in characters now assumed by men? Or, in other words, will Minstrelsy and Burlesque wed?" (*New York Clipper*).

Stage show burlesque, as understood during the late-nineteenth century, seems to have been a blurry amalgam of farce comedy and the theatrical display of shapely women in elaborate, revealing costumes. The wedding of burlesque and African American minstrelsy was consummated by Sam T. Jack's Creole Burlesque Company. As James Weldon Johnson recalled: "The *Creole Show* gave great prominence to girls and . . . had none of the features of plantation days; nevertheless, it was cast in the traditional minstrel pattern. There was a minstrel first part, differing, however, from the regular minstrel show in that the girls were in the center of the line, with a female interlocutor, and the men on the ends . . . Notwithstanding, it was the start along the line which led straight to the musical comedies of Cole and Johnson, Williams and Walker and Ernest Hogan."[4]

The Creole Burlesque Company's white proprietor, Sam T. Jack, was profiled in the December 26, 1891, edition of the *Clipper*:

> Mr. Jack was born in the Western Foothills of the Allegheny Mountains near Pittsburg, Pa, and when but a small child was taken to Oil City, when that mountain-cradled and oleaginous gem of the Allegheny River was the main emporium of the kerosene trade. Young Sam grew up as rugged as the oaks that lined the mountainsides around his home, until an indulgent father sent him away to college, from which, in due time, he was graduated with honors. It was Mr. Jack's first intention to follow civil engineering and oil speculation, but the knowledge of that world outside of his native hills, which he got a glimpse of in college days, soon influenced him to seek a wider field to operate in. As he was a born showman, he took to the white tents and red wagons like a duck goes to water. We next find him traveling with the Golden Menagerie (the old Van Amburgh Show). After one Summer season—having met with an accident—he quit the circus business. We next find him manager of the Oil Regions Circuit of Theatres. This was in 1872–3. While this proved highly successful, there was not life enough in it for him, so the seasons of 1874–5–6 we find him with a large flotilla, or Floating Opera House, with his Marine Minstrels playing all towns between St. Louis and New Orleans, Cairo and Pittsburg, on the Ohio, Mississippi, Red River rivers and Bayou Teeche [*sic*] (and it was here that he promulgated his plans and conceived the idea of a Creole Burlesque Co.). Mr. Jack was at once captain, manager and general high flyer . . . [T]he dangers that he met with from lawless and reckless daredevils in river towns were many, and his audiences often gained the levee to the tune of "Hey, Rube!" . . . He always wound up the performance with a military afterpiece, in which

the performers carried real guns instead of "props," and carried them loaded, too, because, oftimes, the major portion of his audience was apt to be in a like condition, and might possibly require a little persuasion to have them depart in peace. During the travels of the flotilla three fusillades occurred—at New Madrid, Mo., Osceola Park, Ark., and Friars Point, Miss. In this venture he made money, and finally sold the outfit to a Missourian, who is now a wealthy resident of Kansas City. Mr. Jack came East and reestablished the Oil Circuit, managing it successfully from 1877 to 1880, when he sold it to Wagner & Reis . . . His next venture was the management of the late Alice Oates for three years. After that he took the Lilly Clay Co., which is today a leading burlesque attraction. In this organization the late Alice Townsend (whom Mr. Jack married in 1880) was the leading actress up to her death, which occurred March 24, 1890, at Pittsburg, Pa . . . Mr. Jack was always an originator, and the number of innovations which he has produced up to the present time are astonishing. His trademark is "The Survival of the Fittest," and well he survives. The season before last Mr. Jack "sprung" his Creole Burlesque Co. on the public, an innovation at once startling and novel.

If the idea of a Creole Burlesque Company had come to Jack while piloting a minstrel troupe along Bayou Teche, he also appears to have had a vision of the River Nile. In the spring of 1890, with his white "Lilly Clay" Company in full bloom, Sam T. Jack announced plans for an "Oriental Sensation" Company. The most sensational thing about it was Jack's claim to be recruiting performers in Egypt.

It would appear that Sam T. Jack melded his idea for an Oriental Sensation Company into the concept of "Creole Burlesque." The woman pictured in the Oriental Sensation advertisement became the promotional symbol for Sam T. Jack's Creole Burlesque Company, and the image of "young Egyptian women" lingered in the Creole Burlesque Company's presentations.

• ***July 19, 1890:*** "Manager Sam T. Jack arrived in [New York City] July 14 and will commence [July] 21, at Boston, rehearsals of the Sam T. Jack Creole Burlesque Co. This is the first troupe of its kind ever organized and is composed of fifty people, thirty of whom are Louisiana Creoles, the remainder being young Egyptian women. The Egyptian contingency arrived from Europe last week under the charge

New York Clipper, *April 26, 1890.*

New York Clipper, *October 11, 1890.*

of G. W. Gallagher, who went to the other side to bring them over... The season opens Aug. 4 in Massachusetts. A purely Egyptian burlesque will be done, the costumes of which will be correct and in Oriental magnificence" (*New York Clipper*).

Note: The percentage of true "Louisiana Creoles" in Jack's company was probably about the same as the percentage of "young Egyptian women," i.e., not many. A later report said that the company was "made up of many New York City girls."

• ***September 20, 1890:*** "Sam T. Jack's Creole Burlesque Co. recently opened at London Theatre, New York City. The show commenced with a very pretty first part, attractive groupings of shapely femininity. Tropical revelries, Florence Brisco was first conversationalist; Florence Hines, the greatest living female song and dance artist, second and Mrs. Sam Lucas third. The olio sketches were very fine and called for numerous encores. The burlesque, 'The Beauty of the Nile, or Doomed by Fire,' by William R. Watts, is fine. It is cast as follows: Nafra, Sadie D. Walfa; Choep, Florence Hines; Grip, Burnell Hawkins; Zeno, Irving Jones; Isis, his queen, Sarah La Rue; Amasis, King of Thebs, Florence Brisco; Karmack, Mammie Laning; Dinon, Eloise Pousett; Amon, Nina St. Jean; Zoilous, May Vorshall; Yeason, Miss Valja; and Mr. and Mrs. Sam Lucas, musical sketch artists" (*Indianapolis Freeman*).

Note: A standout in this first edition of Sam T. Jack's Creole Burlesque Company was pioneer black minstrel comedian Sam Lucas. At the time of Lucas's death in 1916, *Freeman* columnist Sylvester Russell noted, "It is stated by good authority that he was the first actor who conceived the idea of a creole company and induced Sam T. Jack to put out the original creole company."[5] Then there was the newcomer, "premier knock about song and dance comedian" Irving Jones, in his first major role. It was during the next three seasons with Sam T. Jack's Creole Company that Irving Jones's remarkable abilities as a black vernacular song composer first drew notice.

• ***January 24, 1891:*** "Manager Sam T. Jack's... Creole forces gained a new recruit in Mlle. Hortense, a burlesquer of much local note in Georgia" (*New York Clipper*).

• ***February 20, 1891 (Kansas City, Missouri):*** "Kansas City, has been entertained by a company of prominent colored artists vis; Creoles. Some prominent gentlemen are grieving and longing for the sight again, they were so captivated by the charming beauties that they are already sighing for their return" (*Kansas City American Citizen*).

• ***May 16, 1891:*** "Florence Briscoe was compelled to leave Sam Jack's Creole Co. at Milwaukee, Wis., recently on account of the grip. Upon her recovery she did sketches with Ben Hunn, at Kohl & Middleton's Museums at St. Paul and Minneapolis, Minn. She complains of unprofessional treatment at his hands. She is now in this city [New York]. Miss Briscoe is a fine singer" (*New York Clipper*).

• ***June 6, 1891:*** "Gossip Of The Stage," "The Latest Combination in the Variety Line—Sam T. Jack's Creole Burlesque Company," "Except in the minstrel line the Afro-American has held a very small place on the stage. It has been a number of years since Haverly put the first Georgia Minstrels upon the boards, which for a time forced recognition of worth and appreciation the world over. But minstrelsy had its day and for the past four or five years has been on the wane. The stars, McIntosh, Kersands, Banks, Lucas, the Bohee Brothers, 'Judge' Crusoe and many others having divided their forces or retired from the stage, is probably the cause of this lack of public interest. Mr. Cleveland [the white manager of Cleveland's Colored Minstrels] has tried with some success to revive the colored minstrel business, and while he has a few of the original merry makers, Tom McIntosh being the manager, his company is made up mostly of new talent . . .

The latest combination seen around New York in this line is Sam T. Jack's Creole Burlesque Company. This company is composed of all Afro-Americans and the program contains many names familiar to the musical and theatre going public. The company is what they call in theatrical circles a variety company and is made up of many New York city girls. They played to full and appreciative houses last week at Hyde and Behman's Theatre, Brooklyn. The performance commenced with a tropical revelry, introducing an excellent array of artists. The curtain rose amidst the singing of a beautiful melody, and displayed a galaxy of artists in graceful poses, with the customary end men to make the fun. Misses Florence Briscoe, Florence Hines, May Bohee and Mrs. Sam Lucas, as conversationalists and soloists, gave a new impression of the possibilities of our girls in the variety business. Miss Bohee is a daughter of one of the Bohee Brothers and is destined to attain much prominence among theatricals as a serio comic singer. The De Wolf Sisters in sunset melodies, George Westerner and Fred Piper, punsters, Jones, Norris and Grant, fun makers, Irving Jones, Premier knock about song and dance comedian, the four Creoles and Mr. and Mrs. Wesley B. Norris kept the audience highly amused for over an hour. The veteran Sam Lucas and his wife are splendid entertainers. Mrs. Lucas, besides playing many musical instruments, has developed into a contralto singer of much merit. Miss Florence Hines impersonated a male character in a manner that would do credit to any variety actor on the stage. The prize dancing by Burrell Hawkins, Irving Jones, Burt Grant, Wesley Norris and Miles, Marie Valerie, Stacciona and Stabolo, with George Weston as banjo accompanist, was a feature that elicited much applause. 'The Beauties of the Nile,' or 'Doomed by Fire,' an ancient Egyptian burlesque, by twenty young women, nobles, soothsayers, fire worshippers and Nubians, was a gorgeous display of physical development. The grand Amazonian March, under the direction of Miss Florence Hines, with a superb tableau, concluded the performance. The entire company is well drilled and perform their respective parts with much exactness and precision" (W. L. M. Chaise, *New York Age*).

Note: Florence Briscoe and Florence Hines, two of the most popular female stars of the first show to "glorify the coloured girl" and give "a new impression of the possibilities of our girls in the variety business,"[6] have been practically forgotten in modern scholarship. Yet these pioneering female performers had an impact on the manner in which blues singing was introduced on the black vaudeville stage by the blues women of the 1910s and 1920s. Hines's male impersonations provided the standard against which African American comediennes were compared for decades. She may have directly inspired such blues-era performers as Lillyn Brown, "the original" Bessie Brown, and Alberta Whitman. Florence Hines died in San Jose, California, on March 7, 1924.[7]

Florence Hines.
justly termed the "Black Vesta Tilley," has for years held, and is still the owner of the title—"Leader in her line." She was for seven seasons a prominent feature in Sam T. Jack's Creoles; two seasons with "Darkest America"; and at present a feature in the olio of the *Big* Minstrel Festival using a repertoire of original songs such as "A Millionare's Only Son," "I Can't See My Money Go That Way" and "For I'm the Lad That's Made of Money."

Freeman, *December 30, 1899.*

• ***August 8, 1891:*** "Sam T. Jack's . . . Creole Burlesque Co. will begin rehearsals Aug. 11, at Gilmore's Central Theatre, Philadelphia. The Creoles will begin their tour at that house [August] 24" (*New York Clipper*).

• ***August 15, 1891:*** "The Creoles include the De Wolfe Sisters, May Bohee, Mrs. Sam Lucas, Marie Velerie, Maud Ash, Maud Tazewell, Dora Drew, Bell Davis, Mamie Riley, Cora Ray, Annie Bogus, Bessie Tucker, Rhoda Fulton, Hazel Bellwood, Ollie Russell, Essie Lemon, Hada La Rue, Della Fanning, Dora Harris, Pauline Blackburn, Elfa Titians, Josie Herland, Louise Herland, Marie De Voe, Sam Lucas, Burill Hawkins, Irving Jones, Billy Farrell, Wesley B. Morris, Fred Piper, Coles and Staples, Burt Grant, Mr. Byrd, Wm. Banks, Mr. Palley, F. R. Jacoby, leader; Chas. Hill, assistant stage manager; Chas. H. Duprez, business manager and treasurer; John Isham, advance, and Sam T. Jack, manager and stage director" (*New York Clipper*).

The advance agent for Sam T. Jack's Creole Burlesque Company, John W. Isham, has been described as a light-complected African American who "frequently passed for white and thereby was able to secure responsible positions with various show companies which allowed him to acquire valuable experience in the management and advertising end of the business."[8] Much of Isham's early experience was with circus organizations.[9] Isham became an increasingly powerful figure in Sam T. Jack's new enterprise.

One measure of Sam T. Jack's Creole Company's success is the many clones it inspired. When their second season commenced in the fall of 1891, at least two other unrelated Creole companies also took the road. Famous bandmaster Prof. Henderson Smith, formerly of

Cleveland's Colored Minstrels, made a bid for independence during the season of 1891–1892, when he and his wife took a "Creole Specialty Company" on an adventurous tour of the upper Midwest, as far as the Dakotas. It appears things did not go as expected, and members of Smith's Creole Company were soon availing themselves of the region's abundant wild game.

• ***October 17, 1891:*** "Notes from Smith's Creole Co," "We opened our season at West Suspension, Wis., Sept. 21, to a packed house, and the verdict was 'a great show.'... Our band and orchestra is a great feature... We close our show with a funny afterpiece entitled, 'Don't you dance, if you do you will bust your religion,' by James Waco. We are now touring Dakota and Minnesota, and will soon be in Iowa and Missouri" (*New York Clipper*).

• ***November 14, 1891:*** "Notes from Smith's Creole Co," "We have entered our tenth week, and, although many incidents have taken place since our opening, we continue to do a good business. We were surrounded a week by forest fires in Minnesota, and last week at West Duluth the Opera House caught fire from an oil stove, which exploded, ruining the scenery and spoiling our wardrobe. Mrs. Jerry Mills was taken suddenly ill last week, and we were compelled to leave her behind. We are now headed for the Southwest. Our manager, Mr. Smith, has made arrangements for eight of the boys to go out Saturday after the show and hunt deer until Monday, as the game law is over, and the boys have game fever. Wm. De Wolf joined us last week, and he is quite a favorite in the musical turn. The ghost makes his regular appearance every Tuesday morning at 10 o'clock, and if you walk easy in the halls you can hear the click of his tread" (*New York Clipper*).

• ***December 5, 1891:*** "Notes from Smith's Creoles," "Henderson Smith has disposed of his interest in the company, and returned to West Superior, to take charge of the city band. Our boys, while out hunting at Rice Lake, were fortunate enough to kill three deer, which brought them $45 for their trouble, and quite a supper was served after the show. We were sorry to part with Mr. Smith, but his property and business compelled him to sell his interest" (*New York Clipper*).

Downing's Creole Company, the second clone company to take the road during the fall of 1891, had slightly more success. Despite a very shaky beginning, they were still on the boards in early 1893.

• ***September 19, 1891:*** "Roster of Downing's Creole Co.: W. W. Downing, proprietor and manager; Billy Young, Harry S. Eaton, John Green, James White, Alex. Marshall, W. H. Day, Lew Ewing, Joe Raverzee, John Robinson, H. Woodby, John Bell, Gertie Revels, Zoe Ball, Anna Brown, Ella Spencer, Carrie Johnson, Stella Martin, Jennie Foster and Chette Crawford" (*New York Clipper*).

• ***November 1, 1891 (Topeka, Kansas):*** "Among the Sports," "The Creole Company is in bad luck. Their manager skips out and leaves the troupe to hustle for themselves. Since Billie Young and Harry Eaton left, the show has done poorly, and was forced to disband" (*Topeka Weekly Call*).

• ***November 8, 1891 (Topeka, Kansas):*** "Stage Notes," "The act of the Creole company, last week has a great affect on other colored companies hereafter. If they continue beating their board bills they may get in trouble" (*Topeka Weekly Call*).

• ***January 28, 1893:*** "W. W. Downing's New Orleans Creoles will open Feb. 1. Wanted, all kinds of Colored Talent, both Male and Female; also Colored Band of Six Pieces, White Leader who can Arrange" (*New York Clipper*).

Sam T. Jack's Creole Burlesque Company ultimately outshone all pretenders. However, they had to begin the season of 1891–1892 without one of their "Creole beauties."

• ***August 15, 1891:*** "Mary Louise Purcell, a member of Sam T. Jack's 'Creole' Co., died at the Victoria Hotel, this city [New York], Aug. 4, under circumstances which called for a coroner's investigation. The girl took the part of Queen last season, and was known on the stage as Larue. She was a native of Charleston, S.C., and the daughter of a quadroon and a Cuban. Her big black eyes and clear white skin made her noticeable on the stage in contrast with some of her comrades. After finishing at the Standard, Miss Purcell, with half a dozen others, stayed in this city. On July 30 she slipped and fell down stairs at the hotel where she stayed. The fall was followed by peritonitis, which caused her death. Dr. P. A. Johnson attended the woman, with two other colored physicians. When the board of Health were notified of the death, they declared that because of the fall it was a coroner's case, and refused to give a burial permit. Deputy Coroner William A. Conway made an autopsy Aug. 6 and found no evidence of criminal practice. The funeral was held at an undertakers, and burial was made at Evergreen Cemetery. The Rev. W. T. Carr, of the Shiloh Presbyterian Church (colored), conducted the service, and members of the company sang hymns" (*New York Clipper*).

• ***August 22, 1891 (Chicago, Illinois):*** "Robert Cole and John Staple's refined team of nine instruments have joined Sam'l T. Jack's famous Creole company, at Philadelphia, for the season; the only colored artists of the kind on the road" (*Indianapolis Freeman*).

• ***September 12, 1891:*** "Billy Farrell, of Sam Jack's Creole Co., writes that he is now abjuring the use of cork in his specialty" (*New York Clipper*).

• ***October 4, 1891:*** "Stage Notes," "Sam T. Jack's Creole Co. turned away people at their opening performance at the Ninth Street theater in Kansas City" (*Topeka Weekly Call*).

CREOLE BURLESQUE COMPANY

A Successful Organization of Theatrical Talent.—Traveling in Their Own Pullman Car.

Philadelphia, Penn., Special to The Freeman.

The Hon. Samuel Jack's Creole Burlesque Company played at the Central Theatre the week of August 24th, to 28th. The theatre was filled every evening. The performance commenced with Tropical Revelries, introducing the following array of artists: Miss Maud Tagewell, conversationalist, Messrs Burt Grant, and Piper Fred—punsters; second edition, Miss R. M. Brooks, conversationalist, Jones and Noms, fun makers; the costumes were fine and costly. Ben Hun and Billy Farrell, comedians; fourth edition. Mrs. Sam Lucas, conversationalist, Sam Lucas and Burrell, Hawkins, courtiers, Jones and Noms, comedians, DeWolf Sisters, 4 Creoles, 4 gavotte and grand Ensemble Medley by company. Mr. and Mrs. Sam Lucas entertainers, challenge dancing contest, Messrs Burrell, Hawkins, Jones, Grant, Noms and others, Grand Amazonian March, by young ladies, a superb tableau. This is the only colored company on the road. Mrs. Sam Lucas' musical entertainment was fine. Mrs. Lucas' cornet, violin, and banjoline solos, Mr. Lucas' guitar, DeWolf Sisters, singers, cannot be excelled. Next week they will play in Baltimore.

The company has also a private car built by the Pullman Palace Car Company, with a con-

S. T. JACK, MANAGER.

venient dining room, place to sleep; has also cook and waiters. When they are refused on account of color, they have their own car in which to eat, sleep and be merry. Of the Philadelphia beauties belonging to the company are Misses Bessie Tucker, Christie Cooper and Stibb. After each play, they go immediately to the car, expect some relation in the city; Sam Jack travels with the company. We appreciate Mr. Jack for his kindness to the race; we hope that this may induce others to pattern after him.

Freeman, *September 5, 1891.*

• ***October 31, 1891:*** "That hustling and wide awake manager, Sam T. Jack, has signed for a nineteen weeks' tour of California and the Pacific Coast with his Creole Burlesque Co. The company will play only the best houses" (*New York Clipper*).

• ***November 11, 1891:*** "The Pullman Palace car in which Manager Sam T. Jack houses his beauteous Creoles is thus described by a CLIPPER correspondent, who recently visited it: 'At the right, near the door, is the manager's private office, fitted up in regal style . . . On the left is an immense heater, which furnished the heat for the car. Next we come to the ladies' toilet and wardrobe, which are models in their way. A few steps more bring one into the grand saloon, which is furnished in elegant manner. It is about twenty-five feet in length, and contains three double sections on each side, with moveable tables in the centre. Each section is draped with rich, damask curtains . . . and are upholstered with red velvet plush. At the end of the saloon are the linen closets. The next apartment is the manager's stateroom . . . It contains a large and eloquent sofa, and a double and single berth. Adjoining is the manager's private bath room. Next to this is another stateroom, occupied by the male quartet of the company, which is entirely separate from the other portions of the car. Last but not least we come to the kitchen . . . It is fitted up with every convenience imaginable . . . The car is sixty-five feet long, and . . . equipped with every known modern invention. It is finished throughout with black walnut . . . The Creoles are certainly to be congratulated on having such eloquent and commodious quarters in which to travel about the countryside . . . The car is in charge of Charles H. Duprez, Mr. Jack's efficient treasurer . . . Mr. Duprez is of the old time minstrel managers, Duprez & Benedict' " (*New York Clipper*).

• ***November 22, 1891:*** "Stage Notes," "Sam T. Jack's Creole show are playing week stands in the east" (*Topeka Weekly Call*).

• ***November 28, 1891 (Philadelphia, Pennsylvania):*** "Sam T. Jack's Creole Burlesque Company is playing the Central Theatre direct from the Standard Theatre, of New York City. The cast introduces a brilliant array of artists, including the DeWolfe Sisters, Mary Bohee, Jones, Farrell and Borell, Mrs. Sam Lucas, Sam Lucas and many others of equal merit. They go from here to fill a fifteen weeks' engagement on the Pacific coast" (*Indianapolis Freeman*).

• ***December 5, 1891:*** "Leader Orchestra Wanted at Once for Sam T. Jack's Great Creole Co. Must be a Brilliant First Class Leader. Strictly temperate, reliable, steady and capable to arrange . . . We play only one and two weeks' stands in the larger cities. Salary sure weekly but must be moderate. Apply by letter . . . Care Olympic Theatre, Harlem, N.Y. week of Nov. 30; Hyde & Behman, Brooklyn, N.Y., week of Dec. 7" (*New York Clipper*).

• ***January 9, 1892:*** "Florence Briscoe (soubrette), having closed her engagement with Sam T. Jack's Creole Burlesque Co., has joined hands with her old time partner, Ben Hunn, to play dates at the leading vaudeville houses of this country . . . They will put on a new act, entitled 'Hanton Culled Sassiety' " (*New York Clipper*).

• ***February 12, 1892 (Kansas City, Kansas):*** "The Creoles," "May Bohee, the DeWolfe sisters, Rhoda May Brooks, Florence Hines, Marie Valeric, Marie Roberts, Dora Painter and the pseudo-named young ladies—Miles, Stacciopa, Stabole, Delvin, Lylan, Irien, Filliott—and Billy Young, Billy Farrell, Burrill Hawkins, Chas. E. Johnson, Irving Jones, Harry Eaton, Fred Piper, Geo. McGowan, Geo. Williams, Walter Smart, Billy Schott, W. S. Burnett and others—in all about 32 people—are the *ensemble* of Sam T. Jack's Creole Burlesque company, which closed a profitable week's engagement at the Ninth street theatre last week, beginning Sunday, January 31st.

The company as it now stands is a creditable one, but not so good and as variegated as when it was first seen in Kansas City. We now miss the faces of Sam Lucas and wife, Florence Briscoe and 'Hon.' Ben Hunn; and by the absence of Florence Briscoe, that bright, particular and vivacious gem, will be noticed also the absence of the celluloid-collared 'Johnnies,' who swarmed the theatre to see her and no one else. Ben Hunn was a propounder of very ancient jokes, but for all that he was a pronounced favorite and a drawing card. He and Miss Briscoe are now 'doing' variety theatres in joint companionship. Mr. and Mrs. Lucas are sojourning in Providence, R.I., Mrs. Lucas' home. And then, by the by, we (I mean the theatre-going public) miss Heath and DeShattio, very excellent, admirable and finished lightning change and gun-drill artists, who are also conspicuous figures on the variety stage.

Singing and dancing characterizes the ability of Jack's present company of performers. The comedians are *not* above the average. The jokes are all stale and are heard every day by our street gamins and the *canaille* of the slums. The songs—with several exceptions—are moss-covered and were dropped some years ago by the Hyers sisters and Fiske's jubilee singers. Billy Young's recitations are original and acceptable, but old. Dan McCabe, Billy's former partner, is doing an immense business with his minstrels in Havana, Cuba, both financially and entertainingly. Fred Piper has an exquisite and a melodious some kind of a voice and sings descriptive songs in an irreproachable manner. Miss Bohee's warbling is superb, and the DeWolfe sisters' vocal duet exhibitions are far superior to anything of the sort I—and a good many others—have ever heard. Billy Farrell is a good performer as is also Burrill Hawkins, but Burrill should ring off on 'Elegant Barney' and get a new song. Geo. Williams, Geo. McGowan and Walter Smart (late of Taylor and Smart) make a good acrobatic trio. Harry Eaton can hold a chestnut about as long as any comedian I know of. Chestnuts are his 'hobby.' W. S. Burnett has a deep and sure enough bass voice, but its symphoniousness is doubted. Chas. E. Johnson as 'The Black Ward McAllister' is right there and with a little more practice will have Geo. H. Primrose, John Coleman and Barnet Fagen to look to their laurels. Irving Jones is the gallery gods' god and his facial distortions are very much Kersands-like. He would 'take' well in Lawrence, Kansas. Jones is funny 'in spots'—this with an apology to *The New York Clipper*. Marie Roberts and Florence Hines have good voices and sing 'The Picture that is Turned toward the Wall' in the first part with marked effect; and the latter as a male impersonator is perfection itself. Improvement on Florence Hines' part is out of the question. Marie Valerie's wing-dancing is good and her skirt-dance is alright as far as the skirt is concerned. Dora Painter's wing-dancing is equally as good as that of Marie Valerie. Rhoda May Brooks is traveling undoubtedly on her good looks, conversational ability and Venus-like form. The lesser lights, or the 'ornamental fringe,' haven't any particular huge feat to perform. They have huge feet to show in the challenge dancing contest, however.

The show draws well and, of course, coins money. The company is well costumed on and off the stage. They travel in a special car, with cooking and sleeping apartments, and therefore haven't any insults to put up with. Jack's Creoles have been playing for the past six months only week stands, with an occasional drop-off in some one night stand town. He has been more successful with this aggregation of comedians and comediennes than have William Foote with his All Star African Concert company or

W. S. Cleveland with his Colored Carnival minstrels. Cleveland, with Tom McIntosh, Jim Bland, John Brewer and others, didn't coin a red cent during '91, and he dropped 'em.

It seems as though these shows that go abroad expecting to roll on wheels of gold usually strand. For instance: C. E. [*sic*] Hicks and A. D. Sawyer went over to Australia with a minstrel troupe three years ago and half of them didn't get back. Wallace King, Jack Evans, Irving Sayles, Charlie Bruce and others are still there. William Foote's All Star African Concert company went to Germany some months ago and half of them didn't get back. Madame Selika, Geo. Jackson and Frank Broom are eating limburger cheese. Grace Hawthorne went over to London, England, five years ago to play 'Uncle Tom's Cabin' with colored support. Harry Williams, of Cleveland, is speaking 'Hinglish has she is, doncherknow.' The Bohee brothers drifted to Australia from London and are there now. Florence Williams, of New York, who contributed considerably to the New York *Age*, went to the West Indies with a company of singers, but they haven't been heard from.

Sam T. Jack is in the United States of America. And what's he doing? Why rolling on wheels of gold. Has he any imitators? Of course, but no equals. Longevity of life to Sam T. Jack and his Creole Burlesque company!" ("I. McCorker," *Kansas City American Citizen*).

Note: Among those of the Hicks-Sawyer troupe left stranded in Australia, it was noted in the *Freeman* of May 23, 1914, that "Irving Sayles, of the once famous Sayles Brothers . . . who went to Australia with Hicks & Sawyers' Minstrels, several years ago, died recently at New Zealand." Among the refugees from Foote's Afro-American Specialty Company, George Jackson was "seriously wounded" while "playing an engagement in one of the music halls" in Leipzig, Germany, in 1896. According to the July 18, 1896, edition of the *Cleveland Gazette*, Jackson "got into an altercation with an army officer, who had insulted Jackson's wife (white)."

• ***April 16, 1892:*** "Billy Farrell, of Sam T. Jack's Creole Co., has a new specialty, which was put on for the first time in Baltimore. He calls it the leg laying dance" (*New York Clipper*).

• ***April 30, 1892:*** "The following people closed with Sam T. Jack's Creole Co. at Philadelphia April 23: Billy Farrell, Irving Jones, Anthony Byrd, Mrs. Sadie Jones, Wright Deloines, Ella Cole, Ruby Smith and Venie Mason" (*New York Clipper*).

• ***June 4, 1892:*** "Manager Sam T. Jack, surnamed the Invincible, has, it seems, shaken the dust of the road from his feet, and . . . the public . . . will see him now only at his mascot house, the Madison Street Opera House, Chicago, Ill, except semi occasionally, when he will visit his road companies" (*New York Companies*).

For most of the summer of 1893, when traffic at the World's Columbian Exposition in Chicago was at its peak, Sam T. Jack's Creole Burlesque Company was strategically located at Chicago's Madison Street Opera House.

• ***July 8, 1893 (Chicago, Illinois):*** "Madison Street Opera House," "Manager Jack is attracting all the business his house can hold, and is accordingly content. His Creole Burlesquers held attention last week, and will remain for an indefinite period. The olio engages Chas. E. Johnson, Smart and Williams, the De Wolf Sisters, Irving Jones, Billy Farrell, and Mr. and Mrs. Tom McIntosh" (*New York Clipper*).

• ***August 5, 1893:*** "Madison Street Opera House," "Six women from Honolulu, dancing what manager Jack styles the Hullu-Hullu gavotte, are this week added to the drawing powers of his Creole Burlesquers. This will be their first American appearance. The Creoles, who began their sixth week [July] 30, have still an indefinite hold on the stage" (*New York Clipper*).

• ***August 5, 1893 (Chicago, Illinois):*** "Madison Street Opera House," "Manager Jack's Creole Burlesquers, with the Hulu Hulu Dancers and other new features go into their last week [August] 20" (*New York Clipper*).

At the end of their hugely successful World's Fair stand in Chicago, Sam T. Jack's Creole Burlesque Company made a southern tour that stretched through the fall of 1893. Route listings in the *New York Clipper* preserve these dates:

> St. Louis, Missouri, September 10–16; Fort Smith, Arkansas, September 20; Hot Springs, September 21; Pine Bluff, September 22; Little Rock, September 23; Greenville, Mississippi, September 25; Vicksburg, September 26; Jackson, September 27; Natchez, September 28; Monroe, Louisiana, September 29; Shreveport, September 30; Dallas, Texas, October 2; Sherman, October 4; Fort Worth, October 5; Waco, October 6; Austin, October 7; San Antonio, October 9; Columbus, October 10; Brenham, October 11; Houston, October 12; Galveston, October 13–14.

Apparently, the Creoles were in or near Louisville, Kentucky, on November 11, 1893, when Irving Jones "rejoined" with an important new song and dance.

• ***November 25, 1893:*** "Irving Jones rejoined Sam T. Jack's Creole Co. Nov. 11. He is making a success with his new song, entitled 'The Parsamala Dance' " (*New York Clipper*).

Note: This is the earliest known historical marker of the black vernacular dance song known as the "Pas Ma La," a signal indicator of the impending ragtime revolution. As a popular race composer of the late 1890s and early 1900s, Irving Jones demonstrated great skill in ameliorating the coon song genre. As the star comedian of the 1900–1901 edition of Black Patti's Troubadours, Jones was described as "the very best interpreter of the modern ragtime ballad and one of the most accomplished composers of songs of that class."[10] Jones's early compositions were recorded by numerous Race recording artists of the 1920s.[11]

• ***December 2, 1893:*** "Bob Cole has joined Sam T. Jack's Creole Co" (*New York Clipper*).

Note: Bob Cole may have been the most important performer to come through the ranks of Sam T. Jack's Creoles. In 1898 Cole and then-partner Billy Johnson produced and starred in "A Trip to Coontown," which was, in critic Sylvester Russell's opinion, "the first modern legitimate Negro musical comedy ever produced in America."[12] James Weldon Johnson agreed it was "the first Negro show to make a complete break from the minstrel pattern, the first that was not a mere potpourri, the first to be written with continuity and to have a cast of characters working out the story of a plot from beginning to end; and therefore, the first Negro comedy."[13] In 1901 Bob Cole took James Weldon Johnson's younger brother, J. Rosamond Johnson, for his new stage partner, and they coproduced two "true operettas," "The Shoofly Regiment" (1906) and "The Red Moon" (1908), and coauthored such enduring song hits as "Oh, Didn't He Ramble," "Congo Love Song," "My Castle on the Nile," and "Under the Bamboo Tree." Cole's life ended tragically on August 2, 1911, when he walked into a creek in Catskill, New York, and was drowned: "It is believed his act was deliberate, for he had been ill and despondent recently."[14]

• ***December 9, 1893 (New York City):*** "London Theatre," "Sam T. Jack's Creole Co. opened to good houses on Monday, Dec. 4. The attraction is composed mostly of a collection of dusky hued beauties, who at the rise of the curtain are scattered about the stage in picturesque poses . . . The usual end gags and songs are introduced by the eight end men . . . The olio is a good one. First on the bill were the Mallory Brothers, singers and dancers . . . The De Wolff Sisters, singers, came next, and rendered some popular ballads in good voice. A combination march, ballet and combat was then presented . . . 'The Porter's Dream,' a picture of the South, was applauded. Irving Jones, in a single comedy act, raised much laughter. His turn is followed by another march and a gavotte. Smith and Johnson, in banjo songs and dances, are next, and 'Aunt Jane's Wooden Wedding,' incidental to which the dancing contest is introduced, concludes the show" (*New York Clipper*).

• ***December 9, 1893:*** "Notes from Sam T. Jack's La Belle Creole Burlesque Co," "Among the leading features with this company are Alex. May, in his original creation of Little Shortly, in 'Aunt Jane's Wooden Wedding,' in which he is said to score a hit everywhere. The other stellar attractions are Irving Jones, in his Posmala Dance; the Mallory Bros., in their mandolin songs and dances and musical melange; Bob Cole, descriptive vocalist; the De Wolfe Sisters, in vocal duets; Smith and Johnson, banjoists, etc.; Chas. E. Johnson, the London swell; Fatima, the Midway Plaisance danseuse, and 'Simply' Doc Sayles, the comedian" (*New York Clipper*).

• ***December 30, 1893:*** "Variety and Minstrelsy," "Charles E. Johnson and Bob Cole will soon be seen in their new act, 'Colored Aristocracy,' with Sam T. Jack's Creole Co. Cole won the silver plate at the 'Creole ball' in Boston, Mass., defeating fifteen other buck dancers" (*New York Clipper*).

• ***March 17, 1894:*** "Chas. E. Johnson and wife, of Sam T. Jack's Creole Co., are doing a new grotesque song and dance" (*New York Clipper*).

Note: Charles E. Johnson and his wife, Dora Dean, became the Creole Company's particular cake-walking stars. Dora Dean was originally from Indianapolis, and according to one report, her given name was Luella Babbage.[15] By all accounts stunningly beautiful, she was idolized in an early Williams and Walker song that took her stage name for its title.[16] From Sam T. Jack's Creole Company, the team of Johnson and Dean went on to an incredibly long and successful international career. News came from Germany in 1902 that "Ernst Hellman, one of Germany's foremost artists, has finished a life-size painting of Dora Dean . . . posed in a cake walk attitude. The picture will be hung in the spring exhibit of the German Academy. Miss Dean is the first colored woman to be honored with a sitting by a European artist. She with her husband . . . initiated the German public into the peculiar poetry and motion of the American 'coon song.' "[17] A late 1930s newspaper ad proclaims, "After 50 Years, Johnson & Dean Still Going Strong . . . The first act of its kind to appear at Carnegie Hall, New York, Nov. 27, 1937. They introduced popular songs, did their old fashioned Cake Walk, climaxing with Truckin, Souzie Que and the Boogie Woogie that absolutely rocked Carnegie Hall."[18]

• ***April 7, 1894:*** "The Mallory Bros. are said to be meeting with success in their imitation of a colored brass band, with Sam T. Jack's Creole Co" (*New York Clipper*).

• ***July 28, 1894:*** "Walter Smart, late of Smart and Williams, has joined Bob Coles [*sic*]. The team has signed with Sam T. Jack's Creole Co" (*New York Clipper*).

For the season of 1894–1895, Sam T. Jack leased the Creole Company to his advance agent John W. Isham.

• ***July 28, 1894:*** "Creole Show Notes," "Sam T. Jack's Creole Co., under lease to John W. Isham, will open the season Aug. 19, at Sam T. Jack's Opera House, Chicago, Ill. Many new features added during the vacation are calculated to strengthen the hold this attraction has on the popular fancy. A number of pretty and talented performers have been recently engaged, and they will appear in entirely new and original acts, including a series of sensational terpischorean features never before presented. Manager Jack has stipulated that the entertainment of the

Creole Co. shall be kept up to the high standard of excellence already attained... A number of perfect models have been engaged especially for the presentation of living pictures. The company is pretty well booked up with week stands, and, after a two week's engagement in Chicago, will embark on an extended tour of the United States and Canada" (*New York Clipper*).

• ***August 11, 1894:*** "Creole Show Notes," "John W. Isham, manager Sam T. Jack's Creole Co., has just rehearsed a new first part, which is calculated to prove the feature of that company's entertainment next season. The scenery is of handsome design, representing a picturesque tropical scene, and introducing the ladies of the company in entirely new costumes, patterned after the soft, diaphanous raiment worn by the natives of the tropics, securing perfect freedom of movement. In this connection, Mr. Isham, among other dances, will introduce 'The Moonlight Minuet,' with an efficient *corps de ballet*, and all the mechanical and scenic effects calculated to insure success. 'The Moonlight Minuet,' which has never been presented on any stage, is a dance of joy, supposed to celebrate the close of the wet season in the tropical or equatorial latitude, in which the natives are said to indulge with an abandon of which the average terpischorean artist is seldom capable, and yet with a grace that is entrancing. This dance, for which the surroundings of the new first part are peculiarly adapted, Mr. Isham believes will take its place among the sensational terpischorean diversions of the day" (*New York Clipper*).

• ***August 18, 1894:*** "Roster of Sam T. Jack's Creole Co..... Tom McIntosh and wife, Irving Jones, Tom Brown, 'Doc' Sayles, Mallory Bros., Alex. May, George Williams, Charles G. Johnson [*sic*], [Walter] Smart and [Bob] Cole, Harry Singleton and wife, Belle Davis, Dora Dean, Sadie Jerry, Viola Jones, Marie Roberts, Stella Wiley, Kitty Brown, Mattie Wilkes, Nellie Williams, Merrill Hursh, Maggie Brooks, Annie Ross, Rose Harper, Annie Smith, Mlle. Annette D'Yone, Mlle. Marie D'Este and Mlle. Alicia Favette" (*New York Clipper*).

• ***August 25, 1894 (Chicago, Illinois):*** "Sam T. Jack's Opera House," "Sam T. Jack's Creole Burlesque Co. opened the season and began their tour [August] 18. The house was filled completely... Chas. E. and Dora Johnson, Geo. Williams and Alex May, Belle Davis, the Mallory Brothers, Walter Smart and Bob Cole, Irving Jones [and] Mr. and Mrs. Tom McIntosh provided the olio numbers, which followed the opening burlesque and found an ending in a series of a dozen living pictures" (*New York Clipper*).

• ***December 8, 1894:*** "Notes from Sam T. Jack's Creole Co.," "Our route for week of Nov. 19 was: Flint [Michigan] 19, Pontiac 20, London [Ontario, Canada] 21, 22, Brantford 23, St. Catherines 24... The impression the company made in this somewhat doubtful and puritanical territory is strong evidence of its faultless entertainment. Week of Nov. 26 they played the Academy of Music, Toronto. The company has been out fifteen weeks under Mr. Isham's management and has not had one losing week" (*New York Clipper*).

• ***January 12, 1895:*** "Notes from Jack's Creole Co.," "Among the new features recently added to this company is a novel dance, entitled 'La Danse Electrique,' in which the native belles, attired in rich and fascinating costumes, disport themselves in 'Under the Mistletoe Bough.' Credit is due the Mallory Bros. for 'La Danse Electrique.' The company played three performances at the Palace Theatre, Boston, Dec. 31, including a midnight matinee, to very satisfactory houses" (*New York Clipper*).

On April 27, 1895, shortly after the Creole Burlesque Company closed its touring season, Sam T. Jack announced through the *Clipper* that

John W. Isham would "in no way be connected" with future editions the company. The following week's *Clipper* broadcast the fact that Isham was putting out a Creole Company of his own.

• ***May 4, 1895:*** "Isham's Creole Opera Notes," "John W. Isham's Creole Opera Co., a new aspirant for public favor, will open its season in New York, Aug. 24. The organization will be made up of colored people. Mr. Isham promises to present an entertainment that will be, in every sense of the word, a new departure" (*New York Clipper*).

According to one retrospective account, Isham had "obtained the right and title to Sam T. Jack's Creole Company, under royalty."[19] Contemporaneous reports suggest something more on the order of a coup d'etat, in which Isham absconded with Jack's original name and concept, plus half of his top performers, including the Mallory Brothers, Belle Davis, Mattie Wilkes, Tom Brown, and Tom McIntosh. Apparently, a struggle ensued between Jack and Isham over rights to the "Creole" trademark; finally, Isham informed, in the May 18, 1895, edition of the *Clipper,* that, "Owing to the number of inferior companies under the title, 'Creole,' I have decided to call my new organization John W. Isham's 'Royal Octoroons.' "

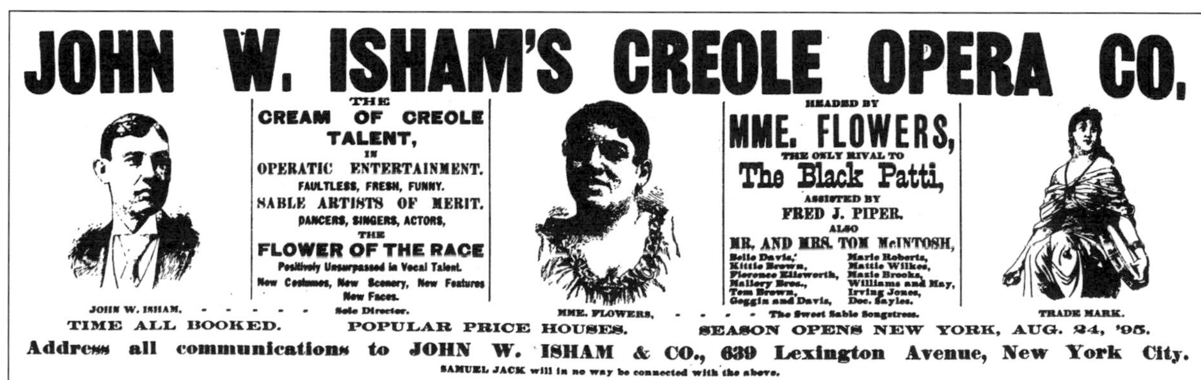

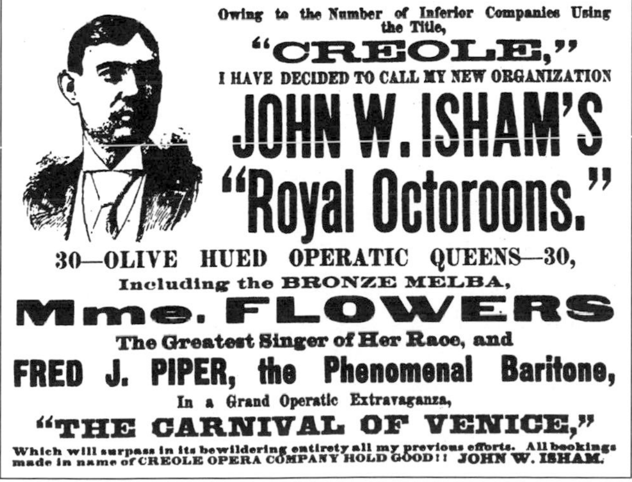

Isham's Creole Opera Co., New York Clipper, *May 4, 1895.*
Isham's Royal Octoroons, New York Clipper, *May 18, 1895.*

• ***August 17, 1895:*** "Notes from Isham's Octoroons," "The engagements for this company are now complete and include: Madame Flowers, Fred J. Piper, Mr. and Mrs. Tom McIntosh, Madah Hyers, Mattie Wilkes, Mallory Bros., Tom Brown, Belle Davis . . . Billy Johnson . . . The season will open at the Olympic Theatre [New York City], Aug. 24" (*New York Clipper*).

• ***December 14, 1895 (Cleveland, Ohio):*** "The 'Octoroons'," "Isham's Octoroon Company at the Star this week is by all odds the very best show of its class that has ever come to Cleveland. . . . The musical act of the well known dancers and comedians, the Mallory Brothers, was fine and thoroughly up to date . . . The 'Twentieth Century Swells,' Brown, May and Furber's 'The Dago and the Monkeys' and 'The Spanish Serenade and Ballet' acts were thoroughly novel . . . Johnson and Shipp, conscientious descriptive vocalists, win their audiences almost instantly. Tuesday evening they were attacked by a crazy fellow (white) who climbed upon the stage from the audience. He was jailed, and promptly, too. Shipp broke a cane over his head . . . Tom McIntosh and wife . . . keep the house in a continual uproar of laughter . . . Tom is funnier than ever and his mouth seems if anything larger. As vocalists of superior ability, the Misses Hyer, Mattie Wilkes, Belle Davis, Mamie Roberts, Mazie Brooks and Fred Piper need no extended mention. With the company chorus . . . Madame Flower and the ladies and gentlemen named simply astonished the audience in their selections from the operas, 'Cavaleria Rustanica,' 'Travatore,' 'Bohemian Girl,' 'Erminie' and 'Princess Bonnie.' The 'Red Hussar' march and chorus, like everything else, was indeed fine" (*Cleveland Gazette*).

Note: Jesse A. Shipp went on to become a conspicuous contributor to the famous Williams and Walker Company productions of the early 1900s.

• ***December 21, 1895 (New York City):*** "London Theatre," "John W. Isham's Octoroons made their first appearance on the Bowery, to crowded houses, Monday afternoon and evening, Dec. 16. The company had been widely heralded as an unusually strong aggregation of talent from the colored profession, and the unanimous verdict accorded them was 'a great show.' The singing part of the programme is exceptionally harmonious, the chorus, composed of many attractive dusky belles and beaux, being well trained. 'The Blackville Derby' opens the performance. It shows life at a race track in many amusing ways. The incidental songs and choruses are cleverly arranged and executed. Frank Mallory, Billy Johnson, Shortly May, Ed. Furber, Fred L. Piper, Ed. Mallory, Tom Brown, Tom McIntosh, Florence Ellsworth, Willie Ford, James A. Gross, Wm. Sheers, Edward Walters, Louis [*sic*] Hyer, Alice Mackey, Belle King, Mamie Stella Dorsey and Musette Fisher took part, Frank Mallory, the Holiday [*sic*] Sisters, Tom McIntosh, Mazie Brooks, Billy Johnson and Mrs. Tom McIntosh contributing solos and a duet. 'Rehearsing for the Coon's Cake Walk,' a character song, introduced by the entire company, was prettily rendered and repeatedly encored. The specialties followed. First on the list was Maude Hyers, singer. The Mallory Brothers followed in their singing and dancing entertainment. The Twentieth Century Swells, a character specialty, showed novel costumes with pretty electrical effects. Tom Brown, Shortly May and Ed. Furber, as 'The Dago and the Monk,' executed many funny antics and danced well. A Spanish serenade, with mandolin and guitar accompaniment, was put on with good effect. Johnson and Shipp, character vocalists, portrayed peculiar scenes and incidents. Mr. and Mrs. Tom McIntosh, the well known team of entertainers, gained well merited applause by their clever work and musical selections.

A novel entertainment entitled 'Thirty Minutes Around the Opera,' closed the show. The central figure of this part of the programme was, of course, Madame Flower, whose fine voice filled the auditorium and created unbounded pleasure among her hearers. Fred J. Piper, in duets with Mme. Flower and in his solos, was also applauded. The principal solos and choruses from several popular operas were well rendered, the tower scene from 'Il Travatore' being the *piece de resistance*, and being boisterously redemanded. 'Cavalleria Rusticana,' 'Bohemian Girl,' 'Red Hussar,' 'Diletto' and 'Erminie' were drawn on for vocal effects with success. The scenes were artistically reproduced, the costumes were handsome, and the entire production deserves unstinted praise" (*New York Clipper*).

Note: Among the members of the 1895–1896 edition of Isham's Octoroons, Mazie Brooks married Ed Mallory, and Gracie Halliday, one of the Holiday Sisters, married Frank Mallory. Both spouses became valuable additions to the Mallory Brothers' "musical melange," Mazie as a harpist and Gracie as a singer and violinist. When Gracie Halliday died in 1906, it was noted that she had studied violin under New Orleans' legendary music professor William Nickerson.[20]

While Isham's Octoroons continued to captivate the most discriminating big city audiences, Sam T. Jack's Creole Burlesque Company opened its 1895–1896 touring season on August 24, 1895, at the Madison Street Opera House in Chicago, under Jack's exclusive management. With Irving Jones, Doc Sayles, Bob Cole, Stella Wiley, Dora Dean, and others returning to the fold, and with newcomers like "Jube" Johnson added to the mix, the roster was at least as strong as before Isham's defection.

• ***August 24, 1895:*** "Roster of Sam T. Jack's Creole Co.—May Bohee, Florence Hines, Kitty Brown, Madge Darlington, Mlle. Sanchez, Vi Jones, Laura Hilton, Sadie Terry, Mlle. Theodora, Connie Anthony, Marie Irvine, Emma St. John, Lizzie Scott, Madge Kyle, Glassy Monroe, Clara Ford, Gertrude Baxter, Lou Donaldson, Bertie Golden, Dora Dean, Stella Wiley, Bertie Allen, Annie Ross, Pauline Preston, Maggie Louise Johnson, Mamie Parson, Henrietta Clay, Maggie Kelley, Dorothy Blackburn, Hattie Betta, Chas. Hunn, Irving Jones, Chas. E. Johnson, Bob Cole, Walter Smart, Wm. Hersey, Doc Sayles, Wm. Gauze, Geo. Williams, Julius ["Jube"] Johnson, Smith and Johnson and Goggin and Davis" (*New York Clipper*).

• ***September 21, 1895 (New York City):*** "London Theatre," "Sam T. Jack's Creole Company opened to midsummer audiences afternoon and evening of Sept. 23. The sable hued performers present an interesting programme. The curtain rises on the usual first part tableau, after a preliminary chorus . . . The olio presents Smith and Johnson in banjo variations; Williams and Jones, comedians; Florence Hines, impersonations; Cole and Wiley, duettists and dancers, and Goggin and Davis. 'Under the Weeping Willows,' a series of medleys and marches, was applauded. 'The Southern Sunset,' with buck dancing accompaniment and a cake walk, concluded the performance" (*New York Clipper*).

• ***November 9, 1895:*** "Bob Cole and Stella Wiley are doing their new dancing specialty with Sam T. Jack's Creole Co" (*New York Clipper*).

• ***November 23, 1895:*** "The week's business in Rochester, N.Y. was big . . . On Saturday night, and during the first part, Wm. Hersey was married to Lottie Bell, of Binghamton, and the marriage was witnessed by the audience. The regular Creolean marriage ceremony was performed. The affair of the week, however was the celebration of the birthday of Doc Sayles, who on [November] 16 was forty-one years old . . . Every member of the company was present on the occasion, including Cole and Wiley . . . Irving

Jones and wife . . . Jube Johnson [and others] . . . Bob Cole was spokesman, and in his pleasant mood caused the affair to be the grandest treat of the season" (*New York Clipper*).

The Creole Burlesque Company was still on the road when Sam T. Jack died in 1899. During its first four years of existence, 1891–1895, the Creole Company had given rise to some of the greatest black stars of the era—Irving Jones, Bob Cole, Dora Dean, etc.. Among the Creole Company's less remembered veterans were Ed and Frank Mallory. The Mallory Brothers had been professionally active since 1881.[21] On the strength of their "mandolin songs and dances and musical melange," they rode the crest of African American minstrelsy throughout the 1890–1895 period: from Richards and Pringle's Georgia Minstrels, seasons of 1890–1891 and 1891–1892, to W. A. Mahara's Minstrels, season of 1892–1893; Sam T. Jack's Creoles, seasons of 1893–1894 and 1894–1895; and Isham's Octoroons, season of 1895–1896.

The Mallory Brothers crossed into the twentieth century as members of the celebrated

Mallory Brothers' Concert Orchestra, Jacksonville, Ill.
Ready for all occasions—Church, Socials, Weddings or Special Engagements. Orders filled promptly.
Front row, reading from left to right: Frank Mallory, Ida McC ee, Edward Mallory.
Standing: C. H. Burghardt Mazie Mallory, Bertha Mallory, Ollie Mack, Wm. Cooper.

Freeman, *March 16, 1912.*

Williams and Walker Company, to which they contributed "a great song entitled, 'Coon Blood is Bound to Show.'"[22] They spent the remainder of their career in "high-class vaudeville." Struck by their remarkable versatility, a mainstream newspaper reporter noted in 1902: "They are good singers and lively dancers, but their principal charm is their inherent Southern power to conjure melody. The harp, piano, staff, hand and chime bells are played with telling effect... Comedy brightens without detracting, and their imitation of a colored brass band, in which every one is a leader, and depiction of a nocturnal raid upon a chicken coop by darkies, is a gem of pantomimic and musical comedy."[23]

The "imitation of a colored brass band, in which every one is a leader" had been one of the Mallory Brothers' features with the Creole Company back in 1894. The intention, it seems, was to mimic the raucous polyphony of a stereotypical nineteenth-century black community brass band.

It was announced in the *Freeman* in 1907 that, "After twenty-five years of success on the stage, the Mallory brothers have quit the road and gone into the real estate and loan business at their home, Jacksonville, Ill."[24] Apparently, they were as successful in business as they had been on the stage; in 1913 "the once famous theatrical team" was invited by Booker T. Washington to "make a talk" at a National Negro Business League convention in Philadelphia.[25] With their road-show years behind them, the Mallory Brothers and their wives maintained a community orchestra that proclaimed itself "Ready for all occasions." Frank Mallory died in 1917.[26]

Developments in "authentic" black minstrelsy during 1891 reflect real advancements. However, the gathering energies of a new, all-inclusive African American minstrelsy wouldn't culminate until the emergence of popular ragtime, a half-decade later. In retrospect, 1891 might be seen as a year in which the stage was set for the

A LIFE SKETCH OF THE MALLORY BROS.

The life of a nation or of a race is, for the most part, but the composite history of the individuals making that nation or race. The Negro race is really just beginning to make its history and at this stage of racial development, the record of each individual is of paramount interest. Too often it happens that

"Full many a gem of purest rays serene
The unfathomed depths of ocean bear;
Full many a flower is born to blush unseen
And waste its sweetness on the desert air,"

and many of our people, whose lives and achievements would prove a stimulus and an intentive to greater effort on the part of the younger members of the race, live in obscurity and are unknown. However, from such as come under our observation we may learn a lesson, and if we are "wise in our day and generation" we will profit by the same.

With just this purpose in view it gives us much pleasure to set forth the almost spectacular career of the "Mallory Bros." of recent theatrical fame.

These two young men (and they are still young men) took their first engagement "on the road" with Hastings Missouri Minstrels when they were mere lads. This engagement, which was secured for them through the kindness of the late George Tichner, a one-time minstrel favorite, lasted just two weeks and they had gone as far as Albia, Ia., when the company went to pieces and they were left to get back home in the best manner possible. As a matter of fact the salary received for this engagement was "nil."

Not discouraged by the disastrous failure of their first engagement they soon secured another place. This time they were booked with "Lew Johnson's King Laugh Makers," which engagement lasted through half a season and for this work the team received $7.00 per week. From this on, their advance in their profession was steady, both as to quality of the companies with which they traveled and the salary received by them. As "song and dance artists" and "end men" they filled engagements lasting from one to several seasons with the following companies: Richard and Pringle, Georgia Minstrels, Mallory Bros., "Crombraugh Minstrels, Billy Kersand's Minstrels, Hicks and Sawyer, Mahara Minstrels, Callander's Minstrels and Halliday's Minstrels.

There are few of the theater-loving world who are unfamiliar with the reputation of these "boys" in this work. Leaving this line and taking up music more particularly they filled engagements with Sam T. Jack's Creoles, Isham's Octoroons, Williams & Walker Co. and the Fenberg Stock Company (white). At this time they, with Miss Mazy Brooks, formed a musical team known as Mallory Bros. and Brooks, and entered the field of polite vaudeville. Miss Brooks afterwards became Mrs. Ed. Mallory and Frank Mallory married the late Miss Gracie Halliday and the organization became Mallory Bros., Brooks and Halliday.

The music given to the public by these people was of an exceptionally high class kind and was far above the average produced by similar teams. The name of Mallory Bros. on the bill board was ever a drawing attraction and when their number on the program was reached, the habitue of the theatre settled himself in his seat to enjoy a real musical treat, nor was he disappointed in his expectations.

In this capacity these men played practically all the largest vaudeville houses in the country, viz.: Hammerstein's and the following circuits: Proctor's, Keith's and Williams. They played in thirty-seven different theaters in Greater New York City alone, which record, we believe, has not been made by any other Negro team.

The crowning of all their efforts was to have been a tour through Europe, where we have no doubt their reception would have been as enthusiastic as it had been in their own country; and to this end contracts were signed and arrangements completed, but this pleasure was denied them, as they were forced to cancel the engagement because of the illness of Mrs. Frank Mallory, nee Gracie Halliday.

It had been their intention to retire from the show business at the close of their European engagement and to enter the mercantile world. As has been said they were compelled, on account of sickness, to return home earlier than they had expected to do, but they at once began to cast about for a suitable mercantile business in which to embark.

At least after much discussion, as their capital was small, they rented a room on the second floor of a business block in this city and opened a small stock of mens and womens second hand clothing, the value of which was $350. From this beginning after a period of seven years their stock covers the whole of two floors in a large building and they handle everything from stoves to diamonds. Their watchword is "buy everything, have everything, sell everything."

Financially these men have been no less successful than along other lines. In their theatrical changes and rise their salaries increased from $7 per week to $250 per week. In the mercantile business their small stock valued at $350 in a rented room on the second floor, has in seven years increased in value to $5,000. They own the building in which their business is housed and the value of this building is $8,000.

These men were two boys in a family of ten children, and while yet but mere lads the question was how could they best help father and mother at home. It was decided they would assume the responsibility of paying the house rent. The writer boasts of an almost lifelong intimate acquaintance with this family and it is her certain knowledge that that father and mother had paid their last house rent.

Not long after this the boys learned to dislike the "paying rent" idea and decided they would buy a house and lot which would serve the double purpose of making a home for father and mother and giving greater independence in their own work by making them less afraid of being "fired" (which event we are glad to say never happened.) It was not long before other pieces of property were added to this one and today the aggregate value of their residential property is $6,500. In addition to this they own their own automobile and have a modest balance in one of the largest banks of the city.

They are the organizers of the Local Business League and are members of the national body. They take an active part in all things religious and secular, civic and social, in the life of their city and their race. They are prominent members of the Knights of Pythias.

Neither of these men boasts a college or even a high school diploma, but their natural ability, aided by sterling worth and unswerving integrity, has won for them fame in their professional world, has made them an important factor in the business and civic life of their home town, and has gained for them an enviable reputation among both white and black as men of solid character and a credit to their race.

Freeman, *December 26, 1914.*

monumental ragtime minstrelsy of the late 1890s. When ragtime did appear, the apparatus for its full professional exploitation was firmly in place, as were many vernacular motifs and practices that connected the nineteenth and twentieth centuries by providing the basic vocabulary of blues, jazz, and gospel music.

Compromises in Jubilee Singing: Thearle's Nashville Students, Wright's Nashville Students, and the Canadian Jubilee Singers

The swelling popularity of authentic Afro-American minstrelsy led to a pronounced shift in the constitution of professional African American jubilee troupes of the 1890s. With a few notable exceptions, itinerant concert companies of vocalists who made jubilee choruses the centerpiece of their entertainment were rapidly becoming a thing of the past. The demand for variety dictated a different approach.

The Nashville Students

It was reported in the December 7, 1889, edition of the *Indianapolis Freeman:* "There are two companies of Nashville Students now on the road, and both travelling in the state of Missouri." The two companies were H. B. Thearle's Original Nashville Students and P. T. Wright's Nashville Students. Neither company was comprised of students; nor did they have any known connection to Nashville. The "Nashville Students" cognomen was intended to reflect the spirit of Fisk University and "the Original Jubilee Singing." Before the end of the century, however, a different spirit would prevail.

Thearle's Nashville Students were an "old style" jubilee troupe, a concert company, organized in 1878. During their 1883–1884 season, Thearle's Nashville Students reportedly traveled "from Maine to California" under the exclusive agency of the prestigious Redpath Lyceum Bureau. At that time, H. B. Thearle credited the success of his Nashville Students to their capacity for "retaining the old Southern style, and giving a truthful representation of the negro as he appeared in the days of slavery."[27] The daily *Louisville Courier Journal* of March 21, 1886, notified that Thearle's Nashville Jubilee Singers sang "jubilee songs, plantation melodies, and a few concert pieces of the ordinary class of music. They have cultivated voices and claim to represent the characteristic music of the negroes of the South. It is not a minstrel company, but a concert company, and their work is valuable, not only for the pleasure it gives, but as a record of a people whose former characteristics are fast dying away. At each entertainment a musical sketch will be given, introducing the company in plantation characters."

Thearle's Nashville Students made at least one early concession to "variety," a dramatic sketch in rustic plantation garb—overalls, calico dresses, and bandannas. In 1886 they produced a "Musical Sketch" titled "Rasper's Birthday, or the 'Possum Supper."[28] A printed program for the season of 1890–1891 indicates they were performing another skit, titled "The Exodusters," in costumes.

Harry B. Thearle, the white proprietor of Thearle's Original Nashville Students, was an all-around entertainment businessman. By 1890 he was, in addition to fielding the Nashville Students, running a theater in Chicago and managing British entrepreneur James Pain's "Pyrotechnic Spectacles," fiery outdoor stage extravaganzas in the guise of historical reenactments, such as "The Seige of Sebastopol," "A Night in Pekin," and "The Storming of Vicksburg."[29]

• ***July 6, 1889:*** "H. B. Thearle, of Chicago, will shortly take out the Original Nashville Students for their eleventh consecutive season. Manager Thearle will also open one of the finest little theatres in the West at Englewood (Chicago), New Year's Eve" (*New York Clipper*).

• ***October 25, 1890 (Cleveland, Ohio):*** "Thearle's original Nashville Students will appear at Case Hall November 1. The company of first class vocalists among the number being Miss Cora Lee Watson, formerly of Cincinnati, and Prof. Z. A. Coleman, a few months ago a resident of this city" (*Cleveland Gazette*).

• ***November 1, 1890:*** "Thearle's Original Nashville Students . . . appear in Case Hall tonight. Joe Hagerman, the 'Lion Basso' is also with this organization. They sing the plantation songs just as they are sung in the South at camp meetings, etc. . . . Go and hear them sing 'Inching Along,' 'You Rock When I Rock,' and other songs. They appear 'in costume' in the second part" (*Cleveland Gazette*).

• ***November 8, 1890 (Cleveland, Ohio):*** "Thearle's Nashville Students drew a large audience to Case hall. Among those in attendance was Mr. Fred Loudin . . . who came all the way from Toledo to hear them" (*Cleveland Gazette*).

• ***November 29, 1890 (Cincinnati, Ohio):*** "The Nashville Students Jubilee Singers sang in this city on last Saturday at the Odeon. A large audience greeted them. The company is composed of the following: Cora L. Watson, Miss Clara Bell Carey, Mr. and Mrs. William Carter, Miss Gertie Heathcock, Joseph Hagerman and John M. Lewis" (*Cleveland Gazette*).

In the fall of 1892 the *Cleveland Gazette* announced that Thearle's star basso, Joseph Hagerman, had formed a new company in partnership with baritone Ollie C. Hall.[30] At this point, Harry Thearle appears to have turned the bulk of his attention to white acts connected to his theater enterprise.[31] In the late 1890s the

TO-NIGHT'S PROGRAMME

- - AS RENDERED BY - -

THEARLE'S

Original Nashville Students

12th Season.

H. B. THEARLE, Proprietor, CHICAGO, ILL.

H. K. McLELLAN .... MANAGER
MILTON GUNCKEL .... BUSINESS REPRESENTATIVE

NOTE.—The members of this company are trained vocalists, capable of rendering in an artistic manner the most difficult and exacting music, but they confine themselves in their public concerts to the music of their race, making a specialty of Camp Meeting, Cabin and Plantation Songs.

PROGRAMME

PART I.

Piano Solo .... Mrs. Carter
Opening Chorus .... Nashville Students
"Jubilee Greeting" .... Miss Gertie Heathcock
"Jolly Times" .... Fred. T. Carey
Melody (selected) .... Miss Cora L. Watson
"Dar's a Jubilee" .... Miss Clara Bell Carey
Bass Solo (as requested) .... J. A. Hagerman
"Ding Dong Bells" .... John M. Lewis
"De Massa Ob De Sheepfol" .... William Carter
"Swing Dem Gates Ajar" .... J. A. Hagerman
"Gospel Train's Arrival" .... Miss Heathcock and Company

PART II.

Nashville Male Quartette .... (2n Selections)
Soprano Solo (selected) .... Miss Cora L. Watson
Fred. T. Carey .... (In his Album of Vocal Gems)
Tenor Solo (selected) .... J. M. Lewis
Miss Clara Bell Carey, the Nashville Nightingale .... (In Selections)
Baritone Solo (selected) .... W. Carter
"The Exodusters" (Duet in Costumes) .... Miss Gertie Heathcock and J. A. Hagerman

PART III.

"Good-Bye My Honey, I'm Gone" .... Fred. T. Carey
"Daniel Saw the Stone Roll" .... W. Carter
"The Christmas Dinner" .... Miss Clara Bell Carey
"Pick Up De Young Lambs" .... Miss Gertie Heathcock
Jubilee Song (selected) .... Miss Cora L. Watson
"We Got a Debt for to Pay" .... J. A. Hagerman
"Day Light's A Breaking" .... John M. Lewis
"The Salvation Army" .... By Company

During the first intermission, Song Books containing Words and Music to the most popular Jubilee Melodies will be offered for sale. Price 15 cts. each, or two for 25 cts.

For Terms and Dates for Concerts by this Company, apply to H. B. THEARLE, 524 Pullman Building, Chicago.

"Programme," Thearle's Original Nashville Students, n.d. (courtesy Fisk University Library, Special Collections)

name "Thearle's Nashville Students" surfaced again.[32] Chicago-based *Freeman* critic "Tom the Tattler" noted in his column of July 28, 1900, that "Thearle's Nashville Students returned to [Chicago] last Sunday, after a trip covering nearly a year, in which time they sniffed the briny breezes of. . . the Pacific."

The other company of Nashville Students, P. T. Wright's Nashville Students, was reportedly organized in 1888,[33] but by 1892 they were claiming a nineteen-year continuous history, seemingly attaching themselves to the heritage of the Fisk University Jubilee Singers. However, P. T. Wright's Nashville Students wasn't a jubilee company; it was a minstrel-variety show. Before the end of 1891 Wright's Nashville Students added a band and orchestra to their roster.

P. T. Wright, the African American proprietor of this talented, financially successful company, was born in Mexico, Missouri, and raised in McComb, Illinois, but was living in Kansas City when he organized his Nashville Students.

• ***September 13, 1890:*** "The Nashville Students comprise the following people under the management of P. T. Wright: Willard Smith, Charles Johnson, John Pomplin [*sic*, Pamplin], Mamie Andrews, Maggie Peterson, John Owens, Mrs. P. T. Wright, Cordelia Scott, C. B. Estes and Bradley Bros" (*New York Clipper*).

• ***May 9, 1891:*** "The Nashville Students, under the management of P. T. Wright, will not close this Summer, but will tour Michigan, Minnesota and Dakota. Billy Johnson joined at Sterling, Ill. Mme. Pauline King has also joined" (*New York Clipper*).

• ***June 20, 1891:*** "Wright's Nashville Students will close a prosperous forty-four weeks' season at Excelsior Springs, Mo., June 27, and will only lay off about six weeks at Kansas City" (*New York Clipper*).

• ***July 24, 1891 (Kansas City, Missouri):*** "Mr. P. T. Wright, the successful manager of the Nashville University Concert Troop is engaged in organizing for his fourth annual tour. Mr. Wright probably stands at the column of Negro concert managers, having made his effort successful in both a financial and a musical sense. He is ably assisted in the work by his accomplished wife. He is desirous of securing for the company a lady who is a soprano soloist, any one fitted for such work will do well to address P. T. Wright, 1733 Tracy avenue, Kansas City, Mo." (*Kansas City American Citizen*).

• ***August 22, 1891:*** "The Nashville University Students and P. S. [*sic*] Wright's Colored Concert Co., with brass band and orchestra, open Aug. 29 at Lee's Summit, Mo. The roster: P. S. Wright, manager and proprietor; Will J. Smith, advance representative; Billy McClain, Willard Smith, John Pamplin, Ida Delyour, Mamie Vaughn, Mrs. P. S. Wright, Prof. J. W. Bohanon, leader of band and orchestra; Baxter Reynolds, Albert Brown and Fred Ford" (*New York Clipper*).

• ***September 26, 1891:*** "The old and original Nashville University students and P. T. Wright's Grand Colored Concert Company were enroute September 13:

> Brunswick, Missouri: September 21, 1891
> Miami, Missouri: September 22, 1891
> Norborne, Missouri: September 23, 1891
> Harding, Missouri: September 24, 1891
> Camden, Missouri: September 25, 1891
> Liberty, Missouri: September 25, 1891
> Kansas City, Missouri: September 26, 1891

Personnel of Company: Billy Johnson, stick dancer; Mlle. Pauline King, leading soprano; Ed Harris, specialist + banjoist; Miss Josie Anderson, old woman impersonator; Jeff. Davis, comedian; Mrs. P. T. Wright, contralto; Prof. John Owens, Musical Director; Master Albert Brown, slack wire performer and juggler; Will J. Smith, business mgr." (*Indianapolis Freeman*).

• ***November 14, 1891:*** "Goggin and Davis, formerly of the Electric Three, are now doing their act in white face, with Wright's Nashville Students" (*New York Clipper*).

• ***February 27, 1892:*** "Reached the top at last. Wright's Nashville Students and Grand Colored Concert Co., with Uniform Brass Band breaks the record. 29 nights in Nebraska to the biggest business ever done by a colored company... Standing room only at every town. Managers in Kansas write for us if you want to fill your houses" (*New York Clipper*).

• ***February 27, 1892:*** "Roster of Wright's Nashville Students: P. T. Wright, manager; Joe Becker, business agent; J. Bohannon, leader of band; Jas. White, Billy Cook, Mamie Gadie Rodgers, Vaughn Sisters, Baxter Reynolds, John Owens and Jas. Wilson" (*New York Clipper*).

• ***March 5, 1892:*** "The Nashville Students enjoyed quite a day's sport at Lebanon, Kas., where P. T. Wright, Jas. Wilson, Billy Cook, Jas. White, Baxter Reynolds and Joe Hunt and his greyhounds had a rabbit hunt" (*New York Clipper*).

• ***April 16, 1892:*** "George Bailey and Le Pain, of Fort Scott, Kan., paid P. T. Wright's Nashville Students a flying visit to attend a banquet given to James Wilson, juggler. Lash Gideon, leader of the band, was master of ceremonies" (*New York Clipper*).

• ***November 19, 1892:*** "The Nashville Students and P. T. Wright's Colored Concert Co. are reported as doing good business. James White and Master Albert Brown are scoring in their specialties. The company will tour Iowa, Illinois, Missouri, Kansas and Nebraska" (*New York Clipper*).

• ***April 8, 1893:*** "The Nashville Students report poor business for the past ninety days. They look forward to better business now. The company: P. T. Wright, manager; Joe Becker, advance representative; Alf. White, Gertie Revels, John Andrews, James White, Anna L. Lepalan-Clemens, S. B. Foster, Master Albert Brown, Ida Lee Wright, Billy Bradley, Geo. W. Lee and Billy Johnson" (*New York Clipper*).

• ***June 10, 1893:*** "The Nashville University Students and Wright's Colored Concert Company and Uniformed Band," "This old and well known musical organization now entering its

WE DON'T LAY OFF FOR ELECTIONS.

A Guaranteed Attraction. Merit Deserves Success. Nothing Like It. New Paper, New Ideas, Everything New and Original, Everything That's Gay. Houses Too Small. Turning Them Away Nightly. Stop Us, Head Us Off. Larger, Grander and Better Than Ever. THE

NASHVILLE UNIVERSITY STUDENTS,

AND P. T. WRIGHT'S GRAND COLORED CONCERT COMPANY,

With Silver Cornet Band and Orchestra, Headed by the Coming Young Comedian, JAMES WHITE.

BILLY BRADLEY, VOCALIST, COMEDIAN AND OLD MAN IMPERSONATOR.	**ANNIE LEPOLO CLEMENS,** THE GREATEST SOPRANO ON THE AMERICAN STAGE.
PROF. S. B. FOSTER, LEADER BAND AND ORCHESTRA, E-FLAT CORNET AND VIOLIN.	**ALBERT BROWN,** SLACK WIRE PERFORMER AND JUGGLER. THE WONDER OF ALL SLACK WIRE PERFORMERS.
MISS P. T. WRIGHT, SOLO. ALTO AND SOUBRETTE PARTS.	**GEO. BAKER,** MUSICAL DIRECTOR, PIANIST AND SIDE DRUM.
G. W. LEE, SOLO B CORNET IN BAND AND ORCHESTRA.	**BAXTER REYNOLDS,** BARITONE SOLOIST AND DOUBLE BASS.

THE GREATEST COLORED SHOW ON EARTH.

Do you want us? Write us as per route in N. Y. CLIPPER. The best of colored talent always in demand. Address all communications to P. T. WRIGHT, Manager, or JOE BECKER, Business Manager.

New York Clipper, *November 19, 1892.*

19th season . . . are about finishing up a most successful return trip from the great West and Northwest, via the Black Hills . . . Some one has said 'give me to write the songs of a people, and I care not who make their laws,' and in that sense, those who are gifted to interpret the melodies of a race, that like the Afro-American, has tasted sorrow's bitterest cup, has felt to its fullest, man's inhumanity to man, are richly worthy the pen of the chronicler, and the record that guards against oblivion. P. T. Wright, Esq., the accomplished and successful manager, is in full possession of those prerequisites of experience and judgement, through which only success can be obtained. The *Black Hills Times*, of a recent date, thus speaks of one of their performances:

'The programme presented by the Nashville University Students at the Opera House last night was the best of its kind ever given in the city; no exceptions. Every one of the performers are artists in his or her line. All are better than the average in singing, and in dancing they can hardly be excelled. James White is a whole show in himself. He sings well and dances a grotesque wing dance that cannot be duplicated . . . Miss Clemons, the leading soprano . . . sings with feeling and expression.

At the conclusion of the programme the troupe were tendered a very elegant banquet at Kemp & Kerchival's restaurant by the better class of the colored people of the city' " (*Indianapolis Freeman*).

• ***August 5, 1893:*** "Variety and Minstrelsy," "P. T. Wright's Nashville Students will open their season Aug. 21 at Macomb, Ill. The roster includes the Eldridges, Jas. S. Crosby, Alice Clark, Jas. Wilson, S. B. Foster, Mrs. P. T. Wright, P. G. Lowery, Nettie Gauff, Sam More, Baxter Reynolds, P. T. Wright, manager and proprietor, and J. F. Penington, agent" (*New York Clipper*).

• ***November 11, 1893:*** "P. T. Wright's Nashville Students closed Oct. 28, after nine weeks' bad business. They may open later in the season" (*New York Clipper*).

• ***February 10, 1894:*** "James Crosby, of Wright's Nashville Students, reports the success of his new songs, 'She's My Best Girl' and 'The Cat's Dead.' Ida Lee Wright is making a hit in her serpentine dance. Roster: P. T. Wright, manager; Joe Beckett, advance; Ida Lee Wright, Jas. L. Crosby; S. B. Foster; Gurtie Revels; John Owens; Albert Brown; L. F. Giedaeu; Lagan Halvey and Baxter Reynolds" (*New York Clipper*).

• ***August 18, 1894:*** "Roster of P. T. Wright's Nashville Students: P. T. Wright, manager; Al. Watts, stage manager; Mrs. Ida Lee Wright, Smith and Johnson, Albert Brown, P. G. Lowery, Prof. S. B. Foster, Mme. Cecil Smith, Miss Fogg and P. Woods" (*New York Clipper*).

Note: Madame C. C. Smith was Kansas City's bright, particular black prima donna.

• ***September 29, 1894:*** "The Nashville Students report doing a good business. They will play the Black Hills Circuit to Billings, Mon. Ida Lee Wright, Smith and Johnson, P. G. Lowery and Al. Watts are prominent members of the company. The new opera house at Custer, S.D., will be opened by this organization" (*New York Clipper*).

• ***March 23, 1895:*** "Roster of P. T. Wright's Nashville University Students—P. T. Wright, manager and proprietor . . . Smith and Johnson, Jas. Crosby, Mme. Hattie Rider, Emma Fogg, John Stewart, E. O. Green, P. G. Lanery [*sic*], Al. Watts, S. B. Foster and Ida Lee Wright . . . P. G. Lowery has been seriously ill with pneumonia, but is able to work again" (*New York Clipper*).

• ***May 11, 1895:*** "Just in time—Not too late! Wanted, for P. T. Wright's Grand Colored Co., a no. 1 good singing comedian and a tenor singer that sings. Nothing too strong for this show . . . We carry no 'star,' but all 'stars.' Address P. T. Wright, Manager of Nashville University Students and P. T. Wright's Grand Colored Co., Macomb, Ill., May 9. Permanent address, Unionsville, Mo." (*New York Clipper*).

• ***July 6, 1895:*** "P. T. Wright's Nashville Students and Colored Comedy Co. opens early in August and will tour Indiana, Ohio and Kentucky. The company is completed and some novelties have been added. Josh White and Jalvan have signed" (*New York Clipper*).

• ***July 20, 1895:*** "P. G. Lowery, the cornet soloist, Frank Kirk and Al. Watts have signed with the Nashville Students" (*New York Clipper*).

• ***August 17, 1895:*** "The Nashville Students opened Aug. 3 to good business. Roster: P. T. Wright, proprietor and manager; Al. F. Watts, stage manager; Ida Lee Wright, Madame Smith, Nettie Goff, Jas. White, J. Stewart, E. O. Green, Jackson H. Hearde, Pete Woods, F. T. Viccas, P. G. Lowery, leader of band; C. F. Alexander, leader of orchestra" (*New York Clipper*).

The 1895–1896 edition of Wright's Nashville Students included many upcoming stars of ragtime minstrelsy and vaudeville. Among them, Frank Kirk found long-term success as "the Musical Tramp," performing on a variety of homemade instruments. With the Georgia Minstrels in 1923, Kirk "played tunes on a 'tin can fiddle' with a broomstick for a bow; gave a banjo solo, a take-off on a Scotch bagpiper and impersonated Barnum's Steam Calliope with a wooden instrument which he peddled with his feet."[34]

P. G. Lowery, one of the greatest young stars of his generation, had joined Wright's Nashville Students in 1893, just two years into what proved to be an illustrious fifty-year-long career in show business. Lowery left Wright's Nashville Students in the spring of 1898, and he spent the latter part of that year as a featured cornet soloist at the Trans-Mississippi Exposition in Omaha, Nebraska.[35]

When P. T. Wright died unexpectedly on March 15, 1898,[36] his wife Ida took over management of the show. The following season Ida Wright placed P. T. Wright's Nashville Students "in alliance with L. E. ["Lash"] Gideon's Grand Afro-American Mastodon Minstrels."[37] By 1902 this alliance was simply known as "Gideon's Big Minstrel Carnival."[38]

In the spring of 1899 P. G. Lowery made his momentous move to the leadership of the "colored contingent" of the sideshow with the Forepaugh-Sells Bros. Circus. When the circus

P. T. WRIGHT.

Proprietor and Manager of Wright's Nashville Students' and Colored Comedy Co.

He was born in Mexico, Mo., 1857. His parents were owned by Quincy Daniels, 5 miles from Mexico. Right after the rebellion, his parents moved to Illinois and made McComb (McDonald Co.), their home. There he entered the public school (being the first colored child to enter). During his evenings and nights he learned the barber trade. His first appearance in the show business was with T. H. Bland's Carolinian's in 1874, as a basso profundo. He advanced on for years, until he finally found out that singing did not pay, so he located in Kansas City, and was appointed a detective (the only colored man in the West), and stands to-day the only colored man a member of the Kansas City Metropolitan Relief Association. Not liking that business, resigned and entered the profession. To-day Mr. Wright stands the only colored manager that has an undisputed reputation and traveling in his own $10,000 palace car. His only assistant being his wife, Ida Lee Wright.

Freeman, *December 25, 1897.*

IDA LEE WRIGHT.

Serpentine Dancer With Wright's Nashville Students.

The portrait above is that of Mrs. Ida Lee Wright, the estimable wife of Manager P. T. Wright, of the famous Nashville Students. Mrs. Wright is a native of Paola, Kan. She enjoys the distinction of being the first colored lady to do the serpentine dance. She is also the possessor of a rich contralto voice.

Freeman, *December 25, 1897.*

closed its season at Aberdeen, Mississippi, on November 3, 1900, Lowery joined promoter W. I. Swain to form Swain's "Original Nashville Students" featuring "P. G. Lowery, the cornet soloist, in his burlesque band."[39] Between seasons with circus sideshows, Lowery carried the old "Nashville Students" cognomen well into the twentieth century.

The Canadian Jubilee Singers

The wedding of black brass bands and orchestras to jubilee concert companies was a consolidation that favored both promoters and musicians. Beginning in the late 1890s, the *Freeman* regularly published "Musicians Wanted" ads, which always included openings for "good singers who can double on brass." The Canadian Jubilee Singers and Imperial Orchestra was a successful black company that combined choral and orchestral capabilities. Composed primarily of black Canadian nationals, the troupe was formed in Hamilton, Ontario, in 1879. Having spent five years touring Great Britain during the 1880s, they divided the rest of their time between tours of the United States and Canada.

The mixed troupe generally consisted of ten members. From their versatile roster, the Canadian Jubilee Singers and Imperial Orchestra were able to field a first-rate jubilee chorus and orchestra. A male vocal quartet was also prominently featured, along with a soprano soloist, plus bass solos by the celebrated "Boy Basso" James E. Lightfoot, who also served as orchestra director and mandolin virtuoso. Other highlights included guitar and mandolin duets and various instrumental solos, including an ophicleide specialty by slide trombonist Nathan Warner.

• ***March 30, 1895:*** "Notes from the Canadian Jubilee Concert Co," "We are meeting with big success on tour through Iowa and Nebraska. Ollie C. Hall, the colored baritone vocalist, is . . . singing Guss Davis' latest songs, 'Gone, but Not Astray' [and] 'Sing Again the Sweet Refrain.' The original Magnolia Quartet are traveling with this company, also . . . Louis Lucas and Ollie Hall, proprietors and managers" (*New York Clipper*).

• ***June 1, 1895:*** "We are now in our thirty-eighth week . . . not missing a night since Sept. 3, 1894. We have been traveling in New York, Pennsylvania, Ohio, Indiana and Michigan, and our season closes July 25, in Detroit . . . Roster of company: William Carter and wife, proprietors and managers; Jimmie Lightfoot, boy basso and leader of orchestra; J. A. Cockbin and wife,

W. T. Cary and wife, Fanny Stewart, Hattie Butler; Nathan Warner, slide trombone soloist, and James Thomas" (*New York Clipper*).

Note: William Carter and his wife were identified as members of the 1890 edition of Thearle's Nashville Students. Upon his death in 1906, it was stated in the *Freeman* that Carter "had been connected with the Canadian Colored Concert Company" for "nearly twenty-five years." His body was shipped to Hamilton, Ontario, Canada, for burial.[40]

• ***August 3, 1895:*** "We closed a successful season of forty-seven weeks in London, Can., July 26. There has not been a change in the company during the entire season, and the man in white never missed a Monday morning [i.e., 'the ghost walks'] . . . Mr. Carter, proprietor and manager, presented each member with a week's salary and a ticket for home . . . Mrs. Carter, the pianist . . . and Jimmie Lightfoot (the boy basso) will spend their vacation at their homes in Hamilton, Can." (*New York Clipper*).

• ***September 14, 1895:*** "We have been rehearsing at Hamilton, Ont., and opened our season Sept. 9. Jimmie Lightfoot, boy basso, has signed, making his fifth season with the company. Roster: Wm. Carter, proprietor and manager; Mrs. Carter, Mr. and Mrs. N. T. Cary, Mr. and Mrs. Cockbin, Miss F. Stewart, John Carter, Nathan Warner, James Thomas and Jimmie Lightfoot" (*New York Clipper*).

• ***September 28, 1895:*** "Notes from the Canadian Jubilee Singers and Imperial Orchestra: We are having success so far, although we were compelled to cancel two dates at Warsaw, N.Y., on account of an epidemic of diptheria. The Board of Health ordered all schools, churches and places of amusement closed. J. V. Carter is meeting with success as a tenor soloist. Nathan Warner, slide trombone soloist, is doing better work than ever, and is a leading feature of the programme. Jimmie Lightfoot, boy basso, is surprising the people in the East and receiving much applause nightly" (*New York Clipper*).

The Canadian Jubilee Singers remained in demand for many years. It seems they had come up with a practical formula for stability and longevity on the road. On July 9, 1897, "The Canadian Jubilee Singers and Imperial Orchestra . . . closed a very successful season of forty-two weeks and four days, missing only two days out of the entire season."[41] Ten years and six days later, on June 15, 1907, they closed "a successful season of forty weeks at Omaha, Neb."[42]

The Canadian Jubilee Singers and Imperial Orchestra.

The above shows the pictures of the Famous Canadian Jubilee Singers and Imperial Orchestra of the world that will appear at Allen Chapel, Tuesday January 30, 1900. It is the only rare treat of the season for the people of Indianapolis. Admission 25 cents; reserved seats 35c. Buy your tickets at once, reserving a seat for yourself and wife or company. A great rush is on.

A. L. MURRAY, A. B. Pastor.

Freeman, *January 20, 1900.*

Selected, Annotated Chronology of Music-Related Citations, 1891

• ***January 2, 1891 (Detroit, Michigan):*** "The Cantata Christmas Night," "The delightful cantata of 'Queen Esther,' was given under the auspices of St. Matthews Lyceum at Fraternity hall on Christmas night. The attendance was large and hence the Lyceum must have netted a neat sum as the results of their efforts. Some of the principals in the cast were the same as those who participated in the same some time ago, but there were quite a number of new voices, who while lacking in the power of voice almost made it up in sweetness of tone. Despite mistakes here and there, such as a principal singing out of tune, the pianist in error, and long waits, the presentation was as creditable as could be expected from the short time that was spent in preparation. The chorus was unusually good. Miss E. Azalia Smith made a very pretty queen and sang as sweetly as she always does . . . After the cantata dancing formed the chief amusement" (*Detroit Plaindealer*).

• ***January 3, 1891 (Indianapolis, Indiana):*** "Artistic Concert," "There will be a grand artistic concert at the Second Baptist Church . . . Among those who will participate are Mr. Joseph Sims, the glass eater, who . . . has a national reputation for eating and walking on glass with his bare feet; Mr. Thomas Gilbert, musician; Mr. Alonzo Smith, the celebrated guitarist; the Upper Ten Quartette, and many others" (*Indianapolis Freeman*).

• ***January 3, 1891:*** "The students of Hampton Institute gave a concert in New Bedford, Mass., last week. The singing by a quartet of students was excellent. A collection was taken after the concert, for the benefit of the Institute" (*Indianapolis Freeman*).

• ***January 3, 1891:*** "Miss Patti Malone, one of the original Jubilee Singers, has just had erected a palatial residence in Athens, Ala. It cost $1,400" (*Indianapolis Freeman*).

• ***January 17, 1891:*** "The colored tragedian, R. Henri Strange, appeared at the Academy of Music [January] 12 as Shylock, supported by a cast of colored actors. The proceeds will be devoted to a fund for the erection of a theatre in this city for colored actors. The site has already

GEORGE E. BARRETT.

A Brief Sketch of the Leading Tenor of the Famous Fisk Jubilee Singers.

Mr. George E. Barrett is one of the most successful tenor singers of the day. He was born in Baltimore, Md. He showed great taste for music while quite young and his father secured him a musical instructor. He was a brilliant pupil and took great interest in his work. He was quite advanced, when death took from him his beloved father. After the death of his father, he came to New York City, in 1875. He joined the Lyric Swan Club the same year. The principal object of the organization then was music in

which Mr. Barrett took an active part. He, however, found he could not afford to continue his musical education, and therefore he returned home. He became a successful teacher and leader of music. Mr. Trotter has him recorded in his book, as a great worker among the people of Baltimore and excellent in conducting concerts and musical entertainments. His influence was remarkable.

Mr. Barrett tells us, that on one occasion he gave an operatic concert, which had never been done before in Baltimore. He engaged Madame Lucy Adger, the celebrated soprano of Philadelphia; Mr. C. Samuel Adger of the same city, as accompanist; Mr. Thomas Boston, leading baritone of Washington, D. C., and the Baltimore Monumental Orchestra. They were assisted by home talent. The concert was advertised for 8 o'clock sharp, and on the evening of the entertainment, there were nine hundred people assembled. On the appearance of Mme. Adger in her song "Nearer, my God, to Thee," by Holton, she was greeted with rounds of applause. The audience was very enthusiastic. The papers stated that Mr. Barrett deserved much credit, as such an entertainment had never been given there before.

Mr. Barrett returned to New York City in 1878 and was engaged by Prof. George L. White, as leading tenor of the famous Fisk Jubilee Singers, who were about to begin their seventh season. He has traveled over the United States and Canada and has crossed the Atlantic four times. He has sung to delighted audiences in England, Ireland, Scotland, France and Belgium. He has been entertained by the royal families of Europe, and had, on one of his visits, the honor of singing in a concert with Ole Bull. The success that Mr. Barrett has attained in his artistic career has not been without many and arduous struggles and his present position is a well earned triumph over difficulties.

New York Age, *January 17, 1891.*

been selected. It is on the west side of Thirteenth Street, between Lombard and Pine" (*New York Clipper*).

• ***January 19, 1891:*** "The Odd Fellow's Masquerade," "The masquerade ball at fraternity hall New Year's night was given by the ladies of the Household of Ruth and Zach Chandler lodge [and] was a very interesting affair, it being the first masquerade of the season. Owing to the frequent heavy showers of rain which prevailed during the day the hall was not crowded but a goodly number was present. The costumes worn were unique and grotesque and the wearers occasioned considerable mirth by their many comical pranks. Prof. Finney's orchestra furnished the music" (*Detroit Plaindealer*).

• ***January 24, 1891:*** "The Nashville Tennessee Jubilee Singers, under the direction of Prof. J. H. Jones, gave an acceptable concert on Thursday evening, last week at Little Zion Church, Harlem" (*New York Age*).

• ***January 24, 1891:*** "The Sad Ending of Blind Tom's Eventful Career—Where Is His Money?," "Poor 'Blind Tom,' the musical genius, is driveling away the remaining months of an eventful life at a private retreat in St. Mark's place. He has been for some time an idiot, and now consumption has set its iron grasp upon his once tough frame, and his days are numbered. 'Blind Tom' earned in his day something like half a million dollars. Today he is comparatively a pauper, and the wonder is what has become of the fortune he made, as he was always in charge of a guardian and was never allowed to spend it.

Judge Andrews, of the Supreme Court, confirmed a report of referee Jerome Buck allowing the estate of Daniel P. Holland $3,000 for services rendered and necessaries furnished the mad musician during the life-time of Holland. Mrs. Elise Bethune, the committee having charge of Tom, vigorously opposed the confirmation of the report. The Judge observed that it was sadly apparent that there would be nothing left for the maintenance of the unfortunate pianist after all claims were paid.

The musician's real name is Thomas Wiggins. He was born in Virginia [*sic*] about forty-six years ago. His mother was a slave. From the time he was able to toddle Tom displayed wonderful powers as a musician. He could play on any kind of instrument, and yet never had an instructor. With the surrender of Lee at Appomattox, Tom became a free man, or rather a free boy. An alert, enterprising Southerner, J. W. Bethune, saw his pecuniary value and got an order from a Virginia court appointing him a committee for the maintenance and safety of Blind Tom. Bethune took him out on the road to every city, town and hamlet from Boston to San Francisco. Tom proved the best card of his time. In those days Tom earned for his manager from $2,000 to $4,000 a week. His mother, Charity Wiggins, thought that she ought to get hold of some of his earnings and fought in the courts for the possession of her son. There were speculative people behind her who supplied her with the needed cash to get legal and bodily control of Tom. Bethune won in every fight. The courts decided that she was not a proper person to have control of such an erratic genius as Tom.

When Bethune died a few years ago he left Tom to the care of his wife, Elise. She, in time, was appointed a committee by the court to maintain Tom. Soon, however, he broke down in health, became dangerously insane and was placed under restraint. All last summer Tom had delighted audiences in the house adjacent to his retreat in St. Mark's place. He played incessantly upon the piano, guitar and other melodious instruments. He can play no more.

The wonder is what has become of the money which Bethune was obliged, by mandate of the court, to deposit for Tom's maintenance. It was supposed to be twenty-five per cent of the net proceeds of the entertainments given. That would give Tom at least $125,000 in his own right. There is now, it is authoritatively stated, less than $5,000 in the exchequer. The $3,000 judgment entered will make an awful gash in the fund" (*Cleveland Gazette*).

Note: A variation of this article had appeared in the January 17, 1891, edition of *New York Age*, where it was credited to the mainstream *New York Morning Journal*. Despite continuing press reports that he could "play no more," that he had been committed to an insane asylum, and that he was about to die or was already dead, Blind Tom lived, traveled, and played the piano until 1908.

• ***January 31, 1891 (St. Louis, Missouri):*** "There is an old maxim that music is a true gauge of the progress and character of a people. Granting such to be the case, it readily accounts for the very prosperous people and polished society that one meets in St. Louis, for we will venture to say that no city in the United States contains so much musical talent in all branches, both vocal and instrumental, and in almost every house you will find an elegant piano—not for show—for here is always one or more of the family that are excellent players. Some of the leading instructors whose abilities are second to none, are Profs. J. M. Harris and J. D. West, violinists; Prof. Bell, instrumental and vocal; Mr. J. Arthur Freeman and Mr. Williams, vocalists, whilst the artists in both branches of music are innumerable. The high stage that musical culture has attained in this city is due, in a large measure to the Luca Musical Society, embracing both branches, and numbering at one time 185; the Mozart Conservatory of Music, and the Home Club. Let the good work continue.

It was our pleasure to receive an invitation to a musicale, given in Prof. Lucky's Academy, Washington Ave, Sunday afternoon, by the 'Luca'. . . About one hundred of the leading musical people of the city were present. The orchestra of 13 pieces, Prof. Harris, leader, rendered four choice selections; Miss Nettie Wilkerson recited an ode from Cleopatra . . . [She] is destined to make her mark as an elocutionist. Miss T. Thomas played a very beautiful piano solo . . . Prof. J. H. Harris played a violin solo, accompanied by Miss Thomas on the piano" (*Indianapolis Freeman*).

• ***January 31, 1891 (Kimmswick, Missouri):*** "The Kimmswick brass and reed band gave a concert Saturday night; it was a success in every respect. At seven o'clock the band met and paraded the streets. The encouraging words the band boys heard, 'the music sounds so sweet.' They marched around the town and to the city hall, where the band boys had agreed to give quite a social ball. Every thing showed that the ball would be a success, and every member did his best. When up in the hall, the leader selected a new piece of music that no band had ever played before. Lonnie our tuba player looked at the girls with a smile, as much as to say, 'Young ladies, I will see you later.' Our tenors and baritones played prominent parts, but it was our altos and clarionets that won the ladies' hearts" (*Indianapolis Freeman*).

• ***February 7, 1891:*** "Stage," "Prof. Z. A. Coleman, the basso profundo, formerly of Donovan's Jubilee Singers, has been stopping in Helena, Montana for the past few months, trying to get the Helena people stuck on his style, but they didn't stick, he finally gave them a cool shake and married a white lady, and embarked for Great Falls, taking with him his new wife and her $3000. We wish the Prof. success, esp. as long as the $3000 lasts" (*Indianapolis Freeman*).

• ***February 7, 1891 (Albany, New York):*** "The concert given by the champion solo singers, Prof. M. S. Simmons and Henry Tate, at Israel A.M.E. Church, Thursday evening was well attended. Prof. Simmons has traveled in twenty-eight States of the Union and also extensively in Europe. Whoever hears the bass solos rendered by him acknowledges him to be a singer of merit. The fine soprano of Mr. Tate is something wonderful. He assumes female costume and imitates the part with perfection" (*New York Age*).

• ***February 7, 1891:*** "Association Hall, Brooklyn, was crowded to its utmost capacity last Monday evening, at the concert given for the benefit of Siloam Presbyterian Church . . . The overflow of Brooklyn's music loving people was a splendid tribute to Miss Flora Batson, the famous mezzo-soprano . . . The concert was opened with a piano solo, 'Racing Down the Rapids,' by Mrs. Wilson . . . Mrs. Robert W. Conner . . . is an accomplished elocutionist, and kept the audience in a perpetual uproar. As she had never appeared before an audience of like complexion before, perhaps, the appreciation with which she was received must have been an agreeable surprise to her . . . Miss Batson sang 'Scene E Cavatina' from the opera 'Atilla' in which the vast improvement she has made in operatic singing as against her fame as the queen of ballad soloists was remarked" (*New York Age*).

• ***February 14, 1891 (Talladega, Alabama):*** "J. Street and Alonzo Connor have organized a Minstrel and Operatic Concert and will soon take the road with Talladega's favorite band led by Prof. Orr with 25 minstrel stars" (*Indianapolis Freeman*).

• ***February 14, 1891 (Zanesville, Ohio):*** "Miss Sadie Hall received a $40 gold watch—1st prize for selling the largest number of tickets for the concert given at Black's music hall by the Tennessee Warblers. Miss Hall sold $58 worth" (*Cleveland Gazette*).

• ***February 14, 1891 (Chillicothe, Ohio):*** "In 1865 we had a good colored brass band, also a band wagon, but most of its members are dead now. At present we have no brass band in the city that is fit to fill an engagement" (*Indianapolis Freeman*).

• ***February 14, 1891 (Talladega, Alabama):*** "Prof. Felix Gay's String Band filled the city with sweet music on last Friday night. Talladega is booming; a good place for a colored doctor or lawyer" (*Indianapolis Freeman*).

• ***February 14, 1891 (Brooklyn, New York):*** "Bills and cards, to which, with others, were attached the names of Messrs. Geo. A. Slater, Geo. E. Thompson and W. I. Stanley, announced a cake walk on Feb. 12, but as these gentlemen regret the use of their names and deny having any sympathy with the affair, it may be safe to say that cake walks form no portion of their social provender" (*New York Age*).

• ***February 20, 1891 (Washington, D.C.):*** A review of a local concert noted, in part: "The concert was largely advertised and Miss S. Labelle Anderson, we were told was the 'colored Patti' and supcradded to the treat of hearing a 'Colored Patti' we were promised several selections by the 'Inimitable Powell Quartette of Phila.' and to fill our measure to overflow, the celebrated [Will Marion] Cook's orchestra, Prof. John T. Layton and Miss Lula Hamer, all local talent were to add to the occasion . . . A few minutes after eight o'clock Cook's orchestra struck up a classical overture before a select and critical audience which would have inspired a more doubtful troup. Following the orchestra came the quartette, then soloist and 'Shylock's Soliloquy' by Mr. Downes . . . From an artistic standpoint the concert was a disappointment. Miss Anderson unfortunately chose pieces too difficult and lost the effect which her voice evidently could have produced. The range of her voice is high and her tones are sweet but not strong and had she chosen a ballad, doubtless she would have scored a decided hit, but as it is she has lost her last chance. The quartette introduced so much of the comical that it was encored several times and were it not for the fact that comedy is a common possession of the race, they would deserve some credit in that line. The greatest disappointment was in the elocutionist. Such a miserable murdering of Shakespeare's masterpiece would certainly have brought the old bard from his grave had he been buried in this continent. With however the appearance of the orchestra, Prof. Layton and Miss Hamer, everybody left with the appearance of having spent a pleasant evening" (*Detroit Plaindealer*).

• ***February 21, 1891 (Knoxville, Tennessee):*** "Banjos Make A 'Merry Hit,'" "Marringhill and McCorkle, the banjo wonders and song and dance artists, are making a 'great hit' in our city" (*Indianapolis Freeman*).

• ***February 21, 1891 (Louisville, Kentucky):*** "The latest dance in the way of a quadrille is 'The She.' The dance is perfectly new and is prepared by Prof. J. R. W. Riley, colored, of Louisville. The dance contains four figures and with waltz time" (*Indianapolis Freeman*).

• ***February 28, 1891:*** "To Dance or Not to Dance—That's the Question," "At the recent meeting of colored divines of Indianapolis at the Second Baptist Church, the sentiment against the 'dance' and dancing church members was very pronounced . . . Rev. E. N. Hayden wished all ministers of God to shut the doors of the church against people who danced . . . Rev. George A. Sissle . . . said that people argued that dancing was not wrong, and such arguments had to be met. The Rev. Mr. Martin, of Corinthian Baptist Church projected a bombshell into the serenity of the meeting, by charging that the church itself was much to blame for winking at and indulging in practices and entertainments, that belonged more to the theatres than the house of God" (*Indianapolis Freeman*).

Note: Among those who spoke out on the subject of dancing, Rev. George A. Sissle was the father of Noble Sissle, of the well-remembered twentieth-century vaudeville team Sissle and Blake.[43]

• ***February 28, 1891:*** "The young men of Louisburg, N.C., have organized a brass band" (*Indianapolis Freeman*).

• ***February 28, 1891:*** "McDonald's Orchestra, of Sacremento, Cal., now consists of the following young men: Violin, D. W. McDonald, dir.; flute, Eugene Burris; cornet, Henry Meadows; trombone, Julius B. Purse; drum, George Fisher; piano, Chas. Persons" (*Indianapolis Freeman*).

• ***February 28, 1891:*** "A few weeks ago Madame R. Robinson, R. R. Thompson, C. T. Moseley, Miss Katie Johnson and others went to Jamaica, West Indies, under the management of the Dominion Concert Troupe. They are meeting with splendid success, from reports in the Jamaica Post, which says of Madame Robinson, that when the song, 'Sing Sweet Bird' was sung, her reputation as one of the queens of song was assured" (*Indianapolis Freeman*).

Note: This is probably the same Katie Johnson who was with the troupe of Tennessee Jubilee Singers that toured the West Indies in 1890.

• ***February 28, 1891:*** "The Stage," "Miss Ednorah Nahar, of Boston, the elocutionist, has been charming large audiences in North Carolina and other Southern States" (*Indianapolis Freeman*).

• ***March 7, 1891 (Petersburg, Virginia):*** "Christmas Evans," "Petersburg's Wonderful Musical Prodigy—Another Blind Tom," "People outside of this city are not aware of the fact that we have here in Petersburg, Va. a most wonderful musical prodigy in the shape of a blind colored boy, 20 years of age. He has lived in Petersburg, where he was born, all of his life and comes from respectable parentage. His name is Christmas Evans.

From the time he was eight years old he has shown a fondness for music and displayed surprising powers as a musician. He has never had an instructor, yet he plays with wonderful proficiency on the piano, organ, guitar, harp, melodian, and other musical instruments. For the past two or three years he has been employed by the most cultivated and refined families in Petersburg to attend private entertainments and perform on various instruments.

The artist's character and exquisite finish of his renditions are remarkable, and his audiences which are oftimes composed of first class musicians go fairly wild with delight. He can imitate most any kind of musical instrument and has only to hear a piece played once or twice before he is able to reproduce it almost to perfection. With the harp or mouth organ he has few, if any rivals. In fact with a mouth harp, he is at home and one fairly thrills with delight when he plays on his instrument his favorite pieces such as: 'Margurette,' 'The Last Rose of Summer,' 'The Mocking Bird,' the imitation of the famous bands he has heard, the moving train, the piccolo, the bugle, the bagpipe, etc." (*Petersburg Lancet*, quoted in *Richmond Planet*).

Note: This marks an early appearance of the term "harp" to designate a harmonica. Christmas Evans's "imitation of a moving train" reverberates in the repertoire of race and hillbilly "harp" soloists on 1920s recordings.

• ***March 21, 1891 (Cincinnati, Ohio):*** "The Carmen double quartette is making preparations for an entertainment at Union M.E. Church this month. The following composed the club: Messrs. Charles Hinson, Grafton Jones, W. W. Staton, Harry W. Smith, C. A. Gradison, Chas. Bushlong, Thos. R. Jones, C. N. Johnson. Mr. Chas. Trotter is pianist. Under the direction of Mr. Fred Burch they have attained high musical excellence" (*Cleveland Gazette*).

• ***March 21, 1891 (Kansas City, Missouri):*** "Kansas City possesses something that is a rarity in most cities, and that is a female quartette. They are all members of the upper circles of K.C. society, and have appeared recently before several white ladies' societies and received much praise for their excellent renditions. It is composed of the following ladies: Miss Ella Thompkins, soprano; Miss Nettie Benton; Mrs. Prof. S. I. Lee, alto; Miss Cordelia Moore, basso; Mrs. Mattie Tetters, pianist" (La Beau, *Indianapolis Freeman*).

• ***March 28, 1891:*** "Kansas City News," "The Oberlin minstrel troupe has returned from their tour in an excellent, healthy condition, but bankrupt" (*Cleveland Gazette*).

• ***March 28, 1891 (Staunton, Virginia):*** "Rev. Silas Smith of Bedford city is in the city. He has given several benefits for the National Brass Band since his arrival here . . . There will be a grand concert given by the National Brass Band at the Opera House, April 2, 1891. Proceeds for the benefit of the band. They will give a grand street parade at 3:30 P.M. Admission to the gallery, 25cts., lower floor 50cts" (*Richmond Planet*).

• ***April 3, 1891 (Kansas City, Kansas):*** "Monday evening, the Ladies Aid Social gave their Easter egg-breaking and apron sale. The Exemplar band entertained the audience with delightful strains of music, among some of their selections we noticed 'Nearer My God to Thee,' 'Come ye Disconsolate,' 'Flee as a Bird,' 'What a friend We have in Jesus' and 'In the sweet bye and bye.' The egg banks were broken and contained $83.50" (*Kansas City American Citizen*).

• ***April 4, 1891 (New Haven, Connecticut):*** "The National Brass Band held their promenade concert Easter Monday night at the Masonic Temple . . . The band was assisted by the mandolin orchestra . . . The affair was a success, the net proceeds being $45" (*New York Age*).

• ***April 4, 1891 (New York City):*** "The Johnson Brass Band is destined to fill a place in this city which is much needed. Since their inaugural concert in December last the number has been increased to twenty-four musicians, and by constant practice they have attained a high proficiency" (*New York Age*).

• ***April 18, 1891 (Philadelphia, Pennsylvania):*** "Bergen Star Concert, at the Academy of Music, April 2nd, in the aid of Bethel A.M.E. Church building fund: Miss Flora Batson, soprano; Miss Fannie Hall, B. F. Lightfoot and Henri Strange, in dramatic and humorous recitations; W. I. Powell, baritone, W. F. Miller, basso; J. W. Wallace, conductor of the Wallace and Miller quartet, Mme P. Adelee Montgomery, W. A. Miller and R. H. Robinson, accompanist; W. I. Powell was stage manager. The Academy being the largest hall in the city every seat was occupied with pleasing spectators. Quartet, 'The Midnight Alarm,' Miller's quartet; recitation, 'Pilot Story,' R. Henri Strange; recitation, 'The Modern Cymon,' solo, 'Gallants of England,' W. I. Powell, and several other solos, quartets and recitations were heard. The Bergen Star Concert was a great success" (*Indianapolis Freeman*).

WANTED, GOOD SPECIALTY PEOPLE,
FOR OPENING, MAY 4, FOR
W. J. Armstrong & Co.'s
OUT O' SIGHT MUSEE AND THEATRE,
EVANSVILLE, Ind.
Break your jumps now between St. Louis and Louisville. Work at all times for specialty people; also novelties and freaks for curio hall.
Address W. J. ARMSTRONG, Manager, Evansville, Ind.

New York Clipper, *April 25, 1891.*

• ***May 1, 1891 (Detroit, Michigan):*** "The Wayne Glee club, composed of 21 employees of the Wayne hotel, have gained a reputation for giving some very pleasing entertainments, and their effort of last Friday evening at Fraternity hall was up to their usual standard...

A large number were in attendance and after the entertainment enjoyed dancing to the strains from Finney's orchestra" (*Detroit Plaindealer*).

• ***May 2, 1891 (New York City):*** "On Tuesday evening the Apollo Social Club gave their first stag party. The club room was brilliantly illuminated with electric lights and the club's colors, blue and white. The party opened with a lively address by president Wm. H. Nimor, followed by a banjo solo by Mr. Fred A. Stevens, the popular treasurer. Boxing by Mr. Geo. Townsend and Mr. Edward Anderson showed that the club was not lacking in pugilistic sport. The violin selection by Mr. Woodley was highly rendered. The solo by Mr. Steven Morris was very fine. The quartette by Messrs. Morris Stevens, Townsend, Dyer and Bell was received with high glee... Checkers, chess and dominoes were indulged in... Supper served at 12 o'clock" (*New York Age*).

• ***May 2, 1891 (New York City):*** " 'The Beautiful Slave,' announced as a new play, but in reality a jumble of nearly all the incidents in 'The Octoroon,' 'The White Slave,' 'Fate,' and 'Uncle Tom's Cabin,' was acted at Niblo's Garden April 27, by a company hastily organized... Lack of rehearsals was painfully apparent... there were some clever jubilee songs, dances, etc., by a dozen or more colored people" (*New York Clipper*).

• ***May 11, 1891:*** "The general public is hereby warned against the fraudulent representations of a troupe styling themselves the 'New Orleans University Glee Club,' under the management of a Mr. F. S. Thomas, which is said to be raising funds for an industrial school in the South. The faculty and trustees of New Orleans University know nothing of such a troupe. They have fraudulently assumed our name and are gulling our friends, especially in the North. All friendly exchanges please copy.

A. E. P. Albert, President Board of Trustees, New Orleans University" (*Southwestern Christian Advocate*).

• ***May 22, 1891 (Detroit, Michigan):*** "The Lone Star quartette that sang to such advantage last week at Whitney's with the Uncle Tom's Cabin company is composed of Will Homer, leader, Dennis Walts, tenor, Daniel Shivers, baritone and Wm. Currie, basso" (*Detroit Plaindealer*).

• ***May 22, 1891 (Detroit, Michigan):*** "George Dorsey, who was with the Peck and Fursman company, has been with them two seasons. He was with the Draper Uncle Tom's Cabin company in the title role during the seasons of '88 and '89 when the Hyer sisters played 'Topsy'" (*Detroit Plaindealer*).

• ***May 23, 1891:*** "The J. M. Blowe brass band, of Vicksburg, Miss., furnished the music for the annual parade of firemen in Jackson, Miss. On May 15 they played a similar celebration at Meridian" (*Indianapolis Freeman*).

• ***May 23, 1891 (New York City):*** "The Delph Club Picnic," "Sulzer's Harlem River Park, which since last season has undergone considerable alterations, on Thursday evening last week was the scene of the fourth annual picnic given by the J. T. Delph Social Club... At 12:30 the Twilight Quartet appeared and were greeted by tumultuous applause. Many old fashioned songs were sung by the quartet and encored. The chief feature of the evening was the prize waltz. This began at 1 P.M.... The prizes were a Scotch pug dog and a gold headed silk umbrella... The affair was attended by over 500 people and was a financial success. Prof. Craig's orchestra played the music" (*New York Age*).

• ***May 30, 1891:*** "Hampton Normal & Agricultural Institute," "Hampton, Va., May 21, '91—The twenty-third annual commencement exercises were celebrated at the Normal School today... A number of beautiful plantation songs very sweetly sung interspersed the exercises... One of the interesting features of the programme was Hampton's song 'Girdle Round the World' represented by students of nine different races attired in race costume with National songs from the Hampton book" (*Richmond Planet*).

• ***May 30, 1891 (Providence, Rhode Island):*** "The Apollo Club celebrated its 15th anniversary. All had an enjoyable time and the merriment prevailed until morning. Just at the hour of twelve the club drank to absent members and then sang 'Nearer My God to Thee'... The Banjo Quartet acquitted themselves nicely" (*New York Age*).

• ***May 30, 1891 (Pine Bluff, Arkansas):*** "Great Cake Walk," "The Ne Plus Ultra club gave a grand moonlight picnic and ice cream supper Friday night, at the residence of Mr. J. O. H. Thompson, for the benefit of the new A.M.E. Church... after which a fine two story cake was put up for the couple that could walk the most stylishly... [with] music furnished by Prof. Jacob's string band. The walkers for the cake, which were not less than twenty-five couples got their Sunday's graceful step, and did their best walking for the cake; after a continuous march of twenty-five or thirty minutes, the music ceased and the jury retired and soon brought back a verdict in favor of Mr. W. H. Bell and Miss Emma Arlington, as being the most graceful walking couple in the march, which entitled them to the cake" (*Indianapolis Freeman*).

• ***May 30, 1891 (Indianapolis, Indiana):*** "Out Of Sight," "The Oriole May And Musical Festival At Simpson Chapel Monday Night—A Great Success." Among the many offerings, "'The Charcoal Man'—a recitation by Mrs. Mattie Sissel, was a finished effort, clean cut and of good conception. Mrs. Sissel is very conscientious in all of her public efforts, and while making no pretense to histrionic ability, we have few, if any amateur readers, amongst the many good ones of the city, who are more desirous than she to give the correct portrayal of the intents of the authors she recites from. And this is true reading.

The bass solo sung by Mr. Wm. Coleman, was a finished and dignified effort...

The rendering of 'Nearer My God to Thee,' by Prof. [Henry] Hart and daughters, Myrtle,

Willie and sweet little Hazel, the seven year old wonder, was an execution of superbest technique and finish . . . The Prof. in his place as lead, Willie at the violincello, Myrtle behind the royal harp, and petite Hazel holding the second violin like any master under her baby chin, was a sight that carried the great audience away from itself, as leaves are swept by the storm. The encore offered with a will was greatly responded to by Prof. Hart and his obedient slave the 'Old Cremone,' and then we did hear a rendition of that sacred hymn, then through the insinuating witchery of music's dulcet melody, we were drawn nearer indeed to God, and farther away from the perishable and sordid things of life. All mankind, the savage as well as the civilized, kneels at music's soothing shrine. All Indianapolis should be thankful that Henry Hart is with us. His life, unassuming, modest, upright, as he has lived it in this community, his great gift always glorified, never abused, has exerted such an influence and inspiration for good for every one of us, in the estimation of the whites, and in our own hearts that it may be that we will not fully realize it until it be taken from us" (*Indianapolis Freeman*).

Note: "Mattie Sissel," who gave such a "true reading" of "The Charcoal Man," was Noble Sissle's mother.[44]

• ***June 5, 1891 (Terre Haute, Indiana):*** "The Four Ace quartette will leave June 15, for Hamilton park under contract for the Summer" (*Detroit Plaindealer*).

• ***June 6, 1891:*** "Stage," "A challenge from the 'Boss Quintette' of Mobile, Ala. has been made public to sing for $100 a side with any quintette in the South" (*Indianapolis Freeman*).

• ***June 6, 1891 (Pittsburgh, Pennsylvania):*** "The concert given by the 'Old Jubilee Singers' in Lafayette Hall Wednesday evening was very successful. After the concert, dancing was indulged in until 1:30" (*Cleveland Gazette*).

• ***June 6, 1891:*** "George Cheatham says whenever he goes after a man in dead earnest that man is his meat. He keeps a private grave yard of his own, and every few months adds a fresh grave to his rare collection. When George tells you that so and so will happen you hadn't better bet against him" (*Indianapolis Freeman*).

Note: Here is an early manifestation of the "graveyard of my own" motif, which fell into the blues tradition.

• ***June 11, 1891:*** At New Orleans University's annual commencement exercises, one of the musical interludes was "Miss Eloise Bibb, 'Sebastopol,' guitar concerto" (*Southwestern Christian Advocate*).

Note: The novelty piece "The Siege of Sebastopol" was played in an open tuning which became widely used in later blues and gospel and still bears the name "Sebastopol." This citation demonstrates that "Sebastopol" tuning was being used by black guitarists as early as 1891.

• ***June 13, 1891:*** "The Musical Chorus," "It has been observed that a race's progress is most surely indicated by its growing taste for music and the arts. Cultivated music we mean . . . In the days when the banjo was the race's musical instrument or the mere 'fiddler,' the musician of our people, these primitive tastes, were not to be scoffed at, but years [of] opportunities, associations and education has produced a change. The cultivated 'brother in black,' is looking up, his ear has become more sensitive, and his love and devotion to the high and cultivated, in music especially, is a very gratifying sign of the times. Mark the prediction there will yet come a day, when the world's greatest prima donna will be a colored woman; and when the Paganinnie's the Rubistein's and Campaninie's of the music loving world will have sprung from Negro parents, and will execute such divine melody, as the world has never listened to" (*Indianapolis Freeman*).

• ***June 13, 1891 (Sedalia, Missouri):*** "There will be given on Main street, Thursday evening, June 19th, a grand entertainment by the Sedalia Brass band. All kinds of refreshments in abundance. No pains spared to make this an evening of enjoyment. Plenty of music rendered by the band... The Sedalia Brass band gave a musical entertainment on Main street, Thursday night, for the benefit of the band, and realized quite a neat little sum" ("Ireland," *Indianapolis Freeman*).

• ***June 13, 1891 (Fulton, Missouri):*** "Samuel Fate died at Mexico, Mo., June 4th, after a short illness. His remains were brought home for burial. Samuel was a natural humorist; He was a notorious cloggist; could play the banjo, sing comic songs, play two tin whistles at once, could make the chromatic scale on a tin whistle with but six holes, crack jokes, etc, in a manner that seldom failed to bring the house down. He was also a great favorite of the railroad brakesmen and conductors" ("H. O. B.," *Indianapolis Freeman*).

• ***June 20, 1891 (Detroit, Michigan):*** "The original Fisk Jubilee Singers will give a concert June 26th at the YMCA Hall. Among the members of the company this season is Mrs. Maggie Porter Cole, Detroit's highly esteemed vocalist" (*Indianapolis Freeman*).

• ***June 27, 1891 (New Orleans, Louisiana):*** "The Excelsior Brass Band, which by the way is one of the finest colored bands in the country, is making great hits as an orchestra and the players of classical music; in fact they tackle anything. Prof. T. V. Baquie [*sic*], is their leader" (*Indianapolis Freeman*).

Note: T. V. Baquet, leader of the Excelsior Brass Band, was the father of jazz clarinetist George Baquet.

• ***June 27, 1891 (Detroit, Michigan):*** "The last sad rites of one of Detroit's most highly esteemed and respected ladies, was solemnized the 20th, at St. Matthews church... Mrs. Ellen Eliza, wife of Theo. Finney... succumbed to the iron grasp, after a lingering illness. The deceased was born in Cincinnati, O., March 10, 1836, and came to Detroit on 1857. For over thirty years she had been pianist of Prof. Finney's orchestra" (*Indianapolis Freeman*).

• ***June 27, 1891 (Boston, Massachusetts):*** "A testimonial and public reception to Hon. and Rev. T. C. Campbell was given at Ebenezer Baptist Church, on the 23rd... Messrs. Sydney Woodland [*sic*, i.e., rising tenor star Sidney Woodward], G. W. Sharper, R. A. Allen's fife and bugle corp and the Newbury male quartette contributed their talent to the entertainment" (*Richmond Planet*).

• ***June 28, 1891 (Topeka, Kansas):*** "City News," "B. Craige, H. Williams, Wm. Spencer, Sloan Edwards and John Davie are with Dr. Tomlinson's medicine company. They give excellent entertainments at Marshall's bandstand every evening" (*Topeka Weekly Call*).

• ***July 4, 1891 (Indianapolis, Indiana):*** "A Grand Time," "The members of the Antioch Baptist church under the direction of their pastor, will run an excursion consisting of fifteen coaches to North Salem [Indiana] tomorrow. This will be one of the grandest excursions of the season ... Addresses will be made by silver tongued orators upon interesting subjects among which are: 'Damned Hot Day,' 'Dry Bones in the Valley,' 'Change Your Clothes,' 'A Wheel in a Wheel.' Fare 50 and 25 cents" (*Indianapolis Freeman*).

• ***July 4, 1891 (Kansas City, Missouri):*** Announcement for an upcoming entertainment sponsored by the Aeolian Society promises to include "The Athletic Quartette, which is considered the best male quartet in the West; also our famous Female Quartette (of K.C.) will render selections. Admission: 15 cents. Mrs. Mattie L. Tuter—Musical director; Prof. A. R. Harris, business manager" (*Indianapolis Freeman*).

• ***July 9, 1891:*** "Mr. F. S. Thomas and Mrs. Tillie Jones Thomas, managers of the Glee Club, which we published as a fraud some weeks ago, because it assumed the name 'New Orleans University Glee Club,' explain their connection with that name as follows: 'We are managers of a company known as the New Orleans University Singers, and travelling on our own merits, since we finished our mission in the interest of LaTeche Seminary, under Dr. Godman, ex-president of New Orleans University. We finished our work with him in 1881, and have been travelling since upon our own merits.' We would not do Mr. Thomas and his troupe any injustice, but it is just to the University and its friends that the fact be known that the New Orleans University has no troupe giving concerts for its benefit in the North" (*Southwestern Christian Advocate*).

• ***July 10, 1891 (Detroit, Michigan):*** "The recital given Tuesday evening by Mr. Richard Harrison and the Young Ladies' Amateur orchestra was unexceptionally fine. The orchestra includes Miss Azalia Smith, leader" (*Detroit Plaindealer*).

• ***July 11, 1891 (Indianapolis, Indiana):*** "A race riot on a small scale occurred Monday between three Macon, Ga., cadets, who are in the encampment here, and Tom Brown, who is home from his tour with the minstrels. They made some smart remark as Brown was having his shoes blacked. He returned as smartly, which nettled the southern bloods, who, possibly forgetting they were *not in Georgia*, set upon him. He felled two of them and took refuge in an Afro-saloon on Kentucky avenue where the most independent of colored characters congregate. The cadets were foolish enough to follow in and were speedily thrown out and severely beaten. One's lip was completely severed to the chin; another's head was badly battered with a billiard cue, and the third was badly bruised and '*horribly mortified by having been assaulted by a Negro.*' Brown was cut about the head" (*Cleveland Gazette*).

Note: Between 1890 and 1895, Tom Brown toured with Richards and Pringle's Minstrels, Sam T. Jack's Creole Company, and Isham's Octoroons, and he went on to appear in several major black musical comedies of the early 1900s, including the 1909 Bert Williams vehicle, "Mr. Lode of Koal."[45] In 1917 Brown went into the music publishing business with fellow African American composers Lew Peyton and Tom Lemonier.[46] Brown died in Chicago on June 20, 1919.[47] It may be by sheer coincidence that Brown's 1891 fighting incident is echoed in the ragtime song "Tom Brown Sits in His Prison Cell," recorded in 1929 by black singer-guitarist Luke Jordan:

> *Tom Brown sat in his prison cell, he could not sit outside,*
> *To pay his little fine, to raise it he had tried,*
> *Was out with a minstrel troupe, were caught up in a fight,*
> *He telegramed his baby for some coin on Saturday night.*[48]

• ***July 11, 1891:*** "Billy McClain and Billy Eldridge have joined hands and are touring Missouri with the Shaker Herb Co." (*New York Clipper*).

• ***July 11, 1891:*** A report from Cleveland's Minstrels: "A sketch, entitled 'Ebonyville Aristocracy' came next, with the following cast: Peter Jackson, John Queen; Lucy, Mr. Lyon; Ike Simpson, Phil E. Baer, Aunt Sukey, Fred Russell, Uncle Medium, Jas. E. Rostrum. Peter Jackson as the intruding colored dude, made matters interesting at the colored picnic and the audience smiled" (*New York Clipper*).

Note: Peter Jackson was a famous black boxing champion who turned to the stage and earned a certain reputation for his portrayal of "Uncle Tom." This early venture finds him in company with famous white minstrel John Queen, author of the turn-of-the-century ragtime song hit "Just Because She Made Dem Goo-Goo Eyes."

• ***July 18, 1891:*** "The Boston Creole Co. closed its Summer season July 11. Their regular season will open about July 27 at Peotone, Ill. They will carry a brass band and orchestra with thirty-five people. G. W. B. Brown is sole owner and manager, with R. C. Pugsley, advance agent" (*New York Clipper*).

Note: Here is yet another "Creole Company."

• ***July 25, 1891 (New Orleans, Louisiana):*** "The Mexican Band of forty-five pieces of the 5th Mexican regiment are playing a very successful engagement at the West End, giving open air concerts, etc. It has come to the knowledge of the writer that two of the best musicians in said band are American Negroes who have regularly enlisted" (*Indianapolis Freeman*).

• ***July 25, 1891:*** "Delaware News," "The Twilight Male Sextet of Norfolk, Va. gave a concert recently at the A.U.M.P. Church" (*New York Age*).

• ***July 25, 1891 (Baltimore, Maryland):*** "Camp meetings, excursions and picnics have reached their height, and the daily exodus of the colored people from this city to the fields, the forest and the seashore is enormous . . . There are not so many excursions as in former years, but there are enough of them; and it is possible that the loss in numbers is made up in the rowdyism and general immorality which invariably accompanies many of them. Even among those given by the churches, lodges, Sunday schools and other respectable organizations, no efforts are seemingly made to keep back the disorderly element from the slums of the city. As an instance, last Monday, your correspondent . . . went to Irving Park, a pleasure ground mid-way between this city and Washington, where the A.M.E. Sunday schools of Washington, Annapolis and Baltimore were having their annual union picnic . . . More than five thousand people were on the grounds—men, women and children, of all ages, sizes and descriptions; of all colors creeds and conditions; of all degrees and shades of moral and intellectual worth—those of good character and those of no character, coming from all the walks of life, the titled divine and the chaste maiden, the lordly libertine, the heartless gambler and the inhabitants of the city's brothels, all mixed in one seething mass. A sight more unlike a model Sunday school picnic cannot be imagined. Dancing was indulged in—at a Methodist picnic, too—all day, and the music was provided by a band which must have been engaged for that purpose, as it was used for but one half-hour in any other way. The seductive games of 'sweat' and 'crap' were in full blast from morning til night, your correspondent counting more than two dozen tables, just outside the park, devoted to this nefarious business . . . The fountain of alcoholic beverages flowed freely . . . and as a result, two victims are reclining upon the hospital couches awaiting the healing of bullet wounds . . . [P]arents and guardians would do well to keep their children home, and not place them in reach of the 'modern Sunday school picnic.' The managers seem to have more regard for the price of a ticket than for the protection of the chastity of the girls, and the safety of the lives of their patrons. Any one who had the requisite 50 cents was welcome. There were some redeeming features about this gathering. The music rendered by the schools of Washington and Baltimore, under the leadership of Profs. J. T. Layton and J. Jas. Dungee, respectively, was highly creditable; the sack race was amusing, and the game of ball would have done credit to Louisville and Washington—'the tail-enders' of the American Association" (*Indianapolis Freeman*).

• ***August 1, 1891 (Coshocton, Ohio):*** "At the meeting of the McKinley club of this city, last Friday evening, the Golden Tip Quartette was chosen as the McKinley quartette. They are L. S. Yager, first tenor; T. B. Carr, second tenor; Isaac C. Dorsey, baritone; Jerome Nichols, bass. The Golden Tip singing club and the Coshocton String band, both managed by Lewis Yager, are gaining quite a reputation" (*Cleveland Gazette*).

• ***August 1, 1891:*** "The Jennie Jackson Concert Company," "Wherever the famous Fisk Jubilee Singers have appeared the name of Jennie Jackson is familiar. Jennie Jackson, now Mrs. DeHart, has organized a fine sextette of colored singers after the model of the original company of Jubilees, and has personally trained them for their work . . . It is worth any price to hear Mrs. DeHart sing 'Way down upon the Swanee River' " (*Richmond Planet*).

Jennie Jackson DeHart. (courtesy Fisk University Library, Special Collections)

• ***August 7, 1891 (Sedalia, Missouri):*** "Emmet Webster, is a fine pianist. This boy is only fourteen years of age and plays excellently.

Miss Minniola M. Jackson the fifteen year old daughter of Rev. J. Will Jackson performs beautifully on the piano. In fact her ability is mentioned in nearly every house in Sedalia. We are sorry that we did not have an opportunity to hear the blind man, Smith perform on the piano while we were in the city. We have heard much about him" (*Kansas City American Citizen*).

• ***August 8, 1891:*** "From the careful manner which Manager Lew Johnson of California has followed in selecting his concert troupe it will, when ready to appear, be one of the finest concert jubilee troupes in America. Everyone selected is an artist in his particular role" (*Indianapolis Freeman*).

• ***August 8, 1891 (New York City):*** "H. Sylvester Russell, the operatic soprano of Orange, N. J. and H. W. Scott of Boston, basso profundo, left the city to join Hicks & Sawyers Minstrels at Philadelphia" (*New York Age*).

Note: During the early 1900s, Sylvester Russell established himself as the first full-time professional music critic of African American descent. Russell's weekly "Chicago Notes" column in the *Indianapolis Freeman* survives as an essential chronicle of entertainment activity in black Chicago during the decade 1910–1920. During the 1890s, however, Russell was consigned to the minstrel show routes as an "operatic male soprano." The troupe he is identified with here was a "domestic" branch of the Hicks-Sawyer Minstrels, under Charles B. Hicks's ex-partner A. D. Sawyer.

• ***August 15, 1891 (Cleveland, Ohio):*** "The concerts given by the Hall Jubilee Singers at Cory Chapel . . . were well attended and seemingly enjoyed. The singing was not of the first note quality, but was well rendered. It consisted mostly of southern plantation melodies" (*Cleveland Gazette*).

• ***August 15, 1891 (Jefferson City, Missouri):*** "The Big Six Concert company left for Herrman, Mo., on the morning of the 4th, inst., arriving at the aforesaid city at 1 o'clock in the afternoon. At 7 o'clock P.M., people were thronging around the music hall... At 7:30 o'clock the doors were opened and the performances began at 8. The declamations, 'Toussaint L'Overture' and 'The Gladiator' were well rendered... A big hit was made with the comic solo, 'Hear Dem Bells'... Lewis and Williams received great applause on 'Massa's in the cold, cold ground.'...The company will be in Tipton [Missouri] three nights, beginning the 12th" (*Indianapolis Freeman*).

• ***August 22, 1891 (Gloucester, Massachusetts):*** "Drownded [*sic*] At Gloucster," "B. F. Lightfoot, the Colored Elocutionist The Victim," "B. F. Lightfoot of Providence was drowned at Magnolia Beach while bathing.

Mr. Lightfoot has been giving a series of readings at the summer hotels, and gave an entertainment at the Hesperus house early in the afternoon. In company with two or three others he started to battle on the beach [*sic*] a little before 4 o'clock. He had just ventured a few feet out beyond his depth when he was seized by a chill. He made an outcry, but before assistance could reach him he was drowned...

Mr. Lightfoot was 26 years of age and had resided in [Providence, Rhode Island] ever since childhood and was a well known and very prominent member of the colored society of this city" (*Indianapolis Freeman*).

• ***August 28, 1891 (Keokuk, Iowa):*** "Thursday afternoon the Grand Lodge headed by the Fields Brothers Band, turned out in full force and paraded the principal streets of the city and presented a fine appearance. The Fields Brothers Band is a fine organization, composed of fourteen young men, the youngest of whom is fourteen years old. They are nearly all related to each other. Four of them are the sons of Mr. and Mrs. Austin Bland, and three are the sons of Mr. and Mrs. Fields. The others are members of different families. This Band has been organized about sixteen months, but in that time under the instructions and leadership of Mr. Fred Fields, a most gentlemanly and talented young man, they have developed into one of the finest musical organizations in the city... and both white and black are justly proud of them. These boys are an honor to Keokuk; they are an honor to the race every where.

Thursday evening at 8 o'clock the G.A.R. hall was filled with a large and fashionable audience to witness the installation of the Grand officers for the ensuing year. At 9:30 the Grand Lodge marched into the spacious hall and formed a circle in the center thereof while Field's band discoursed some rich music... Refreshments of the season were served in the dining hall, and the main hall was left for promenading, and later in the evening it was turned over to what Rev. Sherwood would be pleased to term 'the hoppergrasses, who cut the pigeon wing to the sound of music.' This was a first class entertainment" (*Kansas City American Citizen*).

• ***August 29, 1891 (Lakewood, New York):*** "The concert given by the waiters of the Sterlingworth on the 18th was a grand success... Mr. Frank Crane was the favorite of the evening. His rendition of the comic song entitled 'Charcoal,' carried the audience by storm. Mr. Henry Forbes was especially good in Negro Minstrelsy... Mr. E. H. Leonard captivated all by his clever remarks in a stump speech... Mr. James Randolph rendered the familiar song 'Old Black Joe'; Mr. W. H. E. Hall recited Tennyson's 'Bugle Call'; Prof. Mitchell entertained the audience by a rendition of the Carnival of Venice upon the piano" (*New York Age*).

• ***September 4, 1891 (Detroit, Michigan):*** "Miss Ida Griffin, who spent her vacation traveling with the Fiske Singers, will be with them again next season . . . The fact that she will be chaperoned by Mrs. Porter Cole is a guarantee of her success" (*Detroit Plaindealer*).

• ***September 5, 1891:*** "Wanted—Vocalists—A first class soprano and tenor for the Fisk-Tennesseans Jubilee Singers. Address Robert Day, Jr. business manager . . . Pittsburgh, Pa." (*Cleveland Gazette*).

• ***September 5, 1891:*** "The Great American Colored Minstrels, reorganized by Barnes & Farquharson, sailed from this city [New York] Aug. 29 for Glasgow, Scotland, where they open their season. The company includes Prof. C. R. Wallace, D. W. Sanders, Fred Newman, Ball and Jackson, Dick Cousby, Joseph G. Stevens, Jas. D. Johnson, Frank Johnson, C. Berry, Albert Wilson, Alf. Thomas, Geo. B. Lee, Henry L. Harris, Geo. Tichner, Major Jacque, C. Carr and others" (*New York Clipper*).

• ***September 12, 1891 (St. Louis, Missouri):*** "James W. Grant has composed a new dance entitled, 'la Julienelle.' It is a new combination round-square dance. Mr. Grant was prompted to write the dance from the fact that there are very few pieces of music to which one form of dancing can be strictly confined, hence many time sets are not in harmony, owing to different sets, dancing different forms. This new dance does away with this fault; the music is by Charles S[umner] Byron, who, considering his age, has no superior as a pianist in the west" (*Indianapolis Freeman*).

• ***September 26, 1891:*** "Billy McCann [*sic*], Cordelia Scott and Ollie Ferguson made such a hit at Madison, Mo., last week, that Manager J. E. Cannibaugh gave a supper in their honor" (*New York Clipper*).

• ***September 26, 1891:*** "Billy Windom is with Carncross' Minstrels, Philadelphia. He is a popular comedian, and is making quite a hit singing 'Little Fannie McIntyre.' He will shortly be heard in 'Little Nora Malone'" (*New York Clipper*).

Note: Carncross' Minstrels were white. As *Freeman* critic Sylvester Russell accurately reflected in 1903, "During the season of 1891, William H. Windom was singing in the Concross [*sic*] White Minstrel Company running at Eleventh Street Opera House, Philadelphia, Pa. He had formerly toured the South [with McCabe and Young] as a colored minstrel . . . George Primrose, on hearing Windom sing, quickly decided that Billy had the voice he wanted and at once signed him, regardless of his race, and featured him as the star vocalist in the 'first part' of his [white] minstrel company . . . Mr. Windom is of very light complexion, [but] hardly light enough to pass for white by close inspection."[49] Nevertheless, he continued to "pass" as a member of the white Primrose and West Minstrel Company for the next three seasons, and when George Primrose and John T. West launched Primrose and West's Black and White Minstrels in 1894, Windom was assigned to the white contingent.

• ***September 26, 1891:*** "Sylvester Russell, the male soprano, has closed with the Hicks-Sawyer Minstrels, and expects to appear in concert at Philadelphia Oct. 15" (*New York Clipper*).

• ***October 1, 1891 (Chicago, Illinois):*** "There is a drum corps on the South side of the city that is rapidly making a name for itself. It will soon be recognized as one of the greatest nuisances that is being tolerated on the South side. Every time the drum major, or high-cock-a-lorum of this most profound nuisance takes it into his head that he must parade he calls this 'mess' together, and through the streets they go, like a pack of idiots, pounding drums and blowing horns with such force and discord as would make a pack of Fiji islanders turn green with envy . . . Some of these fine afternoons or evenings you will be 'called down' by the authorities as a public nuisance, then your howl will be: 'Oh, yes! It's the same old story; they do it because we are colored'" (*Detroit Plaindealer*).

• ***October 2, 1891 (Pleasant Hill, Missouri):*** "The colored band of this place is progressing finely under the leadership of Mr. Fount Woods" (*Kansas City American Citizen*).

Note: Trombonist Fountain B. Wood became a conspicuous figure in the history of African American minstrel show bands. In 1902 he was a member of the band with Mahara's Minstrels, under W. C. Handy. In 1927 he was the leader of the band with the legendary Silas Green from New Orleans Company.[50]

• ***October 3, 1891:*** "McKanlass' Colored Comedy Co. are doing well in 'Shooting Craps,' according to all reports. The company have been playing the comedy continuously since the opening of their season at Clarinda, Ia., May 15. The roster: W. H. McKanlass, A. L. Sales, W. T. Mines, W. B. Watts, Master Willie McKanlass, Little Adeline Patti McKanlass, the Reese Twin Sisters, Beatrice Sylvester, Susie Griffin and a band and orchestra" (*New York Clipper*).

• ***October 3, 1891:*** "Miss Batson in New Haven," "Sep. 28—Mrs. Flora Batson-Bergen . . . gave a concert at the Dixwell Avenue Congregational Church last Tuesday evening. A large audience gathered within and in front and around the sides of the church . . . During the concert an accident occurred outside but no one was hurt. The desire to see and hear Miss Batson caused the people to build a temporary stage with benches, which gave away with a crowd on it. The Flower Song from 'Faus' [*sic*] by Miss Batson scored a complete success. She afterward sang as an encore a selection from 'Il Trovatore' in baritone. . . Miss Batson is now and has for some time been under the training of Sig. Farini of New York, the famous Italian teacher, who pronounces her a mezzo soprano of wonderful range and compass, covering three octaves which baffles the vocal efforts of this age" (*New York Age*).

• ***October 3, 1891:*** "Mrs. Flora Batson Bergen, 'Queen of Song,' and Mrs. Matilda Jones, the rising star, supported by New York and Brooklyn talent, will be heard at Bridge Street Church, Brooklyn, Thursday evening Oct. 8 and at Bethel Church, New York, Monday evening, Oct. 12. A word to the wise—go early" (*New York Age*).

• ***October 4, 1891 (Topeka, Kansas):*** "Stage Notes," "The Hyers Sisters Great Comedy Co. will visit Topeka Tuesday Oct. 6. This is the only colored comedy on the road, every one should see them and hear George Freeman, the great cornetist" (*Topeka Weekly Call*).

Note: George Freeman, the "great cornetist," was a product of Topeka's extraordinary community brass band milieu. During the course of his tenure with the Hyers Sisters Company, Freeman was briefly married to Emma Hyers.

• ***October 10, 1891:*** "Wanted, Colored (Black) Performers. Banjo Players who are Good Singers, Comedians who Sing, Quartets that can put on acts, Bone and Tambourine Players, Magicians, Whistlers, Contortionists, Jubilee Singers, Ministers who can preach, for our West India Companies. Long engagements and good salaries to steady, reliable men. Address Healy & Bigelow, 521 Grand Avenue, New Haven, Ct." (*New York Clipper*).

• ***October 10, 1891 (Worcester, Massachusetts):*** "Maj. Alex. H. Johnson has one of the best drum corps in the country, a profession he has followed ever since he came from the war. The corps consists of twelve pieces, and is second to none in the state" (*Indianapolis Freeman*).

• ***October 10, 1891 (Shelbyville, Kentucky):*** "Tom Martin's band was out in the west end serenading Saturday night . . . The Shelby Cornet Band rendered music at the Bellvue house for those who delight in dancing . . . Prof. W. H. Thomas is the musical instructor of the Shelby Cornet Band, which is the best colored band in the state of Kentucky, and the only colored band in the country that plays orchestra music on brass. Prof. Thomas began the study of music in February 1875, under Prof. Robt. Jones then from Prof. Birgess, then from Prof. J. R. Cunningham, of Louisville, and thorough bass from Prof. W. H. Dana. He has taught several bands besides his own. He is also one of the few men white or colored who arranges music for brass band and orchestra. He arranged the orchestra parts of the opera 'Chimes of Normandy' and played the cornet part for the company of fifty voices, conducted by Miss Cecelia Eppenhans" (*Indianapolis Freeman*).

• ***October 10, 1891 (Richmond, Virginia):*** "The Colored Fair," "The Trades' Parade last Thursday morning, under the auspices of the Virginia Industrial, Mercantile and Building Association was a success.

It was nearly 11 o'clock before the procession moved. A squad of police headed it...

A large number of young men were upon horses. Then followed the Anderson Guards, consisting of little boys attired in blue suits and caps to correspond. Richmond Locomotive and Machine Works employees with the motto 'day light and night' were under the command of Robert R. Taylor.

Fitchier Band of Lynchburg were under the leadership of William B. Booker. The Plasters' Union in their white overalls...looked well.

The Excelsior Broom Makers bore aloft brooms and attracted much attention by their unique appearance...

The Virginia Normal and Collegiate Institute Band, U. S. G. Patterson, leader, surprised all. They discoursed sweet music and were handsomely uniformed.

Booker's Drum Corp (fife and drum) William Booker leader.[51]

Mayo's Factory hands were under the leadership of David Broaddus and Athan Green.

The Teamsters' Club...bore carriage whips...

The line rested on 19th street. Coming up Main street, cheer after cheer rent the air. It was evidence direct that the Negro is coming" (*Richmond Planet*).

• ***October 10, 1891 (New Orleans, Louisiana):*** "[M]embers of the Mirth Club assembled at the invitation of their president, Mr. Alphonse Ledoux and his amiable wife at their beautiful residence on [St.] Ann street of the 7th district. The table fairly groaned under its weight of the most choice and most toothsome of the season...Speeches, jokes, songs, instrumentals, toasts and repartees were the order of the evening. Prof. Harry Lambert's fine band stationed among the foliage discoursed sweet strains of music to the enjoyment of all present. The party was held on the spacious lawn of the host" (*Indianapolis Freeman*).

• ***October 11, 1891 (Topeka, Kansas):*** "Stage Notes," "George Freeman, undoubtedly the best colored cornetist in the country, and manager of the Hyer Sisters, gave a concert at the Copeland hotel while here.

Irine Hart, the colored actress with Kate Castleton's Company, reports a big business and a very pleasant trip on the coast...

Albert Brown, of this city, is today the best colored slack wire walker in the country, is with Smith's Big Colored Specialty Company, and will play east this season" (*Topeka Weekly Call*).

• ***October 17, 1891:*** "Bergen Star Concerts," "On Thursday evening, Oct. 8, a Bergen Star concert was given at the Bridge Street Church, Brooklyn...Long before the program was commenced the church was crowded, and at 8:25 when the choir sang the opening chorus, chairs had been placed in the aisles, and many were obliged to remain standing throughout the evening...

Mrs. Flora Batson Bergen and Mrs. Matilda Jones were the stars of the evening. Mrs. Bergen has lost none of her entrancing power...Her descriptive song titled 'The Bridge' was rendered in a manner which cannot be surpassed. Mrs. Jones was greeted with great applause . . . This was her first appearance in Brooklyn" (*New York Age*).

• ***October 17, 1891 (New York City):*** "The concert given October 11th for the benefit of Bethel A.M.E. Church was a grand success and a crowded house greeted the stars, Mme Flora Batson Bergen and Mme Mathilda S. Jones. This was Mme Jones' second appearance in New York since her return from her tour through the West Indies and South America, where she met with great success. Her voice is something wonderful. They were supported by local talent" (*Indianapolis Freeman*).

• ***October 17, 1891:*** "The Original Tennessee Colored Specialty Co., under the management of G. Osborne Grant, are meeting with reported success through Pennsylvania and New Jersey. They will also tour the provinces. Sylvester Russell is the star of the company, which includes, besides Frank De Lyon, the Silver Lake Quartet (Potts, Dixon, Sawer and Johnson), Billy Green, Otis H. Ball, Lit. Jones and others. Frank De Lyon is stage manager" (*New York Clipper*),

• ***October 23, 1891 (New York City):*** "Personal," "We are natural vocalists. We sing almost as naturally as Shelly's 'skylark.' We need not the elaborate culture of European conservatories to be able to touch the tenderest chords of human sympathy. In our church choirs all over the country there are soprano, alto, basso and tenor voices almost angelic in purity of tone and expression the possession of which by a white person would be worth a snug fortune; but just now there is small space on the operatic stage for black interpreters of classic sonatas. But the triumph is coming. These natural flowers from Nature's musical garden cannot always 'waste their sweetness on the desert air.' It is contrary to the usual and regular order of things . . .

Ever since she appeared here a half decade ago in ballad parts Flora Batson has been a prime favorite . . . She has been a hard conscious student of voice, method and stage presence. As a consequence her voice has gained flexibility and strength . . . In the two concerts given in New York and Brooklyn recently Miss Batson astonished the audiences with a bit of acting in the 'Bridge Song'. . . Hard study will tell in the work of any artist, and it tells very perceptibly in the work of Miss Batson.

Madame Jones has more of a reputation as a singer in the West Indies than in the [States] . . . the last one under contract with Miss Florence Williams, who still has a company in the West Indies. When in Hayti Madame Jones and the company sang for President Hippolyte in the palace at Port-au-Prince and received $500 in gold as a mark of his appreciation . . . In operatic parts she appears to good advantage. She was received with great favor and if all the conditions were equal there is no question but that she would in time become as great a favorite in the United States as she is in the West Indies" (T. Thomas Fortune, *New York Age*).

• ***October 24, 1891 (Indianapolis, Indiana):*** "City News," "The Magnolia Quartette is the name of a new musical organization, composed of the following gentlemen: Thos. Pittman, soprano; Silas Fisher, baritone and specialist; Paul Floyd, tenor; Charles Poole, bass. The organization made its first public appearance and scored a great success. Mr. Fisher the specialist of the quartet, is an artist of high degree" (*Indianapolis Freeman*).

• ***October 24, 1891:*** "The Original Tennessee Colored Specialty Co. is in the midst of financial trouble at Philadelphia, caused by a series of unprofitable one night stands through Pennsylvania. Manager Grant's company, however, are loyally standing by him, and the tour will be resumed if the necessary capital can be secured" (*New York Clipper*).

• ***October 30, 1891 (Kansas City, Kansas):*** "Wanted," "At Once two or three good Musicians, and Comedians who can play Mandolin, Guitar or Banjos, and, who can sing loud. A good Organist and Vocalist wanted one who reads music. Apply at Ryus Hotel . . . Salary sure to the right men.

N. B. Monte, bunkers, lurkers, crap shooters and would be's need not apply" (*Kansas City American Citizen*).

• ***October 31, 1891 (Greenville, Alabama):*** "We have a fine string band here that cannot be excelled in this state, conducted by Mr. Raymond Oliver" (*Indianapolis Freeman*).

• ***October 31, 1891:*** "Our Musical People," "The Richmond Jubilee Singers have headquarters at Philadelphia . . .

The Louisiana Jubilee Singers are the attraction at the corn palace at Sioux City, Iowa.

The New Orleans University singers were at the Zion Wesley A.M.E. Philadelphia Church Oct., 14th.

The Famous Glenn Family or Georgia Warblers are making a great hit at the London Musee, State Street, Chicago" (*Indianapolis Freeman*).

• ***November 1, 1891:*** "Stage Notes," "Heyer's Sisters are playing to good houses in Nebraska.

S. B. Hyers, the only colored musical comedy company, are playing week stands in the East. Among their plays are, 'Out of Bondage,' 'Blackville Twins,' and 'Colored Aristocracy' " (*Topeka Weekly Call*).

Note: S. B. Hyers was father to the famous Hyers Sisters. The three of them had worked together in the original 1870s production of "Out of Bondage." At this time, however, the father and his daughters had two separate companies.

• ***November 1, 1891 (Topeka, Kansas):*** "Brothers please quit singing that song, 'Take all the world and give me Jesus.' That talk used to go, but it don't go now" (*Topeka Weekly Call*).

• ***November 6, 1891:*** "The entertainment given at Ellis, Kansas, by the 'Union Pacific Quartette club,' last Thursday evening . . . was a grand success . . . Mr. J. Drake made a great hit in his song, 'A stitch in time saves nine.' Mr. E. Rector, of Kansas City, Mo., made a lasting impression on the people of Ellis, with his songs and dances. Mr. A. Bates will be remembered as having a very sweet voice. His ballad, 'Worlds Fair in 93,' was well rendered. After the concert, the young people enjoyed themselves by tripping the light fantastic toe, until the early morning, after which the club boys made one rush for the Depot, feeling well paid for their nights festivities" (*Kansas City American Citizen*).

• ***November 7, 1891 (Cincinnati, Ohio):*** "Walker's Merry Makers, the great southern trio . . . have just closed a seven week engagement at Kohl & Middleton's museum. Great credit is due these gentlemen, for the artistic manner in which they render their music, vocal and instrumental" (*Cleveland Gazette*).

• ***November 7, 1891 (Glasgow, Kentucky):*** "The Non Musical Quartette were out last Friday night and made the stillness of the night melodious with fine music rendered by them" (*Indianapolis Freeman*).

• ***November 8, 1891 (Topeka, Kansas):*** "Stage Notes," "Hyers Sisters are only doing fair through Iowa . . .

Irine Hart was here with Kate Castleton Co., Monday and Tuesday nights. She is the same Irine, pleasant and graceful as ever. This is her third season with Kate Castleton" (*Topeka Weekly Call*).

• ***November 14, 1891 (Evanston, Illinois):*** "The Tennessee Jubilee Singers gave one of their characteristic concerts in Evanston on Tuesday evening the third to a large audience, and were encored a number of times. Their programme, for the most part, was very good, especially the songs by the male quartette; the solos by Miss Zoe Ball, and the old Negro preacher, delineated by Mr. Wise" (*Indianapolis Freeman*).

• ***November 14, 1891 (Cincinnati, Ohio):*** "The Carmen double quartette, composed of the best male talent in Cincinnati, will concert during the holidays. Messrs. Johnson and Bushong are the best bass singers in the city. The quartette has rendered music of a very high standard. Such an organization of young men has never before existed in this city" (*Cleveland Gazette*).

• ***November 14, 1891:*** "Roster of S. B. Hyers' Colored Comedy Co.: S. B. Hyers, manager, Chas. T. Small, stage manager; Coke. Newman, advance agent; the Mines, Bob and Gussie, Thos. W. Davis, Mrs. Nellie Small, May C. Hyers, Barney Gardner. Business good and everybody happy" (*New York Clipper*).

• ***November 20, 1891 (Lawrence, Kansas):*** "The entertainment given by the ladies of Mt. Maria Tabernacle, at National Bank hall, Nov. 5th, was indeed a grand affair. Its principal features was walking for a cake" (*Kansas City American Citizen*).

• ***November 21, 1891:*** "The Olympian Quartette, comedians and vocalists, are making a great hit in Texas" (*Indianapolis Freeman*).

• ***November 22, 1891 (Topeka, Kansas):*** "Stage Notes," "Doc Saylers [*sic*] is with the Turner Medicine Co., and doing well" (*Topeka Weekly Call*).

• ***November 28, 1891 (New Haven, Connecticut):*** "Mr. John Godette, Jr. gave one of his popular concerts Thursday evening Nov. 12, at the Atheneum with a full house of New Haven's best people, of whom one half were whites . . . The Elm City Quartet produced in addition to their special selections, some of those quaint old plantation songs which received prolonged applause" (*New York Age*).

Freeman, *December 19, 1891.*

Note to illustration above: J. H. "Harry" Fiddler rose to national prominence as a comedian, playing opposite Billy Kersands in late-1890s editions of Richards and Pringle's Georgias. He eventually turned to vaudeville, and from 1907 to 1917 he was the stage partner

Freeman, *February 26, 1910.*

of ragtime piano pioneer Ruby Shelton. According to the March 1, 1913, edition of the *Freeman*, Fiddler and Shelton had been "playmates in school in Indianapolis." The *Freeman* of April 10, 1915, noted, "Class and art are displayed every moment in the Fiddler-Shelton act... Harry Fiddler does not need the assistance of cork... to make him funny... He has complete control of the facial muscles and distorts and contorts them into any desirable position or shape. He has many rivals as a Chinese impersonator, but it is safe to say that Harry stands at the head of the list." Fiddler remained active as a "single" into the late 1920s, at least.[52]

• ***December 4, 1891 (Kansas City, Kansas):*** "Happy Hours sandwiched between Thanksgiving and Xmas. A Grand Musical and Promenade will be given by the Oriole Orchestra, at Vineyard's Hall, Wed. Eve., Dec. 9th. Good order will be maintained during this evening of enjoyment, for young and old. Refreshments served in the hall. Admission 50 cas [*sic*]. Tickets for sale at Simpson's Barber Shop on 12th St." (*Kansas City American Citizen*).

• ***December 5, 1891:*** "The Tennessee Jubilee Singers, under the management of Lew Johnson, are in California" (*Indianapolis Freeman*).

• ***December 5, 1891 (Cincinnati, Ohio):*** "The Carmen Double quartette gave their first concert in Allen Temple, November 26. Mr. Clarence N. Johnson, the bass singer of the Carmen quartette, has joined the concert company of Mrs. Jennie DeHart" (*Cleveland Gazette*).

• ***December 19, 1891:*** "Stage," "The Hyer sisters will start for the Pacific slope in January...

The Bohee Brothers, specialists, will make the season in Australia" (*Indianapolis Freeman*).

• ***December 19, 1891:*** "The Hearne Academy Choral Union will travel next year in the interest of the school" (*Indianapolis Freeman*).

• ***December 19, 1891:*** "Sylvester Russell Angry," "I was surprised when I picked up last week's *New York Clipper* and saw my name advertised as a member of the Tennessee Minstrels. I sang at two performances with this company last October, while waiting to appear at a star concert at the Academy of Music in Philadelphia" (Sylvester Russell, *New York Age*).

The Texarkana Minstrel Company and the Jefferson Davis Monument Fund: "The Thing Is Unnatural"

• ***July 30, 1891:*** "A Monument for Jeff. Davis." "I clip the following from the [New Orleans] *Times Democrat* of July 21: 'Texarkana, July 20.—The colored people who came originally from the ante bellum home of Jefferson Davis, in Mississippi, will give an entertainment at Ghio's Opera House, Wednesday night, the proceeds of which are to go to the benefit of the Jeff. Davis monument fund.'

This is an outrageous shame! What has Jefferson Davis done for the colored people that they should want to help raise funds to help build a monument for him? The cause for which he fought, and spent his life, I should say, left enough monuments on the backs of the poor fathers and mothers, to satisfy any people... The charitable thing for our people to do is to try to forget such men as Jeff. Davis. The white people of the South would respect us more for it. They know as well as we, that no people honestly feel like building monuments for anybody that fought to keep them in slavery, under the lash, and that sold their children, parents, and husbands and wives from each other. The thing is unnatural" (*Southwestern Christian Advocate*).

Note: The author of this letter, Alice R. Albert, was the wife of the editor of the *Southwestern Christian Advocate*, Rev. A. E. P. Albert.

• ***August 8, 1891 (Texarkana, Texas):*** "Awfully Dissatisfied," "We are awfully dissatisfied and will be more than obliged to you if you will publish this in your paper, which is a thorough statement as to how the great story got out concerning our Minstrel show. We signed a contract to give a performance at the opera house on Thursday, July 30th, and the gentlemen that we signed with were to pay all expenses and give us 40 per cent of the gross receipts and he had the bills, advertising the show, printed to suit himself; he had Jeff Davis' name put on the bills for the purpose of getting a crowd at the opera house. We were surprised and hated to see Jeff Davis' name on our bills but were too late getting to the printing office and seeing the bills before they were distributed about the streets. We had signed the contract to give the show before the bills were printed. We did not get a penny of our 40 per cent" (*Indianapolis Freeman*).

• ***August 13, 1891:*** "The Texarkana Minstrel Company and the Jefferson Davis Monument Fund," "The sharp criticism which Mrs. A. E. P. Albert administered to the colored minstrel troupe which was announced to give a performance at the opera house in Texarkana, Texas, for the benefit of the Jeff Davis monument fund, has raised a considerable flurry in the troupe, and they have united in a letter in which they seek to exonerate themselves. They claim that they performed for 40 per cent of the proceeds and that 60 per cent went to the contractor...

This, to say the least, smells rather suspicious, and makes it appear as if somebody was quite willing to go into partnership, into any kind of co-operation, so long as 'our 40 per cent' was not at all diminished. Smooth it over as you will or may, the thing looks worse the more the young troupers seek to explain it. Under the circumstances, we are not at all surprised to learn that 'the colored people of Texarkana were raging mad with them,' for they profited from the use of Jeff Davis' name equally with the contractor and were accessories to the fact, in that they performed and shared the profits under that representation.

The troupe is composed of Dave Jackson, Will Dyson, Isaac Mingo, James Benson, Cary Daughtry, Scott Soplin [*sic*], John Adams, Pleasant Jackson and Hugh Garner. Their action dishonors their race and curses the memories of John Brown, Abraham Lincoln, Wm. Lloyd Garrison, Calvin Fairbank and the host of abolitionists that fought and bled that they might enjoy the privilege of organizing such a troupe" (*Southwestern Christian Advocate*).

Note: Typesetting error notwithstanding, here lies the earliest-known printed reference to Scott Joplin.[53]

Two Southern Brass Bands in New York City: Becker's Brass Band from Kentucky and the Onward Brass Band from Louisiana

In New York City during the summer and fall of 1891, while Johnson's Military Band of twenty-four pieces catered to the band needs of black society, Prof. J. M. Becker's Brass Band—six pieces from southern Kentucky—carved out a living from church and fraternal functions among the emerging black middle class. Another southern brass band visited New York that summer when the Onward Brass Band of Reserve, Louisiana, was invited to participate in a national convocation of Knights of Pythias. It is tempting to suppose that these southern, community-based bands demonstrated regional peculiarities of vernacular style. Within the next few years, ragtime minstrelsy would exact a profound homogenization of black musical culture.

• ***January 3, 1891:*** "The Onward Brass Band of St. John, La., have signed a contract to play for the Grand Conclave of Knights of Pythias in New York City during August, 1891. So in order to properly equip themselves they propose giving a series of prize entertainments, and respectfully request the assistance of their many friends" (*Indianapolis Freeman*).

J. M. Becker's Brass Band.

Here for the Season! A first class Colored Brass Band from Southern Kentucky are prepared to furnish Music for Excursions, Picnics, Festivals and Receptions. We earnestly ask the patronage of Churches, Lodges and Music hunters in general. We are six in number and will endeavor to give you perfect satisfaction. Give us a trial. Address, J. M. BECKER, 929 Sixth Avenue, Top floor, Or 453 Seventh Avenue.

New York Age, *June 13, 1891.*

• ***July 4, 1891 (New Orleans, Louisiana):*** "The excursion to New York that leaves here on the 30th of July, will stop over at Cincinnati and Washington, and returning stop over at New Port [*sic*], R. I., Boston, Philadelphia, Brooklyn and other important cities. Hercules Division No. 4, V.R.K. of P. and the Creole Onward brass band and Supreme Chancellor, Major General and Staff, and two Grand Chancellor's families and other excursionists are among those who will be along. Train leaves over the Q and C.R.R. The Crescent City gang are 'heart breakers' so beware, ye beaux of the North and East!" (*Indianapolis Freeman*).

• ***July 25, 1891 (New Orleans, Louisiana):*** "The great New York excursion leaves here on the 31st . . . They give a public review and picnic the day prior, at Spanish Fort. The brass band [along with] officers and members of the division will show their Northern friends what a Southern division can do" (*Indianapolis Freeman*).

• ***August 8, 1891:*** "Knights of Pythias Meet," "The Supreme Lodge K. of P., N.A.S.A., E., A. and A. held its sixth biennial session in this city at Wendel's Assembly Rooms this week . . . a welcome reception was tendered to the Supreme Lodge by the Grand Lodge of New York . . . The concert which followed was of a very high order; the performances of Misses Joseph of New Orleans, demonstrated them artists of the first class. The Onward Brass Band of St. John, La., also contributed worthy numbers to the program. The features of the program, however, were the numbers given by Mrs. and Miss Preston of Detroit, Mich. The Delsartean Pantomime by Miss Preston and selection 'Le Partate' stamped her a young woman of unusual culture and an artist of exceptional power . . . On Wednesday evening the Knights held a musical and literary entertainment at Bridge Street A.M.E. Church, Brooklyn . . . The musical part of the program differed little from the one rendered the previous night in New York City. The Knights were to have a clambake and encampment at Flushing Thursday and wind up their festivities with a street parade Friday" (*New York Age*).

Note: Prominent black New Orleans lawyer J. Madison Vance was one of the principal speakers at this Knights of Pythias convention, and he probably accompanied the Onward Brass Band to New York. To think that the Onward Brass Band was upstaged by a "Delsartean Pantomime!" "St. John" may refer to St. John the Baptist Parish, which is just upriver from New Orleans and includes the riverside town of Reserve. New Orleans jazz clarinetist Edmond Hall is quoted in *Hear Me Talkin' To Ya* (1955) saying: "My father was a musician. His name was Edward Hall. As a matter of fact he was a member of the Onward Brass Band that came to New York from New Orleans, in 1891." Hall mentioned this again in a 1957 interview, adding that the band was led by "Jim Humphries," the legendary itinerant brass band instructor and patriarch of the Humphrey family of New Orleans jazzmen.[54]

• ***September 5, 1891 (New York City):*** "Mt. Olivet Excursion," "The 11th annual excursion of Mt. Olivet Baptist Church took place on Thursday, Aug. 27, to Grand View Park on Long Island. The steamer *Pavonia* and barge *Warren,* which were chartered for the occasion, comfortably accommodated the large number that embarked for a day's pleasure . . . A pleasant sail of a few hours was had up the East River . . . Meanwhile, J. M. Becker's Brass Band discoursed sweet music, which had an inspiring effect on those who desired to trip the light fantastic toe on the barge. The refreshment tables were under competent attendants and were well

Becker's Brass Band,
having concluded to remain in the city, desires to inform the public that it can be hired at very reasonable terms. Satisfaction guaranteed. Address,
J. M. BECKER, 9[illegible]9 Sixth Ave,
TOP FLOOR, OR
GEO. H. WASHINGTON, Manager, 453 7th Ave.

New York Age, *September 26, 1891.*

patronized. Nothing unpleasant transpired until the Grove was reached, when one of the young men anxious to land so as to secure a table on the grove, unintentionally jostled against a white deck hand, who cut him badly on the left temple and in turn was severely thrashed by the young man's friends and was not again seen during the day on the boat. At the grove the excursionists set their tables and ate their dinners in the open air. The band in the meantime had marched at the head of a large procession to the platform, playing lively airs, which amused the younger portion of the assemblage very much, and then they danced there" (*New York Age*).

"Rags" in Tennesseetown, 1891

The word "ragtime" is not known to have appeared in print until 1896. As early as 1891, however, the word "rag" was being used to describe a certain type of social dance affair currently popular among a class of folks in eastern Kansas.

• ***August 16, 1891 (Topeka, Kansas):*** "City News," "The Jordan hall 'rags,' which are held in Tennessee town weekly, are a nuisance and should be abated" (*Topeka Weekly Call*).

Note: This is the earliest yet-discovered appearance of the word "rags" in a seemingly music-related context.

Tennesseetown, scene of the notorious "Jordan hall 'rags,'" had sprung up on the western edge of Topeka during the 1870s as an "Exoduster" enclave, the final destination for hundreds of African American refugees from deteriorating racial conditions in the South, mostly from Tennessee and Mississippi. During the 1890s, "living conditions in Tennesseetown were substandard by any criteria."[55] Further complaints about the "Jordan Hall nuisance" and cryptic comments about Tennesseetown and its inhabitants give some notion of the general ambience.

• ***October 4, 1891 (Topeka, Kansas):*** "The Jordan Hall nuisance must be stopped at all hazards, and without violence or loss of life" (*Topeka Weekly Call*).

• ***October 4, 1891 (Topeka, Kansas):*** "Those 'shin-digs' who were passing through Tennesseetown going home from a dance Monday night, ought to have muzzles on their mouths so they will not annoy people who wish to sleep" (*Topeka Weekly Call*).

• ***October 11, 1891 (Topeka, Kansas):*** "Last Monday evening the Patrol wagon was called out to Jordan's [Hall] to quiet a row" (*Topeka Weekly Call*).

Apparently, just as things were heating up at Jordan's Hall, a certain folksong became popular with Tennesseetown girls.

• ***October 18, 1891 (Topeka, Kansas):*** "A certain class of girls in Tennesseetown sings a song called 'Proctor Knok' [*sic*] from sun rise until sun set. Girls you must be fond of this song. We wonder if your parents ever heard you sing it" (*Topeka Weekly Call*).

• ***November 8, 1891:*** "They Say," "Misses Electro P. and Minnie E. are very fond of singing 'Proctor Knot [*sic*].' They sing it to the boys at festivals and entertainments" (*Topeka Weekly Call*).

James Proctor Knott was a prominent Kentucky politician during Reconstruction. The popular folksong, however, was not about a man, but a famous racehorse named Proctor Knott. An article in a 1913 edition of the *Journal of American Folk-Lore* preserves a version of "Proctor Knott" reportedly collected from "country whites" in Mississippi in 1909:

> *Bet your money on Proctor Knott!*
> *He's a horse of mine.*
> *Done quit runnin';*
> *He's gone to flyin',*
> *All the way from Little Rock*
> *Bet your money on Proctor Knott.*
> *Proctor Knott run so fast*
> *You couldn't see nothing but the jockey's ass.*[56]

An anecdotal human-interest article in a 1909 edition of the *St. Louis Post-Dispatch* associated the folksong "Proctor Knott" with the origins of ragtime:

> A negro woman, whose name is unknown to fame, is declared to have invented ragtime in St. Louis in 1888, in a house, now fallen, at Broadway and Clark avenue . . .
>
> It was the day of Proctor Knott, a famous racehorse, and he was the theme of an epoch-making ballad which she sang. One stanza has been preserved:
>
> "I-za a-gwine tuh Little Rock, Tuh put mah money on-a Proctuh Knott."[57]

Another informative, tantalizing "Jordan's Hall item" appeared in the "Social and Personal" column of the *Topeka Weekly Call* on December 14, 1895: "Jordan's dancing academy opens at Jordan's hall r170 Lincoln street, Dec. 20. A. R. Eagleson, instructor, Simon Jordan, assistant, W. A. Jordan, business manager."

Chapter Four

1892

Cake Walks in Context

"No one who has never seen a cake-walk can imagine what it is."

—Detroit Plaindealer, 1892

During the spring of 1892 a rash of cake-walk extravaganzas broke out in several big cities of the Northeast and Midwest. By some contemporaneous accounts, these cynically promoted cake walks were spectacles of the ridiculous, undermining and corrupting an African American tradition "for the amusement of the white people, who look down on them, in every sense of the word, from the galleries." At their worst, these commercial cake-walk ventures served to "minstrelize" black *identity*, exploiting a rustic slave custom which, in some of its earliest manifestations, may have been provided on demand for the amusement of plantation masters and their guests.[1]

The cake-walk controversy of 1892 was triggered by an immensely successful "Grand Cake Walk" held on the evening of Wednesday, February 17, at Madison Square Garden, the largest commercial entertainment venue in New York City. The *New York Age* carried a small advertisement for the event and extended a seemingly reluctant endorsement: "Madison Square Garden will be the scene of a novel style of entertainment for that place, notwithstanding the varied shows that have sought public patronage on that spot . . . It is announced as a 'grand cake walk,' which the management proposes to conduct with strict propriety and under respectable auspices. It is thought that under these conditions it will prove a drawing card."[2]

One week before the Grand Cake Walk took place, a meeting was held at Bethel A.M.E. Church on Sullivan Street, and a local community leader "spoke in the most pronounced terms of the manner in which the race was caricatured at the elevated stations in the advertisements of the Madison Square Garden cake walk."[3] Though the *Age* appears to have refrained from reviewing the event, the local dailies were quick to weigh in. According to a morning-after review, on February 18, 1892, in the *New York Press*, "spectators went fairly wild over the great exhibition of style, elegance and grace." However, the *Press* went on to note, without explanation, that the judges of the cake walk "took their places with a shame faced look."

The *New York Times* turned its review into a more general discussion of "the institution of the cake walk":

> The proud Caucasian is apt to sneer at the institution of the cake walk, although in that institution there are expressed, in a manner most interesting to the philosopher and most touching to the philanthropist, the aesthetic yearnings of the African race . . . Now the cake walker does at least attempt, for the space during which he walks for a cake, to convert himself into a work of art. One would expect that the representatives of what boasts itself to be a superior race would cheer him on this effort. As a matter of fact they do nothing of the kind. Cake walks, as they have been known heretofore, are attended by whites exclusively for the purpose of guying the cake walker and, if possible, breaking him up in his stride. Indeed, it is often the design of the white spectators of the baser sort to break up the whole cake walk, and this intention is frustrated only by the superior numbers of the African race and their promptness with the lethal razor. The cake walk is commonly given in comparative secluded quarters and intended for the race to which the cake walkers

belong. When the largest place of entertainment in New York was secured for the cake walk last night, and the utmost possible publicity given to the enterprise, it was not an unreasonable suspicion that the intention was not to hold out the cake walkers as models for the reverent imitation of the spectators, but to expose them to the derision of an unsympathetic concourse of whites.

This is all very wrong. The African race is comic mainly for the reason that it is imitative, but the cake walk is an institution evolved from the African intellect . . . The Assyrian sculptures and the Egyptian mural decorations prove that in those ancient days there was a sense of "grace, style and execution," which are the qualities in which the contestants of last night competed. Nay, it has been justly observed that the frieze of the Parthenon itself is the representation of a Pan-Athenaic cake walk.

Instead of jeering at the cake walkers, therefore, we ought to do them homage for keeping alive the regard for graceful locomotion to which we pay so little heed. It is, indeed, unlikely that the modern sculptor would find inspiration in a cake walk for a rivalry with the carved processions of antiquity. His search for grace and style might be impeded by his painful consciousness of a too prognathous jaw or a too protrusive heel. The more credit is due to the performers who, more or less in spite of nature . . . exhibit a dignified indifference to the guyings of spectators in the boxes, who would themselves cut a very indifferent figure on the floor.[4]

Within a couple weeks of the Madison Square Garden cake walk, a similar event was held in Cincinnati, Ohio.

• ***March 4, 1892 (Cincinnati, Ohio):*** "A Cincinnati Cake-Walk," "Feb. 29.—Great preparations are being made here for the coming cake-walk and the local cake-walkers may be depended upon to put their best foot forward to prevent the valuable prizes which are to be given going to any outsiders. The champions from other states are all entering for the big walk.

A Cincinnatian who witnessed the recent cake-walk at Madison square, New York, says a

THE "CAKE WALK" A BIG SUCCESS

A Novel Scene Witnessed at Madison Square Garden.

The Walkers Were Very Much in It, but Not More So Than Little "Old Folks" and Miss Blizzard in "Buck" Dancing.

Long before the time set for the opening of Madison Square Garden for the great cake walk last night seats were at a premium. A line of people extended for blocks down Madison avenue and the Fourth avenue entrance was besieged with colored beaux and belles who had been practicing for weeks to win the coveted "cake" and the first prize—a grand piano. "Polo Jim" was master of ceremonies.

At 9 o'clock the walkers appeared, led by that prince of walkers, "Polo Jim," who, with his beautiful partner, dressed in a cream colored brocaded silk, trimmed with crepe de chene and a train yards in length, fairly "took the cake" in the estimation of the spectators. Mr. Nichols, chef of the International Hotel, also came in for a great share of the applause, and by his graceful, elegant style in turning the corners evidently had a cinch for first prize.

After the promenade the lanciers was danced. Only about fifteen couple appeared for the grand walk. The small number was somewhat dispiriting to the spectators, but they made things easy for the judges by discarding the concealed weapons with which they had provided themselves. The Gorham Base Ball Club sextet then sang and were appreciated.

The judges took their places with a shame faced look, and a scene such as the Garden never saw before followed. The spectators went fairly wild over the great exhibition of style, elegance and grace.

"Nobby" Ned of Brooklyn and his dusky partner, and "Dandy Jack" came in for a great share of applause. Luke Blackburn and his partner, Martha James, won many encomiums for their walking and were included in the "finals." The "buck" dancing took the crowd in great shape and "Little Old Folks" sent the audience wild. When Miss Lizzie Blizzard danced the "Mobile Buck" the roof came off the Garden, and Diana herself did a few steps.

Luke Blackburn and Martha James were awarded the first prize, Bill Proctor and Mary Clifford the second, Dandy Jack and Mrs. Frank Hoy the third.

[Daily New York] Press, *February 18, 1892.*

large number of fashionable people in the packed auditorium went with the view of ridiculing the affair, but soon after the walk began they joined in the general applause and admiration.

No one who has never seen a cake-walk can imagine what it is, and no one who has seen one can possibly describe it. It must be seen to be appreciated or understood. More than one thousand of our 400 [i.e., the black community's society elite] have already bespoken seats, and it is evident that standing room will be at a premium on that occasion even in the vast Music Hall.

The following prizes will be awarded for beauty, grace, style or eccentricity to those participating in the walk:

First Prize—a $400 grand upright piano... A gold-headed cane and a mammoth cake representing a cake-walk...

Second Prize—A double cased gold watch and silver swinging ice pitcher.

Third Prize—A gold-headed cane and a double cased watch.

Fourth Prize—A double cased gold watch and a fancy clock.

These prizes are to be seen in the windows of Messrs. Oskamp, Nolting & Co., southwest corner of Fifth and Vine streets" (*Detroit Plaindealer*).

The Cincinnati cake walk provoked a rancorous response from representatives of the black community; this set the tone for a unified African American press position on cake walks.

• ***March 18, 1892 (Cincinnati, Ohio):*** "The management of the cake walk fiasco used every endeavor to try and make it appear as if that performance would be given by the 'elite' Afro Americans of this city... Notwithstanding these efforts, not a dozen Afro-Americans in the whole city were degraded enough to lend themselves as foolish tools to perpetuate a degrading practice...

There was not even a respectable Negro in the audience. They are letting white men play the 'Nigger' now, and nearly 2,000 of them turned out to do it. The men who engineered this cake walk affair are the ones who aid and abet immorality among Afro-Americans and then point to it as a racial weakness" (*Detroit Plaindealer*).

• ***March 19, 1892 (Chicago, Illinois):*** "The malicious misrepresentation of colored society by the daily papers is disgraceful, and to have heard the denouncements of cake walks would have shocked the most vigorous cake walker of the nineteenth century. Rev. J. P. Jenner, of Quinn Chapel, in his prepared sermon of last Sunday, denounced cake walking and sought to discourage any cake walkers within the sound of his voice, and demonstrated the ridiculous spectacle" (*Indianapolis Freeman*).

• ***March 25, 1892:*** "A colored preacher in Chicago thinks the cake-walks disgraceful to the colored race. They make themselves cheap and ridiculous for the amusement of the white people, who look down on them, in every sense of the word, from the galleries. He hopes they will show more self respect than to join in them. In Detroit the recent cake walk was a failure simply because of the refusal of the colored people in this city and vicinity to make a show of themselves for the pleasure of the whites" (*Detroit Plaindealer*, reprinted from the *Detroit Journal*).

• ***April 1, 1892 (Grand Rapids, Michigan):*** "The 'cake walk' given at Hartman hall Monday night was not a success artistically or financially. It was evident that the Afro-Americans of this city took no stock in the affair, as the walk proper had less than half a dozen participants, which were of the lowest class" (*Detroit Plaindealer*).

• ***April 22, 1892 (Milwaukee, Wisconsin):*** "It is rumoured that the K. of P's are soon to give another of their pleasant entertainments... One thing we would suggest to them . . . that is, to be a little more particular whom they invite . . . If the respectable people of any community deserved to be distinguished from the disreputable class, they can not be too strict in drawing the social line. During the progress of the 'cake walk' gang through the country, our people set up a great howl of indignation because the daily papers called the participants in the cake walk the 'elite of colored society,' etc. . . . But how can we expect the Anglo-Saxon to classify us if we do not endeavor to classify ourselves. If we admit disreputable people to our entertainments, associate with them on the streets, we must not blame the whites when they think we are one and the same so far as our social standing is concerned" (*Detroit Plaindealer*).

• ***May 6, 1892 (Springfield, Ohio):*** "The so-called cake walk came off on the 28th ult., and it was indeed a disgrace to those who took part, but we are glad to say that none of the better class of our people were there. The parties who got up this enterprise tried their best to persuade our young girls to take part, but Rev. Ransom denounced it from his pulpit in time to save our people from being disgraced and ridiculed by the white people, for they were there in full to make fun of us as a race, and they were very much surprised in not seeing our best people there. This so-called cake walk has been denounced by the colored press throughout the country. All that have been gotten up were by the lower and not the better class of the race" (*Detroit Plaindealer*).

Plans for a Madison Square Garden–style cake walk in Indianapolis, Indiana, during the spring of 1892 were met by such a well-coordinated fury of protest from the local black community that promoters were forced to cancel. This inspired the mainstream daily *Indianapolis News* to offer some "Complimentary Words for Indianapolis Colored People," which were reprinted in the *Freeman:*

> We congratulate the colored people of this community that the proposed "cake walk" has been abandoned. They have honored themselves and this city by making this the first protest against such a thing. Starting in New York, cake walks have occurred in many cities. It has been left to the sturdy good sense and self-respect of the colored people in Indianapolis to properly characterize such a thing, and to do it in a way powerful enough to stop it. Under proper conditions a cake walk is a proper thing. It is childish, but in its essence it is an expression of an endeavor of an improvement. To an ignorant, down-trodden enslaved people a cake walk—an endeavor to cultivate a seemly carriage—is what the practice of gymnastics might mean to an enfeebled race . . . But to make this a public spectacle is as inherently degrading as gladiatorial scenes which devoted the valor of slaves of barbarians to entertainment, with the difference that in this there was by its nature an abdication of manhood. It is worthy of remark and felicitation that our colored people were proof against it. They have asserted their self-respect.[5]

By way of response, the *Freeman* stated, "Next to being proud of the action of our own people in this matter that the *News* refers to, we feel thankful that we live in the midst of a community, the whites of whom, of which the *News* is a shining precursor and mouthpiece, do not desire us to be plantation hands and 'niggers' in our habits and manners, in order to respect and praise us." Another *Freeman* columnist noted, "The complimentary editorials which have appeared in the columns of the *News* and *Journal* relative to the stand taken by the colored people of the city against the proposed 'cake walk' would indicate that the Negroes of Indianapolis possessed a higher average of 'race pride' and good 'horse sense' than the majority of colored communities, which is a fact, and one that we are more than proud of."[6]

A theme that runs through the cake-walk commentaries in the African American press of

1892 is class pride, or class identity, and the desire of some African Americans to impress class distinctions upon white people and distance themselves from the behaviors of "disreputable" and "lower-class" blacks. It seems that cake walks, by their very nature, as well as in the way they were promoted, challenged these distinctions.

Many image-conscious, aspiring African Americans viewed white people's fascination with cake walks and other quaint "befo' de wah" expressions as a socially regressive trend in mainstream culture. The contradictions were redoubled when members of the white society elite began to engage in cake walking. The *Baltimore Afro-American* described a cake walk at an aristocratic gathering near White Plains, New York, in 1898, led by " 'Willie K.' Vanderbilt, a scion of that great house of that honored name . . . What with 'coon songs,' banjo picking and 'cake walks,' the white people are picking up what the better class of colored people are trying to get away from. Are the white people degenerating in their tastes?"[7]

The cake-walk craze provides an eloquent portrait of the bitter equivocation that characterized the ascendancy of black cultural expressions during the late nineteenth century. Despite the unanimity of editorial condemnation in the African American press of 1892, the Madison Square Garden Cake Walk became an annual event;[8] cake walking became a major feature of every black minstrel company on the road; and many minstrel performers leapt into national prominence as particular cake-walking stars.

Beneath the din of the great cake-walk controversy of 1892, at least two black southern community correspondents to the *Freeman* made mention of cake walks in the context of everyday reportage, as a seemingly ordinary community activity, along with literary society meetings, funerals, etc. The combination "rag

NOTICE TO MANAGERS.

"The Cake Walker's Dream,"

Introducing the Cake Walk with which I won the Championship at Madison Square Garden, New York. The hit of the season at Miner's Eighth Avenue Theatre this week, with FLYNN & SHERIDAN'S BIG SENSATION.

ONE BILLY FARRELL,

Assisted by Miss Willie Farrell.

New York Clipper, *October 12, 1895.*

social" and "prize grand march" conducted at an Americus, Georgia, fraternal lodge for the benefit of a local A.M.E. Church, reported on February 27, 1892; and the competitions carried out in Gretna, Louisiana, reported on December 17, 1892; may have respectfully commemorated a tradition-rich folk practice.

• ***February 27, 1892 (Americus, Georgia):*** "Rag Social," "The Rag Social entertainment given at Odd Fellows' hall . . . for the benefit of the A.M.E. Church, was a grand success . . . The most interesting part was the prize grand march by the participants in rags. After a close observation by the judges, it was decided that John T. Calhoun and Mrs. Annie L. Dixon were the winners of the prize, as they were the most ragged of all the competitors. The prize was a very fine cake with a sum of money in it" (*Indianapolis Freeman*).

Note: There is no readily apparent etymological relationship between this particular kind of "rag social" and ragtime music. The relationship between cake walks and "prize grand marches" seems more obvious.

• ***December 17, 1892 (Gretna, Louisiana):*** "Preached for a Cake," "Last Sunday night several preachers preached for a handsome cake. They realized $5.45 also there was a cake walk at Gasper's hall. Lewis Badger took the cake" (*Indianapolis Freeman*).

African American newspapers in eastern Kansas document a particular rivalry between two regional cake-walking stars of the 1890s, "Doc" Brown of Kansas City and Mr. Daisy Harris of Leavenworth. The tendency toward sarcasm in the reportage is somewhat betrayed by an underlying sense of community pride.

• ***May 5, 1893 (Kansas City, Kansas):*** "'Doc' Brown famous cake walkist gave an exhibition of his pastry pedestrianism Monday evening at the Charlotte street Baptist Church, during the May party. This distinguished (?) gentleman said to a CITIZEN reporter, 'I spec's to go to de world's fair and awgernize one av de biggest cake walks dat ever wuz an I will bring back all de big prizes to Kansas City and dat will make her de ledin town av de country.' Of course, we hope the famous doctor (?) will keep his word for we are very anxious that Kansas City may secure some distinction at the World's Fair, if it be only the honor of having 'taken the cake' from such villages as New York, Boston, Philadelphia and the rest of them" (*Kansas City American Citizen*).

• ***July 14, 1894 (Leavenworth, Kansas):*** "'Doc' Brown of Kansas City and 'Daisy' are going to walk for a cake in this city August 1. This will be an event worth going thousands and thousands of miles to see" (*Leavenworth Herald*).

• ***August 4, 1894:*** "Daisy Harris was the daisy at the cakewalk. Doc Brown will never be in it when Daisy takes the floor. The square-cornered turn of Daisy's makes Brown turn green with envy and the head of every member of the Sunflower club swell with pride. Since Daisy has embarked upon the field of cakewalking, may he ever bring the cakes to Leavenworth" (*Leavenworth Herald*).

• ***August 4, 1894:*** "Leavenworth Takes the Cake," "Kansas City wallows around in the soup—Daisy Harris wins easily—Doc Brown's 'Kangaroo Hop,' 'Elephant Squat' and 'Liza Jane' were nothing in comparison with Daisy's 'Featherfoot Fudge'—Daisy had a lead pipe cinch on Brown from the start—The doctor, like the colonel, simply put his foot in it" (*Leavenworth Herald*).

• ***December 15, 1894:*** "Mr. Daisy Harris, the professional cake walker and high roller. . . will go to Richmond, Mo., Dec. 23 to take part in a wide open shuffle cakewalk, and will receive $25, win or lose" (*Leavenworth Herald*).

Doc Brown also generated commentary in the mainstream daily *Kansas City Star*. During the fall of 1894 the *Star* paid close attention to Kansas City's new "Priests of Pallas Carnival," a three-day bacchanalia with mammoth street parades featuring dozens of floats; brass bands; a grand ball; a fireworks display; and, finally, a "night for pandemonium," in which "all restraint will be thrown aside and people will do very much as they please as long they do not break each other's heads or set fire to the city."[9]

From October 1 to October 4, 1894, tens of thousands of people roamed the streets of Kansas City in outlandish masks and costumes, blowing tin horns, banging on pots and pans, and howling into the wind. The *Star* observed a certain level of black participation: "Three negro boys, whom nature had made as black as interior African society would require, came prancing down the street in the garb of women, jangling a cow bell. They evidently were not satisfied with the hue of nature, so they had blackened their faces. . . Several negroes were masquerading as white people, with white masks on their faces, but they invariably forgot to make the deception any way near complete by covering their hands, and they would show in laughable contrast to their faces."[10]

Descriptions of the immensely popular "Doc Brown 'Cake Walk' float" were included in two different *Star* reviews of the "Priests of Pallas" parades. In the first review the *Star* reported:

> There were many happy and proud persons in the day parade, but "Perfesser" Doc Brown, the

champion cake walker of "Little Africa," was a trifle the happiest and the proudest mortal in line. He had a float to himself and he "cake walked" from start to finish. He exhibited all the styles of walking. Between bows and scrapings, he would walk the "knee-joint wobble" from the grand stand to the quarter post; then to the half he would go in a "hen wallow shuffle" and down the stretch he would come like a house afire, hitting sparks from the rocks in a "grape vine twist." The dignified, the plantation free and easy, the watermelon lope and the possum trot—all were shown by this past master in the art of cake-walking.[11]

In the second review the *Star* reported:

"Doc" Brown was monarch of all he surveyed. He was cheered from the time the parade started until it broke up. A very large float was devoted to his special use, and his efforts to execute his famous cake walk while the wagon was jarring along over the stone pavement between the car tracks on Walnut street and at the same time recognize the applause he was receiving were picturesque. He kept his high silk hat in his hand most of the time while he bowed to the crowd and tried to give a cake walk without falling down on a platform that seemed to be moving in every direction at once. A big crowd of negroes had gathered on Twelfth street, and as he approached they saw him a block away and began to yell: "Heah comes Doc Brown. Go foh it, Doc. Dat's right, Doc, you's right in it. Ole Doc's outer sight," and other expressions equally encouraging to the gallant Doc, who wore a grin that covered his whole face.[12]

Later reports in the *Star* make it known that, in addition to his cake-walking skills, Doc Brown was a walking encyclopedia of courtly bows and other stylized gestures of "p'lite susiety." He was commemorated on sheet music by the 1899 hit, "Doc Brown's Cake Walk," and as late as 1943, some forty years after his death, Doc Brown was still "green in the memory" of Kansas City's "older citizenry."[13]

Noticeable by its absence from the various black and white press reports on Doc Brown and Daisy Harris is any mention of female cake walking partners. It appears these two "Champions of the West" represented a male solo development in the ancient art of cake walking.

Toward a Black National Anthem: "John Brown's Body"

The year 1892 witnessed new levels of racial violence in the American Southland. Four hundred years after Columbus discovered himself in America, lynch mobs filled the headlines of the African American press. The refusal of a Chicago congregation to sing "America" at an anti-lynching rally that spring and the fact that "John Brown's Body" was sung instead characterize black America's sense of absolute disenfranchisement. There was the problem of how to express deep-felt patriotism in the face of institutionalized white racism. It seemed more appropriate to summon the spirit of the martyred abolitionist than to sing the empty line about a "sweet land of liberty."

"John Brown's Body" was one of the most popular songs to come out of the American Civil War. An early printed document of the lyrics to "John Brown's Body" appeared, with brief but passionate commentary, in the August 17, 1861, edition of the *National Anti-Slavery Standard:*

One of the favorite Massachusetts songs, sung by the regiment under Fletcher Webster, son of Daniel Webster, which has just passed on to join the army, commences as follows:

John Brown's body lies a-mouldering in the grave,
John Brown's body lies a-mouldering in the grave,
John Brown's body lies a-mouldering in the grave,
His soul's marching on!
Glory Hallelujah! Glory Hallelujah! Glory Hallelujah!
His soul's marching on!

The stanzas which follow are of the same wild strain:

> *2. He's gone to be a soldier in the army of the Lord, etc.,*
> *His soul's marching on!*
> *3. John Brown's knapsack is strapped upon his back, etc.*
> *His soul's marching on!*
> *4. His pet lambs will meet him on the way, etc.,*
> *His soul's marching on!*

Who could have dreamed of this while Webster lived? Who could have dreamed of it when John Brown died? Fletcher Webster would doubtless be glad to have his soldiers sing less violent abolition songs; but neither himself nor his father's ghost can stop the rolling wave. John Brown's ghost is too powerful for them . . . Months ago, a large premium was offered for a new national ode, but it must have nothing "sectional" in it. Aye, there's the rub; with this fetter on her wing the Muse will take no lofty flight. Money cannot make poetry; least of all patriotic poetry; and we should not wonder if, after all the labors of the Patriotic Committee in examining manuscripts, it should be found that the soldiers will still give the preference to the rough, wild strains that represent John Brown's spirit as leading them on to battle and to victory.

Subsequent reports in the *National Anti-Slavery Standard* suggest how quickly and completely "John Brown's Body" spread through black America. In the fall of 1862 a war correspondent stationed in "Little Washington," Virginia, mentioned that he often heard slaves at their work singing the John Brown chorus.[14] In the spring of 1863, an observer at the Magnolia Plantation in Louisiana, just downriver from New Orleans, noted that "the old John Brown song 'Marching On'. . . is universal here and westward among the negroes, and is sung here at their churches in New Orleans on Sunday at service."[15] When the black Fifty-fifth Massachusetts Regiment reached Charleston, South Carolina, in the spring of 1865, they marched into town singing "John Brown's Body," complete with the verse about hanging Jefferson Davis from a sour apple tree.[16] Several weeks later, at a freedmen's celebration in Charleston, "John Brown's Body" was sung by 1,800 black school children, and the "hang Jeff Davis" verse was said to be their favorite.[17]

In November 1879, Loudin's Fisk Jubilee Singers sang "John Brown's Body" to John Greenleaf Whittier in Whittier's private study at his home in Amesbury, Massachusetts. The "Quaker Poet" was proud of his abolitionist record. After hearing the Jubilee Singers' rendition of "John Brown's Body," he went upstairs and brought down a copy of a "document for immediate emancipation" which had been adopted by an abolitionist convention at Philadelphia in 1833. Whittier's name was one of the sixty-two signatures.[18]

The collapse of Reconstruction and the increasingly violent manifestations of Jim Crow during the 1890s brought new vitality and deeper meaning to "John Brown's Body." Consider this scathing report in the May 20, 1892, edition of the *Detroit Plaindealer*, submitted by a popular black columnist who called himself "The Bystander":

> In more direct connection with recent outrages [i.e., the unprecedented rash of lynchings and burnings in the South], a meeting of about 1,000 Negroes was held in an African Methodist church in Chicago [one of several "indignation meetings" reported in connection with the lynchings]. When the hymn "America" was given out including the words "sweet land of liberty," the congregation refused to sing it, and "John Brown's body" had to be substituted . . . Not a few, especially of the editors of the "religious" press, animadverts with some severity upon the congregation of colored Christians who refused to sing "America."
>
> It is very comical this demand of the "religious" journals that a Christian congregation should tell a lie to please God and show Christian citizenship. There is not an editor among them who does not know, if he knows anything beyond the silly flapdoodle of bigotry, that the country is not free.

No man who advocates and believes in equal rights for all men without regard to race or color, is "Free" to speak his sentiments and labor for their adoption in one-third of the States in this Union. What is the use of lying to God about it? . . . The Bystander remembers how heartily we used to sing this vain-glorious lullaby of self-approving vanity when over half the land the slave cringed under the driver's lash and the mountains echoed with the bay of the hounds on the track of the fugitive . . . A lie is not less a lie because it is sung, and no truer when addressed to God than if told to man . . .

The congregation of colored men and women did their duty as patriots and Christians; did bravely and intelligently, and thoroughly, and there is no doubt that their action was the precursor of a demonstration which is destined to be one of the most impressive in the history of free government . . . In the meantime, [the Bystander] desires to express the hope that the "Battle Hymn of the Republic," a much grander and nobler anthem, pulsating in every line with the impulse of liberty and Christ, may for the present at least take the place of "America" in the patriotic worship of the colored Christians of the United States.

In 1892 "John Brown's Body" was sung by African Americans at both church and community gatherings.

• ***June 3, 1892 (Cincinnati, Ohio):*** At a "Day of Fasting and Prayer" at Allen Temple, "The music was excellent and was furnished by the choir of Allen Temple, under the direction of Prof. Joseph Henderson. The meeting was opened by singing 'Nearer My God to Thee.' . . . The meeting closed by singing 'John Browns' Body'" (*Detroit Plaindealer*).

• ***September 9, 1892 (Topeka, Kansas):*** "The song of John Brown will be sung at the celebration, in honor of the slaves, Sept. 16, '92, Burlingame, Kansas. F. L. Jeltz, commander of the Bruce clubs, will lead it and the Young Deserters will join in the chorus. Also, 'Freedom Forever' will be sung and led by the Osage City Bruce club. This celebration is to be one of the grandest ever held in the state; all the young

SATURDAY, JUNE 1, 1895.

"JOHN BROWN'S BODY."

After the execution of John Brown at Harper's Ferry, in December, 1859, a song was adopted that speedily became a part of the marching music of the armies of the north. Its catchy phrases were not only familiar around the firesides of the country, but in all public gatherings where music was wont to inspire the multitude. It relieved the tedium of camp life, and as it resounded through columns of men tramping patiently along the dusty highways it lightened the weariness of their footsteps.

It is said that the words, with the exception of the first stanza, were written by Mr. Charles S. Hall of Massachusetts, but long before the war the air, wedded to other words, was familiar on every plantation in the south. It was the favorite camp meeting melody of the negroes, and few spectacles were more inspiring than when, with grotesque gestures, they joined in singing (the women first):

Say, my brudders, will we meet yo'?
Say, my brudders, will we meet yo'?
Say, my brudders, will we meet yo'?
On Ca-ni-yun's happy sho'?

Then the men responding:

Ya-a-s, my sistern, we will meet yo',
Ya-a-s, my sistern, we will meet yo',
Ya-a-s, my sistern, we will meet yo',
Where partin is no mo'.

CHORUS.

Glory, glory, hallelujer! Glory, glory, hallelujer!
Glory, glory, hallelujer! On Ca-ni-yun's happy sho'.

The war song is as follows:

John Brown's body lies a-moldering in the grave,
John Brown's body lies a-moldering in the grave,
John Brown's body lies a-moldering in the grave,
His soul is marching on.

CHORUS.

Glory, halle-halleluiah! Glory, halle-halleluiah!
Glory, halle-halleluiah!
His soul is marching on!

He's gone to be a soldier in the army of the Lord (thrice),
His soul is marching on.

John Brown's knapsack is strapped upon his back (thrice),
His soul is marching on.

His pet lambs will meet him on the way (thrice),
As they go marching on.

We will hang Jeff Davis to a sour apple tree (thrice),
As they go marching on.

Now, three cheers for the Union (thrice),
As we are marching on.

Glory, halle-halleluiah! Glory, halle-halleluiah!
Glory, halle-halleluiah!
Hip, hip, hip, hurrah!

Richmond Planet, *June 1, 1895.*

gents and ladies from afar will be there; don't forget to curl your hair" (*Kansas State Ledger*).

The desire for an appropriate, eloquent Negro national anthem was finally satisfied in 1900 when James Weldon Johnson and J. Rosamond Johnson published "Lift Every Voice and Sing."

"Colored Pattis" and "Queens of Song," 1892

In 1892 the competition between Marie Selika, Flora Batson Bergen, and Matilda Sissieretta Jones for recognition as the country's "greatest black prima donna" reached a boiling point. Sissieretta Jones's successful showing at Madison Square Garden in May 1892, her subsequent contract with mainstream concert promoter Major James B. Pond, and her fall tour with white cornet master Jules Levy mark the point at which she stepped beyond her competitors to become the era's undisputed black "Queen of Song."

Amidst the fanfare, new community-based "Queens of Song" such as Rachael Walker and E. Azalia Smith came to the fore. According to one of her biographers, E. Azalia Smith had attended a Black Patti concert at a church in Detroit in 1889, and considered it a turning point in her musical career; she also met Edwin Hackley at that concert, and they were married in 1893.[19] As E. Azalia Hackley, she became famous during the decade before World War I for organizing huge choirs in the African American communities of various cities and presenting them in the context of "Negro Folk Song Festivals."

• ***March 5, 1892 (Washington, D.C):*** "The Race's Patti," "Mme. M. Sissieretta Jones, the justly titled "colored Patti" of the United States, appeared for her first time before a Washington audience, at the Metropolitan [A.M.E.] church, Fifteenth and M streets, Monday evening, February 22, and was greeted by a large and appreciative audience. She is the happy possessor of an extraordinary musical voice, with an abundance of sweet tones, which she imparts to her hearers in the most pleasing manner. Madame Jones, by previous appointment, appeared before the chief executive of the nation, President Harrison and family and the guests of the white house, on Wednesday morning, and rendered the following selections to the delight of those present: 'Cavatina,' by Meyerbeer; 'Suawanee River,' waltz, by Pattison; and 'Home, Sweet Home' " (*Cleveland Gazette*).

• ***May 7, 1892:*** "Mme Sissieretta Jones, the 'Black Patti,' who has been attracting attention in the Negro jubilee at Madison Square Garden during the past week by her wonderfully good singing, is to be heard in concert at the academy of music . . . She will sing some operatic selections and some plantation melodies" (*Cleveland Gazette*, reprinted from the *New York Sun*).

• ***May 20, 1892 (New York):*** "A Patti With A Soul," "New York Goes Wild Over the Wonderful Voice of an Afro American Nightingale," "May 16, (Special). The 'Black Patti,' otherwise Miss Sissieretta Jones, has taken New York by storm. Her name was certainly enough to do that, but, if you smile broadly over the decidedly Ethiopian cognomen, your smile dies away when you have heard her sing. There are the most wonderful possibilities in that flexible, bird-like voice of remarkable compass, that it possesses what Adelina Patti's has always lacked—soul. The soul of a nightingale seems to have lodged in that throat. She sings with remarkable passion and depth of feeling, while the brilliant fiorature which embellishes her singing—Well, her execution is perfect. The Black Patti's gowns are in excellent taste. When I heard her the other evening she wore a simple gray dress, with gloves reaching the shoulder, that fitted her shapely young figure well. Her expression is decidedly intelligent and pleasing. It is rather pitiful to think of the way in which her career might be hampered because of her race—not because of prejudice exactly, but she certainly cannot appear in opera, in which she would undoubtedly succeed, unless one were especially written for her, and then almost insuperable difficulties would attend its production. She will be limited to concert, and even there, after the novelty has died out, her color will be an unpleasant circumstance to those over-fastidious people who demand an angel in face as well as in voice for their delectation at a public performance.

Lafcadio Hearn, in his works on the West Indies, celebrates the beauty of the natives there, and here occasionally one sees in the street an Afro-American of remarkable beauty, descended, doubtless, from one of those straight-nosed, thin lipped tribes existent in Africa. The artistic eye sees this beautiful statue with just as much pleasure as if it was delicately tinted, but the vulgar and uneducated eye is blind to the perfection of form and feature merely because of the color.

But if, after the canaille has sated its curiosity it forsakes the 'Black Patti' to run after some pink and white singer of opera bouffe, or the next sensation, whoever she may be, Miss Jones may be sure she will be able to secure an audience of true music lovers as long as she keeps that glorious and thrilling voice, the wonderful gift of God to this young woman—this raven that is yet a nightingale" (*Detroit Plaindealer*).

• ***June 18, 1892:*** "Mme Selika and husband have returned to this country. The company they went abroad with [William Foote's Afro-American Specialty Company] went under" (*Detroit Plaindealer*).

• ***July 1, 1892:*** "A musical festival recently held in Indianapolis, was a great success. Miss Rachel Walker, of Cleveland, the prima donna, was the attraction of the evening. The musical critic of the Indianapolis Journal, wrote of her as follows:

Her voice has all the cultivation that beautified that of Emma Abbott, and is certainly more voluminous than was that singer's voice.

Her perfect control of it permits her to imitate flute trills, as well as the most difficult upper runs on the piano. Her high registers are just as clear, sweet, and voluminous as the lower ones. The audience was first astonished and then spell-bound. Miss Walker has certainly a bright future in the musical world, as she is quite a young lady for her present attainments. There was no voice at the May Musical festival, that could claim any merits not possessed by that of Miss Walker" (*Detroit Plaindealer*).

• ***July 2, 1892 (Pittsburgh, Pennsylvania):*** "Madame Selika—the most renowned vocalist of the race, gave an entertainment in Wylie Avenue church . . . The house was packed, and the applause which followed each selection fairly shook the house. She was accompanied by her husband. Local talent assisted" (*Cleveland Gazette*).

• ***August 5, 1892 (Cincinnati, Ohio):*** "The sacred concert given at Allen temple last Sabbath afternoon, was well attended . . . The beautiful vocal solo by Miss E. Azalia Smith and the well executed piano solos by Miss Mabel Hill and Mr. Eric Dixon, would have been followed by one continuous round of applause, had not custom prohibited any outbursts at these concerts" (*Detroit Plaindealer*).

• ***September 6, 1892:*** "Who is the Jenny Lind of the colored race? Some say she is Flora Batson Bergen, but those who are prejudiced against Batson because of her marriage to a white man say she is found in the person of Madame Selika, and those who don't understand Selika's Hungarian warbles, English ballads, French

FLORA BATSON,

The Peerless

QUEEN OF SONG.

AT BETHEL CHURCH

Napoleon and Hastings street.

Thursday Evening, Sept. 8.

Supported by Popular Talent

VOCAL,
INSTRUMENTAL,
HUMOROUS
AND DRAMATIC.

J, G. BERGEN, MANAGER.

DOORS OPEN AT 7. CONCERT AT 8:15.

The Patti of her race.—*Chicago Inter Ocean.*

The Peerless Mezzo-Soprano.—*New York Sun.*

A Mezzo-Soprano of wonderful range.—*San Francisco Examiner.*

A sparkling diamond in the golden realm of song.—*San Jose (California) Mercury.*

Worthy to rank among the great singers of the world.—*Portland Oregonian.*

Has sung her way into hundreds of thousands of hearts.—*Philadelphia Sentinel.*

Her progress through the country has been one continuous triumph.—*Denver Rocky Mountain News.*

All her numbers were sung without effort—as the birds sing.—*Mobile (Ala.) Register.*

A voice of great range and of remarkable depth and purity.—*Louisville (Ky.) Courier-Journal.*

The sweetest voice that ever charmed a Virginia audience.—*Lynchburg (Va.) Advance.*

Her articulation is so perfect her renditions seem like recitations set to music.—*Kansas City Dispatch.*

A highly cultivated mezzo-soprano, of great sweetness, power and compass, and of dramatic quality.—*Charleston (S. C.) News and Courier.*

No other singer has ever drawn such audiences in New Orleans so many (seventeen) successive nights. —*New Orleans Standard.*

The indescribable pathos of her voice in dramatic and pathetic selections wrought a wondrous effect.—*The Colonist (Victoria, British Columbia).*

She scored a complete success as a vocalist of high ability, and fully justified the favorable criticisms of the Eastern press.—*San Francisco Examiner.*

Her voice showed a compass of three octaves, from the purest clear-cut soprano, sweet and full, to the rich round notes of the baritone register.—*Pittsburgh (Pa.) Commercial Gazette.*

She electrified the vast audience, 12,000 people, at the (Mormon) Tabernacle service on Sunday by her marvelous rendition of the 27th Psalm.—*Deseret Evening News (Salt Lake, Utah).*

She wore a crown, heavily jeweled, and diamonds flashed upon her hands and from her ears. Her singing at once established her claim of being in the front rank of star artists, and there is a greater fortune than that already accumulated in store for her.—*Providence (R. I.) Dispatch.*

She sings without affectation, and has an absolute command of her voice from the highest to the lowest register. Her execution is firm, her notes correct, and her enunciation perfect. She was a surprise to every one present, and established a reputation that will guarantee her full houses at her future engagements on the Pacific coast.—*San Francisco Call.*

Her voice is rich in the qualities most valuable to a singer. The range is wonderful. It is clear and resonant, exceedingly flexible and pure; her articulation is perfect, and she sings with a freedom of effort seen rarely, except in the most famous singers. The tones of her voice are powerful and thrilling. It is rather dramatic than emotional. Her renditions last night covered an extraordinary versatility and range. —*Nashville (Tenn.) American.*

She wore her jeweled diadem with a self-poise and humility that a princess might have envied, and convinced the critics with her first selection, the "Huntsman's horn," as the sonorous amplitude of her rare voice resounded like a silver bugle cheering the hounds to pursuit of game, that she possessed an organ magnificent in respect of sound, and in the use of which there is little the European masters will find to correct. In response to an encore, she gave a selection from "Il Trovatore" in baritone, showing the extraordinary range of her voice, and producing a melody like the low tones of a pipe organ under a master's touch.—*San Diego (California) Sun.*

TICKETS 50 CENTS. CHILDREN 25 CENTS.

Detroit Plaindealer, *August 12, 1892.*

thrills [*sic*] and Arabian halloos say the person is some one else. The latest singing phenomenon of the colored race has been found in the person of Madame Sissieretta Jones of the west indies or somewhere. Did you ever notice that a colored phenomenon is discovered almost every year? In days gone by we had 'The Black Swan' and some other 'duck,' later we had the Hyers sisters and Georgia Gordon and others. Now we have Batson, Selika, Jones, etc. Just who is the Jenny Lind of the colored race will be hard to tell until the singing critics get together and decide on one person" ("I. McCorker," *Topeka Weekly Call*).

• ***September 10, 1892 (Buffalo, New York):*** At a "possum supper banquet" given by managers of the "Southern Exhibit" at an "International Fair," "The representative of the *Gazette* was the only Afro-American guest present . . . [The possum] was nicely cooked and tasted very much like roast pig. While the feast was in progress the jubilee singers sang a number of plantation songs. Mayor Robinson [of Buffalo] was toastmaster . . . After the banquet the guests adjourned to the main building where Mme Sissieretta Jones sang one of her best solos. She was received with great applause and was encored three times" (*Cleveland Gazette*).

• ***September 17, 1892, (Cleveland, Ohio):*** "The greatest of all colored singers, Mme Marie Selika, in a grand benefit concert for the building fund of St. Andrews Episcopal Church, at Music Hall, Sept. 27. General admission is 25 cents; reserved seats: 35, 50 and 75 cents . . . assisted by the renowned Mr. Velosco (her husband), the Hawaiian tenor-baritone" (*Cleveland Gazette*).

• ***September 18, 1892:*** "Mme Sissieretta Jones sang to nine thousand people at Congress Party, Saratoga Springs" (*Topeka Weekly Call*).

• ***October 1, 1892:*** "Madame Sisseretta Jones, the 'Black Patti' has been at the exposition all week, singing. Levy's band is there also. She will concert with the band this season. Madame Selika, the 'Brown Patti,' sang to 5,000 people in the Cleveland, O. Music hall Thursday evening. The famous Excelsior Cornet band (Editor H. C. Smith, director) gave two numbers on the same programme. Besides these, Mr. Smith gave a cornet solo . . . The following is from Tuesday's 'Dispatch,' a local daily newspaper: 'The main hall of the Exposition building was uncomfortably crowded last night to hear

Miss Sissieretta Jones, the Black Patti, sing. The young colored woman sings like Patti, without the slightest visible effort; her voice is well cultivated, her high notes enable her to effectually render the most difficult compositions, and her low tone is peculiarly deep, intense and cultivated, of profound insight into the spirit of her art. Yet she sings intelligently, wholly without affectation and with sound musical feeling. Her voice coming from a skin as white as her teeth would be counted the wonder of all lands—it is a strong and beautiful voice, that sounds with the steadiness of a trumpet. Though it does not ring with passion, it shakes the heart, not your ears, with the pathetic warmth that marks all negro singing . . . She entirely captivated her magnificent audience last night, and her every performance this week will likely attract just such a crowd as she entertained last night' " (*Cleveland Gazette*).

• ***October 22, 1892 (Washington, D.C.):*** " 'Brown' And 'Black Pattis,' " "Their Singing—Selika the Best—Madame Jones a 'Great Singer.' " "Of Mme. Selika the world has spoken, and in her favor. Time nor rivals can wrest from her laurels so richly won; but she is not the Selika of yesterday, and the fact is most apparent when she sings with another whose share to public favors is deserving because 'tis compensating. Selika is a finished artist who appeals to the technical society lights particularly, but they cannot support any first-class concert for the reason they are too few. In the rendition of the staccato notes Mme. Selika has not been excelled, even by Patti, and her shading is so smooth and even that you cannot but commend it. Mrs. Jones is a great singer; she is not the 'greatest singer in the world,' nor is she a black, blue or green Patti. She is no sense a Patti. If Mrs. Jones would remember that Mrs. Greenfield, the Black Swan, made for herself a name without the need of styling herself the Black Jenny Lind, then she will know that she can succeed to as great an eminence without having to share the success with a white woman who would feel dishonored in wearing the title the White Black Swan. Afro-Americans need to impress their children that their race develops geniuses and heroes whose deeds can be emulated and perpetuated with everlasting profit; thus declaring our patriotism. We need more race pride! Our public men and women must exhibit it! *Mme. Jones is a great singer; Mme. Selika is the greatest colored singer. You hear Mme. Jones with pleasure; you hear Mme. Selika with profit*" (J. E. Bruce ["Bruce-Grit"], *Cleveland Gazette*).

• ***October 22, 1892 (Pittsburgh, Pennsylvania):*** "Mme Sissieretta Jones pleased thousands at the exposition during the week, with her magnificent singing" (*Cleveland Gazette*).

• ***October 22, 1892:*** "There is much anxiety in our musical world to know which is the greater singer, Mme Selika or Mme Sissieretta Jones, whom Maj. Pond (white) the great amusement caterer, has made the vocal soloist with the Levy military band for its tour this season . . . We are anxiously awaiting Madame Jones' appearance in this city, that our readers may be given the *Gazette's* opinion" (*Cleveland Gazette*).

• ***October 29, 1892 (Washington, D.C.):*** "Some months ago Mme [Sissieretta] Jones, the singer, sang before the president at the executive mansion, and he was so well pleased that it is said he sent her a magnificent floral tribute when she appeared at the Metropolitan A.M.E. Church during the recent G.A.R. encampment and so successfully sang her way into the hearts of Washington people" (*Cleveland Gazette*).

• ***November 19, 1892 (Pittsburgh, Pennsylvania):*** "The *Pittsburgh Weekly Mirror* says of Mme Sissieretta Jones' wonderful singing at the exposition in that city: 'The Black Patti saved the exposition management from bankruptcy, but they did not give her any medal. They ain't built that way'" (*Cleveland Gazette*).

• ***November 19, 1892 (Cleveland, Ohio):*** "Black Patti," "Grand Concert, indeed!—that of last Monday night at Music hall . . . The greatest of all cornet soloists, Jules Levy, Madame Jones (the Black Patti), and the band certainly met and surpassed the most sanguine expectations of all. Mrs. Jones . . . has a singularly sweet, yet powerful soprano voice, with lower tones that are superbly rich and sonorous. One would think her an exceptionally gifted contralto to hear her low tones. Her high ones are taken with ease, and yet are strong—even powerful—and wonderfully sweet. Her first number, Meyerbeer's cavatina, 'Robert toi que Jaime,' secured her a hearty encore. She returned and sang 'The Cows are in the Clover' in such a manner as to captivate the audience. Her other programme number, a concert 'Valse,' by Pattison, named 'Patti Song,' is just such a pretty, catchy, yet meritorious selection as pleases the general run of public audiences . . . To this Madame Jones received a double encore, singing upon her third appearance 'Swanee River,' with a taste and feeling that won her all the applause the large audience of five thousand persons was capable of giving. Cleveland has never had such a 'cornet' treat as Levy gave . . . We honestly believe that no cornet soloist alive would, *if he could*, play in one concert, substantially three solos and almost twice as many encores, giving as the latter even more difficult selections than he does for the former . . . His taste, expression and all that goes to make him the 'king of cornetists' is, of course, the best—perfect, as far as our limited judgement goes . . . Levy's Great American band ranks with the best . . . The Black Patti–Levy combination is really an exceptionally strong one" (*Cleveland Gazette*).

• ***December 24, 1892 (Cleveland, Ohio):*** "Miss Rachel Walker sang at the Spiritualistic meeting last Sunday. The manager of the affair advertised her as Cleveland's 'Black Patti.' This reminds us that Maj. Pond has taken the Levy band off the road, and now sells the Black Patti's services to concert managers who desire her to sing" (*Cleveland Gazette*).

Lizzie Pugh Dugan: "God Never Gave a Human a More Beautiful Voice"

During the summer of 1892 an itinerant black prima donna named Lizzie Pugh Dugan made her way to Cincinnati, Ohio, to conduct a series of concerts in local churches. Her appearances were advertised and noted in the Cincinnati news columns of the *Detroit Plaindealer*.

• ***June 17, 1892 (Cincinnati, Ohio):*** "Event of the Season of 1892," "Madame Lizzie Pugh Dougan [*sic*], Queen of Song and acknowledged Prima Donna, will sing in one Concert at Zion Baptist Church, Friday, June 24. This concert is for the benefit of the Kentucky State University, whose Chapel was destroyed by fire last December. They are making strenuous efforts to rebuild, and one of their efforts is by starring Madame Dougan . . . Admission 25 cents. Reserved seat tickets 35 cents. J. H. Garnett, D. D., Manager" (*Detroit Plaindealer*).

• ***June 24, 1892 (Cincinnati, Ohio):*** "Mrs. Lizzie Depugh [*sic*] Dugan will sing at Brown chapel on the evening of June 28. Mrs. Dugan is said to be the sweetest singer of the race and large audiences have welcomed her wherever she has traveled. It is seldom that singers of Mrs. Dugan's ability can be heard at any church and this opportunity is one rarely offered. That a large and appreciative audience will greet her is assured. Don't miss hearing, not only our best, but one of the best singers of the day" (*Detroit Plaindealer*).

• ***July 1, 1892 (Cincinnati, Ohio):*** "The grand concert given by madame Lizzie Pugh Dongan [*sic*] assisted by local talent, was poorly attended. The program will be repeated" (*Detroit Plaindealer*).

In 1893 a blurb in her hometown Indianapolis paper placed Dugan in company with the era's top three Queens of Song.

• ***July 1, 1893:*** "Our Musical People," "Said a movement is on foot, coached and encouraged by a syndicate of capitalists, to secure Madame S. Jones, Mme. Selika, Flora Batson, Lizzie Pugh Dugan, with accessory voices, male and female, for a season of grand concerts in Chicago" (*Indianapolis Freeman*).

The final months of 1894 found Madame Dugan on the road.

• ***October 26, 1894 (Kansas City, Missouri):*** "Lizzie Pugh Dougan, the famous soprano soloist of Indianapolis, will positively appear at 5th Street Opera House next Monday night, ably assisted by local talent. Admission 25 cents" (*Kansas City American Citizen*).

• ***December 15, 1894:*** "Mme Lizzie Pugh Dugan, of Indianapolis, Ind., soprano soloist, is giving concerts in the South and West" (*Indianapolis Freeman*).

During her lifetime, Madame Dugan appears to have garnered little recognition in the African American press. However, a remarkable retrospective on Lizzie Pugh Dugan and her workaday career as a "Queen of Song" appeared in the *Freeman* of May 1, 1909, written by a hometown Indianapolis-based observer who signed his name "Siwel":

> I must confess that Indianapolis has not sent out any great colored women, at least in recent days . . . Lizzie Pugh Dugan was of the old school, but one of the most gifted women that ever lived. This is in no sense an exaggeration; God never gave a human a more beautiful voice. When she sang she lifted completely out of herself into some higher sphere, and sang from this new eminence . . . And what's more, and to her a hurt, she only sang thus when fully under the influence of intoxicants—fully, I say, and in no sense of ridicule, but as a truth that's worth knowing . . .
>
> Lizzie had some little musical education; she had no reason to have much, since she was a great big girl before she knew that she was much of a singer . . . Why didn't she do more? She did much. She traveled the country over for years, doing nothing but singing, and that was at a time when Negroes were not so popular on the stage.
>
> She was blessed with a voice and execution, but most unfortunately was without education. Consequently she could not do the great things. The most she could do was commit a few pages of the best music; not whole operas—an impossible thing without the aid of note knowledge. She did not know what she possessed. She rejoiced that she was able to leave common labor and live the life of refinement and ease. Of course, she did not drink at the outset; but it was perhaps due to the leisure which she did not know how to use . . . Indianapolis knows her yet, the present Indianapolis, since it has not been so long since she sang. She has been dead for something like two years.

In the following week's *Freeman*, "Siwel" was compelled to reiterate:

> Since writing of her some have taken exception to the statement that she did her great work when fully intoxicated. I expected the same, and will state the situation more comprehensively. Lizzie Pugh, I say again, was one of the gifted women of the earth when it came to the matter of voice. No one had a greater gift. So great, that without any cultivation except that caught up here and there by singing teachers . . . , she was able to sing as a matter of livelihood before this latter day of opportunity . . . She did not know Italian, French, as Madam Selika did . . . She was blessed beyond her knowledge . . . Remember she was no jubileer; no coon song shouter; sang straight [*sic*] from the beginning . . . Her managers found it convenient to turn her into immediate gold . . . Thus was she coined away, until she felt the exhaust on her life and attempted to supply the deficiency as so many do—by indulgence in intoxicants . . . Her position in the song world has never been known. Many felt

that she was an ordinary one-horse singer, because her opportunities were one-horse; and had they been better, the woman would have perhaps fared no better, owing to the chances of a Negro singer of worth. Look at Selika, the most cultivated of them all—a great artist in the world sense, with all of the requirements, finally reduced to want. However, from her throat bursted no note like that from the throat of our Dugan.

Selected, Annotated Chronology of Music-Related Citations, 1892

• ***January 1, 1892:*** "Detroit Department," "The 'Society orchestra' has engaged Miss Azalia Smith as pianist for the season. The orchestra is under the direction of B. B. Tanninholz, who is the youngest orchestra leader in the city, being only 19 years" (*Detroit Plaindealer*).

• ***January 2, 1892 (Helena, Arkansas):*** "A Colored Ventriloquist," "Wm. Cleveland, the colored ventriloquist, in company with Dr. McNeal, was in the city on the 15th performing on the public square. He is known as the best colored ventriloquist in the South" (*Indianapolis Freeman*).

• ***January 2, 1892 (New York City):*** "A Christmas dinner and parlor concert given by Mrs. Charles Davidson at her residence in West Tenth Street . . . was one of the most unique and pleasant entertainments of the holiday season . . . Mr. and Mrs. Blackwell rendered a duet, 'The Magnolia of old Tennessee,' and several other choice selections . . . Mr. Gus L. Davis enlivened the company with his comic songs" (*New York Age*).

Note: Gussie L. Davis was the famous composer of "The Lighthouse by the Sea," "In the Baggage Coach Ahead," "Maple on the Hill," "The Fatal Wedding," "Little Footprints in the Snow," "Irene, Good Night," etc.

• ***January 2, 1892 (Decatur, Illinois):*** "Colored Dramatic Company," "'Dixie in costume and songs' was rendered at Powers grand opera house on Friday December 18th by colored talent. The vast audience held their breaths at the coming of the 'Black Phalanx' in chorus and song, 'Don't you see the black clouds rising over yonder' followed by the charge on Port Hudson [*sic*], the receiving of President Lincoln with 'Say darkies did you see old massa.' Thus ended the first attempt of the colored people of Macon county to give a concert in an opera house where hundreds would and did witness the performance" (*Indianapolis Freeman*).

• ***January 2, 1892:*** "The American Jubilee Singers and Colored Concert Co., composed of most of the members of the defunct Great American Minstrels, are reported to be doing well in their tour of Scotland. The company is under the management of George B. Lee, and includes James D. Johnson, Albert Wilson, P. R. Berry, Fred Lee and the Black Diamond Quartet" (*New York Clipper*).

• ***January 8, 1892 (Terre Haute, Indiana):*** At a meeting of the Union Literary society, there was an "Address by T. E. Gutherie; banjo solo, Mr. Grant Crowe; oration, Prof. C. F. Stokes; mandolin solo, Mr. Watson Lewis; address, Mr. Manuel; after which refreshments were served" (*Detroit Plaindealer*).

• ***January 9, 1892:*** "Jalvan's Spanish Dancers are rehearsing at Chicago Ill. The company will be headed by Nellie Brown. This troupe will consist of thirty first class singers and dancers, and two fine comedians. The company will be ready for the road about Feb. 1, and will tour Indiana, Ohio, Kentucky, Pennsylvania and Maryland . . . J. Jalvan is proprietor and manager" (*New York Clipper*).

• ***January 16, 1892 (New York City):*** At the installation of officers of John A. Andrew Post No. 234, at their headquarters, 208 Bleeker Street, "The singing by the Southern Twilight

Quintet Club . . . was most heartily enjoyed" (*New York Age*).

• ***January 16, 1892 (New York City):*** At a reception marking the twentieth anniversary of the Railroad Porters' Mutual Protective Union, "Those present were delightfully entertained by the sweet and animated strains of Prof. Craig's orchestra, and for the most part whirled in the mazes of the dance" (*New York Age*).

• ***January 16, 1892:*** "Blind Tom is still exercising his remarkable faculty around the country. He has been killed off by the newspapers a great many times, but hangs on to earth with great tenacity" (*Cleveland Gazette*).

• ***January 23, 1892:*** At a "Union Concert" at St. Mark's Church, New York City, "The Calliope Quartet appeared twice and each time was uproariously applauded, and responded to several encores" (*New York Age*).

• ***January 29, 1892:*** "Negro Religion," "The Negro does not go by the bible he goes by tradition, prejudice, feeling and a host of errors. This is not true of all Negroes, but it is true of a majority . . . The average Negro thinks the chief thing about religion after conversion is 'how you feel.' Hence among the average the only good things in religious service are 'feeling sermons,' 'feeling songs,' 'feeling prayers,' 'feeling testimonies,' and 'feeling meetings.'

. . . 'Feeling meetings, songs, prayers, sermons, etc.,' are alright if the 'feeling' is the right sort. Right here comes the point, the 'feeling' the people talk about is the wrong sort of feeling. What sort of a 'feeling' is it that makes the heels fly up and send the body spinning up and down the aisle? At the time one is shouting he don't know what is going on around him; he don't hear the song or sermon or testimony . . . When the 'shout' is over, 'all is over,' and the person is just like he was before, only a little out of breath and a few pin and buttons less well off. Now, tell me, what good has been attained by that kind of feeling?" ("*Plaindealer*," quoted in *Kansas City American Citizen*).

A GRAND CONCERT
WILL BE GIVEN BY THE
Southern Twilight Quintette,
AT
BETHEL CHURCH,
Sullivan Street, New York,
Rev. THEO. GOULD, Pastor,
On Friday Evening, Jan. 22 1892.
The Quintette will be ably supported by
Mrs. MARGUERETTE CHURCHILL,
The California Nightingale.
Mme. R A. ROBINSON,

The New York Song Bird and Celebrated Soprano, who has just returned from a successful trip through the West Indies laden with medals and press opinions, and others.

Accompanists.—Mme. J. E. ROBINSON and Mr. WALTER LAWRENCE.

The Southern Twilight Quintette consists of Thomas Jackson, 1st tenor; Wm. E. Dorsey, 2nd tenor; Wm. H. Nimor, baritone; J. C. Owens and Wm. R. Dean, basso.

"The 'Southern Twilight Male Quintette' gave one of their musical entertainments in Brooklyn to an audience of eight hundred people, on a wet night, and received encore after encore. They began promptly at 8 o'clock, and their fine assimilation of tone and delicate balancing of voices was very noticable."—*Brooklyn Eagle.*

Admission, ... 25 Cents
Children, ... 15 Cents.
Doors open at 7:30. Exercises begin at 8.

THERE WILL BE
A GRAND CONCERT
GIVEN AT
ZION BAPTIST CHURCH,
(Formerly Shiloh Presbyterian)
167 West 26th St., Rev. G. H. BOSWELL, Pastor,
On Tuesday Evening, Jan. 26, 1891.

This Concert will be given by the **HAYDN MUSICAL and MUTUAL SOCIETY** of New York, under the auspices of the King's Daughters of said Church. **ADMISSION, 25 CENTS.**

SOLOISTS.—Mrs. M. A. Jackson, soprano; Mrs. A. M. Taylor, soprano; Miss M. E. N. Barnett, mezzo soprano; Mrs. M. J. Adams, contralto; Mr. A. Wright, baritone; Miss J. G. Carter, elocutionist; Miss E. B. Magnan, accompanist.

Doors open at 7:30. Commence 8 P. M.

New York Age, *January 16, 1892.*

• ***January 30, 1892:*** "Roster of Billy Jackson's Colored Specialty Co.: Gertie Jefferson, Bobby Green, Bethal and Jones, Will Tidings, Frank D. Lions, Billy Wilson, Lillie Russell, Pastor Panalvor, Ike Randolph, Annie Weathers and

Billy Jackson . . . Mr. Jackson's songs, 'Coon with the Big Thick Lips' and 'A Seat Up Dar for Me,' are said to be hits" (*New York Clipper*).

Note: Two years later, Billy Jackson's Colored Minstrels, starring Ben Hunn and Florence Briscoe, made show business history at Worth's Museum in New York City.

• ***January 30, 1892:*** At an entertainment given by Integrity Lodge 1768, G.U.O. of O.F., in Worcester, Massachusetts, "Guitar solos by Mr. Hawkins and Miss Cooper were well rendered," and Mr. Hawkins also gave a harmonica solo which "was well received" (*New York Age*).

• ***January 30, 1892 (Erie, Pennsylvania):*** "Free Scholarship," "Afro-American One of Four Successful Competitors," "Special to the *Freeman*—Mr. Harry Burleigh returned from New York today and is a subject for the congratulation of Erie musicians, as well as of others who admire worthy ability and excellent character.

A short time since the National Conservatory of Music in New York, over which Mrs. Thurber presides with a corps of the finest musical instructors in the country, announced free scholarships for a four years' course as the rewards of a competitive examination, Mr. Burleigh who entered with 250 other competitors, is one of the four winners and is now entitled to the four years course or till sooner completed. He spent four days in the examination under the best teachers in New York City. He was examined in writing, music, solfeggio or scale singing, singing songs, ballads, oratorio, etc. Signor Romuldo Sapio, who gave him a very rigid examination, informed him that while he did not profess an uncommon voice, it was above the average, and that his abilities and musical intelligence entitled him to the favor of the academy. He will leave next week to commence his studies, which he hopes to complete in two or three years.

The course comprises introduction in singing, harmony, counter-point composition, oratorio, opera, history of music, the Italian language, contra bass, fencing and every accomplishment that is associated with the profession.

Mr. Burleigh—an Erie boy and son of Mrs. John Elmendorf—began to sing first in the High School, from which he graduated with honors; he sang at St. Paul's Episcopal Church for several years, was soloist at the synagogue and the Park Presbyterian Church, and is now singing in the First Church choir" (*Indianapolis Freeman*).

• ***February 6, 1892:*** "The [Theodore] Drury Opera company . . . gave its first concert of the season at Adelphi Hall . . . A full house greeted the company and showed its appreciation by loud and long applause . . . Special mention is made of the Brilliant Quartet, it being the only one comprised of ladies, in the city. After the concert dancing was indulged in to the music furnished by Mr. Miles Terry" (*New York Age*).

• ***February 6, 1892 (Danville, Virginia):*** "Piedmont Church Rousers," "There was—so say the old citizens—the grandest entertainment given at the Loyal Street Baptist Church last evening that has been in Danville for many years . . . The Piedmont Church Rousers assisted by several of our best ladies gave the entertainment . . . The Piedmont Church Rousers is a Danville Company of young men who have made quite a name for themselves in singing the finest sheet music.

Mr. Whitlock Williamson sings the soprano equal to any lady you have ever listened to, while Master David Adams, a member of the highly musical 'Robt. Adams' family,' sings alto with a smooth soft voice that wins and holds the closest attention. Mr. Joseph Fountain fully merits the general praise given him for so fine a tenor voice. Mr. Howard Woolridge sings bass with one of the finest voices we've ever heard. At times his voice runs up high, touching the clouds just above your head, then gradually descending with cadence most pleasing in effect; it recedes and rolls and mellows like deep rumbling thunder playing on chimes" (Ed Stylus, *Richmond Planet*).

• ***February 13, 1892 (New York City):*** "A Wheelmen's Stag," "A number of New York and Brooklyn wheelmen gathered at the 'stag' given by the Claremont Bicycle Club on Saturday evening, at the residence of the redoubtable captain of that club . . . A feature of the evening was the presentation of a long clay pipe to each guest as he entered, which he proceeded to fill with choice tobacco and emit volumes of smoke. Cards was the favorite pastime while the music of a guitar, banjo and mandolin added pleasing harmony to the merry gathering, until the guests were moved to indulge in the Virginia reel and old-fashioned choruses" (*New York Age*).

• ***February 13, 1892 (New York City):*** "An After Concert Supper," "On each evening of last week the Southern Jubilee Singers and the Southern Twilight Quintet, both under the management of Mr. Wm. R. Dean, were engaged in concerts across the bridge. Each concert proved of course a success. Although both companies belong in New York their numerous Brooklyn friends seem inclined to have them in Brooklyn all the time. The troupe after returning to headquarters Friday evening were entertained until a very late hour by their successful and genial manager. At the supper there were Mr. and Mrs. Wm. R. Dean, Mrs. E. Small, Miss Victoria Scott, Mr. and Mrs. Hammock, Messrs. W. R. Butler, Thos. J. Jackson, Wm. E. Dorsey, J. E. Owens, Walter Dean and W. Henri Nimor" (*New York Age*).

• ***February 20, 1892 (Portsmouth, Virginia):*** "Jan. 22, 1892—We, the Lime Kiln Club, No. 2, do propose to present to any band a fine cornet, that will take part and compete for the above piece of music specified [i.e., that "fine cornet"]. No band will be allowed to play but three pieces of music on the stage and the band that plays the three pieces of music the finest will be presented with the above piece specified and the band that comes in to be the Second best will be presented with a fine Plume. No band admitted to have but 13 pieces to play on the stage that night in the time of the race. The judges will be from the Soldiers Home. No Italians or Dutch admitted to play in either band that takes part in this presentation. This is only for colored bands individually, no mixed people required to be in any band that takes part in this presentation. We have sent notification to . . . publish this in the PLANET to all bands in the vicinity and ask them if they will take part . . . It will come off on the 22nd of March 1892, at Oxford Hall, Portsmouth, Va., on High St. Doors open at 7 o'clock P.M., performances to commence at 8 o'clock sharp.

Norfolk, Va., Feb. 4, 1892 . . . Gentlemen—Your invitation of January 22 . . . was duly received and after much consideration we submit the following answer: Our terms for playing is (80) dollars per day or (8) dollars per hour and should you need our services for that or any other occasion we would gladly offer them at the rates above named. So under existing circumstances with many thanks we respectfully decline your invitation. It has been remarked that the gentlemen of Portsmouth, Va., doubts our ability to compete with Portsmouth's bands.

We are not seeking competition, but should the above be facts we herewith issue a challenge to play any colored band in the state for a cash prize of $150 to $200. For further information concerning challenge apply or call at stall no. 25, City Market.

Yours respectfully,
Excelsior Brass and Reed Band,
M. Goodrich, Cap't." (*Richmond Planet*).

• ***February 20, 1892 (New York City):*** "The New Orleans University singers gave a concert on Tuesday evening at the Johnson street A.M.E. Church to a good sized and appreciative audience. The troupe consisted of seven persons, three sopranos, two altos, a bass and a tenor. Mr. F. S. Thomas is the sole manager of the troupe, Miss Tillie Jones Thomas is the leading star. This troupe has traveled extensively throughout the country with much success having raised several thousand dollars for the institution. They are now on their own resources and have just closed a long engagement in Philadelphia" (*New York Age*).

February 26, 1892: "Mr. Frank L. Hamilton, of Chicago, is so much pleased with the violin playing of Mr. Will Cook that he is arranging for a series of concerts in St. Louis and other cities, in which Mr. Cook will star" (*Detroit Plaindealer*).

• ***March 4, 1892 (Youngstown, Ohio):*** "Objected To The Ball," "Feb. 26.—Society circles are stirred up here by reason of an incident which occurred at the A.M.E. Church, where a revival is in progress. The Colored Cornet band, in order to replenish its treasury gave a masquerade ball, which was very successful, nearly all the colored people attending.

Rev. Lee objected to the ball, . . . [and he] expressed the wish that the floor would give way and leave the maskers to their sins. The band boys are up in arms and do not spare Mr. Lee in their criticism of his unchristian-like prayer. They claim that in the past they have largely aided in sustaining the church" (*Detroit Plaindealer*).

• ***March 4, 1892 (Findlay, Ohio):*** "Feb. 29—The Silver Leaf quartet returned home Friday night and report that they had a good house at Van Liew. They expect to visit several small towns in the near future" (*Detroit Plaindealer*).

• ***March 5, 1892 (Lansing, Michigan):*** "There was some disappointment manifested because Mrs. Maggie Porter-Cole was not with [Loudin's] jubilee singers. When the manager was asked for an explanation he said: 'Mrs. Cole sang with us for a long time. When we went abroad my former manager organized a new Fisk jubilee company, and there are now two companies traveling under this name, each of which contains some of the original singers.' The fact is well known that Mrs. Cole was with the Loudin's company and is now with a [different] jubilee company. Hence a popular mistake arose, which was much regretted by the local public" (*State Republican*).

• ***March 5, 1892 (Richmond, Virginia):*** "Ho for a grand concert given by the Hopkins Quartette at and for the benefit of the Second Baptist Church, Tuesday evening, March 8, 1892 . . . Mr. T. H. Hopkins, the silver-toned tenor, who has recently returned from Europe, where he has been singing to crowned heads in the old world will appear for the first time before the public, supported by some of Richmond's best talent . . .

"Admission: Lady and Gent, 25c. Single person, 15c.

"H. B. Burwell, Man. & Pianist" (*Richmond Planet*).

• ***March 11, 1892:*** "James M. Trotter, one of the prominent Afro-American men of Massachusetts, died at his home in Hyde Park Feb. 26, from consumption following malaria fever caught while in Washington. He was appointed by President Cleveland Recorder of deeds for the District of Columbia . . . Mr. Trotter's childhood was passed in the State of Ohio . . . In Massachusetts, prior to the war, he was a teacher. Soon after the breaking out of the war he enlisted as a private in the 55th Massachusetts Regiment, colored troops, and was promoted until he became a lieutenant. Upon his return to civil life he was appointed one of the secretaries of the committee of One Hundred of Boston, and was active in support of the nominees of the democratic party. He was interested in musical matters, and for a time acted as manager for Mme. Selika and other singers. This led to his publication of the 'Lives of Prominent Colored Singers' " (*Detroit Plaindealer*).

Note: James Monroe Trotter's "Lives of Prominent Colored Singers" was published in 1878 under the title *Music and Some Highly Musical People*. In her *Biographical Dictionary of African and African-American Musicians*, Eileen Southern cites Trotter's book as the "first survey of American music published by anyone, black or white."

• ***March 11, 1892 (Kansas City, Kansas):*** "An Elopement," "Quite a stir was caused early the past week by the local daily newspapers announcing the elopement to this city of Tillie Oswald (white), an accomplished young lady from Mt. Oliver, near Pittsburgh, and an Afro-American by the name of Bazine, who, it seems, was Tillie's guitar teacher" (*Kansas City American Citizen*).

• ***March 12, 1892 (Gallatin, Missouri):*** "Our A.M.E. Sunday school is one of the foremost in the state in point of interest and activity. It has . . . Prof. N. C. Smith as chorister. Prof. Smith has organized an orchestra in the school with himself as violinist; Miss Hattie Rowland, organist; and C. H. Maupin, cornetist . . . The Gallatin Colored Cornet band is growing efficient under the leadership of Prof. Smith, and they are in constant demand at entertainments, theatres and socials" (*Indianapolis Freeman*).

Note: This was Prof. N. Clark Smith.

• ***March 12, 1892:*** "Stage," "The Williams family, blind singers, are touring Virginia" (*Indianapolis Freeman*).

• ***March 12, 1892:*** "Stage," "George Barrett, tenor of the Fisk Singers, has resigned on account of ill health" (*Indianapolis Freeman*).

• ***March 12, 1892 (Jacksonville, Florida):*** "Female Orchestra," "The Euterpe female orchestra gave an entertainment here, recently, which was a signal triumph. The ladies appeared in uniform and presented a grand sight. Imagine two little misses beating a triangle, one the tamborine, another performing on the snare drum and still another on the bass violin with the violin also in the hands of a young lady, and all the instruments in the hands of young lady artists" (*Indianapolis Freeman*).

• ***March 19, 1892:*** "Sig. Farini, who sang with Parepa, Nilsson and Lucca, is training a troupe of singers of African descent for the grand opera stage. Selika, the Afro-American soprano, who is famous in Europe, was a pupil of Farini and the bold idea of training Afro-Americans to the highest flights of musical genius was inspired in Farini's bosom by Selika's beautiful, sympathetic, and marvelously melodious voice" (*Cleveland Gazette*).

• ***March 19, 1892 (Dayton, Ohio):*** At a local community entertainment, "Mr. Paul Dunbar spoke Longfellow's 'Bridge' with piano accompaniment" (*Cleveland Gazette*).

Note: This was Paul Laurence Dunbar.

• ***March 26, 1892 (Cleveland, Ohio):*** "Miss Hattie Gibbs, director of the conservatory of music at the Eckstein-Norton Institute, is in town . . . A musical company, consisting of Miss Gibbs, solo pianist; Miss Willa Chambers, soprano; Miss Lula Childers, alto; A. L. Smith, tenor; and W. B. Hayson, bass; has been organized, and will give concerts in the interest of the school. The company will appear in Cleveland. . . .

"The main building of Eckstein-Norton university burned some weeks ago and the teachers of that institution have organized a musical company, which it is hoped will do much to secure funds to rebuild it" (*Cleveland Gazette*).

Note: Eckstein-Norton Institute was located in Cane Springs, Kentucky, near Louisville.

• *March 26, 1892:* "Roster of the Hyers Sisters' Comedy Company: Billy McClain, stage manager; Geo. Freeman, manager and leader of band; Charlie Moore, Louise Bedford, Joe Brooks, Ky Taylor, Cordelia McClain, Miss Mada, Hannah Hyers and Louise and Freeman Hyers. Chas. Callender is at the head" (*New York Clipper*).

• *April 2, 1892 (Lebanon, Ohio):* "The Jennie Jackson DeHart Concert Company sang at the Opera House Monday night (28th) to a large audience. The singing was excellent. Mrs. DeHart's solos were highly complimented" (*Cleveland Gazette*).

• *April 8, 1892:* "Walter Pollock tells of an operatic performance at which he was present, at Martinique, in the West Indies. Opera was 'Lucia de Lammermoor,' and the chorus was entirely composed of native talent, the Negroes being arrayed in Highland kilts and bonnets" (*Detroit Plaindealer*).

A GRAND BENEFIT!!
THE EVENT OF THE SEASON
—:o:AT THE:o:—
TRUE REFORMER'S HALL.
MONDAY EVENING, APRIL 25, 1892.
BRASS BAND CONCERT
A GRAND PROGRAMME:
Instrumental and Vocal Selections, Latest Overtues, Selections, Descriptive Pieces, Solos on Different Instruments with full Band Accompaniment. THE LATEST HIT, the boy who plays on NINE different Instrum nts. The great DUAL PERFORMANCE on the Cornet and Piano by one person at the same time.
A GRAND STREET PARADE.
GENERAL ADMISSION, 35CTS.
U. S. G. PATTERSON, DIRECTOR. A. J. HARRIS, PIANIST.
Tickets For Sale at Anderson's Book Concern, 222 E. BROAD STREET.

Richmond Planet, *April 2, 1892.*

• *April 9, 1892:* "B. F. Thomas, highly respected, wherever known, died in Salina, Kansas on last Thursday (April 2) afternoon. The deceased was widely known in the musical world, and was at the time of his death, manager of the 'Original Fisk Tennesseans,' who were making an extensive tour throughout the country. After reaching Salina he was attacked with pneumonia. This lasted two months, when death came to his relief. The deceased was a member of the Odd Fellows and was buried under their auspices. A wife, and a host of friends mourn his demise" (*Cleveland Gazette*).

Note: B. F. Thomas was a member of the original Fisk Jubilee Singers, singing in the interest of Fisk University, though it appears he never attended Fisk. Born in slavery in South Carolina, Thomas was inducted into the Fisk Jubilee Singers before their second European tour, which began in May 1875. One year later, he left the troupe in England mid-tour and returned to the United States. In November 1877 Thomas rejoined the Jubilee Singers in Germany and completed their European tour with them in July 1878. He was a member of George L. White's independent troupe of Fisk Jubilee Singers and then F. J. Loudin's Fisk Jubilee Singers until late 1883. He went on to sing with Maggie Porter Cole in Mumford's Fisk Jubilee Singers in 1886 and subsequently became associated with a company known as the Fisk-Tennesseans.[20]

• *April 9, 1892:* "Billy McClain and George Freeman, of the Hyer Sisters' Co., are developing into adepts at sparring" (*New York Clipper*).

Note: Ten years later, McClain managed Australian heavyweight boxer Peter Felix.

• ***April 15, 1892:*** "The Messiah which was to be rendered April 15th by the Mozart society of Fisk university, has been postponed to the 22d to await the arrival of Mr. T. W. Talley from Rodney, Miss., to take the leading bass part" (*Detroit Plaindealer*).

Note: Thirty years later, Thomas W. Talley published his seminal study, *Negro Folk Rhymes*.

• ***April 15, 1892 (Detroit, Michigan):*** "The Baptist Lyceum," "An appreciative audience assembled at the Young Men's Christian Association hall, last Wednesday evening, to listen to the distinguished poet and reader Mr. J. Madison Bell, of Toledo, Ohio. Mr. Bell's selections, 'Creation Light,' 'Banishment of Man from the Garden of the Lord,' the 'Ode to Lincoln,' and the 'Future of America in the Unity of the Races' elicited hearty applause. Mr. Bell was assisted by Miss E. Azalia Smith and Messrs. Geo. Owen, John Johnson and Fred Stone of this city in vocal and instrumental selections" (*Detroit Plaindealer*).

• ***April 22, 1892:*** A letter to the editor complains about "so-called musicians" and "would-be stars" who "monopolize the entire hotel in which they are guests":

"As some . . . readers may never have been so unfortunate as to come in contact with any of these picked-up companies at a hotel, I trust they will give me the benefit of the doubt, . . . for I have been doubly afflicted the past few days, and oh! how I have suffered.

'Ye crying baby in church evil' can last but an hour or two during services, while the piano thumpers, horn blowers and ever-ready-to-give-you-a-little-of-their-business-specialty people crowd you at every turn for days at a time.

. . . As I have said before, I have had several days of it now, and the only consolation is that our misery is certainly not as aggravated as that of those who pay their hard-earned sheckels to listen to these 'Original Georgians' and 'New Orleans Creoles,' composed of the favorite would-bes from the neighboring cities" (*Detroit Plaindealer*).

• ***April 22, 1892:*** "St. Paul, Minneapolis and neighboring cities have had a surfeit of jubilee music this past season, there being no less than five 'grand choruses,' of from 50 to 200 voices each, that have sought the patronage of the general public, each and every one advertised to 'sing the melodies of slavery days with all the quaintness of the plantation Negro.' That the failures outnumbered the successes goes without saying.

St. Paul people claim to have the best church choir singing in an Afro-American church in the West. Prof. John Lucca [*sic*], one of the great musical family of that name, is the director and leader" (*Detroit Plaindealer*).

Note: John W. Luca was the oldest of four sons of a "free" shoemaker and chorister of New Haven, Connecticut, who moved "into fields hitherto untrodden by members of their race" when they began touring as a professional vocal and instrumental quartet, around 1850.[21] The Luca Family Singers remained active until 1860. In a 1909 letter to the *Freeman*, John W. Luca recalled having gone on to join the Hyer Sisters as musical director and stage manager around 1870: "remaining with them until I was obliged to give up the business on account of rheumatism. I came to St. Paul, where I remained, and have directed the Methodist choir for twenty-five years."[22] Luca died in 1910.[23]

• ***April 29, 1892 (Detroit, Michigan):*** "One of the attractions at Wonderland next week will be the celebrated Eureka quartet, Tyler, Kennedy, Cummings and Watts, who have been so successful during the past season. Tyler and Kennedy will be remembered as former members of the late Cleveland Minstrels. On a recent visit here with that organization they both scored hits, Tyler in one of his own compositions, and Kennedy in the 'Convict and the Bird'" (*Detroit Plaindealer*).

• ***April 29, 1892:*** "Mrs. Maggie Porter Cole, who is again with the Fiske Singers, will sing next Sunday at the Mormon Temple at Salt Lake City. This temple, which is said to have a seating capacity of 10,000, contains the largest and the finest toned organ in the world and has a choir of 350 trained voices" (*Detroit Plaindealer*).

• ***April 30, 1892 (Richmond, Virginia):*** "V.N. & C.I. [Virginia Normal & Collegiate Institute] Band Concert," "A large crowd greeted the V.N. & C.I. Band Monday night, April 25th at the True Reformer's Hall . . . The selections rendered by the band . . . reflected great credit on them and also showed the ability of their musical instructor, Mr. U. S. G. Patterson . . . It is not our intention to show partiality but the laughing song and 'I've been some, haven't you' which was so well sung and acted by Mr. U. S. G. Patterson . . . deserve special mention . . . The selection on the piano and the cornet at the same time and by Mr. S. J. Harris, Jr., will long be remembered by those who witnessed it . . . The Jubilee Quickstep, introducing cornet and drum solos, hurrah, pistol shot, marching, Hayfoot and Slewfoot[24] was the finest of its kind we have ever witnessed and added greatly in making the whole one of the best musical entertainments ever presented at the True Reformers' Hall since its erection . . .

Whenever colored talent is put on the stage in Richmond, the occasions are characterized by extreme disorder on the part of some members of the rising generation, and instead of diminishing, it seems to be increasing. It is a pity that some of our people cannot show their appreciation of talent manifested among the race in the right manner.

Hereafter some step should be taken to preserve order so that others can enjoy the benefit of the performances" (*Richmond Planet*).

• ***May 6, 1892 (Kansas City, Kansas):*** "The Ministers Alliance met with the Rose Hill Baptist church, Monday May 3rd . . . President G. W. Dickey . . . lined hymn 236 'Am I a soldier of the cross,' etc., and announced the meeting open and ready for business" (*Kansas City American Citizen*).

• ***May 13, 1892 (Kansas City, Kansas):*** "George Hampton and Eddie B. Love are the names of two wonderful young colored men who are stopping at Gordon's hotel. The former is a premier banjoist and the latter is a premier guitarist, and they are marvels in their adopted professions. They are here with Dr. W. W. Watkins' specialty and concert company, which gives a series of refined, moral and high class entertainments, *free*, on the corner of Minnesota avenue and 6th street. These entertainments will be *recherche*, judging from the opening performance Wednesday night. You should not fail to see and hear Hampton and Love as they are two of the greatest colored performers on the continent" (*Kansas City American Citizen*).

• ***May 14, 1892 (Cleveland, Ohio):*** "Three male quartets will sing at Mount Zion [Church]" (*Cleveland Gazette*).

• ***May 20, 1892:*** "Afro-Americans of Fort Worth, Texas, have one lawyer, three hotels, two saloons, five churches, six carpenters, four groceries, six expressmen, two shoeshops, two newspapers, five blacksmiths, three restaurants, nine secret orders, four barbershops, one silver cornet band and a population of 6,670. Four second-hand clothing stores, one fruit and confectionery stand, a public free school with eight teachers" (*Detroit Plaindealer*).

• ***May 20, 1892 (Lockland and Wyoming, Ohio):*** "The Silver toned quartet is an organization that is an honor to our people. It is home talent, and consists of H. F. Fox, 1st tenor; B. M. Fox, 2nd tenor; A. Roberts, baritone and M. V. Roberts, bass.

It is a rare treat to lovers of music to hear them sing. Their singing shows the results of careful training. Their harmony, volume of tone and enunciation are almost perfect and it is no exaggeration to say that they compare favorably with any quartet that has ever visited our village" (*Detroit Plaindealer*).

• ***May 20, 1892 (Richmond, Indiana):*** "Musical Items," "The Brotherhood Brass band gave a grand social festival at G.A.R. Hall, Monday evening, and the selections rendered by them were simply excellent. The band has made wonderful progress under the able tutorship of Mr. Henri Heck [*sic*] . . .

On May 14th, 1843, Thomas Morehead our celebrated inventor first saw the light, and on last Saturday he turned his 49 wheels and in honor of this event the Brotherhood Brass band turned out enmass and proceeded to his residence, where they serenaded him with many beautiful selections" (Detroit Plaindealer).

• ***May 20, 1892 (Cincinnati, Ohio):*** "The picnic given by Wilson division, No. 6, at the Highland House, Thursday night was a hummer, good order prevailed. The music by Prof. Johnson's band was excellent. A large crowd was present" (*Detroit Plaindealer*).

• ***May 20, 1892 (Richmond, Indiana):*** "Musical Items," "The female brass band, of Indianapolis, are giving some very fine concerts" (*Detroit Plaindealer*).

• ***May 20, 1892 (Richmond, Indiana):*** "Musical Items," "Paul S. [*sic*] Dunbar will give a select reading at Bethel A.M.E. in two weeks. Mr. Dunbar is one of the greatest readers in this nation" (*Detroit Plaindealer*).

• ***May 20, 1892 (Richmond, Indiana):*** "Musical Items," "Joseph Blakey, of Indianapolis, and W. H. White, of Muncie, are both claiming the state guitar championship" (*Detroit Plaindealer*).

• ***May 20, 1892 (Milwaukee, Wisconsin):*** "May 16 . . . The concerts managed by Messrs. Jones and Brown were fairly well attended and highly appreciated by those who did attend. Miss Hallie Q. Brown gave an exhibition of extraordinary talent as an elocutionist. Her selections were all interesting and appropriate. Mr. W. M. Cook is a most accomplished violinist and won merited applause. Misses Hughes and Carter did their share on the program entertainingly. The Jubilee singers, well, they helped to fill out the program. Taking all in all the concert was well worth the money and both Messrs. Jones and Brown, deserve credit, they are evidently 'hustlers'" (*Detroit Plaindealer*).

• ***May 27, 1892 (Cincinnati, Ohio):*** "The Calico Hop," "The Iolanthe Social Club organized for the purpose of advancing the knowledge of its membership in the terpsichorean art gave a 'Grand Calico hop,' as a fit closing for the season's meetings . . .

The ladies were all handsomely attired in very stylish costumes. The Gentlemen wore full dress. The music, as furnished by Prof. Hamilton's orchestra, was excellent" (*Detroit Plaindealer*).

• ***May 27, 1892 (Hudson, New York):*** "The Gold Leaf Club gave their annual concert and variety entertainment Wednesday evening. It was largely attended and the program was as follows:

"Song, 'Down on the Farm,' by Club; recitation, 'A Pack of Cards,' F. Bohite; duet, 'Going to the Woods,' Lottie and Cora; recitation, 'Never Despair,' Miss Grimes; guitar duet, Miss Robinson and Mr. Groomer; song, 'The Picture that is Turned Toward the Wall,' by Club; recitation, 'What Is Time,' Miss Lottie Jackson, 'Black Sir Ralph,' Miss G. L. Robinson; Bar Bell Calisthenics; bone solo, Mr. J. Grimes; recitation, Miss Cora Livingston . . .; scene, 'The Levee'" (*Detroit Plaindealer*).

• ***May 27, 1892:*** "Kansas' Leader," "Hon. C. C. James, the David of Negro Israel," "Hon. C. C. James born in Peru Township, Cass County

Michigan, Feb. 20, 1846, being the first colored male child born in the county. He is the great grandson of John James, of Connecticut, who was a drummer in Washington's army during the Revolutionary conflict . . . Unquestionably he is the leader of the Republican Negroes in Kansas" (*Kansas City American Citizen*).

• ***June 3, 1892:*** "Mr. J. B. Morris, of New York, the only Afro-American student of the Knickerbocker conservatory of music, that city, has been offered the position as baritone soloist in the Episcopal church (white), situated on E. 146th street. He has the distinction of being the first Afro-American to be offered such a position" (*Detroit Plaindealer*).

• ***June 11, 1892:*** "An Afro-American Tenor," "Mr. Harry A. Williams, a Cleveland boy, for several years tenor of St. Paul's church, with Mrs. C. S. Ford and others of the excellent quartette choir, who some years ago went to Paris to study under Sbrigilia and other eminent teachers, is rounding off a career abroad that is most creditable to the city of his birth, himself and his race (Afro-American). After completing his course in Paris, where he often appeared in concert and at private musicales he went to London. In one of the Paris musicales he sang with Madame Nevada, the famous American soprano, and was highly complimented and encouraged by her. In London among the many able musical critics, he won warm friends, perhaps the strongest of these being [Luigi] Denza, the eminent English professor of music and songwriter, well known in this country, where his compositions are very popular with the higher class soloists. With Mr. Denza's influence and his own ability, Mr. Williams won success after success in concerts in England, finally joining a well known company of artists in several successful tours. Upon the 23rd of April, Mr. Williams was added to the faculty of the London conservatory of Music, of which Mr. Denza is a director and professor. This is indeed an honor as well as a renumerative position. The conservatory secures a thoroughly competent and exceptionally well prepared teacher of vocal music in Mr. Williams, and is to be congratulated. His many friends in Cleveland will be pleased to learn of his success and that the assistance and encouragement given him before his departure abroad have not been in vain" (*Cleveland Gazette*, written by *Gazette* Editor H. C. Smith for the June 4, 1892, issue of *Cleveland Examiner*).

• ***June 17, 1892 (Springfield, Ohio):*** "The Hod Carrier's moonlight picnic was a grand affair. The Alma Band furnished the music and Dame Nature failed to show up a fair moon to the delight of the participants" (*Detroit Plaindealer*).

• ***June 18, 1892 (Rome, Georgia):*** "The Silver Star Quartette Commedians [*sic*], under the management of F. M. Dozier performed here recently at I.O.O.F. Hall. The singing was splendid, and the commedians kept the audience convulsed with laughter . . . They sang several popular songs with great effect" (*Indianapolis Freeman*).

• ***June 18, 1892:*** "A Fisk jubilee company now traveling in the west has among its members: Mrs. Maggie Porter-Cole (soprano) of Detroit; C. W. Payne, Geo. E. Barrett, tenors; J. N. Fowler, J. N. Caldwell, bassos; Miss Cora Cole, contralto; and Harry P. Guy, of Zanesville, O., pianist and organist. The company was in Denver, Colo. recently" (*Cleveland Gazette*).

• ***June 24, 1892 (Springfield, Ohio):*** "There will be a camp meeting held in Clark county fair ground beginning Sunday June 10, and continuing until July 24, conclusive, conducted by North Street A.M.E. Church . . . This will not be a Sunday picnic or a summer outing but a good, old fashioned camp meeting . . . Excellent music will by furnished by North Street choir . . . The singing evangelists, Rev. Luke White, of Mount Vermont, Rev. C. P. Herrington, of Sandusky, will be present singing old time Methodist hymns and the sweet [songs of the] colored race" (*Detroit Plaindealer*).

• ***June 24, 1892 (Richmond, Indiana):*** "Brotherhood Brass Band have improved wonderfully in the past three months, and they are making some good music. This band is under the tutorship of Prof. Henry Hack, an old professional band man, of Zanesville, Ohio. Mr. Hack has played in the best bands of St. Joe, Mo., Zanesville, Ohio, Kansas City, Sells Bros. circus and other places. Mr. Thomas Morehead, solo B cornet; Mr. Sharp, B cornet; Walter Alexander, solo alto; Dallis Polk, 1st tenor; Sherman Bird, 2nd tenor; John Carter, baritone; W. F. Patterson, the late lead violinist of Muncie city orchestra, Siption pro Hack tice orchestra [*sic*], Shaffroth and Clarks minstrels, Patterson and Robbins Superb concert orchestra and other good companies. He is playing Tuba; Will Thornton, tuba; Alexander Griggsby and drums [*sic*]" (I. T. E., *Detroit Plaindealer*).

• ***July 2, 1892:*** "Mr. Frank Carter, formerly of [Cleveland], now in Fostoria, directs the Washburn Guitar, Mandolin and Banjo Club. One of the special features of the club's concert is the guitar quartette's rendition of the 'Modulating Polka,' Mr. Carter's latest composition. The club also plays a fine march by him" (*Cleveland Gazette*).

• ***July 2, 1892:*** "If our people ever expect to rise by their own merit and ability they must discontinue the objectionable habit of styling their singers as the 'Negro Sankeys;' its ministers, evangelists 'The Colored Moodys;' its gifted singers as 'The Black Pattis;' or the 'Brignolis in Black.' It is just as honorable, and will bring just as many ducats to use our own names, and stand upon their own attainments. No white man ever thinks of calling himself the 'Fred Douglass' or the 'John M. Langston' of the race. He would scorn the idea and we should never be less manly than our fellows" (*Cleveland Gazette*, reprinted from *Pittsburgh Mirror*).

• ***July 9, 1892:*** "E. O. Rogers opens in August with his mammoth 'Uncle Tom's Cabin' Co., with fifty people. Mrs. Rogers will play Topsy for the first time in four years. The band will be one of the features. It will number twenty-two men in beautiful uniforms. The usual amount of dogs, ponies, donkeys, etc., will be carried, and a colored concert company of twelve singers, shouters, dancers, etc." (*New York Clipper*).

• ***July 16, 1892 (Youngstown, Ohio):*** "Remember the Sunday camp meeting of the A.M.E. Church will begin at the fairgrounds . . . Good vocal and instrumental music by a celebrated jubilee choir" (*Cleveland Gazette*).

• ***July 16, 1892:*** "The Stage," "Prof. C. W. Jones, late of Sells Bros. and Barret Circus but recently of the Great Texas Medicine Company will lead the Original Georgia, Ill. [*sic*], Minstrel in September" (*Indianapolis Freeman*).

• ***July 16, 1892:*** "The Stage," "Charles Winter Wood is home in Chicago after a year of college work" (*Indianapolis Freeman*).

• ***July 16, 1892:*** "The Stage," "Sylvester Russell appeared as Paul Jones in an operatic concert at New Brunswick New Jersey, June 8th. The Students from Rutgers College attended the performance in a body" (*Indianapolis Freeman*).

• ***July 22, 1892 (Ann Arbor, Michigan):*** "The musical and literary entertainment given at the Second Baptist church last Tuesday evening was very successfully carried out. The program was as follows: Instrumental solo by Mrs. Shewcraft; vocal solo, Miss May Green; reading, 'Did Job have warts on his nose,' Miss Maggie Johnson; vocal solo, 'Anchored,' Rev. E. L. Scruggs; reading, 'The wicket little boy,' Miss Emily Jones; guitar solo, Mr. Wm. Thomas; vocal solo, 'Break the news gently,' Miss Mary Fisher; recitation, 'Asleep at the switch,' Mr. Wilkerson; vocal duet, 'Tis evening brings my heart to thee,' Miss Beulah

Johnson and Rev. E. L. Scruggs" (*Detroit Plaindealer*).

• ***July 22, 1892 (Springfield, Ohio):*** "The famous and popular Alma cornet band have purchased a fine set of silver instruments costing $300 and few bands of this city are more fitted to meet the demands as a brass band than does this one. They play the latest and most difficult music, and is composed of young men of personal worth and character. Anyone wishing to secure this band can engage them for any reason desired. The following is the band as they appear: Harvey Moore, leader; Chas. Bizzell, first B flat; Chas. White, E flat cornet; Ben Ford, E flat alto; John Boone, baritone; Henry Nelson, E bass; Hudson Clemons, B flat tenor; Grant Love, first E flat alto; Obediah Viney, bass drum; George Hines, snare drum. These young men range from 18 to 23 years of age" (*Detroit Plaindealer*).

• ***July 22, 1892 (Lockland, Ohio):*** "The Lockland cornet band is going to Hamilton Tuesday to play for the Odd Fellows picnic. . . Augustus Gray, who recently joined the band and was given an alto horn is making great headway with his instrument. The rest of the band boys will have to 'hump' themselves for Augustus is coming" (*Detroit Plaindealer*).

DRAWING THE LINE.

Party On Left—"No sir; being manager of a band of "Jubilee Singers," you could hardly expect me to be present at a mere church musicale."

Freeman, *July 30, 1892.*

• ***July 22, 1892 (Topeka, Kansas):*** "Two blind men were seen on the streets last week playing and singing for their living; they went from here to Lawrence" (*Kansas State Ledger*).

• ***July 29, 1892 (Kansas City, Kansas)***: "Don't miss the greatest event of the age at Brown's Park Aug 1st. There will be a political joint discussion, subject: 'How should the Afro-Americans vote in the future to best protest his political interests?'. . .

Quartette and Mandolin contest at the night exercises" (*Kansas City American Citizen*).

• ***July 30, 1892 (Rome, Georgia):*** "The G U O of O F of Seven Hill Lodge 3066 gave a steamboat excursion last Monday to Cirton's grove. The Rome Star Guards were in full uniform and displayed fine drilling. Music was furnished by the Hill City string band and dancing was the leading feature. A fine barbecue was served" (*Indianapolis Freeman*).

• ***August 5, 1892 (Kansas City, Missouri):*** "Don't fail to attend the grandest event of the season at Vineyard Hall 7th inst., given by the Cuban Trio, Joe Javlin the world renowned Egyptian Juggler, George Cathin the celebrated Chinese impersonator [and] H. G. Hutchison the Slide trombone soloist of great fame, having just finished a tour through Mexico and Cuba" (*Kansas City American Citizen*).

• ***August 5, 1892 (Youngstown, Ohio):*** "The harmonica band made a fine display at Greenville Tuesday in their new uniforms" (*Detroit Plaindealer*).

• ***August 5, 1892 (Wyoming, Ohio):*** "A banjo for sale, in good order; thirty two brackets, seventeen frets—Price $5.00. Apply to Lillie McDonald, Wyoming, O., Vine st." (*Detroit Plaindealer*).

• ***August 6, 1892 (Mayslick, Kentucky):*** The Jubilee Singers of Eckstein-Norton University "were here on the 30th of June and won many laurels" (*Indianapolis Freeman*).

• ***August 12, 1892:*** "Mr. Sam Lucas, the well known comedian, and his wife, sailed on the *Cephalonia* from the port of Boston last Saturday, for Europe to be gone three years. They have been sent for by Mr. Warren and Signor Zarini, the celebrated instructor of Mme. Adelina Patti, and of whom Mme. Marie Selika also received instructions" (*Detroit Plaindealer*).

• ***August 13, 1892:*** "When Barlow Bros.' Minstrels were at Canton, O., Aug. 5, Mr. Ferry, the frog imitator, was visited by three other frogs, viz.: Zella, Frank Halter and the originator of all frog imitators, Wm. Delhaur. The quartet had a very pleasant time, and a frog supper was the order of the evening" (*New York Clipper*).

• ***August 18, 1892:*** "Billy Jackson, of Jackson and Jones, the author of 'The Coon with a Big Thick Lip' and 'A Seat Up Dar For Me,' has completed a new song, entitled 'It's Nobody's Trouble But Mine,' and dedicated it to Dick White of the Creole Concert Co." (*New York Clipper*).

• ***August 20, 1892 (Blocton, Alabama):*** "Coal Miner's Band—Excursion," "This is a small town in the Cahoba Coal Fields, with a population of about three thousand. Out of this number there are about eight hundred Afro-Americans, all engaged in mining coal for the Cahoba Mining Co. We have a silver Cornet Band of which all the members are coal miners. The band run an excursion from here to Chattanooga, Tenn., July 29th, over the East Tennessee, Virginia & Georgia R'y, and it was the most enjoyable affair of the season" (*Indianapolis Freeman*).

• ***August 20, 1892 (Washington, Pennsylvania):*** "The Quartette club gave a very pleasant serenade last Thursday evening at the residence of A. A. Stewart. Their selections were grand. The club is composed of Reuben Baker, Jr., James Carroll, Boston Brown, William Wright" (*Cleveland Gazette*).

• ***August 20, 1892 (Coshocton, Ohio):*** "S. L. Yager, one of our ablest jubilee singers, has gone to Trinway, to assist the camp meeting choir there" (*Cleveland Gazette*).

• ***August 26, 1892 (Athens, Ohio):*** "Rev. G. W. Curry, accompanied by the Athens Jubilee Singers, left here on the 12th for the purpose of holding a camp meeting at Enterprise. Rev. Curry will return sometime during this week to make preparations for the camp at Buckeye Park next Sunday" (*Detroit Plaindealer*).

• ***August 26, 1892 (Covington, Kentucky):*** "Rev. Dodds is carrying on a campmeeting in Ostenburg. Apparently it promises success. Last evening the ground was covered with all people, and they were pleased with the African Zulu chief, Mata Mon Zaro, and his New York company, who entertained the audience" (*Detroit Plaindealer*).

• ***August 27, 1892:*** "Crumbaugh & Mallory Bros. Minstrels opened their season at Columbus, Mo., Aug. 12, to a large house. The show scored a hit. The roster is: J. E. Crumbaugh, manager; R. M. Hockaday, treasurer, and Mallory Bros., directors of amusements, with Tom Brown, Billy Johnson, Billy Eldredge, Olli Ferguson, James Wilson, Geo. Bailey, Will Hayden, E. J. Deverin, William Johnson, L. W. Payne, Chas. A. Johnson, P. G. Lowery, Joe Ravise, Hardy Jones, W. A. Halton and Paul Redon" (*New York Clipper*).

• ***August 27, 1892 (Richmond, Virginia):*** "The Excelsior Band of Norfolk Serenades the Richmond PLANET," "A throng of anxious listeners congregated in front of the *Planet* office, Monday evening August 22, to witness a serenade by the above named corps of artists as a compliment to the Richmond PLANET... The band had come to the city on an excursion given by them... This Excelsior brass and reed band under the talented leadership of Mr. Matthew Goodrich rendered several choice selections, which captivated the listeners and placed them in the front rank of Afro-American musicians. This grand and noble feature was heartily enjoyed by all in the vicinity of this establishment both white and colored" (*Richmond Planet*).

• ***September 3, 1892:*** "Mr. and Mrs. Sam Lucas will open shortly in London. They are the guests of the Black Swan Trio" (*New York Clipper*).

• ***September 3, 1892:*** "James Bland, the minstrel, is still in London, England" (*Cleveland Gazette*).

• ***September 9, 1892 (Springfield, Ohio):*** "The Alma band of this city furnished music for the Ninth battalion, at Newark, last week. The band was crowned with honors by the white citizens. An electric car was sent out near the camp grounds Monday night to take the band to town, when at the request of the white citizens, a grand musical concert was given in the presence of a large number of citizens. The *Newark Tribune,* when making mention of the concert says: 'The band is the very best. Good for the boys'" (*Detroit Plaindealer*).

• ***September 16, 1892 (Detroit, Michigan):*** "The Bergen concert at Bethel A.M.E. Church last Thursday night was something new in the way of concerts in more ways than one . . . First, it commenced almost on time; secondly, nearly every person was in their seat before half past eight; and thirdly, it was ended at 9:40, about the usual time that concerts have been opened. The *Plaindealer* hopes that the patrons and performers in future concerts and entertainments will take pattern after this one.

A great deal of interest was aroused in the Bergen concert . . . and it netted a handsome sum for both manager and Bethel church. Mrs. Bergen had been well advertised, and the church was crowded to its utmost capacity. Despite the fact that she is advertised as a ballad singer, and one who excels in her line, there was some disappointment on the part of some of the audience that her singing was not operatic. Mrs. Bergen deserves nearly all of the praise that has been given her, and among Afro-American singers her equal in her line of singing has not been seen in Detroit. She has a voice of great range and versatility. She easily jumps from high soprano to a rich contralto, and her music loses nothing of its charm. She puts power and feeling into her songs and invokes the enthusiasm that prompts her hearers to manifest their delight by strong outbursts of approval in seeking encores, and Mrs. Bergen graciously acceded to their wishes. A well satisfied audience left the church after the concert was over.

Now that Bethel church has opened the season with a first class entertainment The *Plaindealer* hopes that this will not be the end, but that it and other churches of the city, striving to unload a debt, will give some attention to the demands of the people for such entertainments, as was evidenced by the crowd at Bethel, and will follow the example. Flora Batson Bergen is not the only singer of note whose services can be secured on the same or easier terms, than what her manager brought her here for. There is Madame Selika . . . Rachel Walker . . . and . . . our own Maggie Porter Cole, [who] created the furor at the Afro- American league concert two years ago. The people like her, and she would draw crowded houses, and without doubt, if properly advertised, fill the old Detroit rink.

Ten thousand or more Afro-Americans in Detroit—just think of the places we ought to fill in every sphere of business. Just think how hard it would be to fill such places if they were opened to us all at once, then let us ask ourselves and each other—Whose is the fault?" (*Detroit Plaindealer*).

• ***September 17, 1892:*** "The Meadow Brook Quartet are on their way East. Two benefits were tendered them on their departure from 'Frisco by some of the leading colored people of the city" (*New York Clipper*).

• ***September 17, 1892:*** "Mrs. Jennie Jackson-DeHart visited Nashville last week, in quest of singers for her company" (*Cleveland Gazette*).

• ***September 17, 1892:*** "Ollie C. Hall, late of W. S. Cleveland's Colored Minstrels, is now musical director of the Carolina Concert Co." (*New York Clipper*).

• ***September 23, 1892:*** "Among the contestants in the Amateur band contest at the Exposition at Minneapolis was the Harris Military Band of Duluth, composed of Afro-Americans. They drew the first place in the parade for which they got $50, but came out a little behind in the contest for prizes. They were the best uniformed band present" (*Detroit Plaindealer*).

• ***September 30, 1892 (Lexington, Kentucky):*** "The event of the season to Lexingtonians has come and passed. For many years the Colored Fair has been a source of interest and pleasure to Afro-Americans of this vicinity. This year, which will probably be the last of its existence, the managers and directors surpassed themselves and gave to their patrons four days replete with enjoyment and instruction . . .

Four bands contributed excellent music to the day's pleasure. And to the credit of the large numbers present, each day the order was perfect, although 75,000 people passed the gates" (*Detroit Plaindealer*).

• ***October 1, 1892 (New York City):*** "Mr. Harry T. Burleigh, of Eric, Pa., who has begun his second year in the Conservatory of Music in this city, passed his examination last week, making 100%. He has a four year scholarship, but at his rapid rate of progress will finish his course in 3 years. He sang in Washington this week with Mme Selika, Mme Jones and other artists" (*Cleveland Gazette*).

• ***October 1, 1892 (Newport, Arkansas):*** "The Newport Climax Glee Club has organized as follows: W. W. Walker, soprano; R. H. Wise, tenor; L. S. Slaughter, baritone; F. B. Bates, basso; and James McGhee, guitarist. They are meeting with great success" (*Indianapolis Freeman*).

• ***October 1, 1892 (Cleveland, Ohio):*** "Mr. J. G. Shelton has withdrawn from the position of chorister of Mt. Zion Church, feeling the work to be too heavy and taxing for him through all sorts of weather in his present state of health. The music committee has elected Miss Rachel Walker chorister and the choir reorganized with quartette and chorus" (*Cleveland Gazette*).

• ***October 7, 1892 (Toledo, Ohio):*** "Those who saw the beautiful Queen Esther, the grand cantata played at Third Baptist church, Tuesday and Friday evening . . . pronounce it the best attempt yet made to render this play among our Citizens in Toledo . . . An invitation has been extended to all those who took part in the play, to render it at an early date, in one of the white churches. The audience was largely composed of the white friends at the Third Baptist and they were too well pleased" (*Detroit Plaindealer*).

• ***October 7, 1892 (Detroit, Michigan):*** "The *Plaindealer* is glad to note the spirit of activity in the churches, and the disposition they are beginning to show towards having concerts of exceptional merit . . .

As suggested . . . a few weeks ago, that celebrated singers, or talent be engaged by churches and other organizations, that seek to draw money from the public purse. The *Plaindealer* is pleased to note that the services of our own sweet singer, Mrs. Maggie Porter Cole have been secured by Bethel church, and preparations are now under way for a concert that will be equal to, if not surpass in merit the Bergen concert of a few weeks ago. Mrs. Cole is a different style of singer from Mrs. Batson, she has not appeared before a Detroit audience for some time, and the place where the concert is to be held should be crowded. Certainly the people ought to patronize home talent as well as outside, when the attraction is equal in merit, as this will be.

As an illustration showing that it pays to engage the best singers of the race, even if a large sum has to be paid for their services, the *Plaindealer* cites this: Mme Selika, sometimes called the Brown Patti, sang for St. Andrews Mission, of Cleveland, last week, to an audience of 5,000 people, at the music hall, price of seats ranged from fifty cents to one dollar" (*Detroit Plaindealer*).

• ***October 8, 1892 (Cleveland, Ohio):*** "The new choir at Mt. Zion, under the leadership of Miss Rachel Walker, starts off finely. It is hoped to have a quartet and chorus. The singing last Sabbath was spirited and edifying. We wish the new choir large success" (*Cleveland Gazette*).

• ***October 8, 1892:*** "Roster of the Silver Bow Colored Specialty Co.: R. B. Merritt, proprietor; G. H. Watkins, manager; Henry Wise, stage manager; A McKinzey, master of transportation; Harry Moore, advance representative; Frank Johnson, bandmaster; G. H. Wirkman, leader orchestra; C. W. Washington, H. Goodman, W. E. Dorsey; Thos. Myers, A. Johnson, Chas. Mills, Lina Mahony, Mamie Rodgers, Ida Smith and Lulu Davis" (*New York Clipper*).

Note: Stage manager Henry Wise is almost certainly the same "Hen" Wise who appeared with Billy Jackson's Colored Minstrels at Worth's Dime Museum in New York City in 1894 and went on to Australia with Orpheus McAdoo's Georgia Minstrels and Alabama Cakewalkers in 1899. The *Freeman* of January 12, 1901, noted he was back in the States from Australia via Honolulu; two years later he was "still on God's green soil, reaping golden shekels, booked solid for 20 weeks in the Northwest, playing two houses per night."[25] In Chicago in 1913 Wise organized a twenty-five member "Bronze Review" for a tour of Hawaii and Australia, but they "disbanded after a short season on the island." On May 14, 1917, Hen Wise "died of a complication of diseases" at Queens Hospital in Honolulu.[26]

• ***October 14, 1892 (Staunton, Virginia):*** "Prof. J. A. Draper, our talented comedian and ballad singer, left yesterday for Charlottesville on business" (*Detroit Plaindealer*).

• ***October 14, 1892 (Canton, Mississippi):*** "Serenades are the latest fads in Canton" (*Detroit Plaindealer*).

• ***October 21, 1892 (Staunton, Virginia):*** "One of the pleasantest features during the fair at Charlottesville was the concert at Ebenezer Baptist church, under the management of Prof. J. A. Draper of our city" (*Detroit Plaindealer*).

• ***October 21, 1892:*** "Prof. Christmas Evans, a well known young man of Pittsburg [*sic*, i.e., Petersburg, Virginia] who was born blind, is the best harpist in the United States. He is a perfect genius, and can play on the spur of the moment any thing upon his harp that he hears any one

TENTH YEAR AND TRIUMPHANT TOUR OF THE STANDARD AND ONLY BIG CITY "UNCLE TOM'S CABIN" CO. IN EXISTENCE, STETSON'S BIG SPECTACULAR PRODUCTION OF

UNCLE TOM'S CABIN

Under the Management of LEON W. WASHBURN,

Now playing to the capacity of the houses. and turning hundreds away nightly. Election excitement creates no opposition for this standard attroction. Look at the financial record through that hotbed of politics. Central New York:

HUDSON, N. Y., $359. GLOVERSVILLE, $563. SCHENECTADY, $530. LITTLE FALLS, $394. JOHNSTOWN, $324. UTICA (Mat. and Night), $1,202.

A FEW OF THE MANY FEATURES:

KATE PARTINGTON, the only Topsy; PROF. BERGMANN'S GOLDEN CORNET BAND OF 14 PICKED MEN, LEWIS HUNTER'S COLORED BAND OF 10 SOLO ARTISTS, THE ONLY PACK OF GENUINE SIBERIAN BLOODHOUNDS, THE GORGEOUS TRANSFORMATION SCENES---OHIO RIVER BY MOONLIGHT, and EVA'S ASCENT TO THE GOLDEN REALMS (Calcium Lights carried for these scenes); THE LONE STAR QUARTET, THE MANDOLIN STUDENTS.

A HOST OF REFINED AND PLEASING SPECIALTIES INTRODUCED THROUGHOUT THE PLAY.

Gorgeous street Parade daily, with Positively the most expensive uniforms used by any traveling company, bar none. Time all filled.

Wanted, Good Musical Team, Both Must Double Brass.

Address all communications L. W. WASHBURN, 201 Centre Street, New York.

READ PRESS NOTICES.

THOUSANDS SEE "UNCLE TOM."—The engagement of Stetson's "Uncle Tom's Cabin" Company at the local theatre yesterday fully demonstrated the fact that the old time play is still popular, especially with the children. The matinee was the largest ever held at the Opera House, over 1,300 ladies and children attending. Last evening the house was packed, and the crowd numbered close to 1,700 people. Standing room was not available after 8 o'clock. and many were turned away. The company presented the play in an acceptable manner.—UTICA SUNDAY TRIBUNE, Sept 18, 1892.

UNCLE TOM'S CABIN.—Stetson's "Uncle Tom's Cabin" Company was greeted with crowded houses, both at the matinee in the afternoon and at the evening performance, Saturday. This company plays in both large and small towns, and the popularity of the play does not seem to wane in the least, judging from the large audiences which it draws. The Lone Star Quartet was a feature of the entertainment, and was applauded on each appearance. The play, as a whole, seemed to give good satisfaction to those present.—UTICA DAILY PRESS, Sept 9, 1892.

New York Clipper, *October 15, 1892.*

else play. He has traveled much in the States and has received from audiences and newspapers the merited reputation of being the equal of Blind Tom" (*Detroit Plaindealer*).

• ***October 21, 1892 (Lansing, Michigan):*** "Mr. T. J. Davis and Theo Thompson, have re-organized their orchestra, and are prepared to furnish music for any occasion. The orchestra consists of Mr. T. J. Davis, violin; J. Allen, violin; B. Parker, bass viol; J. Thompson, piano; G. V. Allen, cornet; Wm. Rue, clarionet; Theo. Thompson, P. Taylor, trombone. Mr. Davis is leader and manager, and Mr. Thompson, musical director" (*Detroit Plaindealer*).

• ***October 21, 1892:*** "A Novel Idea," "Mr. Cook Presents One for the Columbian Fair," "To the Editor of the Plaindealer:

Dear sir: In the grand display now in preparation, of what America has accomplished, the Negro, although so important a factor in the development of this country, has been entirely omitted. Although for two hundred and fifty (250) years in the most abject state of bondage, closely following which subject to barriers of prejudice, and oppression that tended to retard his advancement, the Negro has made most wonderful strides in the progress of civilization.

Any display in which he is omitted, must be, and therefore is, incomplete. By such omission there is also a great injustice being done an hitherto inferior and oppressed people.

After much study and careful consideration, I have formed a plan which is now submitted to you for your earnest examination and which, I hope, will receive your approval and assistance.

The Negro's greatest achievements have been in art, literature and music, hence, he would appear to best advantage in a display of these talents.

It is my ambition to collect all of the most capable of the race, by reason of both talent and culture in vocal and instrumental music, for the purpose of presenting Italian, English and Negro opera.

The question will doubtless arise, what is 'Negro Opera.' I have now in preparation the Libretto and score, for the opera of *Uncle Tom's Cabin,* all of which, together with the special scenery, will be executed by Negro talent. This opera together with the various English and Italian operas will be given during the entire six months of the 'World's fair.' There will also be special Plantation Concert nights, on which Jubilee music will be sung, and classical concert nights on which only the best classical music will be rendered. In this way the great progress and ability of the Negro can be seen and better appreciated.

This, as I have outlined to you only more fully elaborated upon and thoroughly explained, I have submitted to the Musical Bureau of the World's Columbian exposition, which has the matter now under advisement. Dr. Ziegfield, of the Chicago Temple and College of music, has thoroughly examined my plans and gives them his hearty endorsement.

If you have heard the wonderful voices of Selika, Siseretta Jones and Loudin, or the exquisite skill of the violinists Jose De Brindes or Joseph Douglass, you must certainly be convinced of the feasibility of my plans. Since the time intervening between now and the accomplishment of my purpose is so short, you will confer a great favor upon me by making an immediate reply through the columns of your valuable paper.

Very respectfully yours,

Will M. Cook

Student of Royal Conservatory of Music, Berlin, Germany.

Address, No. 3123 Dearborn street, Chicago" (*Detroit Plaindealer*).

Note: Cook's letter also appeared in the November 12, 1892, edition of the *Freeman.*

• ***October 28, 1892 (Frankfort, Kentucky):*** "On last Friday evening, a number of pleasure-seekers and givers gathered at the residence of Miss Lizzie Mordecai for the purpose of surprising Miss Martha Craig, of Versailles, Ky. At 10:30 P.M. the crowd with vehicles extending about four squares, proceeded to the residence of Mrs. Armour Blackburn. Before entering the house the string band played one of its charming pieces which gave enchantment to those who quietly waited for the next piece, which was a march and all in a line made an attempt to enter the house. On entering each was greeted and received with that pleasant smile which is always characteristic of Miss Craig. Suddenly there was heard in the rear, music which called from the parlor all who enjoy skipping the light fantastic toe . . . At mid-night Mrs. Blackburn gave a cordial welcome to all to prepare for supper, as the string band played, all marched into the spacious dining room . . . All enjoyed themselves and in the early hours of the morning the sweet notes of Home Sweet Home was heard making its way through the house and notified all that the time of adjournment was near at hand" (*Detroit Plaindealer*).

• ***October 29, 1892:*** "Hagerman's Success—A Cincinnati Basso Part Proprietor of a Concert Company Singing In The West," "Prof. J. A. Hagerman, for 7 years basso for the Donavin's Original Tennesseans, and one year with Donavin's Hyers sisters Comedy Company, and three years with Thearle's Original Nashville Students, is now half proprietor and manager of a company consisting of eight people, known as the Carolinian Colored concert company. Mr. Hagerman's partner is the popular baritone, Mr. Ollie Hall, formerly vocal director of Cleveland's colored minstrels. These gentlemen have a good company and are doing good business through the state of Iowa . . . It would be well if more of our colored talent would club together and make money for themselves instead of building mansions for the opposite race. Go ahead, Messrs. Hagerman and Hall, may you long continue is our hearty wish" (*Cleveland Gazette*).

• ***November 5, 1892:*** "Sylvester Russell, the tenor, will hereafter do his act in boy characters, and will discard female characters and full dress suits" (*New York Clipper*).

• ***November 12, 1892:*** "The Carolinian Concert Co. are now in their fourth week under the management of Jos. A. Hagerman and Ollie C. Hall. The company are heading for the Northwest . . . The roster: The Calliope Quartet, Chas. Lewis, Gilmore Hayes, Mrs. Ollie C. Hall, Mary Morgan, Lulu Cobb, Etta Lewis and G. A. Shaughnessy" (*New York Clipper*).

• ***November 12, 1892 (Winchester, Virginia):*** "Pugsley Bros. famous Tennessee Warblers appeared here at Odd Fellows' Oct. 31st and November 1st, under ausp. I.O.O.F. Lodge #1461 . . . Ruby Shelton, pianoist [*sic*]; [Major] Daniels, the phenomenal basso; and Will Hunt, the unequaled baritone, have created quite a stir in the Eastern musical world" (*Indianapolis Freeman*).

Note: R. Byron "Ruby" Shelton was, by every indication, a ragtime piano pioneer. While touring with several important black road shows of the mid to late 1890s, he appears to have also made a point to play for church-related events in his Indianapolis hometown. With Al G. Field's Negro Minstrels in 1898, he teamed with ragtime coon-song composer Sidney Perrin to put on a "hot original musical act."[27] In 1907 Shelton ventured into vaudeville with comedian Harry Fiddler, and a 1915 review of their act informed, "Ruby Shelton is a splendid baritone singer and a phenomenal pianist, playing the popular ragtime selections or the classics with equal facility."[28] In the fall of 1917 the *Chicago Defender* reported, "Ruby Shelton, late

R. BYRON SHELTON.

The above portrait needs no introduction to the many readers of "The Freeman" throughout the United States, especially in this state. Mr. Shelton has been very prominent in musical circles for several years and as a pianist stands second to none among the race. Mr. Shelton has been a member of the following well-known companies: Puggsley Bros., Isham's "Oriental America," Shelton's Stars, and Al G. Field's Colored Minstrels. Mr. Shelton will appear in the Fourth Annual Musical Festival in Allen Chapel June 22-23. Indianapolis.

• • •

Freeman, *June 11, 1898.*

of Fiddler & Shelton, has accepted the lucrative position of musical and amusement director for the Astor theatre in [Indianapolis] . . . He will have a five-piece orchestra at the Astor."[29]

• ***November 19, 1892 (Winchester, Virginia):*** "H. H. Hunt, a Hoosier boy, was in the city with

Wanted Quick, for
C. W. Kidder & Co.'s Big Spectacular "Uncle Tom's Cabin" Co.
TRAVELS BY ITS OWN SPECIAL TRAIN.
We want Actors for every part, Good Colored Quartet that double in brass, Musicians of all kinds, Trap Drummer, Good Drum Major to double in drama. NO FARES ADVANCED. Boozers and kickers will not be tolerated. OPERA HOUSE Managers in Ohio send open time. Kittanning, Pa., Nov. 17, Tarentum, Pa., 18, Leechburg, Pa., 19, Apollo 21.

SNYDER & ZIMMERMAN'S
COLOSSAL COLORED CARNIVAL.
Wanted, a Few More Good Musicians, Song and Dance People and Comedians.
Managers of opera houses in Pennsylvania, New York, New Jersey and New England, send in your open time at once if you want to play the big minstrel boom. Wire or write to Richmond, Va., instead of Hagerstown, Md.
SNYDER & ZIMMERMAN.

E. O. Rogers' Original "Uncle Tom's Cabin" Co.,
The oldest, the largest, the most successful organization in the world. Thirteenth year under the same title. Six monster Siberian and Cuban Bloodhounds, smallest Trick Donkey, eight Colored Jubilee Singers, eight White and Colored Bands; Beautiful Special Scenery; the Best Billed Show in America; a Company of recognized Artists headed by the Peerless Topsy, LILLIAN ROGERS; Eighth week of the present season; houses packed at every performance. Managers in the East having open time for the above address care of
POST-EXPRESS PRINTING CO., Rochester, N. Y.

New York Clipper, *November 19, 1892.*

the Tennessee Warblers . . . The company consisted of the following. They are considered the finest troupe that ever visited our city: L. E. Pugsley, C. H. Pugsley, M. W. Daniels, W. H. Hunt, R. N. Shelton [*sic*] and R. C. Pugsley" (*Indianapolis Freeman*).

• ***November 19, 1892:*** "The Alabama Quartette," "Says A Denver, Colo, exchange: With the A. M. Palmer 'Alabama' company, playing at the Tabor Grand last week, was a colored quartette of high musical calibre. Messrs: Underwood, Frazier, Brown and Du Pree comprise the quartet, and their singing is by no means an unimportant feature of the splendid entertainment provided by the 'Alabama' company. The quartette is a Chicago production, and under the leadership of Mr. B. F. Underwood, is making its mark on the road" (*Cleveland Gazette*).

• ***November 19, 1892 (Cincinnati, Ohio):*** "Jennie Jackson-DeHart, Laura Wells, Marie Bell, Richard Conner, the boy alto; and Mr. Johnson the baritone, left last Saturday to join the Mumford-Fisk Company at New York—They will be absent until May" (*Cleveland Gazette*).

• ***November 19, 1892:*** The author of a column titled "Rounder's Chat" told of a visit to New York: "I sought my friend Mr. H. T. Burleigh, who is a student of the National Conservatory of Music, and found him in its commodious building on Twenty-seventh street. Mr. Burleigh is about the only Afro-American student at this famous institution at present and his standing there is most creditable indeed—at the head of his classes. The faculty, headed by the famous foreigner and finished musician and author, Dvorak, and the presiding genius of the conservatory, Mrs. H. K. Thurber, are both pleased to note my friend's splendid progress. Our people in New York City and Brooklyn appreciate Mr. Burleigh, too, and show him every attention, social and otherwise. He is in constant demand for concerts, etc., possessing a strong, broad and yet sweet baritone voice which he uses artistically" (*Cleveland Gazette*).

• ***November 19, 1892:*** "The colored people of several Southern cities so far forgot themselves as to permit their children to take part in a side show celebration of 'Columbus Day' by the public schools... From McMinnville, Tenn., comes the report of the most flagrant outrage to self-respect. The white children marched in one gate, and were seated on the northern side of the park, and the exercises proceeded without waiting for the colored children. When they did arrive, prayer was being offered, so the master of ceremonies rushed toward them, drove the colored band, which was gaily playing 'Hurrah for the Red, White and Blue' out of the procession and roughly ordered them to go by as they had not come at the appointed time. They were afterward seated at the rear of the park, where they could neither see nor hear anything that was said; every speaker had his back to them. They marched there to sing 'My Country Tis of Thee,' and were not allowed to do even that" (*New York Age*).

• ***November 24, 1892:*** Concerning LaHarpe Street Methodist Episcopal Church in New Orleans, "This is a progressive congregation, largely Creole. The singing was exceptionally fine, especially the French rendition of the beautiful hymn, 'I Need Thee Every Hour' " (*Southwestern Christian Advocate*).

• ***November 25, 1892 (Windsor, Ontario):*** "The O'Banyon jubilee troupe gave a concert in A.M.E. chapel November 21 to an overcrowded house... The O'Banyon troupe intend to complete their tour through Ontario, after which their manager will take them to Great Britain and Africa" (*Detroit Plaindealer*).

• ***November 26, 1892 (Boston, Massachusetts):*** "Mr. Sydney Woodward... [is] considering an offer from an Afro-American company through Mr. Will M. Cook, to sing in opera at the World's Fair. In Boston we consider Mr. Woodward a superb tenor and modest gentleman. He has also promised to assist at a memorial to be given to the dead poet Whittier in December by the colored collegians of Boston" (*Cleveland Gazette*).

• ***December 2, 1892 (Springfield, Ohio):*** "Nov. 29.—The following program was rendered at the North street church Thanksgiving night. The opening song by the company was the 'Old Ark's Moving;' recitation, 'She stood at the bar of justice,' by Miss Belle Bailey; dialogue, 'Stage struck' by Clarence Jackson, John Jackson, Josie Nelson and Annie Turner; song, 'Swing low, sweet chariot,' recitation, 'The mischief whiskey has done,' by Josie Thomas; recitation, 'The Quaker of Olden Times,' by Nathan Hunt; recitation, 'The woman was old' by little Willie Dickson; recitation, 'Have you heard of the Golden City,' by Mamie Jackson. The entertainers closed with a tableaux representing Hope, Faith and Charity by Grace Henderson, Hattie Allen and Josie Thomas" (*Detroit Plaindealer*).

• ***December 2, 1892:*** "Walnut Hill Notes," "The Young Men's Juvenile orchestra, of Walnut Hills, put quite a feather in their crown on Thanksgiving night at Delhi, by playing some of their choice music at the concert of Mr. Samuel Bush. The members of it are, Albert Smith, leader, first violin; Edward Washington, second violin; George Austin, cornetist; and James Elder, bass viol" (*Detroit Plaindealer*).

• ***December 2, 1892:*** "Detroit News," "It is not strange that such deep interest is developing lately in this community in good music. It is a mark of high culture. The Bergen, Porter Cole, and [Blind] Boone concerts have been real brain and soul food" (*Detroit Plaindealer*).

• ***December 9, 1892 (Amherstberg, Ontario):*** "The concert given by the O'Banyoun [*sic*] concert troupe was well attended, and netted those interested $42.70" (*Detroit Plaindealer*).

• ***December 9, 1892:*** "Cincinnati Department," "The Queen City Social Club have concluded to give a full dress hop at Wubeler's hall, Dec. 30. Professor Hamilton's quadrille band will furnish the music" (*Detroit Plaindealer*).

• ***December 9, 1892:*** "Detroit Department," "The second concert given under the management of Mrs. Porter Cole was held at Ebenezer Church last Wednesday and though many of the chorus and Mrs. Cole herself labored under the disadvantages of illnesses from which they were not entirely recovered, they scored another success. The choruses selected tested the versatility of the singing and in several lines a marked improvement over their first work was shown. The best and most finished number, though not the most popular was 'Shades of Evening,' where the blending and harmony of the voices were notable features. 'The Song of the Triton' and the favorite 'Italia' were received with marked favor by the audience which was responded to by encores.

Of the other numbers 'Dear Heart' by Mr. Wm. Abernethy, 'Committed to the Deep' by Mr. George Owens and the male chorus 'Bill of Fare' were especially well done. It is hardly necessary to speak of the solo work by Mrs. Cole. She is always in voice, always indefatigable in her efforts to please her audience and always successful in winning their favor. Her work Wednesday evening was up to her usual standard and the 'chorus' expressed their gratitude and esteem for her work with them by sending up a lovely selection of flowers. Of her numbers the 'Winter Lullaby' was the most excellent and the 'Creole Love Song' the most popular. The next concert by the chorus will be given for the Second Baptist church and an effort will be made to surpass either of the preceding concerts. The first regular rehearsal will be held at the residence of Mrs. Cole, Friday Dec. 16, and the attendance of all the old chorus and such others of the young people as are desirous of improving in vocal work is especially requested" (*Detroit Plaindealer*).

• ***December 9, 1892:*** "Cincinnati Department," "Charles Winter Woods [*sic*], of Chicago, who has recently graduated from Beloit college, as an actor of some merit, has organized the Winter Wood dramatic company and will soon produce 'Damon And Pythias' at Freeberg's Opera house, Chicago" (*Detroit Plaindealer*).

• ***December 9, 1892 (Xenia, Ohio):*** "Dec. 5.—The Democrats had a turnout on Wednesday, the 29 ult. The procession was three blocks long, filled with comically dressed fellows, mostly boys, one beer wagon, eight carriages and 38 boney horses looking for the fertilizer factory, a few common looking country girls with red caps on and red sashes tied around them. They resembled the Arab tribe of Barnum's circus in a place where water was scarce. They were headed by our colored famous Brass band which was employed for the occasion. Further on was a one horse country band playing a tune entitled 'The fun is all over.' We thought so, too. At night they set fire to two cords of wood in the center of the public square, gave a display of fireworks. If the Democratic administration for the next four years is as poor as their demonstration was in Green county not much will be done" (*Detroit Plaindealer*).

• ***December 9, 1892:*** "New York boasts of the largest surpliced colored boy choir in the United States, and, so far as is known, in the world. Such choirs are not numerous, and are to be found only in large cities. There are two in New York—one belonging to a Roman Catholic and the other to a Protestant Episcopal church. The latter is the one here meant . . .

St. Phillip's church in West twenty-fifth street, between Sixth and Seventh avenues, is one of the oldest colored congregations in America. . . . Up to a few months ago the music at St. Phillips was furnished by an ordinary mixed choir of colored singers. Some months before Easter it was decided to change to a boy choir, such as are to be found in Trinity, St. Agnes', St. Andrew's and other more or less 'high' churches in the city. The present organist, Mr. E. B. Kinney, was engaged to organize the choir, and the first services under the new order of things were heard on Easter Sunday. Mr. Kinney, however, found the task of organization a difficult one. He discovered that, so far as the constant desire to have fun and play pranks with one another is concerned, there was not much difference between colored and white boys. And as the choir consisted of thirty boys, in addition to twenty men, he had to keep his eyes open. In time the youngsters began to submit fairly well to discipline and are now quite tractable.

Of course there was no trouble with the men.

The colored race is essentially musical, both in ear and voice, and this fact has caused the choir of St. Phillip's to be reckoned among the best boy choirs in the city. Once the youngsters are interested they enter upon the work with an earnestness that would put many a white boy to the blush. In the choir there are several remarkably good soprano voices . . . The ages of the boys range from nine to sixteen years.

Mr. Kinney says that as far as he knows he is the only white person connected with the church" (*Detroit Plaindealer*).

Note: Edward B. Kinney was a student of Dr. Antonin Dvorák at the National Conservatory of Music in New York. In 1893 Kinney and his "colored boy choir" took part in a famous concert directed by Dvorák at Madison Square Garden.

• ***December 10, 1892 (Dayton, Ohio):*** "The newly organized choir of Wayman chapel consists of W. H. Pendleton, chorister; Missess Mamie Jones and Della Akers, sopranos; Miss Bessie Findley and Mrs. Frank Mitchell, altos; Mr. Frank Mitchell, tenor; Mr. Paul L. Dunbar [the poet], bass; and Mrs. W. H. Pendleton, organist" (*Cleveland Gazette*).

• ***December 16, 1892:*** "Paul Dunbar, of Dayton, Ohio, gives a reading of his own poems, Dec. 28. He has recently received a letter of congratulation from James Whitcomb Reilly . . . Dunbar . . . will issue a volume of his poems in a few weeks" (*Detroit Plaindealer*).

• ***December 17, 1892:*** "Notes from Sutton's 'U.T.C.' Co.: Since our opening, Nov. 8, at Aurora, Ill., we have literally flown Westward, and are now in Montana . . . Our 'auction scene,' introducing banjo playing, laughing songs, negro dancing and patting, is quite a feature" (*New York Clipper*).

• ***December 17, 1892 (Helena, Arkansas):*** "The Male Triple Quartet gave an entertainment, at Centennial church" (*Indianapolis Freeman*).

• ***December 17, 1892:*** "A colored opera company has been organized at Philadelphia, Pa. The musical director and manager is Geo. W. Frisby. The stage is under the management of W. H. Cole and A. H. Jackson. They will produce 'The Pirates of Penzance' at the Academy of Music, that city, Jan. 25, and are also studying

'Patience,' 'Pinafore,' 'Olivette,' etc." (*New York Clipper*).

• ***DECEMBER 17, 1892 (CHARLOTTESVILLE, VIRGINIA):*** "A grand Union Concert Thursday evening December 22, 1892, First Baptist Church, an evening with Prof. J. A. Draper, the traveling chorister and . . . ex-teacher of sixteen choirs. One of the greatest musical trainers of his race and natural born actor, supported by talented artists of this city" (*Richmond Planet*).

• ***DECEMBER 24, 1892 (SHARON, PENNSYLVANIA):*** "The Hyer Sisters played in the opera house the 17th and 18th and were highly praised" (*Cleveland Gazette*).

• ***DECEMBER 24, 1892:*** "The only member of the Digby Bell Opera Company drawing salary the year round is the little colored boy, Edwin Forest Jones. He is probably the only actor in America who gets his salary the entire year, play or no play" (*Indianapolis Freeman*).

• ***DECEMBER 24, 1892 (WILLIAMSPORT, PENNSYLVANIA):*** "The Alma Banjo club, of which Mr. H. Molson is director, will leave January 13th for Philadelphia, to take part in the 2nd prize banjo and guitar concert" (*Cleveland Gazette*).

• ***DECEMBER 24, 1892 (WASHINGTON, PENNSYLVANIA):*** "Rev. J. B. Chapman, the blind musician, whose performances are said to excel those of 'Blind Tom,' gave a concert" (*Cleveland Gazette*).

• ***DECEMBER 30, 1892:*** "St. Louis Leading Lights," "The leading violinist of St. Louis is Mr. J. H. Harris . . . Prof. J. Arthur Freeman is considered the leading tenor soloist . . . The St. Louis Military Band is led by Henry Williams, a promising and bright young musician . . . Mr. J. W. Grant is the leading stage manager and general conductor of entertainments in St. Louis . . . Master Charles Sumner Byron is St. Louis' boy pianist and the composer of the music of J. W. Grant's dances, La Julienelle and Belleloule" (*Detroit Plaindealer*).

• ***DECEMBER 30, 1892 (NEW YORK):*** "Dec. 21.—Jenny Bishop, the 'Black Jenny Lind,' has an engagement with the Union Square Panorama Company, Nineteenth street and Fourth avenue, where she made her debut last night. Her specialties are old plantation songs. Her mother was a slave and picked cotton in Virginia. Miss Bishop has an excellent range of voice and doesn't appear to have any trouble in hovering around high E. Her singing is strong and clear . . . and it is evident that she has had good training.

Miss Bishop handles the old plantation songs pleasingly, but there is lack of feeling in her work. Her notes are bell-like in fullness, but seem to fail to touch the sympathetic nature of a person. Miss Bishop was cheered repeatedly last night and she will appear again today" (*Detroit Plaindealer*).

• ***DECEMBER 31, 1892 (MEMPHIS, TENNESSEE):*** "Dec. 17—Nearly two thousand people assembled here last night at Avery Chapel, the leading A.M.E. Church of this city. The occasion being a celebration of the 85th anniversary of the great anti-slavery poet, John Greenleaf Whittier. The exercises were held under the auspices of the Memphis Whittier Club, a literary organization of Afro-Americans of this city . . .

"The Memphis Orchestra Band, assisted by a chorus of twenty voices, interspersed sweet music" (*Richmond Planet*).

• ***DECEMBER 31, 1892 (RICHMOND, VIRGINIA):*** "Banner Contest," "The contest for the banner of the Union, which was given at the First Baptist Church, 12th inst., in which eleven scholars were entered for the ascendancy, was filled with interest throughout. The singing was grand. The Central Glee Club and other clubs were at their best . . . but Prof. Q. W. Moon of Manchester was the favorite of the evening . . . and his rich voice seemed to set the audience literally wild in 'You cannot laugh like me' " (*Richmond Planet*).

Barber-Musicians

There was a tradition of barber-musicians in Elizabethan England. Elizabethan literature makes occasional references to the playing of stringed instruments in barber shops, and the famous Restoration diarist Samuel Pepys referred to amateur music-making in general as "barber's music." Whether or not there was a direct transmission to American shores, the American barber-musician tradition is distinguished by the fact that, in the States, the barber trade was historically delegated to African Americans. Under the caption "Colored Society," an editorial in the December 21, 1889, edition of the *Freeman* glanced backwards at the tradition of African American barber-musicians:

> When it was considered a menacing danger to the Republic to educate the Negro or allow him to educate himself, when many good men with Christian hearts seriously doubted his ability to receive education and instruction outside of the tum-tum-tum of the banjo or guitar, before the reign of the pedagogue, doctor or lawyer had commenced, or was thought would ever commence, it was something of great eclat and distinction to be a barber. And if to that then highest accomplishment conceded to our race was united the other one of strumming the "light guitar," great Scott, men, stand from under! Then gazed upon you a Negro possessing a talismanic key that gave him the entree to society's most goody goody and exclusive circles . . .
>
> Presto, chango! The barber has disappeared as a bright, particular character in the changing horizon of society. The strolling guitar player is remembered but seldom seen. New "lions" have appeared upon the arena. Frequently old faces in new adjuncts and garbs. The knight of the razor has become the savant. His razors are rusting with disuse. The smell of cytronila and cheap perfumes no longer assails with horrid pertinacity one's sensitive olfactories. In a word, the old regime has passed.

If African American "knights of the razor" were losing status by 1889 and "parlor guitar" styles had become passé in the black community, press reports suggest that black barber-musicians remained a factor on the American musical landscape for many decades. The African American barber-musician tradition wasn't limited to the playing of stringed instruments for pastime. Because Jim Crow segregation laws denied African Americans access to "normal" facilities, the black barbershop, like the black church, played an extended role in the life of the community. Black neighborhood barbershops came to serve as social halls, conservatories and rehearsal studios for local singers and musicians of every description.

• ***DECEMBER 20, 1890 (CHICAGO, ILLINOIS):*** "Prof S. W., East 21st street, proprietor of the 'Little Jem Palace' is not only a knight of the razor, but controls the oldest and largest colored orchestra in Chicago. Any number of pieces can be secured on short notice for entertainment, receptions, etc. Address above number" (*Indianapolis Freeman*).

• ***FEBRUARY 7, 1891 (ST. LOUIS, MISSOURI):*** "James Henry Harris, St. Louis' Greatest Violinist," "The subject of our sketch was ushered into existence at Russelville, Alabama, thirty-eight years ago. At nine years of age, he with his parents moved to Memphis. After one year's residence in the Bluff City, his parents died, leaving him an orphan in the Bluff City. At the age of seventeen he conceived a violent taste and talent for music, and his choice was the king of instruments, the violin, of which to-day he is master. He began his first studies under one of the celebrated professors of Memphis, now in Europe.

In the year 1870, he came to St. Louis with the intention of entering the conservatory of music, but was denied admission on account of color. Notwithstanding these disadvantages his indomitable will enabled him to slowly, but surely improve his time and talent. After almost despairing of finding a teacher, an eminent professor at the risk of his business, agreed to teach him, provided he would come to his residence.

Returning to Memphis in 1873; he still pursued his studies with a determination that won for him the admiration of his friends. Returning to St. Louis in 1879, after much persuasion he signed an engagement with the Hyer Sisters Combination as orchestra leader and solo violinist, visiting the principal cities of the east and Canada, where he acquitted himself with honor. Upon returning to St. Louis, music was in a chaotic condition. He immediately set to work to improve the art and bring it to its wonted standard. Though meeting with discouragement, he established himself in the West End as the J. H. Harris Orchestra, and to day ranks as one of the finest violin players of this country. Several nice waltzes have been composed and published by him. Prominent among them are the 'Memphis Waltzes' dedicated to Miss Mamie Thompson, of Memphis which became very popular. He also teaches violin, violincello and brass instruments. Among his pupils are Profs. Henry Williams, violinist and musical director of the Luca Conservatory of Music, and N.A. Wilkerson, cornet soloist, whose charming tones and effectiveness in simple and classical music has received commendation from all lovers of the art.

The J. H. Harris Orchestra, of which he is justly proud, is composed of the best talent in the city, tutored by himself, numbering eighteen men, and are kept busy furnishing music for the elite of the West End. He is one of the founders of the Luca Conservatory, the first of its kind in the west, and which bids fair to stand second to none in the country as regards to excellence.

In addition to this, Mr. Harris has a well established tonsorial parlor for ladies, gentlemen and children. He also has a study connected therewith where music can be taught daily from 9 A.M. to 3 P.M., and where orders for music can be left" (*Indianapolis Freeman*).

• ***June 13, 1891 (Columbia, Missouri):*** "Levi King, our city barber, is making rapid progress on the clarionet" (*Indianapolis Freeman*).

• ***June 13, 1891 (Bryan, Texas):*** "Wade Hamilton, a highly respected barber, also band instructor and violinist, was fatally stabbed Monday by Amos Thornton, another barber" (*Indianapolis Freeman*).

• ***July 24, 1891 (Atchison, Kansas):*** "The Colored People Of The Town Are Highly Prosperous," "This article shall . . . in a small way give the Africanized side of Atchison . . . There are about 3,000 colored persons in Atchison represented by two schools and ten teachers . . . two physicians . . . one lawyer . . . one real estate agent . . . three grocery stores . . . four church buildings . . . [and] eight secret societies . . . Mr. W. A. Lett, a young man 28 years of age, who was born in Detroit, Mich., owns the finest tonsorial parlors in the town . . . He has five chairs manned by five professional tonsorialists two of whom are his brothers; these three young men are also excellent musicians. Mr. Lett not only controls the barber business in Atchison but with the aid of his brothers sets the society cantor of the place. Their music keeps the town merry at night and their razors are busy in the day" (*Kansas City American Citizen*).

• ***October 10, 1891 (Worcester, Massachusetts):*** "The population of this city is about 90,000 inhabitants, consisting of all nationalities, about 15,000 of whom are colored, of which I aim to mention here . . .

J. W. Dorris, 213 Main street, Worcester's renowned bass soloist, and pronounced king of whistling soloists, both of England and America, has [a barbershop with] three chairs, with ladies' and children's hair dressing room" (*Indianapolis Freeman*).

• ***January 15, 1892 (Adrian, Michigan):*** "At No. 5, East Maumee street is the well known barbershop of Messrs. Jackson and Reid. Their parlors are fitted up with handsome chairs and other accompaniments to a first class business, and it is one of the handsomest shops in the city. They are skilled workmen and enjoy a large and deserved trade. At the rear of these parlors is a small room which has been fitted up with glass cases which are filled with a fine collection of musical instruments. Mr. B. F. Jackson, the proprietor, gives instruction upon 10 or 12 instruments, and has at present 25 or 30 pupils. He and his three children furnish music for many of the best entertainments given in the city" (*Detroit Plaindealer*).

• ***February 12, 1892 (Adrian, Michigan):*** "The local lodge of Good Samaritans gave a very fine musical and literary entertainment at their hall Feb. 3rd. Their programme embraced 12 numbers, each of which was creditably rendered. Special mention is due the Jackson family, composed of Mr. B. F. Jackson [of Jackson and Reid's barbershop] and three children, who rendered several selections upon the guitar and mandolin in magnificent style, also Mrs. Hattie Reid and Mrs. Emma Washington, soloists. There were over 225 people present. After the entertainment refreshments were served. The order cleared about $35" (*Detroit Plaindealer*).

Note: A photo of the Jackson Family band is reproduced, along with a bio from an unidentified source, in Arthur LaBrew's *The Afro-American Music Legacy in Michigan* (1987).

• ***January 21, 1893 (Decatur, Illinois):*** "Plays in a White Orchestra." This article describes one of "Decatur's men of integrity," J. W. Anderson, "the popular tonsorial artist. He came to Decatur less than three years ago, opening a barber shop and hair dressing parlor, where he has continued to prosper until his trade, both white and colored, became so large that it was necessary to seek a larger room. He purchased the present site, 319 North Water street, the principal thoroughfare of the city. He is also an expert with stringed instruments, such as banjo, guitar, mandolin and violin. He is also a member of the opera house orchestra (white)" (*Indianapolis Freeman*).

• ***August 26, 1893 (Helena, Arkansas):*** "John H. Washington, the pleasant and gallant director of Amps Bros.' Orchestra and brass band is prepared to take all messages at his barber shop either for an engagement or the world's best journal, The *Freeman*" (*Indianapolis Freeman*).

• ***November 2, 1895 (Monroe, Louisiana):*** "J. W. Frost, barber and musician, runs the best shop in the city, located on Desaird street near railroad crossing" (*Indianapolis Freeman*).

Noticeably missing from collected African American press reports of 1890–1895 are specific references to vocal quartets in connection with

AN ADVANCED TASTE.

Man.—"Who's jelus? You's a fool; I'm just mad. I tole you to leab de house when dat barbah nigger cum dar wid his banjo, kase I doan want er enkerege a lub fer dat coase music in yer br[illegible]s. Jelus! Humph."

Freeman, *July 23, 1892.*

black neighborhood barbershops. However, there is no dearth of recollection. W. C. Handy remembered brass bands and vocal quartets rehearsing in a barbershop in Florence, Alabama, in the late 1880s.[30] Recalling vocal quartets attached to black barbershops in Jacksonville, Florida, during the mid-1890s, James Weldon Johnson identified the "Barber Shop Chord" as a black musical invention that white quartet singers later appropriated.[31]

Mandolin Clubs

At the dawn of the ragtime age, mandolin playing seems to have been an especially popular pastime and a highly developed art form among African Americans. One particular black community outlet for mandolin playing and male camaraderie was the mandolin club. A typical mandolin club consisted of from three to eight men. Unlike mandolin orchestras, which were exclusively devoted to the mandolin family of instruments—mandolas, mandolinos, etc.—mandolin clubs also included guitars, banjos, and sometimes a cello. They differed from the average string band, however, in that mandolin clubs appear to have eschewed the use of fiddles.

African American press reports suggest that mandolin clubs abounded throughout black America during the 1890s. In a single 1894 edition of the *Cleveland Gazette*, community correspondents mentioned mandolin clubs active in Wellsville, Steubenville, and Columbus, Ohio.[32]

• ***December 6, 1890 (Indianapolis, Indiana):*** "A Grand Entertainment will be given at the Vermont Street Church, Thursday Evening, Dec. 18. The program has on it the names of some of the best musical and literary talent in the city. . . There will also be a Grand Serenade by the Alfred Taylor Mandolin Club" (*Indianapolis Freeman*).

• ***March 28, 1891:*** "Kansas City News," "The Silver Leaf Mandolin and Guitar Club is the best in the city and consists of the following gentlemen: Clun James, Fred Spencer, George Clay. They are open for engagements for balls and entertainments" (*Indianapolis Freeman*).

• ***June 6, 1891 (Richmond, Virginia):*** "The Bijou Concert," "Last Saturday night, the Bijou Concert Company of Washington, D.C., gave a performance at True Reformers' Hall. . . The singing was excellent and the mandolin club covered themselves with glory. They are masters of the guitar, mandolin and banjo. . . The Zephyr Quartette sung various selections. . . The Mandolin Club is composed of Chas. West, Harry West, Eustice Johnson and Eugene Minor. The Zephyr Quartette: Wm. Cowan, Baritone; G. T. Johnson, Tenor; Robert Fox, 2nd Tenor; W. H. Bright, bass" (*Richmond Planet*).

• ***May 13, 1892 (Cincinnati, Ohio):*** "A Mandolin Club has been organized in this city for the purposes of self and public entertainment. The meetings are held every Tuesday evening at 486 Central avenue. The following named persons constitute the club: W. F. Anderson, Dan. A. Rudd, Cyrenus Grandison, Robert and William Blakstone, P. S. Marchand, Blackstone Rankins, Robert Troy, Jr." (*Detroit Plaindealer*).

• ***June 10, 1892:*** "The 'Silver Leaf' Mandolin club furnished music for the 'Three Star' club, of Independence, Mo., last Tuesday evening. They were accompanied by the Hon. Tom Logan who had charge of the floor, which is a sufficient guarantee that the affair was a decided success" (*Kansas City American Citizen*).

Note: Tom Logan was a well-known professional minstrel entertainer.

• ***July 15, 1892 (Kansas City, Missouri):*** "Mrs. Frances Starks ably assisted by Mrs. Lillie Alexander gave her many friends a reception

Thursday evening at her residence 609 Oak street. An elegant lunch was served after which the Silver Leaf Mandolin club (James, Spence, Grisham and Edwards) discoursed their sweetest music to Tom Logan's 'shouting' and 'the light fantastic toe' was tripped until the wee small hours" (*Kansas City American Citizen*).

• ***November 26, 1892 (East Liverpool, Ohio):*** "The mandolin club furnished excellent music at the Phoenix literary society" (*Cleveland Gazette*).

• ***March 24, 1894 (Parsons, Kansas):*** "Local and Personal," "Roberts' mandolin club is becoming quite popular... W. B. Roberts' new guitar is a 'bird.' Now Billie, we expect some rich productions" (*Parsons Weekly Blade*).

• ***June 1, 1894 (Topeka, Kansas):*** "City, County and State News," " 'Sweet Marie' is the latest popular song which is engaging the barbers and ribbon counter young men at Wichita. The Lawrence mandolin club will have 'Marie' in about ten days" (*Kansas State Ledger*).

• ***August 11, 1894:*** "Social Brevities," "A surprise party was given in honor of Etta White's 16th birthday... Etta was very much surprised on her return home from calling at the crowd which greeted her. Dancing was the principal feature of the evening. The music was furnished by Atkinson & Dennis' mandolin club of Topeka, Kan." (*Topeka Weekly Call*).

• ***September 8, 1894 (Steubenville, Ohio):*** "This beautiful little city can boast of the best mandolin club (Excelsior Mandolin club) in the state. The leader is Bart Guyder. Other members are Ed. Fisher, Harry Taylor, James B. Norris, Clarence Murray, C. A. Bowman and Jas. Bell" (*Cleveland Gazette*).

• ***September 15, 1894:*** "The grandest entertainment of the season was given by the Knights of Pythias Excelsior lodge No. 3 at their castle hall Thursday evening... The programme was opened by music by the Mandolin club... The grand march was led by Mr. James Jones and Mrs. Robert McKeen, followed by about fifty couples entered the dancing hall, marched around the room several times and took their positions for dancing... They danced until about 10:30, and then the young ladies and their escorts had thirty minutes for supper, after which they danced until 1:45 A.M. The crowd returned home at a very late hour with happy hearts, and dreamed that they were dancing all the next day" (*Topeka Weekly Call*).

• ***October 20, 1894:*** "Euclid Lodge No. 2 and Mt. Moriah No. 5 A. F. and A. M. are preparing for a grand reception to be tendered by the Templars visiting Topeka during the Knights of Templar convention on Oct. 29th. The Alhambra Mandolin club has been engaged" (*Topeka Weekly Call*).

• ***November 2, 1894 (Topeka, Kansas):*** "Miss Jones' Party," "A very enjoyable affair was the dancing party given last Friday evening by Miss Lela Jones at her home on Hancock St.... Enlivening music was furnished by the Tuxedo Mandolin Club, Geo. J. Weaver, director. The other members of the club are Melville Weaver, Oscar Over, James Noland" (*Kansas State Ledger*).

• ***November 3, 1894 (Steubenville, Ohio):*** "The Clover Leaf Mandolin Club of Wheeling would positively be here... to assist in the 'opening and stag reception' given by the Excelsior Mandolin club at their parlors... The Clover Leaf boys are 8 strong, and are led by the well-known artist Joe Verse" (*Cleveland Gazette*).

• ***February 2, 1895:*** At a private party in Leavenworth, "Dancing was the feature of the evening ... Music was furnished by the Manitou Mandolin Club" (*Leavenworth Herald*).

• ***February 23, 1895 (Painesville, Ohio):*** "The Mandolin club and orchestra, which was organized some time ago under the management of J. E. Johnson, is progressing, and playing good music. W. F. Tompkins, who leads the club with

TWO MANDOLIN CLUBS.

The "Opening and Banquet" a Great Success—Social and Personal Matters.

STEUBENVILLE, O.—The "opening and banquet" given by the Excelsior Mandolin and Guitar club was the finest affair ever given by our people of this city. The musical critics were all there, and it was unanimously voted that the musical end of it could not be beaten. The Wheeling boys (Clover Leaf Mandolin club) arrived at 2:40 p. m. over the P. W. & Ky. railroad and were immediately escorted to the club house. Wheeling was never better represented than she was on this occasion by Messrs. Verse, Jackson, Jones, Irington, Alexander, Mason and Yates. They are all pleasant gentlemen and withal good musicians. The exercises at the club house started promptly at 4 p. m., the first number of the programme being rendered by the "Clover Leaf." The "Excelsior" followed, and then Prof. Meyers, a former instructor of the "Clover Leaf," elicited rounds of applause by several pleasing selections on the banjo and the mandolin. He was accompanied by Prof. Retter on the guitar. Both gentlemen are members of the "Le Premier" club, the crack organization of this neck of the woods. The music was kept up incessantly until 7 p. m., when an adjournment was had to the banquet hall, where for the next two hours a "feast of reason and flow of soul" were the only indulgences. The musical festivities were resumed at the close of the feast and kept up until the "wee sma'" hours, when all retired, wishing Thanksgiving came oftener. The visitors left for home at 6:40 a. m. Friday. A return visit was their only demand, and the Excelsior boys will most likely go. The membrs of the Excelsior desire, through the columns of THE GAZETTE, to thank all those who voluntarily donated any assistance toward making the affair a success and assure them that an effort will be made to return the favor at an early date.

Cleveland Gazette, *December 8, 1894.*

first mandolin, is very competent indeed... Geo. Derby, second; J. E. Johnson, third; Sam Derby, 1st guitar; Theodore Smallwood, second; Wallace Ormes, cello" (*Cleveland Gazette*).

• ***May 11, 1895 (Plainsville, Ohio):*** At a "reception and ball given by Garfield lodge... Johnson's Mandolin club rendered a few fine selections... Johnson's Mandolin orchestra serenaded last week... Among those who were serenaded was G. W. Alvord, Esq., who generously responded with a check for five dollars. The boys will more than likely go again. There will be a lawn fete at W. H. Thompson's Thursday evening. There will be refreshments, and music by Johnson's Mandolin orchestra. This organization furnished music for the YMCA quarterly reception last evening. W. F. Thompkins has sure made a hit with his mandolin" (*Cleveland Gazette*).

• ***June 15, 1895 (Lawrence, Kansas):*** "Mrs. J. H. Johnson has located her dining rooms and bakery two doors west on Warren street... The removal was celebrated by a grand opening. Music was furnished by Mr. James Strode's Mandolin Club" (*Leavenworth Herald*).

Note: An ad in the April 21, 1894, edition of the *Leavenworth Herald* indicates that, in addition to his mandolin club, James H. Strode ran a barber shop on the corner of Henry and Vermont streets in Lawrence.

• ***June 21, 1895 (Lawrence, Kansas):*** At an informal reception for Ida B. Wells, "Music [was] furnished by J. Strode's mandolin club" (*Kansas City American Citizen*).

• ***December 7, 1895 (Richmond, Virginia):*** "On Friday night, the 22nd the palatial parlors of our popular Dr. and Mrs. Dismond were thrown wide open and alight... A Special programme was carried out. Dr. R. E. Jones as master of ceremonies... A mandolin and guitar duet by Miss Hattie and Walter Wallace was

Notice! Notice!

The following program will be rendered by the Orpheus Mandolin Club Monday evening, Sept. 9th at Bethel A. M. E. church. It is something new and will be a rare treat. Come and hear it:

Vogel's Glee — — Alcazar Quartette
Mandolin Band March, Orpheus Mandolin Club
La Primrose Mazurka, A. A. Taylor, Wm. Childs, Jas. Nicholson and A. Bridges.
New Danube Waltz — Alcazar Quartette
Sleigh Ride Polka — Orpheus Mandolin Club
Harwood Gavotte — Orpheus Mandolin Club
Gloria — — — — Alcazar Quartette
Nordica Waltzes — Orpheus Mandolin Club
True Love, Gavotte — A. A. Taylor, Wm. Childs, Jas. Nicholson.
Denver Mining Exposition March — Orpheus Mandolin Club.
Sweet and Low — — Alcazar Quartette
Dance of the Brownies, — Orpheus Mandolin Club.
Rose Waltz — Orpheus Mandolin Club
Liberty Bell March, Orpheus Mandolin Club

Freeman, *September 7, 1895.*

well rendered . . . Mr. Jones, a Specialty Artist gave many solos with guitar accompaniment which were very good, his dialect negro melodies were excellent. Music by the Eureka Mandolin Club, ushered the guests into the spacious dining hall" (*Richmond Planet*).

• ***December 21, 1895 (Baltimore, Maryland):*** "Gypsys are Coming! Hurrah! Hurrah! Encampment! At St. John Temple, Lexington Street, near Pine . . . One hundred and fifty Ladies and Gentlemen in ancient Gypsy costume. Thursday night, Dec. 19th, grand musical concert. Amphion Glee Club and Howard University Mandolin and Guitar Club, of Washington, D.C. . . . Admission to Camp, 10 cents" (*Baltimore Afro-American*).

The black communities of eastern Kansas seem to have been especially amenable to mandolin clubs. The most noted mandolin players to come out of eastern Kansas were the Renix Brothers, who "spent their boyhood in Topeka."

• ***August 4, 1894:*** "The famous Mandoline club of Des Moines, Iowa, composed of the three Remix Bros. [*sic*], arrived in Topeka, Monday night July 30, and received a very warm welcome from eager friends. The boys are very finely developed in their music and have the recommendation of being the best club of its kind in the west. We heartily commend the boys as being from among our colored race belonging to our grand old commonwealth. Wish them a bright future and a great success through life" (*Topeka Weekly Call*).

• ***May 18, 1895:*** "About the best attraction that ever appeared in our city was that of the 'South Carolinian Jubilee Singers' at the opera house last Saturday evening, under the personal direction of the Renix Bros. Everybody was so well pleased that by special invitation they were induced to play Monday night, but there were not a very large attendance, owing to the bad weather. Tuesday night they played for a select dance at the opera house. The Renix brothers, three in number and Mr. Parquette, we feel safe to say that they cannot be beat in playing the mandolin and guitar. Mr. Parquette has but few equals in acrobatic dancing and singing. They left Wednesday morning for McGregor and everybody was sorry to see them go" (*Iowa Herald*, quoted in *Topeka Weekly Call*).

• ***May 18, 1895:*** "The Renix Bros. spent their boy hood in Topeka and first started out as amateur musicians from this city. They have a number of friends here who will be glad to learn of their success" (*Topeka Weekly Call*).

• ***May 24, 1895 (Topeka, Kansas):*** "Renix Brothers, In Iowa State, Meeting With Success," "It has been many months since the Renix Brothers were playing with their distinguished quartette company in this city. However, occasionally we can hear from them. Last week they sent this office a copy of a paper of their success, where they were giving concerts and meeting with success in many Iowa towns. We wish the boys good luck in future and if they come this way we will make it pleasant for our old schoolmates" (*Kansas State Ledger*).

• ***November 8, 1895:*** "Race Cullings," "The Renix brothers are playing a two week's engagement at the Atlanta Exposition. Their musical ability and gentlemanly qualities are fast bringing them into prominence" (*Kansas City American Citizen*).

The Renix Brothers made their way into the twentieth-century entertainment arena as headliners of a "plantation show." The *Freeman* of January 20, 1900, noted: "Renix Bros.' Carolinians continue to crowd them to the doors . . . [F]eatures of the program [include] the numbers rendered by the Renix Bros.' Concert Mandolin Club, and the comedy of A. L. Renix which is decidedly quaint and amusing." A note in the *Freeman* of September 22, 1906, said, "The Renix Brothers Old Plantation Show is now on the Great Cedar Valley Fair Circuit and making good . . . The roster [includes] the Renix Brothers, A. L., J. W. and J. L."

It is difficult to understand what undermined the penchant for mandolin that is so evident in late-nineteenth-century African American music, particularly in light of the brilliant ragtime and blues playing heard on the extant recordings of black mandolinists of the 1920s and 1930s.[33] Whatever the explanation, the demise of all forms of parlor music and the ascent of "country blues" saw a commensurate rise in black guitarists and decline in mandolin playing.

W. P. Dabney

One of the most notable musicians in Richmond, Virginia, during the early 1890s was Prof. Wendell Phillips Dabney. Dabney was born near Richmond on November 4, 1865. After graduating from a local high school, "he attended Oberlin College. He was a teacher in the public schools of Virginia for nine years and began playing the guitar when he was seventeen years old, after receiving general directions in ear-play."[34] During the early 1890s, Dabney and his Richmond Banjo and Guitar Club participated in community stage productions of *Uncle Tom's Cabin* and *Unc' Remus' Birthday Party,* both of which featured plantation melodies, jubilee singing, vernacular dancing, and string band music.

• ***August 31, 1889:*** "We acknowledge the receipt of a copy of W. P. Dabney's beautiful new 'March Overture' for piano, sent by W. H. Anderson, music and news dealer, 222 East Broad street, Richmond, Va. The composer was a student at Oberlin in 1885. Every one of our pianists should possess a copy of this new composition, if for no other reason than that Mr. Dabney is a member of the race" (*Cleveland Gazette*).

• ***November 21, 1891 (Richmond, Virginia):*** "Uncle Tom's Cabin," "Uncle Tom's Cabin is completed and will be open to the public for inspection during the coming week. This great religious and spectacular drama is a unique and unrivalled representation of American slave life and no colored man, woman or child should miss seeing a faithful portrayal and accurate delineation of the most important epoch of Negro History. This first drama, by colored people in Virginia has been arranged for presentation regardless of cost—A new stage scenery and all paraphernalia incident thereto—Richmond Sextette under Thomas Washington—Indep't Orchestra directed by Prof. Dabney.

A corps of Terpischorian artists. Prof. D. Webster Davis—Uncle Tom" (*Richmond Planet*).

• ***November 28, 1891 (Richmond, Virginia):*** "Uncle Tom's Cabin," "It was clearly proven last Monday night at the True Reformers Hall that the people of this city will support places of amusement, managed and controlled by our race, since they can obtain first class accommodations.

The magnificent Music Hall of the True Reformers was crowded to its utmost capacity . . . the occasion being the rendition of Uncle Tom's Cabin.

At prompt 8 P.M. the curtain rose and numerous darkies could be seen on the plantation plying their several vocations. Prof. D. Webster Davis as 'Uncle Tom'. . . acted his part to perfection.

Mr. Henry Braxton delighted the audience with his fantastic dancing . . .

The Phantasmagoria Waltz, composed by the eminent Banjoist [Dabney?], was magnificently rendered . . . by the Richmond Banjo and Guitar Club under the leadership of Prof. W. P. Dabney.

The singing was magnificent. Messrs. James Washington and Lee Mar held the audience spellbound with their song and dance act. The Independent Club's Orchestra was a grand feature . . . It was composed of Messrs. W. P. Dabney, Christopher Jackson, Granderson, Sydney and Thaddeus Mayo, Peyton Davis, Wm. B. Smith and Ben. Chapman . . .

Messrs W. H. Anderson and W. P. Dabney were the managers and deserve credit for the excellent entertainment" (*Richmond Planet*).

• ***May 28, 1892 (Richmond, Virginia):*** "True Reformers' Hall, May 30, 1892, a Grand Concert, Illustrative of the Past and Present, for the benefit of the Independent Club Orchestra. Plantation Scenes, Jubilee Songs, Solos, Duets, Trios, Quartettes, Vocal and Instrumental. Under the auspices of the Richmond Banjo and Guitar Club, Prof. W. P. Dabney, Director . . . Dramatic Selections: Prof. D. W. Davis, William Mitchell, Edward Clay, Vocalist. Specialty Artists: James Washington, the Original Dan Duffy, R. Lemar Williams. Thirty Guitars and Mandolins in Popular Ballads, &tc. . . . Messrs. Ben. Chapman, Ed. Page, Walter Brigg, Andrew Claibourne, Charles Robinson, Hez. James, William Johnson, Andrew Walker, Lewis Thomas, Frank Nelson, Chas. Washington, Dick Branch, Edward Wills, Charles Campbell, Charles Hampton, Geo. Lawson, J. N. Bailey, Ed. Walker, Andrew Mann, John Mann, Fred. Goodman, Ike Fields, Pey Davis, Thaddeus Mayo, 'King' Mayo, William Smith, Robert Dabney, Christopher Jackson, Thomas Miles, J. M. Dabney, form the brilliant guitar chorus. Admission: Reserved seats, 50 cents; Orchestra, 35 cents; Balcony, 25 cents . . . W. P. Dabney, Manager" (*Richmond Planet*).

• ***June 4, 1892 (Richmond, Virginia):*** "Richmond Banjo and Guitar Club Concert at True Reformers' Hall," "A grand concert by the above named corps of artists under the leadership of their accomplished musical director, Prof. W. Phillip Dabney, was presented Monday night May 30th, at the above named place to a very fine audience.

"The First Battalion Band, Mr. Moses Johnson, Leader, was present, and discoursed fine music.

'Unc' Remus' Birthday Party,' a plantation scene was a splendid representation of ante bellum days, intersected by Jubilee Songs by the Independent Club Quartette and dancing by Mr. James Washington and Henry Braxton. The auto harp and zither duet, by Messrs. Charles Campbell and Grandison Mayo, can be classed among the finest. Waltz, Fair Dreams, on thirty Guitars and Mandolins, was rendered to the satisfaction of all. 'The Picture that is Turned towards the Wall' was sung by the popular quartette of the Independent Club; namely Messrs. Sidney and Thaddeus Mayo, Thos. Miles and Christopher Jackson . . . The Richmond Banjo and Guitar Club in the McCabe and Young March cannot be surpassed . . . The

Quartette, 'I'll Whistle and Wait for Katie'... was a striking resemblance of minstrelsy. Guitar and Mandolin duet by Messrs. R. F., and W. P. Dabney will long be remembered by the music lovers of Richmond" (*Richmond Planet*).

• ***April 15, 1893 (Richmond, Virginia):*** "Uncle Tom's Cabin, a religious spectacular was given in the True Reformers' Hall on the evenings of the 10th and 11th last to a large and appreciative audience by amateur artists of our race...

There was some very fine acting...The farewell of Eliza and George by Mrs. I. Jackson and Mr. John O. Lewis was exceedingly impressive and had the stage been more capacious it would have been a perfect scene, especially when Eliza made her escape...But we feel that too much praise can not be given to Mrs. Sallie Jenkins (Topsy) for she, using common parlance, was 'out of sight'...

We congratulate the managers: Messrs. J. O. Lewis, D. W. Davis and W. P. Dabney...

This entertainment while financially benefitting the Colored Missions...was also a source of amusement and instruction to our people" (J. F. R., *Richmond Planet*).

• ***September 16, 1893 (Chicago, Illinois):*** "Prof. W. P. Dabney, the well known Afro American composer, has composed a song entitled 'The Old Leather Trunk.' It will be rendered by Haverly's Minstrels in this city" (*Cleveland Gazette*).

In March 1894 Dabney relocated from Richmond, Virginia, to Cincinnati, Ohio, where he immediately engaged himself in the social, political, and musical life of the city. By the end of 1894 he "had a studio in Wurlitzers [a local music publishing company], where he gave lessons on guitar, banjo, mandolin and bandurria. He taught in the very wealthiest families, had two string orchestras, one white, one colored."[35]

While bringing readers up to date on Dabney's progress in Cincinnati, a February 23, 1895, article in the *Richmond Planet* recalled some incidents of his earlier career, including a personal meeting with Antonin Dvorák:

• ***February 23, 1895:*** "W. Philips Dabney," "The Accomplished Guitar Soloist in Ohio," "Splendid Record—Richmond Proud of Him," "Prof. W. Philips Dabney, formerly of this city [Richmond, Virginia], but now residing in Cincinnati, seems to be meeting with great success.

THE TRIBUNE of that city in speaking of the Stamina League says:

Prof. W. P. Dabney...has composed a piece of music called 'The Stamina March,' and dedicated to this club. The title page, in addition to the name, has a large facsimile of the seal of the club. It is said to be a beautiful piece of music, and will be played in public for the first time at the State League Convention of Republican clubs of Ohio, on February 12th.

Since his arrival in [Cincinnati], Mr. Dabney has been very busy composing for his favorite instrument, among his compositions being a ballad, 'Lonely To Night,' 'Star of the West March,' 'The Stamina March,' and a progressive guitar method, besides a large quantity of mandolin and guitar music. He contemplates going to Europe in a short time for a course of serious musical study...

About six years ago he began the study of the banjo in Newport, R.I. and progressed by his own efforts. He never had a lesson on that instrument in his life, but was offered a lucrative position in Europe by Col. Wm. E. Foote, Man. of Haverly's Theatre, but was compelled to decline through family considerations. He enjoys the personal friendship of such men as Colonel R. T. Ingersoll, Hon. Robert Winthrop, ...Major J. B. Pond, Wilson Barrett the tragedian, and a host of citizens prominent in art and society.

An appointment was made for him with Dr. Dvorak in New York City by [a representative of] the National Conservatory of Music. His piquant interview with the doctor, who has since made the negro and creole melodies of slavery famous by embodying them in his latest symphony, 'From the New World,' is best related in Mr. Dabney's own words:

At the time designated I called on Dr. Dvorak in his office. After a few moments conversation, in which he inquired relative to my musical qualifications, &c., I brought in my guitar, as he was anxious to hear what kind of instrument it was, and what it sounded like. I played several selections—Kowski's Serrenada, "O Thou Sublime, Sweet Evening Star," Rubenstein's melody in F, &c., but he said nothing, apparently paid not the slightest attention. Discouraged by his seeming lack of interest, and reckless at his nonappreciation of pieces numbered among the best in my repertoire, I began playing a little plantation melody of my own composition, known as "Uncle Remus," written in E minor. To my surprise, he suddenly began running his fingers through his hair, paused a moment, rushed to the piano, and taking a sheet of music paper, wrote rapidly for a few minutes. Then seating himself, began to play the air from the notes he had written. After playing it several times he called one of the teachers, a lady, and they conversed in a foreign tongue several moments. He then asked me would I like to come to school and study, at the same time informing me that he would teach me harmony at any time, free of charge. On my informing him that circumstances prevented my availing myself of this kind offer, he invited me to call at his home that evening, which I did, carrying my banjo, and there surrounded by himself and children, I whiled away the hours playing the many melodious minor airs for which the banjo is the instrument most conveniently adapted'" (*Richmond Planet*).

Dabney spent the remainder of his long, productive life in Cincinnati. In 1907 he "published a great march song, dedicated to the Negro soldiers, entitled, 'You Will Miss the Colored Soldiers.' The song and a picture of the colored troops at San Juan Hill, with valuable information of the record of Negro soldiers, is making a decided hit."[36] He also published method books for guitar and mandolin, and in 1926 he authored a book entitled *Cincinnati's Colored Citizens*. However, the real focal point of Dabney's life in Cincinnati was the *Union*, a highly personal, crusading, race weekly that he founded in 1907 and ran almost single-handedly for the next forty-five years.[37]

According to W. C. Handy, it was Dabney who inspired him to write his indispensable autobiography, *Father of the Blues*: "In 1933 Wendell P. Dabney (editor of the *Union* and author of *Cincinnati's Colored Citizens*) accompanied by the late Arthur A. Schomburg, curator of the 135th Street branch of the New York Public Library, sat up all night at my home trying to convince me of the importance of writing my life's story and offering to collaborate."[38]

At least one contemporary source has reported that Dabney was an uncle of pianist, band leader, and jazz recording pioneer Ford Dabney.[39] Wendell Phillips Dabney died in Cincinnati on June 3, 1952.

"Monarchs of the Light Guitar"

Writing in the mainstream music magazine *Cadenza* in 1896, a white guitar and banjo instructor who had been raised on a plantation in northern Alabama declared, "[I]n all my experience I have never met but one Negro who could play the banjo with any skill . . . The guitar is the favorite instrument of the negroes, which some of them play with rare skill."[40] African American press reports of the early 1890s suggest that during the previous two decades there had been a "golden era" of guitar playing among African Americans.

The following brief retrospectives were penned by *Freeman* editor George L. Knox, who had migrated to Indiana from Tennessee in 1864. These recollections seem to describe a period from the 1870s to the early 1880s.

• ***February 11, 1893:*** "We recall the time when the 'guitar players' of the race were like the sands of the sea shore in number, but the 'guitarist' is no longer a fad, a more formidable one seems to have risen in its stead. The 'elocutionist' is with us . . . The 'guitarist' is lonely, there are few left who knew him in his grandeur, when every parlor was open to him" (*Indianapolis Freeman*).

• ***July 1, 1893:*** "Our Musical People," " 'Ed' Rector, 'Dave' Ray and Prof. Bogardos were in the 'old days' monarchs of the 'light guitar.' Where they are, what has become of them, we do not know" (*Indianapolis Freeman*).

The phrase "light guitar" may be little more than a literary ornament, but one authority has raised the possibility that it derived from early-nineteenth-century guitar maker Edward Light.[41] The musical career of "light guitar monarch" E. M. "Ed" Rector dates from the earliest days of black stage entertainment. He was reportedly connected with a "concert party" headed by "The Hamilton Brothers (Dave and Jake)" as early as 1860, and with a minstrel company headed by Lew Johnson in 1870.[42]

The *Freeman* may have lost track of Ed Rector, but the *Detroit Plaindealer* kept him in sight. Detroit was Rector's home base throughout the 1880s and 1890s, during which time he appears to have gotten caught up in the popular transition from string band music to brass and wood-wind–dominated dance orchestras. Articles in the *Plaindealer* trace Rector's Cornet Band back to 1883 in Detroit and document his subsequent association with the most popular local outfit of the early 1890s, the Detroit City Band.[43]

"A Model of Community Service": John W. Johnson and the Detroit City Band

The Detroit City Band was the creation of John W. "Jack" Johnson. Johnson first came to Detroit from his home in London, Ontario, Canada, in the early 1880s. Once in Detroit he joined Rector's Cornet Band. Rector and Johnson were also associated with another local Detroit outfit, the Peninsular Band. With other members of the Peninsular Band, possibly in 1884, Johnson joined the Moxley Brothers Band and traveled with them in Carver's Wild West Show.

Reportedly in the spring of 1885, Johnson joined the band with a troupe of Georgia Minstrels[44] and toured with them for two consecutive seasons. He then returned to London, Ontario, and became leader of the Forest City Band. In 1889 Johnson went out again with the Georgia Minstrels, then resettled in Detroit in 1890 and organized the Detroit City Band.

As John W. Johnson's early movements suggest, the distinction between touring professionals and community-based musicians became blurred during the 1889–1895 period, marked by a heightened interchange of musical values and ideas between the stage and the community. At the community level, African American string bands and brass bands provided entertainment for all sorts of engagements on both sides of the race line. This heightened interaction stirred the development of ragtime.

Reports in 1890s editions of the *Detroit Plaindealer* place John W. Johnson at the center

A PLEASING EVENT.

The Musical and Reunion of the Detroit City Band.

The first musical of the Detroit City Band given at Fraternity hall last Tuesday evening was an event of which they may justly feel proud. The class of music offered was excellent and the rendition very creditable.

In their announcement the management expressed their intention to furnish an entertainment which would attract audiences of taste and culture and their program proved the honesty of the assertion. Any person interested in music must have been gratified at this exhibition of Detroit's possibilities in that line.

But one thing marred the complete success of the entertainment, the understandstanding that dancing would follow the regular program drew, as it always does, a class of patrons who from lack of ability were incapable of appreciating the excellent features of the program and by their restlessness and inattention showed a want of respect for the performers and were annoying to those who desired to hear. It will yet come to pass that managers in love with their art, will see the fallacy of catering to this element and depend for success upon those who appreciate their work.

The program, a trifle long anyway, was rendered more so by the good natured desire to encore the favorites. That the large audience were interested and entertained to the finish is of itself complimentary to the performers.

The band numbering 15 pieces under the direction of Mr. John W. Johnson won the favor of their hearers by their first number, an arrangement of the "Helena waltzes," and kept it through out the evening, the movement of the last number "Tourists. Galop" being especially fine. The double bass obligato by Mr. William Pfeiffer and the ballad "Under the Acorn Tree" by Mr. Edward Hawkins won encores which were given. Mr. Richard Harrison substituted for his Shakesperian reading "Learning Elocution" which was well received and later on did the best work he has ever done in "Fra Giacomo" which was deservedly encored. Miss Smith is a favorite with Detroit audiences and in her two selections "The Blind Girl to Her Harp" and "L'Estasi" displayed her usual taste. She declined an encore. Besides acting as director Mr. John W. Johnson sang a bass solo "The Arabian Love Song" and gave a cornet solo "La reve d'amour" which with Mr. Smallwood's clarionet solo and Mr. Tannenholz violin solo were the gems of the evening. Mr. Crane in his tenor solo "The Lone Grave" was slightly handicapped by the orchestral accompaniment to which he was unaccustomed, but he pleased the audience and sang as an encore "Farewell Marguerite." Other creditable numbers were the euphonium solo with band accompaniment by Mr. Wm. Stone, the bugle solo by Mr. Thos. Moxley and Prof. Rector's guitar selections. Mr. Fred Stone was an ideal accompanist.

A pleasing feature of the entertainment was the flowers sent up to Mr. Johnson after his vocal solo by the choir of Bethel church of which he is a member.

Detroit Plaindealer, *March 13, 1891.*

of a genuine brotherhood of local bands and musicians. Detroit's African American bandleaders were valued both for their dependable character and for their musical talent. They were public figures who, in a formal sense, represented their communities both out of town and across the color line. Johnson and his Detroit compatriots also made a cause of training local young players, often in youth bands. Johnson's illustrious career exemplifies the spirit of service in African American community-based musical activity.

• ***December 26, 1890 (Detroit, Michigan):*** "Several of the younger musicians of the city have organized a band under the caption of the 'Johnson Cornet Band.' Mr. John W. Johnson is their instructor. They hope to have uniforms soon and take rank among the best bands in the city" (*Detroit Plaindealer*).

• ***May 22, 1891 (Detroit, Michigan):*** "Mr. Monroe Weiner of the Detroit City band has just received his new uniform and initiated it last Monday night at C. H. Stone's.

The musicians, Will Finney, John Johnson, Fred Stone, John Smallwood and Frank Mosby will play on the steamer *Kirby* this season.

The Stone brothers hold their dancing school on Friday evening now at Good Samaritan hall, corner of Woodward avenue and Larned street" (*Detroit Plaindealer*).

Note: The Stone brothers, pianist and composer Fred S. Stone, tuba player William M. Stone, and trombonist Charles H. Stone, formed the community cornerstone of the Detroit City Band. In 1899 Fred Stone's composition "Ma Rag Time Baby" became a huge sheet-music success of the early ragtime movement. Will Finney was the son of Detroit bandleader Theodore Finney.[45]

• ***September 4, 1891 (Detroit, Michigan):*** "The Detroit City Band, organized last fall, has, under the instruction of their capable leader,

RAILWAY PORTERS' UNION.

The Railway Porters' Union was organized June 7th, 1890, and incorporated June 15th, 1891, in the city of Montreal, Canada, and is now in a thriving and progressive condition, comprising a number of the oldest and most experienced sleeping car porters in America. We have a membership of 45. The Union had a special invitation from the Trades and Labor Council to participate in a parade and picnic on Labor Day. We employed the City Band of Detroit to furnish us music on this occasion, and are proud to say they gave every satisfaction. Comprising the different organizations too numerous to mention, there were forty thousand men in line. This feature of parade was a novel success in this city. As we turned out to a man we were well received and enthusiastically cheered along the route. On the evening of the 7th we were hospitably banquetted by His Honor, Mayor James McShane, at his residence, and after the Mayor's cheerful address, although diminutive in numbers, we felt strong at heart, and confident of success in the future. We went from the Mayor's residence to our city assembly rooms, and tripped the light fantastic toe till the wee, sma' hours brought us to a close.

B. P. L.

Detroit Plaindealer, *October 1, 1891.*

Mr. J. W. Johnson, been steadily improving... The band leaves here Saturday to fill an engagement in Montreal and will return in time to play for the Porters' Union in the Labor Day parade" (*Detroit Plaindealer*).

• ***October 8, 1891:*** "Detroit City Band," "The second concert and ball by the Detroit City Band will be given Friday, Oct. 16. The management announces to those having invitations that they intend to make this an exceptional affair. The best talent of the city has been secured, among whom are Prof. Theo Finney, Mr. R. B. Harrison, Mr. Ben Tannenholtz, T. H. Moxley, J. W. Johnson, Fred Stone, John Smallwood, Prof. Rector, and Miss Azalia Smith and Miss Kate O. Taliafiero. The proceeds of this concert are to be used to pay for the uniforms recently purchased by the band. Invitations have been issued, and friends of the club receiving them are invited to ask their friends. Those desiring invitations can get them by applying to Mr. Wm. Pfeiffer" (*Detroit Plaindealer*).

Note: John W. Johnson and vocalist Kate O. Taliafiero (or Talliaferro) were married in 1893.[46] The *Plaindealer* of January 1, 1892, called violin soloist B. B. Tannenholz (or Tanninholz) "the youngest orchestra leader in the city, being only nineteen years old." Also note the participation of young E. Azalia Smith (Hackley) in the Detroit City Band's first programs.

• ***October 23, 1891:*** "Detroit City Band," "The second concert and promenade given by the Detroit City Band, under the management of their young and popular leader, Mr. John W. Johnson, was a fine entertainment...

The soloists of the occasion were Mr. Fred Stone, who gave an Euphonium solo...; Mr. R. B. Harrison, in the 'Court Scene,' from 'Merchant of Venice;' Mr. Moxley, cornet solo, 'Sea Flower;' Miss Kate Taliaferro, solo for soprano, 'Stella;' Mr. John B. Smallwood, clarinet solo; Mr. J. W. Johnson, bass solo; Mr. B. Tannenholz, violin solo, and Miss Azalia Smith, soprano solo, 'Friends.'... Miss Taliaferro, who has not before been heard in concert here, has a high, sweet soprano voice which she used very effectively... Beautiful flowers were sent up to her, and she sang an encore very prettily. It is complimentary to all of the participants that they held and pleased their audience throughout the performance. Young people invited to dance are apt to exhibit some impatience at a musical performance which threatens to shorten the hours for their favorite pleasure, but though the concert began late and closed later, and dancing programs circulated through the audience with every number filled, the excellence of the selections atoned for any disappointment experienced by the delayed dancing. The band are to be congratulated on the success of their entertainment, and their leader especially complimented on the proficiency they display" (*Detroit Plaindealer*).

• ***March 4, 1892:*** "Detroit Department," "The Young Men's orchestra, a number of whom have before contributed their aid to Bethel Church, will show their respect and affection for Rev. John M. Henderson by a testimonial benefit concert on March 22. They are under the leadership of Mr. John W. Johnson, whose services in the church choir are highly appreciated by the membership and those who know his ability and energy are confident of the success of the entertainment . . . held in the church parlors. The price of admission being only 15 cents" (*Detroit Plaindealer*).

• ***April 22, 1892:*** "The Band," "To the list of members of the Detroit City band given last week should be added Messrs. Jas. C. Moore and James Turner. Mr. Moore, who plays 1st alto, is now travelling with Richard and Pringle's Georgia Minstrels, but will be with the band during its summer engagements. Mr. Turner, snare drum, . . . was formerly of the Cleveland band" (*Detroit Plaindealer*).

• ***June 3, 1892 (Detroit, Michigan):*** "The Bazar for the benefit of St. Matthews Church, held at Foresters hall for four days commencing Tuesday May 24th passed off very pleasantly . . . Tuesday evening opened the fair and music was furnished by the Detroit City Band and the Newsboys Band . . . Thursday a pleasing concert was given under the direction of Miss Lulu Owen, and Friday, perhaps the best attendance of the week, enjoyed another arranged by Miss E. Azalia Smith" (*Detroit Plaindealer*).

• ***July 15, 1892 (Detroit, Michigan):*** "A Midsummer Concert," "The Midsummer night

Their Annual Review.

At their annual review next Thursday evening, March 31, at Gaines' hall, the Detroit City band will present their leader, Mr. John W. Johnson, a gold and silver cornet. An excellent program has been prepared, aside from the selections by the band, Mr. Fred Stone will be heard in numbers for the piano and euphonium. Mr. Johnson and Mr. Moxley in solos for cornet, and Messrs Griffin and Johnson in duos for cornet, and Mr. J. Chew and J. Griffin in vocal solos. Refreshments will be in charge of the ladies of Bethel church. Admission 25 cents.

A Pleasing Affair.

The Young Men's orchestra made their bow. Tuesday evening, March 22, to a large audience, in spite of about as bad a specimen of weather as March has produced. Their selections were well chosen and given with that perfection and taste which one expects naturally from their talented young leader, Mr. John W. Johnson. The program was varied by a vocal number, "My Mother's Farewell Kiss," composed by Mr. Johnson and sung by Mr. John Chew, a piano selection by Miss Edith Hawley and a selection by Master Willie and Miss Leona Griffin. As a first effort the concert was an unqualified success, and the gentlemen of the orchestra may feel assured of liberal patronage for future concerts. Refreshments were served by the young ladies of the Ready Workers society. The following gentlemen compose the orchestra: Mr. Wm. Johnson, double bass; Mr. John Ward, slide trombone; Mr. Frank Smith, cornet; Mr. Joseph Johnson, clarionet; Mr. John Denney, flute; Mr. David Brown, piano; Mr. Milton Johnson, violin; Mr. John W. Johnson, violin and director.

Detroit Plaindealer, *March 25, 1892.*

THE CITY BAND.

Something of its Organization, itr members and its Leaders.

When an experiment has been tried several times and failure has as repeatedly resulted there from wise people shake their heads at any further attempt to propitiate the gods in that direction. Wise people shook ,their heads eighteen months ago when sixteen young men with from more or less to a smattering of musical training organized under the leadership of John W. Johnson as the Detroit City Band. The graveyard of dead ventures contained a goodly number of headstones memoralizing and com memorating the early demise of bands and that were bands and bands that were not bands. And the idea had become firmly established that the genius cornetalia including the species tubarating the early demise of bands and that were bands and bands that were not bands. And the idea had become firmly established that the genuis cornet alia including the species tubarlum, slidetrombonium etc., was not indigenous to that particular soil and moreover couldn't be cultivated. There is nothing more satisfying than to see one of these pet ideas get a corker in the fifth rib from the shoulder of a lusty enterprise which lives to shame the croakers and to point the way to the more timid. It proves that success is still around for those who know how to hunt for it. The flowery bed of ease and the silver spoon were both out on a vacation when the City Band was born. Its hard knocks came from the start. And when after feeding on hope and wearing what it could for several months, the new organization came out St. John's day, 1891 with its new suit of clothes they couldn't have played a dead march over Pope Leo himself. Since then the band has been quite successful. The rules of the organization have been strict, the practices have been religiously attended and the character of the music which it has rendered makes a few sketches of its members thoroughly deserved and of interest.

Mr. J. W. Johnson, director, commenced his musical carear in London, Ont. Coming to Detroit he joined Rector's Cornet Band and became leader of the Penunsular Band. With a part of the latter he joined Carves Moxley's band and followed the Wild West show; led Milligans Museum Band; toured Canada with fortunes of the Georgia Minstrels for two years. Returning to London, he became leader of the Forest. City Band and won first prize at Hamilton from the colored bands of Canada and 3rd prize at Listowell at a white band tournament. The Georgia ministrels engaged him as cornet soloist for one year; the next he settled in Detroit and became leader of the pres-

JOHN W. JOHNSON.

ent organization. Besides his work on the cornet Mr. Johnson plays the trombone, clarinet and violin, and has a bass voice of robust quality which is very much admired. He is director of the Young men's Orchestra and the Bethel church choir. He is a strict disciplinarian, a painstaking instructor and a hard worker.

John J. Griffin, 1st B. flat cornet, is a native of Detroit and a musical genius. He plays an excellent cornet, the violin, piano, guitar, banjo and double bass. He started with the Moxley brothers and has travelled with some good companies.

Thos. H. Moxley, solo B. flat cornet, commenced with Moxley's cornet Band in Hagerstown Md., and has had much experience as band leader in travelling companies in including Coup's circus. He furnished music for Milligan's Museum in this city, can play the violin and blow that musical curiosity the key bugle to perfection.

Frank Smith 2nd B. flat cornet and expert guitarist was a pupil of Warner's and is filling his position very creditably.

Branch Johnson, 3rd B. flat cornet, got a good start under the instruction of the late lamented John Wilson and is an exceedingly promising member.

Monroe Wainer, solo alto, was a former member of a band in Port Huron. Mr. Wainer plays 1st violin in orchestra music, but when it comes to bands he and the solo alto are inseparable.

Prof. E. M. Rector, 2nd alto is well known as an instructor in the guitar, banjo and mandoline. He has had considerable experience as a band master, having organized Rector's Cornet Band in '83 and directed its successor, the Peninsular. He is very versatile, playing double Bass violin and piano. For the past six months he has played second alto and his wide experience makes him valuable man.

Fred S. Stone, euphonium comes of a family of musical geniuses and takes to all sorts of instruments like a duck to water. He is equally at ease with alto, trombone and euphonium and is considered the finest orchestral pianist in the city.

When Wm. M. Stone squares himself aright and gives one good blast out of his tuba there is an atmospheris commotion beside which the blast of an ocean steamship becomes a mere echo of tit willow. His artistic bellows has been devoted to the tuba since Mr. Rector's Band played in 1883. He also plays the double bass, piano and trombone and is considered an excellent musician.

Chas. H. Stone trombone, also started with Rector's Band, has been playing that instrument ever since. He is a good player.

John Ward, slide trombone began under the instruction of John W. Johnson 18 months ago, is making good progress and promises to be very successful with that prominent instrument. He is also a member of the Young Men's Orchestra.

Wm. Pfeiffer, bass drum, and tuba, made his first appearance in the band business with the newsboys a few years ago, and since that time has developed into a first class musician, his principle instrument being the double bass.

The band has filled some important engagements and has a promising future before it.

Detroit Plaindealer, *April 15, 1892.*

concert given at Bethel church Tuesday night, drew out a large audience, as the exercises and entertainment were given exclusively by gentlemen, who wished to assist the members in their efforts to pay off the debt on the church. Nearly all of the participants were novices on the stage, so a little allowance for stage fright was in order. Several of them, however, acquitted themselves with credit. Notable among them were Mr. Charles Hill, who caught the audience with his recitations of the old man's prayer at Charleston . . . , Lawyer Barnes' reading of Whitman's "What Is Death" and Mr. John W. Johnson's topical song, "Am I Right." Mr. Johnson's local hits were universally regarded as 'all right' " (*Detroit Plaindealer*).

• ***September 9, 1892 (Detroit, Michigan):*** "The Detroit City Band returned home Wednesday evening from Montreal, Que. They took part in the Labor day celebration which was held in that city, they escorted the Colored Porter's Union in the parade, and also furnished string music for the concert and promenade in the evening. The boys were delighted with their trip and reported a good time in general" (*Detroit Plaindealer*).

Note: This was the band's second annual appearance at the Pullman Porters Union's Labor Day celebration.

• ***September 30, 1892:*** "Local," "An event in musical circles will be the grand concert to be given under the management of Mrs. Maggie Porter Cole and Mr. John W. Johnson, for the benefit of Bethel Church. The best local talent has been invited to assist . . .

At a meeting held by the Detroit City band, it was decided to invite all the interested citizens to be present, with them for a few minutes on Sunday, Oct. 2nd, between the hours of 3 or 4 o'clock P.M. Their purposes is the starting of a uniform fund by which they may obtain new

The Band Review.

On Thursday evening, March 31, the Detroit City band, under the management of Mr. John W. Johnson, gave their third concert, and again scored a gratifying success. At their first concert the management, following a a custom which is unfortunately too to that element of society whose support can only be won by the promise of dancing when the regular program has been finished. A large audience of this class was present, with a sprinkling of those who came to encourage what they considered a worthy enterprise and to enjoy the promise of a good musical program. Both classes were pleased. The concert was excellent and the dancing which followed repaid those who had endured the first part that they might partake of the latter part of the evening's enjoyment. But the manager, Mr. Johnson, is an artiste, and while like all others who cater for the pleasure of the public, he is pleased with the announcement, "every seat taken," he prefers that they sould be taken for the purpose of enjoying his music rather than enduring it. At the second concert therefore, invitations were issued to the members of the various social clubs with the hope that while many would be as free to come for the promise of the dancing, which was also arranged for, among the number would be many who would appreciate the quality and kind of music which would be rendered. The result of this second effort was so satisfactory that at the third concert it was decided to dispense with dancing and rely for patronage on such as would appreciate a well rendered program by an organization of young people who, by careful training, persistent study and constant practice, are striving for excellence in their profession. That the entertainment was so largely attended is creditable alike to the citizens of Detroit and the young men of the band. And yet in point of numbers the audience fell far short of what it should have been. Every enterprise of that sort is an emblem oif promise, not alone to the few interested in it, but to the whole people. Its success is the success of all, and to promote it by liberal patronage should be the duty of all who have the welfare of the race at heart. Lack of space prevents the Plaindealer from giving the program at length. The most interesting feature was the presentation of a beautiful silver and gold cornet to the leader, Mr. Johnson, who, during the eighteen months he has been connected with the band, has given his services as leader gratuitously. The presentation was made by Mr. Charles Stone, and responded to in a few well chosen words by Mr. Johnson, who for his next number used the beautiful instrument in a solo for cornet, which completely enraptured the audience and an encore was insisted upon. Mr. Fred Stone, whose skill as a pianist is pretty well known by lovers of the "graceful art," on this occasion gave a number which proved him no less an adept with classical music, and he also was compelled to respond to an encore.

Detroit Plaindealer, *April 8, 1892.*

CITY BAND ANNIVERSARY.

The second anniversary concert and promenade of the Detroit City Band given at Fraternity hall last Friday evening, was interesting, both for its social and musical efforts. Mr. John W. Johnson, the successful young director, has added another to the many laurels he has already won. An important feature of the evening's entertainment was the selections by the News Boys Band, under the direction of Mr. Geo. W. White. The fine selection rendered by the Young Men's Orchestra was arranged especially for the occasion by Mr. John W. Johnson. Mr. Johnson also contributed to the evening's pleasure by a bass solo and an exquisite rendition of "Souvenir de la Suisse," by Liberati, for the cornet.

Mr. John Smallwood was at his best in his clarionet solos. Mr. Wm. Abernethy sang a beautiful tenor solo, entitled, "Molly and I and the baby." Mr. James Anderson, formerly of Philadelphia, was the "Pederewski" of the evening. Mr. John J. Griffin gave a very pathetic rendition of "The Tramp." The Schubert Quartet, Messrs W. Baird, Ed. Haug, Charles Cramm and L. Ling, gave choice selections on the violin, mandolin and guitar. After the concert an orchestra of 14 pieces furnished music for those who desired to further enhance the pleasure of the evening by dancing.

The new uniforms for the band will cost five hundred dollars and it is very gratifying to know that the concert was a financial as well as artistic success.

Detroit Plaindealer, *March 17, 1893.*

uniforms. And aside from this they wish to give a short entertainment to all interested in the band" (*Detroit Plaindealer*).

• ***March 24, 1893:*** "The Detroit City Band have purchased new uniforms, and the boys are now hustling to attend the World's Fair in them" (*Detroit Plaindealer*).

A GRAND OPENING,

APRIL 29, 1893.

J. B. BROWDER will remove to his new place, 308-310 West Fifth Street, between Central Avenue and John Street, North side.

We have spared neither time nor expense to make this one of the finest places of its kind in the city. It will be fitted up with new fixtures made by Mess. Huss Bros. and furnished with all modern improvements including a Peerless Beer Pump.

Yourself and friends are cordially invited to attend this Grand Opening.

Music by JOHNSON'S STRING BAND.

Detroit Plaindealer, *April 21, 1893. It's unclear whether the "Johnson's String Band" advertised to play for this tavern opening was associated with John W. Johnson.*

FRED S. STONE.

The above is a good portrait of Mr. Fred S. Stone, who is now manager of Finney's orchestra, of Detroit. He has composed and published a number of waltzes and marches and receives a handsome royalty therefrom. One of his most popular compositions is the piece called "Ma Rag Time Baby." Fred has just recovered from a severe illness and if nothing serious happens he will be seen at his old accustomed place, viz: the piano.

Cleveland Gazette, *September 16, 1899.*

JNO. W. JOHNSON.

Readers of The Gazette will recognize the above likeness as that of Mr. John W. Johnson, leader of Detroit City band and first cornet with Finney's orchestra. Jack has composed and published several pieces of music and you will hear one or two of his latest productions during the dance. He will also render one of his latest and most difficult solos on the cornet during the concert.

Cleveland Gazette, *September 16, 1899.*

• ***May 12, 1893:*** "The Detroit City Band gave a dance Wednesday evening to raise funds to help defray the expenses of their new uniforms" (*Detroit Plaindealer*).

• ***May 19, 1893:*** "The Detroit City Band have their new uniforms, and present a fine appearance when on parade" (*Detroit Plaindealer*).

Note: It took the Detroit City Band more than seven months to finance their new band uniforms, which cost $500. It was stated elsewhere that John W. Johnson drew no salary for his work directing the Detroit City Band.

The Excelsior Reed and Brass Band of Cleveland, Ohio

The Excelsior Reed and Brass Band of Cleveland, Ohio, was another outstanding African American community-based band. By 1889 the Excelsior Reed and Brass Band had been serving the musical needs of Cleveland's African American community for "ten or fifteen years." The band's formidable leader, H. C. Smith, was also the editor of the *Cleveland Gazette*. Smith was glowingly profiled in the March 23, 1889, edition of the *Freeman:*

> The well known subject of this sketch was born in Clarksburg, West Virginia, on the 28th of January, 1863. He was taken to Cleveland, is present home, in 1865. Here he attended the schools of the city from an early age, passed through all the grades and finished in 1882. During the next year he devoted his entire time to the study of band and orchestral music . . . The result that as a young man of scholarly attainments, of comprehensive views, as a journalist and musician—especially a cornetist—he stands to-day facile princeps among the first of the colored citizens in the State of Ohio. In addition to his editorial duties Mr. Smith is leader and musical conductor of the Excelsior Reed Band. His compositions have found ready sale, especially his song and chorus, "Be True, Bright Eyes," now known throughout the country. . . He is the author of several pieces of music for the guitar in addition to composition for the voice and piano.

Since the leader of the Excelsior Reed and Brass Band also ran the local black community newspaper, there was a ready-made outlet for news of the band's activities. On February 15, 1889, the Excelsior Reed and Brass Band gave a concert at the Gesangverien Hall in Cleveland, for which they received a characteristically positive review.

• ***February 23, 1889:*** "The Excelsior Reed and Brass Band concert at Gesangverien Hall Wednesday evening was a conspicuous success, as all others have been. The following is the program as rendered:"

Overture, 'Hemichbar,' Boston's Orchestra; Medley, 'Plantation Melodies' (Reichart), Excelsior Reed and Brass Band; Cornet Solo, 'King Polka' (Peitee), Geo. H. Turner; Tenor Solo, 'The Last Watch' (Pinsuti), H. A. Williams; Alto Solo, 'Illusion Polka' (Boyer), John W. Thomas; Medley Overture, 'Yankee Tickle' (Hartmann), Excelsior Band; Tuba Solo, 'Big Horn' (Ripley), W. Fenton Taylor; Cornet Solo, Selected (Schubert), H. C. Smith; Selections from 'Lucretia Borgia' (Verdi), Excelsior Band.

"The selections by the band were all pleasing . . . Mr. Smith gave Schubert's Andante and Cavatino, accompanied by Mr. Williams at the piano. Without a doubt, the gems of the evening were Mr. Williams' vocal numbers, 'The Last Watch' and his encore selection, 'My Sweetheart, When a Boy.' He accompanied himself at the piano. The splendid music rendered by Boston's orchestra was applauded many times during the evening. There is a very marked improvement in this organization. Mr. H. C. Boston has greatly strengthened it by adding Prof. Murray, of Columbus, who is an excellent violinist" (*Cleveland Gazette*).

During this time a conflict arose among the band members over how to relate to a local, white-controlled group called the Musical Association, which appears to have functioned, in part at least, as a sort of booking agency or "clearing house." The first hint of a clash appeared on January 5, 1889, in an article describing a young lady's lawsuit against local white "dancing master" Jules E. Heywood, who had "excluded her from his dancing classes because she was a colored girl." The article went on to note:

> A number of the colored members of the Musical Association are talking of withdrawing from it. If the Association continues to meet in Heywood's . . . Hall, after tomorrow, *all should*, and many will. Heywood discriminated, and doubtless does yet, against colored people in his business, and colored men of principle should refuse to contribute a cent directly or indirectly toward the support of this fellow . . .
> The Association's renting his hall (by the year) helps Heywood to pay his rent. This is just what the colored members should vigorously object to, and rather than consent to it, *leave the Association*. It is not any too popular with colored musicians anyhow, because of many good reasons which all know full well.

On March 12, 1889, the Excelsior Brass and Reed Band held its annual election of officers and elected H. C. Smith as leader and director of the band. The March 16, 1889, edition of the *Gazette* related further proceedings of the March 12 meeting:

> [T]he majority of members so voted as to rebuke the few members who seemed determined to drag the band, whole or in part, into the disintegrating ranks of the Musical Association, to be used as this latter named organization, controlled by a few ignorant, poor white men, desired. Colored men must learn to conserve their own interests. By effecting union (sticking to one another in preference to uniting in part or whole, with any other class), is the only way of doing this. Those Afro-Americans who would conserve their own personal interests in preference to the race's interests, are renegades and traitors, and should be so looked upon by all members of the race of intelligence . . . In conclusion THE GAZETTE desires to inform *all* our organizations that the Excelsior is prepared to furnish band and orchestra music for *all* occasions at *reasonable rates*. The exorbitant charges made at periods during last year *are of the past*.

An update appeared on April 6, 1889, under the headline, "The Band To Be Reorganized":

> The Excelsior Reed and Brass Band, after remaining organized ten years or more, a credit to

our people of Cleveland and about the only musical organization of any consequence we have, is about to disband. A *minority* of its members have sought to control it and make it subservient to an organization controlled by white men. Failing in this, they (the minority) last Sunday took steps to disband the organization. The same minority endeavored to defeat the election of the band's present officers a few weeks ago, but being outvoted, they failed. Other attempts were made by these disorganizers which failed because of a *majority's* opposition . . . This contention will doubtless terminate in the organization of a new band led by the editor of THE GAZETTE, which will in addition to containing harmony have *social status*, the Excelsior Reed [and Brass] Band lost and never could gain, because of the presence of several of this minority, who have always been a drag on it, from a social standpoint. More anon.

The story was concluded in the April 13, 1889, *Gazette*:

Last Sunday the Excelsior Reed and Brass Band, after a life of ten or fifteen years, was disbanded because of a most disagreeable minority, led on by men controlled by petty jealousy, meanness and a few poor white men, officers of the Musical Association . . . This minority was led by men who, while members of the band, were seldom seen doing their duty as members when it was in parades or went from the city to fill engagements. Our readers know well who they are without further mention. After a disgraceful wrangle the Excelsior Reed and Brass Band disbanded, and the majority of its members immediately organized the Excelsior Cornet Band, electing H. C. Smith, leader . . . The minority kickers can have the satisfaction of knowing that they are not wanted, were never much use to the band, and that a better band than our people of Cleveland have ever had will be the result.

This story of "petty jealousy, meanness and a few poor white men" illustrates the necessity for developing an independent black entertainment business establishment. The new, independent Excelsior Cornet Band of Cleveland, Ohio, was able to resume the work of furnishing "band and orchestra music for *all* occasions."

• ***June 15, 1889 (Cleveland, Ohio):*** "The funeral of the late Patterson Ware was held from his residence, 32 Parkman street, Sunday, at two o'clock P.M. It was under the direction of the Odd Fellows and the Household of Ruth. Rev. T. H. Jackson delivered comforting remarks. The music was furnished by a vocal quartette composed of Misses Rachel and Mollie Walker, Messrs. Clarence Williams and Ernest Osburn . . . The remains, escorted by the order, headed by the Excelsior Cornet Band, were interred at Woodland cemetery" (*Cleveland Gazette*).

Note: The vocal quartet at this funeral included Cleveland's future "Colored Patti," Rachel Walker.

• ***June 29, 1889:*** "The Excelsior Cornet Band has made all necessary improvements in the platform and attended to other matters needing improvement, and about July 11 will give their second lawn fete upon the grounds of Mr. Richard Scott No. 30 Quebec street. Both band and orchestra music will be had and every thing done to increase the pleasure of those who attend. Provisions have been made to have plenty of cars at the conclusion of the promenade programme. The splendid crowd at the first one held a few weeks ago, will attest its entire success and guarantee the increased success of the one to be given July 11. Garden street cars carry you to the grounds" (*Cleveland Gazette*).

• ***December 16, 1892 (Cleveland, Ohio):*** "The Excelsior cornet band concert, given at Excelsior hall last Thursday evening was a grand treat. The whole affair was a credit to the musical talent of H. C. Smith, who is the leader of the band, and the originator of the concert" (*Detroit Plaindealer*).

Benjamin L. Shook: A Community-Based Musician

Benjamin Lothair Shook was born around 1876,[47] in Nashville, Tennessee, but his parents moved to Cleveland when he was six months old, and he attended the public schools and graduated from high school there. Shook's career portrays a bridge over deep American musical traditions. The *Cleveland Gazette* documents his youthful participation in the musical life of the local community, particularly his background in male quartet singing. Ben Shook was about thirteen years old when he helped organize the Young Star Quartette.

Recreational quartet harmonizing was very popular during the 1890s, especially among young black men. For generations into the twentieth century African American males formed harmony quartets almost as a matter of course. The Star Quartette and the Young Star Quartette were active in the social and political life of Cleveland's African American community throughout the 1890s. The Star Quartette, featuring basso Sam Moore, was singing in the 1880s. They performed in a surprisingly wide range of venues, for audiences of both races. They were enmeshed in local politics and in church and community affairs, and they were mentioned occasionally in the local news columns of the *Cleveland Gazette*, beginning with the earliest extant edition of January 5, 1889.

• ***November 29, 1890 (Cleveland, Ohio):*** " 'The Win, Tie or Wrangle' Club gives a ball in Gesangverein Hall Christmas night. The Star Quartette sings a number of the best selections at this entertainment" (*Cleveland Gazette*).

• ***October 31, 1891 (Cleveland, Ohio):*** "More Color Prejudice Shown," "The Star Quartette accompanied John Rice, Secretary of the

Thearle's Original Nashville Students, with Miss Cora Lee Watson, of Cincinnati, and Prof. Z. A. Coleman in the company, appear in Caso Hall to-night. Joe Hagerman, the "Lion Basso," is also with this organization. They sing the plantation songs just as they are sung in the South at camp meetings, etc. Go and hear them sing, "You Rock When I Rock," "Inching Along," and other songs. They appear "in costume" in the second part.

Boston's orchestra gives a ball at Jayne's Hall next week. See dodgers.

Look out for diphtheria, scarlet and typhoid fevers.

The ball at Gesangverien Hall Wednesday evening was a success.

Miss Rachael James is visiting her mother in Greencastle, Pa.

Mrs. Wallace, of 14 Judd street, will soon make her future home in Kane, Pa.

The old sport (Jason Tilley) and his cabinet certainly gave a successful cake walk and ball Wednesday evening. The hall was crowded and Mr. Harry Stewart and Miss Cora Lockwood succeeded in winning the cake. Mr. John McKee (Nobody's Claim) was a very successful floor manager and the Star Quartette captivated the large audience. Sam Moore is a great basso.

There will be a broom drill and a literary entertainment at Cory chapel Tuesday and Wednesday evenings. Some novel features will be introduced.

Manager and Mrs. Flora Batson Bergen on their return trip from California, sang in St. Paul five nights last week and will appear at Farwell Hall, Chicago, Nov. 25. Their Chicago address will be 2714 Dearborn street, from Nov. 14 to 25.

Remember to go to Hull's rubber store for the best bargains.

Have *you* sent in a *year's* subscription for THE GAZETTE? If not, do so at once and receive it through the mail.

Watch and wait for the event of the season. The Young Elks will positively give their grand prize ball on the 10th of November at Gesangverein Hall, 174 Ontario street. First-class music will be in attendance. Grand march at 8:30 p. m., sharp. Come everybody and compete for the prize for the best lady and gentleman dancer in the grand waltz and quadrille. The committee of arrangements are H. T. Thomas, F. C. Brown and E. J. Fields.

Cleveland Gazette, *November 1, 1890. Notice of the Star Quartette's participation in a local "cake walk and ball" was surrounded by reports of local appearances by Thearle's Nashville Students, Flora Batson and Loudin's Fisk Jubilee Singers.*

county Republican executive committee... into the Hollenden House barroom last Saturday evening for liquid refreshments. The bartender refused at first to give the quartette anything to drink unless they agreed to step behind a screen. This Sam Moore, a member of the quartette, refused to do and started in to lecture the bartender, telling him he drank wherever he pleased, when he had the price, here in Ohio, long before the said bartender left the old country. Meanwhile, Sam was pounding the counter and seemed in a fair to demolish things in general. Messrs. Akers and Rice told the man in charge that unless the quartette was served, they wouldn't accept anything and never would darken the doors of the Hollenden again. The rest of the party concurred, and immediately all were properly served" (*Cleveland Gazette*).

• ***December 1, 1894:*** "Local," "The Foraker club attended Anti-Lynching League meetings in a body last Monday at St. John's Church. The Star quartet had joined the club, and will bear its name" (*Cleveland Gazette*).

• ***November 12, 1898:*** "At the Foraker meeting at the Armory Saturday evening County Clerk Harry L. Vail referred to Sam Moore's quartette as the 'Snowball' quartette. This slur, it seems, displeased greatly the Afro-Americans in the audience and has been generally discussed since. We have not heard how the quartette liked the new name. That a man of Vail's supposed intelligence would make such a 'break' is what surprises us. Black people are now to be called 'Snowballs' by our county clerk, we presume. How do you like it, reader?" (*Cleveland Gazette*).

• ***November 19, 1898 (Lima, Ohio):*** "The Star quartette sang several beautiful selections at the Second Baptist Church Thursday evening and at the A.M.E. Church Wednesday evening and expects to give a concert at Grace Church (white) in the near future" (*Cleveland Gazette*).

The Star Quartette is an early example of a community-based black quartet singing organization, in many ways similar to the African American gospel quartets that flourished during the twentieth century and survived until the close of the century through the Fairfield Four, Dixie Hummingbirds, and others.

The Young Star Quartette, inspired in name at least by the older Star Quartette, was singing in public by the spring of 1889. Cleveland's music lovers took note.

• ***March 2, 1889 (Cleveland, Ohio):*** "The Young Star Quartette," "The benefit which was tendered at Weisgerber's hall last Tuesday night to the young Star Quartette was a success. The performers were: Miss Bulah Griffin, soloist; Warren Cosey, first tenor; Joseph Lucas, second tenor; Johnnie Cossey, first bass; Bennie Shook, second bass. Misses Maud and Jessie Turner gave a pretty piano duet and Messrs. George Ross and Joseph Carroll a violin duet. The entertainment closed with a ball, Boston's orchestra furnishing excellent music. Miss Bulah Griffin and Master Bennie Shook did exceptionally well in their solos... The Quartette sang 'Bright Eyes,' [*Cleveland Gazette* editor] H. C. Smith's song and chorus, Master Shook taking the solo part, and it was one of the gems of the evening" (*Cleveland Gazette*).

• ***March 9, 1889:*** "The Young Star quartette return thanks to the committee who tendered the benefit concert, also to the persons who contributed their services in any way, and to the friends who gave us such a hearty reception. The Young Stars have become an organized body with Miss Bulah Griffin as soloist. All arrangements for future engagements must be made with B. M. Shook, business manager. They will sing at Doan's Armory, East End, Tuesday evening, March 12th for the G.A.R." (*Cleveland Gazette*).

Note: Business manager B. M. Shook was Ben Shook's father.

• ***October 19, 1889 (Cleveland, Ohio):*** "The concert given by the drill corps of the Ezekiel Commandery Thursday evening was a decided success. Little Miss Fannie Shook made her debut as a pianist and proved a very promising one... Master Bennie Shook is improving greatly as a vocalist, and sang 'Mother will keep the gate ajar' and H. C. Smith's 'Be True Bright Eyes,' very well" (*Cleveland Gazette*).

• ***November 21, 1891 (Cleveland, Ohio):*** "The Young Star Quartette concert at Excelsior Hall December 2. Tickets for sale by members of the quartette, or at the door. A good orchestra in attendance" (*Cleveland Gazette*).

• ***November 28, 1891:*** "Young Star Quartette to appear at Fall Leaf Social Club entertainment at Cleveland city armory" (*Cleveland Gazette*).

• ***December 5, 1891:*** "The concert given Wednesday at Excelsior hall by the Young Star quartette was quite a success indeed, both from an artistic and financial standpoint" (*Cleveland Gazette*).

• ***December 19, 1891:*** At the Fall Leaf Social Club entertainment: "The Young Star Quartette sang well... a little fair criticism will but help this organization, and we offer it here in the shape of two or three suggestions. One of the tenors, Master John Cossey, should aim to sing more naturally, and not 'pucker up' his mouth quite so much, in imitation of some vocalists. His brother forces his voice too much, and it sticks out prominently above the others. Master Joseph Lucas should exercise a trifle more care in his effort to sing, so as to harmonize entirely with the other voices. The best voice in the quartette and the one deserving the least criticism is Master Ben Shook's. He has a remarkable basso voice for one so young, and with care and study, it will make many a dollar for him, when fully developed and trained. His parents will do well to place him under Prof. Underner, at once. Our suggestion to Master Lucas can be taken by Master Shook and the other two members of the quartet with profit. However, the organization is the best one of the kind the younger element of the city has ever produced" (*Cleveland Gazette*).

• ***April 30, 1892 (Cleveland, Ohio):*** "Knights Templars Gala Times," "The joint entertainment given by the Red Cross Commandary No. 7, K.T., and Ezekial No. 3, K.T., was a very unique affair. Aside from the inspection and review, a short programme was observed, participated in by [Ben Shook's father] B. M. Shook, Eminent Commander, who delivered an address; H. T. Eubanks, our elocutionist; Miss Rachel L. Walker, prima donna, and the Young Star Quartette" (*Indianapolis Freeman*).

• ***October 1, 1892 (Cleveland, Ohio):*** At the annual Emancipation Day celebration, "The Young Star quartette, and another quartette (white) sang splendidly" (*Cleveland Gazette*).

• ***October 21, 1892 (Cleveland, Ohio):*** "The Young Star quartet, led by John A. Cossey of Cleveland, Ohio, is a valuable auxiliary in the present [election] campaign" (*Detroit Plaindealer*).

While retaining membership in the Young Star Quartet, Ben Shook also became associated with a "jubilee club" led by Mabel Lewis Imes, an outstanding contralto singer and former member of the original Fisk University Jubilee Singers. Mabel Lewis had retired from itinerant jubilee singing around 1881, when she married Martin Imes and settled in Cleveland.[48]

• ***March 25, 1893 (Cleveland, Ohio):*** "Mrs. Mabel Lewis Imes, one of the 'original Fisk Jubilee Singers,' has organized a company of jubilee singers of young people. The members are: Mrs. T. W. Walker, pianist; Mrs. Ida Walker, soprano; Miss Nettie Jones, contralto; Mr. W. Scott Brown, tenor; and Mr. Benjamin Shook, basso. The company made their debut in a

BE SURE TO ATTEND THE

GRAND MASS MEETING

OF

Colored Republicans of Northern Ohio,

Under the Auspices of the Colored Republicans of Cuyahoga County, at

MUSIC HALL, MONDAY EVENING, OCT. 10, 1892.

SPEAKERS:

HON. JOHN R. LYNCH,

Of Mississippi, the Fourth Auditor of the Treasury at Washington, D. C.

COL. O. J. HODGE,

OF CLEVELAND.

MR. CHAS. A. COTTRILL,

OF COLUMBUS, O.

THE FAMOUS EXCELSIOR CORNET BAND

AND THE

Young Star Quartette

Will Furnish Excellent Music for the Occasion.

Hon. Jere A. Brown, Chairman of the Meeting. Messrs. George A. Myers and Ray F. Johnstone, Permanent Secretaries.

The Meeting Will be Called to Order Promptly at 8 P. M.

THE LADIES ARE SPECIALLY INVITED TO BE PRESENT.

"Colored Republicans of Northern Ohio," Cleveland Gazette, *October 8, 1892. It was noted in* Detroit Plaindealer *of October 21, 1892 that, "The Young Star quartet, led by John A. Cossey of Cleveland, Ohio, is a valuable auxiliary to the present [election] campaign."*

concert given by Mrs. Imes in the Educational and Industrial rooms. The rooms were filled, and the music enjoyed by all present... The concert was in every respect a grand success" (*Indianapolis Freeman*).

• ***March 25, 1893:*** "Was Born A Slave," "[Mabel Lewis Imes] sang a number of selections with excellent taste and expression. She was assisted by a number of her friends and a very pleasing programme was rendered, the old slave songs of the south being given with characteristic power and sweetness. Mrs. Imes' voice is very winning and her friends hope that she may receive other opportunities of displaying its capacities in the interest of her commendable plan. Those assisting her were Mrs. Hattie Walker, pianist; Misses Ida Walker, Nettie Jones, Masters B. L. Shook, Jr., Scott Brown and Little Florence Imes, who also sang, and Miss May Brown, elocutionist" (*Cleveland Gazette*).

• ***April 21, 1894:*** At what was described as an "Imes complimentary concert at Mt. Zion church," featuring Rachel Walker: "The mixed quartettes, the first composed of Miss Walker, Mrs. Imes, Messrs. Brown and Shaw, and the second Mesdames Seelig and Trues and Messrs. Brown and Shook, were very well received" (*Cleveland Gazette*).

Possibly under the influence of Mabel Lewis Imes, Benjamin Shook enrolled at Fisk University in 1894. The *Cleveland Gazette* of April 27, 1895, noted, "Mr. Ben Shook, now attending Fisk University at Nashville, was on the road last week with a glee club of that institution." In the fall semester of 1895, Shook traveled to Detroit, Michigan, with a quintet of singers to represent Fisk at the annual meeting of the American Missionary Association. The quintet also included the great Fisk jubilee contralto Agnes Haynes (later Agnes Haynes Work). The *Fisk Herald* politely noted in its account of the annual meeting that "The music of the quintet was a marked feature and added quite materially to the interest of all sessions."[49]

Shook left surprisingly few footprints during his three years at Fisk (1894–1897). School catalogues of that time don't list him in the Music Department, and he may not have been fully engaged in Fisk's musical life. He is not listed among the members of the Mozart Society, nor was he enrolled in school-sponsored vocal music classes. It is possible that Music Department politics curtailed Shook's music career at Fisk. The head of the Music Department, Jennie A. Robinson, was not an appreciator of jubilee music. Shook's intensive training in vernacular quartet singing may not have been appreciated either.

Leaving Fisk before the end of 1897, Ben Shook returned to Cleveland and reactivated the Young Star Quartette. They "filled several engagements" during the week before Christmas and remained active into early 1898, at least.[50] By the fall of 1898, Ben Shook was singing with another local group.

• ***September 17, 1898:*** "The Amphion Quartette, composed of Messrs. Walter Revels, 1st tenor; J. Clarence Brown, 2nd tenor; Walter Randolph, 1st bass and Benjamin S. Shook, 2nd basso, and Mr. Charles Burroughs, the well-known Detroit tragedian, will assist in making the Detroit City band concert at Army and Navy hall Monday evening, September 26, the finest affair of the season. Mr. Burroughs has never appeared in Cleveland" (*Cleveland Gazette*).

At the above-described concert, the Amphion Quartet sang " 'Best of All' (Moir)" and the Scottish ballad-turned-barbershop anthem, "Annie Laurie."[51] At the end of the nineteenth century, black quartets were singing a mixed repertoire that included jubilee songs, but many of them seemed to prefer more up-to-date popular songs and semi-classics. Despite the "secular" inclinations of the 1890s generation of black male harmony singers, contemporaneous documentation raises compelling parallels with procedural formalities, community service functions, and musical considerations associated with black community gospel quartets of the twentieth century.

• ***November 26, 1898:*** "Local," "Benj. Shook, Jr. made a decided hit at Hull & Dutton's daily musicale last week and the week previous, singing, 'Be True, Bright Eyes,' accompanied at the piano by George Solomon. He has a good bass voice and uses it well" (*Cleveland Gazette*).

• ***April 8, 1899:*** "Local," At St. John's Church, "Mrs. Smith sang a beautiful solo entitled, 'Hail, Easter Morn,' with a violin obligato by Ben. F. Shook, Jr." (*Cleveland Gazette*).

• ***May 13, 1899:*** "Under the head of 'An Accomplished Boy,' the daily *Press* gave the following one evening last week. 'The elevator boy at the McWatters-Dolan Co. clothing store speaks five languages. He has English, German, French, Bohemian and Italian, and also reads Latin and Greek. The name of this much learned elevator boy is Benjamin L. Shook, and he lives at 11 1/2 Maple street. He comes of one of the oldest colored families in the city. Benjamin M. Shook, the boy's father, is the engineer in the Standard Building. Ben Shook, the elevator boy, was born in Nashville, Tenn., but his parents brought him to Cleveland when he was six months old, this being their former home. He is a graduate of the high schools in this city, and only lacks one year of graduation in Fiske university. In addition to his other accomplishments, he is a talented musician and ranks as one of the best amateur violinists in the country' " (*Cleveland Gazette*).

It seems strange that Ben Shook's violin playing skills weren't mentioned in the *Cleveland Gazette* until 1899. Nevertheless, Shook's musical talent must have been known in Detroit, because he was enticed from Cleveland to assume leadership of the celebrated Finney Orchestra of Detroit, replacing Theodore J. Finney, a singularly prominent figure in Detroit's musical world, who died of heart failure on April 17, 1899.[52] One of Shook's last musical functions as a citizen of Cleveland was to sing at the funeral of twenty-two-year-old former Young Star Quartette associate George Solomon.[53]

• ***June 3, 1899:*** "Local," "[Benjamin Shook has gone to Detroit] to succeed Prof. Finney (deceased) for the summer, at a weekly salary of $18—he said. Ben will play first violin in the orchestra" (*Cleveland Gazette*).

• ***September 9, 1899 (Cleveland, Ohio):*** "Mr. Ben Shook will be here with Finney's Orchestra as leader and conductor. Let everybody turn out and give the Cleveland boy a rousing greeting" (*Cleveland Gazette*).

Settling in Detroit, Ben Shook found long-term success in the band music business: "By 1918 Shook was considered the biggest single music contractor in Detroit, with over 100 musicians performing in three separate orchestras, some playing in other Mid Western cities, including Chicago at the Edgewater Beach Hotel."[54] It seems Jelly Roll Morton was briefly employed by Ben Shook, perhaps around 1916.[55]

The *Chicago Defender* of June 18, 1921, reported that Ben Shook, "well known in theatrical circles," had purchased a theater at 2814–2816 Hastings Street, for the purpose of presenting black vaudeville shows. In 1927, after having "slipped out of the game several years ago to engage in other lines," Shook became "active again, holding several contracts for big music jobs in the motor town. He . . . organized three units of 9, 10 and 11 men. They open soon at the Granada park, the Roseland and the palatial pleasure boat *Tashnee.* Ralph Brown and George Duff, Jr. of Chicago are playing in Mr. Shook's bunch."[56]

According to the *Pittsburgh Courier* of September 21, 1929, the "Detroit Serenaders, Benjamin Shook, director, classy dance orchestra of Detroit, . . . will play at the Pythian Temple . . . for a big fall ball. The Detroit musical stars are en route to play a five week's engagement at Roseland Ballroom, New York City. The Serenaders play opposite McKinney's Cotton Pickers at the Greystone Ballroom in Detroit."

Shook lived long enough to be interviewed by Rudi Blesh, who was collecting data for *They All Played Ragtime*. Shook's career evokes the changing landscape from nineteenth-century jubilee singing and other pre-ragtime music forms to the advent of the jazz age.

Chapter Five

1898

The Dvorák Statement—"As Great as a Beethoven Theme"

The world renowned Bohemian composer came to the United States in 1892 to head the National Conservatory of Music in New York. His famous pronouncement about the future of African American music originally appeared in an article titled "The Real Value of Negro Melodies," in the May 21, 1893, edition of the mainstream daily New York *Herald*. In the June 3, 1893, edition of the *Cleveland Gazette* it took the headline "Negro Melodies":

New York City—In a recent interview in regard to the opinion he had formed regarding a national school of musical composition in this country, Dr. Antonin Dvorák, the Bohemian composer, who has been posted at the head of the National Conservatory of Music located here in New York, and who has given the music of this country especial study during his residence here, is quoted as expounding himself as follows:

I am now satisfied that the future music of this country must be founded upon what are called the Negro melodies. This must be the real foundation of any serious and original school of composition to be developed in the United States. When I first came here last year I was impressed with this idea, and it has developed into a settled conviction. These beautiful and varied themes are the product of the soil. They are American. I would like to trace out the individual authorship of the Negro melodies, for it would throw a great deal of light upon the questions I am most deeply interested in at present.

These are the folk songs of America, and your composers must turn to them. All of the great musicians have borrowed from the songs of the common people. He gets into touch with the common humanity of his country.

In the Negro melodies of America I discover all that is needed for a great and noble school of music. They are pathetic, tender, passionate, melancholy, solemn, religious, bold, merry, gay, or what you will. It is music that suits itself to any mood or purpose. There is nothing in the whole range of composition that cannot be supplied with themes from this source. The American musician understands these tunes and they move sentiment in him. They appeal to his imagination because of their associations.

When I was in England one of the ablest musical critics in London complained to me that there was no distinctively English school of music, nothing that appealed to the British mind and heart. I replied to him that the composers of England had turned their backs upon the fine melodies of Ireland and Scotland, instead of making them the essence of an English school. It is a great pity that English musicians have not profited out of this rich store. Somehow the old Irish and Scotch ballads have not seized upon or appealed to them.

I hope it will not be so in this country, and I intend to do all in my power to call attention to this splendid treasure of melody which you have.

Among my pupils in the National Conservatory of Music I have discovered strong talents. There is one young man upon whom I am building strong expectations. His compositions are based upon Negro melodies, and I have encouraged him in this direction. The other members of the composition class seem to think that it is not in good taste to get ideas from the old plantation songs, but they are wrong, and I have tried to impress upon their minds the fact that the greatest composers have not considered it beneath their dignity to go to the humble folk songs for motifs.

I did not come to America to interpret Beethoven or Wagner for the public. That is not my work, and I would not waste any time on it. I came to discover what young Americans had in them and to help them express it. When the Negro minstrels are here again, I intend to take my young composers with me and have them comment on the melodies."

And saying so, Dvorák sat down at the piano and ran his fingers lightly over the keys. It was his favorite pupil's adaptation of a southern melody.

"The Dvorák Statement," as it came to be known, directly influenced the development of music in America for decades to come. No other critical commentary on African American music has made so profound an impact. Predictably, the statement provoked a raft of protest from mainstream musicians and critics.[1] Their cries were duly noted in the African American press.

• ***June 3, 1893:*** "The prediction that the American school of music is to be built upon what are commonly referred to as 'Negro' melodies seems to be a bitter pill indeed for many prejudiced musicians (white) to swallow. In Boston, the minority of those from whom the *Herald* requested opinions cry out against Dr. Dvoràk's prediction" (*Cleveland Gazette*).

In fact, the same point had been made more than twenty years earlier, when the Fisk Jubilee Singers first introduced slave spirituals to the American concert stage. Following a concert in January 1872, a New York clergyman pronounced the Fisk Jubilee Singers "living representatives of the only true, native school of American music...the genuine soul music of the slave cabins."[2] There was the feeling in certain circles that Dvorák had merely stated the obvious. The March 24, 1894, edition of the *Freeman* quoted an article from the *New York Sun*, which observed, "It is a rather curious thing... that we needed Dvorák to tell us what we have known very well during the past 40 years."

With the advent of ragtime, the Dvorák Statement achieved the aura of prophecy. James Huneker, a colleague of Dvorák's at the National Conservatory and "one of the few men who did not like the 'New World' Symphony...probably envious...wrote an obituary when Dvorák died in 1904 in which he says that Dvorák's influence on young American composers was thoroughly detrimental because it is owing to him and others like him that these young composers now listen to ragtime and think it is music!"[3]

Seemingly in support of Huneker's logic, if not his opinion, *Indianapolis Freeman* critic Sylvester Russell took the opportunity of Dvorák's death to emphasize the influence of the Dvorák Statement on African American composers of popular ragtime music: "Stepping down now to a lower grade of Negro catchy music; what a promise of encouragement [Dvorák] has set in Rosamond Johnson, Sidney Perrin, Shepard Edmonds and others of the folk-lore race of American songwriters."[4]

In 1911, as blues and jazz were beginning to reverberate from black southern vaudeville stages, Sylvester Russell wrote:

> Dvorák, the great European composer, who first firmly established the procedure of Negro folk-lore as the only genuine original American music, which he had extracted from the Slavonic melodies of the jubilee and syncopated two-step of the guitar and banjorine, so skillfully used in early stages of buck dancing, was hardly aware that he had handed his name down to posterity sacred to the memory and gratitude of the Negro race in the annals of American musical history. And in Dvorák's contention of the past, the present argument waxes strong, re-enforced by the recent declaration of Signor Giacomo Puccini, grand opera composer in London, England, when he said: "There is no such thing as American music. What they have is Negro music, which is almost the savagery of sound."...Puccini's mind had probably wended its way back toward the jungles of Africa. He had probably forgotten that the American Negro, like the Indian, is living in a day when the war cry has ceased and the natives live quiet on the reservation...The only thing that can be said to be savage in the classical development of American (Negro) music, is when composers migrate from the treatment of jubilee,

back to the raw dispassionate theory of ragtime lore.[5]

It seems doubtless that Scott Joplin's rags, W. C. Handy's blues, and the compositions of Will Marion Cook, James Reese Europe, Duke Ellington, etc. reflect the influence of the Dvorák Statement in African American music. All of these composers were working to reconcile the innately artful aspects of an evolving black "folk" music with established standards of "legitimate" composing: the folk elements would be a basis for creating a new national or racial music culture.

When Dvorák first came to the National Conservatory of Music, it was thought that he would hold many concerts in New York City, but in fact he only gave one, a benefit concert sponsored by the *New York Herald*, staged in the concert hall of Madison Square Garden on January 23, 1894:

> It was a unique programme. Each soloist, with one exception, belonged to the colored race. The idea was due to Mrs. Thurber [Jeanette M. Thurber, the National Conservatory's chief administrator]. She threw open the doors of her excellently equipped musical education establishment to pupils of ability, no matter what their race, color or creed. Emancipation, in her idea, had not gone far enough. Bodies had been liberated, but the gates of the artistic world were still locked.
>
> Her efforts in this direction were ably seconded by Dr. Dvorák.[6]

Dvorák repeatedly chose to focus on African American musicians. The grand concert at Madison Square Garden was an opportunity taken by Dvorák and the redoubtable Mrs. Thurber to afford an appropriate setting for featured guest soloist Sissieretta Jones, "the Black Patti." The other soloists on the program were all students at the conservatory. Accompaniment was provided by the full orchestra of the conservatory and the "colored boys choir" of St. Phillip's Church, under the direction of Edward B. Kinney, a pupil in Dvorák's famous composition class.

In her first appearance on the program, Sissieretta Jones sang the soprano solo in the "Inflammatus" from Rossini's "Stabat Mater," accompanied by the St. Phillip's Church Boys Choir, which immediately captivated the *New York Herald's* reviewer:

> When the audience entered the hall last night the first thing which attracted attention was the gallery at the back of the stage, a gallery fitted with a chorus composed entirely of colored pupils. It was an interesting sight, and one not without its pathetic side, for there was a look of earnestness upon the faces of the members so intense as to cause a feeling of sadness.
>
> And how they sang when the time came! Their very lives might have depended upon it. As the shrill voices of the boys of St. Phillips colored choir rose in Rossini's "Inflammatus," voices with the curious tonal color which is one of the characteristics of the colored race, you were compelled to admit that had the National Conservatory of Music done nothing more than to open wider to them music's unlimited resources of enjoyment it would have achieved a noble work.
>
> There was one little fellow who attracted everybody's attention. He had no sheet music, but he apparently needed none, singing with an evident enjoyment that showed how deeply he was interested in the work. He never took his eyes from the conductor's baton, and at every attack he made a funny little convulsive start as though he said, "Now for it!"
>
> His ardor was shared by every individual in the choir. Their attention was riveted upon the affair in hand. The proof of this was found in the fact that every attack was as unanimous as though it were sung by one huge voice.[7]

The highlight of the program was the premiere of Dvorák's arrangement, for two solo voices and choir, of the Stephen Foster favorite "Old Folks at Home," sung "entirely by negroes"—the St. Phillip's Boys Choir with soloists Sissieretta Jones and Harry T. Burleigh.

Of the song itself Dvorák said: "It is a folk song and a very beautiful one, too. The only difference it has from what usually comes under that head is that we know the composer's name... American music is music that lives in the heart of the people, and therefore this air has every right to be regarded as purely national."[8]

In choosing to spotlight Foster's unfailing chestnut, Dvorák seems to have intentionally blurred the rigid distinctions between folk, popular, and classical composition. According to music historian Charles Hamm, "Perhaps Dvorák's most important contribution to American music was his foresight and audacity in suggesting that contemporary, commercially produced popular music could be the national song of the United States."[9]

Dr. Dvorák's pupil and friend Harry T. Burleigh served as his facilitator regarding the spiritual "songbook." It has been noted that "Once after Burleigh had sung 'Go Down, Moses,' Dvorák exclaimed, 'Burleigh, that is as great as a Beethoven theme!' Another of Dvorák's favorites was 'Swing Low, Sweet Chariot,' the second and third measures of which, as Burleigh often pointed out, Dvorák used almost note for note in the second theme of the opening movement of the symphony 'From the New World.' "[10]

The Dvorák Statement had importance as an inspiration and a prediction. A new American music which drew its vitality in large part from the sources Dvorák identified did rise to guide the world's aesthetic vision through the twentieth century. However, it was not achieved through the agency of any presumed-to-be-superior, classical music, but through the continued progressive development of the folk music by the musical sons and daughters of the slaves who had spawned it. Dvorák's vision of an African American model for an American national music was realized through the evolution of ragtime, blues, jazz, and black gospel music.

Black Music in the White City: African Americans and the 1893 World's Columbian Exposition

"To the colored people of America, morally speaking, the World's Fair now in progress, is... a whited sepulcher."

—Frederick Douglass, 1893

The 1893 Chicago World's Fair, known as the World's Columbian Exposition, was one of the largest, most pretentious events of its kind ever produced. "The White City," as the central exhibition was called, featured an architectural display of unparalleled grandeur and extravagance, and the adjacent "Midway Plaisance" was the most influential amusement phenomenon of the era. This was an affair not to be missed, and between May 1 and October 31, 1893, more than 21.5 million admissions were paid.[11]

Conflict and controversy surrounded the prospects for African American participation in the World's Columbian Exposition, and the pertinent news coverage was contradictory and political. In the end, the course of African American music was affected in roughly equal measure by the cultural-artistic-political confab created by the fair and the racist policies which were imposed by fair officials. These forces helped set a path for the emergence of ragtime.

Several bold new realities of the entertainment marketplace were manifest at the fair. In late May 1893, less than a month after it opened, the fair's director of music, Theodore Thomas, was forced to resign. Thomas was the celebrated conductor of the Chicago Symphony Orchestra, but the fair crowds demanded popular music, and an editorial in the *Chicago Daily Tribune* cut to the quick: "If, as the advocates of popular music claim, the people want Ta-ra-ra, Boom-de-ay and such, cheap bands can play this class of music just as well as expensive bands."[12]

Quoting from Thomas's letter of resignation, the *Chicago Daily Tribune* noted: "He recognizes that a reduction of expenses is of vital importance to the interests of the Fair and notifies the committee that he has cancelled all engagements with foreign and American artists and musical organizations and abandoned all festival performances. Having taken this action he recommends that the Fair music hereafter shall not figure as an art at all, but shall be treated merely on the basis of amusement, and suggests that the two bands shall be divided into four and the Exposition orchestra into two small orchestras, 'which can play such light selections as will please the shifting crowds in the buildings and amuse them.' "[13]

By August the *New York Tribune* was able to report, "Financial matters of the Exposition are looking brighter," and the *Chicago Daily Tribune* of August 19 wrote, under the headline "Crowds Coming Now": "Since the Columbian Exposition opened only one thing has been lacking to make it in every respect a complete success—the number of paid admissions. The people now are commencing to come in multitudes. The attendance has been increasing steadily for two weeks. What influence has been brought to bear to bring them? W. E. Curtis, Frank D. Millet and Lieut. Wells say it is the outdoor amusement features that have taken the place of the indoor orchestra and choral concerts. There seems to be no doubt that this 'Barnumizing' scheme has become popular."

"Outdoor amusement features" referred to informally staged spectacles such as swimming races between the various nationalities represented at the fair as well as open-air "international concerts" such as the one recorded in the *Chicago* Daily Tribune of August 22, 1893, under the heading "World's Fair Music":

> The musical portion of the international program given in Festival Hall yesterday afternoon attained a value decidedly lacking upon the occasion of the first concert, the singing of the Hawaiian Quartet and the concerted performance on the marimba by four Guatemalans being both unique and interesting from a musical point of view. The Hawaiians accompanied their numbers upon two guitars, a taro patch, and a ukelele. The latter instruments, on the guitar order, are respectively five and four stringed. The voices of the quartet are sweet, and in the case of the first tenor, Malpinepine, especially melodious. The charm lies in the naturalness. The "Wind Song," given as an encore, as well as their music throughout, is strongly tinged with the gentle pathos and rhythm of the negro melodies.

There was even some minimal, anonymous black participation in the new amusement features. On the evening of August 22, a "naval parade" was staged in the World's Fair lagoons. It included "the canoes of the Indians... Penobscot, Apache, Arawac and Sioux paddled beneath canopies of swinging lanterns," followed by "three Eskimo kiakas... and a needle-pointed Dahomey moussaing with red fire burning on either end." Then "the air was filled with old familiar strains of music. Two yawls canopied in bright lanterns and filled with negroes, came sailing by, and 'Old Kentucky Home,' sung with rare effect set the people along the shores to shouting demands for more. Throughout the length of the canal and Grand basin the singers made the air sweet with the melodies of Dixie." Finally, the Guatemalan marimba quartet "moved about on the water, dividing the musical honors with the dusky singers."[14]

The 1893 World's Columbian Exposition proudly claimed to embody the accomplishments and aspirations of all mankind. As described by William S. McFeely, in his biography of Frederick Douglass: "The fair was designed to be a metaphor for human progress. Harlan Ingersoll Smith, an assistant to Harvard anthropologist Frederick Ward Putnam, the man in charge of the ethnological exhibits, declared that 'from the first to the last . . . [they] will be arranged to teach a lesson; to show the advancement of evolution of man.' Otis T. Mason, the curator of the Smithsonian Institution's Bureau of American Ethnology, proudly announced, 'It would not be too much to say that the World's Columbian Exposition was one vast anthropological revelation.' "[15]

Frederick Ward Putnam's chief assistant, anthropologist Franz Boaz, supervised an extensive Northwest Coast Indian exhibition housed in the Anthropological Building in the White City. Other ethnographic exhibits, including those on the Midway Plaisance, were nominally under Putnam's administration but were beyond his scientific influence, and sometimes had the character of an entrepreneurial freak show: "Crowded under G. W. G. Ferris's 250-foot-high wheel were 280 Egyptians and Sudanese in a Cairo street, 147 Indonesians in a Javanese village, 58 Eskimos from Labrador, a party of bare-breasted Dahomans in a West African setting, Malays, Samoans, Fijians, Japanese, Chinese, as well as an Irish village with both Donegal and Blarney castles and a reconstructed old Vienna street. The official ethnological exhibition with its handful of Kwakiautl, Navaho, and Arawak was reduced to insignificance. Only the most unusual or bloodcurdling Kwakiutl demonstrations could match the erotic Egyptian dancers and other *succes de scandale* of the Midway."[16]

While Chicago was hosting the 1893 World's Columbian Exposition, the American South was exhibiting a bloodcurdling "anthropological revelation" of its own. As documented in Ida B. Wells's "World's Fair Pamphlet," more than one hundred human beings were murdered by lynch mobs during the first six months of 1893.

If the 1893 World's Columbian Exposition was a tableau of late-nineteenth-century culture and civilization, it did not aspire to be a window into the future in matters of race relations. Seemingly in harmony with prevailing attitudes, President Benjamin Harrison appointed 208 members and alternates to the National Board of Commissioners for the Fair—not a single black person among them. According to F. L. Barnett, writing in Ida B. Wells's "World's Fair Pamphlet:" "The President willfully ignored the millions of colored people in the country and thus established a precedent which remained inviolate through the entire term of Exposition work . . . the Nation's deliberate and cowardly tribute to the Southern demand 'to keep the Negro in his place.' . . . it remained for the Republic of Hayti to give the only acceptable representation enjoyed by us in the Fair."[17]

The government of Haiti appointed "the grand old man" Frederick Douglass, former ambassador to Haiti, to preside at the Haitian Exhibit of the World's Fair. Douglass was joined there by Ida B. Wells and Paul Laurence Dunbar. These three unforgotten spirits were accessible for conversation in the reception room and executive offices of the Haitian Exhibit. Ida B. Wells was busy distributing the "World's Fair Pamphlet," a collection of essays which she had contributed to, edited, and brought to publication. The idea for the pamphlet was first suggested by Frederick J. Loudin of the Fisk Jubilee Singers in an open letter published February 25, 1893, in the *Cleveland Gazette*:

> We have been boycotted by the World's Fair in that no Negro is permitted to fill any position of honor or profit, with the exception of the action of one or two states; and now to add to the insult the management . . . ask us to state when we apply for accommodation that we belong to the proscribed race, in order that, in accord with the jim crow legislation of the southern states we may be consigned to the "nigger quarters," which they seem to have been mindful to provide, and that, too, in a city where the hotels do not discriminate.
>
> Let us then compile the accounts of the lynchings, the shootings, the flogging alive, the

> burnings at the stake, and all the kindred barbarous acts and print them in a book or pamphlet form for *free* distribution at the world's fair.

The *Cleveland Gazette* accompanied Loudin's letter with a lengthy editorial in support of the pamphlet: "We endorse it with all our heart and stand ready to contribute service, and our limited means, to further such a project . . . and therefore urge the Hon. Mr. Douglass and Miss Ida B. Wells to take the matter in hand at once and develop something along the line so plainly and forcibly drawn by our friend Mr. Loudin."

Ida B. Wells was able to produce a useful and enduring document. As she recalled in her *Autobiography*:

> I had joined hands with Frederick J. Loudin of Jubilee Singer fame and Mr. Douglass in an appeal to the colored people of the United States for funds with which to publish a pamphlet for circulation at the coming World's Fair . . .
>
> It was a clear, plain statement of facts concerning the oppression put upon the colored people in this land of the free and home of the brave. We circulated ten thousand copies of this little book during the remaining three months of the fair. Every day I was on duty at the Haitian building, where Mr. Douglass gave me a desk and spent the days putting this pamphlet in the hands of foreigners . . . It is very interesting to record that echoes from that little volume have been received by me from Germany, France, Russia and faraway India.[18]

Colored Folks Day

As early as October 1892, Will Marion Cook had begun to publicize what the *Cleveland Gazette* of January 21, 1893, called "A Great Scheme":

> An opera, the music composed by an Afro-American, and the cast to include only members of the race, it is said, will be one of the unique attractions at the world's fair. The opera will be a new version of "Uncle Tom's Cabin." Its composer is said to be Will M. Cook, who studied violin about a year in Berlin. Frederick Douglass presented Cook to President Harrison, so current report has it, and told him that he wished to have represented at the fair some exhibition of the progress made by our race in music. President Harrison wrote to the director of the world's fair, who at once gave permission to present this opera within the grounds of the fair. Mr. Cook promises to secure a great deal of talent to help him in his scheme. The tenor, he says, will be Mr. Harry Williams . . . and the soprano, Madame Sissieretta Jones . . . Mumford's Fisk Jubilee Singers, Mrs. Jennie Jackson DeHart, Mrs. L. Hamar [*sic*, Lula Hamer], of Washington, and Mr. Harry Burleigh, of Erie, Pa. . . . A concert will be given February 13, under the patronage of many society women in New York City, to enable Mr. Cook to raise a fund sufficient to secure a large chorus also.

Somehow, Will Marion Cook's idea of a special concert was co-opted by World's Fair officials, as one alluring aspect of their otherwise unappealing plans for a "Colored Folks Day" at the fair. Those associated with the Colored Folks Day initiative included Philadelphia musician and composer Joseph B. Adger, Washington music teacher and choir master J. T. Layton, and Washington lawyer Charles S. Morris, husband of Frederick Douglass's twenty-eight-year-old daughter Annie.

William McFeely's explanation of the advent of this "special day" posits an unduly harsh interpretation of Frederick Douglass's motives: "Will Marion Cook . . . had been urging that there be a special day at the fair when young black artists like himself and his friend Joseph Douglass—a grandson in whom [Frederick] Douglass took great pride—should perform. He had pled with Douglass to support such an event, and the commissioner, charmed by the young artists who had congregated in the city, overcame his doubts. He knew what such a day was likely to turn into, but he still had sufficient vanity to look forward to being the centerpiece of a celebration, and he overrode the objections of other black leaders."[19]

On March 3, 1893, this ominous report appeared in the *Detroit Plaindealer*: "It is said that the Colored World's Fair Opera company will produce *Uncle Tom's Cabin* at the great fair, and instead of having Uncle Tom die from the lash, he will be burned to death as was Smith recently in Paris, Texas. An effort is to be made to make the scene as realistic as possible, so as to give the people a general idea of this late piece of barbarity. This determination having come to the ears of certain Southern Democratic journals, has caused great excitement and indignation, and they are calling upon the World's Fair management to not permit this scene to be enacted."

The reference is to the February 1, 1892, Paris, Texas, lynching of Henry Smith, a deranged black man accused of the murder of a four-year-old white child. At least ten thousand spectators cheered on as Smith was slowly tortured and burned alive, in one of the most infamous demonstrations of communal barbarism in American history. The newspaper account of Will Marion Cook's plan to use his operatic adaptation of *Uncle Tom's Cabin* as a vehicle for exposing this barbarism may have been disinformation planted by opponents of the Colored Folks Day program; the atmosphere was heavy with distrust and antagonism.

Sissieretta Jones, the celebrated Black Patti, was ultimately denied the opportunity to sing Cook's "Uncle Tom's Cabin," which she declared "to be the most beautiful music she'd ever heard."[20] In fact, she was prohibited from participating in the Colored Folks Day activities altogether. Jim Crow limits would soon be imposed on her professional horizons.

Early in 1893, under the personal management of Major James B. Pond, one of the most powerful mainstream American impresarios of his day, Sissieretta Jones reached the pinnacle of her career. It was during this time that she entered into a series of benefit concerts for Will Marion Cook's ill-fated World's Fair Colored Opera Company: "The object of these concerts is to raise funds to enable the World's Fair Colored opera company to produce the opera of *Uncle Tom's Cabin* at the World's Fair, to show the advancement of the race since abolition of slavery."[21]

It was reported that three thousand people heard the Black Patti at Carnegie Hall in New York City on February 13, 1893, in the first of this series of benefit concerts. Also involved in the benefit concerts were Ednorah Nahar, the elocutionist, and Charles S. Morris, who acted as Sissieretta Jones's unofficial manager for the concert series. The black community press described Black Patti concerts under the management of Morris or Nahar at different locations in Ohio and Illinois during February and March 1893. Not all of them were financially successful. According to the March 21, 1893, edition of the *Detroit Plaindealer*, the Black Patti gave a concert at the Board of Trade Auditorium in Columbus, Ohio, after which the local agent "skipped with the receipts."

Regardless of her enthusiasm for Will Marion Cook's opera, Sissieretta Jones's benefit concerts were in conflict with her exclusive contractual agreement with Major James B. Pond. Pond's response was to bring a lawsuit against her, which he won. The *New York Times* reported on June 27, 1893:

> Sissieretta Jones, the "Black Patti," got a severe lecture yesterday from Judge McAdam of the Superior Court on the evils of ingratitude. Incidentally, she was enjoined from singing under any other management than that of Major James B. Pond.
>
> On June 8, 1892, the Major made a contract with the "Black Patti" for a year. He was to pay her $150 a week, furnish all accommodations for her, and pay all travelling expenses. Some time ago the Major and his colored star disagreed, and they have been contending in the courts for several months

over a clause in the contract which gave the manager the privilege of reengaging the singer for an additional two years under the same terms provided for the first year's work.

The "Black Patti" wanted to engage in business for herself, and Major Pond applied to Judge McAdam for an injunction. In granting the motion, the court said yesterday of Sissieretta:

"She feels now as if she could get along without her benefactor and she has thrown down the ladder on which she ascended . . . Every sense of gratitude requires her to be loyal to the Manager who furnished her with the opportunity for greatness . . . Talent is of little value without opportunity."[22]

Colored Folks Day was announced for August 25, 1893. The African American press was united in its opposition to Colored Folks Day. After denying African Americans any place of honor, it was felt that fair officials were throwing them a crumb to entice them to turn out in large numbers and spend lots of money. Then a story began circulating that these same officials had arranged to have watermelons strewn around the grounds especially for Colored Folks Day. Ida B. Wells asserted in a July 22, 1893, letter to the *New York Age* that "The horticulture department [of the Exposition] has . . . pledged itself to put plenty of watermelons around on the grounds with permission to the brother in black to 'appropriate' them."

It is possible the watermelon story was a ruse designed to discredit Colored Folks Day. It appears that watermelons were not actually scattered around the ground, but were said to be prominently displayed by vendors. In any event, with all the unfavorable publicity, Colored Folks Day did not enjoy great attendance.

The special concert turned out to be a saving grace of a generally unwelcome day. A report in the *Chicago Tribune* of August 26, 1893, described it: "All the morning a great crowd of colored people had been gathered about Festival Hall.

NO "NIGGER DAY" WANTED.

We are opposed to a "nigger day" at the Columbian Exposition. We have begged, argued, threatened in vain for the clean, respectable non-lowering recognition due us as a wronged and hindered people, anxious to let the world know how, in the face of every opposition, we have accomplished something out of our own brawn, brain and will force, but being denied, hooted, laughed at, trifled with as though we were a race of gulls and simpletons, we would be the veriest gulls and simpletons indeed, did we now, like a wilderness of monkies instead of dignified rational men and women, indorse this Massachusetts idea of a special day for 'colored people'' at the coming Exposition. There is no accounting for taste however, and if the colored people of the "Old Bay State," backed by one or two Negro Bishops with time on their hands, desire to have such a distinction, may the Lord have mercy on their foolish souls, for they know what they do, but let it be distinctly confined to Massachusetts, and the race in general be spared the humiliation of the thing.

Freeman, *February 25, 1893.*

Many of the men had brought their families . . . At 3 O'clock, 2,500 people were in the hall, two thirds of them negroes. Fred Douglass was greeted with applause as he walked across the stage to take the chair. With him was Isabella Beecher Hooker, sister of Henry Ward Beecher and Harriet Beecher Stowe. She wore an old-fashioned dress of gray silk . . . Along the side sat half a dozen prominent colored men, most of them afterward taking part in exercises."

TO TOLE WITH WATERMELONS.

A Novel Way to Increase the World's Fair Attendance—"Colored Folks' Day."

One of the important points in Mr. ——'s letter is that he is in favor of the pamphlet one dollar's worth. It will be especially needed to offset the effect of "Colored Folk's Day" at the world's fair, which will be August 25. Some colored men have promised to get two hundred thousand colored excursionists there that day, and the officials of the exposition have been published as highly in favor of the idea. The horticultural department has already pledged itself to put plenty of watermelons around on the grounds with permission to the brother in black to "appropriate" them. The secret of the kindness (?) of the world's fair commissioners is that the attendance at the fair has been very poor all along, and the colored brother has been especially conspicuous by his absence. This "Colored Folks' Day" is to be an extra inducement to have him come. He has been shut out of any other participation in the fair except to spend his money there, and as he has not been doing that very freely, a cordial invitation to do so is given at the eleventh hour. Because colored men are urging this scheme to put thousands of dollars in the pockets of the railroad corporations and the world's fair folks who thought no Negro good enough for an official position among them, it will succeed. The self-respect of the race is sold for a mess of pottage and the spectacle of the class of our people which will come on that excursion roaming around the grounds munching watermelons, will do more to lower the race in the estimation of the world than anything else. The sight of the horde that would be attracted there by the dazzling prospect of plenty of free watermelons to eat, will give our enemies all the illustration they wish as excuse for not treating the Afro-American with the equality of other citizens.—Ida B. Wells' Chicago letter to the N. Y. Age.

Cleveland Gazette, *July 22, 1893.*

THE WATERMELONS ABSENT.

"Colored Folks' Day" (yesterday, August 25) at the world's fair was a farce. Hardly one of the prominent persons advertised to participate—to speak, sing and play—was present. Even the promised watermelons were conspicuously absent. Joseph Banneker Adger, of Philadelphia; Will Cook and Charles Morris, of Washington, D. C., ought to ashamed of their connection with the alleged affair. It looks very much as if they would sacrifice the dignity and manhood of the entire race if only they could make a few paltry dollars as a result of it. Prominent world's fair authorities, who have studiously avoided recognizing the Afro-American in any but a menial capacity, and who hoped to realize from such a "day" thousands of dollars for the needy treasury of the exposition, played upon the credulity of these and other Afro-Americans with the result stated in our opening sentence. The self-respecting, manly and womanly Afro-Americans all over the country have denounced the effort and the "day," and their good work has been crowned with the success it surely merited. We don't mean to say that there were not some of our people at the world's fair yesterday in attendance upon the "Colored Folks' Day" exercises, because there were the few who were misled as well as those who will do anything once. Such persons are found in all classes of people. "Colored Folks' Day" at the world's fair was a farce, nevertheless. That is all sufficient. It will show the fair managers and the country that our people will not be sold for a "mess of pottage," even by members of our own race, and that we can resent insults, etc., as well as other classes.

Cleveland Gazette, *August 26, 1893.*

One of the "prominent colored men" present was the remarkable Bishop H. M. Turner. He was perhaps the only African American chaplain in the army during the Civil War, having been appointed to that position by President Lincoln. During Reconstruction, he was elected to the Georgia Legislature. Bishop Turner later served as President of Morris Brown College, in Atlanta, wrote books, and edited magazines. He is best remembered as a leading advocate for the recolonization of Africa by American Negroes.

Before the musical program began, Frederick Douglass delivered an extemporaneous speech so powerful it altered the context of Colored Folks Day. He said, in part:

> That we are outside of the World's Fair is only consistent with the fact that we are excluded from every respectable calling, from workshops, manufacturies and from the means of learning trades. It is consistent with the fact that we are outside of the church and largely outside of the state.
>
> The people who held slaves are still the ruling class at the South. When you are told that the life of the negro is held dog cheap in that section, the slave system tells you why it is so. Negro whipping, negro cheating, negro killing, is consistent with Southern ideas inherited from the system of slavery.[23]

Douglass went on to define "the problem": "Men talk of the negro problem. There is no negro problem. The problem is whether the American people have honesty enough, patriotism enough to live up to their own Constitution."[24] The speech evoked an apology from Ida B. Wells, who had protested Douglass's decision to take part in Colored Folks Day: "As I read a report of it next day in the papers—for I was among those who did not even go to the meeting—I was so swelled with pride over his masterly presentation of our case that I went straight out to the fair and begged his pardon for presuming in my youth and inexperience to criticize him."[25]

The musical portion of the Colored Folks Day program was entirely classical. According to a morning-after review in the *Chicago Herald*, "There was not a clap-trap selection" in the entire presentation. Lazy reporting in certain mainstream dailies, including the *New York Times*, gave the false impression that Sissieretta Jones actually did participate in the concert. The *Chicago Herald* correctly stated that the audience was "charmed with a substitute," mezzo contralto Madame Deseria Plato (a.k.a. Mrs. Boardley), who "sang Meyerbeer's 'Lleiti Signor.' "[26] In addition, Hallie Q. Brown recited "The Black Regiment," and Paul Laurence Dunbar "read an original ode to 'The Colored American,' " which he "composed especially for the occasion."[27] Joseph Douglass played "a violin fantasie from 'Trovatore,' " baritone Harry T. Burleigh sang "the Toreador's song from 'Carmen,' " and tenor J. Arthur Freeman sang "Buck's recitative and aria, 'The Shadows Deepen.' " All were accompanied on piano by Maurice Arnold Strothotte, an African American student at the National Conservatory. The program's musical highlight was delivered by tenor Sidney Woodward of Boston, "a tall and very black young negro."[28] "His first number was Verdi's 'I Due Foscari.' His execution was excellent, the audience . . . demonstrative in its recalls. He responded, and even then his hearers simply insisted that he should repeat the encore. They pounded the chairs and cried his name aloud."[29]

Notable by its absence was Will Marion Cook's opera of *Uncle Tom's Cabin*. According to the *Chicago Herald's* seemingly trustworthy review, only an excerpt was sung, a duet by Sidney Woodward and Harry Burleigh, which came toward the end of the program.

By most accounts, it was as a result of Will Marion Cook's enterprise that Colored Folks Day was conceived, a fact that did not resound in his favor in the midst of the controversy the event provoked. It appears Cook's opera fell victim to the poisonous racial environment surrounding the World's Columbian Exposition.[30]

At the conclusion of the August 25 Colored Folks Day concert, Charles S. Morris made a public apology for the nonappearance of the Black Patti. According to Morris, "opponents of colored American day at The Fair had written and misled her and her husband in regard to the good character of the celebration. This was done after her manager, Major Pond, had signed an agreement for her to make three appearances here for the sum of $800, of which $300 was paid by telegraph."[31]

In a contradictory statement, Major Pond explained that "his star did not appear because the guarantee money reached him by wire . . . too late to get word to her at Asbury Park in time to catch the last train to Chicago."[32] There is something disingenuous about both explanations—coming from the two primary antagonists in the Black Patti–World's Fair debacle.

On May 20, 1892, a foresighted commentator was quoted in the *Detroit Plaindealer*: "It is rather pitiful to think of the way [Sissieretta Jones's] career might be hampered because of her race—not because of prejudice exactly, but she certainly cannot appear in opera . . . unless one was especially written for her." Now, an opera had been written for her by Will Marion Cook, but the opportunity to appear in it had slipped away. Strictly as a matter of popular prejudice, Madame Jones was "kept in her place," and perhaps a certain precedent had been established. Three years later, Sissieretta Jones abandoned the concert stage and became the titular head of The Black Patti Troubadours, a successful minstrel troupe which was owned and managed by white men.

On September 27, 1893, a month after the controversial Colored Folks Day had come and gone, Sissieretta Jones sang under Major Pond's management in the Assembly Hall at the Columbian Exposition Woman's Building. She was assisted by Madame Neal Gertrude Hawkins, soprano; Madame Deseria Plato, contralto; and Joseph Douglass, violin. Madame Jones's appearance was neither publicized nor announced until the day it took place.[33]

The Midway Plaisance and the Dahomean Village

"Not until the 'midways' of our recent expositions stimulated general appreciation of Oriental rhythms did 'ragtime' find supporters through the country."

—*Etude*, December 1898

The Midway Plaisance at the 1893 World's Columbian Exposition stretched for nearly a mile, offering a melange of amusements and cultural exhibits that constituted an uneasy marriage of popular anthropology and voyeuristic sideshow. To one modern analyst, the Midway Plaisance demonstrated "purposeful confusion" and "deliberately constructed chaos . . . [a] kaleidoscopic passing of scenes, appearing quickly and discouraging valuation or judgement."[34] Another commentator proposed that it "provided a patently unself-conscious, eclectic, and noisy relief from the idealism of progress and unity so pervasive elsewhere on the fairgrounds. In any case, millions of Americans came and enjoyed themselves on the Midway and, for many of them, it was the memory of their experiences there that they most cherished."[35]

The main constituent of the Midway was the native village exhibits, which displayed foreign nationals in native garb, demonstrating aspects of their peculiar lives and cultures. One of the most elaborate and popular exhibits on the Midway was the "Streets of Cairo," which included a reported sixty shops, manned by Egyptians, Sudanese, and Nubians. Another North African exhibit was populated by Algerians and Tunisians. These exhibits contained theaters that featured native music and dance. Prominent was the "belly dance" and its most famous practitioner, Fahreda Mahzar, known as "Little Egypt." Paul Olah's Gypsy Band entertained at a Hungarian cafe, and musical performances highlighted many other cultural exhibits.

Various early commentaries suggested that the potpourri of international music heard on the Midway Plaisance in 1893 stimulated creative exploration among visiting African American musicians. Writing in the *Illinois Record* in 1898, Will Marion Cook offered this rather curious description: "During the World's Columbian Exposition at Chicago, the 'Midway Plaisance' was filled with places of amusement where the peculiar music of the 'muscle dance' was continually heard, and it is worthy of note that after that time the popularity of the 'rag' grew with astonishing rapidity and became general among Negro pianists."[36]

The role of exotic and erotic dance in the emergence of ragtime and jazz deserves more consideration than it has yet received. Shifting musical styles were invariably linked with new dancing trends. Frederick W. Putnam, director of ethnographic exhibits at the 1893 World's Fair, intended that exotic dance should have a prominent place. "In defending the great anthropological lessons of the Fair, Putnam at one point suggested that a certain tolerance had been installed where dance was concerned, due to the great variety on display in Chicago."[37]

"Tolerance" was not the universal response to exotic dance. Members of the Board of Lady Managers of the World's Fair were more or less scandalized by the dances performed in the Egyptian, Algerian, Persian, and Turkish theaters on the Midway Plaisance. Their grievances were aired in the *Chicago Tribune* of July 4, 1893, under the headline "Want Midway Dances Stopped. Lady Managers at the Fair Think They Are Offensive":

> Some of the lady managers have been down on Midway Plaisance. They told their experiences in the board meeting yesterday afternoon. They were not pleasant experiences. In fact, the women went so far as to say several harsh things concerning certain features of the street of nations . . .
>
> Mrs. Baker's unpleasant experiences. "I will take second place to no one in missionary work," she said, "But I went down on the plaisance yesterday impelled by a sense of duty. (Applause and laughter). I never have been so grieved or shocked in my life as at the things I saw . . . I consider it our duty . . . to enter a protest against them and demand that the places where they perform should be closed . . ."
>
> Then Mrs. Baker sat down and cried as if her heart would break.

A few outraged critics, oddly suggestive of Elvis Presley's early detractors, spoke out against the introduction of international dances like the hula, first presented by Sam T. Jack's Creole Company during their World's Fair engagement at the Madison Street Opera House. Resistance to the popularization of exotic dance was sometimes couched in the blindly ethnocentric, fervidly racist rhetoric of the day: "The other day a low class place of amusement imported dancers from the islands of the Pacific Ocean; and a few observers of amusements were invited to see a rehearsal of the Hawaiian national dance. And what did the improvised jury of experts see? Half a dozen semi-savages, whose color did not permit them to blush in the Caucasian fashion; but whose human instincts made them to cover themselves, and made them shrink from the excesses of their aboriginal exercises. These simple barbarians were ashamed of themselves."[38]

Of all the Midway Plaisance attractions, it was the Dahomean Village that insinuated itself most prominently into American musical lore. The village housed some sixty-seven men, women, and children imported from the African slave coast nation of Dahomey. Like everything else racial in nature at the World's Columbian Exposition, the Dahomean exhibit was controversial. The African American press was cynical from the outset.

In his speech at Colored Folks Day, Frederick Douglass protested that the officials of the Exposition "apparently... want us to be represented by the music and by the civilization of Dahomey ... They have filled the Fair with the sound of barbaric music, and with sights of barbaric rites, and denied the colored American any representation."[39] One contemporary writer expressed that "bringing Dahomeyans to Chicago would teach them just how overwhelmingly powerful the whites were."[40] As described in Eugene Levy's biography of James Weldon Johnson, "The popular reaction to the lightly clad Dahomans was part amusement, part repulsion. One journalist probably caught the feeling of most white onlookers when he wrote that their barbaric display represented the Afro-American in his natural state."[41]

A *Chicago Daily Tribune* reporter's description of the May 3, 1893, arrival of the Dahomeans on the Midway Plaisance drew a cunning parallel which tends to confirm Levy's assertion:

> The new arrivals formed the strangest procession that has yet moved down the plaisance. Black as the shades of night, every one of them, they shivered from the cold, raw air and groaned along under heavy trucks, which they balanced on their heads with as much skill as the Southern negroes "tote" smaller bundles.
>
> The women carried the heaviest loads, and that was the only way in which the sexes could be distinguished... [The women] were Amazons, hideous with battle scars and with the lines of cruelty and determination on their faces...
>
> The Dahomans have been in route for two months and reached their camp worn out. A number of them were suffering from the cold, although through an interpreter they said the Chicago climate was much better than that of Paris, where they were on exhibition for a week. They squatted about in the unfinished houses in their camp and devoured canned corn-beef with a relish. The Amazons went to sleep under whatever covering they could find, while the other women were put to work. The men just stood around and shivered until Mr. Gravier, one of the French managers of the show, secured some stoves and built fires for them.

If anything, the *Chicago Daily Tribune's* dehumanizing assessment of the African visitors was slightly more sympathetic than most. Ben C. Truman, in his 1893 *History of the World's Fair*, offered this succinct appraisal: "The [Dahomean] men are uglier than chimpanzees ... A more horrible-looking set of men and women it would be hard to find than these Dahomeyans and every effort has been made to illustrate their customs and peculiarities."[42]

J. W. Buel's World's Fair opus, *The Magic City*, included a photo of two Africans with the caption "Representatives of the Dahoman Cannibals ... in times of great scarcity of food it is common to kill and eat their own kin."[43] Virtually every account of the Dahomean visitors mentions their lack of appropriate warm clothing and the discomfort they experienced as a result. According to J. W. Buel: "[The Dahomeans] picked up several expressions, among which a request for 'Chicago beer' was most frequently used in their limited conversation with visitors; but when the pinching weather of October winds and frost attacked their bare limbs the Dahomans lost interest in everything except desire to return to their native country."[44]

Buel's brand of levity was of a recognizable stripe. According to anthropologist Curtis M. Hinsley, "Most distinctively, the exposition produced a humor that revealed deep uneasiness and uncertainty about boundaries. It was a humor evidently intended to encourage sympathy with the exotic and simultaneously to keep a certain ironic distance."[45]

In order to effectively "illustrate the steps of progress of civilization,"[46] Exposition planners erected the Dahomean village as an example of a degraded and underdeveloped culture, against which the accomplishments of modern Western man could be measured. The shameful inhospitality, lack of humane concern, and general ridicule to which the Dahomean visitors were subjected seriously undermined the Exposition's pretentious "metaphor for human progress."

Though Exposition planners cast them at the bottom rung of an assumed evolutionary ladder, the Dahomeans brought unexpected cultural attainments to the fair, attainments which helped point the way into the twentieth century for American popular music. Their singing and drumming inspired several contemporaneous observations. Amidst a discussion of "the plantation melodies as sung by the Hampton students," an article in the November 1893 issue of the journal of Hampton Institute, *Southern Workman*, noted:

> A visit to the Dahomey Village in the "Midway" followed by an evening at a Negro revival meeting anywhere in the South might throw some light upon the origin of these "spirituals." The chorus of wild Dahomeyans singing in response to their leader's solo and keeping time by rhythmic beating of the feet, swaying of the body, clapping of the hands, show, in many ways, the same characteristics that we note in the singing of the American Negroes; but the sweetness, the strange harmony, the soul, is lacking. The music is only a rude chant.
>
> In the revival meeting, we find an audience growing more and more excited as the service proceeds. Prayers that at first were uttered in every day speech change to a musical recitation. Responses, that at the beginning were few and monosyllabic, grow longer and more rhythmical, until, at last, the leader of the meeting becomes the leader of the shout, and the whole congregation, with rhythmic and musical response, supports the chorus of a harmonious song. The transition from speech to song is so gradual that it is impossible to tell when the line has been passed, where prayer and responses end and song and chorus begin. This then is the second stage of development of the Negro "spiritual." It is born out of the natural instinct of the race under stress of great religious excitement, and is as different from, and also as like to, the wild chant of the Dahomey as the Christian American Negro is different from and yet like to the savage Dahomeyan. Slavery and its sufferings, Christianity and its hope, have produced, out of certain characteristics peculiar to the race, this distinctive American music.

A far more detailed, "scientific" account of the music of the Dahomeans was supplied by musicologist Henry Edward Krehbiel in the August 20, 1893, edition of the *New York Daily Tribune*. Under the title "Songs and Dances of the Dahomans," Krehbiel spoke of "Revelations in Drumming" and "African Relics in American Slave Music." He noted, in part:

> The harp player in the village seems to be an excellent representative of the minstrels of whom travellers tell . . . He sits beside his little hut all day. . . , strums an unvarying accompaniment upon his instrument and sings little descending melodies in a faint high voice . . . His instrument . . . is at once primitive yet considerably developed. It has eight strings accurately tuned diatonically, but omitting the fourth of the major scale . . . The most interesting feature of the minstrel's song is the fact that he accompanies it with harmony. . . With his right hand he plays, over and over again, a descending passage (dotted quarters and eighths) of thirds; with his left hand he syncopates ingeniously on the highest two strings . . .
>
> That the Dahomans have a knowledge of harmony may be learned at the Fair from another source than the harping minstrel. The chief occupation of the villagers is to give exhibitions of their dances, which are accompanied by choral song and the beating of drums and bells. The song is sung by the men and women in unison; the harmony, singularly enough, is supplied by the band of percussion instruments. It is a triad which is broken up in a most intricate and ingenious manner . . . The fundamental tone comes from a drum made of a

The inhabitants of the Dahoman Village, as pictured in Halligan's Illustrated World's Fair, *1894.*

The "Arabian Orchestra" in the streets of Cairo, Midway Plaisance, in Halligan's Illustrated World's Fair, *1894.*

hollow log, about three feet long, with a single head, played by one who seems to be the leader of the band, though there is no giving of signals. This drum is beaten with the palms of the hands. A variety of smaller drums, some with one, some with two heads, are beaten variously with sticks and fingers. The bells, four in number, are of iron, and are held mouth up and are beaten with sticks. The players have the most remarkable rhythmic sense and skill . . . The fundamental effect in respect of rhythmical form is a triple accent against the double accent of the singers, either thus:

or as indicated in the quick marching song of which I shall speak presently. But it is impossible to convey an idea of the wealth of detail achieved by devices of syncopation, dynamics, etc., except by scoring the part of each instrument.

A large contingent of the King of Dahomey's army is composed of women . . . There are twenty-one women in the Dahomey village who play the part of Amazons in the dances, which take place several times a day . . . The dances which I witnessed seemed all to be war-dances and were pantomimic in character. The dancers formed in line and moved with measured steps, keeping admirable time . . . The actions of cocking the guns, aiming and firing, made up part of the pantomime. The songs consisted of frequent reiteration, at intervals filled with the drumming (which was incessant so long as a performance lasted), of short phrases. I am indebted for two specimens to Mr. Heinrich Zoellner, the conductor of the Leiderkranz, who is . . . profoundly interested in folk-music . . . Two dances were performed while Mr. Zoellner was in the village . . . To the first the dancers sang the following slow melodic phrase from thirty to fifty times, while the band drummed in double time and the dancers advanced and retreated without particular regard to the rhythm, some individuals indulging in fancy steps ad libitum.

Then there came a change of tempo and rhythm and also in the manner of singing and dancing. The drummers changed from double to compound triple time, the singers separated into two choirs, sang the following antiphonal allegro phrase and began to keep step with absolute precision:

In this little melody there is a characteristic feature which I am strongly inclined to think has been transplanted into the slave music of the United States. In what key is it? Not C minor, as the prevalence of C, E-flat and G would seem to suggest at first sight. The A is too disturbing for that. But if one might conceive the phrase in the key of F the explanation is at hand. Then it will be seen that it illustrates, or at least points to the origin, of the great predilection which our slave melodies show for a flat seventh in major melodies. A great many slave tunes might be cited in evidence, but I take a single one, because of its familiarity—the much-admired "spiritual" "Roll, Jordan, Roll."

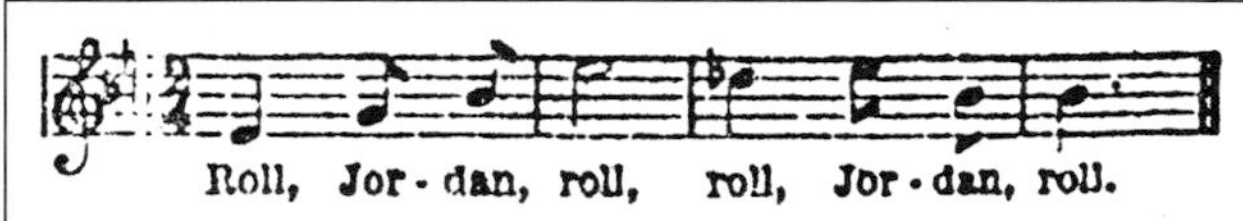

It is obvious from the structure of the African melodies which have been noted down for us by travellers that they grow out of . . . a latent sense of harmony. It is too early to attempt to tell why, but the fact is that while the negroes . . . use the pentatonic scale by preference, they do not always eschew the seventh, but use it as a diminished interval. In the cases before us they combine it with the tonic triad, and thus show, unconsciously, appreciation of the fifth relation. They seem to feel the tone as the essential element in the dominant-seventh chord of the under fifth. Some times they resolve it properly enough into that key, as in the case of the song, "There's a Great Camp Meeting in the Promised Land," which was adduced at the recent Musical Congress in Chicago as a striking illustration of the prevalent use among the slaves in America of the flat seventh.

In that song the first division closes with a perfect cadence in F major. The next phrase begins as abruptly as the third measure of the Dahoman example, with E-flat. The American negroes, however, in this case, having been for a long time directly under the influence of European music, resolve the chord properly into B-flat. The Dahomans seem satisfied in the last measure to treat the E-flat as a grace-note, and find sufficient sense of repose in the F major triad. In "Roll Jordan Roll," our own singers have as little compunction about going straight back to their tonic triad . . . There are other survivals of African elements in our slave songs, though perhaps none of them is so striking as this. It deserves to be noted in connection with this that the interval is treated the same, whether it be major or minor. Singing in the latter mode our slaves are wont to introduce a major or a sharped sixth, as is exemplified in the following camp-meeting song . . . which I have from a lady who learned it fully fifty-five years ago in Boyle County, Kentucky:

The scientific study of folk-music may be said to have just begun. It will not have proceeded far along the lines that have been recently marked out before we shall have learned many things which till now have seemed to be mysteries.

Rudi Blesh and Harriet Janis wrote in *They All Played Ragtime*:

The World's Columbian Exposition had, in fact, prepared the way for ragtime, even though a few years elapsed before its publication started. While the sensational dancing of Little Egypt is likely to be remembered by old-timers, the Dahomean Village was an equally sensational attraction. Between the two of them a spate of exotic dances became the talk, from the hootchie-cootchie to the bombashay.

The village was uniquely authentic amid the spurious curiosities of the Midway. Its native occupants entertained all day with drumming and chants. They came from the African West Coast, where America's slaves had once been captured, and the rhythms of the drum batteries and the haunting chord-chains of their chorales held in their essence the transforming contribution that the Negro has made to American music.[47]

Neither Rudi Blesh nor Harriet Janis had been present at the 1893 Chicago World's Fair to witness the Dahomean singers and drummers firsthand. Their high opinion of the Dahomeans' music came in large part from a reading of Henry Edward Krehbiel's 1914 book, *Afro-American Folksongs*, in which Krehbiel reiterated some of the observations he had made in his 1893 essay. Krehbiel reproduced Heinrich Zoellner's transcription of the Dahomean "March time" war song "illustrating the employment of the flat seventh and cross-rhythms between singers and drummers," and he reconfirmed that "The players showed the most remarkable rhythmical sense and skill that ever came under my notice. Berlioz in his supremest effort with his army of drummers produced nothing to compare in artistic interest with the harmonious drumming of these savages."[48]

It wasn't Krehbiel's intention to establish an evolutionary link between the Dahomean drummers and the appearance of ragtime, a music he held in low esteem. Blesh and Janis, however, had another agenda: "The general public first heard ragtime on the Chicago Midway."[49] They went on to note:

> At least one newspaper account attests the impact of Dahomean rhythm on popular music. The *Chicago Chronicle* in 1897 reviewed a new song, *There's No Coon That's One Half So Warm*, as follows: "M. B. Garrett, during the World's Fair, long before the 'coon' song epidemic became prevalent, was impressed one day during a visit to the Dahomey Village with a melody in strict 'ragtime' played by the natives. He jotted down the notes, filed them away and forgot about them. When the rage for Negro songs commenced. . . . he at once set about arranging it into a song. *No Coon Is One Half So Warm* is now one of the most popular sought-after songs of the popular order before the public."[50]

LEADER OF THE DAHOMEY ORCHESTRA.

New Orleans Daily Picayune, *June 15, 1893.*

When the World's Fair closed, the European managers of the Dahomean Village arranged to mount their exhibit at various festivals and parks. On September 1, 1894, the World's Fair Dahomeans began a two-week encampment at Troost Park in Kansas City, and on September 3 they were the subject of some "comparative ethnology" in the mainstream daily *Kansas City Star*. An unnamed reporter claimed he could see little difference between the Dahomean "savages" and "the civilized Negro . . . About the only thing the white man has taught the black brother is to wear clothes and play the slide trombone":

> As far as the black man's music goes, he has apparently the same tunes in Africa that he has here in America. The same recurring minor strains, the same delicious syncopations occur in the music of the war dance, as it is heard at Troost park, that one hears at a negro camp meeting where the negroes sing their own songs. Of course there is more din, more beating of tom toms and blowing of horrible bone horns and more rings of jangling bells among the savages, that may be expected, but as they let their voices rise in unison, and naturally drop into the four parts and swell the chorus the same cadences are heard that thrill the Caucasian on the outskirts of a camp meeting crowd when some old brother lilts his voice and starts the ancient hymn . . . In executing their dances it is easy to see where the American negroes get their grace and perfect ideas of time. The barbaric instruments of course carry no tune and only mark the time—something as negroes "pat" for each other to "rag."

The author of this report was no H. E. Krehbiel. His "comparative ethnology" was intended to amuse white readers at the expense of black citizens. What is notable is that, unlike the distinguished ethnomusicologist, this white Kansas City reporter already knew to use the word "rag" to describe black dance.

Only someone with a disposition to believe could take the *Kansas City Star* reporter's jaundiced observations as evidence that the World's Fair Dahomeans played anything equivalent to ragtime. Regardless, the Dahomean Village and its singers, dancers, and drummers were an important part of the residual image of the World's Fair in the eyes of several hundred thousand African American visitors. As Blesh and Janis wrote, "The Dahomeans were not quickly forgotten."[51] One imprint may be Bert Williams and George Walker's 1902 musical comedy hit, *In Dahomey.* Two men who had been personally involved with the Columbian Exposition, Will Marion Cook and Paul Laurence Dunbar, wrote the music and lyrics for *In Dahomey.* The plot centers around two young men who travel to Dahomey and gain control of a colony of emigrants from the state of Georgia. George Walker becomes the King of Dahomey and Bert Williams the Prime Minister.

In 1908 black Chicago-based newspaper columnist William "Juli Jones" Foster coined the nickname "Dahomian Stroll" for the booming black theater and cabaret district on State Street between Twenty-seventh and Thirty-fifth Streets,[52] another probable imprint of the Dahomean Village at the 1893 World's Fair. The popular nickname was soon shortened to "the Stroll," and it stuck for many years.

Jazz historians have traditionally accepted the notion that ragtime—and, by extension, jazz—emerged from various sources agglomerating at the Columbian Exposition, yet the connection may not be as straightforward as has often been supposed. While it seems to be accepted as a matter of faith "that some form of ragtime made an appearance at or around the 1893 Chicago World's Fair,"[53] no convincing evidence has yet been presented that ragtime was actually heard at the Columbian Exposition.

The Midway Plaisance offered "a more spontaneous kind of amusement" than found within the Exposition grounds proper, but contemporaneous documents give no indicatation that it provided a place for informal, make-shift entertainments, or for homegrown or itinerant black pianists.[54] Nevertheless, it has been asserted that "When the fair opened . . . pianists from all over the central United States converged on the amusement thoroughfare called the Midway, as well as the huge Chicago red-light district. Few were the players who went unemployed as the thousands of visitors poured into the Windy City, and all amusements, both licit and illicit, flourished."[55]

Histories of the city of Chicago attest to the expansion of the notorious First Ward Levee District at the time of the World's Fair, as the city reportedly opened wide to meet the demands of entertaining so many out-of-town guests. It is easy to believe that budding African American piano "professors" and other musicians were attracted to Chicago by the heightened atmosphere of celebration surrounding the World's Columbian Exposition, but there are no firsthand accounts of music in the levee district, so the particulars remain *out of sight.* Romanticized narratives routinely mention the presence of black musicians:

> [T]he wheels clicked merrily and the brothel doors stood ajar. Concert saloons blossomed out with extravagant shows, panel houses opened in the principal streets, freak shows and dime museums pandered to the lowest public tastes, new bordellos and cribs shacks sprang up, and hundreds of sharpers, pimps, and strong-arm men lurked in

every Levee street and alley to separate the visitors from their money. The entire Levee seethed with the most abandoned orgy of vice and crime the city had seen. Elaborate new saloons and brothels were built up in an area south of the Levee proper between Eighteenth and Twenty-second Streets which became known as the Tenderloin and which shortly exceeded the old Levee itself. . . In the brothels beer flowed, champagne corks popped, the "professors" and Negro bands played gay tunes, and the girls worked double shifts.[56]

Among the professional road shows that descended on Chicago during this time, Buffalo Bill's Wild West Show set up on a spacious open lot just one block away from the Exposition grounds and opened on April 26, 1893: "Annie Oakley, Johnnie Baker and Col. Cody are the chief exponents of marksmanship, while Mexican, Cossack, Syrian and Arabian horsemen intermingle their equestrian feats with those of the more or less noble red men."[57] The show's manager was Nate Salsbury, who later promoted the "Black America" extravaganza in New York. However, there is no evidence that the 1893 World's Fair edition of Buffalo Bill's Wild West Show included any African American performers.

Buffalo Bill's Wild West Show reported good business over the entire run of the fair. Prospects were not so sanguine for many local theaters, as the *Clipper* reported on July 8, 1893: "The first month of the Fair brought out a mere sprinkling of strangers, and when, with the days of June, the influx began, our managers gave their hopes a new lease of life, but results have shown that our provincial friends are here to see the Fair and do the labyrinth of amusements the Midway Plaisance affords, but have little desire to push their coin through the box office windows of local play houses."

In the face of repeated complaints that "the Fair has brought nothing but sorrow to a majority of our amusement providers,"[58] one Chicago theater manager reportedly enjoyed "all the business his house can hold."[59] Road-show operator Sam T. Jack leased the Madison Street Opera House and presented his groundbreaking Creole Burlesque Company of African American entertainers for two full months during the fair's late-summer peak.

• ***July 22, 1893 (Chicago, Illinois):*** "Madison Street Opera House," "'This is the house that Jack built' is an apt line in Manager Jack's billing this week, and if one may judge by the great catch of hot weather patronage his Creole Burlesquers are attracting, it would take more than 'all the king's horses and all the king's men' to pull it down again. These dusky entertainers began their fourth week [July] 16, and have still an indefinite hold on the stage" (*New York Clipper*).

The black community weeklies published numerous reports of special concerts by African American artists in Chicago during the World's Fair summer of 1893. In August the *Freeman*'s Chicago correspondent described a program at Bethel Church which featured Madame Marie Selika, Sidney Woodward, Harry T. Burleigh, and Will Marion Cook. Cleveland soprano Rachel Walker also appeared in concerts in Chicago, as did the black queen of ballad singers, Flora Batson.

An outstanding concert company known as Edith Pond's Midnight Stars organized in Chicago and drew from the excess of talent gathered around the Colored Folks Day program.[60] According to the *Cleveland Gazette* of August 26, 1893, the Midnight Stars included popular "dramatic reader" Ednorah Nahar, Rachel Walker, Joseph Douglass, Willie Bensen, and William C. Elkins. Edith Pond's Midnight Stars toured the Midwest for a couple of months but disbanded in December after several financially disappointing programs. William C. Elkins went on to direct the quartet, chorus, and glee club of the famous Williams and Walker

Company. During the 1920s he directed his own jubilee singing groups on commercial recordings for Paramount, Okeh, Gennett, Cameo, QRS, and Brunswick.

Conclusion

Chicago held the nation's attention throughout the run of the Exposition. Irrespective of racial issues, nearly every American wanted to view the 1893 World's Fair. Among the famous African Americans whose biographies include a footnote on the fair is Mary Church Terrell, founder of the National Association of Colored Women, who described visits with Frederick Douglass and Paul Laurence Dunbar in her book *A Colored Woman in a White World*. George Washington Carver, at the time an anonymous college student, had a painting on exhibit at the Art Palace.[61] James Weldon Johnson, then a student at Atlanta University, worked at the World's Fair as a "chair boy," pushing visitors around the grounds in wheelchairs, for a fare of 75 cents an hour. He was said to have been one of just thirty blacks out of one thousand "chair boys."[62] Robert S. Abbott, future founder and editor of the *Chicago Defender*, then a student at Hampton Institute and a member of the Hampton Quartette, also visited the fair.[63]

A variety of commentators with vastly different focuses agree that a most important function of this Exposition was as a gathering place for emerging black leaders in all fields. The backward, repressive social atmosphere of the 1893 World's Fair must have lent a sobering air to their palaver.

The 1893 World's Columbian Exposition was, among other things, an exhibition of the unabashed official rejection of the principle of racial equality. This blatant authorization of discrimination closed the book on the matter for the rest of the nineteenth century at least. Moreover, the conduct of the World's Fair made clear the uselessness of continued appeals for equal treatment based on demonstrations of merit or talent.

For the prior thirty years, public exhibitions of talent and high character had been a prevailing tactic in the struggle for equal justice and opportunity. This kind of thinking underlied the Original Fisk University Jubilee Singers' successful tours of the 1870s. Under the influence of the Fisk singers and other such groups, the spiritual singing tradition was recognized as a dignified attribute of African American culture, deserving of respect. Spiritual singing became associated with high cultural and "spiritual" values and aspirations, as well as a kind of self-conscious pride of racial heritage. Many African American community leaders of the period felt that effective political appeals could be made from this high moral platform. It was this approach that W. E. B. DuBois evoked in this *Detroit Plaindealer* essay of May 5, 1893: "[L]et us go to the World's Fair, and sing—what? Bach, and Beethoven, Handel and all the white music we can find? To some extent, if you will, if you must, but above all, let us sing the jubilee songs as God never heard them sung before, with solo, semichorus, full-chorus and orchestra, to bring out for once the full brave beauty of the only original music of modern times. Then would visiting Europe gain a respect for the American Negro that would be of untold value."

By the 1890s the political environment had degenerated to a point where this message no longer resonated. Hell-bent on "keeping the Negro in his place," and conditioned by a half-century of "Ethiopian minstrelsy," the white, mainstream public was unprepared to accept any black music that entailed respect. African American musicians who visited the World's Columbian Exposition were confronted by a stark contrast between the inaccessibility of a legitimate platform on the fairgrounds and the economic opportunities readily available in the wide-open atmosphere of the "Levee sin-district."

Moreover, the forced resignation of Theodore Thomas as musical director of the fair manifested the popular rejection of *all* music seen as projecting "aspirations" rather than entertainment. "High culture" in America was already becoming somewhat obsolete.

The impending ragtime revolution opened venues to African American performers and established the black popular music profession on a full-blown basis. The ground rules which dominated its rise were somehow crystallized at the 1893 Chicago World's Fair. Anthropologist Curtis M. Hinsley has identified a powerful economics lesson that was imparted by public perceptions of the fair:

> The Chicago experience clarified some disturbing truths. The temptation of the dark energies of the Street in Cairo or the Midway is made all the more alluring by the knowledge that the sensual feast can be bought . . .
>
> The process of commodification rested on the premise that at the bottom everything is for sale and everyone has a price—that the world, no matter how bizarre, is reducible to cash terms . . .
>
> Chicago suggested that wherever we traffic in the world, there are those market informants who understand the commodity premise and are prepared to authenticate their cultures accordingly . . . the market vision prefers these "reasonable others."[64]

The commercialization of black secular music came as a result of this newly negotiated, unspoken Faustian agreement. Conditioned by fifty years of minstrelsy, white audiences of the "Gay '90s" demanded "coon" travesties as a necessary accompaniment to their ragtime. African American performers of the ragtime era struggled with the harsh realities of doing business and making art in a substantially racist society.

The artistic expressions of the rising generation of African American entertainers did not

RAG TIME MUSIC.

It is said that "rag time" music is going out of fashion. We are glad of it. More lies have been sprung over the footlights in rag time than otherwise. Take the vile lie, "All Coons Look Alike to Me," and that other "Every Race Has a Flag but the Coon." One of "our companies" of the "Coon" sort advertised recently in a Savannah (Ga.) newspaper that a certain part of the theatre would be "reserved for coons." The Afro-Americans of Savannah were fighting mad over it and they were right. We have Irish drama in abundance, but no Irish dramatist or impersonator ever uses the weaknesses of his race to disgrace his race. The Afro-American dramatist and impersonator are perhaps the only creatures in all the world who do it and grin over the profits of the depravity of it.

The music of rag time is tolerable, but most of the sentiment of it is false, degrading and intolerable. We want our men and women on the stage, but we want them in a decent and honorable way.

We are glad the prevailing rag time music is gasping for its life.—Nhe New York Age.

Yes, and we are glad that the "rag time" business is on its last legs. There has nothing happened since the war that did so much to show up Negro weaknesses as that very thing of "rag time" music. Everything that Negroes ever did, or ever will do, or ever can do was told during that late exciting epoch of "rag time." Negroes had no scruples against allowing the white people know just what their life meant while they sang and grinned away about "Ma Baby Loo" and "Ma Honey."

The truth of the whole business is there was a wholesale letting down of the racial standard, whatever that might have been. Talk about "racial depravity" "and some of us" and such; why there was not a Negro chick and child in America that did not sing of "Ma Baby," "I'd Dress My Baby Like a Swell White Lady." What right have we to dress our "babies" like swell—like anybody if we are not married to them? And, mind you, they are applauded. Our children sing it. The writer's children sang it, poor innocent fools. Their age and innocency is all that saves them. But what about those that are in the receptive mood, in that dangerous period when such sentiment is gulped down? Those songs told of open and notorious depravity, and the good people aided and abetted the sentiment because it came from the stage. We need no witnesses. Even the whites were becoming inocculated, but remember the songs did not refer to them. They gave the shekels to hear us sing away our honor, and we sang.

Freeman, *March 16, 1901. This article expresses a popular editorial consensus of the African American press regarding coon songs and, by association, ragtime music in general. If it betrays a certain snobbery, its observation of the "wholesale letting down of the racial standard" that aided and abetted ragtime's commercial ascendancy is remarkably candid.*

project mainstream aspirations, but a new sense of liberty, license, and abandon. Soon, African Americans found effective means to assert control of their public cultural image. No more than a dozen years after the World's Columbian Exposition, Robert T. Motts converted his beer hall at Twenty-seventh and State Streets into the Pekin Theater, the first commercially viable black-owned theater featuring black entertainers and welcoming black and white audiences. Motts' Pekin Theater became a model and inspiration to a new, independent black vaudeville industry that would soon blanket the Midwest and South with little theaters. Once the dynamic context of black theater entertainment for a black audience was in place, the stage was set for an American cultural revolution.[65]

Hard lessons learned at the 1893 World's Fair cleared the way for the imminent appearance of ragtime, and, one step further down the road, the emergence of more fully self-directed black music styles such as blues, jazz, and gospel. In regard to all of these things, the 1893 World's Columbian Exposition, the "whited-sepulchre," was a landmark in American music history and a watershed in African American cultural history.

PAUL LAWRENCE DUNBAR.

A Young Man Whose Poems Have Attracted Wide-Spread Attention and Comment.

Master Dunbar, a fair outline portrait of whom we give above, was born in Dayton, June 27, 1872—the son of Joshua and Matilda Dunbar, both of whom had been slaves in Kentucky. His mother was widowed when he was very young, but bravely took up the task of educating her three sons—Paul and two half-brothers—and it is to her nobility and indomitable courage that the first named owes whatever of success he may achieve. He entered the common school of Dayton at the age of six and, with the exception of constant ill health, passed through it much as do other boys, entering the high school in his fourteenth year. While there Paul was twice a winner of prizes offered for literary articles and graduated in 1891 with no honor or distinction save that of class poet. After graduating he accepted a very humble position, but began writing short stories for the A. N. Kellogg Newspaper Company, from which he drifted back to his first love—poetry—and began to write for the Chicago News-Record. In June of last year the Western Association of Writers met in Dayton, and being invited he read before them a couple of his poems, which were enthusiastically received. Attention was thus drawn to him and his writings were widely copied by the press. Then a New York paper began paying for his verses. The Chicago News also decided to remunerate him and others followed the example thus set. A stranger in Canada, learning his condition and having read some of his poems, presented him with twenty dollars' worth of books, and letters of congratulation have poured in from all over the country. Master Dunbar has also been presented with membership in the W. W. A. by Dr. Ridpath and decorated with the historian's own badge. He still holds his humble position. About Christmas time a volume of his verses was published. Paul says that he "will not depend upon literature for a living, but that the law or journalism shall be his profession."

Our portrait above does not indicate his complexion, which is usually termed "a dark brown skin."

His position as elevator boy in one of Dayton's business blocks pays him but $4 a week.

Cleveland Gazette, *January 7, 1893.*

Selected, Annotated Chronology of Music-Related Citations, 1893

• ***January 12, 1893:*** An obituary for a member of the choir of Mt. Zion Church in Glencoe, Louisiana mentions that, on her deathbed, she requested visiting members of her choir to sing "We Will March Down To Jordan" and "We Will Anchor By-And-By" (*Southwestern Christian Advocate*).

• ***January 13, 1893:*** "Mr. Walter F. Craig, of Brooklyn, is gaining fame as a musician. Of him the *New York Age* says: '. . . Mr. Craig has done much to break down the barriers of caste. He was the first musician of the race to be admitted to the Musical Union; he achieved a national reputation as a virtuoso of high order at a concert given in the Boston Music Hall, and has been recently elected a member of the great Dvoràk's orchestra, of which he has been placed by the master himself, among the prime violins'" (*Detroit Plaindealer*).

• ***January 14, 1893 (Chicago, Illinois):*** "Central Music Hall—Sissieretta Jones gave four concerts, [January] 5–7, assisted by Ariel Nichols, Adele V. Holman, Amelia Haden, Marie Haden, Wm. Sherman Baxter and, to large audiences" (*New York Clipper*).

• ***January 20, 1893 (Detroit, Michigan):*** "Mme Sissieretta Jones, 'The Black Patti,' will sing in the auditorium Feb. 9th, under the management of Mrs. Maggie Porter Cole . . . 'I want all the best people in Detroit to hear Miss Jones sing,' said Mrs. Cole. 'I want to show them that the talents of colored people are not confined to cake walks and dance halls, but that our race has produced one of the greatest singers of the age'" (*Detroit Plaindealer*).

• ***January 20, 1893:*** "Bazoo and Bootjack," "There is one thing I have noticed here which is in keeping with my observations everywhere. That is the proneness of Afro-Americans to make monkeys of themselves. Once, while on the Pacific slope, I went on a pleasure trip. I was hardly seated before a band of hoodlums began to sing jim crow songs to the great amusement of the whites. I turned away in disgust and the white people eyed me as a curiosity. They couldn't conceive of an Afro-American, who could be entertained by reading or conversation on the popular subjects of the day in preference to listening to jig songs. They had always pictured him as a jim crow being and those fellows were helping to confirm their belief. I would have felt more comfortable if the whole lot had been pitched overboard. The fellows were showered with small coins while not one of the donors would have thought it profitable to have patronized one of the concerts given by Afro-Americans of talent.

Not long after that I was at a public gathering where patriotic sentiments pervaded the whole meeting, but the omnipresent jim crow Negro was there and it wasn't long ere a crowd of them got together and commenced their unearthly yell. I slipped quietly away, cursing my fate, not that of my race connections, but that so many of them with whom I am identified, continue to make such blankety blank fools of themselves, and make this foolishness so conspicuous at all times" (*Detroit Plaindealer*).

• ***February 4, 1893 (Johnstown, Pennsylvania):*** At a concert at Free Will Church, "the chorus 'Live Humble,' given in regular Baptist style, brought down the house" (*Cleveland Gazette*).

• ***February 4, 1893 (Huntsville, Alabama):*** "The Terrell Band, composed of Messrs. Bob and Alonzo Terrell, Tard Birdman, Prior Johnson, John Robinson and Prof. James Turner, paid Decatur a visit and made many friends" (*Indianapolis Freeman*).

Note: The "Prof. James Turner" mentioned here could be the legendary Jim Turner, whom W. C. Handy talked about in *Father of the Blues*.

• ***February 11, 1893 (Rochester, New York):*** "There will be a mandolin contest here soon, for a purse of $2000, between Prof. A. L. Lancheir, colored, and Mr. D. W. Jones, white, of Detroit Mich. The judges will consist of one Afro-American and one White man, together with one of our leading ministers. Each contestant is expected to play five pieces of the most difficult music" (*Cleveland Gazette*).

• ***February 11, 1893 (Williamsport, Pennsylvania):*** "Mr. H. Molson, leader and teacher of the Alma Banjo club of this city, was the only representative of our race at the contest given at Academy of Music at Philadelphia last month" (*Cleveland Gazette*).

• ***February 17, 1893 (Detroit, Michigan):*** "The most important events of the season were the 'Black Patti' concerts of last week. . . .

The work of the chorus was excellent and deserves commendation. Its numbers were enthusiastically encored and great credit is due Mrs. Cole for her skill in bringing it to such a state of perfection in so short a time. Mrs. Cole sang well, seldom better, and her reception was almost as warm as that accorded to Mme Jones. No comparison can be drawn between Mme Jones and Mrs. Cole, because their voices and method are so dissimilar. Neither had any difficulty in filling the vast auditorium with their voices, despite the fact that the hall has such a bad reputation for singing purposes. . . .

The only poor part of the concerts was the attendance of Afro-Americans. It was poor, very poor, when the high character of the concert and the great reputation of Mme Jones is taken into consideration. Had it not been for the whites who largely outnumbered them the enterprise would have been a big financial failure. Instead of the three hundred colored people present the first night and about two hundred the second, there should have been a thousand each night . . . If Madame Jones ever makes a reappearance in Detroit the *Plaindealer* hopes that members of the race will endeavor to make amends for their failure of last week.

While the concerts were not a financial success, great credit should be given to Mrs. Maggie Porter-Cole for her enterprise in bringing Mme Jones to Detroit" (*Detroit Plaindealer*).

• ***February 18, 1893 (Johnstown, Pennsylvania):*** "The first appearance of Chapman's F. C. [*sic*] Troupe was not altogether a success. The music was good. The first chorus led by Prof. Scott, the quartette by Messrs. Scott, Cooper, Banks and Turpin, and the lovely tenor and bass duet, 'No Hope Beyond' by Messrs. Cooper and Scott, were worthy of notice. Warrick and Prunsley are successful fun-makers, and almost surpass themselves, but it is almost time for our people to cease blacking themselves and making clowns of themselves for the amusement of White people" (*Cleveland Gazette*).

• ***February 24, 1893:*** "The Happy Home club of Bay City [Michigan] is a temperance club which has branches all over the state. They hold weekly meetings and have a literary department consisting of the best vocal and instrumental talent of the city and they render a fine program every Monday evening. There are no colored members at present, but 'Tolbert and Christopher,' the colored banjo and guitar artists of Bay City, have kindly accepted the invitation of assisting the club in their entertainment and made their third appearance at their hall last Monday evening introducing trick banjo and guitar playing, and met with success" (*Detroit Plaindealer*).

• ***February 25, 1893 (Rochester, New York):*** "WON THE PURSE OF $2,000—In the Mandolin Contest—The Winner Accepts the Challenge of a London Professor," "The great mandolin contest took place last week Thursday evening for a purse of $2,000. Prof. A. L. Lanshire, an Afro-American, of Boston, and D. W. Jones (white), of Detroit, Mich., were the contestants. The judges were A. W. Lewis, of Syracuse, professor of music; Rev. Dr. Jones, of Hamlin, and Prof. W. W. Whitmore, the great guitarist of Scranton, the only Afro-American. Each contestant rendered four selections, and the judges decided in favor of Prof. Lanshire, because he kept the best time and played the highest grade of music. Both played beautifully. After the contest a telegram was read from Prof. A. W. Griffin, of London, England, challenging the winner for a contest in Boston next May for $2,500 a side. It was immediately accepted by the victor" (*Cleveland Gazette*).

• ***March 3, 1893 (Adrian, Michigan):*** "A company of local talent recently made a trip to several of the main villages in the Hoosier state. But, alas! were stranded with an elephant on their hands" (*Detroit Plaindealer*).

• ***March 3, 1893 (Cincinnati, Ohio):*** "A Winter Baptizing," "Yesterday morning about 11 o'clock, after the regular Sunday morning services were completed, Rev. Foster, the minister of the Cumminsville, colored Baptist church, baptized four of his flock in the Miami canal, at the head of Division street. The affair was witnessed by fully 2,000 colored and about 500 white people. The whole colored congregation sang and shouted and great religious fervor prevailed... Rev. Foster, the minister who conducted the baptismal exercises, is 88 years of age, being said to be the oldest minister in the state" (*Detroit Plaindealer*).

• ***March 3, 1893:*** " 'Eplethelia' [*sic*] the opera in three acts by Harry L. Freeman, at Denver, Colo., was a grand success. This is the first opera ever written by a colored man and should be appreciated" (*Kansas City American Citizen*).

Note: The Denver premier of Harry Lawrence Freeman's opera *Epthelia* was also noted in the February 9, 1893, edition of "the *Rocky Mountain News*, a major Denver newspaper of the time."[66] Freeman went on to play a vital role in the black musical comedy movement of the early 1900s, serving as musical director of Ernest Hogan's *Rufus Rastus* Company and Cole and Johnson's *The Red Moon* Company. He remained musically active into the 1940s.

• ***March 4, 1893 (Pittsburgh, Pennsylvania):*** "C. P. Stinson has returned from Youngstown where he was meeting with success. Mr. Stinson is known the world over as a champion banjoist, having won a few years ago, a championship medal in a contest in Kansas City, Mo. He was the only Afro American contestant. He has also crossed the waters several times and played before the queen. Mr. Stinson can be found holding a very creditable position in one of our largest music stores" (*Cleveland Gazette*).

• ***March 11, 1893:*** "Woman's World," "Mme S. Jones sang at the residence of Judge Andrews, on Fifth Avenue, N.Y. before a party of 30 ladies, among whom were Mrs. Hicks Lord, Mrs. C. Fields, Mrs. Vanderbilt, Mrs. Stevens, and Mrs. Astor, at whose house Mme Jones will sing next week. The chief justice of India, who was present, presented the singer with a valentine which, when opened, contained a check for $1000... The ladies pronounced the singing superior to Patti's" (*Indianapolis Freeman*).

• ***March 11, 1893 (Richmond, Virginia):*** "Jubilee Songsters," "The Jubilee Songsters of Bethlehem have come for public favor and rightly do they deserve the same. Under the leadership of the well-known J. H. Binford, they are paving the way to success. They have given a series of Concerts in the various churches... They sing jubilee songs, which fills the audience with enthusiasm. The following compose the singers:

James H. Binford, Leader, David Cottriel, James Burton, Tobias James, Percy J. Wallace, Henry Gaines, Robert C. Burke, Golden Taylor, Alex. Hines.

They will give one of their grand concerts at the 6th Mt. Zion Baptist Church, Monday night, March 30, '93" (*Richmond Planet*).

• ***March 11, 1893 (Helena, Montana):*** "The 'Bucket of Blood' is doing good business. Levy Sikens, the proprietor, is a man well thought of and well fitted for the business. Will Allen, proprietor of the 'Mascot' is also doing good business. It must be remembered that Mr. Allen is one of the best piano players in Helena" (*Indianapolis Freeman*).

• ***March 17, 1893 (Topeka, Kansas):*** "Musicians of Rare Ability," "Geo. Freeman, one of the greatest cornetists living, and the famous Hyer sisters are in the city. Mr. Freeman is, without doubt, the finest Negro soloist on the American stage, is a thorough Kansan, having been born in Lawrence, Kan. He started his musical career at an early age, and is now an artist who stands at the head of his profession. The Hyer sisters, the great musical prodigies, have been before the public a number of years. Their songs have delighted the most fastidious, and as actresses, they bear enviable reputations. The mere mention of their names, brings to mind the old-time Billy Kersands, Wallace King, Sam Lucas and Bob Smart. Geo. is the son of Mark Freeman, the celebrated chef de'cullinaire, at the Copeland hotel of this city" (*Kansas State Ledger*).

• ***March 24, 1893 (Emporia, Kansas):*** "There will be a harp contest at this place on the 23rd inst., between the Emporia and Osage City fellows. A concert will be given in connection with the contest" (*Kansas State Ledger*).

Note: This "harp contest" was, most likely, a harmonica contest.

• ***March 25, 1893:*** "Eaton and Weathers, colored vocalists and comedians, gave a second entertainment at Excelsior Assembly Hall [in New York City], March 14 . . . Besides the above performers . . . [the] Calliope Quartet [and others] appeared" (*New York Clipper*).

• ***March 26, 1893:*** "Colored Prima Donnas as 'Black Pattis,'" "The west can rejoice that it is not being afflicted with the 'Black Patti' business. Kansas, fortunately, hasn't the 'black fever.' Missouri, unfortunately, has. In this state there is a 'Black Emmet' running around loose. In most cases there is more color than music. After a while some fool will call Tom Fortune the 'Black Henry Watterson' and Frances Harper the 'Black Anna Dickinson.'

"In every case our singers carry this black business to extremes. Flora Batson, who has a white husband and who delights in calling herself the 'Black Patti,' should not do so. Wonder if Patti has ever thought of calling herself the 'white Selika?' Of course she hasn't. Then why does Madame Selika call herself the 'Brown Patti?' Then there is Madame Sissieretta Jones with a name that you can't get on a bill-board, who is also the 'Black Patti.' If M. Jones wants to shorten her name she should simmer it down to 'Sis.' That's euphonious and somewhat classical. 'Sis' should make her own name a great fixture among glittering stars. We thought that when the 'Black Jenny Lind' or the 'Black Swan' tumbled off the earth we were safe, so far as disgusting pseudonyms were concerned; but, bless the Lord, we have Patti in three different colors—white, black and brown. After a while we will hear of a 'Red Patti.' Mark the prediction" (*Topeka Weekly Call*).

• ***March 31, 1893 (Findlay, Ohio):*** "Mr. Ben Williams is the most expert performer on the guitar in the city. He is the composer of several beautiful productions" (*Detroit Plaindealer*).

• ***March 31, 1893 (Emporia, Kansas):*** "The harp contest which was given at the skating rink last Thursday night, was quite a success. Mr. Witty, of Osage City, went off with the honor of the championship. The concert which was given in connection with the contest was very lengthy and interesting" (*Kansas State Ledger*).

• ***April 8, 1893 (Louisville, Kentucky):*** "The great singer Mme. Jones sang at Masonic temple. She sang to the 'nigger' roost; it was full to the hatch hold where colored people were crawling in. The lower part was empty, by the absence of the good, nice white folks, for whom it was reserved. Strange to say, there is nothing that these theatre managers can do to keep the colored people away from them; every time the curtain goes up at 8:00 o'clock, over $50 of the black man's money has passed through the hands of Marse John, for the privilege of laughing on top of the house" (*Indianapolis Freeman*).

• ***April 14, 1893:*** "In Pythian Circles," "The presence of brass bands at funerals and anniversaries should be stopped. It is not only a useless expenditure of money, but it brings out a class of followers that one would rather not see" (*Detroit Plaindealer*).

• ***April 21, 1893:*** "It is seldom the case that the three races prominent in the United States—the Caucasian, Indian and Negro—are banded together as equals, where one feels as though he were no more or no less than his companions, but this is a fact with the Utopian quartet, of Bellevue, Neb. In this quartet of singing are one Indian, one Negro and two Caucasians, all of whom look to each other as a necessity to the organization" (*Detroit Plaindealer*).

• ***April 22, 1893 (Decatur, Illinois):*** "William Moore will leave soon for Peru, Ind., where he will join the Wallace Cornet band as slide trombone player. Mr. Moore made a tour of the United States last season" (*Indianapolis Freeman*).

• ***April 28, 1893 (Dayton, Ohio):*** Paul Laurence Dunbar gives his impressions of Detroit: "April 18—My first impression of Detroit was that the city was a haven of rest for foot, eye and ear. Such a smooth level expanse of streets and avenues; such a modest quietness of color; such a harmony of sounds as is seldom seen in any city...

A circumstance that is fresh in my mind occurred one cold night when we were going home late. As we all neared a certain corner, a strain of music broke upon our ears. My friend listened a moment and then exclaimed, 'Ha old fellow, you shall see our "Arkansaw Traveler."' As he spoke a figure rounded the corner and approached us with a swift swinging step. It was an old colored man and he was fiddling and singing for dear life, playing the 'Arkansaw Traveler.' He passed us without a glance, apparently absorbed in his music. Just think of it, in the cold dead of night... this old man innocent of overcoat or gloves going along the street playing and singing. The strange character and strange music as it died away in the darkness with the old man's form, brought a creepy weird feeling over me and I involuntarily edged a little closer to my companion. On the night following, I was to deliver a couple of my poems before the Newsboys Association. I went there prepared to meet a noisy, disorderly crowd of dirty ragamuffins, who would jeer me when I appeared and probably hoot or egg me from the stage. Instead... The boys were dressed neatly and comfortably and disorder was the exception rather than the rule. They have an excellent band of twenty-five pieces, and their playing would shame many more pretentious organizations that I have heard. In addition, I not only had the pleasure of observing the workings of the phonograph, but also of listening to an interesting talk about its inventor, by his life-long friend Col. Thomas" (*Detroit Plaindealer*).

Note: One month earlier the same Detroit Newsboy's Band, under the direction of George W. White, had participated in the second annual concert of the popular black Detroit City Band.

• ***April 29, 1893 (Philadelphia, Pennsylvania):*** "At the Academy of Music, Broad and Locust streets, was held the Championship contest and Festival of Music and Tragedy, under the auspices of Bethel A.M.E. Church, Thursday evening, 13th, inst. The contest was between the Pugsley Brothers, the Tennessee Warblers, of Nashville, and the Hyzer Quartet, of New York City" (*Indianapolis Freeman*).

• ***May 6, 1893 (Charleston, South Carolina):*** "The Odd Fellows of Charleston celebrated their 50th anniversary in grand style April 26th, the line was formed in front of their hall as follows: Chief Marshall, R. G. F. Gibson, mounted; . . . Prof. Clark's Brass Band, eighteen men;... Eclipse Brass Band, fifteen men;... they paraded through the principal streets to

Mt. Zion Church, where the Rev. Welch preached the finest oration ever heard on Odd Fellowship" (*Indianapolis Freeman*).

• ***May 7, 1893:*** "The Afro-American band, of Lincoln, Neb., has accepted a proposition from the merchants of the city to give concerts in the post office square this summer, the season begun May 1st" (*Topeka Weekly Call*).

• ***May 25, 1893 (New Orleans, Louisiana):*** The musical interludes at the annual commencement exercises at New Orleans University included "Guitar solo, 'Imitation of Banjo,' by C. A. Ridley of Houma" (*Southwestern Christian Advocate*).

• ***May 27, 1893 (Helena, Montana):*** "Tom Thumb Wedding," "The auditorium contained a large audience May 11th to witness the Tom Thumb wedding given for the benefit of the A.M.E. Church. The wedding was the point of interest, although there were plenty of good things on the program . . . The Quartette of Messrs. Dorsey, Henderson, Howard and Mitchell sang beautifully . . . The solo, 'Spider and the Fly,' was rendered most charmingly. The duet, 'New-Boom-de-ay,' by Masters and Johnson was splendid" (*Indianapolis Freeman*).

• ***June 3, 1893:*** "Now Booking for Seasons of 1893–94, Parsons & Pool's Famous Ideal 'Uncle Tom's Cabin' Co. and Tennessee Jubilee Singers, in a Legitimate and Complete Version . . . No kickers or drunkards wanted" (*New York Clipper*).

• ***June 3, 1893:*** "Mrs. Helena Brayton, of the South Carolina Board of Woman Managers of the World's Fair, is organizing a band of Negroes to sing plantation melodies at the Exposition" (*Indianapolis Freeman*).

• ***June 10, 1893:*** "Blind Tom No. 2, a sightless Afro American pianist, of Columbus, Ga., is making a tour in the east. He is a wonder also" (*Cleveland Gazette*).

• ***June 10, 1893:*** "Mr. Harry T. Burleigh, of Erie, Pa., and Paul Bolin of Poughkeepsie, N.Y. are the Afro American students at the National Conservatory of Music" (*Cleveland Gazette*).

• ***June 23, 1893:*** "The Blues,"

" 'What's the matter with you today, are you down hearted?'

'I've got de blues.'

'The blues—what do you call the blues?'

'I deavor to tell you or in odder words to splanify de blues to you. You see de blues am dis: when you git up in de mawnin you feel worse, you put you clothing on, mope about and you feel wus, den go down to yer brekfust and you can't eat, and den you feels wuser, you den goes upstars to comb yer har and on looking in de glass you's struck wid de black prospect dats a fore you and den you am worserever den eber.'

A BIG BLACK BOOM. A BIG BLACK BOOM.

THE GRANDEST AND LARGEST AFRO-AMERICAN PRODUCTION EVER PRESENTED TO THE AMERICAN PUBLIC,

SLAVERY DAYS.

75 ARTISTS. 75

Comprising the leading lights of the Afro-American profession; traveling in their own SPECIAL HOTEL PALACE CAR, carrying A CAR LOAD OF SPECIAL SCENERY and intricate mechanical effects, presenting a series of startling and novel surprises, introducing the GRAND MOONLIGHT SCENE ON THE LEVEE, the most original realistic PLANTATION COTTON PICKING SCENE ever presented on any stage.

30 CREOLE BEAUTIES 30

20 WELL KNOWN AND CELEBRATED COMEDIANS 20

Introducing the Original and Only BEN HUNN.

25 Of the Greatest and Most Wonderful Buck and Wing Dancers of the Present Century 25

All of the Above headed by the World's Famous

ECLIPSE QUARTET, the celebrated HARRIS SISTERS, and the original ARKWRIGHT FAMILY.

This will positively be the most novel production presented the coming season. Every sheet of paper used will be absolutely new and special and ALL LITHOGRAPH WORK. The assortment second to none of any enterprise before the public. The above production under the personal supervision of MAJOR BEN F. PAYNE. Managers having open time for this stupendous aggregation address immediately, as time is filling rapidly.

J. ED. HURST,
General Manager of the
ABE SPITZ AMUSEMENT CO.,
Owners and Managers.

Home office:
673 Washington St., Room 4.
Boston, Mass.,

Also of the
BIJOU THEATRE, Lowell, Mass.
MUSIC HALL, Lynn, Mass.
GAIETY THEATRE, Brockton, Mass.
DUPREZ AMERICAN FOLLY CO.,
Now organizing for the coming season.

The name selected by the ABE SPITZ AMUSEMENT CO. for which a prize of $25 was offered is the AMERICAN FOLLY CO., suggested by H. J. FOLSOM.

WANTED, Colored Artists in All Branches.

Address as above.

New York Clipper, *June 10, 1893.*

Dear reader did you ever have 'de blues? I pity you if you ever get them" (*Kansas City American Citizen*).

Note: Here is evidence of the currency of the word "blues" in the 1893 vernacular of what is indicated by the dialect as a substratum of black society.

• ***July 1, 1893:*** "Our Musical People," "One of the most accomplished musical families in the race are 'the Harts' of Indianapolis. The father, Henry, is a virtuoso . . . also a composer of Negro music . . . author of 'Carve Dat Possum,' 'Dafney, Do You Love Me,' etc." (*Indianapolis Freeman*).

Note: "Carve Dat Possum" is more generally associated with Sam Lucas, whose name appears on the published music.

• ***July 1, 1893:*** "Our Musical People," "Prof. Ruby Shelton, pianist, late of Pugsley's Tennessee Warblers, severed his relations with that company, in Philadelphia, and is now resting at his home in Indiana" (*Indianapolis Freeman*).

• ***July 1, 1893 (Vicksburg, Mississippi):*** "Odd Fellow's Day was well conducted by Pedestal, Brotherhood Lodge No. 1844, gave a grand celebration and street parade Thursday, June 22nd, headed by Prof. J. M. Blowes Cornet Band . . . The procession formed at Bethel A. M. E. Church Hall [and marched to the Odd Fellows Hall] . . . At night, a musical concert was given under the management of Mrs. S. P. Dozin, Prof. M. F. Reynolds, cornetist; W. M. Killy clarionetist; R. H. Brooks, violinist; Mrs. S. P. Dozin, pianist" (*Indianapolis Freeman*).

• ***July 1, 1893:*** "Our Musical People," "Blanche D. Washington, teacher of piano, guitar, banjo and singing, is proprietor of a school of music, 120 W. 26, N.Y." (*Indianapolis Freeman*).

• ***July 29, 1893 (Houston, Texas):*** "The late [*sic*] 'Sin Killing Griffin' expects to build a $4,000 church soon in 1st ward to be known as Independent Baptist church. He is invited over by Rev. E. Lee to conduct a sin killing revival at Mt. Vernon. Rev. Griffin is attracting much attention among white and colored. You can hear the Negro 'Spurgeon' on market square every Saturday evening" (*Indianapolis Freeman*).

• ***August 11, 1893 (Mexico, Missouri):*** "Mexico is only a city of the third class but her people are strictly of the first class and can take care of a crowd of strange visitors to perfection.

"The 23rd Annual Session of the grand lodge of Missouri United Brothers of Friendship and Sisters of Mysterious Ten, convened in this city last Tuesday morning at Hiner's Hall . . . The early part of the week was devoted to the transaction of business . . . A grand celebration and picnic was tendered the 'Grand Lodge' on Friday the 4th. The picnic . . . was held in a beautiful grove 1/4 mile east of the public square. On the morning of the picnic at 10 o'clock, a special train from Columbia bearing over four hundred excursionists arrived.

"About one hour later another came in from Moberly bringing over three hundred people. Each regular train on both the Wabash and C. and A., brought in visitors by the score from all points of the state. About noon, the procession . . . paraded the principal streets of the city thence to picnic ground. The participants in the parade arranged as follows:

"Mexico Cornet band, followed by members of the Mexico Star Lodge, next came the Sturgeon Band followed by visiting lodges after which came the Huntsville Band . . . On the picnic ground every-thing was extremely pleasant. The three bands furnished splendid music during the day . . . There was plenty of music and dancing . . . There were games of base-ball between Mexico and visiting teams. We did not learn the exact score, however, Mexico 'got there' at night. Mexico's celebrated, 'out of sight' second Gilmore band, arrayed in uniform . . . assembled on the public square and treated a great throng of people to several choice musical selections . . . The band then marched to Hiner's hall where a magnificent entertainment was given in honor of the installation of grand officers" (*Kansas City American Citizen*).

• ***August 11, 1893:*** "A Days Outing," "A Party of our Society young people spent a day at beautiful Fairmount Park last week and report having had a very enjoyable time under the shade of the many wide-spreading Oak and Elm trees . . . The most enjoyable feature of the entire affair was the elegant luncheon served at 5:30 P.M. by the ladies . . . although deprived of the pleasures of the Beach on account of color, after seeing the other attractions of the Park well watched with interest the bathers until the sun had sank to rest in the West, and the dim shades of twilight darkened into night and the moon had risen over the treetops in the distance casting a silver ray of mellow light upon the lake when all were reminded of home by hearing the soft strains of music 'The old folks at home' the sound floated out upon the night winds with a wonderful effect. Upon investigating we found a colored quartette present from K.C. seated in front of the 'Great Crystal Maze' where they rendered some excellent music, as the echo of the song 'My old Kentucky Home' died away all were leaving for home, feeling much improved by the days outing" (*Kansas City American Citizen*).

KNIGHTS OF PYTHIAS

GRAND CONCERT

AT

BETHEL CHURCH,

Cor. 30th and Dearborn Sts.

Wednesday Eve., August 16, '93.

For benefit Hannibal Lodge, No. 6, K. of P.

ARTISTS:

MISS RACHEL WALKER,

Soprano, Cleveland, Ohio.

Miss Valetta Winslow, Delsartist, San Francisco, Cal.

Miss Ednorah Nahar, Reader, Boston, Mass.

Miss Gertrude Jackson, Pianist, Chicago, Ill.

Mr. H. T. Burleigh, Baritone, New York City, N. Y.

Mr. Joseph Douglass, Violinist, Washington, D. C.

Mr. W. A. McCormick, Whistler, Riverside, Ill.

PAGE'S MANDOLIN ORCHESTRA, Englewood, Ill.

The Uniform Ranks of Knights of Pythias have been invited to attend the concert in full uniform.

CLEOPATRA

will be given by Miss Nahar in gorgeous costume, assisted by the Orchestra and Whistler, the same piece that was given at Philadelphia at the Academy of Music Nov. 17th, 1890, before 5000 people.

Admission 50c. Reserved Seats 75c.

Sale of seats will begin in the Church, Saturday, Aug. 12.

Freeman, *August 12, 1893.*

• ***August 19, 1893 (Manchester, Virginia):*** "Prof. Francis Nelson, who has won for himself great fame as a tenor songster, will leave for Newark, N.J. with his quartette, 26th inst., where they will remain ten days. From there they go to Boston, and on the way back they will stop at the cities of New York, Philadelphia, Baltimore and Washington.

Mr. W. H. Bailey, who has had great experience as a traveling man, has been chosen manager of the singers and will join them at New York. This quartette is composed of the most advanced singers of this city, and have the honor of being called the best in the state. Wherever they have competed with others they've carried off the laurels . . . Messrs. A. Q. Powell, basso; W. H. Hatcher silver-tongued baritone; N. G. Robinson, soprano; Miss Mollie Gaines, sub soprano; Mrs. Margaret Harris, alto; Mr. Francis Nelson, tenor. Nor can too much praise be given Mr. Nelson who is endowed by nature as a songster and instructor" (*Richmond Planet*).

• ***August 26, 1893:*** "Variety and Minstrelsy," "The McKanlass Colored Specialty Co., No. 1, opened July 20 and report good business through Wisconsin. They enter Minnesota this week. The roster: Prof. W. H. McKanlass, manager and proprietor; Trixie Sylvester, Fannie Mack, Maggie Johnson,

Chas. Miller, J. H. Ross, Prof. Sartoli, pianist, and Edwin Paterson, advance" (*New York Clipper*).

• ***September 1, 1893:*** "W. L. Eagleson, a colored man, thinks that the craze for celebrations, street parades, and brass bands has already lasted too long, and that the leading colored men, especially the ministers of the gospel, should protest earnestly against so many picnics, excursions, and emancipation celebrations. With the winter near at hand and no work to be had, men standing around unable to get work, it is a crying shame to induce them to spend what little money they may have on some excursion or celebration by advertising that Fred Douglass, Langston, Bruce and others will speak at such and such a place, when money-making is the only object those men have in mind, utterly indifferent as to whether these poor people freeze or starve later on" (*Topeka Daily Capital*, reproduced in *Kansas City American Citizen*).

• ***September 16, 1893:*** "Mme. [Sissieretta] Jones sang to 300,000 at the Buffalo Exposition, who stood in chairs and cheered the great artist. At Hayti during the revolution, Mme. Jones quelled a turbulent mob of 10,000 people, merely by the singing of 'Nearer my God to Thee'" (*Indianapolis Freeman*).

• ***September 23, 1893 (Selma, Alabama):*** "Chathan [*sic*, Cheatham] Bros.' Black Face Concert at Zion Hall on Green Street Monday September 11. For the benefit of the I. B. and C. Lodge with 14 stars was quite a success" (*Indianapolis Freeman*).

• ***September 29, 1893:*** "Missouri Items," "The Clinton Military Band is certainly a worthy institution. The members of the band are going to give an entertainment to raise funds and they haven't attacked 'Ye Old Folks Concert,' a 'Dream of Ancient Greece,' 'The Union Spy,' 'A Banker's Daughter,' the 'Broom Drill,' or 'The Tennessee Scout.' It will just be an old fashioned concert and the boys will play 'Number 113,' 'Clayton's March,' and a few of the old timers that bring joy to the old fashioned heart" (*Kansas City American Citizen*).

• ***September 30, 1893 (Cleveland, Ohio):*** "Last week Thursday evening Mr. and Mrs. Charles L. Seymour and his two little daughters and brother were very finely serenaded by the 'Clover Leaf' quartette. The singing was very fine, and Mr. and Mrs. Seymour regretted exceedingly that the lateness of the hour prevented their inviting them in and entertaining them in a manner which their kindness suggested. However, if the quartette will notify Mr. Seymour of their next intended visit, he will be prepared to entertain them in royal style" (*Cleveland Gazette*).

• ***October 7, 1893 (Yellow Springs, Ohio):*** "A Harmonica society has been organized by the young people" (*Cleveland Gazette*).

• ***October 14, 1893 (Philadelphia, Pennsylvania):*** "At the Baptist Pastor's meeting, on Monday, the reverend gentlemen, after they had concluded their debate, were entertained by the St. Bartholomew Colored Quartette, of New Orleans, La. On Monday evening there was given at Zion A. M. E. one of the most interesting entertainments that any Afro-American would desire to attend. It was the concert given by Prof. Nutlos' choir, supported by Mme. M. S. Jones, the famous 'Black Patti' of the Negro race. 'Blind Tom No. 2,' under the management of Rev. Manly, was far inferior to our 'Blind Tom,' the original. The Manly instrumental trio did very clever work. Mr. [Christmas] Evans, son of the late Senator, Jos. P. Evans, of Petersburg, Va., made the audience roar with his imitations on the Harmonica of different instruments, and an exact imitation of Gilmore's famous band" (*Indianapolis Freeman*).

• ***October 21, 1893:*** "Mr. and Mrs. Al. E. Anderson, of the 'Slavery Days' Co., report having met with success since the opening of the season. Mr. Anderson has produced a new big four song and dance, entitled 'Four Night

Ramblers,' introducing Jerry Mills, Henry Winfred and Frank Sutton. The act consists of tumbling and high kicking. Mrs. Mamie Smith is . . . singing 'Do, My Huckleberry, Do' and 'Two Little Girls in Blue.' The show is *en route* west" (*New York Clipper*).

Note: This is not the Mamie Smith who recorded "Crazy Blues."

• ***OCTOBER 28, 1893:*** "A mass meeting of citizens was held at Lake Charles, La., Oct. 18 and the following resolutions were passed: '*Resolved*, That the citizens of Lake Charles do publicly and solemnly protest against the wanton insult heaped upon the name of Louisiana's daughters by a certain wandering troupe of negro female half breeds, who are advertising themselves as "The Creole Beauties," and thus casting a slur upon the name of the Creole families of Louisiana that have always been the pride of the State. We urgently request all fair minded citizens who are unwilling thus publicly to pronounce the fair daughters of Louisiana as of mixed blood to resolutely turn their backs on this slanderous show. . . No violence was shown the company here, but at New Iberia the situation was so threatening that they jumped their engagement. At Lafayette they were waited upon by a committee, headed by the Mayor, who informed them that they could not play there and had better leave the town at once. A mob collected around the car in which the alleged Creoles were, and there were threats to burn it if they did not leave. The manager decided it best to get out of Creole country at once, and left for New Orleans. They have concluded it safest not to appear in Louisiana'" (*New York Clipper*).

Note: Especially in Louisiana, the word "Creole" has had a history of antagonistically different meanings. The defenders of the "fair daughters of Louisiana" were of the opinion that "creole" defined Louisianians of exclusively European descent, and this meaning has not died out. However, it is more commonly applied to Louisianians of African descent whose "New World" language and culture were originally French.[67]

• ***NOVEMBER 4, 1893:*** A lengthy review of a "star concert" in Chicago notes, in part: "The National Conservatory of Music, New York City, has appointed one of its Afro-American pupils, Mr. Harry T. Burleigh, of Erie, Pa., to a position as teacher of vocal music in one of its departments. The fame of the young man's distinction preceded him, and when he appeared in our midst as a concert singer, much was expected from him. His stage presence somewhat cooled the ardor of our expectations, for the nonchalance of his bearing is quite detracting. The fact of a careful vocal training, however, is established at once by the manner in which he treats such songs as Massanet's *Vision Fair*, and the *Torador's Song* by Bizet. Mr. Burleigh has a robust baritone voice, of wide range, and good quality, especially in the middle register. The best wishes of us all accompany him in his new work" (*Cleveland Gazette*).

• ***NOVEMBER 4, 1893:*** "The Queen of Song," "A Fair Criticism of Mrs. Flora Batson Bergen and Others of Our Leading Vocalists," "If a sweet, resonant voice, and popular applause be the criterion, then Madame Flora Batson deserves the name, 'Queen of Song.' For during the past summer she has sung her ballads with as much feeling, and to as large audiences as when her fame was new. Ballad singing has its own proper place in music, and accordingly there is a certain standard for judging it. By this alone must ballad singers be judged, as long as they carol their simple songs. But when they step out of their sphere into the realm of the opera and oratorio, then are they made liable to severer criticism. Now I would not for a moment take ought from the glory of Madame Bergen's success, but since she assays to sing such songs as *Fleur des Alpes*, whose technical difficulties are much too much for her powers of execution, one must deplore the fact that she has not braved the severe requirements of voice culture, but has been so easily contented to wear laurels won almost without an effort" (*Cleveland Gazette*).

• ***November 4, 1893:*** "World Players," "Edmond Dede, of Paris, Fr., was among the rescued passengers of the steamship *Marseille,* which went ashore at Galveston, Tex., Oct. 19. He is a full blooded negro, and was born in the city of New Orleans in 1827. He left New Orleans forty years ago, and has since then made his home in Paris and Bordeaux. His card introduces him as a composer of music and a chief of orchestra of the Grand Theatre of Bordeaux, a member of the Society of Authors and Composers of Dramatic Music, and a professor de violin. Among the many works composed by him are 'Ellis Nebaha,' 'Les Faux Mondains,' 'Le Senstire,' 'Apics le Mice,' 'La Noyes,' 'Diane et Acteon,' and 'Triomphe de Bacchus.' In all he has composed over two hundred waltzes, operas, ballets and other different musical compositions. He was on his way to New Orleans when the *Marseille* foundered. He lost his baggage and many valuable pieces of music of his own composition, but succeeded in saving his violin . . . He is the guest of his cousin during his stay at Galveston" (*New York Clipper*).

• ***November 4, 1893:*** "The Colored Professional Club, of [New York City], gave a social on the evening of Oct. 29 in honor of their President, Ike Hines, in which many noted colored performers participated. Among those present were: Ike Hines and wife, Tom McIntosh and wife, Billy Jackson and wife, Gussie L. Davis, Harry S. Eaton, Billy Young, George Bailey, Florence Hines, Mocking Bird Rube, Sissieretta Jones (the Black Patti), Wm. Mack, Bert Loder, Jube Johnson, M. Porter and others" (*New York Clipper*).

Note: According to a 1906 *Freeman* retrospective, Isaac "Ike" Hines was born in 1850 in Baltimore, Maryland, entered "the profession" as a member of the original Twilight Quartet, and founded his Professional Club in 1886.[68] Ike Hines's Professional Club eventually acquired legendary proportions. As Perry Bradford recalled in his 1965 autobiography, *Born With the Blues,* "The originator of the hot spots, afterwards called cabarets and known today as night clubs, was Ike Hines, a Negro entertainer who was a former banjo player with Hicks and Sawyers Georgia Minstrels . . . Ike's new style of entertainment was started in the basement of an old Greenwich Village house . . . Ike's place had become so popular in 1884 that he hired a manager and changed the name to Ike's Professional Club."[69] James Weldon Johnson identified Ike Hines's Professional Club as the model for the "club" described in his *Autobiography of an Ex-Coloured Man.*[70]

• ***November 18, 1893 (Cleveland, Ohio):*** "A Splendid Concert," "Mt. Zion church was pack last Tuesday evening. An exceptionally enthusiastic audience greeted the new race concert company, which until recently was known as 'Edith Pond's Midnight Stars'—a very poor name. The company is now under the management of its excellent reader and has been re-named the 'Ednorah Nahar Concert Company.' Miss Pond's connection with it was severed some weeks ago and it is being run on the co-operative plan. The following programme was rendered:

"Piano Solo, Mr. Fred W. Burch; Baritone Solo, 'The Warrior' (Pinsuti), Mr. Wm. E. Elkins; Soprano Solo, 'O Dolce Concerto' (Kucken), Miss Rachel Walker; Violin Solo, 'Gypsy Melodies' (Sarasale), Mr. Joseph H. Douglass; Reading, 'The Pauper's Story,' Miss Ednorah Nahar; Baritone Solo, 'Thy Sentinel Am I,' Mr. Wm. E. Elkins; Soprano Solo, 'Thou Brilliant Bird' (David), Miss Rachel Walker; Violin Solo, 'Il Trovatore' (Verdi), Mr. Joseph H. Douglass; Reading, 'The Chariot Race' (Wallace),

Miss Ednorah Nahar; Vocal Duet, 'L'Addio' (Donizetti), Miss Walker and Mr. Elkins" (*Cleveland Gazette*).

• ***November 25, 1893 (Nashville, Tennessee):*** "The Tennessee Warblers left for Louisville, Friday 10th. Mrs. Emma L. Pugsley, wife of L. E. Pugsley, the proprietor and manager of the Tennessee Warblers, died Saturday 4th. Madame Bessie Fort Smith, the colored female clarionet blower, gave a successful entertainment Wednesday night, November 15th, at Jackson street Congregational church . . . Mr. Daniels, the bass singer of the famous Tennessee Warblers, was defeated in a contest with Mr. J. W. Johnson, of Georgia . . . The Apollo quartette (double) lives again" (*Indianapolis Freeman*).

• ***December 16, 1893:*** "It was rumored this past week that the Nahar Concert Company was stranded in Springfield, Ohio" (*Cleveland Gazette*).

• ***December 23, 1893 (Chillicothe, Ohio):*** "Some of our boys, between the ages of 12 and 21, who should be attending school, have organized a minstrel troupe and are traveling over Ross County making monkeys of themselves. Last week they gave an exhibition of their talents (?) here, and all who participated had their faces blackened, so it is said, not being satisfied with nature's work" (*Cleveland Gazette*).

• ***December 23, 1893 (New York City):*** " 'Uncle Tom's Cabin,' introducing Peter Jackson in the character of Uncle Tom, is this week's bill at Jacob's Theatre. The opening night audience was fairly large and evinced their appreciation of the manner in which Peter Jackson and Chas. F. Davies assumed their respective roles. During the action of the play Jackson sparred three rounds with Joe Chovinski [*sic*, Choynski]" (*New York Clipper*).

• ***December 30, 1893:*** "The Haxpie Colored Georgia Minstrels opened at Paterson, N.J., Dec. 25 . . . The performance is under the direction of Billy Young, late of McCabe and Young" (*New York Clipper*).

• ***December 30, 1893:*** "Towell and Young and George Wilson joined H. S. Eaton's Afro-American Vaudeville Co. at Albany, N.Y." (*New York Clipper*).

Note: This may be an early reference to singer Jim Towel, who became known in early-1900s vaudeville as a member of the Majestic Trio,[71] and who in 1928 made a commercial recording of the 1894 Gussie L. Davis composition, "I've Been Hoodooed."[72]

• ***December 30, 1893:*** "In spite of hard times, the 'Slavery Days' Co. still keeps moving. Florence Hines, the male impersonator, joined at Philadelphia. Georgia Douglas, leading soprano of the company, was compelled to return to her home in Boston, owing to indisposition" (*New York Clipper*).

"Folk-Lore and Ethnology," "Coonjine" and "Hully-Gully"

At Hampton Institute in the Tidewater section of Virginia, the summer of 1893 was punctuated by lively discussions of the "Dvorák Statement" and the future of "Negro music." Hampton's tenured music professor, F. G. Rathbun, agreed with Dvorák that the slave melodies constituted "the only real American music," but he doubted they could be made "more beautiful in their symphonic treatment and form than now in their old time simplicity," and he warned that, under the influence of "our sight singing teacher, our English teacher and teacher of elocution," the "old time way" of rendering them was "rapidly passing away."[73] The Dvorák Statement and F. G. Rathbun's admonition gave a heightened sense of urgency and mission to efforts already afoot to create a "Hampton Folk-Lore Society."

The prime motivator of the Hampton Folk-Lore Society was Alice Mabel Bacon, a white teacher who was inspired by the recent example of the American Folk-Lore Society.[74] With some twenty members, mostly African Americans, students and recent graduates of the school, the Hampton Folk-Lore Society held its first monthly meeting on December 11, 1893.[75] The group published a statement of purpose in the December 1893 edition of Hampton Institute's monthly journal, *Southern Workman*, and the statement also appeared in the American Folk-Lore Society's *Journal of American Folk-Lore*. Moreover, it was picked up in the January 27, 1894, edition of the *Freeman*, where it acquired the headline, "Plea for Negro Folk Lore—We Must Imitate the Example of Other People's and Preserve from the Rust of Oblivion the Traditions, Habits and Sayings of our Forefathers."

The statement called for "intelligent observers," especially "educated colored people" in the South—preachers, teachers and doctors—whose work "brings them into close contact with the simple, old-time ways of their own people," to assist in the preservation process: "We want to get all such persons interested in this work, and get them to note down their observations and . . . send them into the editor of the *Southern Workman*. We hope sooner or later to join all such contributors together into a Folk-Lore Society and to make our work of value to the whole world, but our beginning will be in a corner of the *Southern Workman* and we have liberty to establish there a department of Folk-Lore [and] Ethnology."[76]

The Hampton Folk-Lore Society's pathbreaking "Folk-Lore and Ethnology" column made its debut in a corner of the January 1894 edition of *Southern Workman*, and it continued in monthly installments for the next six years.[77] The installment of February 1894 told how "During the month preceding an effort had been made to get hold of any strange words used in games or elsewhere, and 'Hully Gully,' 'Oli ola' and 'Coonjine' had been gathered as a nucleus for further study . . . Comparison of notes among members of the society developed the information that 'coonjine' is used on the Mississippi River for a peculiar motion of the body used apparently to lighten or hasten the labor of loading and unloading. 'Hully-gully,' or 'Hull da gull' as it appears in a report from Kentucky, is a phrase used in a game. The player holds up a handful of grain or parched corn, shakes it before his opponent and says, 'Hully gully, how many?' "

This early report points to occupational labor and children's games as particular starting points for African American folklore. The fact that both "hully gully" and "coonjine" evolved into dance songs further illuminates a principal trail of historical continuity in American folk and popular music.

The information in the February 1894 Southern Workman regarding "hully gully" was echoed in an article on "Ozark Mountain Party-Games" in a 1936 edition of the *Journal of American Folk-Lore*: "The game known as 'Hully-gully' is . . . usually played with grains of parched corn, chinquapins or hazelnuts . . . It is really a gambling game . . . One player shakes a number of nuts or grains of corn or whatever . . . in his closed hand, crying 'Hully-gully handful—how many?' "[78]

In 1960 a dance song titled "(Baby) Hully Gully" became a national hit recording for the Olympics, a black rock-and-roll vocal group from California.[79] In their book *Jazz Dance*, Marshall and Jean Stearns classified the "Hully-Gully" with the post-1960 "wave of dances" that "crashed over American dance floors during and after the Twist."[80] It was also a lingering folk motif documented by the Hampton Folk-Lore Society in 1894.

"Coonjine" has been more often cited for its "ancient lineage." For some reason, writers and folklorists have habitually romanticized this idiosyncratic work-motion. The theme of the "coonjining roustabout" comes forth with an unaccounted-for sense of familiarity in the 1931 novel *John Henry*, by Roark Bradford,[81] who may be better remembered for his 1928 collection of "humorous" black folk sermons entitled *Ol' Man Adam an' His Chillun*, upon which the famous play *The Green Pastures* is based. Bradford's *John Henry* is set in the mythical "Black River country" of Louisiana, where the title character is presented as a "cotton-rollin' roustabout" and "coonjinin' fool." Indeed, while loading five-hundred-pound bales of cotton onto a riverboat, Bradford's John Henry *invents* the "coonjine" by putting "a weave in his hips, and a buck in his back" to compensate for the "heave and pitch" of the gangplank underfoot.[82]

In 1939 *John Henry* was adapted as a Broadway musical with Paul Robeson in the title role and a supporting cast that included Josh White as the itinerant songster "Blind Lemon," Leonard de Paur as the "walking boss," and Samuel A. Floyd as one of several "workers."[83]

Folklorist Mary Wheeler's 1941 book, *Steamboatin' Days: Folk Songs of the River Packet Era*, informs that "the words and melodies of the songs [in her book] were taken down from the singing of old Negroes who in their youth worked on the boats."[84] To illustrate that the "life of the steamboat rouster was not an easy one," Wheeler offered this transcription of a "roustabout song":

> *My knee bones is achin',*
> *My shoulder is so'—*
> *When I make this trip*
> *Ain't gonna make no mo'.*
> *Coonjine, nigger, coonjine.*[85]

In her chapter "Dance Songs," Wheeler suggested: "It is possible that the Negro songs known as 'Coonjines' originally referred to the old African dance, the 'Counjai.' But to the 'steamboat nigger' the Coonjine is the combination song and dance that is associated with handling freight. The 'plank walk' springs under a heavy weight . . . To avoid jarring, the feet are dragged along the stage plank, accompanied by a song that takes its rhythm from the shuffling feet and swaying shoulders."[86]

Wheeler's reference to "the old African dance, the 'Counjai' " invokes the 1867 collection *Slave Songs of the United States*, which describes and gives examples of a genre of Louisiana Creole songs that "were sung to a simple dance, a sort of minuet, called the *Coonjai*; the name and the dance are probably both of African origin."[87] When George Washington Cable noted some of the same Creole dance songs in his 1886 article, "The Dance in Place Congo," he gave them a French spelling—"Counjaille."[88]

Wheeler was among the first to suggest a historical link from "Counjai" to "Counjaille" to "Coonjine."[89] The supposed connection between the dance described by Cable and the work movement mythologized by Roark Bradford has, at times, provided excessive leeway for willful conjecture. In *They All Played Ragtime*, authors Rudi Blesh and Harriet Janis described, without recourse to documentation, how, during the mid-1880s, St. Louis, Missouri's "levee apron rang with the . . . shouts of roustabouts coonjining to the plink-plank of banjos," and they boldly concluded that George Washington Cable's "Counjaille" was "the same 'coonjine rag dance' of the levee men and boatmen all up and down the Mississippi, the Missouri, and the Ohio."[90] The provocative conjunction "coonjine rag dance" appears to have been the exclusive product of Blesh and Janis's poetic license.

Lawrence Gushee's 1994 article, "The Nineteenth-Century Origins of Jazz," resurrects an anecdotal account of the origin of ragtime that black Chicago-based sheet-music retailer and newspaper columnist Will "Juli Jones" Foster had put forth in a 1911 edition of the *Freeman*: "Sometime along in the early eighties a triple combination of song, walk and dance by the name of 'Coon Jine, Baby, Coon Jine,' sprang up among roustabouts on the many boats and spread like wildfire. The song and dance found its way to the levee resorts, where all prosperous houses had old hand-me-down square pianos with a half dozen broken keys; yet these instruments were considered jewels in those days, as it only required a few keys to play the 'Coon Jine.' This is where the original ragtime started from—the quick action of the right-hand fingers playing the 'Coon Jine.'"

Conceding that Will Foster's "single-origin theory is obviously inadequate to explain a multifaceted phenomenon like ragtime," Gushee relates it to an observation made by writer-adventurer Lafcadio Hearn in an 1881 letter to musicologist Henry Edward Krehbiel: "Did you ever hear negroes play the piano by ear? There are several curiosities here [in New Orleans], Creole negroes . . . They use the piano exactly like a banjo." Ringing in the alleged "Counjaille" connection, Gushee cautiously "imagines that Hearn's 'Creole Negroes' who played the piano like the banjo had 'Coon Jine' in their repertory," and that "the complex history" of this "particular dance song" just may "involve New Orleans."[91]

By 1893, when the Hampton Folk-Lore Society issued its initial "plea for Negro folk lore," the "coonjine" theme had made its way to the marketplace. "Can't-Yer-Koon-Jine" was published from New York City that year, billed as an "Ethiopian Eccentricity":

Can't yer koon jine, baby,
can't yer koon jine,
Can't yer koon jine good and strong,
Who's a gwan to do my koon-jining
When I am dead and gone.[92]

The "coonjine" theme persisted well into the twentieth century on sheet music and sound recordings. In 1919 the famous blues and jazz composer Spencer Williams put out a song called "Kune-Jine":

Kune-jine Baby Kune-jine,
Kune-jine Baby Kune-jine,
Tra, tra, tra, tra, tra, tra, tra.
Moonshine maybe Moonshine,
Moonshine maybe Moonshine,
Tra, tra, tra, tra, tra, tra, tra.[93]

In 1922 "Kune-Jine" was recorded by Anton Lada's Louisiana Orchestra, with Lada coming in for credit as co-composer.[94] In 1929 a variation titled "Kunjine Baby" was released by race recording stars "Georgia Tom" Dorsey, Tampa Red (Hudson Whittaker), and Frankie "Half Pint" Jaxon, under the unique sobriquet "The Black Hill Billies."[95] That "Coonjine" was taken up by "white hillbillies" is confirmed by fiddler Bill Shepard's January 29, 1932, recording session for Gennett, which included "Coon Jine My Lover" among the unissued takes. A distinguishing feature of the Black Hill Billies' version is its interpretation of the core refrain:

Oh, coonjine, baby, coonjine,
Mama don't allow me to coonjine,
Coonjine, baby, coonjine,
That's my baby now.

Though it is absent from Spencer Williams's version, the "mama don't allow" theme, which informed W. C. Handy's first published blues composition, appears to have also been familiarly associated with "Coonjine." Newman I. White's 1928 book, *American Negro Folk-Songs*, includes a version collected in Cabarrus

County, North Carolina, in 1919. The transcription is skewed, but it is "Coonjine" nevertheless:

Coon shine, ladies, coon shine.
Coon shine on the floor.
O my pa don't 'low me to coonshine
And my ma don't 'low me to try.
Git up in the morning 'fore day,
Coon shine on de sly.[96]

At least four versions of "Coonjine" can be found in the field recordings at the Library of Congress. One is by African American banjo player Sidney Stripling. It was collected by John Work III, of Fisk University, in 1941, at the second annual Folk Music Festival sponsored by Fort Valley State College in Fort Valley, Georgia.[97] Stripling's "Coonjine" is a humorous pastiche of referential phrases:

I'm gwine to build me a new house
Sixteen stories high,
When I get my new house done
I'm gwine to marry a wife.
Mama don't allow me to coonjine,
Papa don't allow me to try,
But every time I get the chance,
Gonna coonjine anyhow.
Hey, baby, coonjine,
Hey, baby, good moonshine,
Mama don't allow me to coonjine.
I'm gwine to build me a new house,
Sixteen stories high,
Every story of my house
Will be made of pumpkin pie.[98]

The "African Prince" Phenomenon, 1891–1895

• ***September 19, 1891 (Yazoo City, Mississippi):*** "Jave Tip O'Tip, the Zulu Prince, (?) a strange young man of some 18 or 20 years, is in the city professing to be a native African of the fearless Zulu tribe. He says that he has been in this country for six years and that he has three sisters attending school at Washington, D.C., from whence he came to travel throughout the country to lecture and acquire means to return to school again. We question his identity and would be glad to hear from the Washington correspondent respecting Jave Tip O'Tip" (*Indianapolis Freeman*).

• ***October 2, 1891 (St. Louis, Missouri):*** "An African Prince," "There is a bona fide Prince royal in the city, though he is not even remotely connected with the illustrious family of Hanover, which is related to every royal family in Europe. In fact, the Prince might be referred to as 'a new coon in town' for the very potent fact that he is of African extraction. He is a full-blooded Zulu from Capetown, Africa, and his full name and title runs as follows: Jave Tip-O-Tip, Victoria Flosse, Zulu, Dungan Omish, son of King Cetowa Totowa . . . A Republic reporter called yesterday afternoon . . . and was ushered into the presence of the Prince, who answers to the prosaic alias of 'Mr. Dempsey Powers' in this country . . .

The following are the first lines of the well-known Gospel hymn, 'Come to Jesus,' which the Prince sang for the reporter in good voice:

Ener Jessebar,
I Quebarlar,
I Aquarmar,
I Adarwar,
I Baouarnar,
Chorus—Sarnar, Sarnar.

The translation of the above lines is as follows:

Come to Jesus;
He will save you;
He is willing;
He is ready;
Won't you trust Him?
Chorus—Just now! Just now!

While not by any means an expert in the use of the Queen's English, the Prince makes himself understood, and says he picked it up during his first six months in this country. He said the Yulas calls a wife a 'mushman'; a husband, a 'gorgman,' their babies, 'pickaninnies'... The Prince will be introduced this evening to the congregation of Wesley A.M.E. Chapel on Wash street, and he will probably remain in the city for two weeks delivering several lectures" (*St. Louis Republic*, quoted in *Kansas City American Citizen*).

• ***October 9, 1891:*** "The *Republic's* African Prince, about whom we published a great deal, turns out to be a first class fraud. The Prince seems to be a South Carolina black man who learned of Africa from a showman... Brother Easton in the Race Problem, his paper published in St. Louis says:

'A grand time was enjoyed Sunday by the large congregation at the reopening of the Chambers Street Baptist church... We were amused when a young man, with whom we have

There is in the city at this time a real copper colored Kaffer African, of the Kaffer Tribe of southeast Africa. He attracted a good audience at St. John's Church Monday evening, despite the cold night. His name is heralded all over the United States. Commonly known as Oskazuma.

The following is what the different newspapers say of him:

The Globe, St. Louis: Oskazuma lectured here at the Seville Museum, which pleased all.

The Defender, Jackson, Miss.: A real live African is in the city and lectured at Representative Hall last night. He is entertaining.

Officers of the Mississippi Penitentiary: Oskazuma interested us all here last night. —T. B. Stone and M. L. Jenkins, wardens.

From Verona, Alabama, News: Oskazuma exhibited and lectured at St. John's Church, West Selma, to a full house. He is an honorable gentldman, and we recommend him to the public. [Signed]

Ministers of Selma.

Mayor of Gunnersville, Ala.: Oskazuma lectured here last evening on the customs and habits of his country. He is certainly wonderful.

B. Coman, Mayor.

Blount Springs, Ala.: Oskazuma lectured here last night to a full house and it was instructive and amusing.—Prop. Blount Springs Hotel.

St. Joe Musee, Bert Martin, Mgr.—I have employed the services of Oskazuma, and will need his services again.

The copper colored Kaffer from South Africa, has been in the United States several years. He attended school in this country three years, and four years in England. Rev. J. C. C. Owens was the first to secure his services in this city, and gave him a good house, considering the inclement weather. He will lecture at all our churches before he leaves the city, and exhibit his articles of curosity, He is to be at B Street Baptist church soon. Look for him, watch for him. See hand bills.

[Topeka] Kansas State Ledger, *February 23, 1894.*

Prof. Ulato Monszaro,
the South African Prince who plays on
Sixty Different Musical Instruments.
Has a voice of wonderful range and compass. Besides the musical treat the audience will be lectured to on
African Custom
by an African in native Garb.

Richmond Planet, *July 22, 1893.*

had some acquaintance, was introduced as a young African Prince, just from Africa. The young man in question was employed by Barnum some years ago to act the "Zulu youth" in "the greatest show on earth," and so well did he learn his part that he concluded he was "just from Africa" sure enough . . . He knows no more about African customs and habits than an unlettered rustic does about Blackstone's Commentaries'" (*Kansas City American Citizen*).

• ***July 1, 1892 (Cincinnati, Ohio):*** "Tip-O-Tip, the Zulu from South Africa who has been attending the Central Tennessee State College, at Nashville, lectured last Tuesday evening at Union Baptist church, on the 'habits and customs of his people'" (*Detroit Plaindealer*).

• ***August 26, 1892 (Covington, Kentucky):*** "Of late the city has been ablaze anent a dissembler under the guise of a Zulu, bearing the title of Tip-O-Tip, whom the *Post* described as a scurulous thief, robber, and assassin. And now appears the real Zulu chief, Mata Mon Zaro, who spots Tip-O-Tip as an Arabian, assuming the nationality of an African. The accounts of Tip-O-Tip have thwarted the success of Count Mata Mon Zaro as a lecturer, and who says that were he to meet him again on his route, he would smack him so that he would feel and know the Zulu's power" (*Detroit Plaindealer*).

• ***January 21, 1893 (Richmond, Virginia):*** "A Full Blooded African," "His Remarkable Performances," "Orlando Gibson, whose African name is Boneo Moskego, a full blooded Zulu is in the city and has been lecturing at several churches here . . . He is the son of the late Zulu Chieftain, Cetewayo, and has with him his mother, who was one of this African king's forty wives . . .

He interests the audience by showing the habits and customs of the natives of Africa. Hymns are sung in the African language and translated into the English. He puts a rope in his mouth and the strongest men are unable to pull it out. All kinds of glass are broken and then trampled upon with his bare feet. He raises a man weighing 186 pounds with his teeth, and puts a glass of water in his hand and defies six of the strongest men in the house to prevent him from drinking it" (*Richmond Planet*).

• ***April 13, 1894 (Topeka, Kansas):*** "Oskazuma," "The subject of this sketch is Oskazuma, the well-known copper-colored African who has been attracting large audiences in this and other countries . . . He was born on the coast in southeast Africa, nearly thirty years ago. He has become famous as a warrior during the siege of 1873 with the English. He was captured and placed on a piratical ship and brought to this country . . . He speaks English fluently, and is considered a well educated man. He has made a contract with Mr. B. L. Bowman, of the Sells and Renfrow circus, which will bid adieu to winter quarters [in Topeka] after the 28th of this month. He has been earnestly requested to give his farewell lecture at a grand concert given by the Busy Bee Club, Thursday evening, April 19th at St. John's A.M.E. Church" (*Kansas State Ledger*).

• ***November 30, 1894:*** "A Letter from the Prince," "Oskazuma, the African prince and warrior, writes a very interesting letter. He has traveled from the Atlantic to the Pacific coast this season, and has at this time retired from the circus and is now exhibiting with a celebrated company of singers" (*Kansas State Ledger*).

Note: Before the turn of the century, Prince Oskazuma, "African Warrior, Lecturer, Mimic, Fire Fiend," had begun touring with Buffalo Bill Cody's Wild West Show.[99]

Prof. Tobe Brown: "Terpsichorean Soiree"

Robert L. Brown, known as T. B., or "Tobe" Brown, was born in Shelbyville, Kentucky, in 1863. He died January 29, 1939, and is buried in Eastern Cemetery in Louisville.[100] Brown was a versatile musician, a cornet soloist, pianist, and music teacher who headed an orchestra that specialized in music for dancing. He arrived in Kansas City, Missouri, from Louisville around 1890, and by 1893 it was the consensus of Kansas City's black society that, "If Brown is going to furnish the music, we will have a good time."

• ***September 30, 1892 (Kansas City, Missouri):*** "A grand concert and Ball will be given by the St. Joseph concert club, Thursday Oct. 6th at Vineyard Hall. Brown's Orchestra will furnish the music for the occasion. Don't fail to attend. Admission 35c" (*Kansas City American Citizen*).

• ***November 11, 1892 (Kansas City, Missouri):*** "A Grand Entertainment," "The many friends of No. 11 Hose Co. Kansas City Fire Department will please take notice that a grand musical and Literary Benefit for this Co. will be given under the auspices of the Attucks Club at Music Hall 6th and Broadway streets, Thursday evening, Nov. 17th, 1892 . . . Admission 50cts . . . Come one, come all.

Literary musical programme, 8:30 P.M.: Overture, Nebuchadnezzer, Verdi, Prof. Brown's Orchestra; Base Solo, 'The old turnkey,' Mr. A. R. Harris; Soprana Solo, 'The Dove,' Miss Eliza Thompkins; Cornet Solo, 'Irie Bravaro,' Prof. Brown . . . ; No. 11 Fire Company March, Smith, Prof. Brown's Orchestra.

Grand March Quadrille . . . Virginia Reel . . . Home Sweet Home" (*Kansas City American Citizen*).

• ***December 16, 1892:*** "One of the most enjoyable events of the season was a party given by the Young Men's Progressive club, at Brown's Dancing Academy, Tuesday evening, Dec. 13 . . . Dancing and card playing were the amusements of the evening. Music was furnished by Brown's Orchestra" (*Kansas City American Citizen*).

• ***April 7, 1893 (Kansas City, Missouri):*** "Prof. Brown has been made a handsome offer to go to Denver, Colo., but he will remain in Kansas City, where he and his wife have made hosts of friends. The Dancing Academy has done much good here. Chicago, New York,

Lessons

IN DANCING AND MUSIC,

—Both—

Piano And Cornet,

GIVEN BY

PROF. T. B. BROWN AND WIFE.

Adult class, Tuesday and Friday evenings; children's class, Saturday aftetnoon from 2:30 to 4. Also private lessons given at any time. All late dances given both square and round, including Oxford Minuet, Prairie Queen, etc. For terms call on or address Prof. Brown or wife, 604 Oak street.

Kansas City American Citizen, *May 6, 1892.*

Boston, nor Washington can boast of no more graceful dancers than Kansas City" (*Kansas City American Citizen*).

• ***April 7, 1893 (Kansas City, Missouri):*** "Grand Soiree," "Wednesday evening, March 29th, 1893 will live long in the memory of K.C.'s high social circles . . . The occasion was the second grand formal reception tendered by the Young Men's Mutual Aid Association . . . at Prof. Brown's Dancing Academy 6th and Charlotte streets . . .

Messrs. Smith and Johnson the colored professional Banjoists now playing at the Ninth Street Theatre were present and gave such remarkable evidence of their musical abilities as won frequent and hearty applause.

The amiable A. W. P. Griffin sang two solos with guitar accompaniment that brought forth the clapping of hands.

At 10:30 P.M. Prof. Brown of the Dancing Academy was seated at the piano. This was the signal for the beginning of the following:

PROGRAMME

1. Grand March (Quadrille). 2. Waltz. 3. Illinois. 4. Saratoga Lanciers (Grand Square). 5. Harvard Gavotte. 6. Rye Waltz. 7. Carola. 8. Oxford Minuet. 9. Prarie Queen. 10. Extras and Home, Sweet Home . . .

The gay company continued to trip the light fantastic toe till the 'we 'sma' hours o 'morn' to music by Prof. Brown, while Mrs. Brown the Professor's amiable wife did the calling" (*Kansas City American Citizen*).

• ***May 20, 1893 (Kansas City, Missouri):*** "Terpsichorean Soiree," "Prof. Brown, the Dancing Master and celebrated cornetist and wife . . . gave their grand closing exercises of their dancing academy at Turner Hall Monday, May 1, 1893. The following was the program rendered by the children's class. First, grand march . . . Second, Saratoga Lanciers . . . Third, Harvard Gavotte . . . Fourth, Irish Bell . . . Fifth, Lanciers Plain . . . Sixth, Fisher's Hornpipe . . . Seventh, Oxford Minuet . . . Eighth, Celurius Ballet . . . Ninth, May Pole . . . Mrs. Prof. Brown then . . . gave the rest of the evening up to the older people who danced till 3 o'clock to the sweet strains of dancing music from Prof. Brown's full orchestra of ten pieces" (*Indianapolis Freeman*).

• ***December 22, 1893:*** "Among The Musical People," "Prof. T. B. Brown," " 'If Brown is going to furnish the music, we will have a good time,' is what is often heard with reference to coming social events, and so it is. For more than two years Brown's orchestra has furnished music for the elite affairs of Kansas City's '400' and it is acknowledged the best to be had. Prof. Brown is a thorough musician. For more than fifteen years he has been actively engaged in this business and his ability as an instructor and musical director is everywhere conceded. He comes from the state of Kentucky and the old Cunningham band of Louisville was for years under his direction. Since coming to Kansas City, however, he has devoted his time to furnishing orchestral music and giving instruction in all the branches, teaching both string and brass. In addition to this in October of last year he opened a dancing school in Masonic hall, corner Sixth and Charlotte streets, and as a result the dancing element of Kansas City was given an opportunity to keep up with the times in the Terpsichorean art. In the person of his estimable wife the professor has an able assistant, especially in the dancing arena. Mrs. Brown is a refined, graceful and accomplished lady and as dancing instructor has few equals in the race. All of latest dances are taught and private lessons are given in both music and dancing by this unique combination at Brown's conservatory" (*Kansas City American Citizen*).

Note: This is the only known account linking Brown to the historic Cunningham Band of Louisville, also known as the Falls City Brass Band.

• ***January 5, 1894 (Kansas City, Missouri):*** "Le Grand Soirree [*sic*]," At a large reception given by the Young Men's Mutual Aid Association in Turner Hall: "Of course Professor Brown's Orchestra *Celebre* with seven pieces was there to furnish the music, and the Professor certainly acquitted himself grandly. . . The programme consisted of 25 numbers, many of

T. B. BRO'VN, MUSICAL DIRECTOR.

Kansas City American Citizen, *December 22, 1893.*

Freeman, *March 11, 1899.*

them being the very latest music obtained by Prof. Brown while attending the Musical congress at the World's Fair, the past fall" (*Kansas City American Citizen*).

Brown eventually left Kansas City and returned to hometown Louisville. The *Freeman* of March 11, 1899, informed that "Prof. T. B. Brown and his orchestra of Louisville, Ky." had recently visited Indianapolis to "furnish music" for a "full dress ball . . . Mr. Brown is a past Master of dance music," and his seven-piece orchestra "is ready to do justice to a Sousa March, a rag or the latest operatic selection." Over the next several years, Brown's Louisville-based orchestra emerged as a regional star in concert settings at fairs and chautauquas. During the summer of 1907 they played for both "the Owensboro Chautauqua, the first Negro Chautauqua in this country," and "the Fern Creek Fair Association, white, and received the same kind of compliments."[101]

Professional African American brass and string bands have a long and illustrious history in Louisville. Classically trained violinist Henry Williams, a free black man, organized a famous band and a dancing school, which he publicized in the *Louisville Public Advertiser* as early as December 29, 1834. Williams's Dancing Academy catered exclusively to whites.[102] Professor Brown's 1890s Kansas City dancing school experience places him in a seemingly important but little-explored tributary of jazz development. In Nashville, Tennessee, during the early 1900s, barber-musician Dock Liner conducted the popular Eureka Dancing Class, and his Eureka Orchestra produced a number of notable musicians, including N. C. (Nathaniel) Davis and his brother C. M. Davis.[103] Trumpet legend Doc Cheatham recalled the Davis brothers giving rudimentary instructions to the church-based band that he started out with as a child in Nashville. Cheatham couldn't recall Dock Liner or the Eureka Orchestra. He said they must have been "a little before my time."[104]

In 1958 trumpet great Willie Hightower told jazz researcher Bill Russell that he and his wife, Lottie, had organized a band in connection with the Eudora Dancing Class, held in Mason Hall at Fortieth and State Streets in Chicago: "The man used to run dancing classes here in Chicago. Every night in the week there was a dancing class somewhere. Well, he had shows, he put on shows, and he . . . built the band right along with it. And that helped both him and what we did, we named the band 'Lottie Hightower and her Eudora Nighthawks Band.' "[105] In 1927 the name was shortened to "Hightower's Nighthawks" for a historic Black Patti label recording.[106]

Blind Boone: "Clear out of Sight"

Itinerant concert pianist John William "Blind" Boone was widely considered to be the successor to Blind Tom. Rumors that he was related to famous colonial frontiersman Daniel Boone attain a certain genealogical credibility in a 1927 *Pittsburgh Courier* report: "Boone . . . traces his descent from Daniel Boone . . . through his great grandmother, daughter and slave of Nathan Boone, fourth son of Daniel."[107]

Blind Boone reportedly began his musical career as a child, playing the harmonica in an "urchin's street band."[108] According to an article in the *Cleveland Gazette* of May 2, 1896, he "was born in the camp of the Seventh regiment of Missouri militia, at that time located at Miami, Saline county, Mo. His mother was the 'contraband' cook of Co. I. When six months old he lost his sight by an attack of brain fever. He was sent to the school for the blind in St. Louis, to be taught a trade, but, neglecting his work for music, he was dismissed. After a short and bitter life as a tramp in St. Louis and vicinity a kind-hearted conductor, Mr. A. J. Kerry, put him on a train and sent him to his mother at Warrensburg. Another kind-hearted gentleman, this time a colored man, named John Lange, put him in the Sunday-school to play [piano] for the children, and gave him the musical education which has fitted him to travel as a musician for the past 16 years."[109]

From his home in Columbia, Missouri, Blind Boone toured extensively throughout the 1889–1895 period. Playing mostly in churches, he fairly saturated Missouri and eastern Kansas. His popularity and financial success no doubt stimulated piano playing in African American communities, where the seeds of new vernacular styles had already begun to germinate.

While there is no hard evidence that Blind Boone performed ragtime before the turn of the century, there are clear signs that he was inclined toward vernacular music expressions. His early-1890s stage repertoire was liberally spiced with "Campmeeting Songs" and "Plantation Songs,"[110] and his published compositions of the period include coon songs, pseudo-spirituals, and other vernacular concoctions, such as "When I Meet Dat Coon To-Night," "Whar Shill We Go When de Great Day Comes," and "Dinah's Barbecue (Song and Break Down)."[111] His 1909 composition titled "Boone's Rag Medley No. 2—Strains from Flat Branch" includes the proto-blues anthem "I'm Alabama Bound."[112]

• ***June 8, 1889 (Topeka, Kansas):*** "Blind Boone in Kansas," "Unquestionably the grandest and most successful musical performances that have ever been given here were those given by the great world's wonder and musical phenomena, Blind Boone...

Boone has been here several times and on every occasion he was greeted by a large, enthusiastic, and appreciative audience...He interprets and executes the most difficult pieces of Lisst and Bethoven [*sic*]...He himself has composed and published about fourteen pieces...

The Negro race can well be proud of Boone. He is under the management of Mr. John Lange ...The other members of the company are Miss Stella [May] Vocalist and Mrs. Ruth H. Lange, Secretary" (P. H. Bray, *Indianapolis Freeman*).

• ***March 8, 1890:*** "Blind Boone, one of the greatest musical prodigies that ever lived, and his concert company, gave a concert at Capitol City Opera House, Des Moines, Iowa to good business" (*Indianapolis Freeman*).

• ***March 21, 1891 (Kansas City, Missouri):*** "Blind Boone, the great pianist appeared at Allen Chapel, the 12th, and the 13th at 10th street Baptist Church. The program was excellent and he was greeted with large audiences at both places. The one at Allen Chapel was for the purpose of purchasing a new piano for the high school, to the proceeds of which Boone generously donated $5.00" (La Beau, *Indianapolis Freeman*).

• ***April 18, 1891 (Jefferson City, Missouri):*** "'Blind Boone,' the musical wonder of Missouri, gave an appreciative concert at the Second Baptist Church...The following program was rendered:

Hungarian Storm March	Liszt
Last Hope	Gottschalk
Campmeeting Song	Boone
Swanee River (With variations)	Boone
Plantation Song	Boone
Schubert March Militaire	Tausig
Song	Boone
Hungarian Rhapsodie No. 6	Liszt
Song (selected)	Miss Stella May
Marshfield Tornado	Boone
Plantation Song	Miss Stella May
Imitation of instruments	Boone

By request Boone played The Blue Danube Waltz. An interesting feature of the evening occurred toward the close of the program. Boone's manager asked the audience to select some one to play a piece, stating that afterwards Boone would reproduce it. Prof. Page's 11-year-old daughter was selected, and played the Sleigh Ride by W. M. Treloar. As soon as she had finished, the blind performer proceeded to give a praiseworthy reproduction that brought forth great applause from the crowded house" ("Ganelon," *Indianapolis Freeman*).

• ***June 13, 1891 (Columbia, Missouri):*** "The Blind Boone Band was out last Saturday and rendered some of their selections under the direction of Prof. W. C. Smith. The boys show excellent training from the simple fact that they have only been organized ten months ... Prof. Smith's Orchestra of fourteen pieces, assisted by some of Columbia's noted singers, will give a grand musical concert on or about the 22d inst... Don't forget the rally at the A.M.E. Church next Sunday" (*Indianapolis Freeman*).

Freeman, *September 5, 1891.*

Note: That a black community juvenile band in Boone's hometown was named after him says much about his reputation and influence. The "Prof. W. C. Smith" who had charge of this band may well have been Prof. N. Clark Smith.

• ***September 5, 1891:*** "The Blind Boone Concert Company," "Here is an organization... that is really a creditable one to the colored race... One pleasing feature connected with the combination is the fact that it is indebted to no white man for its success. It is wholly and entirely a colored affair, managed by a colored man, Mr. John Lange, of Columbus [*sic*], Mo., who has no superior in the country for managerial ability" (*Indianapolis Freeman*).

• ***September 26, 1891:*** "The Blind Boone Concert company, one of the most successful and enterprising Afro-American Concert companies on the road, is now doing Michigan and Canada" (*Indianapolis Freeman*).

• ***October 31, 1891:*** "Our Musical People," "Blind Boone has engaged with O. B. Shephard for a forty weeks tour in Canada next season, for $12,000 clear of all expenses" (*Indianapolis Freeman*).

• ***January 9, 1892:*** "Notes from Archie White's Refined Minstrels—This is our third week in Missouri, and business is way up... A number of the boys visited Blind Boone at his home, Columbia, Mo., Christmas Day, and were royally entertained" (*New York Clipper*).

• ***February 14, 1892 (Kansas City, Kansas):*** "Blind Boone, the musical genius, is to appear at a place called the Tabernacle in this city on the 15th inst. From what one can hear from newspaper reports he is 'out of sight' " (*Topeka Weekly Call*).

• ***July 2, 1892 (Cleveland, Ohio):*** "The Blind Boone Concert Company gave a concert... in

First Congregational church . . . The audience was small but enthusiastic. Mr. Boone's playing is really fine, and several of the numbers were encored. His playing of the 'Marshfield Tornado' was exceptionally good, the roaring of the winds being perfectly imitated on the piano. Thursday evening he played in the Methodist church" (*Cleveland Gazette*).

• ***July 9, 1892 (Cleveland, Ohio):*** "The Blind Boone Concert Company repeated its excellent programme at the Epworth memorial church . . . Boone is blind, but an educated artist. His playing rivals that of Blind Tom in his palmiest days" (*Cleveland Gazette*).

• ***September 10, 1892 (Oberlin, Ohio):*** "Blind Boone gave a concert in College chapel . . . It was the finest of the season and quite an audience was present. Blind Boone covered himself with glory when he imitated the classical piece Prof. Breckenridge of the conservatory played. The imitation was nearly perfect" (*Cleveland Gazette*).

• ***September 10, 1892 (Cleveland, Ohio):*** "The Blind Boone Concert Company drew an audience that completely filled Mt. Zion Church last week Thursday. Miss May's singing pleased very much and Boone simply astounded the people by his wonderful playing . . . Miss Fanny Johnson's piano selection was played by him remarkably well after only one hearing, and his other imitations were equally remarkable" (*Cleveland Gazette*).

• ***September 10, 1892 (Cleveland, Ohio):*** "Blind Boone's shout, 'Change cars for the blue vein city,' during his imitation of a train of cars moving, at his Mt. Zion church concert last week, and the way it was received, staggered two or three of the large audience. It was certainly a 'hurter' " (*Cleveland Gazette*).

• ***November 25, 1892:*** "Detroit Department," "The Blind Boone concert company has been giving a series of entertainments in the various churches of the city. Monday evening the company gave a program for the benefit of the independent Baptist church. A very large and appreciative audience attended. Blind Boone is undoubtedly a musical marvel. His piano playing exhibits wonderful powers of execution as well as a musical genius, while his range of voice is unusually wide and his tones are very pleasing. The other members of the company, especially Miss Stella May add interesting features to the program although it is to be regretted that most of these features are of a minstrel order" (*Detroit Plaindealer*).

• ***February 10, 1893:*** "The Blind Boone Concert Co. . . . of colored artists are in [Kansas City] filling a ten days engagement at the leading churches of the city . . . They played at the following churches this week . . . Tuesday night, 6th and Prospect Christian Church, Friday, Summit Street Christian Church. They will appear on the 11th at the 1st Christian Church, Kansas City, Kansas. 13th, Springfield Ave. Christian Church, 14–15 Liberty St. A.M.E. Church, 16th Allen Chapel, cor. 10th and Charlotte Sts." (*Kansas City American Citizen*).

• ***February 24, 1893:*** "As we predicted, the Blind Boone Concert Company's engagement at Allen Chapel was a grand success . . . It was said by many old citizens present, that it was the largest assemblage of colored people ever seen in Kansas City. Good music, a crowded house of well behaved people . . . The company went to Ottawa, Ks., Friday morning. They will return to Kansas City in May, to fill a month's engagement" (*Kansas City American Citizen*).

• ***March 31, 1893:*** "At the Blind Boone concert given in the Presbyterian church at Parsons, Kansas last week, the colored people were asked to take seats in the gallery, but resented the indignity by returning their admission tickets and going home" (*Kansas City American Citizen*).

• ***May 12, 1893:*** An advertisement for the Blind Boone Concert Company said, "Bring the children they will be benefitted. Blind Boone has been the cause of a great many children falling in love with the piano, they having heard him play at concerts. His music charms them, and gives them brilliant ideas that they could not otherwise receive. We have the testimonials of a number of parents, who give him the credit of their children being artists. Blind Boone will be twenty-eight years old next May. He weighs 225 pounds, is in the best of health, performing on the piano this season as never before. The following engagements have been made for the company in Kansas City, Mo., for evenings next week: Monday at Isaac's Hall, Springfield avenue; Tuesday, Calvary Baptist church, East 9th street; Wednesday, Liberty St. A.M.E. Church; Thursday, First Pres. church, 13th and Oak streets, Friday, Lydia avenue Christian church (W.C.T.U.); Saturday, First Pres. church, 10th and Forrest avenue, May 22nd, Tabernacle, Kansas City, Kan . . . Under the management of Mr. John Lang. Headed by the marvelous Musical Prodigy Blind Boone . . . Prices within the reach of all. Admission 25 cents" (*Kansas City American Citizen*).

• ***May 26, 1893:*** A program rendered by the Blind Boone Concert Company in Kansas City included, "Hungarian Storm March by Liszt, Last Hope by Gottschalk, Camp Meeting Song by Boone, Suwanee River (with variations) by Boone, Plantation Song by Boone, Hollander's March by Hollander, Plantation Song by Boone, Hungarian Rhapsodie No. 6 by Liszt, Song (Selection) Miss Stella May, Schubert's Serenade, Trans. by Liszt, Plantation Song by Miss Stella May, Marshfield Tornado by Boone, Imitations of various instruments, concluding with Dixie, with variations by Boone.

All of which was beautifully executed. Blind Boone was (excuse expression) 'Clear out of sight' " (*Kansas City American Citizen*).

• ***September 9, 1893:*** "Variety and Minstrelsy," "Blind Boon [*sic*], the pianist and composer, has dedicated one of his latest songs, 'Dina's

UNCLE SAM'S DESCRIPION OF BLIND BOONES CONCERT.

"I attended dat blind man's concert
Dat de paper's advertised,
An' de way he played, I tell yo',
Jes' made me open my eyes.
For de way he handled dat insti'ment;
Fingers played upon de keys,
Was a sight I ne'er had witnessed,
An' a sight I could scarce believe;
'Twas as if by magic he teched it
So 'xactly did he execute.

'Peared to me I'd gone to heben,
An' an angel was playin' de keys.
He sat right down to de pi'ner,
An' his fingers were jest at home;
When he placed dem on de keyboard,
Manipulated de keys, I believe,
De first was a March, he called it
Tho' I didn't quite understand,
But I knew it was dreadful pretty
An' how he played it was grand!

An den "De Last Hope" followed
Oh chile, how beautiful 'twas,
I guess 'twas classical music,
Dere's some ob dat kind, yo' kno'.
But I tell yo' after 'twas finished,
An' a plantation melody sung,
I cl'ar forgot myself, dat's sho;
I thought I war Souf agin;
I wish yo'd heard de next one,
'Twas Swanee Ribber he played.

But den he'd added some extras,
Made it de sweetest e'er played.
His next selection, a fine one,
Dis ob his own git up,
An' den he sung a melon song
Which fairly took de house;
Ob course he was enchored,
An' right promptly did he respond
Following dis annudder
Ob dem high fluted ones.

He allus sings for chilluns,
Has a little song for dem,
An' Oh so cute an' simple! that
'Twas 'Mamma buy me dat.'
How I wish yo'd heard dat lady
Wid her voice so rich and fine.
She stood wid grace an' beauty
Dat she won dem people's love;
One ob her songs dat pressed me
Was something 'bout gamblin' an' sich.

'You'd better quit dat gamblin,'
(Now jes gimme time to think)
'Don't yo' eber think 'bout dyin'?'
I can't jes make de rhyme;
She too was enchored, remember,
I tell yo' her singin' took!
For 'Ole Uncle Rufus' was lovely,
But 'Listen to dem Chimin' Bells.'
Den after she'd finished her singin'
His master piece he played.

Next came dat awful Tornado
Which was composed by him;
He played two pieces together
An' imitated a music box,
A fife an' drum, an' incomin' train
An' de tunin' ob a violin.
So if eber he comes agin, now
Yo' mus' go to hear him play—
Yo' mus' hear dat Blind Boone Concert,
Hear de singin' by Stella May.

Virgie Whitsett.

Freeman, *March 28, 1896.*

Barbacue,' to the Mallory Bros., now with Sam T. Jack's Creole Co." (*New York Clipper*).

• ***December 8, 1893 (Topeka, Kansas):*** "The Blind Boone Concert Company gave a wonderful entertainment at the St. John's A.M.E. Church Wednesday evening of this week . . . The Marshfield, Mo., cyclone was displayed amid trembling hearers. It seemed realistic, causing some of the hearers to feel like they only wished an entrance to escape . . . It is reported on good authority, aside from the complimentary tickets at the Blind Boone concert $107.60 were the receipts at the door. $47.40 no doubt, of this lucrative amount will be given to the Church . . . Boone is certainly a wonderful musical prodigy, and deserves much credit for the good work being done being especially favorable to the churches" (*Kansas State Ledger*).

• ***January 18, 1895:*** (Topeka, Kansas): "Blind Boone to Come," "The celebrated singer and pianist, Blind Boone, who is known all over the world as a natural musician and a prodigy of nature, will be here next Friday evening, at St. John's A.M.E. Church . . . Mr. Lang, his brother-in-law, and manager, takes pride in introducing him to this country as the only and real high-toned colored musical prodigy on earth" (*Kansas State Ledger*).

Blind Boone continued to travel and perform until shortly before his death in 1927.

Chapter Six

1894

"Black and White" Minstrelsy

Primrose and West were here this week with an aggregation of white and colored minstrels. This exhibition enables the spectator to contrast the relative merits of white and colored minstrelsy. Such an exhibition conducted as this one is does a great deal to create respect for colored actors. White and colored shows are the greatest drawing cards on the road.

—*Leavenworth Herald*, November 9, 1895

A major breakthrough occurred in the mid-1890s with what was identified in the *Freeman* as the "new fad of mixed minstrelsy," offering African American performers in one portion of the show, and blackfaced whites in the other. This new "Black and White" minstrelsy appears to have foreshadowed the primacy of African American minstrel troupes during the ragtime era.

Freeman critic Sylvester Russell noted in 1903, "While Primrose and West were not the originators of black and white minstrelsy, they nevertheless once had the largest and greatest company of its kind ever put on the road."[1] Reports in the *New York Clipper* confirm that veteran white minstrel show proprietors George H. Primrose and John T. West assembled a model "Black and White" show for the season of 1894–1895. Originally intending to send out two separate companies, they ended up consolidating under the slogan "forty whites and thirty blacks."

• *May 12, 1894:* "Primrose & West will have two big companies on the road next season. Primrose and West themselves, with seventy people, will play the large cities only, while a company of colored performers will play cities and one night stands" (*New York Clipper*).

THE WORLD'S MIGHTIEST MARVELS!

PRIMROSE AND WEST'S BIG MINSTRELS

70 PERFORMERS.

40 WHITES AND 30 BLACKS

A Revelation in Minstrelsy!

Primrose and West's Minstrels

THE COMING SEASON WILL COMPRISE

TWO— Great Companies in One, 40 WHITES and 30 BLACKS —TWO
TWO-- Grand First Parts, Carrying 40 WHITES AND 30 BLACKS —TWO
TWO—Handsomely Uniformed Military Bands, 40 Whites and 30 Blacks—TWO
TWO—MIGHTY MINSTREL PARADES, 40 WHITES and 30 BLACKS—TWO
TWO—Weeks' Stands Played in every Principal City in the Country—TWO
TWO— Specially Appointed Cars, and Carrying —TWO
TWO— Carloads of Scenery —TWO

This Truly Great Innovation in Minstrelsy

WILL REQUIRE

2 Distinct Stage Managers, Electricians, Mechanicians, Musical Directors, Carpenters, Masters of Transportation, 2

AN ILLUSTRIOUS, EXALTED, IMPOSING NOVELTY.

A truly new, actually original, and imperatively great first part. The most elaborate, costly, and beautiful ever beheld in Minstrelsy, differing radically from all our previous effects, and monumentally surpassing in massive effect and bewildering grandeur any similiar effort ever attempted.

MINSTRELSY AS IT WAS AND MINSTRELSY AS IT IS
30 BLACKS WILL BE PRESENTED IN 40 WHITES

SEPARATE STATELY TRANSFORMATION SCENES,

Each in itself a complete revelation, and each resplendently embellished with magnificent scenery, rich paraphernalia, and brilliant vocalisms. The entire representation forming a

SPECTACULAR PAGEANT OF PHENOMENAL BEAUTY.

A scene of bewildering splendor never equalled in Minstrelsy, by the aid of specially painted scenery.

Primrose and West's Modern Minstrels, 40 in Number,

Will, in conjunction with PRIMROSE AND WEST'S 30 true representatives of the colored world, present their own conception of a MODERN MINSTREL FESTIVAL, giving eclat to the closing scene of the MOST ORIGINAL AND STUPENDOUS FIRST PART EVER DREAMED OF.

PRIMROSE AND WEST'S MINSTREL REVOLUTION,

Whose greatest effort is to please the people, and who for years have been the

FIRST FAVORITES OF AMERICA'S HAPPIEST CITIZENS,

Will present to the American public a STATELY ARRAY OF ARTISTIC MARVELS. We have finally reached

The Uttermost Boundary of True Greatness.

The pomp, the pride, the glory of the minstrel stage is ours, and ours alone, and our steadfast friends are faithfully assured of an

UNBLEMISHED, UNEXAMPLED PERFECT MINSTREL PERFORMANCE OF GIGANTIC PROPORTIONS.

TOO GREAT FOR IMITATORS AND TOO STRONG FOR RIVALRY.

Our reason for carrying 40 WHITES and 30 BLACKS is to present to the public MINSTRELSY FROM ITS BIRTH TO THE PRESENT DAY. TWO DISTINCT PERFORMANCES.

40 WHITES AND 30 BLACKS

70 PERFORMERS.

A FEW MORE COLORED MUSICIANS WANTED

Address all communications to

Mr. JOS. P. HARRIS, General Manager, 18 E. 22d St., N.Y.

JOHN W. VOGEL, General Agent.

New York Clipper, *July 14, 1894.*

• ***July 21, 1894:*** "Some immense lithograph work will be displayed by Primrose & West this season with their company of forty whites and thirty blacks. The subject of one stand is 'The Noonday Parade,' displaying very effectively the well known stars seated in a carriage drawn by four gray horses, between forty whites and thirty blacks. Manager Harris says he has the time for the big seventy booked solid, with the exception of about three weeks" (*New York Clipper*).

• ***August 25, 1894:*** "Roster of Primrose & West's Minstrels—Geo. H. Primrose, W. H. West, Jos. P. Harris, Geo. Wilson, Lew Sully, Jos. Garland, Frank Rice, Fred Elmer, Thos. E. Glynn, John L. Howe, Jimmy Wale, Andy McLeod, Wm. H. Windone [*sic*], M. B. Stevens, Harry Gilbert Castle, Arthur La Bord, Robt. E. Carmichael, James Shults, E. E. McKinley, Geo. Dyer, Henry Klepper, Mat Ensign, Harry Hardy, S.M. Ettinger, Horace Bell, Johnny Whalen, F. A. Herting, Geo. L. Bullard, Sheik Hadj Taher's troupe of Arabs, Alf. Weathers, Geo. F. Freeman, Miles Terry, L. S. Hunster, Wm. Hill (the Knickerbocker Quartet), Philip Portlock, Wm. H. Tucker, Sam'l G. Baker, Lewis Shepard, J. A. Shipp, James Wilson, Chas. Johnson, Lewis Frances, George Reese, G. W. Sebastian, Daniel Robertson, M. L. Van Dyke, the Grundy Bros., George Tichner, W. Dickson, Thos. W. Young, Harry Kelly, William Davis and Eddie Carter. John W. Vogel, general representative . . . making the trade mark forty whites and thirty blacks" (*New York Clipper*).

Note: Sheik Hadj Taher's troupe of Arabs appears to divide the names of the white performers from the black, with W. H. Windom passing for white.

• ***September 8, 1894:*** "Primrose & West's Minstrels opened auspiciously Aug. 24 at the Opera House, Utica, N.Y. . . . The street parade in the afternoon was a feature. Seventy performers all dressed in the height of fashion, two handsomely uniformed military bands, a drum corp, fifteen Arabs dressed in their native costume and mounted on prancing steeds, with Primrose and West and their old partner George Wilson, in an open carriage, drawn by four white horses . . . The evening performance went off with the characteristic dash of this organization. The first part was opened by the thirty blacks of the company, who were dressed in the old time style, and who sang 'Nellie Was a Lady,' 'Suwanee River,' 'Kentucky Home' and 'The Virginia Rosebud'" (*New York Clipper*).

• ***November 3, 1894:*** "The parade given by Primrose & West's Minstrels in [New York City], last week, was an unique and novel idea. The permit having been granted by the city officials, Messrs. Primrose & West took advantage of the opportunity to present to the New York public an attraction, such as they have never before been able to show. The line of march was down Eighth Avenue to Fourteenth Street, to Broadway, thence along Broadway to Forty-second Street, to Sixth Avenue, to the Grand Opera House . . . Seventy performers were in line, preceded by a troupe of Arabs, dressed in their native costumes. Behind them came Primrose & West's Military Band, in gorgeous costumes, playing some stirring music, headed by a drum major (Johnny Whalen) . . . Then came the comedians singers and dancers of the forty whites . . . Another troupe of mounted Arabs followed, and then came the thirty blacks, marching in a style that would do credit to a military company. 'Way Down in Dixie' was played by their excellent band of colored musicians, and behind them came another troupe of mounted Arabs. It was an imposing sight" (*New York Clipper*).

• ***November 17, 1894 (New York City):*** "People's Theatre," "A crowded audience gathered here on Monday night, Nov. 12, and partook of three hours' solid enjoyment, if one may judge by the applause and laughter which reigned throughout the night. The Primrose & West minstrel organization was the attraction, and, although this company have been playing in this city and immediate vicinity for six weeks, it is evident that they could play to very profitable business in this city for a still longer time. This troupe, by the way, is the first minstrel organization to visit the People's Theatre in eight years. The morning parade by the full company was a new feature for the East siders . . . The entertainment furnished by this organization this season furnished two types of minstrelsy, the genuine colored performers, who open the show in the first part of the programme, and are succeeded by those who appear in burnt cork, in the second session of part one. The rise of the curtain shows the stage peopled by the genuine black members of the company in full evening costume, who give several distinct types of negro character delineations. They sing all sorts of songs, from 'Sweet Ham Bone' to sentimental ballads, and quartet renditions in perfect harmony. They gave 'The Suwanee River' and 'My Old Kentucky Home,' while pictures of southern plantation life were shown upon canvas in the background with great effect. Their singing was heartily applauded. J. A. Shipp presided, with Alf. Weathers and Ike McBeard on the ends. Then came the second session of part one, with the white members of the organization seated in front of the stage, while the colored forces occupied an elevated space in the rear, with the orchestra in the middle . . . Wm. H. Windom [sang] one of the song gems of the program, entitled 'The Girl I Love,' and responded to a double encore for his sweet vocal efforts . . . Hadj Tahar's troupe of Arabs closed the excellent program" (*New York Clipper*).

• ***January 12, 1895:*** "Primrose and West did not entirely abolish the color-line when they consolidated their two minstrel companies. The whites and Afro-Americans travel in separate special cars en tour" (*Cleveland Gazette*).

Note: There is nothing to indicate which of Primrose and West's two "special cars" accommodated the great singer and songwriter William H. Windom. Windom went on to gain wider fame fronting the Blackstone Quartette, an African American vocal harmony group from Chicago, in "big time" vaudeville. His career was summarized in his obituary in the *Freeman* of September 20, 1913, written by Sylvester Russell:

> William H. Windom, the most famous idolized minstrel ballad singer of his time, according to report, died at Gary, Ind., August 26, 1913, from grief over the death of his wife and son. Windom, whose Christian name was Wisdom, was born in Paducah, Ky., and was forty-seven years of age. His father was a white man and his mother was a colored woman. It was in McCabe & Young's colored minstrels about 1888 that young Wisdom attracted attention with a high sweet alto voice in the song "Ragged Patch." He was later engaged by Concross for his permanent white minstrels at the Eleventh Street opera house in Philadelphia, Pa. About 1892 George Primrose, of Thatcher, Primrose and West's minstrels, discovered him and passed him as a white man in the company. Billy changed his name to William H. Windom and after introducing the song, "After the Ball," his popularity was established. When he and Gussie L. Davis, the colored songwriter, had finished "The Fatal Wedding," Billy's cup of joy was running over, for he was loaded down with flowers every night from strangers. Two more of his greatest successes were "Teach Our Baby that I'm Dead," his own song, and "It Don't Seem Like the Same Old Smile" . . . His big venture in vaudeville under his own name (his new name, Windom), assisted by the Blackstone colored quartette, which included Conley and Dixon, was the best singing quartette then and highest salaried one on the American stage. Windom, who was highly intelligent, had a remarkable personality. He was noncommittal on the color question and did not care or recognize any discussion as to whether

he was black or white. He married a white woman in Chicago who loved him and knew well of his mulatto racial birth. It was rumored that George Primrose, who had passed him as white, did not smile upon his marriage to a white woman. And right here I must retaliate by stating to the world that Windom, who was half white, had just as much right to marry a white woman as he did to marry a black one, and more so, because of obvious reasons. When Windom made his appearance at the Grand theater in Chicago alone last season in a black face nurse girl monologue with a baby carriage, he was recognized by a reception. I met him at the La Verdo after the show. His hair was ashen grey.

In the following week's *Freeman*, Russell amended his account of Windom's life:

William H. Windom . . . it seems, was born in Clarksville, Tenn., according to William Coleman, formerly of the Blackstone Quartet . . . The original Billy Johnson was Windom's first team partner before his minstrel days. Mr. Windom's father is said to have been a white banker at Paducah, Ky., who always recognized his son and even visited Billy's colored mother in Clarksville. Billy also used to visit his mother until she died. Besides a successful career upon the stage, Windom's fortune was estimated to be between fifty and one hundred thousand dollars. He owned a grocery store, conducted by his brother-in-law. He also recently purchased a picture theater in Gary, Ind. I am told that his three sons are alive; but worry over the death of his wife caused his death. He died of brain fever. His age was fifty-two years. He was a member of the White Rats [an early mainstream actors' union], and it is said that a delegation of them was once sent to Clarksville, Tenn., to investigate Billy's ancestry, all of which makes very nice reading matter, now, since the days of slavery.

• ***February 9, 1895:*** "Primrose & West's Big 70 Minstrels gave four complete performances and traveled 545 miles in thirty-two hours last week. The company gave a matinee and night performance in Cleveland, O., Jan. 26, and opened with matinee on schedule time at the Hagan, St. Louis, the following day" (*New York Clipper*).

• ***May 11, 1895:*** "An Unprecedented Victory!!! Primrose & West's Big Minstrels, 40 Whites—70 Strong—30 Blacks, have just closed their regular season at Norwich, Ct., Saturday, May 4" (*New York Clipper*).

• ***August 3, 1895:*** "Geo. H. Primrose and wife are the guests of [business partner] John T. West at Willow Camp, Cayuga Lake, N.Y., rusticating previous to commencing rehearsals with the company, which opens the season at Utica, N.Y., Aug. 17 . . . [with] the addition to the company of a pickaninny band of sixteen pieces, under the direction of an European leader" (*New York Clipper*).

• ***August 24, 1895:*** "Primrose & West Minstrel notes . . . Jos. Garland's new sketch, executed by the thirty blacks, entitled 'Christmas in the South,' a clever construction, characteristic of the negro at Christmas time, introducing the little coon band, is very funny" (*New York Clipper*).

During the summer of 1894, the resilient D. W. McCabe, who had stranded his company in Mexico two years earlier, put a strong "Black and White" minstrel show together with the help of experienced band leader Henderson Smith.

• ***October 13, 1894:*** "Notes and roster from D. W. McCabe's Big Forty Minstrels, twenty white and twenty black—Good business everywhere. Roster: Henderson Smith, Willie McCabe, Prof. E. Elmore, Walker, Thomas and Brown, La Roy Bland [*sic*], John Stone, James Partridge, H. Herman, J. Durrow, Will Pratt, J. Smith, McCabe Bros., Brewer Bros., Collins Bros., Haywood Bros., and the four Jacobs Bros" (*New York Clipper*).

• ***October 20, 1894:*** "McCabe & Young's Minstrel Notes," "We are now in our twelfth week of prosperity, although through Illinois we played to poor business, but since we struck Iowa and Minnesota we have done a nice business. Henderson Smith and wife have purchased the show and D. W. McCabe is now business manager. Prof. Elmore's Band and Orchestra of ten pieces is a feature, and in our noonday parade catches the people. James Partridge has charge of the stage and is giving satisfaction. Our company numbers twenty-two people . . . Thomas and Brown's musical act and Le Roy Bland are the features of the show" (*New York Clipper*).

Note: LeRoy Bland went on to join W. A. Mahara's Colored Minstrels in 1896, and he toured with them for several seasons. His career was interrupted in the fall of 1902 when he was "unjustly charged with murder" and thrown in Chicago's Cook County Jail.[2] He was finally acquitted, after a second trial, in the spring of 1903.[3] Best remembered as a female impersonator, Bland was also known for his "North American Indian characterization—Big Chief."[4] He made his biggest hit in the vaudeville team of Bland and Clayborne Jones. Bland's death in 1912 was noted in the *Freeman:* "John Stone, professionally known as LeRoy Bland, died at his home 2446 Dearborn street [Chicago], Wednesday evening, May 29, 1912. He was born in Nashville, Tenn., October 15, about forty-four years ago, but came North with his people and was reared at Davenport, Ia. Mr. Bland first became known to fame as a female impersonator and character specialty artist with W. A. Mahara's Minstrels."[5]

• ***December 8, 1894:*** "Notes from D. W. McCabe's White and Black Consolidated Minstrels," "Business continues big throughout South Dakota, Iowa and Minnesota. The company is composed

Freeman, *February 27, 1909.*

WANTED INSTANTER, FOR THE GREAT QUADRUPLE AMALGAMATION, THE

W. S. CLEVELAND MASSIVE MINSTREL SHOWS,

ALL NATIONS' GREATEST ARTISTS, NOVELTY FEATURES, ETC., INCLUDING

35 WHITE MINSTREL STARS, COMEDIANS, SINGERS, DANCERS AND MUSICIANS. 35

15 MALE AND FEMALE JAPANESE, JUGGLERS, GYMNASTS, CONTORTIONISTS, BALANCERS, ETC. 15

35 GENUINE COLORED MINSTRELS, MUSICIANS, SINGERS, COMEDIANS, DANCERS, ETC. 35

(Would Prefer Couple of the Smaller Colored Co.'s Organized, and Already on Tour.)

15 MOORISH-BEDOUIN ARABS, ACROBATS, TUMBLERS, EQUILIBRISTS, MUSICIANS, ETC. 15

No "Back Liners," No "Fill Ins," No "Soaks," No "Nihilists," No "Discards" need apply. Address all communications, by mail or telegraph, to

W. S. CLEVELAND, Sole Manager. WIRE Mattoon, Ill., Jan. 24; Paris, Ill., 25; Brazil, Ind., 26. Permanent address, 1,088 Elmwood Ave., Buffalo, N. Y., U. S. A.

New York Clipper, *January 26, 1895.*

of twenty- eight people, fourteen white and the same number of black" (*New York Clipper*).

• ***June 1, 1895:*** "Notes from McCabe & Young's Minstrels," "We are now booking our company from the East, and time is nearly all filled. The company will number twenty-five people, both white and colored, and be under the personal management of the old time minstrel, Lew Benedict . . . We open Aug. 1, and play direct East, then sail for Havana on Jan. 6. We have engaged Black Karl, the magic wonder . . . We shall organize in Chicago and open in Elgin, Ill" (*New York Clipper*).

At the beginning of 1895, white minstrel troupe proprietor William S. Cleveland announced his intention to enter the field of "Black and White" minstrelsy with a new wrinkle, an "All Nations" theme somewhat redolent of the World's Fair Midway.

• ***February 2, 1895:*** "W. S. Cleveland is hurrying forward the enlargement of his minstrels enterprise to mammoth proportions. A white and black minstrel company will compete for honors . . . Besides will be seen troupes of Arabs and Japanese. Three bands of music will enliven the street parade. The curtain will go up on an 'All Nations' first part and fall on a big burlesque, in which an 'All Nations' dance and march will be given" (*New York Clipper*).

• ***March 23, 1895:*** "Roster of the W. S. Cleveland Big Double Minstrels: White contingent: W. S. Cleveland, Lew Benedict . . ., Forest City Quartet . . . [etc.]. Colored members: D. W. McCabe, J. W. Brewer, Dan Palmer, Watson Lewis, Wm. McCabe, Henderson Smith, Harry Singleton, Frank Beebe, Thos. Meyers, Henry Hutchinson, Geo. Bailey, Jas. Patridge, Edward Dorey, Frank Dorey, B. Jackson, Luther Ewing, Alex. Musgrove, Wm. Jones, Horace Lewis, James P. Bell, Felix Ellis, Eli Adams, Georgia Quartet, Theo. Mitchell, Fred Anderson and Norman Paxton, and the troupe of Arabs" (*New York Clipper*).

Note: It appears that, for a while at least, D. W. McCabe's Mastodon Minstrels comprised the black contingent of W. S. Cleveland's Big Double Minstrels.

• ***August 10, 1895:*** "Notes from W. S. Cleveland's Minstrels," "We opened our season Aug. 1, at Erie, Pa. . . . Thirty-three whites, twenty-seven blacks, eleven Arabs and ten Japs . . . The company, entire, are on the stage at one time, not separate or distinct. This is the only company that gives this performance" (*New York Clipper*).

• ***August 10, 1895 (Buffalo, New York):*** "At the Academy of Music W. S. Cleveland's Greater Massive Minstrels broke the Summer lethargy, opening to good business Aug. 5 . . . The noon parade was by far the best thing of the kind yet seen in Buffalo, in its military conduct, costuming and numbers. . . . In the parade the white band came first, then came the principal white performers, then the Japanese troupe in Oriental costumes, the Arabs, the colored performers and the colored band in the order named. Cheers were in order all along from North to Exchange Street, and the eighty-five members of the company and the half mile pageant owned the town indeed . . . [T]he whites against the blacks give a competitive battalion drill" (*New York Clipper*).

At least two more exponents of "Black and White" minstrelsy were identified in the *Clipper*.

• ***May 25, 1895:*** "Casad's Minstrel Notes," "Billy Casad will spend the Summer in Michigan until about Aug. 1, when he will go to his home at Plymouth, Ind., and arrange the opening of his company . . . Our street parade will consist of two brass bands, white and colored. The white band will wear uniforms of various colors of satin, including dress coats and silk hats. The chocolate band will dress as 'rubes,' and with all over-shoulder instruments, the oldest obtainable in this country" (*New York Clipper*).

• ***September 21, 1895:*** "Notes from the Crawford Bros' Big Double Minstrels," "This company of twenty whites and twenty blacks, with two bands in the street parade, will open their season in Chicago, Ill., Sept. 22, playing mostly week stands in the West and coming East later in the season. . . . The white band, composed of fourteen musicians, is directed by Emil Klimert; the white orchestra, by Charles Plimental. The Webster Brother's Colored Band and Orchestra, twelve men, comprise the colored musical contingent, in addition to which there will be singers, buck and wing dancers, acrobats and comedians galore" (*New York Clipper*).

"Black and White Minstrelsy" eventually slipped out of currency, but in the mid-1920s a very similar style of presentation again excited public enthusiasm, and "Black and White Revues" did record business on the mainstream theater circuits. During that time, the *Chicago Defender* expressed the opinion that these racially consolidated shows represented "a step forward which we should all feel proud of."[6] However, "Black and White" shows, whether in the 1890s or the 1920s, didn't signify more racially tolerant attitudes: "Several reasons are recognized as being responsible, chief among them all being the proven drawing power of the Negro acts that have been presented."[7]

"Darkest America": Al G. Field's Real Negro Minstrels

Al. G. Field was the namesake proprietor of a famous white blackface minstrel troupe. In the fall of 1894 he announced his intention to launch a second troupe, "a company of genuine negroes," which came to be known as "Darkest America." Field drew attention to his plan with talk of touring Australia.

• ***November 17, 1894:*** "The Al. G. Field American Minstrels is the title of the company of genuine negroes now being organized for a tour of Australia. Before sailing for the Antipodes a short season will be made, extending from Pittsburg to San Francisco. While *en route* in America the company will use the parlor, sleeping and dining car Columbus, built by Barney & Smith for Mr. Field" (*New York Clipper*).

• ***June 8, 1895:*** "Al. G. Field Notes," "The Al. G. Field Real Negro Minstrels and Troupe of Arabs will open their season in Columbus, O., July 4. The company will number forty people, and will travel in their own train of cars, including sleeper, dining and baggage cars. It will be one of the best equipped colored shows ever organized. The parade is a special feature, the Arabs and four mounted buglers head the parade . . . Clarence Alston's brass band will be gaudily uniformed. The Charleston Shouters will bring up the rear, riding on a typical cotton float. Mr. Field engaged these people in Charleston, S.C., where he heard them at a colored camp meeting. There will be four men, three women and six boys. Their chants and shouts are very peculiar, and they are expected to be a big surprise. The show will not be of the old style of negro minstrelsy. To introduce scenes peculiar to the South will be the aim of the management. First, the beginning, or first part, will be entirely different from the old style first part. It will show a crack colored military company in camp. The action will be made up of funny scenes in camp life. 'The Barbers' Holiday,' a camp meeting scene; 'The Phantom Patrol' and 'The Darktown Fire Brigade' are all new features . . . Oliver Scott will be manager . . . Clarence Alston, leader of the band; Frank Hailstock, leader of orchestra . . . After a tour of Canada the company will make a forty weeks tour of the States, and possibly go to England next Summer" (*New York Clipper*).

Note: Prof. Frank M. Hailstock was one of the most promising young orchestra leaders of late-1890s African American minstrelsy. Born in Akron, Ohio, in 1875, he was eight years old when he "began his study of the violin under Wm. Lantz of Leipsig, Germany." At age twelve he "was selected as principal violinist at the Trinity Lutheran Church (white). He next attended the Dana Musical Institute in Warren, O., and studied violin under Thaddeus Ackley and theory under W. H. Dana." Then "he took up the cornet and . . . became a member of several white bands." In 1894 nineteen-year-old Hailstock joined the band with Whalen and Martell's "South Before the War" Company, and in 1895 he took charge of the orchestra with Al. G. Field's Real Negro Minstrels, and he was still with them in 1898 when they were reincarnated as Oliver Scott's Refined Negro Minstrels. On the road during the early weeks of 1899, Frank Hailstock came down with pneumonia, and on February 20, 1899, he died at his home in Akron, Ohio.[8]

THE LATE FRANK M. HAILSTOCK, JR.

Freeman, *March 4, 1899.*

• ***July 6, 1895:*** "Notes of the Al. G. Field Negro Minstrels," "Rehearsals have commenced in earnest . . . The colored camp meeting shouters serenaded Gov. McKinley recently, and were congratulated by the Governor . . . Fred. W. Simpson, the colored slide trombonist, just returned from Europe, has been engaged for the band . . . The band will render a grand concert on the

State Capitol grounds, Albany, July 4. The roster of the company is as follows: Oliver Scott, manager; Will A. Junker, treasurer; A. P. Scott, general agent . . . Cicero Reed and son, Andy Williams, Barrie McPhail, Edwin A. Winn, Billy Jackson, Wm. H. Redd, Holly V. Robinson, L. Chanalt, Adolph Henderson, John Rucker, Chas. Owsley, C. E. Santagg, Harry Fidler, Ben Moore, Clarence Alston, F. M. Hailstock, Wm. Preston, Rufus Haywood, Geo. Haywood, H. J. Hutchinson, McCarver Bros., Rastus, Lenwood Holland, Willie Jackson, J. H. Gordon, Harry Taylor, Jas. White, Chas. Patterson, Ben Holland, Billy Turner, Frankie Bass, Lem Demus and B. Felton" (*New York Clipper*).

Note: Fred Simpson remained a prominent figure on the minstrel band and orchestra scene. In 1900 he joined the band with Williams and Walker's "Sons of Ham" Company.[9] During the season of 1903–1904 he served in the band and orchestra with Richard and Pringle's Georgia Minstrels,[10] and in 1905 he took over as bandmaster. "Using a gold trombone as a baton,"[11] Simpson led the Georgia Minstrels Band for the next seven seasons.

• ***July 13, 1895:*** "The Al. G. Field Real Negro Minstrels, consisting of forty genuine Southern negroes, representative of Darkest America, opened its season July 4, at Columbus, O." (*New York Clipper*).

• ***July 13, 1895:*** "The Al. G. Field Real Negro Minstrels chose the nation's birthday for their opening at Columbus, O . . . The opening is a bit of tropical character, representing a mansion and flower garden on the Suawanee River . . . Jassimine blossoms were in profusion, and, to add to the effect, the house was perfumed with jassimine by mechanical contrivance. The trees moved as if in a gentle breeze, and the perfume was seemingly wafting from the trees as the curtain went up . . . The first solo, by John Rucker, 'Ringing the Old Village Bells,' was encored . . .

FRED. W. SIMPSON,

Trombone Soloist with Al. G. Fields' Negro Minstrels.

Among the really great wonders in the musical world none are more deserving of meritorious comment than Mr. Fred W. Simpson, a typical Hoosier, born and reared in Indianapolis. To-day he ranks as one of America's greatest trombone soloists, and has been rightfully nom de plumed "The Black Innes." With

FRED W. SIMPSON,

Trombone Soloist, with Al. G. Field Negro Minstrels.

a fair education, received in the public schools of Indianapolis, and with a meagre knowledge of music, he began the study of the slide trombone, and his success has been phenomenal. Mr. Simpson never had a private lesson in his life, which proves conclusively that his ability is wonderful and natural. He has been playing a slide trombone for six years, and has filled some very important engagements. During the seasons of 1893, 1894 and 1895 he was a very valuable adjunct with Mahara's Mammoth Minstrels and made a successful trip with this company through California and the entire West, including British America. Season of '95-'96 he was with the Al. G. Fields' "Darkest America;" the season of '96 he joined Al. G. Fields' Negro Minstrels, which company he is still with. A funny experience in Mr. Simpson's life was when he was learning to play the trombone in a band-room; the professor in charge of the band told him he could never learn to play the trombone, and to give it up and try something else. Not being daunted by the remarks of the professor, he kept on practicing and happily he succeeded, as the world well knows. Mr. Simpson uses a Conn instrument, made especially for him.

The Freeman, *December 25, 1897.*

The Magnolia Quartet sang very nicely, and the Charleston Shouters, at the conclusion of the first part, made a hit, especially McIntosh. It is a new style of stage work and went big, the old camp meeting scene arousing the audience to a high pitch. Prof. Simpson, with a well executed medley solo upon the trombone, opened the olio. Cicero Reed and sons followed in an act entitled 'Let's See You Do It.'. . . Harry Fiddler did a turn of very good imitations, his impersonation of Chinese character being the best . . . Next came the feature of the olio . . . 'The Phantom Patrol.' The stage drapings were black, the performers, some thirty in number, were clad in white, and the marching and drilling was done in perfect time, under the glare of calciums . . . The buck and wing dancing was one of the big hits . . . Andrew Williams did the time honored frog act . . . 'The Dark Town Fire Brigade' was the closing act, and it was a blaze of fun . . . The haps and mishaps of the country firemen were taken true to nature. The watermelon scene was funny enough to make an Indian laugh" (*New York Clipper*).

• ***August 24, 1895:*** "Notes from 'Darkest America,'" "Several new features have been added to 'The Barbers' Picnic' by the McCarver Bros., making it the strongest dancing act before the public . . . Billy Jackson, Harry Fiddler, Billy Caldwell and John Rucker's end work continues to give universal satisfaction" (*New York Clipper*).

• ***September 7, 1895:*** "Roster of Prof Hailstock's Orchestra, with Al. G. Field's 'Darkest America'—F. M. Hailstock, leader; R. Haywood, J. Haywood, G. Haywood, C. Alsten, R. Donge, Wm. Preston, F. Simpson, H. Walters" (*New York Clipper*).

• ***October 19, 1895:*** "Notes from 'Darkest America,'" "We entered the state of Ohio at Piqua . . . Urbana, Bellefontaine, Kenton and Findley followed suit . . . Mrs. Field paid us a visit at Urbana, bringing with her our winter parade coats. They came none too soon, as we were compelled to don them the next day. Our band, under the direction of Prof. C. E. Alston, is in splendid shape, and their daily concerts are a feature . . . The McCarver Brothers take the house by storm in their 'Georgia Cracker Jacks.' Harry Waters' crying specialty is taking three and four encores nightly. Fred W. Simpson astonishes his hearers with his trombone solos . . . George Titchner, comedian and dancer, and Joe Ricks, musician, are recent additions to the big black family" (*New York Clipper*).

In 1897 Al G. Field leased his Darkest America Company to fellow white minstrel-show entrepeneur John W. Vogel, who took full control of it the following year. A review from an 1897 mainstream daily paper provides a summarial description of 1890s plantation minstrelsy:

> "In Darkest America," as presented . . . by Mr. John Vogel's large and in every way meritorious company, was perhaps the best presentation of scenes intended to be depicted, taking the performance in all its details, that could be exhibited. The actors are in the main colored people, and from the fidelity which the scenes of the plantation in slavery times are produced, one would be justified in imagining that they had all served at least a liberal apprenticeship among the slaves of the past. The illusion however is broken by the fact that, while they make up as perfect representations of the "old field niggers," they are all too young to have had such an experience. It is their art therefore, that aids the natural powers of song and mimicry to reproduce scenes that must come, to most of them at least, only through tradition. The corn husking scenes in the barn, the massing singing and the wild antics of the dance in perfect time with the music was a perfect reproduction of the actions of the people they represented both on festival occasions and in a measure at Sunday wood's meetings. All through the program there were glimpses of this natural state of old-time laborers of the South. Even in the more studied music selections which exhibited a perfection of culture impossible to people not naturally gifted,

they would lapse into the real Negro eccentricities, which are only burlesqued in the attempted imitations so common to the burnt cork drama.[12]

Selected, Annotated Chronology of Music-Related Citations, 1894

• *January 6, 1894 (Helena, Arkansas):* "While Abe Amps was at Friar's Point with the brass band, some miscreant set fire to his house about 2 o'clock in the night, destroying everything" (*Indianapolis Freeman*).

• *January 13, 1894 (Richmond, Virginia):* "Calico Entertainment," "There will be a grand calico dress entertainment at Hayes' Hall 727 N. 2nd St. Monday night, Jan. 15th, given by the Peach Bud Club. Two prizes will be given, viz. to the lady wearing the prettiest calico dress and to the best male dancer.

Good music in attendance. Good order preserved.

"All invited. Admission, 25 cts." (*Richmond Planet*).

• *January 13, 1894 (New York City):* "The Colored Professional Club gave a reception recently to the members of the 'South Before the War' Co. and other professional friends. I. Hines, one of the original Twilight Quartet, is president; G. L. Davis, the songwriter, secretary, and Tom McIntosh, vice president. Fred Peper [sic, Piper], Albert Brown, Dan Frizer, Will Siddings, Billy Young, the Calliope Quartet, Unique Quartet, Meadowbrook Quartet, Knickerbocker Quartet and many others belong to the club" (*New York Clipper*).

• *January 13, 1894 (Knoxville, Tennessee):* "On Tuesday evening Prof. W. L. Lindsey gave an entertainment to a packed house. The professor performed on five instruments at one time" (*Indianapolis Freeman*).

BLIND TOM'S STILL A SLAVE.

A Motion to Punish the Committee of His Person for Contempt—His Earnings.

New York City.—A motion to punish Elise Bethune, as the committee of the person and estate of Blind Tom, the pianist, for contempt of court for not obeying an order made by Justice Andrews in January, 1891, was made before Justice Truax, of the supreme court, a few weeks ago. The order of Justice Andrews required her to pay $3,304 to Irene Ackerman, as administratrix of the estate of Lawyer Daniel P. Holland, for legal services to Blind Tom. Lawyer John McGrone, for the motion, said:

"In using the name of Blind Tom in the motion I am about to make, don't let it be thought that I am going to begin another fight for the freedom of that poor old man. Nothing, not even the emancipation proclamation, has ever freed him, and he is held in slavery as strong to-day as before the war."

Blind Tom had been the slave of John G. Bethune, counsel said, before the war, but until away along in 188! was regarded still as the slave of Mr Bethune and his family. At this time it was decided that there must be an accounting for the earnings of Blind Tom, which Mr. Bethune had taken as his own property, and judgment for $8,000 was entered against the Bethune estate. The case was carried by Col. Holland up to the United States supreme court from the courts of Virginia. In 1887 Blind Tom was adjudged a lunatic, and Mrs. Elise Bethune, a daughter-in-law of the deceased master of Blind Tom, was made guardian of his person and estate. Blind Tom has not been too insane to play since he was declared a lunatic. Mrs. Bethune declares that he played on a salary for such concerts as he has been engaged in since she became committee. She says that his salary has been used in his maintenance, and that she did not comply with the order because there are no funds of the estate to pay the Holland claim. It was contended on the other side that Blind Tom has earned about $33,000 since she became committee, and that a large tract of land which Mrs. Bethune has purchased at Navesink Highlands should be credited to his estate. Decision was reserved.

Cleveland Gazette, *February 3, 1894.*

"STANDING ON THE CORNER, DIDN'T MEAN NO HARM."

By GEO. EVANS. Original words and music, the greatest Negro song ever produced, now being sung with great success by

GEO. PRIMROSE, OF PRIMROSE & WEST'S MINSTRELS.

Get it at once and use it, as it is sure to be the greatest hit the coming season. Words and Music sent for 10c. Address the publishers,

J. C. GROENE & CO, 19 Arcade, Cincinnati, O.

New York Clipper, *February 10, 1894.*

Note to illustration above: "Standing on the Corner, Didn't Mean No Harm" is a precedent version of ragtime piano legend Ben Harney's 1895–1896 hit, "You've Been a Good Old Wagon But You've Done Broke Down," popularly identified as "one of the first published ragtime songs."[13] The two songs are structurally, if not melodically related, and they both make use of the famous verse about "standing on the corner." The George Evans version gives this interpretation:

> *Standing on the corner didn't mean no harm,*
> *With my Susan Ann Melinda,*
> *Up came a coon and he grasped her by de arm.*

The blues-like imagery, form, and feeling that distinguishes "You've Been a Good Old Wagon" is also evident in Evans's "Standing on the Corner, Didn't Mean No Harm":

> *Ain't got no money, but I'm going to have some,*
> *My baby, honey,*
> *Ain't got no money, but I'm going to have some,*
> *My darling, my daisy.*
> *I'm going to shoot craps, and if I'm right,*
> *I'll dress my baby out of sight.*[14]

In 1931 Jimmie Rodgers, "the father of country music," used the "standing on the corner" couplet to open his "Blue Yodel No. 9," recorded with accompaniment by Louis Armstrong.[15] Apparently, George Evans's "Standing on the Corner" remained popular enough in its own right to warrant its reissue in 1936.

• ***January 27, 1894 (Austin, Texas):*** "There was a concert given by the Lone Star, Ivy Leaf and Black Mountain Quartettes last week" (*Indianapolis Freeman*).

• ***January 27, 1894:*** "'Wife for Wife' [a mainstream theatrical production] next season will be strictly a comedy drama, with all the name implies; six distinct humorous character creations will be in keeping with the plot of the play. Independent of these specialties, one entire scene will be devoted to a 'Plantation Jollification,' in which buck and wing dancing, sentimental and comic songs and banjo serenades will be introduced by genuine Southern darkies. This will be an extra attraction, featured and billed accordingly. A syndicate of Brooklyn capitalists have secured the attraction, and the tour will be booked by T. H. Winnett, who has the bookings of several first class attractions for next season" (*New York Clipper*).

• ***February 3, 1894:*** "Wm. H. Windom, of Primrose & West's Minstrels, has just completed a new descriptive waltz song, entitled 'The Fatal Wedding,' which he is singing with much effect" (*New York Clipper*).

• ***February 9, 1895:*** "B. L. Bowman, museum manager, has closed contract to take charge and manage the museum and candy stands of the Great Syndicate Shows, this making his fourth season with this show. Mr. Bowman says he will have everything new, using an 80ft. canvas, with a 40ft middle piece, and a large double deck front. He has engaged Prof. Shelry's colored band and jubilee singers" (*New York Clipper*).

• ***February 15, 1894:*** "So long as singing plantation melodies, patting Juba, and scrambling for the pennies flung by Northern tourists among the colored children at Southern depots, continues, the flavor of domestic slavery will continue . . . We should help the colored man to rise; and the way to rise is literally to forget what is behind, and press forward to that which is before" (*Western Christian Advocate*, reproduced in *Southwestern Christian Advocate*).

• ***February 17, 1894:*** "Three Southern Songs!!" "Words and Music by Col. Will L. Visscher. Arranged by W. Herbert Lanyon. Uncle Dan, Aunt Sis Tabb, Where My Honey Sleeps. Each 30 cents, or the three songs, 75 cents.

These are charming, plaintive and characteristic Southern songs, written in dialect and by one 'To the manner born.' Since 'Long befo' the wah,' no songs have been issued that so strikingly portray the melodies and atmosphere of the ante-bellum South.

The songs have existed for several years only in the memory of the composer, who is a noted poet and journalist, and who has frequently sung them on the stage and to the delight of his audiences and winning the enthusiastic commendations of press and public.

Col. Vissher, at the earnest solicitation of numerous friends, now allows these songs to be published for the first time and their popularity is assured. They are published with a beautiful and artistic title page by a famous artist, suggesting in a charming way the subjects of the songs" (*Richmond Planet*).

The Poor! Without Fire Clothing or Food

THERE WILL BE A

Grand Concert

AT THE

First Baptist Church,

Tuesday, Feb. 20,'94

AT 3 P. M.

FOR THE BENEFIT

OF THE POOR

By some of the Best Talent of our city assisted by Students of Hartshorn Memorial College.

PROGRAMME—Part I.

1.—Friendship, Love and Song.......Quartette
2.—Duet—Instrumental.......Mrs. Jones and Miss Southerland
3.—Selection—"Lady Claire".......Miss Mary Rice
4.—Solo "Pictures of Home".......Mr. W. Q. Moon
5.—Recitation "The Pilot's Story".......Miss Annie Taylor
6.—Solo—Instrumental.......Mrs. R. K. Jones
7.—Solo—"The Lover and the Bird".......Miss S. Alice Kemp
8.—Chorus—"The Hammer Song.......Hartshorn Students

PART II.

1. Quartette—Way Over Jordon...Messrs. Bowler, Tharps, Mrs. Cross and Miss Kemp.
2. Reading "The Famine".......Miss Lavinia Carter
3. Solo—"Wrecked and Saved".......Mrs. M. A. Cross
4. Chorus "Hail us Ye Free".......Hartshorn Students
5. Duet—The Pale Moon.......Mrs. Jones and Mrs. Cross
6. Recitation "The Kiss In School.......Miss Geraldine Jordan
7. Duet—Instrumental.......Mrs. Jones and Miss Simons
8. Good Night—Quartette.......Quartette

Admission, - - - - 15c.

Richmond Planet, *February 17, 1894.*

• ***February 17, 1894 (Manchester, Virginia):*** "The Literary Feast given at the First Baptist Church last Tuesday night, 13th inst., by the teachers of the Public School was a grand success . . . Mr. Q. Wm. Moon, Manchester's greatest baritone singer . . . sang 'Pictures of Home,' on which he was encored. He responded and imitated 'Robinson's Brass Band' going down Broad Street [Richmond, Virginia's main thoroughfare]. The imitation was fine" (*Richmond Planet*).

• ***February 17, 1894:*** "The New Orleans University Students report good business. They carry their own band and orchestra, and change their bill three times a week. The roster: Leola Hanson, Mattie Wilkes, Camille Cassell and Kitty Brown, and J. A. Shipp, Ike McBeard, Rob A. Kelley, Prof. Geo. Dulph and his Black Hussar Band, and Prof. Carter B. Lumpkin's Imperial Orchestra. Rob't A. Kelley is the manager" (*New York Clipper*).

Note: This organization of northern stage stars was in no discernible way related to New Orleans University or the New Orleans University Singers.

• ***February 17, 1894:*** "People Wanted for Crumbaugh's Colored Minstrels . . . Cranks, Lushers and Vulgarians save stamps. Write at once to J. E. Crumbaugh, Columbia, Mo." (*New York Clipper*).

• ***February 17, 1894:*** "Ed. Davis' 'Uncle Tom's Cabin' Co. played Charlottesville, Va., recently. The morning after the company was billed most of the paper was painted over with black paint and S.V.C. in large letters, which stands for 'Sons of Confederate Veterans.' Lincoln's picture on the three sheet was entirely painted over with black, while over the big stand of Eliza on the ice followed by blood hounds were the initials again . . . Before the company had left the manager found out who did it and declared he would push the case and punish the offender" (*New York Clipper*).

• ***March 3, 1894 (Fort Smith, Arkansas):*** "The Junior Brass Band of this city, under the management of Prof. Geo. H. W. Stewart gave a grand concert and ball at Murta's opera house in Van Buren, on last Tuesday night 20th inst. Expenses deducted leaving a balance of $55 as cleared. A large number of Fort Smithians accompanied the band to Van Buren. Quite a crowd followed on the next train at 8 P.M. Reaching Van Buren, the band at 3 o'clock paraded the streets. At night, over 300 people attended . . . The program opened with an overture by the band, followed by an address . . . after which the band played 'After the Ball.' Dancing was then indulged in until the arrival of the train at 2 A.M. Among the interesting features of the entertainment was the performance of a wonderful contortionist, Dr. Andrews, a colored man . . . The comic sermon, solos, and quartettes by members of the band and others were well received. The band was organized about four months ago, with Prof. Stewart as teacher, and the boys have made very rapid progress" (*Indianapolis Freeman*).

• ***March 10, 1894 (Wilberforce, Ohio):*** "Old Wilberforce has given rise to the youngest organized concert company now on the road. Their program is selected from the leading musical and literary authors. They will be known hereafter as 'The Seven Wilberforce Students'" (*Indianapolis Freeman*).

• ***March 17, 1894:*** "When Beethoven was writing the 'Moonlight Sonata' for a colored piano player from New Orleans who was making a tour of Germany, he asked the American for a motif that was purely Afro-American; but the only tune that the American knew to be of New Orleans creation was a simple air, sung by the creoles. Anyone who knows the old airs of Provence will find one in the motif of the first part of the 'Moonlight Sonata'" (*Cleveland Gazette*).

• ***March 17, 1894:*** "Notes from the 'Slavery Days' Co." "Mr. and Mrs. Chas. T. Small, formerly of the Heyer Colored Comedy Co., joined this company at Albany last week. Florence Hines, owing to severe indisposition, was compelled to lay off and returned to her home in Chicago. Henry Williams, the flat foot buck and wing dancer, after six weeks at the Mercy Hospital in Pittsburg, owing to a fractured shoulder, joined the company [March] 5. Major Ben F. Payne, associate manager and stage director, is progressing nicely with his new play, 'The Millwright.' 'Slavery Days' will not close this Summer. It is booked solid and working to the Pacific Coast" (*New York Clipper*).

• ***March 23, 1894 (Topeka, Kansas):*** "Phonographical Success," "This wonderful gentleman Prof. E. H. Borton, who has been conducting a fine series of phonographical entertainments at 526 Kansas avenue, is said to have one of the finest and most original talkers now in operation. One can distinctly understand, if they will place the tubes in their ears, and listen attentively. All kinds of good music can be heard, selected and obtained by calling and consulting this gentleman. He is attracting large crowds daily, and all classes stop in to hear the wonderful phonograph" (*Kansas State Ledger*).

• ***March 24, 1894 (Helena, Montana):*** After a lecture "at the auditorium . . . R. Lucas, Al Marshall and Phil T. Simmons rendered 'Sebastopool' [*sic*] on three guitars and were encored" (*Indianapolis Freeman*).

• ***March 31, 1894 (Richmond, Virginia):*** "Thursday and Friday evenings, March 22nd and 23rd, concerts were given in the Second Baptist Church which will long be remembered by pleasure-seekers in Richmond.

The concerts were given by the great Mme. Sissieretta Jones, the Black Patti, supported by Mr. Lindsay, a pronounced musical genius and the best of our local talent, Mr. W. Q. Moon, Mesdames Mildred A. Cross, F. P. Walker and Lena V. Jackson as pianist for the home talent . . .

Too much praise cannot be given Mr. Lindsay, who performed on the guitar, mouth organ and flute. His imitations surpassed anything previously heard in this city, while his whistling 'Listen to the Mocking Bird,' was simply wonderful.

Mme. Jones ably sustained her reputation . . . Her 'Swanee River' was grand and soul-stirring" (*Richmond Planet*).

• ***March 31, 1894:*** "Recently Mme Sissieretta Jones visited Mme Melba, who is classed all over the world with Adelina Patti, as a soprano soloist, at the Hotel Savoy, in New York City, and there sang several selections, which were received with enthusiasm by the great Melba. She immediately told Mme Jones that her voice was grand, and also stated that Mme Jones should go to Paris and finish under her instruction and volunteered her services at the benefit for the same. Mme Jones intends to take her advice, and in a short time, one of the greatest concerts ever given in New York will take place. The main artist will be Madame Melba, and the proceeds will be to finish the musical education of Mme S. Jones in Paris" (*Cleveland Gazette*).

• ***March 31, 1894*** (Winfield, Kansas): "We had the pleasure of meeting Eddie B. Love, female impersonator and vocalist; also Mr. Geo. Hampton, comedian and banjoist. These two gentlemen travel with Dr. Watkins Specialty Co. and are known as Pete and Lize. They are artists of their profession" (*Parsons Weekly Blade*).

• ***April 4, 1894:*** "A BLADE reporter called at Rev. Sin Killer Griffin's church at 8:30 P.M. last Saturday night and found the Rev. instructing his choir . . . and they had quite a conversation while the choir continued singing . . .

Reporter: 'Have you any visiting ministry?'

Rev.: 'Yes, I have both ministers and songsters. I have here with me Rev. Slaughter of Little Rock, and Rev. Burnett of Longview, Rev. Hawkins of Shreveport, La., and also have Geo.

Hawkins, of Little Rock, though he is only a songster. I have with us Miss Jones, of Parish, and Miss Perry, of Bonham. They are my vocalists.'

Reporter: 'Are you realizing many souls for your reward in this meeting, and how long will you run it?'

Rev.: 'Yes, I have in all twelve conversions and seven ready for baptism Sunday. I will run ten days.'

Reporter: 'Who is going to preach tonight?'

Rev.: 'I am going to preach myself to-night, as we are to have a large crowd. I shall mount the steed to-night.'

Reporter: 'Well Rev., you must excuse me for taking so much of your time to-night.'

Rev.: 'Well, just wait five or ten minutes and I will have the choir sing you a song or two.'

So at that juncture the Rev. . . . informed his choir and church that they had with them a gentleman representing the *Parsons Blade,* which some of you take, and I want you to sing two rich songs for him . . . The choir then sang 'I Heard the Savior Say,' and 'Only a Step to Jesus.' Then Rev. Hawkins prayed quite a lengthy prayer. Just about that time the reporter's time was getting precious, so he rose and congratulated the Rev. and his host for the hospitality . . . and contributed 25 cents for the good of the cause, and just as he bowed to them in order to say God bless you, Rev. Sin Killer Griffin said: 'Oh, yes, I forgot to present you with one of my photos.'

The reporter then took his departure, assuring them that he would call again, and in case he failed to meet them again in Denison [Texas] he would be sure to meet them some where about Jordan" (*Parsons Weekly Blade*).

• ***April 7, 1894 (Decatur, Illinois):*** "The entertainment given by the Monitor band was a success . . . The 'Little Link' quartette under the direction of Mr. Slaughter, deserves especial commendation for their trouble in preparing several nice songs which were delivered very effectively" (*Indianapolis Freeman*).

THE BELLS' QUARTETTE

At Blackford Street Church, Monday Night, April 9th.

1.	"Hail us Ye Free,"	Company.
2.	Overture,	R. B Shelton.
3.	"Annie Laurie,"	Bell Quartette.
4.	Soprano solo,	Katie Clay.
5.	Character Duett,	M. W. Daniels, Wm. D. Cook.
6.	Tenor solo,	Chas. H. Lewis.
7.	Selection,	Bell Quartette.

PART II.

1.	Soprano solo,	Duretta Dixon.
2.	Selection—Imitation of Caliope,	Bell Quartette
3.	Tenor solo,	William Cook.
4.	"Vacant Chair,"	Bell Quartette.
5.	Bass solo,	M. W. Daniels.
6.	Imitation of Band.	Bell Quartette.
7.	"Good Night."	Bell Quartette.

Freeman, *April 7, 1894. The presence of Ruby Shelton and Major Daniels indicates that the Bells Quartette was comprised of "ringers." Their concert renditions of calliope and band imitations represent the ancestry of early-twentieth century quartet band imitations and the "human orchestra" horn imitations popularized by the Mills Brothers during the 1930s.*

• ***April 14, 1894:*** "Relative to Harry T. Burleigh's appointment as baritone soloist in St. George's Protestant, Episcopal Church of New York, Dr. Rainsford, the rector, recently said, with much good sense: 'I can see nothing at all remarkable in the fact of Mr. Burleigh's being in my vested choir; he has a very fine voice, we are glad to have him, and if he wishes to do so, why should he not sing in the church of God?' Old prejudices are fortunately growing less, and this instance should cause no surprise' " (*Cleveland Gazette*).

• ***April 14, 1894 (Richmond, Virginia):*** "No More This Season," "The Jubilee Songsters of Bethlehem, who have been giving spiritual concerts at our churches in this city since January 15th . . . have stopped for the season.

They gave their last concert at the Sixth Mt. Zion Baptist Church, Monday night, April 9, 1894. They have had good success and done much good in helping the churches for which they sang. They decided to stop because of the great wave of salvation that is now flowing through our city, for they are great revival workers and want to go into the field of battle and help bring souls to the Lord" (*Richmond Planet*).

• ***April 21, 1894 (Galveston, Texas):*** Included on the program at a local concert was a "selection on mandoline, guitar, triangle and piano by Peachy brothers" (*Parsons Weekly Blade*).

• ***May 5, 1894 (Winfield, Kansas):*** "We learn that Bud Goodseal is traveling with Wadkin's Linament Co., with 'Pete' and 'Lize.' Bud is a good concert man" (*Parsons Weekly Blade*).

• ***May 19, 1894:*** "Prof. Booker T. Washington Taken To Task—Charged With Making a Jest of a Sacred Race Song," "Editor Freeman:

Will you please give me space to defend the songs of our fathers from the fun-poking methods of some of our great men?

I saw a speech made by Prof. Booker T. Washington, President of Tuskegee University, of Alabama, in which he seems to be guilty of the same mistake made by other great men of the race, namely: making a jest of . . . the most sacred songs on earth, produced by any race, of which the Negroes are the originators . . .

He who mocks the songs given our fathers by the spirit of God in the days of slavery, is a blasphemer. No songs on earth are more sacred, at any rate they are the best we have got, and the educated Negro has not been able to give us anything to equal them . . .

Nothing is worthy of our assumed cultured people unless it has something other than a Negro origin. Bishop H. M. Turner, the great and grand man of his race to-day, has well said: 'The young Negroes are the only people on earth who will mock and poke fun at the sayings, songs and doings of their fathers and mothers . . .'

Mr. Washington repeats the same old stale story of our defamers and persecutors . . ., 'That the Negro sings and shouts all night and then goes home to an empty pantry, then the master's chicken roost must suffer.'

We cannot pick up a book of songs that stirs the souls of men, but what has borrowed largely from the Negro idea of jubilee music. Many of the music writers not only use them as a basis for the construction of their music, but use the words and are not ashamed to do so. Whoever heard of a gospel hymn or triumphant song, until the Fisk, Tennessee and Hampton Jubilee singers had by so sweetly singing their father's songs, put a new soul into the world's music. The pathetic touch of the Negro music by black men awakened America, England, France, Germany, India, Austria, Scotland, Ireland and other countries, as no other songs have done. The Negroes are the originators of the best Gospel and Triumphant songs of earth. Think of 'Swing low, sweet chariot;' 'Steal away to Jesus;' 'Been Redeemed;' 'Ten Virgins;' 'Walking in the Light of God;' 'We shall be like Him;' 'The Triumph of Israel;' 'Moses smote the water;' 'Didn't old Pharoah get lost?' 'Halleluah to the Lamb;' 'Nothing but the blood of Jesus;' 'The Lord is of the giving hand, nothing but the blood of Jesus;' 'Over there;' 'Why don't you come to Jesus?' 'Give me Jesus and you may have all the world, but give me Jesus;' 'Elijah's chariot.' I repeat the educated Negroes who mock our songs have not been able to equal the music of their fathers . . . They would mock it out of existence without ability to give us anything as good as they would take away. Our white friends made the improvement needed. They saw great worth and arranged the tunes to notes . . .

"It was not the quaint, amusing features which made it so attractive, but above all was its power to cheer the heart and move the soul. Whether men are rich or poor, whatever stirs their inmost nature and awakens sentiments which lift them towards God will attract them. The Negroes music, when properly sung, does this for every man of any race, and in every country, but some of our select few 'who think everything white is God and everything black is the Devil.' Those who have more education than self respect and good common sense... spurn everything not labelled white or very much bleached. Many of the ministers, professors, choirs and churches look with contempt upon these our only songs and turn to others which they must borrow or steal. Let them give half the attention to our own music, and the harvest will be great and honor awarded to those who reflect credit upon the fathers of the race. God bless old Fisk, Tennessee, Hampton and Prof. J. Loudin.

Yours for the race

J. J. Jones, D.D., First Baptist church, and chief of the Bureau of Organization of Nation Equal Rights Council, Steelton, Pa." (*Indianapolis Freeman*).

• ***June 2, 1894:*** "To The Editor of The Freeman," "Please allow me space in your paper to reply to an article written against Prof. B. T. Washington. In your last issue I noticed that a Mr. Jones had been worked up to a high pitch of excitement over what he called making a jest of the sacred songs of our mothers... What Mr. Washington says concerning the Negro of the South is said in order to picture the need of money to educate the young [of the] race above degradation and crime. In speaking of the 'chicken roost' and the 'empty pantry,' if you were in Mr. Washington's state instead of in one corner of Penn., you would concur with him when you saw the reality in what he said...

The very songs sung by our fathers, spoken of by Rev. Jones, are collected [and] set to music by Prof. Hamilton, and sung with more effect at Tuskegee than any other place in the South. If Mr. Jones would only take the pains to go to Tuskegee and hear those students sing 'Steal away to Jesus,' 'Swing low, sweet chariot,' 'Been Redeemed,' etc., he would find out that he could be taught something about the songs of our mothers...

Respectfully yours for the right,

Lee Roy Robinson, Bessemer, Ala." (*Indianapolis Freeman*).

• ***July 7, 1894:*** "The Monte Carlo Quartet, Harry Prampin, band leader, and Frank M. Hailstock Jr., orchestra leader, are booked with the Howard McCann Operatic Minstrels" (*New York Clipper*).

Note: Harry Prampin remained a popular road-show bandleader throughout the 1890s, and he went on to form a vaudeville team act with his wife, Laura.

• ***July 7, 1894:*** "McCabe's Minstrel Notes," "McCabe's Mastodon Minstrels, for many years known as McCabe & Young's Operatic Minstrels, open their season at Chicago, July 8. They go out under the direction of George H. Abbott, an old timer, who has surrounded himself with a number of old school performers... The company is headed by Dan W. McCabe, who has made himself famous as a minstrel producer and stage manager. The aggregation includes twenty-one well known performers, as follow: John Brener, gun man; the Palmino Family, three in number, the great Hindoo jugglers, their first appearance in this country; Bobby Kemp, William McCabe, A. Denning, Harry Prampkin, Will Preston, Prince McCabe, Maurice Jordan, Frank Patrick, John Pamplin, Walter Dixon, Gorton Collins, George Techner, Ed. Harris, Watson Lewis, Neal Moore Jr., Le Roy Blair [*sic*], impersonator, and Matiena Gonzalives, a Spanish star of note. The old time

Harry Prampin.
Cornetist and bandmaster; entered the profession in the year of 1892, as band master of the Merritt University Students and has since successfully led the bands of McCabe & Young's Minstrels, Davis' Uncle Tom's Cabin company for three seasons: Salter and Martin's Uncle Tom's Cabin company; J. Ed George' Georgia Graduates and in August '98 he joined the Original Nashville Students now combined with L. E. Gideon's Minstrels under the direction of Rusco & Holland. Mr. Prampin is an accomplished cornetist and a promising young bandmaster, using the largest and most classical repertoire of overtures. Permanent address: The Freeman.

Freeman, *December 30, 1899.*

first part finish will be one of the great features of the show, introducing a Mexican bull fight and circus day at Darktown. The olio will consist of the Drum Major's Outing, the Twilight Quartet, song and dance festival, shadow pantomime and living pictures, South before the war. The performance concludes with Dan McCabe's laughable afterpiece, entitled 'The Black Silver King.' At the close of the Chicago engagement the company will tour Michigan, opening at South Haven, July 16" (*New York Clipper*).

• ***July 14, 1894:*** "Notes from Howard McCarver's Operatic Minstrels," "We open season at Atlanta, Ga., Aug. 27. Howard McCarver, proprietor, and under the management of Tony Burch . . . Will give a splendid first part, a novel street parade, and our afterpiece, 'Fun in Hulegan's Club Room,' also the famous Monte Carlo Quartet. Roster: Harry Prampin, Frank M. Hailstock, Jr., Joe Hall, J. R. Easley, Chas. A. Hunter, J. C. Lowery, A. S. Lowe, J. A. Terril, Cheatham Bros., Heard and Knot, Hi Henry Williams, Billy McCarver, Britt Craig, Jas. R. Johnson, Lenona Bros., Ruby Jacks and John N. Anderson. The olio will consist of the Buck Town Quartet, eight song and dance [*sic*], arranged by Will Cheatham, 'Echoes of the Marriage Bells.' The company will tour the northeast" (*New York Clipper*).

• ***July 14, 1894:*** "Al. E. and Mamie Anderson are filling a five week's engagement at the Pavilion Theatre, Grand Island Beach, N.Y. Mamie Anderson is singing with success one of Will H. Fox's late songs, 'It Might Have Been.' The team returns to Boston, Mass., soon for rehearsal with Lanworth's Big Colored Show for next season" (*New York Clipper*).

• ***July 14, 1894:*** "There are many burlesque camp meetings throughout Ohio, controlled by alleged Christians who are conducting these side show minstrel affairs solely for the purpose of making money. It is bad enough for our people to make monkeys of themselves in the usual ways without using the cloak of religion to cover their disgraceful conduct and schemes.

"SWINGING ON DE GOLDEN GATE"

BY PAUL BARNES. The "Hottest" Coon Song ever written.

IT IS NEW AND AN "INSTANTANEOUS HIT."

Come and get it or send 10c. in stamps for professional copy and orchestration.

CRUGER BROS., 30 W. Twenty-eighth Street, New York.

New York Clipper, *July 21, 1894.*

It seems very hard for some people to understand that the days of the camp meeting has long since passed, and that there are now very few places so remote from the outside world that their inhabitants do not look upon the average camp meeting as the next thing to a minstrel show in every way" (*Cleveland Gazette*).

Note to illustration above: When Paul Barnes's "Swinging on de Golden Gate" was advertised again in the *Clipper* of September 15, 1894, the black vaudeville team of Hodges and Launchmere was said to be "making it the hit of their act at the Casino Roof Garden." A version of this pseudo-spiritual, credited to Fred Lyons, was in circulation as early as 1882, under the same title, and with the characteristic chorus:

Den awake me, shake me,
Don't let me sleep too late,
For I am a gwine away in the morning,
To swing on de golden gate.[16]

Sung for humorous effect by both white and black minstrels of the 1880s and 1890s, "Swinging on de Golden Gate" was recorded in 1927 by "hillbilly" artist Fiddlin' John Carson,[17] and in 1933 it was included in an "Album of Fireside Songs" sung by "country" radio and recording artists Frank and James McCravy.[18]

Possibly, "Swinging on the Golden Gate" began as a minstrel parody and evolved into a twentieth-century folk hymn, but perhaps the "wake me, shake me" chorus has grassroots origins and persisted in African American tradition despite the popularity of the parodic versions. In any case, "Wake Me, Shake Me" remained a popular vehicle for both sacred and profane interpretations, through most of the twentieth century.

Black gospel quartet arrangements of the "wake me, shake me" chorus were recorded by the Wright Brothers Gospel Singers of Dallas in 1941 and the National Independent Gospel Singers of Atlanta in 1950. Both quartets waxed engaging, traditional-sounding acappella renditions, not at all comedic in affect. The Wright Brothers' recording may be the clearest representation of a "folk-rooted" version, based on a traditional verse pattern:

I met my mother this morning,
She was climbing up the hill so soon,
She was trying to get to Heaven in due time,
Before the Heaven doors close.
I met my father this morning...
I met my brother this morning...
I met my sister this morning.[19]

The National Independent Gospel Singers' recording of "Wake Me, Shake Me" shares the same verse pattern. Titled "I Met My Elder This Morning," it is likewise authentically folkloric, full of emotional intensity and rousing "down home" rhythms.

In a very different fashion, Billy Guy, the exemplary comedian-harmonist of the Coasters, reached back into the American song bag to concoct a hilarious version of "Wake Me, Shake Me," rendered as a sanitation worker's complaint! One verse contains an irreverent spiritual parody, a very late workingman's update of nineteenth-century minstrel convention:

> *I had a dream,*
> *I had a dream,*
> *I said I looked over yonder,*
> *What did I see,*
> *I see two big garbage trucks,*
> *I said a-comin' after me,*
> *A-picking up cans, I said side by side,*
> *Why don't you swing down sweet garbage truck*
> *And let your buddy ride.*[20]

In 1961 "Wake Me, Shake Me" experienced a resurgence in the black religious repertoire, after gospel singing star Brother Joe May waxed a consciously artistic and decidedly unhumorous reading of the traditional verses and chorus.[21]

• ***July 28, 1894:*** "Billy McClain and wife, Chas. Halker [*sic*, Walker] and wife, Tom Williams and the Arnold Bros. go with Thos. H. Davis' 'On the Mississippi.' Harry McClain goes with Thos. H. Davis' 'Dixie' Co. . . Woods and McPhail have closed with Harry S. Eaton's Colored Sports at Rocky Pt., R.I., and joined Jones, Milbank & Windle's Vaudevilles, playing under canvas" (*New York Clipper*).

• ***July 28, 1894 (New York City):*** "Casino Roof Garden," "The bill presented July 23 and week included . . . Hodges and Larchmere [*sic*], and the Casino Pickaninnies" (*New York Clipper*).

• ***August 4, 1894:*** "The Two Andersons [Al and Mamie] are playing at Austin & Stone's Museum, Boston, this week, doing their Southern sketch, 'Corn Bread'" (*New York Clipper*).

• ***August 4, 1894:*** "A New Play," "C. E. Callahan's comedy drama, 'Coon Hollow,' was produced at Aurora, Ill. . . . Act three shows . . . a Mississippi wood landing, and . . . the race between the Robert E. Lee and Natchez . . . In this scene a plantation dance by twenty darkeys is introduced" (*New York Clipper*).

• ***August 11, 1894:*** "McKenzie Gordon (white) a New York tenor singer, refused last week . . . to appear on the stage in concert at the Monona Lake assembly, Madison, Wis., because Mme Jones, who was the artist of the evening, was to appear. However, the concert went on without the prejudiced fool. 'The Black Patti' is not only the better known and appreciated of the two (herself and Gordon) but she can teach the jackass good manners" (*Cleveland Gazette*).

• ***August 18, 1894:*** Among the titles listed in an ad for "Comic and Sentimental" songs available from New York publisher Spaulding & Gray is "I've Been Hoodooed" by Gussie L. Davis, described as "Decidedly the best 'darky' song Mr. Davis has ever written" (*New York Clipper*).

• ***August 25, 1894 (Cleveland, Ohio):*** "Mr. Walter S. Espy and Miss Emma L. Hyers were married this past week. The former is 'Uncle Tom' and the latter the 'Topsy' of the Davis Company now at the Lyceum" (*Cleveland Gazette*).

• ***September 6, 1894:*** A correspondent from Plaquemine, Louisiana, asserts that "reforms are needed in the manner of conducting, managing and governing our church affairs . . . The habit of jumping, falling over the pews, tearing the clothes, disarranging the toilets, stamping the feet and other undignified things for which so many of churches are noted make us appear in the category of the uncivilized, to say the least of it. This habit is called shouting, which is a misnomer. What is shouting any how? It is to utter a sudden and loud outcry, usually in joy, triumph or exultation . . . Therefore there should be reform in the manner of shouting so

"Billie" McClain.

"Billie" McClain, the minstrel man, was born on Elm street, this city, Oct. 12, 1866. He used to play an E flat cornet in Hayes' Band, but his first appearance in public was in Crone's Garden, in 1881. From an early age he evinced an unusual ability as a mimic and has on many occasions delighted private gatherings. His first professional career began with Lew Johnson's minstrels in 1883, shortly afterwards with Hecks & Sawyer's minstrels and Blythe's Georgia minstrels. In 1886 he joined Sells Bros.' circus, which visited the Hawaiian Islands. In 1880 he took out the Gigantic Comedy Co., which was forced to the wall in Texarkana, Tex. He joined Cleveland's minstrels in '90 and toured the United States and Canada until 1891; had engagements with Lewis Turner's Co, Nashville Students, Hyer Sisters, and lately was with Whallen's "South Before the War." Since May 7, 1894, he has played with Callender's minstrels

"BILLIE" M'CLAIN.

and Jas. Paine & Son. July 28th, Mr. McClain came West for Davis & Kehoe's "On the Mississippi," a comedy drama of unusual proportions. Fifty people are in the cast, and besides, two carloads of scenery, one live alligator and two horses are used in the play. Mr. McClain composes and arranges his own music and is one of the few who have made the stage a financial success. Besides owning property in New York, he lately purchased a property at 955 N. New Jersey street, where his mother will hereafter reside.

Freeman, *August 25, 1894.*

much practiced by our church people. Let them break off this uncouth and irreligious way of serving God. Let them be taught to shout in the true sense of the word, in spirit and truth, if the Holy Ghost moves them to do so. Yes, shout, but shout aright and in a way as not to make the church the place of resort for the ungodly whenever they want a good, hearty laugh" (J. L. Jones, *Southwestern Christian Advocate*).

• ***September 8, 1894 (New Orleans, Louisiana):*** "Last Friday night a serenade was tendered Misses Ophelia Malonson and Mamie Tolmaro, by Mr. A. O. Leavias' string band and the Lilac quartet in honor of their cousins, Misses Ella White and Camille Harrison, of Plaquemine, La., who are spending some times very pleasantly in the city" (*Indianapolis Freeman*).

Note: "Mr. A. O. Leavias" is no doubt Adam Oleavia, remembered by New Orleans jazz historians as a local cornetist and bandleader, "the first to employ both Bunk Johnson and Tony Jackson."[22] On the strength of oral testimony collected from Bunk Johnson, early jazzologists assumed that Adam Oleavia was a downtown Catholic Creole with a French last name—"Olivier."[23] However, descendants of Adam Oleavia have since revealed that he was an uptown Baptist African American whose last name was originally spelled "O'Leavia."[24] Early city directory listings confirm the O'Leavia/Oleavia spelling of this historically underrated New Orleans musician's last name.

• ***September 15, 1894 (Richmond, Virginia):*** "The Jubilee Singers of Bethlehem have filled engagements at the Fifth St. Baptist Church, Fifth Baptist and 6th Mt. Zion churches. They are composed of six singers and sing only scriptural hymns. Fine audiences have greeted them since they have opened the season . . . At the Fifth St. Baptist Church the singing was excellent . . . Belshazzar's Feast, John the Revelator, and Long Time Ago, were favorites with the audience . . . The next entertainment will take place at the Second Baptist Church on next Monday night, Sept. 17" (*Richmond Planet*).

• ***September 15, 1894 (Topeka, Kansas):*** "The famous Little Link quartette serenaded Senator Martin, who had just returned from Washington, Thursday night. Jas. Rivers is the manager" (*Topeka Weekly Call*).

• ***September 15, 1894 (Cleveland, Ohio):*** "The South African Kaffir choir now concerting in the city was the musical success of England and the colonies. It is composed of seven distinct tribes of native Africans. They sang by special request before Her Majesty the Queen, Rt. Hon. W. E. Gladstone, and at the garden party of Baroness Burdett-Coutts. 'The Review of Reviews' of London says: 'There has been no troupe to compare with them since the jubilee singers of Fisk University.' The great and only South African Choir will concert at St. John's A.M.E. Church Friday evening September 21. Admission: 25 cents. This will perhaps be the only opportunity of your life to see and hear such a novel and yet so excellent a musical organization" (*Cleveland Gazette*).

• ***September 15, 1894:*** "Notes from Howard McCarver's Minstrels," "Prof. Joe Hall's brass band of fourteen pieces is making a good impression. Prof. Frank M. Hailstock, Jr., and his operatic orchestra of eight pieces receive applause for fine selections. Terrell, the Egyptian juggler, is a feature and is repeatedly called, as is also Matt Beasly, the contortionist. Heard and Knox, in 'Fun in a Chinese Laundry,' are one of the greatest drawing cards of the season. The famous Cheatham Bros. always get encores, as do the McCarver Bros. Will C. Hayden, Britt Craig, A. S. Lowe, Hi Henry Williams, Prof. Will Jones, D. C. Thomas, Eddy Smith, R. Z. Ellison, J. C. Lowery, Wash Fannagan, Billy Donelo, Harry Raymond, Jomy Silvo and Lou Da Mount are also with the company" (*New York Clipper*).

• ***September 15, 1894:*** "Notes from Crumbaugh's Refined Minstrels," "We are now in our fifth week and are playing to excellent business. George Bailey's trombone solos in our noonday concerts are the feature of our street parade. Our first part evening serenaders arranged by Jas. Crosby is meeting with success" (*New York Clipper*).

• ***September 15, 1894:*** "The Unique Quartet, Messrs. Moore, Settle, Cayson and Delyons, are with 'The Operator' Co., touring the Southern and Western states" (*New York Clipper*).

Note: The Unique Quartet, under the leadership of Joseph M. Moore, was among the first African American artists to make sound recordings. Their initial session reportedly took place in New York City, December 19, 1890. Copies of at least two of their recorded titles from the 1890s, "Mama's Black Baby Boy" and "Who Broke the Lock," survive.[25]

• ***September 15, 1894 (Baltimore, Maryland):*** "'On the Mississippi,' a melodrama by William Haworth, was produced for the first time on any stage at Harris' Academy, Sept. 10 . . . The cast [included Charles Walker, Katie Carter and Cordelia McClain]. The action takes place in the mountains of Tennessee, in New Orleans, in a Louisiana swamp, in a jail at Kelly's Ferry, and finally in Tennessee again. The New Orleans scene includes an elaborate gambling house, a floating theatre and the corner of St. Charles and Canal Streets" (*New York Clipper*).

• ***September 29, 1894 (Topeka, Kansas):*** "The Little Link quartette club assists Dr. Brownfield's concert actors" (*Topeka Weekly Call*).

Note: Dr. Brownfield was a medicine show operator. An ad in the same edition of the *Weekly Call* describes him as "the doctor of doctors . . . His open air concerts bear the name of 'excelsior.' His medicine holds the same. There has been cure after cure for catarrh brought to Topeka, but Dr. Brownfield's catarrh cure excells them all. And what is his cure? The simplest thing on earth; only roots which the doctor has brought from the Sandwich islands."

• ***September 29, 1894:*** "New Plays," " 'Down in Dixie' is among the latest additions to the list of Southern plays, and was presented for the first time at Heuk's Opera House, Cincinnati, O., Sept. 2 . . . Incidental to the plot, there is a serenade by a pickaninny band of sugar cane cutters, some songs by the Florida Quartette, of cotton pickers, and the essence of Southern hoe downs by youthful colored dancers. In one scene, a little coon who is busily engaged in finishing a watermelon drops into a stream, and is swallowed by a monster alligator" (*New York Clipper*).

• ***October 5, 1894 (Topeka, Kansas):*** "The I.X.L. Glee Club is rapidly gaining in popularity under the efficient management of Prof. James W. Rivers, the well known baritone soloist" (*Kansas State Ledger*).

• ***October 12, 1894 (Topeka, Kansas):*** "The Little Link Quartette will give a concert at St. John's A.M.E. Church next Tuesday evening. Quite a number of the latest quartettes, songs, plantation melodies will be rendered. Wm Moore, first tenor; Earnest Kilbro, W. M. James, baritone; James Rivers, base" (*Kansas State Ledger*).

• ***October 12, 1894 (Topeka, Kansas):*** "Mr. Hood Shelton entertained a few intimate friends at a stag party last Saturday evening in his suit of rooms on Kansas Ave. High-five, guitar and mandolin selections and vocal solos, formed the amusements of the evening. Cake and port wine was served" (*Kansas State Ledger*).

• ***October 20, 1894:*** "A colored flambeau club has been organized in N. Topeka with fifty members and a drum corps attachment. They expect to have their uniforms soon. There has been one organized in Tennesseetown also" (*Topeka Weekly Call*).

• ***October 20, 1894:*** "York Anderson, stage manager of the 'Slavery Days' Co., has put on a new act for the company, entitled 'The Colored Barber's Picnic, or Hot Stuff in de Woods' " (*New York Clipper*).

• ***October 20, 1894:*** "Mamie and Al. Anderson have secured four little pickaninnies in conjunction with their Southern plantation sketch, 'Corn Bread' " (*New York Clipper*).

Note: Mamie and Al E. Anderson were a husband-and-wife comedy team specializing in "Genuine Southern Comedy." Their act can be seen as a precursor to the great southern husband-and-wife teams that were the mainstay of independent black vaudeville, 1910–1920.

• ***November 3, 1894 (Richmond, Virginia):*** "The Flora Batson Concerts," "Monday evening last, the Fifth Street Baptist Church was crowded with an appreciative audience to listen to the accomplished and cultured voice of the renowned Queen of Song, Flora Batson . . . She was accompanied by Mme. V. A. Montgomery as pianist . . . At the request of the PLANET man 'Coming thro' the Rye' was sung.

The home talent held up their end of the entertainment, to a remarkable degree . . .

The only and original D. Webster Davis, brought down the house with his plantation dialect composed into poetry. Mr. Davis is an evening's entertainment by himself although he 'stole de breeches to be baptiz' in.'

It is estimated that between 1000 and 2000 people were present.

Tuesday night another large crowd greeted Miss Batson. The home talent at the Second Church also acquitted themselves very well . . . Thomas M. Crump rendered three solos and in company with Wesley Foster sang a splendid duett, entitled 'Cup of Woe.' . . . Prof. H.B. Burrell was pianist" (*Richmond Planet*).

• ***November 3, 1894 (Springfield, Ohio):*** "Mayarzo Fanere Sakie, the young man from South Africa lately adopted by the North Ohio Conference, was in the city this week, as was also the native African choir, of which he was formerly a member. The choir gave two entertainments at the Grand Opera House Saturday (Oct. 27) afternoon and evening, and also assisted at the YMCA (white) meeting at the City Hall, Sunday afternoon. The choir is managed by a white man, whom, Mr. Sakie says, is by no means neglectful of his own interests and who has not fully lived up to his contract in the matter of the singers' share of profits. Mr. Sakie addressed the Tawawa literary society last Monday evening" (*Cleveland Gazette*).

• ***November 3, 1894 (Cadiz, Ohio):*** "Mr. W. H. Lucas has engaged the native African choir to appear here Saturday evening for the benefit of the church. Mr. F. Sackie, formerly a member of the choir, is attending Wilberforce under the patronage of the North Ohio conference" (*Cleveland Gazette*).

• ***November 3, 1894:*** Under the heading "Habits and Associations That Harm the Negro," a Philadelphia-based writer complains that "the Negro does not encourage social and intelligent intercourse in organized bodies and assemblies . . . Especially is this true of the rural districts, and particularly in the South. As our large cities in the North are made up largely of the influx of this rural constituency with its warped and biased intellect malformated and shrunken by ignorance, superstition, heredity and environment, we see the baneful results of our progress, civil and political . . . He meets, truly, but how does he meet? . . . It is on Saturday nights in the stores of the white merchants, who only cares for him for what money he can get out of him, and who will sometimes furnish him with free rum and invariably has a 'nigger' in the fullest sense of the word with a mouth organ, fiddle or accordion to attract attention. They meet in the alleys in the rear of the taverns and hotels where they are renegaded [*sic*] to get their rum, apparently denied the semblance of manhood, to walk up to the bar like men" (Chas. V. Monk, *Indianapolis Freeman*).

• ***November 10, 1894 (Pittsburgh, Pennsylvania):*** "The African choir appeared here last Monday evening in Carnegie Hall. Owing to inclement weather the audience which greeted them was not as large as expected" (*Cleveland Gazette*).

• ***November 10, 1894 (Cadiz, Ohio):*** "The African Choir Fails to Materialize," "The African choir . . . failed to make its appearance. There was promise of the largest house of the season to hear them. 2/3 of all the seats were sold in advance . . . when Mr. Lucas received a dispatch from Pittsburgh saying they could not come. It was a bitter disappointment to the whole town" (*Cleveland Gazette*).

• ***November 10, 1894:*** "Roster of Jackson & Massey's Octoroon Vaudeville Co.—Billy Jackson, Daisy Ivory, Will Betters and Wife, Will Porter, Sis Dixson, Sadie Rollins, Lue Wilmore, Durain Sisters, Laura Brown, Ed. Malary [*sic*], New York Quartet, Cutie Turner, Annie McGill, Maude Smith; Dave Massey, proprietor; Billy Jackson, manager, Luke Pully, leader of orchestra" (*New York Clipper*).

• ***November 17, 1894 (Topeka, Kansas):*** "A large number of people were entertained by the famous Johnson, Eagleson and Moss minstrel company, Wednesday evening at Lukens' opera house. A highly interesting and amusing programme was rendered, and was to conclude with a five round mill glove contest for points between the light weight champion of Kansas, and Jimmie Bell of Kansas City, Mo, but as it was impossible for them to participate, John Abbott and Henry Edmonds were substituted . . . Home talent, in our estimation is always appreciated. This was the best local minstrel show ever witnessed by the people. The state of Kansas can not furnish any better one . . . Dude Moss and the Boston colored swells drilled to perfection" (*Topeka Weekly Call*).

• ***November 24, 1894 (Mobile, Alabama):*** "A quartette is organizing to go out with nothing but sacred music during the holidays" (*Indianapolis Freeman*).

• ***November 24, 1894:*** "Mr. A. U. Craig was in Kansas City last week making arrangements for a series of long distant telephone concerts. Everything is complete and he is now ready to receive dates for the holidays. Concerts will be given in Atchison, St. Joseph, Kansas City and St. Louis. A telephone concert consists of placing a large bell telephone in a hall and having the music furnished at a distant place" (*Leavenworth Herald*).

• ***December 8, 1894 (Nashville, Tennessee):*** At a program at Fisk University Memorial Chapel, "Mrs. Jennie Jackson DeHart, sang 'Old Folks At Home.' Despite the fact that it has been some time since Mrs. DeHart has been connected with the Jubilee Singers, and has, for the most part, retired from the stage, she retains much of her sweetness of tone in the rendition of such songs as 'Old Folks At Home' and jubilee songs" (*Indianapolis Freeman*).

"IN OLD VIRGINIA,"

A MAMMOTH

SPECTACULAR SCENIC PRODUCTION.

30 WHITES, 20 BLACKS

AN IDEAL DRAMA OF SOUTHERN LIFE

THRILLING DRAMATIC CLIMAXES, GREAT CAST OF CHARACTERS, WONDERFUL SCENIC EFFECTS FOR ENTIRE PRODUCTION, GRAND STREET PARADE BY GRENADIER (White) BAND, JUBILEE SINGERS AND PLANTATION SHOUTERS.

A FEW OPEN DATES AFTER DEC. 18.

WANTED, TO COMPLETE CO., A1 Emotional Leading Lady, must be first class and fine looking; Strong Juvenile Leading Man, Soubrette or Ingenue, Woman for Character, one with child six or eight years old preferred, and Man for Heavies. A few Musicians to complete Band and Orchestra, also People for Small Parts that can double in band. Colored Quartette, Jubilee Shouters and Pickaninny that play brass. State full particulars and lowest salary first letter. Management pays R. R. and hotel. Address

F. W. MINDROP, Manager, 35 Emily Street, Cumberland, Maryland.

WM. CRADOC & CO., Proprietors.

New York Clipper, *November 24, 1894.*

• ***December 8, 1894:*** "Roster . . . of Ed. Davis' 'Uncle Tom's Cabin' Co. (Western) [includes] Harry Prampin [and] John Pamplin . . . We carry nine head of stock, a fine troupe of bloodhounds, and transport the show on two cars, sleeper and stock. Have been out twelve weeks . . . At Stillwater, Minn., on Nov. 2, our band gave to the inmates of the Minn. State Prison, a select concert, assisted by members of the company in specialties. The entertainment was highly enjoyed by the convicts, and a bountiful repast, prepared under the direction of Warden Wolfer, was done credit to by the members of the company" (*New York Clipper*).

• ***December 22, 1894:*** "Roster and notes of Ferguson's Colored Concert Co.," "We opened our season at Wyconda, Mo., Dec. 6 to 'S.R.O.,' and everything is running smoothly. The company will tour Missouri, Illinois and Iowa. The roster: Ed. O. Ferguson, sole owner and manager; Hugh Hoskins, advance agent; E. Edwards, pianist; J. Glenn, stage manager; A. W. Conyers, G. Gregory, W. M. Garland, G. Jackson, Richard Lewis, and the Oakland Quartet" (*New York Clipper*).

• ***December 22, 1894:*** "Notes and roster from Edwin F. Davis' 'U.T.C.' Co.: [The troupe's fifty members include] F. B. Wood, Will Grundy, Jim Grundy . . . Will McCarver, Howard McCarver . . . Madah Hyers [and] Emma Hyers . . . The company travels in three palace cars, carrying nineteen head of stock, eleven blood hounds, three brass bands and one drum corps and four gold chariots" (*New York Clipper*).

Note: By the end of 1894, Anna Madah and Emma Louise Hyers were nearing the end of their long, illustrious professional career. After touring with Isham's Octoroons during the season of 1895–1896, they appear to have gone separate ways. Madah went on to participate in the turn-of-the-century Australasian adventure with Ernest Hogan and company. At the end of 1902 she "closed with the Williams & Walker aggregation to go to Sacramento, Cal., to visit her mother."[26]

Disturbing commentary on Emma Hyers appeared in an 1896 edition of the *Leavenworth Herald*, in an article by a New York–based gossip columnist who called himself "The Man Behind The Scenes," ostensibly concerning her late ex-husband, George Freeman: "It is a fact generally known by theatrical colored people that Emma Hyers is a lover of intoxicating liquors, especially whiskey, and it is said that it is a hard task getting her on the stage unless she is in a state of total inebriation. When Freeman and his wife and her sister, Madah Hyers, were traveling together some time ago, he, together with his sister-in-law, often pleaded piteously that Emma Hyers give up the dangerous habit... She became so unendurably bad that Freeman finally got a divorce... It is said that he died of heart failure, but worry really killed him! Worrying about Emma Hyers sent George Freeman to his grave, the same as the whiskey habit is sending her to hers."[27]

Emma Hyers was still on the road in the fall of 1897, when she was identified as a member of the Black Patti Troubadours.[28] She reportedly died before 1900.[29]

A Tour of Conquest and Melody: Prof. W. H. Councill and the Alabama State Normal School Quartette

"I say it is wonderful under these circumstances that the relations between the races are as amicable as they are. The Southland is, indeed a land of miracles which exceeds Galilee."

—William Hooper Councill

Between January 1889 and December 1895 more than one thousand black men and women were murdered by lynch mobs. This reality framed daily life for all African Americans living in the South. Even in the midst of these surroundings, William Hooper Councill was clever and righteous enough to overcome all opposition.

Councill was born in slavery in 1848, and he spent a portion of his youth in the infamous Richmond, Virginia, "slave pens."[30] Despite his hard early experiences, Councill preached a doctrine of inter-racial reconciliation and cooperation; "he cherished no animosity and allowed none to influence his acts in life."[31]

With a singularly adroit and reasonable manner, Councill attracted the support of influential white southerners to his innovative African American education endeavor. As a young man

PROF. W. H. COUNCILL,
President of the Industrial and Agricultural School, Normal, Ala.

Freeman, *December 25, 1897.*

Councill reportedly made a powerful ally of the famous Confederate general and Alabama politician Joe Wheeler. In 1875, with a one thousand dollar appropriation from the Alabama State Legislature, Councill founded the Alabama State Normal School at Normal, Alabama, on the outskirts of Huntsville, and he served as its president until his death in 1909. Still in operation, with an enrollment of some forty-eight hundred students, the school is now called Alabama A&M University.

Loudin's Fisk Jubilee Singers didn't travel in the South during the bloody 1890s, but in 1894 Professor Councill guided a male quartet and two female elocutionists from his school on a reportedly successful "education campaign" through potentially dangerous northern Alabama. Some "Incidents of Their Pilgrimage" are preserved in a series of open letters to the *Freeman*. The first two were penned by Ira T. Bryant, a member of the male quartet.

• ***July 8, 1894:*** "Alabama State Normal Quartette on a Tour of Conquest and Melody," "Mr. Editor . . . I hope you will . . . grant me space in your paper to give your many readers an account of the Educational Campaign, conducted by Prof. W. H. Councill, principal of the State Normal and Industrial school, Normal, Ala. The company consists of a male quartette, and two young ladies of the school. June 25th the company set out with the intention of arousing an educational interest in the colored people. We gave our first engagement in Huntsville . . . The next appointment was at Maysville, we arrived there at 7:30 P.M. June 28th. The church was crowded when Prof. Councill and the quartette arrived. The crowd continued to swell and soon the doors and windows were blocked with eager listeners . . . The program of the evening consisted of renditions from the State Normal Quartette, recitations by the ladies, Misses Hannah Gray and Loula Houston, . . . and an able lecture by Prof. Councill . . .

July 3d we boarded the train for Mooresville; there we met with a cordial reception by the people interested in the advancement of education. Prof. Councill delivered his lecture on 'Hot Potpourri.' Professor pointed out to them the importance of building up their homes, educating their children, and many other things which impede the progress of the race. After the lecture he called for the hands of those who would build up their homes, educate their children and buy land, and who would attend some school next year. Many hands were raised and a live interest was manifested. The attendance was so large that no church or hall in Mooresville had a seating capacity sufficiently large to accommodate the people, hence a platform was erected in the street.

We reached Decatur, the gateway of the South, July 4th . . . On account of the 4th of July picnic and the Decatur Brass Band supper, the Quartette decided to postpone its engagement until July 20th, when we will be through here on our way to Birmingham.

Words are inadequate to express the hospitality shown us by the people wherever we have been. The attendance at each entertainment has been extremely large. White as well as colored people have greeted us at each place. The good people at each point have given us their halls free of charge, and sheltered and boarded the company.

We hope to meet with success throughout the campaign, and arouse the people to their duty to themselves, to God, the church and the nation.

Yours for the race,
Ira T. Bryant."

• ***August 4, 1894:*** "The March Of A Conqueror," "Professor Councill and his Band of Troubadours on their Jaunt Through the Cities of the Southland," "Editor Freeman:

It is now my pleasure to continue my article upon the educational campaign. From Decatur, where we were at my last writing, we went to Trinity. Here we were welcomed by an immense audience of both races... Our next appointment was Courtland, where we were received cordially by the people, both white and black. Filling two engagements here, and accomplishing much good, we departed for Moulton, which is situated sixteen miles from Courtland, through the country. The white people at Moulton were so deeply interested in our meeting that they insisted that we stay over the next night and use the court house, where all could witness our exercises, for the church could not hold the vast throng. We remained and great was the success. Many declared themselves awakened to the great need of education, and promised to enter school somewhere this fall...

From Moulton we returned to Courtland, then boarded the train for Leighton. Here we were ushered to the magnificent home of Mr. Pruitt, one of the wealthiest colored men of his age in the state. Mr. Pruitt acquired a fortune of several thousand dollars within the past five years. The church not being large enough to accommodate the people who were waiting to hear Prof. Councill lecture, and the Quartette sing, we were offered the large grove in front of the white hotel. The strange feature of this occasion was that the whites in the audience were in the majority...

Our next engagements were at Tuscumbia. Here we were given free access to the large city opera house on both nights, and being greeted by throngs of people, we were able to accomplish much good. So aroused were the people that they requested us to stop again on our return. We did so, and believing it possible to better reach the mass of our people, we used the Baptist church. Prof. Councill could not be present on this occasion, and members of the Quartette volunteered to say something along the great lines of education. We were warmly welcomed at Sheffield, and the opera house was offered us, but as it was not seated, and we didn't have time to arrange seats, we used the A.M.E. Church. We next stopped at Florence... A large crowd welcomed us that night... At the close of the exercises there was a rush for the front and many thanked us for the entertainment we had given them... It being our earnest desire to reach our people in the villages as well as cities, we went thence to Barton Station. Prof. Councill was compelled by a press of duties at Normal to be absent, the Quartette feeling the loss of Professor's lecture, attempted to fill the space by listening to remarks made by prominent Bartonians. After our literary and musical program, we listened to the sentiments of our audience. They thanked us for our visit to their town, and encouraged us in our work by telling us they were aroused to their duty... Our next point was Margerum, and we expounded to them the great truth, urging them to a higher and nobler life. There being but few people at Hartsell, we stopped at Flint instead. The young ladies, worn out by their long trip and continued singing and reciting, returned with Professor to Normal, there to rest and enjoy the refreshing breezes of what we call 'Home, Sweet Home.'

Our stay in Flint was indeed pleasant and we believe quite profitable. Our next engagement was at Blount Springs, the splendid summer resort of the South, noted for its many kinds of water. There was no church large enough to seat the people, black and white, who were anxious to see and hear, we were asked to use the Spring yard... From Blount Springs we left for Birmingham. In my next [letter] I will speak of our work in this great city. The Quartette is laboring earnestly for the uplifting of our race. Our songs attract the crowds and amuse, but the great lectures of Prof. Councill arouse, stimulate to action and thought, the thousands who hear him. The white people of the state are in sympathy with our efforts in this direction... More anon,

Ira T. Bryant."

A final report on the tour came from a music teacher at Normal State, Miss H. M. Fayette.

• ***September 1, 1894:*** "They Sung Their Way," "Prof. Councill and his Troubadours," "By Miss M. M. Fayette, Normal, Ala.," "Editor Freeman:

Please allow me space in the columns of your valuable paper to give a further account of the educational campaign in Northern Alabama, as conducted by Prof. Councill and the Normal School Quartette . . .

From Decatur the company went to Trinity, where they received a warm reception from both white and colored . . .

Blount Springs was the next point touched. Here two rousing meetings were held. People came from miles and miles around in order to hear the famous race orator, who was at his best . . .

Birmingham, the 'Magic City,' was then visited. In spite of the strikes which have so demoralized business all over the country, and especially in this place, the very seat of the trouble, Prof. Councill and his quartette held four very successful meetings at the following churches, viz.: A.M.E. Church, Rev. Dr. Banton, pastor; A.M.E. Zion church, Rev. Warner, pastor; South Side A.M.E. Church, Rev. Banks Williams, pastor; Pratt City church, Rev. J. H. Warrick, pastor. The audiences were very enthusiastic, showing their appreciation and approval of the good points made in the lectures . . .

From Birmingham the campaign spread to the 'Model City,' Anniston, where was held one of the most satisfactory meetings of the entire trip. The Congregational church was crowded with a fine assembly of both white and colored . . .

According to arrangements, Gadsden was the next town visited. Here the same enthusiasm which had marked the progress of the quartette from the beginning of their tour, was manifested. Here also a strange thing occurred. Prof. Councill's speech extended over the time for the departure of the cars. They were held over, at the instance of the County Superintendent and the Probate Judge until he had ended his speech. Crowds of whites and blacks then gave them a warm send off, the superintendent of the road, instructing the conductor to charge them nothing to the next station. This is the first instance on record in the history of the South of a train being held over for a Negro . . .

The people of Attalla extended a hearty welcome to the company and a very successful meeting was held . . . At Guntersville we found a large and eager crowd . . . After leaving Guntersville, Prof. Councill and the quartette returned to Normal and spent a pleasant week resting and recuperating, at the end of which they again started on their tour, going first to Scottsboro . . . The next day they took their departure for Stevenson . . . The company then left the state for a short trip in the state of Tennessee, going first to the pretty little town of Winchester . . . Lastly the town of Fayetteville was given a visit . . .

The campaign was from start to finish a complete success, and the object for which it was inaugurated, was accomplished. The colored people were everywhere awakened to their real condition, their needs, etc. . . .

The whites were given a deeper insight into the condition of the Negro . . . 'If the mountain won't come to Mohamet, Mohamet must go to the mountain.' God bless Prof. Councill and his grand and noble work" (*Indianapolis Freeman*).

During the 1890s, Prof. Councill's little school was an island of formal education in a sea of folk culture. A note in the January 1891 edition of the school's monthly journal, the *Normal Index* informed, "The 'break down' given in a near neighborhood the other night, caused 'Uncle Duster' to be up all night guarding his melons . . . We will be able in a few days to give the names of the boys who stole off the

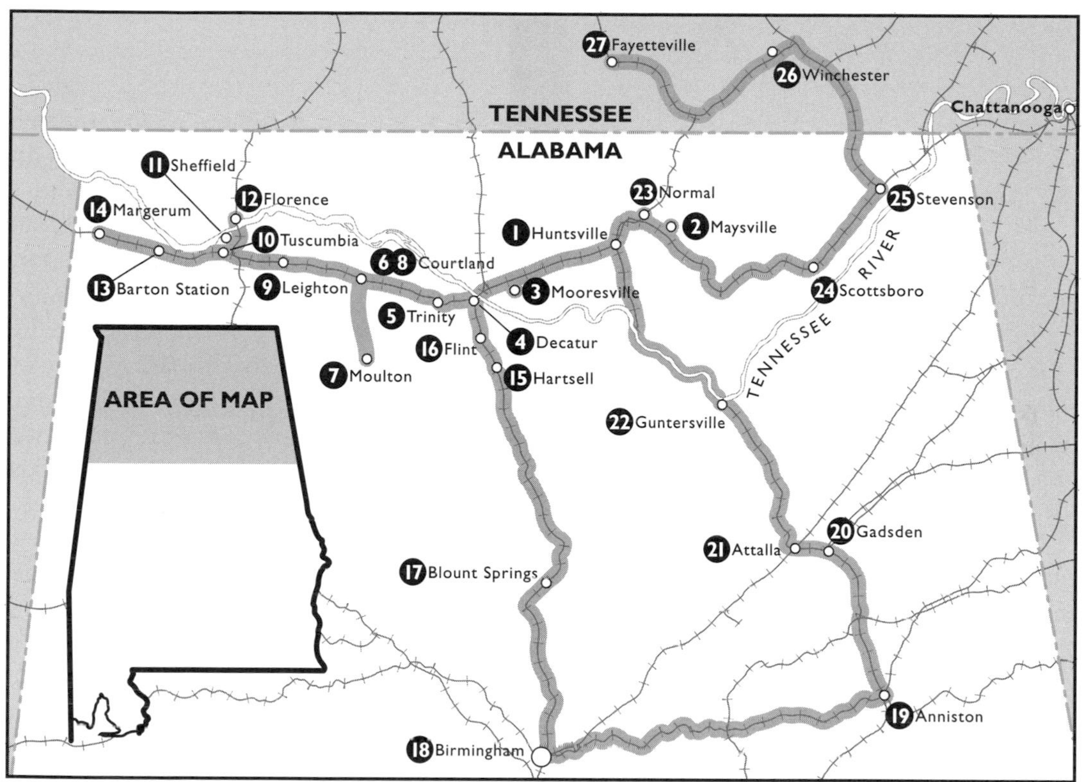

The route of Prof. Councill's 1894 "Tour of Conquest and Melody": 1. Huntsville; 2. Maysville; 3. Mooresville; 4. Decatur; 5. Trinity; 6. Courtland; 7. Moulton; 8. Courtland; 9. Leighton; 10. Tuscumbia; 11. Sheffield; 12. Florence; 13. Barton Station; 14. Margerum; 15. Hartsell; 16. Flint; 17. Blount Springs; 18. Birmingham; 19. Anniston; 20. Gadsden; 21. Attalla; 22. Guntersville; 23. Normal; 24. Scottsboro; 25. Stevenson; 26. Winchester, Tennessee; 27. Fayetteville. (1895 U.S. General Land Office Map of Northern Alabama, Julius Bien and Company, courtesy Craig Remington, Department of Geography, University of Alabama. Special thanks to Joey Brackner, Alabama State Council on the Arts)

grounds to a real old country 'break down' one night last week."

There is a strong legacy of music education at Alabama State Normal College. After visiting the campus around 1894, a mainstream reporter for the *Birmingham Age-Herald* noted, "A brass band belongs to the institution, and the school of music is taught by competent teachers. Pupils and teachers know how to sing. The writer has rarely listened to so grand a concord of human voices. It was inspiring."[32]

One of Normal State's music teachers during this time was W. G. Still, father of the famous composer William Grant Still. The December 1890 edition of the *Normal Index* expressed, "We are indebted to Mr. William Still of Philadelphia for many kind acts on behalf of this school." The next month's *Normal Index* elaborated: "We are now having some excellent music at Sunday morning services. Mr. Still has a first class choir . . . Mr. Still is well pleased with the progress made by his band boys."

Correspondence posted from Normal State to the *Detroit Plaindealer* in February 1893 informed that "our Brass Band is making progress and plays quite well. Much credit is due Mr. W. G. Still for his untiring efforts to make this branch of our work a success."[33] On Easter Sunday 1893, following an "eloquent sermon from Professor Councill," the "quartette, 'Nearer my God to Thee,' by Misses McEwen and Jones, [and] Messrs Stell [*sic*] and Melton was almost heavenly"; and at an evening "musicale" a few weeks later, "many compliments were showered on Professor Stell and Miss Fayette for the progress made by the various music classes . . . The band sustained its reputation in the closing number, 'D. C. Wells' Quick Step.' The classes in vocal music gave us several excellent selections and have made marked progress, both in note reading and expression."[34] When W. G. Still died in 1895, his destined-to-be-famous namesake was only six months old.

In 1900, after hearing him play for a school closing in Sheffield, Alabama, Prof. Councill hired W. C. Handy to take charge of "band, orchestra and vocal instruction" at Normal State. At the time, Handy was between seasons with Mahara's Minstrels. Handy later wrote, "To understand what happened at A. & M. it is necessary to know Professor Councill. Councill was . . . a colorful and eloquent man . . . Where music was concerned he was a stickler for the classics . . . Since he was deeply religious he loved the best forms in sacred music."[35] Handy didn't say whether those "best forms" included Negro spirituals, and it is doubly frustrating that the Normal Quartet's repertoire wasn't mentioned in the 1894 "Incidents of Their Pilgrimage."

Handy recalled in 1941 that when he left Normal to return to Mahara's Minstrels in 1901, "James Wilson, cornetist in our minstrel band, became musical director at A. & M., a position he has held almost forty years."[36] Actually, Wilson was still with the Famous Georgia Minstrels at New Madrid, Missouri, on February 15, 1902, when a racial incident ended in the lynching of fellow bandsman Louis Wright.[37]

The *Freeman* of March 8, 1902, reported: "James H. Wilson, cornetist with the Georgia Minstrels, who was shot while in the orchestra pit during our recent trouble in New Madrid, Mo., has displayed wonderful nerve. He laid all night in jail without the aid of a doctor until the next day and not then until they saw fit to send one . . . We take the very best care of Mr. Wilson as we have with us a man quite handy in that line of work, George A. Swan recently from the Ninth Cavalry. Mr. Wilson is hauled to and from the Opera house nightly and is improving rapidly."

According to a 1903 *Freeman* report, Wilson was born in Nicholasville, Kentucky, December 19, 1880, and "after 'going through' the public schools of that place he finished his education in the public schools of Cincinnati . . . Mr. Wilson has traveled extensively throughout this country and Canada with different well known musical organizations. He is now professor of music at the A. and M. College of Normal, Ala."[38]

In 1906 Professor Wilson took leave from Normal State to tour with Billy Kersands' Minstrels, from whom a note in the *Freeman* that fall assured, "Our band is still knocking ragtime cold with the rag time king and cornetist, Jimmie Wilson, the real author of the recent Pittsburgh hits, 'Drag Lotz' and 'Shame Lotz.' We handle quite a number of Mr. Wilson's rags and some of his marches which are very fine, especially the one entitled 'United.' "[39]

At the end of his 1906–1907 season with Kersands' Minstrels, Wilson returned to Normal State to stay. On April 24, 1909, the *Freeman* reported: "James H. Wilson, trumpeter and bandmaster of the A. and M. College Band and Minstrenola Club of the A. and M. College

Prof. James H. Wilson, Freeman, *January 2, 1904.*

at Normal, Ala., conducted the music for the funeral of Prof. W. H. Councill."

Following the death of Professor Councill, there are signs that Wilson expanded his school music curriculum into vernacular fields. A concert given in 1912 by the "College band" included "Mammy's Shuffling Dance" and "Ragtime Violin."[40] In 1927 a concert by the Normal State Band, Orchestra and Music Lovers' Club began with a trumpet solo by Wilson. A "Girls' Quartette" rendered songs including "Down in the Cornfield." The orchestra selections ranged from "Poet and Peasant" to "Deep Henderson." Spirituals also formed a part of the program.

Students In National Music Week Program

State Agricultural and Mechanical Institute
Band, Orchestra and Music Lovers' Club
In Concert

High School Auditorium

Huntsville, Alabama, May 2, 1927

PROGRAM

Trumpet Solo.........Salute Polka.........*Liberata*
James H. Wilson

(a) Hear Our Prayer ....*Abbott*
(b) Stunt
(c) He Didn't Know But One Piece
Band

Spirituals:
(a) I'm So Glad
(b) O Bye and Bye
(c) Who'll Be a Witness

Overture ....Poet and Peasant ....*Suppe*
(b) Black Bird
(c) March ....Thunderer ....*Sousa*
Orchestra

Little Boy Blue
Down in the Corn Field
I Love You
Girls' Quartette

Descriptive ....The Haunted House.........*Lafferty*
(b) Deep Henderson
Orchestra

Let's Go to Jordan
(b) Jubilee
Every Time I Feel the Spirit
(b) Listen to the Lambs
Glee Club

Finale: March ....Retreat.........The Star Spangled Banner

James H. Wilson, Conductor ...... Elsie Hill, Accompanist

Normal Index, *May 1927. (courtesy of Alabama A&M University Library)*

That Barbershop Chord

By the mid-1890s there were signs of a divergent orientation along the entire spectrum of African American community-based musicians and singers. Piano players, string bands, and vocal quartets were all glancing sidewards, less intent upon aspiring to outdo white musicians at "the white man's music," more interested in exploring the possibilities latent in folk music themes and vernacular music fashions. Their explorations soon produced ragtime.

Among black quartet singers, the litmus test of the new sensibility was the barbershop chord. Though commonly taken for a white invention, "barbershopping" is more likely of African American origin, embracing both the concept of male quartet singing in barbershops and the particular style of harmonizing that came to be known as "barbershop."[41]

In the introduction to the 1867 collection *Slave Songs of the United States*, the compilers noted that, among the "contraband" singers they observed, "There is no singing in *parts*, as we understand it, and yet no two [singers] appear to be singing the same thing . . . And what makes it all the harder to unravel is that . . . they seem not infrequently to strike sounds that cannot be precisely represented by the gamut, and abound in slides from one note to another, and turns and cadences not in articulated notes."[42] "Slides" and "turns" signify what W. C. Handy called a "deep-rooted racial groping for instinctive harmonies."[43] They form the basic building blocks of improvisational barbershop harmony.

Considering the importance placed on vocal music education in Afro-American schools and colleges of the period, the salient difference between barbershop harmonizing and the "cornfield singing" of slavery days *may be* that barbershop harmonizing reflects greater harmonic sophistication and a more conscious approach to vocal arrangement. Although it remained largely unstated, it appears that barbershop harmony was the underlying factor in the sweeping popularity of a new generation of black professional quartets during the 1890s. By 1900 at least one reactionary black newspaper critic was fruitlessly badgering African American stage quartets to "get out of the beaten path of barbershop harmonies."[44]

It is confirmed by a one-sentence report which first appeared in the "Kansas Notes" column of the mainstream daily *Kansas City Star* in early 1894 that barbershop terminology was familiar in eastern Kansas *across race lines*. This most casual comment constitutes the earliest yet-discovered reference to "barbershop" as an American musical style.

• ***February 6, 1894:*** "Kansas Notes," "Although Emporia has a Haydn club it is not above singing 'I found a horseshoe,' with a 'barbershop chord' on the second horseshoe" (*Kansas City Star*).

Eleven days later, on February 17, 1894, this same item appeared in the "Kansas Matters" column of the African American weekly *Leavenworth Herald*. The racial identity of the Haydn Club of Emporia, Kansas, remains unknown.[45]

Another early indication of popular barbershop harmonizing comes forth from this "Kansas Notes" report:

• ***January 31, 1894:*** "The serenading malady which was raging in Russell has been headed off by the frost, and now the young men who sing 'Down Mobile,' 'In de Evenin' by de Moon Light,' 'Come Where the Lilies Bloom,' 'Farewell, Farewell, My Own True Love' and 'Good Night, Ladies' are playing high five in the court house" (*Kansas City Star*).

This anecdotal account of recreational singing among the "young men" of Russell, Kansas, encapsulates the repertoire of popular ballads and "negroid selections" associated with early barbershop quartet singing. "Down Mobile" was a signal vehicle for "cracking up chords." Better remembered as "Way Down Yonder in the Cornfield," it appears to have originated in slavery; its most characteristic verse ("Some folks say that a preacher won't

"With a 'barber shop chord' on the second horseshoe." The "second horseshoe" may have come at the beginning of the second verse, or it may have been an improvised addition, akin to the second "way down" in typical barbershop arrangements of "Way Down Yonder in the Cornfield." There is no clear evidence of barbershop harmony in this 1891 sheet music arrangement of "I Found a Horseshoe."

steal...") is collected in *Slave Songs of the United States*, in a song called "Run Nigger Run." Its popularity with barbershoppers is confirmed by its extensive history on commercial recordings.[46]

African American composer James Bland's "In the Evening by the Moonlight" (1880) is also deeply embedded in barbershop history and lore. Barbershop devotee and music historian Sigmund Spaeth described it as "a song intimately associated with the *Levee* and *Mobile* tunes" of black folk origin, the harmonies of which "are the barber's own whiskers."[47]

In the evening by the moonlight
You can hear those darkies singing,
In the evening by the moonlight,
You can hear those banjos ringing,
How the old folks would enjoy,
They would sit all night and listen,
As we sang in the evening, by the
moonlight.[48]

The "before-the-war" plantation tableaux painted by this barbershop classic illustrates an oppresive tension which was exacerbated by the world of theatrical commerce. The liberal use of black male vocal quartets in 1890s minstrel plantation shows such as "The South Before the War" and "Slavery Days" crystallized a subtly slanderous image of the typical plantation quartet, barbershop harmony and all.

During the 1890s, African American vocal quartets made barbershop harmony the cornerstone of vocal ragtime. Some few black professional quartets of a certain "highbrow" orientation publicly refrained from engaging in barbershop harmony. For the most part, however, improvisational barbershop harmony can be taken for granted in the black male vocal quartet–related newspaper citations of this period.

Quartets to the Fore: The South Before the War Company and Its Plantation Pretenders, 1892–1895

An experimental venture, originally organized for a brief summer tour, "The South Before the War" Company toured successfully for many seasons and inspired a popular reign of plantation shows or, in the slang of the profession, "plant shows." Built around a romantic idealization of plantation slavery, the South Before the War was a new departure disguised as an "ancient oddity."

There was nothing unusual about a plantation setting in nineteenth-century minstrelsy, but the African American men and women of the South Before the War imparted an added sense of *realism* to their plantation recreations. Moreover, the South Before the War was perhaps the first big-time theatrical exhibition of up-to-date, "ragtime-ready" black vernacular music and dance. Through its ubiquitous male vocal quartets and "pickaninny band," the public got its first whiff of emerging ragtime minstrelsy.

The South Before the War Company and the gang of plant shows that followed in its wake formed a bright, particular platform for the commercial ascent of African American quartet singing, and thereby established a new theatrical outlet for the improvisational barbershop harmonizing craze that was sweeping through black America. Despite its landmark status in African American show business history, the South Before the War was a backward-looking stage vehicle, purporting to depict the pleasant side of slavery. The unprogressive imagery that it projected would burden black male quartet artists for decades to come.

The white proprietors of the South Before the War Company, John H. Whallen and Harry Martell, were both experienced professionals.

CLEVER COLORED TALENT

WANTED QUICK.

Ladies and Gents of experience, refinement and culture in Cake Walking, Shouting, Singing, Plantation Melodies, Quadrilles, Wing, Reel and Buck Dancing. Also all Sports of the Ancient and Modern Africans, Colored Orchestra, etc. Telegraph at once for our Spectacular Production of

"THE SOUTH BEFORE THE WAR."

Managers of large theatres, rinks, gardens, parks, etc., wire at once for this Monster Festival Spectacle, with special scenery, set pieces, props and electric, also calcium, effects by the carload. Address

WHALLEN & MARTELL, Buckingham Theatre, Louisville, Kentucky.

JOHN HAMMOND, Agent.

New York Clipper, *April 16, 1892.*

The March 5, 1892, edition of the *Clipper* supplied background information on Whallen:

> Mr. Whallen's birthplace was New Orleans, but Cincinnati and Louisville have been the main points of his labors . . . The stock is Irish . . . At an early age he was thrown upon his own resources, his father dying when the boy was but eight years old . . . He . . . at the age of thirteen, went into the Confederate army . . . Mr. Whallen did not go into the theatrical business until some years after the close of the wars—in fact, not until after his settlement at Louisville. He did detective and police duty, [and] helped to build the Cincinnati Southern Railroad . . . The Buckingham Theatre [in Louisville]—one of the largest, best and complete of its kind—that he and his brother now own, was not put there without many ups and downs . . . Besides the Louisville interest that Mr. Whallen has in theatricals, he is half owner of the Whallen & Martell Mammoth Co.

The April 2, 1892, edition carried a sketch of Martell: "Harry Martell . . . was born in New York City, and entered the profession when a boy . . . In 1878 Mr. Martell first headed and managed the family of acrobats who have since become popularly known as the Martells, and under that name they have played for the past fourteen years with the principal circus and most prominent specialty organizations in America, viz.: Barnum & Bailey, Adam Forepaugh, Sells Bros., W. W. Cole . . . etc. In 1890, he formed a partnership with J. H. Whallen . . . and organized the Whallen & Martell show . . . He has a cozy home in the mountains of New York State, where . . . he spends his Summer vacations."

• ***April 23, 1892:*** "J. H. Whallen, of Whallen & Martin's [*sic*] Specialty Co., and also proprietor of the Buckingham Theatre, Louisville, Ky., is organizing a colored company for a Summer tour. The title of the company will be 'The South Before the War,' and will be composed of regular Southern negroes, male and female. They will introduce the old plantation songs, jigs, buck dancing, etc., prevailing at that time. A feature will be a real cotton picking scene, showing the darkies picking cotton, while singing their melodies. Chas. Howard, the original Old Black Joe, will lead the cotton pickers, and will also act as stage manager. The company opens at St. Louis, April 24. John Hammond will conduct the tour" (*New York Clipper*).

While the vast majority of the South Before the War Company comprised the rising black stars of ragtime minstrelsy, Charley Howard and Billy Williams were white minstrel stars, effectively absorbed into the musical drama. They performed in blackface, portraying "old man" and "wench" characters. Charley Howard was a founding father of blackface minstrelsy. It is noted in the 1911 book *Monarchs of Minstrelsy* that "Howard has been given credit of being the first to represent the aged darkey on stage. At the age of ten years he traveled with Joe Sweeny's company giving concerts in the Southern States, appearing in barns and churches, and traveling by coaches."[49]

• ***May 7, 1892:*** "The Stage," "Billy and Cordelia McClain have left the Hyer Sisters and joined Whallen and Martell's combination" (*Indianapolis Freeman*).

Much of the success of the South Before the War is attributable to Billy McClain, the creative genius of its first two big seasons. The McClains left the South Before the War in 1894, and, with Charles Walker and his wife, joined Thomas H. Davis's "On the Mississippi" production.

• ***May 14, 1892:*** "Whallen & Martell's 'South Before the War' is reported to be meeting with success through the West. The play pictures the pleasant side of slavery, and gives the people an opportunity to introduce their specialties in the second act. The company: Charley Howard, Billy Golden, Ben Taylor, J. H. Boyle, Carrie Graham, Quianitta De Lorme, Sadie Harris, Dutchie Lewis, Katie Carter, Tag Washington, Dan J. Miller, James Carmenelli, Billy McClain, Mlle. Cordelia, Walker's Merry Makers [a vocal trio], . . . the Twilight Quartet and others" (*New York Clipper*).

It is likely the Billy Golden mentioned above is the same Billy Golden who "dominated blackface dialogue records with plotted sketches in the old-time minstrel vein until the early 1920s, recording for every notable phonograph firm."[50]

• ***June 4, 1892:*** "[Billy] Jackson and [Irving] Jones joined Whallen & Martell's 'South Befo' de Wah' Co. May 23" (*New York Clipper*).

• ***June 11, 1892:*** "'The South Before the War' Co., had a smashup on the road, and did not arrive in Detroit until 9 o'clock May 28, when the audience were waiting at the Opera House" (*New York Clipper*).

Whallen and Martell's South Before the War Company concluded its first short season in late June 1892 and commenced its 1892–1893 season about two months later. Route listings in the *Clipper* include the following:

> Cincinnati, Ohio, August 28–September 3, 1892; Indianapolis, Indiana, September 5–10; Louisville, Kentucky, September 12–17; Chicago, Illinois, September 19–24; Milwaukee, Wisconsin, September 26–October 1; Wheeling, West Virginia, October 19; Pittsburgh, Pennsylvania, October 24–26; Columbus, Ohio, October 27–30; Louisville, Kentucky, November 2; St. Louis, Missouri, November 13–19; Memphis, Tennessee, November 23–26; New Orleans, Louisiana, November 28–December 3; Chicago, Illinois, December 5–10; Cleveland, Ohio, December 12–17; Harlem, New York, January 9–14, 1893; New York City, January 16–21; Philadelphia, Pennsylvania, January 23–28; Rochester, New York, January 30–February 4; New Haven, Connecticut, February 13–15; Providence, Rhode Island, February 20–25; Washington, D.C., February 27–March 4; Baltimore, Maryland, March 6–11; York, Pennsylvania, March 13; Frederick, Maryland, March 14; Cumberland, March 15; Wheeling, West Virginia, March 16–18; Cleveland, Ohio, March 20–25; New York City; March 27–April 1; Boston, Massachusetts, April 3–15.

One notable development of the South Before the War Company's brilliant 1892–1893 season was Billy McClain's elevated role in the production of the show. Another portentous development was the addition of a second and third vocal quartet to the roster.

• ***September 3, 1892:*** "Billy McClain of Indianapolis is leading colored comedian and assistant stage manager with Whalen & Martells' 'South Before The War' company, which opens the New Empire Theatre, [Indianapolis] Sept. 5" (*Indianapolis Freeman*).

• ***November 5, 1892:*** "Ferry, the frog man, has joined the Whallen & Martell Co." (*New York Clipper*).

• ***January 7, 1893:*** "Variety & Minstrelsy," "Roster of the 'South Before the War' Co., under the management of Whallen & Martell: Charles Harland [*sic*, Howard], Sheffer and Blakely, Billy McClain, George Thompson, Ferry [the Frog], Mrs. Cordelia McClain, Helene Carr, Twilight Quartet, Eclipse Quartet, Buckingham

Quartet, Katie Carter, Minnie Taylor, Maria Taylor, Walker Trio, Hattie Gear, Charles Smith, Pearl Woods, Maggie Dixon, James Hall, James Anderson, Joseph Hodges, Lew Sheppard and Phil Portlaw. Good business is reported. The company are stationed at the Grand Theatre, Williamsburg, N.Y., this week. Billy McClain's new song and dance, 'Old Schoolhouse Bells,' as interpreted by Katie Carter, is winning much praise" (*New York Clipper*).

Katie Carter was a vernacular dance specialist and an unsung pioneer of early black show business. She was a member of Curtis's Afro-American Specialty Company that traveled to Australia in 1899.

• ***January 21, 1893 (New York City):*** "London Theatre," " 'The South Before the War,' Whallen & Martell's novel attraction, opened Monday, Jan. 16, to good houses. The lovers of the good old Southern pastimes, as indulged in by the colored population of ante-bellum days, found plenty of food for delight in the performance. The genuine buck and wing dance, the darkey shuffle and the different types of dusky mortals were portrayed by genuine colored men and women. A number of good looking colored girls have been engaged, and their picturesque costumes lent much realism to the different scenes. The opening act, 'Under a Southern Sky,' telling of the return of an escaped slave to his Southern home, was done at this theater last Summer. Charles Howard and Buck Sheffer, as Old Eph and Aunt Chloe, differed from the genuine darkeys only in the color of their own skin. Chas. Walter, Geo. C. Thompson, Helene Carr, Cordelia Le Clain [*sic*], Maggie Dixon, Kate Carter, Joe Hodges and Billie Le Clain, were in the cast. Cordelia Le Clain sang 'Old Kentucky Home' and 'Way Down Upon the Swaunee River' very well. Kate Carter in songs and dances, followed the opening sketch. 'Washing on the Levee' introduced Sam Wade, Ben F. Payne, York Anderson and Al E. Anderson [the Eclipse Quartet] in a funny act. This was succeeded by an exhibition of buck and wing dancing by men and girls. Chas. J. Walker, Jim Hall, Ben Gillion, in a number of darkey melodies, sang well, and accomplished themselves on guitars. In the second act of 'the play,' a camp meeting scene, with all its comical probabilities, its exhorters, and a congregation of many types, furnished much amusement. Ferry, the frog man, performed a number of feats in contortion. Sheffer and Blakely followed in their 'Possum and Sweet Potatoes.' The Buckingham Quartet, consisting of Harry Scott, Harry Williams, Anderson White and Henry Winfred, and the Eclipse Quartet appeared in a funny musical act, introducing medleys, etc. The Original Twilight Quartet sang a number of selections with good effect. A cake walk concluded the performance. The staff: Whallen and Martell, proprietors; Ed. F. Snader, business representative; J. H. Almond, treasurer; Chas. Hand, stage manager; Billy McClain, amusement director" (*New York Clipper*).

• ***March 4, 1893:*** "Mrs. Cordelia McClain celebrated her birthday Feb. 26, and was the recipient of many valuable presents from the members of 'The South Before the War' Co. Billie McClain has written a new song and dedicated it to Chas. Howard. Lew Sheppard, of the Twilight Quartet, put it to music. It is called 'De Gospel Pass' " (*New York Clipper*).

• ***April 15, 1893:*** "Whallen & Martell's 'South Before the War' Co. closed the season at Boston, April 15, three weeks earlier than expected, on account of the illness of Mr. Martell. Salaries have been paid in full, and each member of the company has received his or her fare home. The company start out again in August" (*New York Clipper*).

• ***June 24, 1893:*** "Billy McClain, on June 18, began rehearsing the sixty colored people who are to take part in Pain's spectacle, 'The Siege of Vicksburg,' which opens at Manhattan Beach, Coney Island, June 24. At the close of the spectacle, Mr. McClain will resume his position with 'The South Before the War' Co." (*New York Clipper*).

• ***November 18, 1893:*** "Roster of Whallen & Martell's 'South Before the War' Co.: Prof. Anderson, treasurer; Chas. Howard, stage manager; Billy McClain, assistant stage manager; Billy Williams, Ferry, the frogman; Geo. C. Thompson, Jessie Oliver, Mrs. Cordelia McClaine, Ben Owens, Chas. Walker, James Hall, Billy Caldwell, Joe Clark, Eugene Clark, Geo. C. Moore, Willie Murray, Walter Esher, Chas. Smith, Florence Briscoe, Pearl Woods, Titchie Kendall, Lulu Cross, Lola Archmere, Gracie Butler, Anna Hubbart, Annie Scott, and the Twilight, Mandar and Buckingham Quartet" (*New York Clipper*).

Among the many notable performers with this great outfit, brothers Joseph and Eugene Clark were the progenitors of an extraordinary African American musical and theatrical family of Louisville, Kentucky. Eugene Clark was reputed to have been "in the profession since 1879,"[51] and he was active in minstrel and circus annex companies well into the 1920s, at least. A note from C. L. Erickson's Alabama Minstrels in 1912 mentioned, "Our first part opens with overture of burnt cork, which starts the ball rolling with Joe and Eugene Clark with tambourine and bone solos."[52]

At the end of 1893 Whallen and Martell announced plans to expand the South Before the War by incorporating a seemingly more progressive "Negro Evolution" theme, reminiscent of William Foote's 1892 innovation with the Afro-American Specialty Company.

• ***December 2, 1893:*** "Notes from Whallen & Martell's 'South Before the War' Co.," "Messrs. Whallen & Martell have a prominent author at work on the third act, which will serve to show the colored man's advancement since the war, introducing him as the citizen, soldier and statesman. It is predicted that the introduction of the modern negro in the closing scenes of the 'South Before the War' will be as big a hit as those which serve to show him as the slave" (*New York Clipper*).

• ***January 6, 1894 (New York City):*** "London Theatre," "Whallen & Martell's 'South Before the War' Co. is the attraction this week. Chas. Howard and a clever company portrayed scenes in the Sunny South in antebellum days, when the life of the colored folk had its bright moments, although they were slaves. The cast also includes Billy Williams, Charles Walker, Geo. Thompson, Jessie Oliver, William Ferry, Cordelia McClain, Contella Chandler, Miss Lutt, Dancing Charley, Wm. Cottrell, Billy McLean [*sic*], the Clark Brothers and George Moore. The olio consists of Katie Carter, a clever dancer; the Beantown Comedy Quartet in 'Washday on the Levee,' a prize buck and wing dancing contest, Lo La Lauchmere, an importation from Hawaii; Ferry the frog man, in a good act; Billy Williams, comedian, and the Buckingham, Twilight and Standard Quartettes. The performance concludes with a cake walk" (*New York Clipper*).

Company member Jessie Oliver made historically significant cylinder recordings with backing provided by the Standard Quartette. According to a Columbia Phonograph Company promotional letter of March 3, 1894, "Miss Jessie Oliver is the first songstress whose work is both musically and phonographically satisfactory. . . The Standard Quartette have assisted in the chorus of some old-fashioned melodies."[53]

• ***February 10, 1894:*** "Billy McClain is doing well with his new song, 'Hand Down de Robe.' He has also written a new song for Billy Williams, of 'The South Before the War' Co., entitled 'I'se South Carlina Lize'" (*New York Clipper*).

• ***February 17, 1894:*** "Billy Farrell has introduced his new specialty, 'The Cake Walking Coon,' in the last act of 'The South Before the War'" (*New York Clipper*).

• ***February 24, 1894:*** "The Twilight Quartet—J. W. Hodges, B. Underwood, A. D. Brice and Billy Farrell—are said to be meeting with success singing Hodge's Baby Yodel, which will be ready for publication in a few weeks" (*New York Clipper*).

Perhaps "Hodge's Baby Yodel" had some connection to the most popular lullaby-yodel of the day, "Sleep, Baby, Sleep."[54]

• ***June 9, 1894:*** "'South Before the War' Co., Wanted, Three Pickaninny Bands... Two for the United States and one for Europe. Address all communications to J. H. Whallen, Buckingham Theatre, Louisville, Ky." (*New York Clipper*).

• ***June 28, 1894:*** "Billy Williams, the comedian, has been reengaged to play Aunt Chloe in Whallen & Martell's 'South Before the War' Co. for next season. During the Summer he will manage a steamboat running from Newark, N.J. to Buffalo Bill's [Wild West Show] at Brooklyn" (*New York Clipper*).

• ***August 4, 1894:*** "Charley Howard is re-engaged with Whallen & Martell's 'South Before the War' Co., to play Old Eph Clawson for season of 1894–95" (*New York Clipper*).

The success of the South Before the War Company inspired several imitators. In the fall of 1893 white entertainment impresario Abe Spitz put out a large company under the title "Slavery Days"; it included "a moonlight scene on the levee and an original and realistic plantation cotton picking scene showing a real cotton field as it was in slavery days, with the darkies in the field singing and picking the cotton."[55] Whallen and Martell were quick to react.

• ***November 11, 1893:*** "'The South Before the War,' Whallen & Martell's attraction, has not been east this season, although a company, said to be under the management of Abe Spitz, has been billed in Massachusetts and New York State. Whallen & Martell intend on bringing action against Mr. Spitz" (*New York Clipper*).

• ***December 9, 1893:*** "Harry Martell recently visited Patterson, N.J., to see Abe Spitz's production of 'Slavery Days,' which he thought infringed upon his rights in 'The South Before the War.' After seeing the performance he had an interview with Mr. Spitz, during which a mutual understanding was had. Mr. Spitz is now having a new opening sketch written, entitled, 'Uncle Rufe's Dream,' introducing a number of tableaux of Southern life. 'The Slavery Days' Co., both men and women, donned their new ulsters last week" (*New York Clipper*).

Perhaps more vexing to Whallen and Martell than a possible copyright infringement was the fact that Slavery Days had invaded the ranks of the South Before the War and made off with the Eclipse Quartet. Slavery Days prospered into the fall of 1894, at least.

• ***May 19, 1894:*** "Notes from the 'Slavery Days' Co.," "We are yet on the move, heading into the British provinces [Canada] and meeting with unexpected financial success. Major Ben F. Payne, York Anderson, Henry Williams, Chas. Arter, Nellie Smalls and little Mamie B. Payne, at Cambellford, Ont., went on a fishing jaunt. A dinner was served at the Queen's Hotel and a number of fish stories were recited... York Anderson is quite a success singing 'Climbing Up the Hills to Zion.' Little Mamie B. Payne is a great card. Alberta Monette caps the climax in her buck and wing dance" (*New York Clipper*).

• ***October 13, 1894:*** "Roster of 'Slavery Days' Co.—John E. Stokes, manager and proprietor;

NOTICE.

McINTYRE and HEATH,

The oldest and best negro delineators before the public, have a few words to say in regard to a statement made in last week's issue of THE CLIPPER by certain parties who claim that "The South Before the War" is original with them. The title of the play may possibly be. Evidently the parties have forgotten that "The South Before the War" is nothing more or less than

McINTYRE & HEATH'S "'WAY DOWN SOUTH,"

and for the benefit of those who do not know we take this method of informing them that if there are any original ideas they belong to McINTYRE AND HEATH, for in the year of 1885 McINTYRE AND HEATH fixed up a negro comedy, taking parts of "Uncle Eph's Dream," by Chas. White, deceased, and "Scenes on the Mississippi" by Buckley's Serenaders, and a few of their own ideas. They then made an engagement with Hyde & Behman to put them on the road, which they did.

Hyde & Behman christened the play "'WAY DOWN SOUTH." During the season of '89 they also produced the same play with James Hyde Specialty Co. Now, the said parties have taken this same play, omitting one scene, the Cake Walk, and called it "The South Before the War." These are the simple and true facts, which all managers and the public know. During the season of '94 and '95

McIntyre & Heath

WILL PRESENT TO THE PUBLIC ONE OF THE BEST NEGRO COMEDIES EVER PRODUCED, ENTITLED

"DOWN MOBILE,"

With a carload of Beautiful Scenery, Mechanical Effects, New Songs, etc. Address YANK NEWELL, Manager McIntyre & Heath's "Down Mobile," 1,180 Broadway, New York, N. Y.

New York Clipper, *December 9, 1893.*

Mrs. Clara West, musical director; York Anderson, stage manager; Harry Bright, advance agent; Henry Winfred, assistant stage manager; Harry Clifton, master of transportation; W. H. Jacobs, leader of brass band; Jerry Mills, Frank Sutton, Ned West, Perry Tilghman, Nathan Walker, Joshua McNott, John W. Barr, Bob Landrum, N. Turner, Charles H. Bratton, W. Fidbiman, Irene Smith, Rosie Nicholson,

"THIS IS THE STRAW THAT BREAKS THE CAMEL'S BACK."

It was really amusing to read Whalen & Martell's ad. in last week's CLIPPER, and see how hard they were trying to square themselves with the public. 'Twas very funny indeed. They want to know where my TWO STARS,

McINTYRE AND HEATH'S,

originality comes in. Now Messrs. W. and M. YOU ought to know better than anyone, as you have been reaping the benefit of their originality for the past two years Their work, as comedians, for nineteen years shows for itself. And they are unquestionably at the present time two of the greatest negro comedians in their line on the face of the earth. A big thing to say, but nevertheless true. These two artists have not sprung up like mushrooms, they were 19 years ago, as they are at the present day, foremost in their line, originality has been their success and in their comedy

'DOWN MOBILE.'

in which they star next season, they will surpass all their former efforts.

Now, to show these gentlemen what I am kicking about, as they term it, I wish to prove to the Public and Profession that the play, they claim to be original with them, is an appropriation from McINTYRE & HEATH'S play "Way Down South," Mc. & H never lay claim to more than they have done. They took two small sketches, entitled "Uncle Eph's Dream," and "Scenes on the Mississippi," and made them into a successful play, calling it "Way Down South," and which has been taken bodily by you, and called "South before the War."

The first act is word for word, also third act. You have been making bluffs through THE CLIPPER about YOUR ORIGINAL PLAY, and I could not have had a better opportunity to show the public where you got your original play from. You also claim that "Uncle Eph's Dream," the sketch from which Mc. and H. took the foundation of their play, was written by your man, Charles Howard.

THE SKETCH WAS NOT WRITTEN BY HOWARD,

THE AUTHOR OF THE SKETCH IS CHAS. T WHITE, late of Harrigan's Stock Co. He was one of the best negro farce writers in his day. You also claim you have the sketch copyrighted. YOU HAVE NOT, as the book has been in print for twenty years and is copyrighted by Dewitt Publishing Co., No. 33 Rose Street, New York City, and the title page reads as follows: "Uncle Eph's Dream, an original negro sketch, in two scenes and two tableaux, by Charles White. Entered according to act of Congress, in the year 1874, by Robert M. Dewitt, in the office of the Librarian of Congress at Washington."

Now, for Scenes on the Mississippi. You claim it was produced in New Orleans, for the first time in 1868 at the Olympic Theatre. Once more, you are wrong, for here is the proof. Title page reads, "Scenes on the Mississippi, in two scenes by Buckley's Minstrels, arranged by Chas. T. White, as performed at the American Theatre, 444 Broadway, New York, Dec. 14, 1863." Perhaps your star was not in the business at that time. In proof of statements I have made McINTYRE & HEATH send both books to NEW YORK CLIPPER OFFICE

You say you want no more controversy. I would not, either, if I were in your place. Least said now on your part, the better; but don't forget in the meantime the old adage "THE LONGER WE LIVE, THE MORE WE LEARN." I will close by stating that when

'DOWN MOBILE'

Opens its season you may be able to get a few more ideas from McINTYRE & HEATH.

Respectfully yours YANK NEWELL,
Manager "Down Mobile," 1,180 Broadway, New York

New York Clipper, *December 23, 1893.*

DIXIE GRUEL for YANK NEWELL.

After perusing the card in last week's CLIPPER, inserted by embryo manager of colored opera, we must exclaim with Shakespeare, in "The Tempest," "Your tale would cure deafness." In the falseness of its statements it fairly outdoes Gulliver's Gulliver. He declares that "South Before the War" is nothing more nor less than "Way Down South," done in 1885 by a pair of colored comedians, and is their original idea. Then the next second he forgets himself and gives to the amusement world the startling information THAT THEY FIXED IT UP by nabbing "Uncle Eph's Dream"—written by Chas. White, deceased, and "Scenes on the Mississippi" by Buckley's Serenaders. If this is so, on what do they rest their claim of originality? In order to set this wonder on the right tack we wish to declare that "South Before the War" is no part of "Uncle Eph's Dream," and which was NOT WRITTEN by the late Chas. White, the authorship to the same belonging to Mr Chas Howard, who is at present in our employ, and WHO IS THE OLDEST AND BEST NEGRO DELINEATOR IN THIS COUNTRY.

He wrote "Eph's Dream" or "Under a Southern Sun" in June, 1865, at the Palace Variety Theatre, Cincinnati, Ohio. In 1868, three years afterwards, Mr. Chas O. White assumed the role of the Master, for Mr. Howard—that being the first time Mr. White ever saw the piece It was then produced in New Orleans by Mr. Howard at the Olympic Theatre. At that time YOUR PAIR OF STARS WERE NOT KNOWN IN THE BUSINESS. At the Olympic Theatre, same city, Mr. Bob Hart introduced "Scenes on the Mississippi," the race scene between the Robt. E. Lee and the Natchez and the steamboat explosion and NOT THE BUCKLEY SERENADERS WHO USED IT AFTERWARDS. After getting through with these misstatements he goes in even deeper and declares that we had taken this piece and omitted the Cake Walk only, and called it the "South Before the War," when he knows full well, if he knows anything, that we do produce the Cake Walk, and it has been a feature of the "South Before the War" ever since it was organized. We have seen "Way Down South" produced and never saw a Cake Walk in it. However, our friend may have had his specs on. Then, again, "Way Down South" at its best, was only a thirty minutes afterpiece as done by Jas. Hydes' Co. While the "South Before the War" is in three acts and runs for nearly three hours, and is a copy of nothing yet seen in American Amusements.

It is not our intention to enter into any further newspaper controversy in the matter with any one, as we are not looking for notoriety ourselves and will give none. In short "South Before the War" is not "Uncle Eph's Dream" nor "Scenes on the Mississippi," but our original production and we are the first managers to successfully organize a company composed of colored people depicting life in the South in Slavery Days.

THE TITLE, PLAY, AND ALL THE ADVERTISING MATTER used in advertising it is copyrighted, as also is "UNCLE EPH'S DREAM," WE HAVING ACQUIRED THE RIGHT AND TITLE TO IT FROM MR HOWARD, THE AUTHOR. The only notice we will take of scribblers in the future is to ignore them. It is useless to toy with a party who is struggling to place before the public a nigger act stuffed like a Christmas turkey in order to create a play. There is merit and originality in our performance, which is proven in the statement books of every theatre of this country, and we will continue fearless and boldly to supply the amusement market with an attraction worthy of unlimited comment and uncountable dollars.

If "Down Mobile" is not going to be an infringement on "South Before the War," what is this fellow kicking about, any way; and if it is, why we have redress in the courts. Respectfully,

Whallen & Martell.

New York Clipper, *December 16, 1893.*

Ida Winfred, Georgia Douglas, Emma Brown, the Delaware Band and the Eclipse Quartet" (*New York Clipper*).

In December 1893, about the same time Harry Martell and Abe Spitz reached a "mutual understanding" in the matter of the South Before the War versus Slavery Days, James McIntyre and Tom Heath, a well-known team of white "Negro delineators," leveled charges that Whallen and Martell's South Before the War was "nothing more or less" than a copy of their 1885 production, "Way Down South." This provoked a pointed exchange in the *Clipper*.

Toward the end of the summer of 1894, another addition to the growing family of quartet-heavy plantation shows—the Old South Company—was announced.

• ***August 18, 1894:*** "Wanted, for the Old South Colossal Colored Carnival, Aged Darkey Impersonator, Old Wench Impersonator, Colored Quartettes, Buck and Wing Dancers, Colored Lady Vocalists, No. 2 Band (Colored), 8 or 10 pieces" (*New York Clipper*).

• ***September 22, 1894:*** " 'The Old South' opened its season at Gilmore's Auditorium, Philadelphia, Sept. 10, with a matinee performance. The company numbers fifty-three people. Roster: Geo. C. Thompson, Harry T. Leonard, Marjorie Maxwell, Lillian Calef, Harry Pierson, Alabama Pickaninnies, eight in number, Standard Quartet, Meadow Brook Quartet, Old South Quartet, Billy Jackson, Irving Jones, Luke Pulley, Tub Fields, Jim Towee [*sic*], Wm. Hall, Walter Emery, Frank Farris, Kid Bailey, Winn and Miller, Sadie Jones, Mable Wallace, R. L. Scott, Emma Scott, Delia Snowell, Helen Murray, Mamie Moore, Lulu Walker, Nettie Sanson, Jessie Augustus, Nora Randolph, Ella Mathews, Amanda Price, Anna Brown, and a brass band and orchestra of fifteen pieces" (*New York Clipper*).

• ***September 29, 1894:*** "Billy Jackson has joined his former partner Irving Jones, and they are now with the 'Old South' Co." (*New York Clipper*).

• ***September 29, 1894:*** "The Meadow Brook Quartet—D. L. Frazier, B. F. Underwood, Jim Jones and Robert Dupree—have joined 'The Old South' Co." (*New York Clipper*).

• ***October 13, 1894:*** "The Meadow brook Quartet has been dissolved. Ben Underwood is the only member of the quartet remaining with the 'Old South' Co.... Luke Pulley, pianist and vocalist, has joined the 'Old South' Co. as leader of the orchestra" (*New York Clipper*).

• ***February 16, 1895:*** "The Alhambra Quartet has signed with 'The South Before the War' Co. The quartet is made up as follows: John Bell, first tenor; H. Morton, second tenor; Oscar Murray, baritone; and W. Pleasant, basso" (*New York Clipper*).

• ***March 9, 1895:*** "Notes of the Stage," "The famous Standard Quartet of Chicago, that are now traveling with the South Before War Co., H. C. Williams, Ed Moss, R. L. Scott of this city and Wm. Cottrell, of Toledo, O., are making quite a reputation for themselves. Their singing is one of the features of the show" (*Indianapolis Freeman*).

• ***May 4, 1895:*** "Charley Howard, an old darkey impersonator and comedian, died April 28, in Brooklyn, N.Y., from the effects of a fall received March 24 while boarding a train at Evansville, Ind. The deceased was fifty-seven years of age, and was a member of 'The South Before the War' Co. when he received the injuries that resulted in his death. A widow and a son survive him. Interment will occur May 1 at Evergreen Cemetery" (*New York Clipper*).

• ***July 6, 1895:*** "Billy Williams, the comedian, will return to Whallen & Martell's 'South Before the War' Co. next season to play the same part, Aunt Chloe, and manage the stage. They open on or about Sept. 1" (*New York Clipper*).

White minstrel star Billy Williams was a famous "wench impersonator."[56] He appeared in blackface makeup and female attire for his "Aunt Chloe."

• ***September 7, 1895:*** "Business manager Geo. L. Chennele informs us that the season of Whallen & Martell's 'South Before the War' will open Sept. 16 at the Buckingham Theatre, Louisville, Ky. The organization will, he announces, be stronger this season than ever before, the company including fifty people as well as a band of pickaninnies" (*New York Clipper*).

• ***September 14, 1895:*** "The following have signed with 'South Before the War' Co.: The Eureka Quartet (Wm. Hill, Lew Francis, Luke Pulley and H. W. Scott), Mrs. Nora Randolph, Mrs. Annie Scott, buck and wing dancer; Alice Gibson and Mrs. Bertha Pulley" (*New York Clipper*).

• ***October 26, 1895:*** " 'South Before The War' has lost none of the popularity it achieved at its first appearance at the Empire. All 3 floors were filled at each performance. Whallen & Martell are carrying a large company this year without a diminution in the quality of work given. All the old favorites are retained, including Billy Williams, Auntie Chloe, Ferry The Frog, and the four quartets which were so well received last year" (*Indianapolis Freeman*).

• ***November 23, 1895:*** "Martell's 'South Before the War' Co. are now traveling in their new palace car named the Hattie . . . The dancing this season is a feature, also the cake walk" (*New York Clipper*).

The South Before the War Company continued to tour until the end of the century, at least, and it continued to press black quartets to the fore. The August 27, 1898, edition of the *Freeman* noted: "The 'South Before the War' Company opened their third stand this season at Kenosha, Wisc., on the 14th to S.R.O. The following is the roster: Mr. and Mrs. Harry Martell, proprietors . . . the Shattuck Quartette (W. C. Creimer, J. C. Crooms, J. R. Douglass, John A. Milton), Standard Quartette (Wm. Cottrill, Julius ["Jube"] Johnson, J. W. [John Wesley] Jenkins, John Hall), Capital City Quartet (Dave Smith, Dick Robinson, P. Black and Jean Clark) . . . Ben Harney,[57] leader orchestra."

African American quartets had graced the professional stage as far back as the Luca Family in the 1850s, but a new era in black quartet singing began with the plantation shows of the 1890s. In the aftermath of the success of the South Before the War, Slavery Days, and Old South Companies, black quartets became a centerpiece of ragtime minstrelsy and mainstream vaudeville. By the end of the century the public had developed a connoisseur's appreciation of black vocal quartet harmony, and barbershop harmonizing jumped the "race line."

The Twilight Quartet toured with the South Before the War Company during its opening season in 1892 and on through 1893. According to a 1906 *Freeman* retrospective, "the once famous Twilight Quartet" made its "first appearance . . . in New York in high class vaudeville, and later were engaged as entertainers by many of our most exclusive patrons of colored talent. The members of this quartet when first organized were the now famous Joseph Hodges, of Hodges & Launchmore [*sic*], Robert Martin, Isaac Hines and Billy Moore."[58] The Twilight Quartet appears to have been an outrider of the plantation show quartet movement. At New York City's Grand Street Dime Museum in 1889, they appeared in the plantation scenes in a presentation of *Uncle Tom's Cabin.* In April 1891 the Twilight Quartet appeared at Niblo's Garden, New York City, in the cast of the play *The Beautiful Slave,* a "romantic spectacle of Southern life."

The Standard Quartette of Chicago stands out among the many quartets linked to the

South Before the War because they made some of the earliest-known sound recordings of black vocal harmony.[59] Between 1894 and 1897 the Standard Quartette made at least thirty-two different cylinder recordings, ranging from spirituals to sentimental ballads, coon songs, and plantation melodies.[60] Though some of their recorded titles appear to have been conscious throwbacks, intended to recall the flavor of earlier times, several of these same titles were recorded by black quartets in the 1920s. This underscores the persistence of the plantation show repertoire in the evolution of African American male quartet singing.

Thus far, only two of the cylinder recordings made by the Standard Quartette are known to have survived. These century-old recordings preserve hearty, spontaneous-sounding renditions of "Keep Movin'" and "Every Day'll Be Sunday Bye and Bye,"[61] both of which are minstrelized parodies of spirituals. "Every Day'll Be Sunday Bye and Bye" has been credited to Sam Lucas:

As I was running across the field,
Every Day'll be Sunday bye and bye,
A black snake bit me on my heel,
Every day'll be Sunday bye and bye,
I turned around to do my best,
Every day'll be Sunday bye and bye,
My left foot took in a hornet's nest,
Every day'll be Sunday bye and bye.[62]

The Standard Quartette's pioneer recordings do not appear to have gained the attention of the African American press. There was no salient record industry in the mid-1890s; it would have required an extremely farsighted commentator to identify these recordings as anything more than a curious novelty.

According to a report in the *Freeman*, three members of the Standard Quartette originally hailed from Indianapolis.[63] They appear to have participated in a "National Contest" there in 1894, and in 1895 the Standard Quartette highlighted a season of "Quartet Extravaganzas" in Indianapolis, promoted as singing contests between the mightiest of the current generation of black vocal groups. Singing competitions remained an important ingredient of the African American vocal quartet tradition well into the twentieth century.[64]

• ***January 27, 1894 (Indianapolis, Indiana):*** "City Happenings," "A great many white people will attend the contest . . . the masses of the young people are elated over the coming contest . . . Tickets are going very fast for the National contest . . . The YMCA Hall will be crowded . . . February 7, the National Contest between the Tennessee Warblers, the Chicago Quartette and the Hoosier Quartet will be an eventful occasion" (*Indianapolis Freeman*).

It is possible the Chicago Quartette was the Standard Quartette of Chicago. The *Freeman* never did say who won the contest.

• ***February 23, 1895:*** "City Happenings," "The famous Harry New Quartet has been secured for the Herculean Extravaganza. Three of the best quartets in the state take leading parts in the Herculean Extravaganza . . . The Herculean Extravaganza Quartet, second to none in the state, with new and original songs" (*Indianapolis Freeman*).

• ***March 9, 1895 (Indianapolis, Indiana):*** "City Happenings," "Three Quartets for the Herculean Extravaganza: the famous 'Harry New Quartette,' the renowned 'Clay-Gist Hoosier Star' Quartette, and the 'Elliot-Hunter' Quartette, April 2nd at Bethel" (*Indianapolis Freeman*).

• ***May 11, 1895 (Indianapolis, Indiana):*** "City Happenings," "The singing contest between the Standard Quartette of Chicago and Clay Gist Star Quartette of this city, came off at the 21 Baptist Church on last Thursday evening" (*Indianapolis Freeman*).

• ***December 21, 1895:*** "City Happenings," "The famous Standard Quartette at Bethel, Dec. 25th . . . The Standard Quartette stands ready and well qualified for any and all engagements. Irving Hardy is the manager, 64 East Washington Street; J. L. Williams, secretary" (*Indianapolis Freeman*).

Among the quartets who toured with the South Before the War, Slavery Days, and/or the Old South, the Eclipse Quartet left the richest trail of documentation in the *Clipper*. Two of its early members were identified with the Bay City Quartet, trouping through the Midwest in the summer of 1889.

• ***June 29, 1889:*** "The Bay City Quartet (B. F. Payne, A. E. Anderson, J. D. Johnson and A. King) and J. C. Carr (drum major) closed their engagement with the Holmes Colored Concert and Minstrel Co. at Mapleton, Ia., June 22, to join the Shaker Medicine Co. (Dr. Louis Turner's) at St. Louis, Mo., for the tenting season" (*New York Clipper*).

In the fall of 1889, the Eclipse Quartet was making the rounds of various midwestern city dime museums.

• ***September 28, 1889*** (Milwaukee, Wisconsin): "Grand Avenue Theatre and Museum Annex—Curio [Hall]—Morelle (Yankee Whittler), Glass Swimmers, Chief Onowaha and son, and the Dr. Cronin Mystery. Stage . . . Eclipse Quartet and Burton's Dog Circus" (*New York Clipper*).

• ***October 19, 1889 (Chicago, Illinois):*** "Kohl & Middleton's Dime Museum—South Side: Hazel-Zazel Jones, the double headed Indiana baby; Austin, the expansionist; the Eclipse Quartet in Theatre No. 1, and Crolius Comedy Co. in No. 2" (*New York Clipper*).

New York Clipper, *April 9, 1892.*

For at least a year before signing with the South Before the War, the Eclipse Quartet appeared in major vaudeville theaters of the northeastern states and Canada.

• ***June 27, 1891:*** "The Eclipse Quartet—Anderson Bros., Payne and Wade—after a successful season of forty-eight weeks, playing dates, will close at Boston, Keith's Bijou, preparatory to an engagement with Payne's Panacea Co. for next season" (*New York Clipper*).

• ***August 29, 1891:*** "W. S. Purdy's Black Cyclone Minstrels opened their season Aug. 15, at the People's Theatre, Hamilton, Can., to a crowded house. The first part represents the deck of a yacht, with the company dressed in sailor costumes . . . The roster: Harry Gillam, Ben Southold, James Campbell, Geo. Forrester, Jessie Forrester, Nip Clark, Ollie Hall, the Eclipse Quartet, Ed. Harris, Fred Lightfoot, Arthur Barnes, Robert Street, Arnold Mathews and Garnett Barnes. W. S. Purdy is the manager, with Arthur Barnes leader of band and orchestra" (*New York Clipper*).

• ***October 3, 1891:*** "The Eclipse Quartet . . . open at Austin & Haynes' Palace Theatre, Boston, soon, for a two weeks' engagement, after which they return to this city [New York]. Maj. Ben F. Payne is their manager" (*New York Clipper*).

• ***April 9, 1892:*** "The Eclipse Comedy Quartet—Anderson Bros., Payne and Wade—had a pleasant time at Philadelphia week of March 28. At the Ninth and Arch Street Musee York [Anderson] was presented with a handsome diamond ring by the quartet. They are *en route* West" (*New York Clipper*).

• ***May 28, 1892:*** "The Eclipse Comedy Quartet . . . have signed with the Whallen & Martell 'South Before the War' Co." (*New York Clipper*).

"HELP," "HELP," "HELP."
WE ARE STARVING FOR THE WANT OF VACATION.
AFRO-AMERICAN ARTISTS.
THE
AL. E. ANDERSONS MAMIE
ORIGINATORS OF PLANTATION JOLLITY.
"Corn Bread," "Corn Bread," "Corn Bread."

We've got a hot plantation act, for strongest olios, entitled, "CORN BREAD," with plenty of ginger, which we manufacture ourselves and cure all grave yard faces in twenty minutes. No more one night stands, but we are playing dates. Strictly all week stands now. Sorry, but nothing open at present. Write later. Thanks to managers for kind offers with combinations for next season. Yours, respectfully, THE ANDERSONS.
HOME ADDRESS 178 PLEASANT STREET, Boston.
P. S.—Regards to our friends. Knockers and back cappers want to lay dead now and swipe. Got a trunk full of old jokes. Would like to sell the NITS. If this shoe fits wear it. Ha, ha, ha. Now will you use your little hammer papa bought you.

New York Clipper, *June 16, 1894.*

The Eclipse Quartet stayed with the South Before the War for most, perhaps all of the 1892–1893 season, then went out with Slavery Days for the season of 1893–1894. Before the summer of 1894, Al E. Anderson left the Eclipse Quartet to form a team act with his wife, Mamie, and by June, Al and Mamie Anderson were touring with Lanworth's North and South Colored Vaudeville Company.

• ***June 30, 1894:*** "Roster of Lanworth's North and South Colored Vaudeville Co.—Peter Lanworth, proprietor and manager; Gill Pierce, representative; Geo. E. Lanworth, treasurer; Al. E. Anderson, stage manager; Mamie Anderson, Hattie Parker, Florence Hines, William Ritchie, Delma Blakemore, Billy Allen, Emma Allen, Jerry Mills, Yeager and Clifton, Ida Bond, Henry Williams, Albert Manott, Henry Winfield, Irene Smith, York Anderson, Maggie Dickson and the Golden Gate Quartet" (*New York Clipper*).

• ***August 18, 1894:*** "Roster of Lanworth's North and South Colored Vaudeville Co. [includes] H. Winfred and wife . . . and the Golden Gate Quartet. The season opens at Troy, N.Y., in September" (*New York Clipper*).

When Lanworth's North and South Colored Vaudeville Company opened its season of 1894–1895, the roster included a reconstituted Eclipse Quartet under Al E. Anderson's brother York.

• ***September 15, 1894:*** "The Eclipse Quartet—York Anderson, Henry Winfred, Frank Sutton and Henry Williams—have signed with the Lanworth Colored Vaudevilles" (*New York Clipper*).

• ***September 29, 1894:*** "Roster of Lanworth's Colored Vaudevilles and French Creole Possumala Dancers[65]—Peter Lanworth, proprietor and manager . . . Al. E. Anderson, Mamie Anderson, Prof. Fred Johnson, Jerry Mills, Harry Clifton, York Anderson, Harry Williams, Frank Sutton, Ida Winfred, Georgia Douglas, Billy and Emma Allen, and the Eclipse Quartet. The company are *en route* west" (*New York Clipper*).

• ***October 20, 1894:*** "The Eclipse Quartet is no longer connected with Lanworth's Vaudeville Co." (*New York Clipper*).

• ***February 23, 1895:*** "The Eclipse Quartet (Anderson, Fields, Freeman and Miller) have closed a successful two weeks at Austin & Stone's Museum, Boston, Mass." (*New York Clipper*).

• ***September 14, 1895:*** "The following people will appear in Chas. Lovenberg's spectacle, 'New King Cole,' which will be prepared for the Rhode Island State Fair: The Austin Sisters, the Forepaugh Family, Mazzuz and Abbacco . . . the Lovenberg Sisters with a band of pickaninnies . . . and the Eclipse Quartet. There will also be a chorus of one hundred voices" (*New York Clipper*).

• ***November 30, 1895:*** "The Eclipse Comedy Quartet which is filling a two week's engagement at Stone & Shaw's Museum, Boston, Mass., consist of York Anderson, Harry Clifton, Sam Wade and Ben F. Payne" (*New York Clipper*).

With the sole exception of Al E. Anderson, the membership of the Eclipse Comedy Quartet at Stone and Shaw's Museum in November 1895 was identical with that of the Eclipse Quartet that had opened with the South Before the War in the autumn of 1892. During the intervening period, however, the personnel was

FRANK SUTTON.
SHERMAN COATES.
ARTHUR COATES.
HENRY WINFRED.
THE FAMOUS GOLDEN GATE QUARTETTE—with Metropolitan Burlesquers.

Freeman, *December 24, 1898.*

anything but static. Shortly after the departure of Al E. Anderson in the fall of 1894, the Eclipse Quartet included Frank Sutton and Henry Winfred, both of whom would achieve greater fame as members of the Golden Gate Quartette. With Sutton, Winfred, and brothers Sherman and Arthur Coates, the Golden Gate Quartette became one of the most famous of the turn-of-the-century ragtime vocal quartets.

During the summer of 1894, Lanworth's North and South Colored Vaudeville Company witnessed the birth of an incipient combination called the Golden Gate Quartet, which undoubtedly included Henry Winfred. Meanwhile, Sherman Coates and perhaps also his brother Arthur were under the tutelage of the great Billy McClain, as cast members of the "river shows" "On the Mississippi" and "Down on the Suwanee River."[66]

By 1896 the membership of the Golden Gate Quartette was fully congealed, and they came into prominence as rising stars with Sam T. Jack's Creole Company. By the end of the century the Golden Gate Quartette was performing in major mainstream venues such as New York City's Madison Square Roof Garden, and in 1900 they became a "strong feature" with the famous Williams and Walker Company.[67] A later incarnation of the Golden Gate Quartette—the Golden Gate Trio, featuring Henry Winfred—was still touring vaudeville in 1911.[68]

The Eclipse Quartet may not have survived until the turn of the century. The *Freeman* of February 13, 1897, noted, "York Anderson, formerly of the Eclipse Quartette, died at his home at Fall River, Mass., Jan. 28.," at age thirty-one. Then, the edition of June 11, 1898, reported: "Samuel. H. Wade, at one time a member of the Eclipse Quartette (Anderson Brothers, Payne and Wade) died May 26 at his home in Boston, Mass., from consumption." The *Freeman* of August 25, 1900, provided a glimpse at Ben F. Payne's ongoing career: "'The Paynes,' Ben., Susie and Mamie, closed with Boom's Black Diamond Co. at Middleton, Conn., on the 5th inst., and signed with [the premier edition of] 'A Rabbit's Foot Company'. . . Major Ben. F. Payne is holding down Uncle Ebeneezer Duzenberry in the comedy cast of the play." Payne died on the road in Charleston, South Carolina, September 4, 1903.[69]

IN MEMORY OF
MADAME SUSIE PAYNE.

Madame Susie Payne, a well-known performer, departed this life July 23, 1912, in New York City. She was the mother of Mrs. Ella Aiken and Mamie Payne, the latter also a well-known performer. The mother was known for her character work, which was seen in vaudeville, where she was a success, particularly in the east.

Madame Payne was at one time a member of Sam T. Jack's Company, also a member of the "South Before the War" Company. After this she had her picks

MAMIE PAYNE, of Foster and Payne, Playing "Bellboy and the Maid."

with whom she had great success. She traveled very much, touring in Mexico, Cuba, through the States and Canada. She worked both socially and on the stage. For twenty-seven years she was a performer.

Her death has greatly sorrowed the hearts of those who knew her, especially her children—her two daughters. However, she died in the faith; she declared her hope. She called her daughters about her at her departing moment, advised them to make ready for the hereafter in the heavens, where she declared she was going.

She left two daughters, two nephews and a son-in-law to mourn her passing. She was interred in New York City.

Freeman, *July 26, 1913.*

The death of Al E. Anderson in 1925 gave occasion for a brief retrospective on the old Eclipse Quartet:

> Albert E. Anderson . . . died Tuesday, Dec. 8, at his home in Keokuk, Iowa . . .
>
> Anderson was born August 25, 1869 . . . He started in the show business in 1884 with McFadden's "Uncle Tom's Cabin." . . .
>
> After being with several minstrel shows and doing a knockabout song and dance with his brother, Morris, for a while, then with another brother, York, he later joined Ben Payne and George Moore and with another partner formed the Eclipse quartet and worked the variety theaters in the old days and for several years made a name for themselves. This quartet joined the old "South Before the War" company, where they put on the old "Wash Day on the Levee" scene . . . Anderson later joined Sam T. Jack's Creole company, where he met and married Mamie Riley.[70]

A Low and Narrow Pathway of Opportunity in the Circus Sideshow "Colored Annex," 1891–1895

"It is generally understood by the public at large that circus people have a tough time, I deny the assertion and will say for good treatment, equal justice and sure salary, give me the circus."

—P. G. Lowery, *Indianapolis Freeman*, November 9, 1901

Although African Americans barely enter into official circus history, black musicians and performers have always played a part in the success of the American circus. P. T. Barnum appears to have featured a black entertainer in his first "traveling exhibition" in 1836. A review of Barnum's career, published in the *New York Clipper* shortly after his death in 1891, notes:

> Barnum's circus career began in April, 1836, when he connected himself with Aaron Turner's

Show as ticket seller, secretary and treasurer... The company was four in all, the two Turner boys, sons of the proprietor, who were good riders; Joe Pentland, in Barnum's words, "one of the wittiest, best and most original of clowns," and Vivalla [a chair balancer, stilt walker and plate spinner]... When the season and the partnership came to a close in October, Barnum... took with him Vivalla, Sanford, a negro singer and dancer; two or three musicians, some horses and a small tent, and began a traveling exhibition of his own. At Camden, S.C., Sanford suddenly left the company, and, not to disappoint the audience, Barnum blacked himself and sang the songs that had been advertised.[71]

From May through August 1873, a company of nine black jubilee singers, sometimes billed as the Original Jubilee Singers and apparently also known as the Alabama Slave Minstrels, were on tour with the P. T. Barnum Circus in Massachusetts, Pennsylvania, Missouri, Illinois, and Indiana. At Fall River, Massachusetts, Barnum's advertisement in the *Daily Evening News* claimed a jubilee concert was "given in the Grand Hippodrome after each Exhibition by the Original Colored Jubilee Singers for the benefit of students in Southern Schools."[72] Such philanthropic claims should not be taken seriously. Nevertheless, Barnum was obviously inspired by the recent success of the Fisk University Jubilee Singers, who first appeared in New York City in December 1871 and who scored a great hit at the "World Peace Jubilee" in Boston in June 1872.

When P. T. Barnum carried his "Greatest Show on Earth" to London, England, in late 1889, the roster included "Charley and Oscar, Zulus," and "Butler's troupe of twenty-three jubilee singers."[73] Upon their return to the United States in February 1890, the *Clipper* noted, "a few of the jubilee singers... are to remain on the other side to fill special engagements."[74] Later that spring when the roster of Barnum and Bailey's Circus for the coming season was announced, a troupe of "Jubilee Singers" was listed among the "sideshow features."[75]

Jubilee singers were commonly associated with circus sideshows of the 1880s and 1890s. An 1880 advertisement for W. C. Coup's United Monster Shows, a traveling circus, registers Height's Jubilee Singers among its many attractions.[76] Reports in 1889–1895 editions of the *Clipper* document a growing number of black jubilee singers, brass bands, minstrels, and vocal quartets on the rosters of various circus sideshows.

• ***May 18, 1889:*** "Under the White Tents," "Stow, Long and Gumble's Trans-Continental Circus and Menagerie and Balloon Shows opened April 25 at Hawks, O., to good business. They play Columbus, O., for one week, then take the road and make one day stands only. The roster [includes] Side Show people—Max Zimmerman, manager; Lew Zimmerman, assistant manager; John Lewis, sideshow talker; Capt. Lovavovetish, Jasper Zulo, Millie Jasper, Baldwin Allen, Half Horse and Half Man, Lew Smith and Jack Smith's Colored Band of ten pieces" (*New York Clipper*).

• ***June 8, 1889:*** "Notes from the John Robinson [Circus] Show," "Our street parade is a great feature, one of our novelties being the two Zulus in their native costumes... Two water buffalos, driven by Zulus, are among the new attractions in the Hippodrome" (*New York Clipper*).

• ***August 10, 1889:*** "Notes from the Robinson Show," "A band of colored jubilee singers was added to the concert [July] 28" (*New York Clipper*).

• ***August 10, 1889:*** "Wanted, for McClelland's New United Monster Shows and Wild West,... a troupe of Jubilee Singers... Excelsior Jubilee Singers of Baltimore... write or telegraph at once. A long season in the South. Address

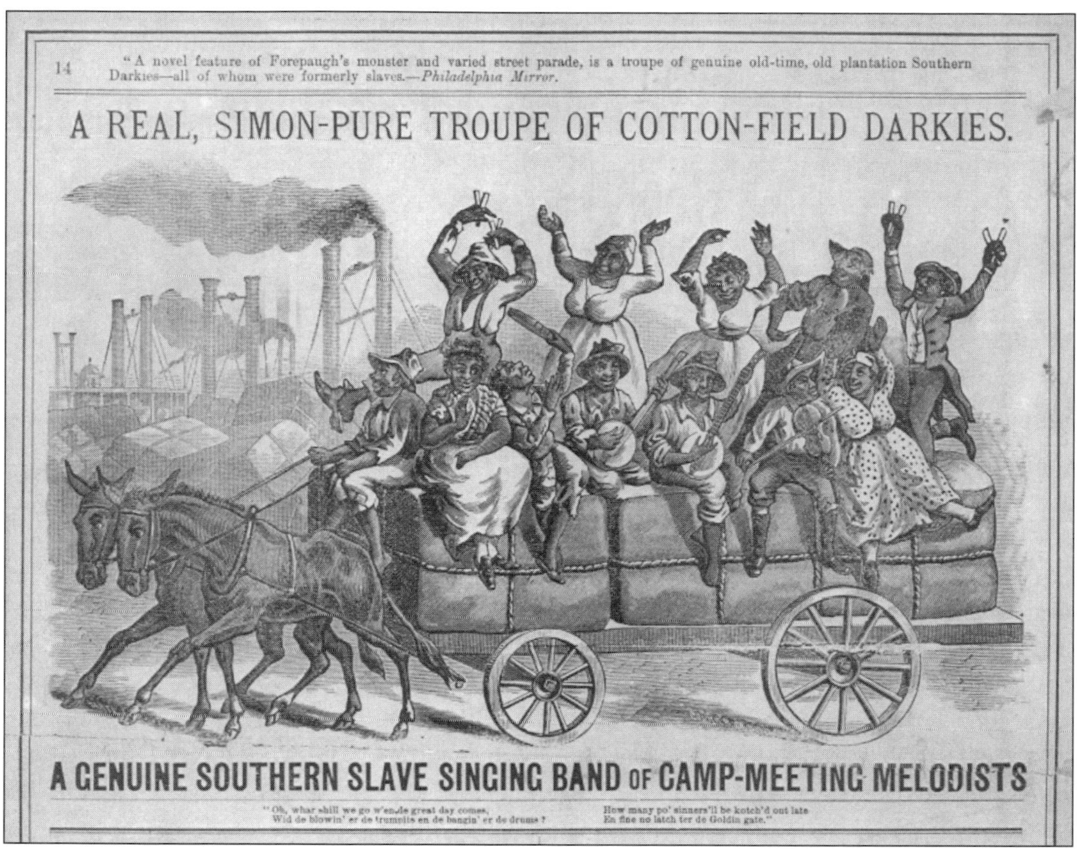

14
"A novel feature of Forepaugh's monster and varied street parade, is a troupe of genuine old-time, old plantation Southern Darkies—all of whom were formerly slaves.—*Philadelphia Mirror*.
A REAL, SIMON-PURE TROUPE OF COTTON-FIELD DARKIES.
A GENUINE SOUTHERN SLAVE SINGING BAND OF CAMP-MEETING MELODISTS
"Oh, whar shill we go w'en de great day comes,
Wid de blowin' er de trumpits en de bangin' er de drums?
How many po' sinners'll be kotch'd out late
En fine no latch ter de Goldin gate."

Forepaugh Circus Magazine, *1883. (courtesy Robert F. Houston)*

Wm. J. McClelland, Brockport, Elk Co., Pa." (*New York Clipper*).

• ***July 19, 1890:*** "Walter L. Main paid the Brazilian Circus a visit at Stapleton, S. I., [*sic*] and is said to have expressed himself well pleased with the performance. He also made a big offer for the fourteen Congo Zulus, which J. S. Hoffman secured last week" (*New York Clipper*).

• ***July 26, 1890:*** "Notes from the John Robinson Show," "Our business through Montana was great . . . The little uptown sideshow, under the management of Millwood & Conlon, is taking in a great deal of the 'long green.' They have a very clever band of Jubilee singers, who make things very lively" (*New York Clipper*).

• ***March 28, 1891:*** "Roster of McMahon's International Hippodrome, Circus and Menagerie—John S. McMahon, proprietor . . . Sideshow [includes] Ten Zenegambian [*sic*] Serenaders and Three Headed Illusion, etc." (*New York Clipper*).

• ***April 11, 1891:*** "Walter L. Main's new Monster R.R. Shows, Double Circus, Roman Hippodrome, Elevated Stage, Menagerie, Museum, Aquarium and Free Horse Show will open at Geneva, O., April 25 . . . The [show includes] four separate brass bands, and a troupe of jubilee singers, a colored brass band [and a] Continental Fife and drum corps . . . Sideshow—Hugh Harrison and wife (second sight), E. M. Vernel (magician and ventriloquist), Chas. Scott (Zulu), Madame Harrison (mind reader), John Jennings (strong man), Geo. L. Stull (lion claw wild man), Geo. Cordozia (tattooed man), Mattie Williams' den of performing alligators, Zano's performing snakes, Zenobia (fire king), Mattenazina's wrestling bears, May Milton (long haired lady), Ina Vernello's troupe of performing birds, Prof. I. O. Nutt's Colored Minstrels, Jubilee's Brass Band and Orchestra, cape vampire (man eating gorilla), birds, monkeys, illusions, [etc.]" (*New York Clipper*).

• ***April 18, 1891:*** "It is Prof. J. O. McNutt, and not I. O. Nutt, who is to furnish the colored brass band and jubilee singers for Walter L. Main's Show" (*New York Clipper*).

• ***April 25, 1891:*** "Roster of Washburn & Arlington's New United Shows, Wild East, Wild West, Circus, Menagerie, Hippodrome and Congress of Nations: L. W. Washburn and Geo. Arlington, proprietors . . . Hassan Ben Said's troupe of twelve Arabs, eight men, two women and two children; Red Fox's band of ten Indians, six bucks, two squaws and two papooses . . ., Prof. McDonald and twelve men (white band), Prof. Simus, eight men (colored band) . . . Ike Hall's Drum Corp . . . and others in the side show. An Arabian village and Indian encampment are features of the show" (*New York Clipper*).

• ***May 9, 1891 (Columbus, Ohio):*** "The past week has been one of enjoyment among the colored people of this city. The first thing occurring was one of the most successful concerts we have attended for quite a while. Those taking part in the concert were Wilbury King, Gus Sherman, the Mendelsohn Vocal Club, Miss Nettie Robinson, J. Wiggins, White's quartette and S. P. White's band; the band mentioned is a band organized for the purpose of traveling with Sells Bros' circus; ten men compose this band—Wm. and Thos. Mays, from Wichita, Kan.; S. Streets, of Jonesville, O.; John Gluff, of Springfield, O., N. Nogae, of Champaign, Ill.; W. W. Walker, of Nashville, Tenn.; Chas. Granaway, N. F. Ridout, Wm. Hedgpath and Solomon P. White are from Columbus . . . W. F. [*sic*] Ridout, with his solo 'Fascination,' won the esteem of all . . . The band left Saturday night, and will be 8 months on the road, returning some time in November; they play in side shows and parade. The quartette, composed of four members of the band, is good. They will sing while out on the road" (*Indianapolis Freeman*).

Note: Bandmaster Solomon P. White was born in Chillicothe, Ohio, in 1867, and began his professional career in 1887 with the band of the S. H. Barrett Circus. In 1888 he joined the sideshow band with the Sells Bros. Circus, and in 1889 he became its leader.[77] A note from Sells Bros.' Circus in the fall of 1897 declared, "The side show band under the leadership of Prof. Sol White is still winning much applause, on parade and under tent, for their excellent music. 'Lucky Jim Jackson's Jubes' also come in for their share of liberal applause for the unrivalled camp-meeting shouting."[78]

White paved the way for the enormous advances credited to P. G. Lowery, who took White's place at the head of the colored band and minstrels with the Forepaugh-Sells Bros.' Circus in 1899. Eleven years later, in a retrospective history of the "circus annex minstrelsy" phenomenon, the *Freeman* declared: "The branch of colored show business known as circus minstrels and vaudeville had its beginnings with P. G. Lowery, the renowned cornetist and bandmaster . . . in 1899 . . . Since Lowery's initiative, all have fallen in line—the little ones and the big ones—until at this time no less than fourteen white tents are giving employment to big colored companies . . . Something like three hundred people—performers and

P.G. Lowery and his Hagenbeck & Wallace Circus Sideshow Annex Band, circa 1916. Lowery is seated in the second row, third from left.

musicians—are employed in this phase of the show business. The number promises to increase."[79]

• ***July 11, 1891:*** "Notes from Dick's Circus," "We are now in our ninth week, and have had a prosperous season . . . Our sideshow is run by Senator Frank B. Hubin, with the following people: Capt. McIntosh (tattooed man), jubilee singers and Prof. Hubin's Punch and magic" (*New York Clipper*).

• ***April 2, 1892:*** "Roster of the Sideshow with Miles Orton's Show [includes] Prof. W. H. Jacobs' Colored Band of eight pieces" (*New York Clipper*).

• ***April 16, 1892:*** "Walter L. Main's Show will open their tenting season of 1892 at Geneva, O., April 23 . . . Sideshow [includes] Mme. Harrison, mind reader; Rena Stillwell, snake charmer, with snakes, armadillos and alligators . . . ; Sheephead Ann, half woman, half sheep; vampires, armadillos, dragons, monkeys, birds, illusions and mechanical inventions . . . [and a] colored band of eight pieces, Baldwin Allen, leader" (*New York Clipper*).

• ***July 2, 1892:*** "Roster of Sideshow with Hunting's Circus and Menagerie [includes] Nip Clark, Bob Landon, Burt Landon and Philip Walker (Congo Band)" (*New York Clipper*).

• ***March 11, 1893:*** "Notes from the Great Wallace Show," "Sideshow [includes] C. W. Jones' colored band, ten pieces; Prince Mungo, Morean chieftan; Princess Julia, snake charmer; Zamora, triple jointed wonder . . . [etc.]" (*New York Clipper*).

• ***July 1, 1893:*** "Walter L. Main's Sideshow Roster [includes] J. T. Kawanda, wild boy; Hughie Stout, fat man; Caddie Clare, fat woman; den of fifty snakes, cages of vampires, birds, monkeys, agoutis, grave diggers, picas and a man slayer ape. Prof. J. O. McNutt's brass band and orchestra and a troupe of jubilee singers supply the music" (*New York Clipper*).

• ***July 29, 1893:*** "The Black Hussar Band and Jubilee Singers are now engaged with Cook & Whitby's English and American Circus" (*New York Clipper*).

• ***February 3, 1894:*** "Sells & Rentfrow's Winter Quarters [in Topeka, Kansas] . . . B. L. Bowman . . . is putting together a fine side show. He will use a 70 × 100 ft. side show canvas . . . Mr. Bowman has engaged a Zulu band of ten pieces for the side show, a number of new freaks and curiosities" (*New York Clipper*).

Note: In nineteenth-century circus parlance, a "Zulu" was an African American performer costumed and portrayed as an uncivilized "wild man" manifestly suitable for exhibit alongside other "freaks and curiosities." "Zulu bands," "Congo bands," etc., were an extension of the "Zulu wild man" theme.

• ***April 28, 1894:*** "Roster of Wolfscale's Algerian Band and Jubilee Singers—James Wolfscale, band master; D. H. Lankford, Ed. Green, Baxter Reynolds, William Moore, James Thompson, Sylvester Bell and Ora Hicks. They are engaged with Sells & Rentfrow's Circus" (*New York Clipper*).

Note: With Barnum and Bailey's Greatest Show on Earth in 1914, bandmaster James Wolfscale had charge of the Black Hussars Military Concert Band of thirty-two pieces, the largest circus sideshow band on the road that season.[80] Their repertoire ran from "Poet and Peasant" to "Dynamite Rag."[81] Wolfscale died in Chicago on October 21, 1921.[82]

• ***August 4, 1894:*** "Roster of Griffin's Annex, with Hunting's Circus and Menagerie [includes] the Congo Quartette" (*New York Clipper*).

• ***August 4, 1894:*** "Cook & Whitby Notes," "Lew Nichols, manager of the side show with Cook &

INTERESTING CAREER OF OLDEST BAND AND MINSTREL MANAGER.

Prof. James Wolfscale a Success in the Business for Over a Quarter of a Century.

Accompanying this sketch is a splendid likeness of Prof. Wolfscale, of the Barnum & Bailey circus. His experience in the show business has not only been with circuses, but with minstrel shows as well, having trooped with such old-timers as P. T. Wright and McCaulis Minstrels. He began his circus career in 1890, and since that time he has been with the following shows: Sells & Gray, Sells & Downs, Cole Bros., Jones Bros.' Wild West, Adam Forepaugh & Sells Bros. and Barnum & Bailey. Prof. Wolfscale has been re-engaged for the season of 1914 with the Barnum & Bailey show, which will make his third consecutive season with "the greatest show on earth." Mr. Wolfscale's success in the show business is due to his legitimate way of doing business, and his making it a rule to carry nothing but gentlemen in his company. For the past two seasons Wolfscale's band, dressed as Egyptians and mounted on camels, was one of the features of the great spectacle "Cleopatra," introduced by the Barnum & Bailey circus during their engagement at Madison Square Garden, New York City. For season of 1914, Prof. Wolfscale will carry a band of sixteen pieces and it will be the largest colored circus band on the road. Mr. Wolfscale

would like to hear from first-class musicians at all times. All mail will reach him at his permanent address, 3212 Wabash avenue, Chicago, Ill. Prof. Wolfscale wishes "a Merry Christmas and a Happy New Year" to his many friends in and out of the profession.

Freeman, *December 20, 1913.*

Sol P. White, Freeman, *October 23, 1897.*

P. G. Lowery, White Tops, *February–March 1943.*

Whitby's Circus, reports good business throughout Canada. The roster [includes] Prof. Jones' Black Hussar Band and Rooster Orchestra" (*New York Clipper*).

• ***September 29, 1894:*** "Mr. William Roberts, formerly of Indianapolis, is traveling now with Sells Bros. Circus, of which he is said to be the leading member of the quartet, which is known as the Silver Leaf. The show is at present 'doing' the Southern states" (*Indianapolis Freeman*).

• ***January 5, 1895:*** "Jones' Peerless Black Hussar Band, allied with the Sunny Brook Quartet, have been re-engaged with the Wallace Circus, making their fourth season with that show" (*New York Clipper*).

• ***January 12, 1895:*** "J. O. McNutt has signed with the W. L. Main Big Shows to furnish the side show band for the next season, with the following musicians: J. O. McNutt, W. S. Brown, J. W. Pleasants, F. D. Powell, Jas. S. Norton, W. T. Enix, C. B. Smith and Chas. E. Enix" (*New York Clipper*).

• ***April 6, 1895:*** "Roster of the Walter L. Main's Side Show for the coming season [includes] four colored jubilee singers, Prof. J. O. McNutt's Colored band of nine pieces, a huge man slayer ape and a monster snake" (*New York Clipper*).

• ***April 20, 1895:*** "Under the Tents," "Roster of Jones' Black Hussar Band, with the Wallace Circus: Ed. Planchard, Will Barnett, D. Brown, Joe Patton, John Duff, Geo. Bailey, C. Gilbert, Wm. Hunter, C. W. Jones and the Willow Brook Quartet" (*New York Clipper*).

• ***June 8, 1895:*** "Roster of N. J. Doris' Side Show—J. Sandrew's Band of seven pieces, Capt. Decoursey, tattooed man; Sandon, strong boy; Inez, electric lady; Miss Julien, snake charmer; Col. McClure's Rooster Band, Mme. Mernorva, mind reader, and Hobi, Mori Chief" (*New York Clipper*).

Note: The term "rooster band" may have referred to a small, black, costumed "country" or "rube" band.

• ***June 15, 1895:*** "Notes from Bonheur Bros.' New Model Show," "Tom Jefferson, from Atlanta, Georgia, a real Southern colored comedian, who has a laugh in his every act and sentence, proves himself a performer of no ordinary talent and ability, and keeping the audience in roars of merriment" (*New York Clipper*).

• ***July 27, 1895:*** "Notes from the Bonheur Bros.' Show," "Business continues good and we turn people away at almost every stand . . . Our troupe of genuine colored minstrels are improving their work and making their acts stronger each day. No other tented exhibition carries such a concert as we give and everyone says so . . . Roster: Howard Bonheur, J. R. Bonheur, managers . . . Tom Jefferson, Sloan Edwards and Jack Cook, singers, dancers and comedians . . . Joseph McCree, old time colored jubilee singer, banjoist and buck and wing dancer" (*New York Clipper*).

• ***August 10, 1895:*** "Notes from Bonheur Bros.' New Model Shows," "At Saturday's Point we turned away three hundred people after the S.R.O. card was hung up. For the first time in the history of this show a Sunday performance was given July 28, for the benefit of Jacob Buher and Samuel Adrisis, who were injured recently in an accident. They are old friends of the Bonheur Bros. A grand picnic was given near the show grounds on this date, at which several thousand people assembled. Members of three broken up show companies were on the ground as guests of the Bonheur Bros. Such a large crowd of people from adjoining towns assembled about noon on the picnic grounds that, with one accord, each and all favored putting up the big top for a Sunday afternoon entertainment. All stray members of the defunct organizations signified willingness to assist in the performances and give a combined show. A few people from Williams and Murphy's Circus, members of Litchfield & Holmes' Comedy Co., and people from Prof. Walker's Oriental Phantasma, together with Bonheur Bros.' colored actors from away south of Dixie's line, made up a novel and successful afternoon performance . . . Le Roy Bland has signed to join at Mantorville. The New Orleans Octoroon Band, of five mouthpieces, are a card that other managers are trying hard to secure. Howard Bonheur is in Minneapolis, Minn., in the interest of the show" (*New York Clipper*).

Resolute performers and musicians such as Sol P. White, P. G. Lowery. and James Wolfscale dedicated their talents and energies to the circus sideshow business. They tried to make the most of this mitigated pathway of opportunity for steady employment and public exposure. Black bands and minstrels were strictly barred from the main circus tent, where a white band invariably dominated. The unyielding Jim Crow segregation of African American entertainers into the sideshow was an unmistakable expression of disrespect. Jubilee singers on exhibit alongside "freaks and curiosities" epitomizes the double-edged equivocality of popular enthusiasm for African American entertainment in the 1890s. Dime museums represented a similar type of platform.

Dime Museums

Dime museums were an urban phenomenon whose heyday lasted roughly from 1870 to 1910.[83] Consisting of a curio hall and a separate theater stage, dime museums catered to the late-nineteenth-century taste for grotesqueries. They ranged "from grand five story buildings that contained theaters accomodating three thousand spectators and curio halls parading upwards of ten thousand curiosities to small storefronts that were converted into exhibition rooms displaying a few old coins, petrified wood, and some living anomalies."[84] Traveling "museums" took this same concept on the road.

A good idea of the layout and accouterments of a state-of-the-art dime museum is preserved in this review of the opening of the Mount Morris Dime Museum in New York City.

• ***May 4, 1889:*** "Mt. Morris Museum," "This new place of amusement, situated on Third Avenue, between One Hundred and Twenty-fourth Street and One Hundred and Twenty-fifth Street, threw open its doors April 29 to bid for the patronage of the upper part of this city. The building is two stories in height, the second floor having a glass front. The lobby is handsomely tiled, and has the word 'Museum' in the centre in blue and white. The box office and walls of the lobby are painted in white and gold, while the transomes are inlaid with colored glass, as is also the front of the box office. A handsome brass chandelier adorns the lobby... Entering the door on the left one ascends a flight of stairs leading into the curio hall. The wall and ceiling of this floor are handsomely papered in red and gold, with gold moulding acting as a frame for panels. It is 25 ft. wide, 95 ft. deep and 15 ft. high. At the rear end is a red plush frame, which will be utilized by marionettes, shadowgraphs and stereopticon. The Punch and Judy box is on the right, while a toilet room occupies the space on the left. The platforms for the curios are placed along walls. They are all moveable, about four feet high, three feet wide and six feet long, and are covered with handsome velvet carpet. In the front a platform extends across the entire width of the building. A flight of stairs on the right lead to the theatre. This is decorated similar to the curio hall and is seated with three hundred folding opera chairs. The stage is 25 × 20 ft., with a proscenium opening 12 × 15 ft. It is well stocked with new and handsome scenery, painted by Harry Deaves. Below the stage are four large and comfortable dressing rooms and toilet room.... A large bill has been provided for the opening week... The curio hall this week presents a moving diorama of the great Centennial parade. It is truly a wonderful exhibition of mechanical skill and ingenuity and is the work of Edwin Deaves, father of Harry Deaves, the manager... The other attractions are: The African dude, Ridder; Circassian tattooed man, two cowboy banjo and bone players, a sleight of hand man, a group of life size mechanical figures, the Hindoo Priest, English Jack, the frog man; Prof. Skinner's Punch and Judy, a fat man and a lady pianist" (*New York Clipper*).

An ad seeking performers for Austin and Stone's Dime Museum in Boston, Massachusetts, suggests the range of exhibits that constituted a bill-of-fare in a dime museum curio hall.

• ***June 29, 1889:*** "Wanted—Season of 1889–90—for AUSTIN & STONE'S MUSEUM, Tremont Row, Boston, the best known and most successful Museum in America, any number of lecture hall performers, who can give short and novel entertainments: Freaks, rare Curiosities, wonderful Mechanical Inventions and Automata, Illusionists, Performing Animals, Fire Kings and Queens, Dwarfs, Fat Men and Women, Giants and Giantesses, Snake Charmers, Tatooed People, Zulus, Bearded Ladies, Glass Dancers, Bellringers, Athletes, Ventriloquists, Contortionists, Ossified Men and Women, Metallic Men and Living Skeletons, Circassions, Heavy Weight Lifters, Lion Tamers, Trapeze Performers, Balancers, Indians, Glass Eaters, Long [Haired] Women, Long Whiskered Men, Sword Walkers, Club Swingers, Musical Novelties, Albinos, Marionettes, Sword Swallowers, Necromancers, Rapid Artists, Paper Kings,

Whistlers, Imitators of Birds and Animals, Elastic Skin Men, Stone Chain and Bar Breakers, Silhouette Artists, Punch and Judy Performers, Ingenious Wood and Metal Workers, Rifle and Pistol Shots, Skeleton Dudes, Performing Snakes and Seals, Aquatic Marvels, Knife Throwers, Wax Works, Trained Dogs and Monkeys, Midgets, Prestidigitateurs, or any other attraction suitable for exhibition in our Curiosity Hall. We also want the very best variety talent for our stage performances" (*New York Clipper*).

A review of the *New York Clipper* reveals that many black jubilee singers, minstrel performers, vocal quartets, and ersatz "Zulus" worked in dime museum theaters throughout the 1889–1895 period. During the off seasons of African American minstrelsy, the larger dime museums provided a platform for some of the better-known colored stars.

• ***February 2, 1889 (New York City):*** "Grand Street Museum," "With an eye always open for attractive features, the management of the Grand have this week put in Mme. Caspers and her four young and attractive spinning maidens; the midget, Hop o' My Thumb; Belle Moody, the human billiard ball; the Martin Sisters, Albinos; La Selle, the water queen; Natator, the man fish; Mme. Rosa, the bearded lady; while in the theatre 'Uncle Tom's Cabin' will serve as the attraction, with Sallie Partington as Topsy, and the Twilight Quartet in the plantation scenes" (*Indianapolis Freeman*).

• ***February 16, 1889:*** "Tom McIntosh, minstrel, and Billy Gauze, a female impersonator, were playing in a St. Paul, Minn., dime museum last week" (*Indianapolis Freeman*).

• ***March 23, 1889 (Chicago, Illinois):*** "Epstein's New Dime Museum," "Convention of cranks, Lang's Meteors in Theatre No. 1, and New Orleans Colored Minstrels in Theatre No. 2" (*New York Clipper*).

• ***April 6, 1889 (Baltimore, Maryland):*** "Johnson's Dime Museum," "Baby Bunting (miniature horse), H. Leon (strong man), Irene Seymour (tattooed woman) and Dolly Liona (Circassian) were new in the curio hall 1. In the auditorium: Murray & Williams' Minstrels and the Bohee Sisters" (*New York Clipper*).

Note: It is likely one of the Bohee Sisters was May Bohee, who was also making appearances in dime museums as a single during this time. May Bohee was a daughter of one of the famous Canadian-born Bohee Brothers of banjo-playing fame.[85] She was known as a "warbler." In June 1891 May Bohee was counted among the performers in the first edition of Sam T. Jack's Creole Company. She became the wife of fellow "Creole" Charles Hunn, and she remained with the company through the season of 1894–1895, at least.

• ***April 13, 1889 (St. Paul, Minnesota):*** "Kohl, Middleton & Co.'s week of [April] 8: Curio Hall—John Miller (half man), Adam Lester (midget), Uri (clay artist), Peter Runyan (fat man), Mme. Rosa (beardless lady [*sic*]). Upper stage—Ray & Hughes' Comedy Co. Lower Stage—Eaton & Farrell's Georgia Minstrels" (*New York Clipper*).

Note: During this time the roster of Harry S. Eaton and Billy Farrell's Georgia Minstrels reportedly included up-and-coming comedian Ernest Hogan.

• ***April 13, 1889 (Baltimore, Maryland):*** "Johnson's Dime Museum," "Blind Tom No. 2 was the only novelty in the curio hall [April] 8, all last week's features being retained" (*New York Clipper*).

• ***April 20, 1889 (New York City):*** "Worth's Palace Museum," "The auditorium entertainments are of unusual worth, and enlist the services of the Excelsior Quartet . . . and others" (*New York Clipper*).

• ***May 11, 1889 (New York City):*** "Grand Street Museum," "Roltair's living mermaid and Blue

Beard's chamber continue to be the drawing features in the curio hall . . . Monroe, the ossified African, also remains a good feature. The new attractions in the curio hall are: Angelo's trained birds, Kanapaloutikake, Queen of the Cannibal Islands; Big Eliza, the fat African, and a mechanical production of 'Life on the Mississippi,' depicting all the phases of plantation existence . . . In the theatorium is Barry & O'Neill's Double Vaudeville Co., presenting Fred Manley, Chas. Hunn . . . and others" (*New York Clipper*).

Note: Minstrel comedian Charles Hunn was a leading player in African American troupes of the 1880s and 1890s. Much of his early work was in partnership with brother Ben Hunn. Their father was reported to have been a Baptist preacher in Atchison and Leavenworth, Kansas.[86] According to his obituary in the *Freeman*, Charles Hunn was born in Leavenworth in 1854 and toured England with Callendar's Georgia Minstrels in 1883. His last tour was with the 1895–1896 edition of Sam T. Jack's Creole Company. He died in Providence, Rhode Island, July 15, 1897.[87] He has been credited, among other things, with writing "the first real coon song . . . 'I'm the Father of a Little Black Coon.' "[88]

• ***July 20, 1889 (Boston, Massachusetts):*** "Austin & Stone's Museum," "An even dozen russet cheeked Creole beauties were placed on exhibition [July] 15. They have been big typed in the leading papers" (*New York Clipper*).

• ***September 28, 1889 (Boston, Massachusetts):*** "Austin's Nickelodeon," "The stage performers [include] the Four Little Coons" (*New York Clipper*).

• ***October 12, 1889:*** "To Museum Managers," "A Sure Winning Card, THE MOREAU CANNIBALS, A Troupe of Wild Africans, six in number, wearing their native costumes, exhibiting their war dances, music and implements of dance and war. This is one of the best drawing cards at present in the country. Have just finished a long season at Doris' and Worth's Museums. They have never played West of New York. Managers desiring this Magnet Attraction, send open time at once to MILLIKEN & CORTISS, Dramatic Agents, 1, 169 Broadway, N.Y." (*New York Clipper*).

• ***December 7, 1889:*** "The Stage," "Good business still attends Mr. and Mrs. Sam Lucas, who are now playing Kohl, Middleton & Co's dime museum circuit . . .

It is strange to me to drop in now and then at a Dime Museum and to note a large number of our people attending a performance, who on the next Sabbath, when the pastor speaks condemnatory of the theator [*sic*], are the first ones to say 'amen.' A great many of them do it from a point of ignorance. Let me say to this class of people that . . . dime museums are the most degrading of theatrical business, the most immoral" ("Trage," *Indianapolis Freeman*).

• ***December 21, 1889 (New York City):*** "Worth's Palace Museum," "The auditorium list is pretentious and [includes the] De Wolf Sisters" (*New York Clipper*).

Note: Just a few months earlier, the De Wolf (or De Wolfe) Sisters had appeared at Dockstader's Theater in New York City, as members of a "colored coterie" that included banjoist Horace Weston and soprano soloist Sissieretta Jones, the Black Patti. The De Wolfe Sisters were known for their "charming" vocal duets. By the summer of 1891 they were touring with Sam T. Jack's Creole Company, and they remained with the Creoles until the end of 1893, at least.

• ***February 22, 1890 (Cincinnati, Ohio):*** "Kohl & Middleton's Museum," "The music that echoed through the Curio Hall was the result of Lizzie Sturgeon's 'feats' upon the piano with her pedal extremities . . . and in the parlor theatre Magilton's Gotham Grotesqueries appeared,

William Ferry, as "Ferry the Frog," Australasia, *August 19, 1899. (courtesy State Library of Victoria and Gary LeGallant)*

introducing . . . Sam Lucas and wife [and others]" (*New York Clipper*).

• ***April 26, 1890 (Boston, Massachusetts):*** "Grand Museum," "Manager Lothrop is constantly presenting his thousands of patrons weekly with something out of the usual run of amusement features. Last week, and for some time previous, he had on the track in the natatorium a dozen young women, contending in a [marathon] walking match . . . On the stage is presented a drama of Russian life, 'A Wife's Honor.'. . ., and in addition there is an olio in which appear Sam and Mrs. Lucas [and others]" (*New York Clipper*).

• ***May 24, 1890 (Minneapolis, Minnesota):*** "Palace Museum (Kohl, Middleton & Co.'s)—Week of [May] 19: Curio Hall—Lottie Grant, Clint Williams and bear and Le Vard (sword walker). Theatre No. 1—Raffin's troupe of performing pigs and monkeys. Theatre No. 2—Seth Earl, the Princess, William Gauze, Gentry and Williams, and Thos. Ripley" (*New York Clipper*).

Note: William Gauze, the paramount African American female impersonator, had just closed out the 1889–1890 touring season with McCabe and Young's Minstrels.

• ***June 21, 1890 (New York City):*** Among the attractions in the curio hall of the Harlem Museum was "William Ferry (boneless wonder)" (*New York Clipper*).

Note: William Ferry was the celebrated "frog contortionist" who toured several seasons with the South Before the War, then toured Australia at the end of the decade with Orpheus M. McAdoo's Georgia Minstrels.

• ***September 6, 1890 (Chicago, Illinois):*** "Kohl & Middleton's Dime Museum—South side—Gypsy Band, Zulu Chieftans and other novelties in the curio halls, the Excelsior Quartet in Theatre No. 1" (*New York Clipper*).

• ***November 8, 1890 (St. Louis, Missouri):*** "McGinley's Museum—J. W. Kennedy (strong man), Grey Eagle (tattooed), Eight Legged Sheep . . ., Bob Webster (darkey), Wm. Delaney (Irish character) . . ., W. M. Edward (black comedian) and the Imperial Quartet this week" (*New York Clipper*).

• ***November 15, 1890 (Philadelphia, Pennsylvania):*** "Ninth and Arch Museum," "The Georgia

Minstrels are in the theatre. In the company are Billy Wilson, Joseph Halmont, Andrew Loud, Robert Kelly, Wesley B. Norris, Joseph W. Hodges, Neal Mattews [*sic*] and the Twilight Quartet" (*New York Clipper*).

• ***December 13, 1890 (New York City):*** "Huber's Palace Museum," "The new faces on the vaudeville programme include . . . the Unique Quartet" (*New York Clipper*).

• ***March 7, 1891 (Chicago, Illinois):*** "Kohl & Middleton's Dime Museums," "South Side—Prof. Woodward's educated seals, Eclipse Quartet Comedy Co. in Theatre No. 1 . . . West Side—Me and Him (boxing skeleton and fat man), Big Alice (fat girl) and a troupe of New Zealanders" (*New York Clipper*).

Note: Between touring seasons, dime museums appear to have been a preferred roost, or venue, for the famous plantation show quartets of the mid-1890s.

• ***April 4, 1891:*** "Notes from Zimmerman Bros.' Traveling Museum," "Everything is all bustle just now on account of the great show that the Zimmerman Bros. will put on the road about May 15. The show starts from Davenport, Ia., under canvas. Our outside attractions will be Prof. R. R. Ritter in his aerial flights and parachute descents . . . Prof. Hugo will have charge of the annex. Our museum at present comprises the half horse and half man, Prof. Hugo (magician and illusionist), Baltimore Jubilee Singers, Joe Brown (cowboy banjoist), seven cages of animals, one cage of monkeys, also trained donkeys and dogs" (*New York Clipper*).

• ***May 2, 1891 (Chicago, Illinois):*** "Kohl & Middleton's Dime Museum," "Bronco Bill's brave boys, comprising ghost dancing Indians and government scouts; the Comets in Theatre No. 1, Ben Hunn's stars in No. 2 and First Prize Ideals in No. 3" (*New York Clipper*).

Note: Minstrel comedian Ben Hunn personally recalled in 1902 that he had started out "in the business twenty years ago."[89] He toured with the 1891–1892 edition of Sam T. Jack's Creoles, and he married fellow "Creole" Florence Briscoe. In 1900 he was a headliner with the first edition of "A Rabbit's Foot" Comedy Company[90]—the legendary Rabbit Foot Minstrels—and in 1902 he was heard singing "Turkey in the Straw" in Ernest Hogan and Billy McClain's "Smart Set" Company production, "Enchantment."[91] He met a violent death in 1908, as chronicled in the *Freeman:* "Ben Hunn, an old comedian, who was shot by one of the members of the Sells Floto Circus, died from the effects and was buried at Kansas City, Mo., Aug. 13."[92]

• ***May 23, 1891 (Philadelphia, Pennsylvania):*** "Ninth and Arch Museum," "Thirty little pickaninnies all in a row, zealously guarded by thirty anxious mammas, occupy the curio stage this week. The prettiest will receive from Manager Brandenburgh $250; the fattest, $200, and the best behaved, $150. This novel contest is an original idea of Mr. Brandenburgh. In addition to the usual assortment of freaks and curios an entertainment is given by the Pickett & Dixon Original Colored Tennessee Minstrels" (*New York Clipper*).

• ***May 30, 1891 (Philadelphia, Pennsylvania):*** "Ninth and Arch Museum," "In addition to the usual array of curios, there is specialty entertainment galore this week. The Georgia Minstrels, including Julius ["Jube"] Johnson, Walter Addis, Robert Lukens, Billy Collender and Sam Lucas, present an interesting bill" (*New York Clipper*).

• ***August 27, 1892 (Cincinnati, Ohio):*** "Kohl & Middleton's Museum," "While improvements are in progress there is no interruption to business, and the performers share the auditorium with the decorators and their scaffolding. The regular season opens Sept. 5. Ulato Mous Zaro and his Zulu warblers were in the curio hall

Aug. 22 with Chau Morris, Kentucky Frank and Wild Nell" (*New York Clipper*).

• ***September 10, 1892:*** "The Hubins—Frank and Millie—close their season with Richards' Circus and will start out with their own travelling Museum and Congress of Wonders. They will have eight people, jubilee singers, special printing and pictorial work" (*New York Clipper*).

• ***September 10, 1892:*** "A. C. Bauscher's European Museum opened their fair ground season at Dodgeville, Wis., week commencing Aug. 22, under favorable circumstances. The roster [includes] the Milwaukee Colored Jubilee Trio, Jess Clinton, Geo. Price and Johnny Osborne; living half lady, aerial suspension and decapitation" (*New York Clipper*).

• ***April 22, 1893 (Chicago, Illinois):*** "Epstean's Dime Museum," "Visitors to curio hall this week will find Gilbert's Performing Wolves the chief factor... On the stage... Bremer & Palmer's Colored Minstrels" (*New York Clipper*).

• ***May 6, 1893 (Cincinnati, Ohio):*** "Kohl & Middleton's Museum," "Evaleen, the water queen; F. D. King, W. B. Mann and John Saunders, the living skeleton, were the cards in the curio hall May 1. Carter's Plantation Quartette appeared on the Bijou stage... Business continues good" (*New York Clipper*).

• ***December 30, 1893 (New York City):*** "Huber's Museum," "On stage No. 1 the Georgia Minstrels introduce Fred Piper, the Knickerbocker Quartet, Billy Wilson, Hunn and Bethel and Jones" (*New York Clipper*).

• ***March 10, 1894 (Philadelphia, Pennsylvania):*** "Ninth and Arch Museum," "Gertie Cochran, an infant prodigy; Peate's trained monkeys... and Schweigerling's marionettes are leading features. In the theatre, Bill Jackson's Colored Minstrels" (*New York Clipper*).

• ***March 10, 1894 (New York City):*** "Huber's Palace Museum," "Sir Chas. Wombell's performing leopards are in the last week of their engagement at this house... Other features on the bill are the Esquimaux Village... and Balbrona, fire king. [Stage acts include] Oura's Imperial Japanese Troupe... [and] Mammie Flower [*sic*]" (*New York Clipper*).

Note: In 1895, ballad singer Mamie Flower was a featured star of "Black America," a famous outdoor summer extravaganza held at Ambrose Park in Brooklyn.

• ***March 24, 1894 (New York City):*** "Harlem Museum... Curio Hall—Asbury's Sunny South Co. of Jubilee Singers [and others]" (*New York Clipper*).

• ***March 31, 1894 (Boston, Massachusetts):*** "Austin & Stone's Museum," "Clever varieties are given on the Stage by the Afro-American Trio,... Imperial Comedy Quartet,... Fred Piper... and others" (*New York Clipper*).

• ***April 21, 1894 (Philadelphia, Pennsylvania):*** "Ninth and Arch Museum," "A female running race is the latest conceit of manager Brandenburgh's fertile think tank. The sprinting is done on machines. The Georgia Colored Minstrels have the theatre" (*New York Clipper*).

• ***May 26, 1894 (New York City):*** "Worth's Museum," "Billy Jackson's Colored Georgia Minstrels began an engagement of one week here on Monday, May 21. This is a new departure in stage performances at this house, and will likely prove a profitable one, as the organization is comprised of many of the most prominent colored performers in the profession, and, besides the regular patrons of the house, there is a large contingent of colored residents in the neighborhood. Roster of the company: Billy Jackson, Ben Hunn, the Knickerbocker Quartet, Florence Brisco, Bethel and Jones, Gertie Jefferson, Hardaway and Phillips, Edward Denton, Charlie Walker, Annie Jones, Henry Wise, William West, Glen Floide, Portlock Tucker, Baker Sheppard and the Gray Sisters" (*New York Clipper*).

Note: Worth's Museum was located on the corner of Thirtieth Street and Sixth Avenue, on the site of the old Haymarket Theater. Between May 1894 and May 1895 Worth's Museum presented many of the most creative young African American performers, including Ben Hunn, Florence Briscoe, Charles Walker, Hen Wise, Billy Farrell, Gussie Lord Davis, Katie Carter, and Irving Jones, along with some of the top vocal quartets of the day, including the Unique Quartet, Standard Quartet, and the Calliope Quartet. These outstanding entertainers were all associated, however briefly, with Billy Jackson's Colored Georgia Minstrels.

The titular head of this illustrious enterprise, Billy Jackson, was known, in the positive sense, as "a hustler"[93] and a potent force in "Negro comedy" in the Northeast. He was a former partner of song-writing genius Irving Jones, and a prolific composer of coon songs and popular ballads in his own right. Jackson's 1890s song creations included such titles as "Coon with the Big Thick Lips," "A Seat Up Dar for Me," "The Hen Roost Inspector," "That Coon Got Lucky Mighty Soon," "My Little Mobile Queen," "Coon That's Noise to Me," "Coon You've Done Me Wrong," and "When the Dew Drops Cease to Fall."[94] By 1897 Jackson and his wife, Madrid, a "champion colored lady pianist,"[95] were appearing on the mainstream vaudeville theater circuits, and it was announced in the *Freeman* of July 14, 1900, that they were booked for leading roles in the debut edition of the Rabbit's Foot Minstrels.

Billy Jackson's Minstrels held the boards at Worth's Museum on and off for the better part of a year, at least. These young black stars demonstrated their combined drawing power to the entertainment establishment at this high-profile midtown New York venue, perhaps suggesting the latent commercial potential in black stage shows for a black audience.

• ***June 9, 1894 (New York City):*** "Worth's Museum," "Billy Jackson's colored Georgia Minstrels . . . have been drawing big houses. Manager C. V. Moore has decided to run them two more weeks or longer. The standing room only signs are out frequently at nine o'clock. Among the performers are Ben Hunn, Fred Piper, Billy Johnson, One Billy Farrell, Hen. Wise, W. Proctor, The Standard Quartet, James Sisters, Annie Jones, Hardaway and Phillips, Bethel and Jones, three Russells, and Emma Jones. The company consists of forty people, with a grand Amazon march by the ladies, all colored, after the minstrel show" (*New York Clipper*).

• ***June 30, 1894 (New York City):*** "Worth's Museum," "The Colored Minstrels closed at this house on June 24, after a run of five weeks" (*New York Clipper*).

• ***July 28, 1894:*** "[Billy] Jackson's Minstrels continue for two weeks longer at O'Connor's Empire Garden, Coney Island. Irving Jones has a new song" (*New York Clipper*).

• ***August 11, 1894 (Boston, Massachusetts):*** "Austin & Stone's Museum," "This is certainly the Gorilla Season at Stone & Shaw's house, and the Gumbo's, Sr. and Jr., are drawing big audiences . . . They are a queer looking pair. The troupe of Southern plantation negroes likewise form a very attractive feature in their plantation songs and dances" (*New York Clipper*).

• ***August 11, 1894:*** "The Original Imperial Quartette are in their twelfth week at Austin & Stone's Museum, Boston, Mass." (*New York Clipper*).

• ***August 18, 1894 (Chicago, Illinois):*** "Globe Musee," "In the curio hall, Martin Seaburger, an Albino; [etc.]. On the stage . . ., Mallory Brothers [and others]" (*New York Clipper*).

• ***August 25, 1894 (New York City):*** "Worth's Museum," "A minstrel performance is the principal feature of the programme this week, Billy Jackson's Georgia Colored Minstrels having possession of the theatre . . . Billy Jackson,

Billy Young, Towel and Hall, the Caliope Quartet, Gussie Davis, Billy Johnson, Henry Wise, Geo. Weston, W. H. Proctor, Katie Carter, Sadie Jones and Eva Phillips, with Trocheroo's Orchestra" (*New York Clipper*).

• ***October 13, 1894 (New York City):*** "Worth's Museum," "The Colored Minstrels continue to cater to the patrons of this house in the theatre, while the museum attractions constitute a varied collection of interesting features of the curio world. Changes are made weekly in stage and museum attractions, the Black Jenny Lind being a new feature of the stage" (*New York Clipper*).

• ***November 3, 1894 (New York City):*** "Worth's Museum," "There is no change of bill here . . . and the colored minstrels appear to have enough drawing power to warrant their retention from week to week. This is, however the closing week of their engagement" (*New York Clipper*).

• ***November 24, 1894 (New York City):*** "Worth's Museum," "The continuous vaudeville show is still in vogue here . . . This week's entertainers include . . . Irving Jones [and others]" (*New York Clipper*).

• ***December 8, 1894 (New York City):*** "Worth's Museum," "The Colored Georgia Minstrels returned to this house on Dec. 3 . . . The principal performers are: One Billy Farrell, Billy Johnson, Hen Wise, Jas. Wilson, W. H. Proctor, Fred Piper, Gussie L. Davis, Jerry Mills, Bob Coles [*sic*], Unique Quartet, The Russells, Jim Russell, Stella Wiley, Roxie Nicholson, Vera, Wilks and Camille Casselle" (*New York Clipper*).

• ***January 12, 1895 (New York City):*** "Worth's Museum," "The Colored Minstrels still continue their profitable engagement here. An innovation this week is the production of a naval first part and a drama entitled 'Good Old Georgia in '49' " (*New York Clipper*).

• ***February 2, 1895 (Chicago, Illinois):*** "Kohl & Middleton's Clark Street Musee," "The curio feature this week will be Nancy Garrison, a negress with long hair. . . . and a bevy of snake charmers . . . For the fourth consecutive week the muscle dancers of the long forgotten Midway will be in possession [of the theater stage]" (*New York Clipper*).

• ***February 9, 1895 (Chicago, Illinois):*** "Kohl & Middleton's Globe Musee," "Aunt Nancy, a colored woman with long hair, is the curio feature this week . . . The stage will be in the possession of Florence Hines [and others]" (*New York Clipper*).

• ***March 23, 1895:*** "Worth's Museum," "The colored minstrel organization seems to be a fixture here in the theatre portion of the building . . . The company is known as C. V. Moore's Colored Minstrels, and is composed of the following: Billy Wilson, Gussie L. Davis, Billy Farrell, Fred Piper, Billy Johnson, Jim Wilson, Spriggs and Grundy, J. Williams, Mr. and Mrs. Wesley Norris, Mattie Wilkes, Lottie Davis, Jerry Mills and his pickaninnies" (*New York Clipper*).

• ***May 4, 1895 (New York City):*** "Huber's Palace Museum," "On the stage . . . Billy Johnson, . . . Unique Quartet [and others]" (*New York Clipper*).

• ***June 1, 1895 (Chicago, Illinois):*** "Kohl & Middleton's Clark Street Museum," "Features for the week include a cake walk, a troupe of Turks and Arabs in native dances, and bronze statuary" (*New York Clipper*).

• ***June 15, 1895:*** "Notes from Mme. Foster's [Traveling] Museum," "Business during the Confederate reunion at Houston, Tex., was exceptionally good. Our exhibition at Houston was the only one of the many in the city at that time that made much money. Shows of all kinds were on each side of us, they dropped their admission fee down to five cents, hired brass bands and jubilee singers, and then did little business . . . We leave Fort Worth, Tex., for Boston, Mass., and other New England cities, carrying a full collection of live reptiles, centipedes, tarantulas, vinegaroons and other deadly creatures" (*New York Clipper*).

• ***July 6, 1895 (Cincinnati, Ohio):*** "Kohl & Middleton's Musee-Theatre," "Yellowstone Vic's curios and Garrett's pickaninny band were in the museum" (*New York Clipper*).

• ***October 5, 1895 (New York City):*** "Huber's Eighth Avenue Museum," "In the theater are... Prof. Meehan's Canine Paradox...and the Unique Quartet" (*New York Clipper*).

• ***December 7, 1895 (New York City):*** "Huber's Eighth Avenue Theatre," "The stage people are: Ben Hunn, Williams and Johnson, the Unique Quartet, Billy Wilson, assisted by several ladies, in a first part and a cake walk" (*New York Clipper*).

C. V. Moore's Colored Minstrels

CREOLES AND PICKANINNIES.

GUSSIE L. DAVIS, - - - Stage Manager

Fred Piper, Ben Hunn, Billy Johnson, Billy Wilson, Jerry Mills, Bethel and Jones, One Billy Farrell, W. H. Proctor, Ben Williams, Ed. Furber, Irving Jones, James Botts, James Williams, Bob Coles, Stella Wiley, Mattie Wilkes, Ben Wise, Unique Quartet, Gussie L. Davis, James Wilson, Wesley Norris, Jas. Russell, Mocking Bird Rube and 20 others.

THE BEST COLORED TALENT FURNISHED FOR ALL OCCASIONS

Now playing the 40th week at Worth's Family Theatre, 30th St. and 6th Ave., New York. Managers will address all communications to C. V. MOORE, care of Worth's Family Theatre, 30th St. and 6th Ave., N. Y.

New York Clipper, *April 13, 1895.*

Chapter Seven

1895

"Black America"

"Black America" was an outdoor environmental theme-park extravaganza, a "Panorama of the Negro, from the Jungles of Africa to the Civilization of America." Installed at Ambrose Park in Brooklyn, New York, during the summer of 1895, it created a mild sensation. Veteran African American road-show performer Tom Fletcher recalled it in his 1954 book, *100 Years of the Negro in Show Business!* "*Ambrose Park*... was transformed into the likeness of a southern plantation. Cotton bushes with buds blossoming, were transplanted. Bales of cotton were brought in and a cotton gin in working order set up. Poultry and livestock were brought in and real cabins built, a large part of the company using these cabins as living quarters for the season. This entire layout provided atmosphere through which the audiences would roam at random before the show itself started."[1]

According to Fletcher, "Black America" was Billy McClain's idea: "Billy served as talent scout and stage manager, a sort of prototype of the modern technical director," with financial backing from "Nate Saulsbury, promoter of large enterprises."[2] Nate Salsbury was the number-two man with Buffalo Bill's Wild West Show. Under Salsbury's management, the Wild West Show had made a successful run at Ambrose Park during the summer of 1894. The summer before that, Salsbury had managed the World's Fair edition of the Wild West Show in Chicago.

"Black America" exploited the heritage of plantation slavery in much the same way that Buffalo Bill's Wild West Show exploited the folk culture of the American frontier, by romanticizing it and encapsulating it in a sort of human zoo. An endorsement of "Black America" in the *New York Times* assured, "The entertainment... brings before the spectators the peculiarities of the Southern negro in a manner that most Northern persons have never been able to observe... Those who take part in the performance... are well qualified to enlighten the Northern white man in relation to a life that will soon be extinct."[3]

• ***May 11, 1895:*** "At Ambrose Park, South Brooklyn, N.Y., Nate Saulsbury, 'Buffalo Bill's' partner in the 'Wild West' show, has erected about 100 log cabins to accommodate the 400 Georgians who are to depict African and plantation life in his 'Panorama of the Negro, from the Jungles of Africa to the Civilization of America'" (*Cleveland Gazette*).

• ***June 1, 1895 (Brooklyn, New York):*** "Ambrose Park," "'Black America,' Nate Salsbury's new Summer attraction, opened its season with two performances here, May 25. The audience was large, both in the afternoon and evening, and the audience very enthusiastic. The programme was a long one, and began with a concert by the Baltimore (colored) Brass Band, and was followed by jubilee singing, a company of Ninth U.S. Calvary, colored boxers, Amazon drill and march; Wood Brothers, vaulters; James Wilson, juggler; Othellins, acrobats, colored jockeys, foot races, Madame Flower; E. Denton, wire juggler; C. Johnson, grotesque drill; J. J. Christian, fancy skater; quadrille on horseback; George Wilson, buck and wing dancing; historical pictures, etc" (*New York Clipper*).

• ***June 8, 1895:*** "Ambrose Park," "'Black America' still continues to draw thousands of people to see what is proving to be one of the best attractions of its kind ever seen in this country. An

Black America

Opens SAT. AFTERNOON, May 25, at Greater New York's delightful pleasure grounds,

AMBROSE PARK, 39th Street Ferry, South Brooklyn.

A Typical Plantation Village of 150 Cabins,

500 Southern Colored People,

presenting Home Life, Folk Lore, Pastimes of Dixie, More Music, Mirth, Merriment for the Masses; More Fun, Jollity, Humor and Character presented in

Marvellously Massive Lyric Magnitude for the Millions

than since the days of Cleopatra

General Admission to Grounds and Covered Seats **ONLY 25 CENTS.**

Special Chairs, 50cts., 75cts. Box Seats, $1.00.

FARE ONLY 5 CENTS, via 39th Street Ferry, foot Whitehall Street, Battery, landing at doors.

TWO PERFORMANCES DAILY, 3 and 8:15 P. M., Wet or Dry.

New York Clipper, *May 25, 1895.*

entire new programme is presented this week... The programme for this week includes the real living scenes in the life of the Southern negro, amid cotton fields and in cabins. A novel exhibition for those who have never been South, and a pleasing sight for those who have; a chorus of voices and soloists, male and female; Negro racers, hurdle riders, gladiators, athletes, banjoists, wing and buck dancers" (*New York Clipper*).

• ***June 8, 1895:*** "A lovely sail, via 39th St. Ferry, foot Whitehall St., New York, brings you to Ambrose Park, South Brooklyn, and to Black America, Nate Salisbury, Director. Every newspaper in New York and Brooklyn enthusiastically declares it to be the greatest novelty ever seen in America! Real living scenes in the life of the real Southern negro, amidst real cotton fields and in real cabins.

An extraordinary exhibition for those who have never been South, and a welcome, gladsome sight for those who have.

Chorus of voices never surpassed in this hemisphere, and soloists, male and female, equal to any of grand opera fame in Europe.

Negro racers, hurdle riders, gladiators, athletes, banjoists, specialists, wing and buck dancers and a perfect presentation of the Old Plantation Darkey.

Admission, 25c. Reserved, 50c. and 75c. Box seats, $1. Every day at 3. Every night at 8.15. Doors open an hour earlier. Performances in wet or dry weather" (*New York Clipper*).

• ***June 15, 1895:*** "Ambrose Park," "'Black America' presents several new attractions this week. Among them is Gilmore's Band, which was recently engaged for the Summer. A chorus of five hundred singing negroes has been secured, and this, in conjunction with the band, under the baton of Victor Herbert, is the chief feature of each performance" (*New York Clipper*).

• ***June 29, 1895:*** "'Black America' becomes more popular with the people as they become better acquainted with the style of performance offered each week... The colored people do not furnish all the good music, as Gilmore's Band, under Victor Herbert, gives a concert before the singing" (*New York Clipper*).

• ***July 6, 1895 (Brooklyn, New York):*** "The past week was not a particularly busy one for the Summer resorts, especially the out of door ones. The cold, rainy and disagreeable weather has caused a very meagre attendance, and has chilled those who had the temerity to defy the elements. During the week just past a party of several hundred colored people from 'Black America' visited the City Hall in this city to sing in a driving rain for the mayor. A crowd, protected by umbrellas, soon gathered and listened to the melodies, while the singers themselves were soaked by the rain. Whether Mayor Scheiren was averse to the singing or the notoriety it caused is not known, but the fact remains that he stayed in his office while the singers were present. At length Alderman Walsh invited them into the City Hall rotunda, and they sang with some degree of comfort. Finally they took their departure without seeing his Honor" (*New York Clipper*).

• ***July 6, 1895:*** "An addition to the vocal forces of 'Black America' made her appearance last week in the person of Bessie Lee, a colored warbler of excellent voice. She sings 'The Old Folks at Home' and 'The Cows Are in the Clover' with a voice that is clearly heard all over the immense park . . . A band of forty tamborine and banjo players are an additional feature on the programme, and share honors with the quaint and fantastic cake walk" (*New York Clipper*).

• ***July 6, 1895:*** "Warning to Al. G. Field, and to everybody and to anybody else who may contemplate using the title of 'Black America:' The title, 'Black America,' is my sole and exclusive property, and I propose to vigorously protect my rights to the fullest extent the law of the land permits in the United States, the Canadas and Abroad . . . Nate Salsbury, Ambrose Park, South Brooklyn, N.Y." (*New York Clipper*).

• ***July 13, 1895 (Brooklyn, New York):*** "The public should bear in mind that this week, beginning July 8, is the last of 'Black America' in this vicinity . . . The program is in three parts. The first is a concert by Ascher's Military Band, with Prof. Emil Ascher as conductor. Part second—The choral portion of 'Black America' company in a grand concert, conducted by William McClain, in which the following take part: Jube Johnson and quartets, Harry Singleton and quartets, Mme. Cordelia [McClain] and quartets, and ends with an old fashioned cake walk. Part third—a company of the Ninth U.S. Calvary, in their musical ride and drill; Charles Johnson, grotesque evolutions; cross country ride, by colored jockeys on thoroughbred Kentucky horses; assault at arms by colored boxers; Madame Flower in ballads, assisted by the quartets; buck and wing dancing and 'Tub' Fields' Sheepskin and Rosewood Orchestra, historical pictures with choral effect by entire company, and ends with 'Home, Sweet Home' by Ascher's Band" (*New York Clipper*).

Note: This lends credibility to Tom Fletcher's recollection that Billy McClain had recruited "63 quartets from all parts of the country" to participate in "Black America."[4]

When "Black America" concluded its stand at Ambrose Park, Billy and Cordelia McClain and others joined the latest "river show," "On the Suwanee River."

• ***July 27, 1895:*** "Rehearsals have begun of 'On the Suwanee River,' the elaborate and novel darkey show that E. J. Nugent is soon to produce. William McClain, Mme. Cordelia and others who figured prominently in 'Black America' are in the cast" (*New York Clipper*).

• ***August 10, 1895:*** " 'Down on the Suawnee River,' with fifty negroes and scenery . . . has its first production Aug. 11 at Whitney's Opera House, Detroit. The scene is laid in the African jungle, then in the South, and then in New York. The negro is shown in savagery, slavery, and Thompson Street civilization" (*New York Clipper*).

"Black America," Illustrated American, *June 29, 1895.*

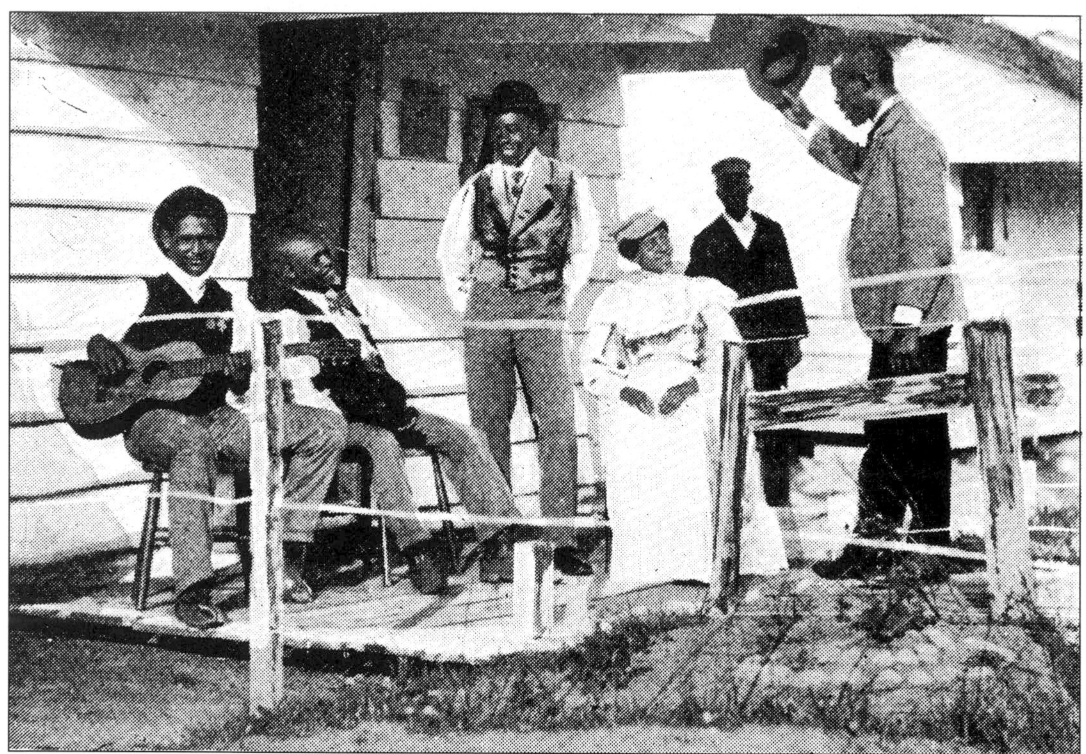

These three "location" photographs are among several that accompanied an article on "Black America" which appeared in Illustrated American *of June 29, 1895. The informal male chorus on the previous page was labeled, "The Laughing Song;" the porch scene with the guitar player was captioned, "Leisure Moments;" and the panoramic scene of couples dancing took the caption, "Way Down South in Dixie." (courtesy Chris Ware and* Rag Time Ephemeralist*)*

• ***December 21, 1895 (Brooklyn, New York):*** "Bijou," "'Down on the Suwanee River,' a new play illustrating the characteristics of negro life, was presented here [December] 16 . . . There are a number of interesting features, including a pie and watermelon eating match, a cake walk and a full brass band" (*New York Clipper*).

Meanwhile, "Black America" broke camp and moved to the Huntington Avenue Circus Grounds in Boston for what was probably its final full-scale, outdoor production.

• ***July 27, 1895 (Boston, Massachusetts):*** "Black America," "Full five hundred sable brothers are in our midst, presenting to us every afternoon and evening, on the circus grounds, Huntington Avenue, quaint pictures of Southern life in *ante bellum* days. The entertainment is unique, the plantation scene being especially attractive, being a good reproduction from actual life" (*New York Clipper*).

• ***August 31, 1895 (Boston, Massachusetts):*** "'Black America,'" "This novel and very interesting delineation of life in the South, as given by the troupe of colored people, on Huntington Avenue, entered upon its last week here [August] 26. The success of the show has been gratifying to the management, and the thousands who have attended the entertainment praised it very much" (*New York Clipper*).

Brass Bands in Kansas

Unlike vocal quartets, with their trademark barbershop harmony, black brass bands do not appear to have deviated palpably from standard Western musical practices, or found a particular outlet to express their independent cultural sensibilities prior to the commercial explosion of ragtime. Eastern Kansas was a prominent producer of African American brass bands, band directors, and horn players. Among the outstanding local organizations of the mid-1890s were the Midland Band of Kansas City, Jackson's Military Band (a.k.a. the Dispatch Band) of Topeka, and the Walnut Valley Band of Parsons, all of whom generated commentary in the local papers.

• ***July 5, 1890 (Topeka, Kansas):*** "A Brass Band Contest," "The biggest event of the season will be a giant Emancipation Celebration under the auspices of the Dispatch Club on August 1st at Topeka. One of the leading events of the day will be a band contest for a prize of $50. This contest is open to all Negro bands. It has been falsely stated that the famous Dispatch Band, of Topeka, would enter the contest, but this is not true. The Dispatch Band is barred. It is hoped that bands from all over the state will be present and participate.

The Dispatch Band under the able management of Geo. W. Jackson is coming to the front, and is looked upon as the finest Afro-American band in the west. The boys are willing to contest for honors with any band west of the Mississippi. They are now preparing 'The Gloria, Excellcis,' accompanied by a chorus of one hundred voices, for August 1st. Come and hear the famous band" ("Fearless," *Indianapolis Freeman*).

• ***June 28, 1891 (Topeka, Kansas):*** "The Masonic Installation at Luken's opera house last Saturday night was a grand success. The hall was filled. The Dispatch Band gave some fine music" (*Topeka Weekly Call*).

• ***July 28, 1891 (Topeka, Kansas):*** "The Dispatch Band, under the instruction of Professor George W. Jackson, has developed into one of the finest colored musical organizations of the West. Professor Jackson, who is an able instructor and intelligent gentleman, deserves great credit for his valuable services to that organization since he took hold of it. From a few selections poorly executed a short time ago the band has now a large number of pieces which are rendered with that precision, harmony and volume of tone which brings delight to the ear of the genuine lovers of music. We trust that the members of the band and our people in this community have a due appreciation of the energy and ability of Prof. Jackson which has brought about this happy result. He and his organization are an honor and credit to the race and we should show an appreciation of the fact by giving them a rousing crowd on the 1st at Garfield Park" (*Topeka Weekly Call*).

• ***September 27, 1891 (Valley Falls, Kansas):*** "Emancipation day was appreciably celebrated here at the park. There was music by the Cactus Blossom Drum Corps and Cornet Band" (*Topeka Weekly Call*).

• ***June 10, 1892 (Kansas City, Missouri):*** "The Midland [Band] . . . will accompany the excursion to Beatrice, Neb., on the 25th inst., to the grand dedication of the Beatrice A.M.E. Church" (*Kansas City American Citizen*).

• ***June 24, 1892 (Kansas City, Kansas):*** "The Governor's Guard is rapidly coming to the front as one of the 'crack' military companies of this state . . . The people of this city are justly proud of the guards and its band. The entertainment to be given by them at the Tabernacle, corner 7th street and State avenue, promises to be *the* event of the season. Their entertainment begins Monday, June 27, with a grand band concert by the Governor's Guard band and the Midland and Central bands of Kansas City, Mo.

Tuesday, June 28, vocal and instrumental selections will be rendered by some of the best talent of the two Kansas Cities. They will be ably assisted by the Oriental Mandolin Club . . .

Wednesday, June 29, there will be vocal and instrumental music, the entertainment to conclude with a competitive drill given by the guards . . .

The guard's band is making rapid progress under the leadership of Mr. Tilford Davis, Jr. It is

HOORAY for the FIRST of AUGUST!

A GRAND EMANCIPATION CELEBRATION,

GIVEN AT

Garfield Park, Topeka,

UNDER THE AUSPICES OF THE

Dispatch Band of Kansas.

There will be a Grand Cancert given by the Dispatch Band at 3 p. m., under the direction of Prof. W. Jackson, at which time the Band will render some choice selections from some of the best operas of the day. The great Coney Island Polka Concert Solo, played by John Ferguson, leader of the famous Dispatch Band of Kansas.

Hon. Lewis Hanback,

Ex-Congressman from Sixth District of Kansas, will deliver an address.

Also, Hon. W. B. Townsend and Hon. B. K. Bruce of Leavenworth; C. Patterson, of Wyandotte; Col. J. M. Brown, Rev. H. B. Parks, Rev. B. F. Foster and S. G. Watkins, of Topeka, are invited and expected to deliver addresses.

GEO. W. SMITH, Master of Ceremonies.

There will be a grand entertainment in the evening at Metropolitan Hall, at which time the visiting Bands will join in and give a Musical Festival, to the delight of all present.

COMMITTEE OF ARRANGEMENTS.

GEO. W. BROWN. GEO. W. JACKSON.
JOHN PERKINS.
GEORGE LOWRY. H. W. DILLARD.
FRED M. STONESTREET, Charm'n. JAMES M. MASON, Marshal of the Day.

Look Out for the Parade at 10 a. m.

Admission to the Grounds, 10c.

Topeka Weekly Call, July 28, 1891.

the only colored *military* band in the state . . . The guards and band will parade at 8 o'clock Monday evening" (*Kansas City American Citizen*).

• ***July 1, 1892 (Kansas City, Kansas):*** "The entertainment given by the Governor's Guard on Monday, Tuesday and Wednesday evenings was a grand success . . . The climax . . . was reached on Tuesday evening when an interesting programme was rendered by the talent of the two sister cities. The young Misses Watts rendered a selection, 'Under the Old Umbrella' . . . Mrs. Mattie Teeters rendered a piano solo from La Somnambula . . . The Midland band . . . rendered several selections in good form . . . The Silver Leaf Mandolin club was the feature for the third night" (*Kansas City American Citizen*).

• ***July 1, 1892 (Kansas City, Kansas):*** "Two colored bands are being organized, one of little girls, if they are successful in perfecting the organization there will be four colored bands in our city. Our people are always on the extreme" (*Kansas City American Citizen*).

• ***July 22, 1892 (Topeka, Kansas):*** "Mr. Joe Raveise, the noted baritone who has won much fame by his good work in the Dispatch Band, will leave the city on the 29th of August to travel with a minstrel company" (*Kansas State Ledger*).

Note: Joe Ravise (as his name was most often spelled) spent the rest of his life with various traveling minstrel companies. Unfortunately, his life was cut short, as noted in the February 17, 1906, edition of the *Freeman:* "Joe Ravise, tuba player with Allen's New Orleans Minstrels, was shot and killed instantly by the sheriff at Dunnellon, Fla., February 5, as the show was en route to Crystal, Fla. He was well-known and was one of the best concert tuba players in the profession. His home was at Pine Bluff, Ark." An eye-witness confirmed in the following week's *Freeman* that Ravise had been "shot and killed for almost nothing by the marshall, a white man, and his body left in the street for over three hours and then thrown in a box, nailed up, hurried away in a wagon and buried and no one dared to speak. But the show was booked here the following day and came back and the K. of P's gave him a lovely funeral; had him dug up, washed and dressed and put in a beautiful casket. The band and all turned out and gave him a swell burial . . . I am proud to say that although they were booked here that night they refused to show."

• ***August 5, 1892 (Topeka, Kansas):*** "The Dispatch band furnished music at the city park from 9 to 12 A.M.; at Garfield park, from 1 to 6 P.M.; at Luken's opera house from 7:30 to 8:00; at the Metropolitan hall, from 8:30 to 10 P.M., on Monday Aug. 1st" (*Kansas State Ledger*).

• ***August 26, 1892 (Emporia, Kansas):*** "The colored citizens of Emporia will celebrate the emancipation celebration and jubilee at Solden's grove, Wednesday, September 21st, 1892. Quite a grand time is anticipated. The procession will start from Ninth avenue and march down Commercial street to the grove, headed by the Emporia Cornet band" (*Kansas State Ledger*).

• ***September 9, 1892 (Topeka, Kansas):*** "The Dispatch Band had a grand success last Monday evening at Lukens' opera house. Their purpose was to raise money to furnish themselves with a new uniform for a trip to the World's Fair, to convene in Chicago May, 1893" (*Kansas State Ledger*).

• ***October 7, 1892 (Topeka, Kansas):*** "The Dispatch Band Dressed Up," "Hundreds of Topeka's people wended their way on last Monday evening to Metropolitan hall, for the dual purpose of seeing the finest uniformed colored band in America, and hearing music rendered by one of the best colored bands in the United States. The people feel proud of the Dispatch Band, and on this occasion they showed it by their long continued enthusiasm, and their exceeding generosity.

The new uniforms are immense: White Prince-Albert coats, trimmed in blue and gold, with blue shoulder knots, blue pants with white stripe, white helmets, with various ornamental trimmings of blue and gold. The suits are made of the best material throughout, and the boys looked at their best. Their wonderful rendition of that famous overture, 'William Tell,' brought forth thunders of applause, that shook the building to the foundation" (*Kansas State Ledger*).

• ***October 21, 1892 (Topeka, Kansas):*** "Geo. W. Jackson and the Famous Dispatch Band," "Since the Dispatch Band has received such high praise from the press and public, we think it proper to give a short sketch of the life of their teacher, to whom much credit is due for the high standard the band has attained as a musical organization. Mr. Geo. W. Jackson is a musician of unusual ability, a good teacher, and a finished musical organizer.

He was born in Washington, D.C., where he lost both mother and father, at an early age. Beginning in 1864, Mr. Jackson entered the service of the U.S. naval department; after serving two years he was placed in St. Martin's seminary, at Washington, D.C., where he attended school from '66 to '70; leaving the school, he went to live with his uncle to learn the trade of cabinet maker. Becoming dissatisfied on account of a family disagreement, he left his uncle's house. Next we find him with Rev. Father Barotti, who had taken quite a liking to Young Jackson, and seeing the musical talent that he possessed, decided to assist in making Jackson a thorough musician. Following up this motive, he placed him under the training of Prof. John Esputi, ex-leader of the U.S. Marine band, and at that time teacher of the Marine Academy, also teacher of St. Augustine's choir, of which Mr. Jackson became a member. A performance of 'The Doctor of Alcantarri,' was given by the choir, assisted by thirty-five members of the Marine band. At this entertainment Mr. Jackson distinguished himself in the interpretation of one of the leading roles, the character of Dr. Parocelses. They played many engagements in Washington, D.C., Baltimore, and Philadelphia. Again he returned to the Marine academy and received instructions in the same class with the well known composer and instructor, J. P. Sousa. Next we find him in Chicago, teaching bands; and running an express business under the name of Carrol & Jackson. The band under his guidance soon prospered, and he secured an engagement for the full band, to travel with Calender's minstrels for the season of 1881. We find him again in '82 with Calender's minstrels, unexcelled as a manipulator of the slide trombone, and an all around musician. Now we have him at Chicago from '86 to '89, playing with Prof. Henderson's band and orchestra. He accepted an engagement in '89 with Schocraft & Clark's minstrels, which left Omaha on August 20th, and arrived in Topeka on September 8th. Here the company stranded, and Mr. Jackson soon joined the Dispatch band, and became leader of the same" (*Kansas State Ledger*).

• ***November 18, 1892 (Topeka, Kansas):*** "The fifth anniversary given in honor of Mr. and Mrs. J. M. Spaulding, 1236 Lincoln street, was the grandest entertainment ever held among the upper tens of Afro-American creed . . . The Dispatch Band gave music for this elaborate ovation, until several well spent hours were consumed in pleasure and enjoyments" (*Kansas State Ledger*).

• ***April 7, 1893:*** "City Locals," "The Famous Dispatch Band of Topeka will give a grand musical concert at Vineyard Hall on Wed., April 9th . . . The Dispatch Band will render the overture of Wm. Tell at Vineyard Hall . . . This overture is said to be the most difficult piece written by Prof. Rossin [*sic*] and is the only colored band in the state that plays it . . . The Dispatch Band will appear in their new uniforms which cost $1000 . . . Admission 50 cents . . . Watch for the Grand street parade of the Dispatch Band at 5 o'clock P.M., April 9th from Union depot to Vineyard Hall" (*Kansas City American Citizen*).

• ***April 15, 1893 (Topeka, Kansas):*** "The Dispatch Band will run an excursion to Kansas City, Kan., on the 19th, and will prove to the Kansas Cityans that Topeka has the finest band in the West. Our famous primadona, Mrs. C. C. Smith, will accompany them" (*Topeka Weekly Call*).

• ***April 21, 1894:*** "Topeka's famous Dispatch Band will give its usual spring reception and promenade concert at Hamilton's hall [in Topeka] on Thursday evening, April 26 . . . Under the very efficient leadership of Prof. G. W. Jackson the Dispatch band stands without rival among colored bands West of Chicago. During the past winter Prof. Jackson has trained fifteen new men, and will bring out at Hamilton hall a full uniformed band of thirty-five pieces. The band will be assisted by Madame C. C. Smith, Kansas's sweetest singer" (*Leavenworth Herald*).

• ***May 5, 1894:*** "Winfield Items," "The Walnut Valley Band has secured Prof. H. Caton as their teacher and they will no doubt come out on the streets in a short time as Mr. Caton is a first class teacher with many years experience" (*Parsons Weekly Blade*).

• ***May 5, 1894:*** "The grand opening concert given in Hamilton's hall last Thursday evening by the famous Dispatch band was in every way a rare musical entertainment . . . While the boys deserved a much larger audience, yet the hall was quite comfortably filled when Director Jackson's men opened upon the march, 'Liberty Bell.' . . . The waltz, 'La Serenata,' was especially good. Madame C. C. Smith, Topeka's 'Queen of Song,' came in for a large share of the honors . . . Perhaps the finest production of the evening was the cornet solo, 'Rocked in the Cradle of the Deep,' by Thomas Lewis . . . The imitation skirt dance by little Harry Dillard was another feature" (*Leavenworth Herald*).

• ***June 9, 1894:*** "The famous Dispatch Band gave a grand concert at Vinewood park Wednesday, May 30. They had a great success . . . The dirge 'Peace, troubled soul,' (to the memory of Geo. W. Lowery, deceased), was grand and enjoyed by all" (*Topeka Weekly Call*).

• ***June 9, 1894:*** "George Wellington Gross, who used to toot a horn of solid gold in the Rise and Shine brass band of Lawrence, has moved to . . . Topeka, where one has to sign an affidavit to get a teaspoon of beer, and where hereafter George will 'discourse beautiful strains' for the Dispatch band. And when a social favorite of Shungannaga or Tennessee Town comes to town for a good time, George, with his ever ready hospitality, will send out invitations" (*Leavenworth Herald*).

• ***June 23, 1894:*** "The colored republicans of the third ward held their latest rally at the primaries, at Stillie's hall last week . . . The Dispatch Band furnished the music" (*Topeka Weekly Call*).

• ***July 6, 1894:*** "City Locals," "The Governor's Guard Band played Tuesday July 3rd in Huron Place to a large and appreciative audience. It is the best colored band in the two [Kansas] Cities" (*Kansas City American Citizen*).

• ***July 7, 1894:*** "Winfield News," "The Walnut Valley band gave an open air concert on Main Street last Friday evening. The boys did well and should have the praise from everybody . . . Some of our would be sporty boys tried to burlesque the band boys when they were on the streets last Friday evening. Now boys we will not call your names this time but if you have not enough raising to act right in company, we will let the public know who you are" (*Parsons Weekly Blade*).

• ***July 14, 1894:*** "An excursion will be run to Kansas City Wednesday, July 18th, under the auspices of the Dispatch Band and Excelsior Lodge No. 3, Knights of Pythias.

The famous Dispatch band which needs no praising, gave a grand concert at St. John's A.M.E. Church on the fourth of July for the benefit of the church" (*Topeka Weekly Call*).

• ***August 18, 1894:*** "The Dispatch band has changed its name, and will hereafter be known as 'Jackson's Military Band'" (*Topeka Weekly Call*).

• ***August 24, 1894:*** "The Dispatch Band of Topeka, the best colored musical organization west of the Mississippi river, has disbanded and reorganized under the name of Jackson's Military Band. Since Topeka already had one Military Band—Marshall's—it is regretted by the friends of Prof. Jackson and his band that they had not taken some other designation. The similarity of dress and similarity of names makes it appear too much as though they were trying to copy after their white brethren. The boys have a fine organization and its name and uniform should be separate and distinct from their neighbor's" (*Kansas City American Citizen*).

• ***September 1, 1894:*** "Social Brevities," "Jackson's Military band now entertains people from two until six at Vinewood park Sunday's. They have a large crowd in attendance" (*Topeka Weekly Call*).

• ***September 8, 1894:*** "Labor Day was highly celebrated by the Topeka citizens. The grand street parade took place about 10:30 A.M. which was considerably better than the greater portion of the people expected. Marshall's Military band entertained the people at Garfield park, and Jackson's Military band entertained the people at Vinewood. The day was pleasantly spent by all and no one was hurt" (*Topeka Weekly Call*).

Note: J. B. Marshall's Military Band of Topeka was rated among the leading white brass bands in the nation.

• ***September 15, 1894 (Topeka, Kansas):*** "The remains of the late George Freeman, the only son of Mr. and Mrs. Mark Freeman, 829 Kansas avenue, arrived in the city Sunday morning from Pittsfield, Mass., where he came to his sudden death caused by heart disease. The deceased has been traveling with musical organizations for the past fifteen years. At the time of his death he was traveling with the famous minstrels of Primrose and West. The late George Freeman was the acknowledged leading Negro cornetist of America. He was in the city visiting his parents for six weeks this summer and at the time of his death had been away from home only two weeks. During his stay in this city he played with Jackson's Military band. At the time of his death he was 31 years, 4 months and 10 days of age. During his trip in Europe he made many friends who will be grieved to hear of his sudden death.

The procession, headed by Jackson's Military band, left the family residence at 3 P.M. and slowly wended its way to St. John's A.M.E. Church, where more than nine hundred people had assembled to pay the last respects to an honored citizen. The band in full uniform were the first to enter the church" (*Leavenworth Herald*).

• ***September 15, 1894:*** "Emancipation Day will be celebrated in Topeka by the G.A.R. at the city park and by the Benevolent society at Vinewood park. Excursions are expected from Osage city and several other points. Jackson's Band and the Osage band will furnish music at the city park and the Lawrence band will be engaged at Vinewood" (*Topeka Weekly Call*).

• ***November 24, 1894:*** "Jackson's Military band will give a grand benefit entertainment Thanksgiving evening in honor of their kind director, Prof. Geo. W. Jackson . . . Admission 25 cents at hall. Grand march at 10 P.M." (*Topeka Weekly Call*).

• ***November 30, 1894:*** "Prof. Jackson," "A meeting was held at the Jackson's Military Band-men's Hall, at which place a solid gold Medal was presented to their leader, G. W. Jackson. The medal was of pure gold, finely finished. It was composed of three parts. The center was in form of a Maltese Cross with a gold wreath connecting the arms of the same. In the center was engraved a Grecian Harp, across which was an Elizabethan scroll, on which music was inscribed: these were surrounded by a wreath of laurel. The whole exquisitely engraved. Around the wreath were the words 'presented by Jacksons Military Band.'

This beautiful and expensive specimen of the goldsmith and engraver was designed made and engraved by Topeka's artist workman, John Radford" (*Kansas State Ledger*).

• ***December 22, 1894:*** "Jackson Military band will give a grand concert and matinee and Ball Christmas afternoon and evening at Hamilton Hall the matinee will be especially for the children and those who do not dance. The military ball will be strictly first class no bad characters admitted . . . come or miss half your life. Matinee, children 5 cents, adults 10 cents, Ball couple 50 cents, single 35 cents" (*Topeka Weekly Call*).

• ***March 2, 1895:*** At the funeral of William H. Slaughter, the procession included "Jackson's Military band, playing softly The Dead March from Saul" (*Topeka Weekly Call*).

• ***May 25, 1895:*** "The Dispatch band accompanied the Topeka baseball players to Leavenworth last Sunday and gave what might be called by some people a concert on the public thoroughfares. The Dispatch band is not near so good as it has been in the past, and, from the fact that every member of the band came here drunk Sunday, it is not surprising that it was no good at all. Nearly all of the society were out to hear the band play, as were also many common people, but aside from the applause which the band received from the Topeka people, who probably came along for that purpose, the music did not receive much attention, presumably for the reason that it was horribly butchered, and for the further reason that the members of the band were in too maudlin a condition to know whether they were blowing through their horns or standing on their heads. It is to be hoped that the band will come here the next time in condition to dispense music" (*Leavenworth Herald*).

• ***June 1, 1895:*** "Local News," "Jackson's Military band gave an entertaining concert at Vinewood Decoration Day in the afternoon. The band had a fair attendance but would have had more if it had not rained in the morning. Mr. Charlie French was out and took the photos of the members of the band. The concert that was to have been given by the band in the evening at Barker's church, was postponed on account of the rain until an indefinite date" (*Topeka Weekly Call*).

• ***July 19, 1895:*** "Band Gets a Medal," "Jackson's Military Band, the well known Topeka colored musical organization, was awarded a gold medal in a band contest at Kansas City last Friday, in which there were ten competing bands.

The leading bands in the contest were the St. Joseph Central band, two bands from Kansas City, and one from Lincoln, Nebraska.

In addition to the gold medal being awarded to Jackson's band the Topeka lodge Knights of Labor was awarded first prize in the competitive drill" (*Kansas State Ledger*).

• ***July 27, 1895 (Topeka, Kansas):*** "Topeka has a brass band viz: Jackson Military Band. They wear white doe skin coats, white helmets and blue trousers. It is second to any colored band in the United States [*sic*]. It has been asked to play at the Mid-Winter Fair at Atlanta, Ga." (*Indianapolis Freeman*).

• ***August 2, 1895:*** "The Pride of Kansas City," "The citizens of Kansas City may justly feel proud of the K.C. Midland Band. Prof. Dan Blackburn, the very efficient instructor and leader, and Mr. Eugene W. Yober, the energetic and able manager, have through their untiring efforts lead their associates to victory. We are pleased to note that this band won the first prize (which was fifty dollars) last week, at Sedalia, Mo. The contestants were: The Clinton, Lexington and Sedalia bands.

We hope that the public will see to it that these young men who have through much sacrifice and hard labor made themselves so proficient in the art of music, are encouraged and well patronized" (*Kansas City American Citizen*).

• ***AUGUST 16, 1895:*** "Topeka Items," "Prof. Jackson's Band is one of the best and most deserving organizations in the city, but how much better would it have been for them, if everyone who paid 75 cents to go on the excursion, had just handed that amount to the manager instead of dividing with the railroad company" (*Kansas City American Citizen*).

• ***OCTOBER 18, 1895:*** "Topeka Locals," "The cornerstone laying of the prospective new colored Baptist church took place here on Sunday last. The Masons and Knights of Pythias did the honors of the occasion. Headed by Jackson's Band they made a very fine parade" (*Kansas City American Citizen*).

No enumeration of Kansas' black band and orchestra prodigies of the 1890s can ignore the very famous trumpeter and bandleader P. G. Lowery, who came out of Reece, Kansas, and its regional brass band milieu. The Kansas press drew attention to Lowery at the beginning of his professional career.

• ***JUNE 30, 1894 (PARSONS, KANSAS):*** "A musical concert is expected in the near future to be given by Prof. P. G. Lowery in the interests of the Walnut Valley Band. Prof. Lowery is known all over the State as one of the best Triple Tongue Soloists in the West. He took second prize at the great contest in this State" (*Parsons Weekly Blade*).

African American musicians who chose not to tour for a living found available opportunities in local communities. In Kansas City, Professor

Nashville Concert Company.

EDITOR FREEMAN:

The company is now in its tenth week and doing wonderful business. The manager, Mr. P. T. Wright, assures us he has the best company he has managed for ten years, making the best colored show on the road. Their comedians, Mr. Al F. Watts and Mr. James White, the latter a native of this city, and the leading feature with Georgia Ministrels are making a decided hit. The company has three ladies this season, Mrs. C. C. Smith, the great prima dona Mrs. Nettie Goff, the lady trombone soloist, and Mrs. Ida Lee-Wright, who last season won a world's reputation as a serpentine dancer, is now doing a wonderful new dance. Their band is the topic of all newspapers in every city they appear. Their band master, P. G. Lowery, the greatest colored cornet solist the world has ever known is well pleased with his band, out of a band of nine he has six soloists without himself. E. O. Green, the trombone soloist, is the feature of the evening's concert and P. A. Woods owing to his masterly powers on his chosen instrument as a baritone solist, he has a clear field. The band master says he can put on any kind of a solo that may be called the limit of his instrumentation. The other soloist that are making hits are Messrs. John Stewart, on tuba and C. F. Alexander as saxaphone soloist, the musical wonder who is master of all the standard musical instruments. The band master, P. G. Lowery, was presented with a beautiful gold badge from the company on the 11th of October, at the company's cost of $25.00 J. H. Hearde, the sword walker, is making a great hit assisted by Jno. Stewart, the wire walker. The orchestra is justly named the Big Four under the direction of C. F. Alexander, the company is comprised of perfect ladies and gentlemen and deserves great credit.

Freeman, *October 19, 1895.*

T. B. Brown furnished orchestral music for all occasions, gave musical instruction "in all the branches," and ran a popular dancing school. Other master musicians, notably Charles T. Watts and William L. Dawson, carried forward Kansas City's extraordinary level of instruction in instrumental music.

Regardless of their stature and accomplishments, Kansas' African American brass band mentors of the 1890s were not particularly known as innovators. By all indications, they kept within the mainstream styles and disciplines, but they were masters of those disciplines, and they were master instructors to a large number of younger musicians who subsequently demonstrated a more adventuresome creativity.

"Kid Bands" in Kansas: The John Brown Juvenile Band and N. Clark Smith's Pickaninny Band

One significant development in the mid-1890s was the rise of African American juvenile bands, more commonly termed "kid bands" or "pickaninny bands." Many early jazz musicians received training in juvenile bands or had their first professional touring experience with one. The John Brown Juvenile Band of Kansas City was organized in 1892. It played for excursions, picnics, and other black community functions.

• ***February 6, 1892 (Kansas City, Kansas):*** "The juvenile brass band of this city, under the leadership of J. Tilman, managed by Messrs. Taft, Bradford and P. C. Thomas, is making [such] rapid progress that the white juvenile band is becoming very jealous" (*Indianapolis Freeman*).

• ***April 15, 1892 (Kansas City, Kansas):*** "The 'Boy' Band Concert," "It was first thought that owing to the continued disagreeableness of the weather last Tuesday evening that the John Brown juvenile brass band concert would be postponed, but the boys and their many friends would not have it so, and the results were a good entertainment and an enjoyable good time . . . The Crescent City Mandolin club entertained while the 'Boy' band made an impression upon the audience that will long be remembered. The financial success was alright" (*Kansas City American Citizen*).

• ***June 10, 1892 (Kansas City, Kansas):*** "Beyond a shadow of a doubt one of the grandest successes

DON'T MISS THIS.

Ho, Ho! For a big time, at the Tabernacle corner Seventh and State Avenue Monday night May 30th in the interest of the John Brown Juvenile band. Hear your boys, encourage our boys, hear the richest program of the age.

Invocation; Rev. Geo. W. Dickey, Nearer my God, by the band, Address subject Which way; Hon. C. H. J. Taylor Quartett, Mandoline club, Kansas City, Mo., Address Prof. W. W. Yates. Duett Miss M. Calaway and G. B. Williams, Cornet solo Bohemian Girl; Prof. W. J. Tillman, Selection by members of the Band, Recitation; Miss Cora D. Nero, Solo Mr. Geo. Teeters, Solo S. Taff, Bass Solo B. S. Stovall, Instrumental Solo Mrs. S. Hartwell, Paper; Mrs. F. J. Jackson, Selection Alamos; by band, Address; Hon. Paul Jones, Solo G. B. Williams. Overture by Band.

Hear the above program. Don't miss it. Captain Louis Thompkins, of the G. A. R. Kansas City, Mo., and other prominent Persons are invited, all societies are cordially invited. Remember the place, at the Tabernacle. Admission 15c or 25c a couple.

Kansas City American Citizen, *May 27, 1892.*

scored in this city this season was that of the John Brown Juvenile band at the M. and O. hall Tuesday evening. The boys were most ably assisted by the 'band of bands,' the Midland band, of Kansas City, Mo . . . The Midland and our Juveniles will accompany the excursion to Beatrice, Neb., on the 25th, inst., to the grand dedication of the Beatrice A.M.E. Church" (*Kansas City American Citizen*).

• ***July 15, 1892 (Kansas City, Kansas):*** "Look out! Look out! for the star light Picnic, the grandest of the season will be given at the Metropolitan church Monday and Tuesday evening July 18th and 19th. There will be served refreshments of all kind there will also be a grand program... music by the John Brown Juvenile band... admission adults 10ct children 5ct" (*Kansas City American Citizen*).

The difference between a juvenile band and a pickaninny band was the difference between functioning within the black community and venturing into the broader commercial entertainment arena. In eastern Kansas the best-known pickaninny band of the mid-1890s was the one directed by the legendary bandmaster, composer, and music educator Professor N. Clark Smith. According to a 1920 retrospective prepared by Salem Tutt Whitney,

> [N. Clark Smith] began his musical career when a boy employed in the publishing house of Carl Hoffman, Kansas City, Mo., and of Lyon & Healy, Chicago. Here he displayed such a talent for music that Mr. Healy, the junior member of the firm, gave him free access to all parts of the large plant to indulge his taste for music. Trying this instrument and that, asking questions here and there, it wasn't long before young Smith could play nearly any instrument in the establishment. Then the employers gave serious attention to the development of the talented lad by sending him to Dr. Ziegfield, president of the Chicago Musical College. Here he was trained in composition and modern orchestration by Felix Borowiski, the Polish composer, theorist and critic. His voice training was entrusted to Prof. J. R. Miller, tenor soloist of the Theodore Thomas Orchestra.

When his famous Pickaninny Band first "came to the front," Smith was based in Wichita.

• ***June 9, 1894:*** "Concerning Kansas," "Prof. N. Clark Smith, formerly of Leavenworth, is a successful music teacher of Wichita, both white and colored people giving him a liberal patronage" (*Leavenworth Herald*).

• ***April 20, 1895 (Wichita, Kansas):*** "The 'kid band' has made quite an impression on the

STILL COMING TO THE FRONT.

The people of Wichita know N. Clark Smith as leader of an orchestra and the colored kid band, but there are perhaps few people in this city who are aware of the fact that this modest young colored man is a composer.

Mr. Smith composed a march which he dedicated to Frederick Douglass that has been published by Brainard and sons, Chicago, and is said to be very fine, 20,000 copies being published and sold so quickly that Mr. Smith's friends here were unable to get a copy.

The publishers wrote Mr. Smith that they will publish another larger edition both in this country and in England and that "Douglass March" promises to become popular. Mr. Smith got a neat little sum of money out of the first edition and he will get a royalty of ten per cent. on all sales hereafter made.

He has composed a song, "Good Night," which the local musicians pronounce a fine piece of music. Professor Sickner pronounces it a most perfect piece of music and says that the harmony is almost perfect. Mr. Smith sang his song with piano accompaniment at Shaw's music store yesterday and those who heard it were highly pleased with the song and music. It will be sent to the Chicago house for publication this week and a trial edition will be issued.

N. Clark Smith is only 27 years old and is a close student. He may become the most noted colored composer in the world and there would be nothing remarkable in that, because Wichita is always coming to the front.—*Wichita Eagle, July 7.*

Leavenworth Herald, *July 13, 1895.*

people recently by their wonderful execution of some difficult music. Prof. N. C. Smith is their teacher and certainly deserves great praise" (*Indianapolis Freeman*).

• ***July 26, 1895 (Wichita, Kansas):*** "For Waller's Benefit," "July 19—N. Clark Smith, the colored composer, is going to John Waller's assistance with a musical composition. He is composing a song relating to Waller's unhappy fate. Mr. Smith's music is quite popular. His Frederick Douglass waltz is now in its third edition.

The basis of his Waller composition is to be a southern negro melody. Some time ago while in Atlanta, Ga., he heard a peculiar melody from the lips of an old colored aunty, 80 years of age. It was singularly fascinating in time and note and Mr. Smith spent hours with the old lady getting the tune, which he transcribed and now has in his possession. He will use it for a theme. The tune, while very pretty, consists of only eight measures. To this the old aunty had adjusted eighty stanzas of her own composition, and she insisted on singing them all to Mr. Smith" (*Kansas City American Citizen*).

Note: John L. Waller was a black citizen of Kansas who had a remarkable political career. In 1891 he was appointed the American minister to Madagascar under President Harrison. His arrest in 1895 by French authorities in Madagascar, and his subsequent eleven-month imprisonment in France on trumped-up charges of treason, made him a *cause celebre* in the African American press. He later led a regiment of Kansas soldiers in Cuba during the Spanish-American War. John L. Waller was also the maternal grandfather of musician and popular song composer Andy Razaf.[5]

• ***October 12, 1895:*** "City Cullings," "Clark Smith and his kid band are taking the Kansas people by storm" (*Leavenworth Herald*).

• ***November 2, 1895:*** "Probably the most attractive feature about the Apple Carnival parade was Prof. N. Clark Smith's Pickaninny Band of Wichita. Sousa, so it is said, calls this band the best kid band in the world. Sousa heard the band play in Wichita last summer, and he ought to know what he is talking about. After Sousa wrote his famous march, 'King Cotton,' Prof. Smith was the first one of his friends to receive a copy. This certainly was a great compliment, and also a recognition of true genius. The band was not here in its entirety, several of the members having gone home to Wichita from Kansas City Sunday night. The band came to Leavenworth at the request of Elliot Marshall of the Burlington Railroad company, he having heard it play in Kansas City last week. Thinking it would be a great thing for the Apple Carnival parade, he sent Prof. Smith a telegram. The band numbers 22 members and is led by Master Willie Smith, who is only 9 years old. It easily surpasses Topeka's Dispatch band, which was here last summer. The band has made such a great success that Prof. George Jackson of the Dispatch band, is also organizing a Pickaninny Band" (*Leavenworth Herald*).

• ***November 30, 1895:*** "City Cullings," "Prof. N. Clark Smith was a very pleasant *Herald* visitor Monday. Prof. Smith and his Pickaninny Band have located permanently in Kansas City, Mo., where both the band and the bandmaster are progressing nicely. We are informed that the band will have forty members next year, and that a tour will be made of Kansas and Missouri and other states. 'Down In Dixie,' a show which has been playing in Kansas City, Mo., this week, has a Pickaninny Band, so we are informed by Prof. Smith. 'The Crackerjack,' which is playing in Iowa also has one. In fact, pickaninnies seem to be all the rage, even a pickaninny preacher having made her appearance in New York. Every pickaninny born nowadays seems to have a bright future. His future is centered in the fact that some day he will be a member of a Pickaninny Band" (*Leavenworth Herald*).

In 1895 Prof. N. Clark Smith was just beginning his varied and distinguished career. In 1899, Smith and his Pickaninny Band traveled to Australia with M. B. Curtis's Afro-American Minstrels. The following year they filled an extended engagement in Honolulu with a company under the direction of Ernest Hogan. In 1903 N. Clark Smith organized Chicago's first black symphony orchestra. Later, he directed the renowned Tuskegee Institute Band, and he spent the last seventeen years of his life (1916–1933) teaching music in the black public high schools of Kansas City, Chicago, and St. Louis.

N. CLARK SMITH VISITS CHATEAU CAFE.

Prof. N. Clark Smith of Wichita, Kansas, who conducted the chorus at Orchestra Hall Monday night, is having a pleasant time circulating among his many friends. Wednesday night he was a supper guest at the Chateau Cafe. He was highly pleased at the service at the new and up-to-date place.

Chicago Defender, *May 16, 1914.*

Perhaps the most prominent graduate of Prof. N. Clark Smith's Pickaninny Band was clarinetist Wilbur Sweatman, who was born in Brunswick, Missouri, in 1882 and came under Smith's wing some time before 1895, when Smith relocated from Wichita to Kansas City.[6] Lionel Hampton credited Professor Smith with inspiring his early interest in music. As a youngster, Hampton played the bass drum with the Chicago Defender Band under Smith's tutelage.[7] Other notable jazz musicians who benefitted from N. Clark Smith's latter-day career as a high school music teacher include pianist Sonny Thompson, who was a member of the Wendell Phillips High School Band; Walter Page, who became the leader of the famous Blue Devils; and alto saxophonist Herman Walder, "widely regarded as an important early influence on Charlie Parker." Recalling his days at Lincoln High School in Kansas City, Walder noted, "I was under Major [N. Clark] Smith . . . Oh, that cat was a masterpiece. Man, I remember, he come by me and I made the wrong note. Man, he took that baton and hit me right on the top of the head . . . till I got it right . . . He was a masterpiece."[8]

"In Old Kentucky"

The most famous juvenile band of the 1890s was the Woodlawn Wangdoodle Pickaninny Band from the play *In Old Kentucky,* which became a fixture and ultimately a legend in black entertainment. *In Old Kentucky* was not in the "plant show" tradition of the South Before the War Company. It was a legitimate dramatic production with an almost entirely white cast. The story revolved around a group of Kentucky mountaineers—hillbillies—and it included moonshiners, revenue officers, a family feud, etc.[9] Though there is nothing in the plot to indicate a place for African American performers, *In Old Kentucky* was nevertheless the vehicle which propelled the craze for "pickaninny bands." A retrospective in a 1910 edition of the *Freeman* explains:

> One of the features of Litt & Dingwall's production of "In Old Kentucky". . . that never fails to make a lasting impression on the auditor, is the Pickaninny Band, a collection of youthful, frolocksome Afro-Americans, whose acting, playing, dancing and comic abilities add much to the fun and jollity of this interesting play, and help to preserve admirably the atmosphere of life in Kentucky, in which environment is located the story and action of the play. When Charles T. Dazey first wrote "In Old Kentucky," the idea of a pickaninny band never entered his mind. The play did provide for a colored band under the title of the "Woodlawn Whangdoodles." The story of the introduction of the juvenile colored musicians in "In Old Kentucky" is interesting, particularly so in view of the great popularity this feature of the performance has assumed in the many years of its success. It was several months following the first revealment of the play that Mr. A. W. Dingwall, on a visit to Minneapolis, ran across a pickaninny band playing in the street. The "boys" were from Indianapolis, Ind., and were touring the country under the direction of and for the benefit of some colored religious and educational institution of the South . . . It did not take Mr. Dingwall long to appreciate the importance of securing a band of this kind for "In Old Kentucky." Negotiations at once ensued, and when "Kentucky" was on its first road tour at Pittsburg a Pickaninny Band was introduced and proved to be one of the most fascinating features in the immediately phenomenal success of this enjoyable play. In the original road revealment of the play the author's idea of the men's band in the piece was much elaborated upon, and for the years of the wonderful success of this popular play the Pickaninny Band, both in outdoor and in stage participation, has remained a popular and appreciated feature.
>
> Prior to the advent of "In Old Kentucky," it is doubtful that more than half a dozen pickaninnies had ever set foot beyond a stage door. But with the advent of "In Old Kentucky," the widespread interest created can best be judged by the statement that there are now perhaps no less than five thousand colored actors struggling for fame. The question is often asked as to where the management secures its unfailing supply of these little, agile Afro-Americans, all of the same age, approximately, and all more or less gifted as musicians. Not from the cotton fields or plantations, but from Indianapolis, that place of residence of the colored man.
>
> John Powell, the leader of the band, lives here in Indianapolis, and during the dozen years or more that it has been his duty to play in the band, direct it, manage it, and especially to reorganize it as soon as the boys grow beyond Mr. Powell's artistic deadline, they have been supplied by other pickaninnies from this city, and the visible supply of them would worry a crop statistician. To belong to "Mistah Pow'l's band of Ol' Kentucky" is in itself most important to the youthful colored lad, and to receive musical instruction at Powell's summer school of band instruction is the prime ambition of all the tender, youthful colored lads of Indianapolis, and it is with regret and sorrow that, as the years go by, they find themselves up against the "deadline" and are forced to resign in favor of some more youthful and smaller sized aspirant for musical and terpsichorean honors.[10]

• ***September 16, 1893 (New York City):*** "People's Theatre," "What in stage parlance is called an 'instantaneous hit' is credited to the first city production of C. T. Dazey's new comedy drama, 'In Old Kentucky,' at this house, night of Sept. 11 . . . In act two, representing the Woodlawn mansion and stables a colored juvenile brass band is introduced with good effect, and banjo playing and buck and soft shoe dancing is

PICKANINNY BAND

"In Old Ky" Company

We are in need of clarionet and cornet players who can handle 3rd and 4th grade music. Must be small, not over 5 ft. 3 or 4 inches in height. Sweatman and Saulters write

JACK POWELL,

2218 S. Meridian Street, Indianapolis, Ind.

Freeman, *July 2, 1904.*

Freeman, *September 24, 1910.*

indulged in by a score of colored attaches of the plantation . . . The act closes with an attempt to burn the stable, which makes a thrilling climax" (*New York Clipper*).

• ***October 28, 1893 (New York City):*** "Academy of Music," "The favorable verdict pronounced when 'In Old Kentucky' was first produced in the metropolis, on the east side, was emphasized on Monday evening, Oct. 23, when it was again presented here at the Academy. Notwithstanding that rain had been falling throughout the day, and the evening was decidedly unpleasant out of doors, the auditorium was filled in every part . . . The role of the heroine, Madge Brierly, maid of the mountains, was cleverly enacted by Bettina Girard . . . The scenic and mechanical effects gotten up expressly for the Academy presentation, were perfect . . . while the realistic effects upon which the piece largely depends for success proved powerful factors. The soft shoe dancing of Burt Grant . . . afforded so much satisfaction that he had to 'oblige' repeatedly, while the 'Woodlawn Wangdoodles,' a baker's dozen of colored lads of all sizes and ages, composing a really excellent brass band, led by drum major Master Walter Brister, fairly electrified the audience, who vociferously redemanded the appearance of the musical pickaninnies. The character of the opening would seem to indicate an extended run for an attraction well seasoned with fun, mixed with pathos, and full of thrilling incidents" (*New York Clipper*).

• ***December 23, 1893 (New York City):*** "Academy of Music," "'In Old Kentucky' entered Dec. 18 upon the ninth week of its metropolitan run. It is still drawing satisfactory houses. There has recently been much sickness among some of its important performers, and in order to prevent contagion one of them was put to death, but as the unfortunate was one of the racing horses the event caused little comment" (*New York Clipper*).

• ***December 30, 1893 (New York City):*** "Academy of Music," "'In Old Kentucky' began the tenth week of its run with a matinee Dec. 25. Its many stirring and sensational scenes, together with the novelty and merit of its Pickaninny Band, have made it one of the most pronounced successes of the season" (*New York Clipper*).

• ***February 10, 1894 (New York City):*** "Academy of Music," "'In Old Kentucky' continues its successful run. It entered Feb. 5 upon its sixteenth week. The Oriole Quartet was an added attraction on that date. They will continue as one of the features of the pickaninny scene" (*New York Clipper*).

• ***March 9, 1894:*** "Last week the Grand did the largest business of the season . . . The play was 'In Old Kentucky' but the attraction was the pickaninnies and the music they made" (*Kansas City American Citizen*).

• ***October 26, 1894:*** "Amusements This Week," "Grand Opera House—One week beginning Sunday, Oct. 28th. In Old Kentucky—Famous Pickaninny Band!!!" (*Kansas City American Citizen*).

• ***November 22, 1895:*** "Since 'In Old Kentucky,' the great Southern play, with the famous 'Wang doodle' pickaninny band made such a wonderful hit in the amusement world, pickaninny bands are in demand all over the country" (*Kansas City American Citizen*).

By the end of 1895, pickaninny bands were an American entertainment institution.

• ***December 14, 1895:*** "'On the Mississippi,' another 'river show' something like 'Down on the Suwanee River,' played to Kansas City all this week to crowded houses. The show, like all river shows, has a Pickaninny Band. There is a marked similarity noticeable in 'In Old Kentucky,' 'In Old Tennessee,' 'Down in Dixie,' shows named after states, and the river shows. Indeed, the similarity forces one to the belief that the river and state shows, which generally have the plantation as the most attractive scene, were written by one and the same man who probably had only one object in view: the Pickaninny Band. Although we are getting tired of the pickaninny business, we should like to see a show, 'In Kansas,' start out with a kid band and some Topeka politicians. It would make a great hit" (*Leavenworth Herald*).

"The Fake and His Orphans": Sherwood's Youth Missionary Band, 1889–1895

One of the most disturbing music-related stories of the 1889–1895 period concerns the itinerant exploits of Rev. William Henry Sherwood and his Youth Missionary Band. Reverend Sherwood has been cited for his 1893 songbook, *Harp of Zion*, "perhaps the earliest book of black gospel tunes now known to exist."[11] The cover of this landmark gospel song collection

Rev. W. Henry Sherwood, as pictured in Harp of Zion.

Front cover of Harp of Zion.

features a photograph of Rev. Sherwood's Youth Missionary Band, comprising twenty-five "Neglected and Friendless Children of the Negro Race in the Black Belt of Virginia."

Little is known of Reverend Sherwood's early life. It can be deduced from some of the brief annotations in *Harp of Zion* that he was born in the late 1850s and spent some of his early life in Florida.[12] An article in the November 15, 1889, edition of the *Detroit Plaindealer* identifies Sherwood as the "pastor of the African Episcopal church at Tallahassee." By this time, Sherwood had published several articles and books. The earliest one known to survive is his *Life of Charles B. W. Gordon, Pastor of the First Baptist Church* (1885), a ninety-nine-page exaltation of the popular young pastor of the oldest and largest black Baptist Church in Petersburg, Virginia.[13]

During the latter part of 1890, Reverend Sherwood and his itinerant Youth Missionary Band were giving open-air concerts in New Orleans and Baton Rouge, and from there they ventured into Kansas and Missouri.

• ***November 8, 1890:*** "In New Orleans, there is a band of colored boys, ranging in age from 7 to 12, who give open-air concerts for missionary purposes. They are called 'Sherwood Missionary Band'" (*Indianapolis Freeman*).

• ***December 6, 1890 (Baton Rouge, Louisiana):*** "Rev. Dr. Sherwood, the Negro evangelist, spent a week with us working up the spiritual tide . . . Dr. Sherwood is a wonderful little man of great talent and he is using it in the right manner, working in the Lord's Vine yard, gathering in the sons and daughters of man. His success this year has been upward of nearly eleven hundred souls. Dr. Sherwood is the proprietor of a wonderful little band of boys who play upon brass instruments; they are truly little wonders of the age. They have travelled through Florida, Georgia, Alabama, Louisiana and Mississippi" (*Indianapolis Freeman*).

• ***April 24, 1891 (Topeka, Kansas):*** "Topeka has enjoyed during the past week in addition to the Salvation Army with banjo and drum upon the street, the music from a full-fledged brass band of colored boys from Florida, who play upon the streets every afternoon to attract a crowd to hear the great colored evangelist who has been conducting a series of meetings at the A.M.E. Church. It seems to be quite a joke on Topeka that it takes a preacher and a brass band all the way from Florida to convert its hardened sinners" (*Kansas City American Citizen*).

• ***May 9, 1891 (Kansas City, Missouri):*** "The Rev. Dr. Sherwood, the noted evangelist and his band of seven small boys have been conducting services at Allen Chapel during the past week; his mission is to raise funds for the Foreign Mission Society; he is having only moderate success; he styles himself the Negro Sam Jones, but we cannot see where the resemblance comes in, unless it is to tell big tales" (*Indianapolis Freeman*).

At this point, a pattern of nagging questions and criminal accusations emerged.

• ***August 15, 1891:*** "Rev. Sherwood, an evangelist, is said to have taken a number of colored boys from an asylum at Omaha, Neb., drilled them and appropriated their earnings, allowing them but 10 cents a day for food" (*Cleveland Gazette*).

• ***October 17, 1891 (St. Louis, Missouri):*** "Rev. Sherwood, who manages the Youth's band is highly indorsed by the leading journals of the country. These youths are properly cared for by its managers and no inducement that you could offer them could ever persuade one of them to desert him. He is not only kind to them but in time some one of this number may achieve great distinction as a musician. If there were more such men as Sherwood, who was willing to help those who could not help themselves [*sic*]" (*Indianapolis Freeman*).

• ***November 7, 1891 (Indianapolis, Indiana):*** "Is This True?" "Little George Johnson, one of the members of 'Sherwood's Youth's Band' [*sic*] that has been giving exhibitions in our streets for the last week, makes some very serious charges against the manager of the organization. He says that the boys are cuffed and kicked at will, that they receive but five cents, on every dollar that they collect, that the 'boss' is making money, by coaxing church members to board them for nothing, and that several of the boys want to quit but are afraid to, and that, in fact he treats them more as slaves than human beings" (*Indianapolis Freeman*).

• ***November 14, 1891 (Indianapolis, Indiana):*** "Sherwood's Youth's Band," "Is Mr. Sherwood Really Going to Establish an Orphan's Home in the South for Colored Children?" "Attention was called in the last issue of THE FREEMAN to Mr. Sherwood, who hails from some point in Louisiana, and who has come from St. Louis, and who has a brass band composed of colored boys ranging from ten to fifteen years in age, and whose mission he claims is to evangelize, and to raise money to build an orphans' home somewhere in Florida.

The article referred to was published from a statement made by one of the boys who left the band, and who came to THE FREEMAN office for work and protection. The boy brought some serious charges against Mr. Sherwood, and THE FREEMAN only asked if they were true. It seems that evangelist Sherwood was greatly incensed at the article, and has made much ado about it. THE FREEMAN only asked a few questions, and Rev. Sherwood has answered them himself. He says that there is no Orphan's Home at Jacksonville, Fla., that neither he nor any member of the band have so stated it; that he, is in no way connected with any orphan's home, and has not in this or other cities sought aid from churches or individuals on such a pretext. He further states that he is an evangelist, and that he hires the boys to play in the band, paying them for their services. He says that this idea of the band, and of raising money on the streets and elsewhere, is his own, and that he is making what he can out of it; and that should he feel so inclined in the future, it is possible that he may invest the money collected in an Orphan's Home somewhere in the South.

When asked if it was in accordance with christianity, or even humanity to take these boys all over the country, whip and abuse them, as they claim, and deprive them of an opportunity to get an education; he said that it was his and their business, and not the public's business. These statements THE FREEMAN gives its readers, who must judge of the merits and demerits of the case. The impressions has obtained in this city and elsewhere that he was raising money for an Orphan's Home, and with this understanding a large number of good families in this city have taken the boys to board and room during their stay here with the understanding that they were helping the church" (*Indianapolis Freeman*).

• ***April 15, 1892:*** "One of the latest sensations in Cincinnati was the appearance on the streets of a band of youthful Afro-American musicians from Pensacola, Florida, orphan asylum. The band is composed of seventeen members ranging from 6 to 14 years of age, whose knowledge of using brass instruments is truly remarkable. The cornet soloist deserves especial mention, not only as a proficient performer, but as a composer of music, many pieces they use being his own composition. They are raising money to build a new orphan asylum" (*Detroit Plaindealer*).

• ***April 15, 1892:*** "Here and There," "In each instance in which His Honor found occasion to exhibit his bitter prejudices last week, his actions were without precedent. Sherwood's Band in their two, and one-half years on the road had never been refused a permit to solicit aid before in any city. And the starving conditions of the laborers from Columbia Tenn., appealed to the sympathies of officials in each city on their route, except Cincinnati. Strange as it may seem, Covington and Newport, Ky., came quickly to their rescue" (*Indianapolis Freeman*).

• ***April 29, 1892:*** "'Dot leedle German band,' with its ta-ra-ra boom-ta-ra, is not in it with the Florida Orphans' band, composed of 17 little Afro-American orphan boys, ranging in age from nine to thirteen years. Rev. Dr. Sherwood, an evangelist of Pensacola, Fla., organized the band about two years ago, and is now touring through the North with his little musicians. Under the direction of Mr. W. H. Pickle, who hails from Tennessee, the boys render some very creditable selections, and attract large crowds in their street parades. It is said they will sail for Europe in June" (*Detroit Plaindealer*).

• ***May 14, 1892 (Evanston, Illinois):*** "On Monday night, the 9th, inst., a grand concert will be given by Dr. Sherwood's youth band, at Lyon's hall, for the benefit of the A.M.E. Church of this place, and the Florida Orphan school. The band is composed of sixteen little orphan boys... Dr. Sherwood preached at the A.M.E. Church on Sunday night, and had his little band with him. The church was crowded to 'standing room only'" (*Indianapolis Freeman*).

• ***July 1, 1892 (St. Paul, Minnesota):*** "The little boy band which is stopping at Hotel De Mink under the management of R. E. [*sic*] Sherwood, is having much success" (*Detroit Plaindealer*).

• ***July 15, 1892 (Toledo, Ohio):*** "The Sherwood band has arrived in our city and is creating quite an excitement among our white citizens, the little fellows being so small. They really play wonderfully" (*Detroit Plaindealer*).

• ***September 24, 1892:*** "There is a colored man who is traveling over the north with a company of boys as musicians. This man claims that he is representing an orphanage concern for Jacksonville, and he is successfully hoodwinking the credulous people of the north. We give our northern and western exchanges notice that this man is a liar and he represents no benevolent work in Jacksonville, but is placing all the 'filthy lucre' in his own bag" (*Cleveland Gazette*, reproduced from the *Southern Courier*).

• ***October 8, 1892 (Atlanta, Georgia):*** "Sherwood Again," "Prof. Sherwood, proprietor of the orphan's band, who claims to be from Jacksonville, Fla., was run from here last spring for immoral purposes. One of his little boys was met on the street this morning selling papers. He is on his way home to his parents in Montgomery, Ala. The little fellow's name is Willie Woods. Sherwood wanted him to play for him at the World's Fair, but he would not. Willie was baritone. When Sherwood got to Chicago he was detected and jailed by a colored detective. He has two from this city who are not orphan children" (*Indianapolis Freeman*).

• ***November 2, 1892 (Richmond, Virginia):*** "Sherwood's Youth's Band" "A Surprising Success—Serenading the *Planet* Offices," "Sherwood's Youths Band arrived in the city last Sunday. They are in charge of Rev. W. H. Sherwood, now of Pensacola, Florida. Seldom has there been greater excitement on our streets than that produced by the appearance of these little colored boys, attired in red coats and blue pants. The ages of these little ones ranges from 5 to 14 years. And the music was splendid. After each rendition with their fine costly instruments under their arms they extended their caps as they made their way through the surging crowd and collected whatever money the populace were open hearted enough to give. This Band is composed of twenty boys who play, 15 of whom are professional players and five in training. They also have an orchestra consisting of 11 violins, violin-cello, base violin and viola, two cornets, clarionet and flute. They play for churches and benevolent institutions. All of the members of this little band are orphans.

"Rev. Sherwood states that he secured only those who had been neglected and apparently cast off. Some were gotten out of the gutters, so to speak. They now play by note and some members of the band write, engrave and play their own music. We regard it as a wonderful thing, demonstrating however that the Negro race can be made proficient in any accomplishment which our favored white race enjoys.

These little musicians serenaded THE PLANET office last Monday morning. The little Drum Major with his gray colored shacco and baton presented an appearance both amusing and satisfactory. Rev. Sherwood stated that they are the main support of the Orphan Asylum now being erected at Pensacola.

The band gives religious concerts for churches, and benevolent institutions, etc. We believe it should be encouraged and have no hesitation in expressing the opinion that it will not be denied admission to any church whose officers have once heard the magnificent strains of the interesting musicians. They played at John Wannamaker's Church at Philadelphia and were given the fine uniforms which they now wear and $500 besides.

The Band is now in the city and can be seen at 318 N. 3rd St." (*Richmond Planet*).

The January 1893 edition of the *Christian Educator*, a quarterly journal of the missionary arm of the Methodist Episcopal Church, included this glowing endorsement of Rev. Sherwood and his work:

> Sherwood's Musical Band of thirteen colored orphans, ranging from six years to fifteen, is perhaps the second musical wonder among colored people. The band was organized by Rev. W. H. Sherwood, of Florida. It is composed of thirteen orphan boys, and they give concerts throughout the country, the money from which goes to build an orphanage in Florida. They play with equal facility upon string and upon brass instruments. Moreover, they change places and instruments at pleasure. Each boy can play any one of five or six different horns. They write their own music, engrave, and print it. Dr. Sherwood himself taught them the art of engraving. The leader of the band, Geo. F. Thompson, fifteen years of age, is a true disciple of Apollo. He composes originally as well as by sound, transposes from key to key, reads by

sight rapidly and accurately, engraves, and directs the orchestra. In a spirited contest against the best cornetists of St. Louis, Mo., he won the gold cornet. He has also written cornet-music for song-books and individuals. He has appeared before musicians and audiences, public and private, of note, with satisfaction. He bids fair to become one of the great musicians of the country.

Apparently, it was during the spring of 1893 that Reverend Sherwood settled in Petersburg, Virginia, and became superintendent of the Sherwood Orphan School at 260 Halifax Street. This development appears to have been directly linked to Rev. Charles B. W. Gordon's ongoing work at the Tabernacle Baptist Church on Halifax Street.[14]

From their new home base in Petersburg, Sherwood's Youth Missionary Band plowed into the northeastern states:

• ***April 29, 1893 (Philadelphia, Pennsylvania):*** "A grand concert was given by the Sherwood's Youth's band, at the Horticultural hall, Broad street, above Spruce, on Tuesday evening, 11th inst., for the benefit of Zion Wesley A.M.E. Church, also the orphans' home, in Petersburg, Pa. [*sic*, i.e., Va.] The hall was quite full. The concert was grand and consisted of orations, recitations, etc. by the boys" (*Indianapolis Freeman*).

• ***August 19, 1893 (Worcester, Massachusetts):*** "The Sherwood Band of Negro orphans, from Petersburg, Va., visited our city on the 7th, inst., and gave a concert for the benefit of their home in Association Hall, YMCA building. One of our wealthy residents presented the little 5-year-old drum major with $25. They also received many other gifts from benevolent friends. They made their headquarters at Zion A.M.E. Church, by request of Rev. F. J. Waters, and were well provided for by members and friends of the church" (*Indianapolis Freeman*).

• ***September 9, 1893 (Worcester, Massachusetts):*** "The Sherwood Orphan Band visited our city for a second time Thursday, Aug. 24th, giving a street parade in the afternoon and a concert in the evening at Association Hall. The band was fitted out with new instruments by the C. G. Conn agency in this city, Mr. Conn himself giving a $500 contribution towards their purchase. They will make a trip to Europe next year" (*Indianapolis Freeman*).

By this time, *Harp of Zion* had made its debut.[15] The September 30, 1893, edition of the *Richmond Planet* declared:

> We have received "Harp of Zion" by W. HENRY SHERWOOD, D.D. This book of gospel songs is published at Sherwood Orphan School, 260 Halifax St., Petersburg, Va.
>
> The selections are the productions of colored persons and are especially adapted for use in churches, Sunday Schools and home circles. In the preface the author says:
>
> "From all parts of the religious world, where there is a church or Sunday school representing the Afro-American Race variety, there cometh a cry for a new and up to date singing book, published for and by men of our race, and adapted to our services. Recognizing the exceedingly difficult task of preparing such a work all of our colored authors have entirely shunned this field; thus creating in the minds of the white men of this country the impression that the Negro in the musical world, is at most nothing more than a mere imitation, and that he must sing in the past age if he sings at all or he must never sing his own song."
>
> The book contains a fine "cut" of Sherwood's Youth Band, those orphan musicians which have astounded the people in so many parts of this country. The price of these books are 35 cents per copy or $3.60 per dozen and may be secured by writing to the address above.

There are actually *two* cuts of Sherwood's Youth Missionary Band in *Harp of Zion*. One shows a brass band comprising twenty-five uniformed boys and young men. Not all of their instruments can be readily identified, but there appear to be at least five trumpets or cornets, four slide trombones and a valve trombone, five baritone horns, two bass horns, a clarinet and a flute, plus a drum major, snare drummer, bass drummer, and cymbal player. A second pose shows the same group in their alternate role as a concert orchestra, with most of the horn players holding violins, a cello, and a string bass.

Harp of Zion contains about 150 songs, including many familiar spirituals, hymns, etc., interspersed with more recent gospel songs by white and black composers. Twenty-eight titles are attributed to Reverend Sherwood himself. Another title, "The Scattered Race," is credited to Sherwood and M. W. H. Branch:

They are going thro' the land,
As a missionary band,
Leading sinners by the hand to His care,
That salvation He may give
As they turn to Him and live
In the pretty world of Love, over there.

Three titles are cited as collaborations by Sherwood and George F. Thompson, the fifteen-year-old leader of Sherwood's Youth Missionary Band; another is credited to George F. Thompson alone; and another is credited to Thompson and Rev. J. H. Manly. That Sherwood's Youth Missionary Band actually played some of these early original gospel songs by black composers is confirmed by a footnote to Sherwood's own "Go and Labor": "Favorite of Sherwoods Youth Missionary Band sliding trombone solos."

One *Harp of Zion* song, "The Lord's Our Rock," by Frank M. Davis, is an early manifestation of the modern gospel standard "Jesus Is a Rock in a Weary Land." When it appeared in the popular 1927 collection *Spirituals Triumphant Old and New*, "Jesus Is a Rock in a Weary Land" was credited to better-remembered black gospel composer William Henry Smith. Also included in *Spirituals Triumphant Old and New* is one of Reverend Sherwood's old *Harp of Zion* titles, "The Church Is Moving On," the only known twentieth-century imprint of his work.[16]

After relocating to Petersburg and publishing *Harp of Zion*, Reverend Sherwood was able to shore up his reputation in the African American press for more than a year.

• ***October 21, 1893:*** "Sherwood's Youth Band in Richmond," "The entertainment by Sherwood Orphan Band at the True Reformer's Hall last Monday night was a decided success that spacious edifice being filled to overflowing. The recitations by the pupils were very creditable while the playing was fine. The sight of the little boys handling with perfect ease the large instruments was inspiring and the audience was indeed generous in its applause.

Rev. W. H. Sherwood, D.D., made stirring remarks. He has written several music books in which are many pieces composed by members of this band. Many of these little ones can write music with ease, and it is surprising to observe what a degree of proficiency has been obtained. The Orphan Training School is located in Petersburg, and this is the most effective means of raising funds for its support" (*Richmond Planet*).

• ***December 2, 1893 (Richmond, Virginia):*** "Sherwood Band," "Last Monday night the True Reformers hall was filled to overflowing the occasion being the Sherwood Orphan Band concert, which was a success. The little boys were seen at their best. The recitations were very creditable and the music was excellent. The boys received applause after applause from the audience.

Rev. W. H. Sherwood, D.D., addressed the audience at the closing of the entertainment. In his address he intimated a desire to soon take charge of the orphan asylum of this city, which he hopes to make a success" (*Richmond Planet*).

34
GO AND LABOR.*
"Go work to-day in my vineyard."
W. H. S.
W. H. SHERWOOD.
1. There's a call for faith- ful la-b'rers in the vine-yard of the Lord,
2. Hark! a cry comes o'er the o- cean, from the is - lands of the sea,
3. But the call for help sounds near-er, in the cit - y's nois - y street—
Where the ruth-less hand of Sa - tan has been scatt'ring tares abroad;
From the heath-en and the sav - age in their dark i - dol - a - try—
From the friend-less and the homeless, who with wea - ry ach - ing feet
'Tis a call that must be answered--are you read - y to be- gin?
"Come and help us in our blindness—clear the mists of sin a - way,
Tread the ways of death un-heed - ed, save by His all- see - ing eye,
Will you spread the glo-rious Gos- pel o'er a world that's lost in sin?
Let the lands that lie in dark-ness see the Gos-pel's glo-rious ray!"
That can count the stars of heav- en, and yet marks the spar-row die!
* Favorite of Sherwoods Youth Missionary Band sliding trombone solos.

"Go and Labor," featuring "sliding trombone solos," in Harp of Zion.

• ***May 19, 1894 (Washington, Pennsylvania):*** "The Sherwood Brass Band, composed of orphan boys ranging from four to fourteen years of age, appeared at St. Paul's church . . . in a musical and literary entertainment, to a large and appreciative audience . . . The boys are from the orphan school at Petersburg, Va. . . . Cornet solos, saxophone solos, select orations, recitations, melodious songs and rousing brass band music was the order of the programme" (*Cleveland Gazette*).

At the end of 1894, allegations of fraud and child abuse again came to dominate the saga of Reverend Sherwood and his orphan band.

• ***December 29, 1894:*** "That fellow Sherwood, who in the last two years has toured the North and South with a brass band of little orphan boys, alleging that he was collecting money for an orphan asylum at different places in the South, is in England 'working the same old racket,' and also trying to discredit Miss Ida B. Wells. It is providential that Miss Hallie Q. Brown and Mr. G. F. Richings are also lecturing in that country. They can and will attend to that traitorous scoundrel Sherwood" (*Cleveland Gazette*).

• ***February 9, 1895:*** "A 'Sherwood' Victim," "To the Editor of *The Freeman*," "I think I should write to let all my people know how badly I have been treated. I came to this country with fifteen other boys. Dr. Sherwood (his right name is Griser) told my mother that he would pay me some money and give me plenty to eat and clothes to wear. He treats all the boys like slaves, and only gives them two meals a day. We walk about the streets all day, playing our music and begging money for him. He gives us rice and soup, and not much of that. If we ask for more he whips us until we cannot stand up. I ran away and got to Birmingham. I found Rev. Mr. Stanford, the colored preacher. He has been very kind to me. Sherwood came to this place to try to get me back, but I would not go. Mr. Stanford said he would not let him or anybody else ill use me. I have written to my mother and am coming back. Mr. and Mrs. Stanford are good people, and they will help me till I come back. Mr. Stanford is very sick. He is a great preacher to the white people. Such a bad man as the man who calls himself Dr. Sherwood is a disgrace to my people. Everybody should know how bad he is. He says we are all orphans, and that he has got a large building in Petersburg, Va., and a big lot of children. I am glad I have got away from him. Please put this in *The Freeman*—it is the truth.

Yours very respectfully, George Fayerman of Petersburg, Va. (age 14 years), January 23, 1895"

Editor *The Freeman,* just a line to say the above letter was written by my instigation, and [I] have no doubt, out of justice to your people, you will find space for same. The Doctor, from what I can make out, is a fraud, but I shall write you further shortly touching the question. George Fayerman, the boy referred to, has been brutally used.

Fraternally yours, Geo. B. Lloyd" (*Indianapolis Freeman*).

Sherwood's questionable behavior caused other orphanage bands to be distrusted as well.

• ***October 5, 1895 (London, England):*** "The 'Fake' and His 'Orphans' Stranded," " 'Rev.' John Jenkins, the alleged president of an orphanage in America somewhere, accompanied by fourteen Afro-Americans, ranging in age from 5 to 10, has made application to the magistrate of the Bow street police court for assistance to return to Charlestown, S.C. He said the boys formed an orphanage band and he had been told by a committee of pastors of the orphanage to bring them to London, where they could perform and thus raise money. He found the laws would not permit children under 11 to perform in public and they were now stranded without money and he feared that they would starve. The magistrate was unable to help the party. The party arrived in England on board the American line steamer *Paris,* which arrived at Southampton on September 4. P. A. Collins, United States consul general in London, said that he could not assist them either" (*Cleveland Gazette*).

" 'Rev.' John Jenkins" referred to in the above citation is Rev. Daniel Joseph Jenkins, founder of the Jenkins Orphanage in Charleston, South Carolina. Reverend Jenkins was anything but a "fake," and his orphan band achieved great fame during the early 1900s. Several jazz musicians of the 1920s and 1930s trace their beginnings to the Jenkins Orphanage.[17] During the fall of 1895, however, Jenkins was being unfairly persecuted because of the Sherwood/"Griser" fraud.

One week after the *Cleveland Gazette* reported Reverend Jenkins's difficulties in London, a Cincinnati, Ohio—based *Freeman* correspondent served notice that Sherwood's Youth Missionary Band was in his town.

• ***October 12, 1895 (Cincinnati, Ohio):*** "Sherwood's Band, composed of small boys will give an entertainment at Allen Temple A.M.E. Church" (*Indianapolis Freeman*).

• ***November 23, 1895 (Cincinnati, Ohio):*** "Sherwood's Boy Band—Abandoned By Him—Given A Benefit," "The little orphan musicians, whose band was abandoned here by one Sherwood a few weeks ago, were allowed to play for the collection at Zion Lyceum Monday evening. The money will be used to purchase them clothing" (*Cleveland Gazette*).

On this pathetic note, newspaper reports on Rev. William Henry Sherwood and his Youth Missionary Band appear to give out. It isn't easy to summarize the debilitating parodox of Sherwood's life history—such as it can be reconstructed from newspaper reports—touching on recurrent allegations of child abuse as well as pioneering work in the field of black gospel hymnbooks. Regardless, Sherwood's Youth Missionary Band was certainly a frontrunner in the increasingly popular African American juvenile band phenomenon.

While little is known about the repertoire and performance style of late-nineteenth-century African American juvenile bands in general, extant reports indicate Sherwood's Youth Missionary Band played "rousing brass band music" in "religious concerts" bent on "working up the spiritual tide." Indeed, they specialized in gospel songs with "sliding trombone solos," long before the emergence of the "trombone shout bands" whose beginnings have been traced to Bishop "Daddy" Grace's evangelical tours of the 1930s.[18]

Further excavations of contemporaneous sources may recover additional information about Reverend William Henry Sherwood, his pioneering black gospel songs and songbooks, and his hard-traveling Youth Missionary Band. It is probably safe to predict, however, that the half will never be told.

Selected, Annotated Chronology of Music-Related Citations, 1895

• ***January 26, 1895:*** "Tim Thompson, a little Negro boy, was asked to dance for the amusement of some white toughs. He refused, saying he was a church member. Jim Sosling, one of the men, knocked him down with a club, then danced upon his prostrate form. He then shot the boy in the hips. The boy is dead and the murderer is at large" (*Topeka Weekly Call*).

• ***January 26, 1895 (Richmond, Virginia):*** "Mr. Sidney Woodward, the World's Greatest Tenor, the man who took the World's Fair by storm in a Grand Concert! at and for the benefit

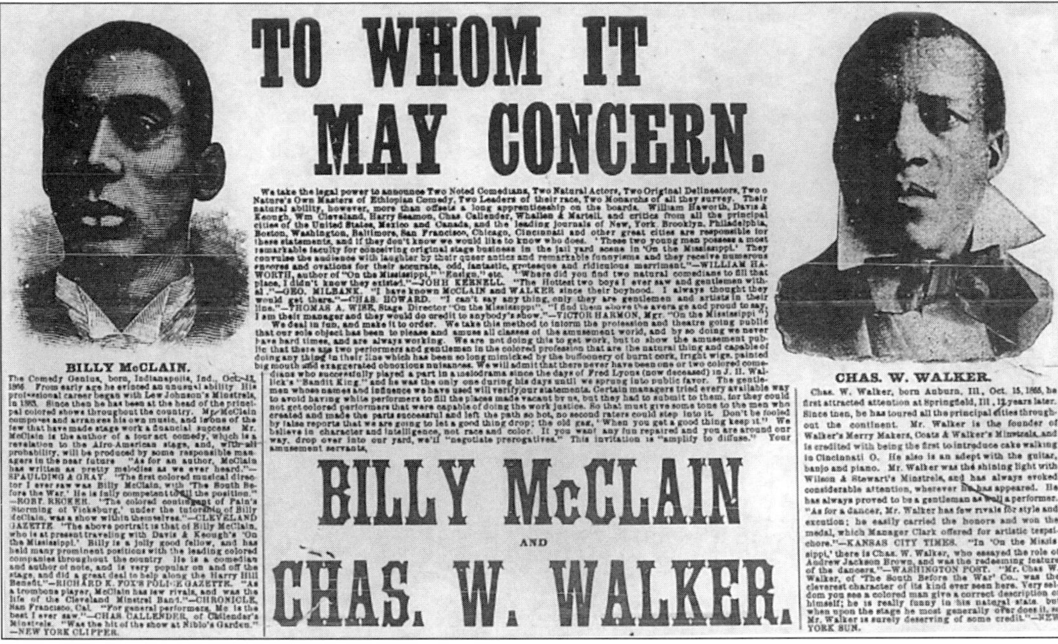

TO WHOM IT MAY CONCERN.

We take the legal power to announce Two Noted Comedians, Two Natural Actors, Two Original Delineators, Two o Nature's Own Masters of Ethiopian Comedy, Two Leaders of their race, Two Monarchs of all they survey. Their natural ability, however, more than offsets a long apprenticeship on the boards. William Haworth, Davis & Keough, Wm Cleveland, Harry Seamon, Chas Callender, Whallen & Martell, and critics from all the principal cities of the United States, Mexico and Canada, and the leading journals of New, York, Brooklyn, Philadelphia, Boston, Washington, Baltimore, San Francisco, Chicago, Cincinnati and other great cities are responsible for these statements, and if they don't know we would like to know who does. 'These two young men possess a most remarkable faculty for conceiving original stage business in the jail yard scene in 'On the Mississippi.' They convulse the audience with laughter by their queer antics and remarkable funnyisms and they receive numerous encores and ovations for their accurate, odd, fantastic, grotesque and ridiculous merriment."—WILLIAM HAWORTH, author of "On the Mississippi," "Ensign," etc. "Where did you find two natural comedians to fill that place, I didn't know they existed."—JOHN KERNELL. "The Hottest two boys I ever saw and gentlemen withal."—GEO. MILBANK. "I have known McCLAIN and WALKER since their boyhood. I always thought they would get there."—CHAS. HOWARD. "I can't say any thing, only they are gentlemen and artists in their line."—THOMAS A. WISE, Stage Director "On the Mississippi". "I find them above the average and proud to say, I am their manager and they would do credit to anybody's show."—VICTOR HARMON, Mgr. "On the Mississippi.")

We deal in fun, and make it to order. We take this method to inform the profession and theatre going public that our sole object has been to please and amuse all classes of the amusement world, and by so doing we never have hard times, and are always working. We are not doing this to get work, but to show the amusement public that there are two performers and gentlemen in the colored profession that are the natural thing and capable of doing any thing in their line which has been so long mimicked by the buffoonery of burnt cork, fright wigs, painted big mouth and exaggerated obnoxious nuisances. We will admit that there never have been one or two colored comedians who successfully played a part in a melodrama since the days of *Fred Lyons* (now deceased) in J. H. Wallick's "Bandit King," and he was the only one during his days until we sprung into public favor. The gentlemen whose names and influence we have used will verify our statements. Certain managers tried every available way to avoid having white performers to fill the places made vacant by us, but they had to submit to them, for they could not get colored performers that were capable of doing the work justice. So that must give some tone to the men who created and made the parts successful and left the path so hot, no second raters could step into it. Don't be fooled by false reports that we are going to let a good thing drop; the old gag, "When you get a good thing keep it." We believe in character and intelligence, not race and color. If you want any fun repaired and you are around our way, drop over into our yard, we'll "negotiate prerogatives." This invitation is "amplify to diffuse." Your amusement servants,

BILLY McCLAIN AND CHAS. W. WALKER.

BILLY McCLAIN.

The Comedy Genius, born, Indianapolis, Ind., Oct. 12, 1866. From early age he evinced an unusual ability. His professional career began with Lew Johnson's Minstrels, in 1883. Since then he has been at the head of the principal colored shows throughout the country. Mr. McClain composes and arranges his own music, and is one of the few that have made stage work a financial success. Mr. McClain is the author of a four act comedy, which is a revelation to the Afro-American stage, and, with all probability, will be produced by some responsible managers in the near future. "As for an author, McClain has written as pretty melodies as we ever heard."—SPAULDING & GRAY. "The first colored musical director I ever saw was Billy McClain, with 'The South Before the War.' He is fully competent to fill the position."—ROBT. RECKER. "The colored contingent of Pain's 'Storming of Vicksburg,' under the tutorship of Billy McClain, was a show within themselves."—CLEVELAND GAZETTE. "The above portrait is that of Billy McClain, who is at present traveling with Davis & Keough's 'On the Mississippi.' Billy is a jolly good fellow, and has held many prominent positions with the leading colored companies throughout the country. He is a comedian and author of note, and is very popular on and off the stage, and did a great deal to help along the Harry Hill Benefit."—RICHARD K. FOX'S POLICE GAZETTE. "As a trombone player, McClain has few rivals, and was the life of the Cleveland Minstrel Band."—CHRONICLE, San Francisco, Cal. "For general performers, Mc is the best I ever saw."—CHAS CALLENDER, of Callender's Minstrels. "Was the hit of the show at Niblo's Garden."—NEW YORK CLIPPER.

CHAS. W. WALKER.

Chas. W. Walker, born Auburn, Ill., Oct. 15, 1865, he first attracted attention at Springfield, Ill., 12 years later. Since then, he has toured all the principal cities throughout the continent. Mr. Walker is the founder of Walker's Merry Makers, Coats & Walker's Minstrels, and is credited with being the first to introduce cake walking in Cincinnati O. He also is an adept with the guitar, banjo and piano. Mr. Walker was the shining light with Wilson & Stewart's Minstrels, and has always evoked considerable attention, wherever he has appeared. He has always proved to be a gentleman as well a performer. "As for a dancer, Mr. Walker has few rivals for style and exeution; he easily carried the honors and won the medal, which Manager Clark offered for artistic terpsichore."—KANSAS CITY TIMES. "In 'On the Mississippi,' there is Chas. W. Walker, who essayed the role of Andrew Jackson Brown, and was the redeeming feature of the dancers."—WASHINGTON POST. "Mr. Chas W. Walker, of 'The South Before the War' Co., was the cleverest character of its kind ever seen here. Very seldom you see a colored man give a correct description of himself; he is really funny in his natural state, but when upon the stage he most generally over does it, so Mr. Walker is surely deserving of some credit."—NEW YORK SUN.

New York Clipper, *January 12, 1895.*

of the Second Bapt. Church, Monday eve., Jan. 28, and at the Fifth St. Bapt. Church, Wed. Eve., Jan. 30" (*Richmond Planet*).

• ***January 26, 1895 (Baton Rouge, Louisiana):*** "We have two brass bands that discourse sweet and classical music, as well as several string bands" (*Indianapolis Freeman*).

• ***February 2, 1895 (Richmond, Virginia):*** "Sidney Woodward," "Mr. Woodward is 28 years of age, a native of Georgia, of a dark complexion, very courteous and graceful. He has been a resident of Boston between four and five years and has spent about three years in a Conservatory of Music in that city . . .

He feels proud of his position in the Choir of the Congregational Church (white) of Boston and is certainly in our judgement worthy of all the popularity he has thus far won in the musical world. His entertainment at 5th Street Baptist Church, Wednesday, Jan. 30th was witnessed by an appreciative audience.

. . . Mr. Woodward was programmed for a solo entitled 'Fleeting days' for which he substituted, the Spanish song 'I Duo Foscari.' In this he was encored vociferously to which he responded with 'He Tied Her Bonnet Under her Chin.'. . . The Auctioneer was then rendered by Mesdames Walker and Price and Messrs. Reid and Taylor. This quartette was a treat and on being encored sang Sweet and Low. . . Mr. Woodward was here programmed for three numbers viz: 'Celeste,' 'Two Maidens,' 'Ah! I Have Sighed to Rest.' For the solo Two Maidens he substituted 'Beware.' At this point Mr. Woodward reached 'C' above the staff" (*Richmond Planet*).

• ***February 9, 1895 (New York City):*** "People's Theatre," "William Haworth's melodrama, entitled 'On the Mississippi,' opened a week's stay here night of Feb. 4. The occasion marked the first presentation of the melodrama in this city. . . The cast is a competent one. . . The colored people in the drama cleverly performed all they were required to do. Led by William McClain, they were prominent in many of the best scenes of the drama . . . The cast [includes] William McClain, . . . Charles W. Walker . . . [and] Cordelia McClain" (*New York Clipper*).

• ***February 16, 1895:*** "Notes from Shea's 'U.T.C.' Co.," "We are spending the week of Feb. 4 on Davis' Lake, La., to very good business. The weather is warm, and the tent is comfortably filled each night . . . The Colwells closed at Vicksburg, going to New Orleans . . . The present roster of the company [includes] . . . Claude Thornton, Doc Sales [*sic*], Jim Wickersham . . . Our old dog Nero died Sunday, and was buried in the Mississippi River" (*New York Clipper*).

• ***February 16, 1895:*** "In an oratorical contest with six white students Saturday, February 2nd, Charles Winter Woods [*sic*], colored, of Chicago, carried off the first prize at Beloits [*sic*] College in Wisconsin" (*Richmond Planet*).

Note: Born in Nashville, Tennessee, in 1870, Charles Winter Wood graduated from Beloit College in 1895.[19] When Richard B. Harrison died in 1935, Wood took his place as "de Lawd" in the popular play *Green Pastures.* Wood spent most of his professional life as a teacher, first at Tuskegee Institute and later at Florida A&M College in Tallahassee. Wood's elocutionary skills were not always so well appreciated. A report from Mobile, Alabama, in the August 3, 1901, edition of the *Freeman* noted, "Prof. Charles Winter Wood tried to give people of Mobile a specimen of his ability for a week and could not get enough people to encourage him to visit Mobile again; elocution was not their fancy." In 1924 Wood recorded four exemplary recitations for the Black Swan and Paramount labels, including his own original dialect poem, "Honey You Sho Looks Bad," and Paul Laurence Dunbar's "When de Corn Pone's Hot."[20]

• ***February 23, 1895 (Richmond, Virginia):*** "Great Variety Entertainment, For the Sole Benefit of the Poor of Our City, at True Reformers' Hall . . . Tuesday Eve., Feb. 26th. No Expenses, all the proceeds for the poor. The following attractions have been solicited and most have consented: Ciceronian Symphony Orchestra, Mr. John L. Alexander, Violinist; Madame M. A. Cross, Madame Georgie C. Price, Madame Fanny P. Walker, Miss S. Alice Kemp, Miss Gertrude Smith, Mr. Conway B. Reide, The Washington Quartette, The 9th St. Quartette, Miss Hattie Wallace, Mr. A. T. Wright, Mr. Joseph G. James, Miss Mazie Myers and Mr. D. Webster Davis in elocution. Miss Octavia Ferguson, Managing Living Pictures and Living Statuary, The Young Thorp's Trio, The Little Princess, The Hartshorn Students, Mr. Thomas M. Crump, Mrs. Rosa K. Jones, Miss Olivia C. Oliver and Mrs. Lena V. Jackson . . . Admission, 15c" (*Richmond Planet*).

• ***February 23, 1895 (Richmond, Virginia):*** "The Public Calls Them Out," "The Jubilee Songsters of Bethlehem who have won such fame among the lovers of spiritual singing will open up the season at the 6th Mt. Zion Baptist Church, Monday eve., Feb. 25. They are too well known to need any comment, as it is known that they are the best scriptural songsters in the South and the best Scriptural rhymers that the South has produced. We think that the people of Richmond should take interest in these young men and patronize them liberally. We notice that in the North and West when they find that there is a band of singers who are trying to make a mark for themselves and bring credit to the city from which they came, the public tries to help and encourage them. We believe that if the people of Richmond would do that with these songsters it would be a benefit to both parties" (*Richmond Planet*).

Note: The phrase "Scriptural rhymers" seems to be peculiar to this citation.

• ***March 2, 1895:*** "A Couple of Warm Babies at Shea's Music Hall, Buffalo, N.Y. this week. Al. and Mamie Anderson, the Two Black Mascots.

Producers of Genuine Southern Comedy. Route: Shea's Music Hall, week Feb. 25; Wonderland Musee, Erie, Pa., March 4; Keokuk, Ia., 11; Eden Musee, Quincy, Ill., 18; Eden Musee, Saint Joe, Mo., 24; Novelty Theatre, Kansas City, Mo., April 1; Olympic Theatre, Chicago, Ill., 8; South Clark St. Musee, 15; Globe Museum, 29. P.S.—A Big Success Everywhere" (*New York Clipper*).

• ***March 8, 1895:*** "Current Events At Wilberforce U.," "Friday night our six Native African Students, organized as the 'Wilberforce Kaffir Choir' rendered a well selected program, singing in English, then in their own native language, giving most interesting and instructive talks upon life in Africa. Particularly so was the story of the 'African Witch Doctor,' and illustrating the manner in which Missionaries must preach to the natives. The Africans have remarkable fine voices [*sic*]; worthy of mention, Mrs. Manye and Mr. Krtiya" (*Kansas City American Citizen*).

Note: In an earlier report from Wilberforce, the *Richmond Planet* of January 26, 1895, noted the "registration of . . . four additional African students . . . Miss Charlotte Amilia Manye, age 24, Basuto tribe, Kimberly, Diamond Fields; Mr. Edward Tolitte Magaya, age 21, Fingo tribe, Craddock, Cape Colony, South Africa; Mr. James Nxanxani N. Kolombe, age 25, Ngqika tribe, Queenstown, Cape Colony South Africa and Mr. John Boyana Radabe, age 28, Fingo tribe, Seymour, Cape Colony, South Africa . . .

"Mr. Moyazo Fanele Sakie, who is about 24 years old and belongs to the Ngqika tribe, living at Grahamstown, Cape Colony, South Africa has exhibited most excellent qualities of mind and disposition during his stay of about three months. These African people, although they have spent nearly two years in this country giving engagements under an American agent, are without means of support and fully merit the charity of the benevolent."

• ***March 9, 1895:*** "Sadie Jones presented her husband, Irving Jones, with a baby boy on Feb. 28" (*New York Clipper*).

• ***March 23, 1895:*** "Miss Hallie Q. Brown in Manchester, England," "On Tuesday evening, Feb. 19th Miss Hallie Q. Brown . . . of Wilberforce College, O., commenced a series of lectures and recitals in [Manchester, England] . . .

February 23rd, saw Miss Brown at Salford under the patronage of Rev. F. Hill (Episcopalian) and the Rev. Jas. Clarke. Again Miss Brown charmed the large audience assembled with her songs and recitations. Her rendering of 'The Elf Child,' 'Aunt Jemima's Courtship,' and the 'Reading Class' being greeted with shrieks of laughter. Her recital of 'Rock of Ages,' which immediately followed was such as we have never heard equalled. Commencing with the 'Wild Woodland' Notes of a fresh girlish voice it gradually changes to those of a woman upon whom 'Life's battle,' is beginning to tell, then to the feeble, tremulous chords of the aged, greyhaired saint, just about to step 'over the border,' and finally we hear them sung over the closed coffin . . .

February 23rd from 5 to 7 o'clock was spent at an 'At Home' given by Mr. W. E. A. and Mrs. Axon to enable Miss Brown to meet a select coterie of friends. Before leaving she was requested to speak on the mode of living practiced by the Negroes on the plantations . . . She then proceeded to Lever St. Wesleyan Schools Picadilly, where she was announced to lecture on 'Women and the Drinking Saloon,' under the auspices of the Manchester and Salford Temperance Union . . . On account of the news of Hon. Frederick Douglass' death having just reached us, Miss Brown begged permission to give a short sketch of his life instead of the lecture arranged and never shall we forget her magnificent eulogy on this great and noble man . . .

The following afternoon Miss Brown gave a short address and sang plantation hymns in the

Miles Platting Mission room, Newton Heath, and in the evening lectured on the progress of Negro education" (*Richmond Planet*).

• ***March 23, 1895 (Richmond, Virginia):*** "The Massachusetts Committee on Mercantile Affairs has been making a tour of a portion of the South, visiting mills and factories . . . [including] Patterson's tobacco factory. Here they were shown how chewing tobacco is manufactured. In the stemming room were a large number of colored persons both male and female.

The singing was inspiring, and when one of the songsters broke forth with 'Marching through Georgia' there was a noticeable change in the northern men" (*Richmond Planet*).

Note: Since the days of slavery, Richmond's tobacco factories had been a particular destination for tourists in search of "authentic Negro singing." Among those who made the pilgrimage in 1849 was William Cullen Bryant.[21]

• ***March 29, 1895:*** "Dr. J. C. Brownfield has a large practice and they still come. His concert of selected and well trained singers will leave soon to advertise his medicines on the road, but the Doctor will be compelled to remain among his patients" (*Kansas State Ledger*).

• ***March 30, 1895 (Piqua, Ohio):*** "A Native's Lecture," "Mr. Sakie, a native of Africa, delivered a very interesting lecture on the customs of his people at the A.M.E. Church Tuesday. He explained their ignorance, superstition, etc., and also delivered the Lord's Prayer in the Kaffir language. He is a student at Wilberforce and has adopted the name of Daniel A. Payne" (*Cleveland Gazette*).

• ***April 13, 1895 (Bryan, Texas):*** "Mr. A. K. Cole has tendered his resignation as manager of the 'Black Diamond' a local ministrel [*sic*]. He has accepted a position with Dr. F. E. King's traveling medicine show" (*Indianapolis Freeman*).

• ***April 13, 1895:*** "Roster of the Colored Sports Co.—Afro-American Trio, Yeager and Woode, Barrie McPhail, Billy Wilson, Tommie Brandon, Rastus, the Numans, Elm City Quartet, Lulu Walker, Ella Payne, Mable Wallace, Little Ruth, Maude Ashe, Freddie Williams . . . We open our Spring and Summer season April 15, at Quincy, Mass.

"Roster of the Haliday Sisters Colored Specialty Co.—Charles Preston, proprietor and manager; Haliday Sisters, Edward H. Winn, Billy Tull, Billy Miller, West Jenkins, Alton Lightfoot, Harry Scott, Sonnie Hall, Charles Mahoney, Gertie McFarland, Jessie Thompson, John Turner, Daisy Mitchel, Billy Porter, J. Newton Europe, musical director" (*New York Clipper*).

Note: John Newton Europe was James Reese Europe's older brother.[22]

• ***April 27, 1895:*** "Marie Selika, the 'Brown Patti,' will appear in concert in Boston, May 9. The 'Black Patti' is in Europe, as is also the white Patti, and the 'Creole Patti' is somewhere in the South. The 'Yellow Patti,' the 'Green Patti' and the 'Red Patti' will break loose shortly" (*Leavenworth Herald*).

• ***April 27, 1895 (South Charleston, Ohio):*** "The Wilberforce National African Concerters will remain over until Sabbath and furnish music for the Shorter Chapel [A.M.E.] Church. Mr. Bayana Radasi, of Africa will preach" (*Indianapolis Freeman*).

• ***May 4, 1895:*** "Madame Jones' Great Success," "Madame Sissieretta Jones, the 'Black Patti' is singing in Germany. She leaves for Berlin, Germany, then for London, England where she will remain about six weeks.

She will return home to fulfill her engagements at Asbury Park, the Pittsburg Exhibition and Saratoga, New York.

After this she will return to Germany to sing for two years . . .

Madame Jones sang for the Emperor of Germany, April 5th. He was so much pleased that he ordered a diamond cross made for her.

It will be a grand thing when finished" (*Richmond Planet*).

• ***May 4, 1895:*** "In the cake walk contest, April 28, at Miner's Bowery Theatre, this city [New York], the cake was won by Frank Mallory and Marie Roberts. Both are members of Sam T. Jack's Creole Co." (*New York Clipper*).

• ***May 11, 1895 (Springfield, Ohio):*** "A phonograph concert was given at the 2nd Baptist Church . . . The instrument used was Edison's 1895 concert phonograph, by means of which all were enabled to hear at the same time. The programme consisted of selections by well-known bands and orchestras, as well as solos and readings by eminent singers and readers. A selection by the church choir was reproduced, to the delight of the audience" (*Cleveland Gazette*).

• ***May 18, 1895:*** "Al. and Mamie Anderson, Southern plantation sketch performers, will arrive at their homes, Boston, Mass., June 2, and close there for the Summer. They will open next season about September, with a new act entitled 'Echoes of de Ole Mississippi' " (*New York Clipper*).

• ***June 1, 1895 (Richmond, Virginia):*** "Come! Come! Come!" "There will be a Grand Musical Entertainment at Asbury M.E. Church, 25th St., between N and O St., on the Electric Car Line, Monday Evening, June 3, 1895, by the Polished Tongue Quartette. Mrs. Francis Cox, Soprano; Mrs. Sophia Dillard, Alto; Prof. W. T. Day, Tenor; Prof. W. H. Russell, Basso; Miss Mildred Anderson, Pianist.

The Polished Tongue Quartette of Lynchburg are the best Musical Singers in the State" (*Richmond Planet*).

• ***June 8, 1895:*** "Mme. Flower, of Piper and Flower, is filling a short engagement at Ambrose Park. Mr. Piper was compelled to cancel an engagement while preparing for his annual Summer tour. They are engaged with J. Isham's Royal Octoroons for next season" (*New York Clipper*).

• ***June 8, 1895:*** "Palmer, the barber had been very ill and looked very much unlike himself as he crept from chair to chair in the shop of McQueen and Co., on 3rd Avenue in Brooklyn one chilly afternoon, when I entered and joined the group of loungers around the stove . . . The topic of conversation on this particular afternoon was music, vocal and instrumental, singers and performers of renown and repute, songs that were new, old songs that would never die . . . Palmer, who had been a silent and attentive listener finally spoke up and said: 'I have travelled very extensively as a tenor singer in minstrels, was also a choir leader in Brooklyn for a good many years. Failing health together with age has caused me to give up these, yet I love to hear good singing with good accent and expression . . . There are two songs that are special favorites of mine . . . and I never tire of hearing them sung. One is: "See that my grave's kept green," and the other one still sweeter is, "Jesus Is Mine." ' He cleared his throat and began to sing with a voice that though somewhat cracked had not lost its sweetness:

'Fade, fade each earthly joy,
Jesus is mine;
Break every tender tie,
Jesus is mine;
Dark is the wilderness,
Earth has no resting place,
Jesus alone can bless,
Jesus is mine.'

His voice was growing husky, there were tears in his eyes. We joined him on the second verse for we too were filled with emotion:

'Tempt not my soul away,
Jesus is mine;
Here would I ever stay,
Jesus is mine;

All that my soul has tried,
Leaves but a dismal void
Jesus has satisfied,
Jesus is mine.'

He could sing no longer, his strength was failing him, and the last line was just a whisper—'Jesus is mine.'... After closing the shop we walked together, Palmer and I as far as Atlantic avenue. There we separated. I saw him no more. A few mornings afterwards... in the hospital was laid all that was mortal of Palmer. The death angel had passed during the night and with icy hand had touched him perhaps with the last line of that favorite hymn upon his lips—'Jesus is mine.' ...

Who knows what atonement he made for a life of sin within those brief hours ...

'See that my grave's kept green.'

Were there no friends or kindred near to heed that request? Not one. This poor wretch whom it seemed the world had turned its back upon, has had quite an eventful career. Born in or near Alexandria, Va., he left home during Grant's first term as President, leaving behind a wife and several children... It is said that at one time Palmer was one of the most popular colored barbers in Brooklyn, that he was a leader of a very popular church choir, that he dressed in the height of fashion and mingled with the elite... Though there be no one to sod and keep that grave green... and though no choir stood around to chant a requiem over the departed leader, the Nightingale will sing a lullaby" ("Jack Thorne," *Richmond Planet*).

• ***June 15, 1895:*** "Eaton & Weather's Pavilion Minstrels are playing a two week's engagement at Kohler's Pavilion Theatre, North Beach, L.I., N.Y. Roster: Eaton and Weathers, Billy Young, Wesley Norris, Jerry Mills, Hen. Wise, Tom Brown, Billy Farrell and (6) Octoroon ladies, in drills, etc." (*New York Clipper*).

Note: From his partnership with Ernest Hogan in 1889 to his partnership with Alfred Weathers in 1895, Harry S. Eaton had been a dedicated, workhorse minstrel performer and entrepreneur. A note in 1898 advised, "Harry Eaton and Alf Weathers have dissolved partnership... Mr. Eaton is managing the Ike Hines' Colored Theatrical Club and Vaudeville Exchange, at 118 West Twenty-Seventh Street, New York City."[23] Upon his death in 1904, the *Freeman* made note that Harry S. Eaton was born in Knoxville, Tennessee, and was "about fifty years of age." It was also asserted that Eaton's career had been haunted by sudden changes of luck, "to such an extent that many managers and performers began to look upon him as a 'Jonah,' and expressed it."[24]

• ***June 15, 1895 (Springfield, Ohio):*** "The South African choir sang at North Street church last Sunday morning. They came up to sing for the mens' meeting of the YMCA which was held at the First Presbyterian church in the afternoon, and also sang at the First Lutheran Church in the evening" (*Cleveland Gazette*).

• ***June 22, 1895:*** "Denton's Genuine Colored Georgia Minstrels will open their Summer season June 24, at Flushing, L.I., under a canvas top, 40 × 80. The company will be under the management of M. M. Lavene, and will number twenty people, with a uniformed brass band. Roster: Billy Young, Edward Denton, Jerry Mills, Hen. Wise, Lew Henry, Billy Bradley, Will Better, Will Hill, Mrs. Wise, Sarah Peachy, Lil. Russell, Mamie Cartwell, Rocksey Nichols, Geo. Fisher, Bertie Smith and Roenia Washington" (*New York Clipper*).

• ***June 22, 1895 (Leavenworth, Kansas):*** "Wednesday morning we saw a white fakir on the streets with a harp in his mouth, a triangle on his head, an accordion in his hands, and a bass drum on his back, playing them all at once, and they made the poorest music we ever heard.

When a white man makes up his mind to quit work, he goes at something that is generally a nuisance to the public" (*Leavenworth Herald*).

• ***July 6, 1895 (Muskogee, "Indian Territory"):*** "Last Monday morning at 11 o'clock representatives from all the F.A. & M. lodges in Indian Territory and Oklahoma met at the Muskogee Masonic hall. They paraded through the principal streets of the city led by the Webbers Fall colored brass band to the fair ground where a large crowd and all the barbecued beef, mutton and pork that could be expected awaited them. The procession was fully a quarter mile long and was one of the greatest colored Masonic exhibitions that has ever been in this city" (*Indianapolis Freeman*).

• ***July 6, 1895 (New York City):*** "Among the many people who turned out with the Colored Theatrical Club on June 27 were Tom McIntosh, H. C. Williams, Tom Brown, Harry S. Eaton, Will H. Young, Bob Cole, Ed. Goggin, Chas. T. Davis, Burt Grant, Cole M. Grant, Billy Johnson, One Billy Farrell, Wesley B. Norris, the Standard Quartet (Ed. De Moss, H. C. Williams, Will Cotrell and R. L. Scott), the Unique, Twilight, Caliope and Symphony Quartets, together with J. J. Christian, James Wilson, Robert Biggs, Fred D. Height, Fred J. Piper, all of whom were headed by the genial boniface, Ike Hines, the steward of the Professional Club Hotel, and Jos. C. Hodges (of Hodges and Launchmere), the only two surviving members of the original Twilight Quartet, and many others who marched to the jubilant music dispensed by Profs. Miles Terry and Bob Frazier's Professional Club's Band. They report having had an excellent time and added much financial gain to their benevolent organization" (*New York Clipper*).

• ***July 13, 1895:*** "A Colored Professional Club has been organized in Baltimore, Md., with the following enrolled as officers and members: H. E. Morton, president; John Davis, vice president; Will Gross, O. Murray, Bob Green, Kid Tolson, Alf. Harden, Tom Cooper, Joe Peterson, Edward Cooper, Hawk Edwards and the Alhambra and Eastern Spring Quartet. The headquarters are prepared for the reception of professionals when they visit that city" (*New York Clipper*).

• ***July 20, 1895:*** " 'A Cracker Jack' Co. goes into rehearsals at Detroit, Mich., Aug. 6, and opens the season at Defiance, O., Aug. 19. This company will be under the management of John C. Fox, and will have as a feature a little darky band of twelve pieces" (*New York Clipper*).

• ***July 20, 1895:*** "The Sylvester Russell Summer Specialty Co., opened at Marshall Hall, Asbury Park, N.J., July 12, with the following people: Clarence Powell, comedian; J. Xertus Jones, contortionist; Irving Scuyler, instrumentalist; Prof. Chas. Halloway, guitarist; Sylvester Russell, contra tenor, and Prof. W. H. Lang, leader" (*New York Clipper*).

• ***July 27, 1895:*** " 'In Old Virginia' will open the season Aug. 19, at Cincinnati, O. [with] the Alhambra Quartet" (*New York Clipper*).

• ***July 27, 1895:*** "Manager Ed. R. Salter, of Salter & Marten's 'Uncle Tom's Cabin' Co., is at present in Peru, Ind., preparing a car for the transportation of his company during the coming season . . . and it is announced that special features of the production will be two horses, two mules, three burros, two oxen, two donkeys, eight Shetland ponies and six bloodhounds; three bands of music, white, colored and ladies' band; a troupe of Georgia shouters, pickaninnies and jubilee singers . . . The tour will begin Aug. 29" (*New York Clipper*).

• ***July 27, 1895 (Boston, Massachusetts):*** "Palace Theatre," "Manager Wm. Austin swings out a catchy bill of fare for the amusement seeking public of the week of [July] 22 . . . [including] a brand new musical sketch, entitled 'Uncle Josh,' in which will appear two female teams

COMPLETE SCENIC PRODUCTION OF THE FOREMOST AMERICAN DRAMA.

INTERPRETED BY A THOROUGHLY FIRST CLASS COMPANY OF DRAMATIC ARTISTS.

PRESENTED IN ITS ORIGINALITY WITH ALL THE ESSENTIAL FEATURES.

AN ORGANIZATION NECESSITATING AN ACTUAL OUTLAY OF TWELVE THOUSAND DOLLARS.

TRAVELING IN OUR OWN CARS, CONSISTING OF SLEEPING AND DINING COACHES, BAGGAGE AND STOCK CARS.

SALTER & MARTIN

MAMMOTH ORIGINAL

"Uncle Tom's Cabin"

CO.

GEO. DORSEY as UNCLE TOM.

WANTED, TO STRENGTHEN JAMES DOLAN'S IMPERIAL BAND AND ORCHESTRA,

30---MUSICIANS---30

White and Colored, who double in brass and orchestra, or stage; Quartets, Shouters, Pickaninnies, First Class Dramatic People, and a Female Band, about eight in number. Also a White and Colored Drum Major. Address
366 SIXTH STREET, DETROIT, MICH.

WE CARRY ALL SCENERY AND EFFECTS,

ELECTRICAL APPARATUS,

MALE AND FEMALE PICKANINNY SINGERS AND DANCERS,

THE GEORGIA SHOUTERS AND JUBILEE SINGERS,

TWO FINELY EQUIPPED BRASS BANDS
(White and Colored),

A SUPERB ORCHESTRA,

AND THE FOLLOWING STOCK FOR THE PROPER PRESENTATION:

Horses, Oxen, Mules, Dogs, Donkeys, Shetland Ponies, Carriages, Carts and Wagons.

Every Sheet of Paper Lithographed and Newly Designed.

Introducing a Parade that for Novelty and Expense has never been Equaled by a Traveling Combination.

New York Clipper, *July 20, 1895.*

in a baseball match; the Ninepin Quartet and a troupe of real Northern darkies in their delineations of 'coon' life to the core" (*New York Clipper*).

• ***August 3, 1895 (Baltimore, Maryland):*** "Our Churches," "Services of the Division St. Bapt. Church," "Our watermelon fest was opened last Monday. It will continue through all the month of Aug. Music by the Crescent Cornet Band on Monday and Thursday, a literary Concert by the Sunday school scholars. On Wednesday Miss Alverta and Jenette Caroll will entertain the audience with one of their famous duets . . . Cards of admission 10 Cts. Watermelon free" (*Baltimore Afro-American*).

• ***August 3, 1895:*** "Master Frezon Deleon, the boy drum major has signed with the 'In Old Virginia' Co. . . . and the Alhambra Quartet and Mlle. Almeda have signed with this company, the latter to play the lady of the plantation" (*New York Clipper*).

• ***August 10, 1895:*** "Notes from the Original Tennessean Jubilee Singers—We have succeeded in completing the roster of our company. . . Rehearsals begin Aug. 15, will take the road about Sept. 1. Our roster: Sam R. Snowden and Phil R. Miller, proprietors and managers; Clara Belle Carey, soprano; Belle Stone, contralto; Jessie Ogdent, contralto; George Conley, tenor; Fred T. Carey, tenor; J. A. Hagerman, basso, and A. B. Johnson, pianist" (*New York Clipper*).

• ***August 17, 1895:*** "Edward E. Nickerson's Colossal Comedy Company, Grand Military Band and Concert Orchestra [white] . . . Mr. Nickerson has also engaged the original Mobile Four, singing, buck and wing dancing pickaninnies" (*New York Clipper*).

• ***August 24, 1895:*** " 'Coon Hollow' opened the season at Wilkesbarre, Pa., Aug. 19. The company [includes] . . . Walter Kelley, the Calliope Quartet, Coon Hollow Quartet, and a troupe of colored buck and wing dancers" (*New York Clipper*).

• ***August 24, 1895:*** "The Old and the Young Negro Compared," "It is becoming shamefully customary for these young, school-sent fellows . . . to be forever and anon harping upon the ignorance and oddities of their fathers and grandfathers . . . The old men, and women too, were up at day dawn Sabbath morning, wending their way to the church of God to prayer meeting

Stowe & Co.'s Colossal "Uncle Tom's Cabin."

LARGEST AND BEST IN THE WORLD.

50 PEOPLE, WHITE AND COLORED, 50

2 full Brass Bands and Pickaninny Fife and Drum Corps. A grand spectacular scenic production. A street parade surpassing anything ever seen, presenting more novel features than was ever conceived by the mind of man. 3 special cars required to transport this, the World's Grandest "U. T. C." Our carload of new special scenery an entertainment in itself. The only company in the world ever presenting a genuine Cotton Gin and Press in full operation. The Wonderful Mechanical Steamboat Scene. The grandest of stage-pictures, and many other new and beautiful stage settings. Clell Cassity, write.

Including a "Pickaninny Fife and Drum Corps," New York Clipper, *August 24, 1895.*

. . . They would often sing, pray, preach, exhort and praise God all night long . . . We have known the old men, even in slave time, to preach with such power that rowdy white fellows, who would go to their meetings to disturb them, would fall under conviction . . . Who among the pimple-headed, mocking preachers of today can do it? . . . The truth is they are not fit to untie the shoe latchets of the old preachers.

When we leave the old Christians and turn to the old sinners, the same grade of superiority is found . . . When they danced, they displayed an agility with their feet, that resembled the wings of a human bird and double shuffled and cut 'the pigeon wing' in a manner that the young generation can no more do than they can fly. Among the old men, were found the finest fiddlers, banjo and guitar pickers, jewsharp blowers, five reed blowers and adepts in all kinds of music, except the piano (which were only owned by one in ten thousand among the whites) that were in the land. But now if there is a first class young fiddler among the Negroes at all, we venture to say, there is not more than one to every million. We have not heard a colored fiddler in fifteen years, who could do much more than scratch the instrument with a bow. The Negro fiddler of today, can no more equal Henry Lester of Abbeville, S.C., Vince Arnold, of Anderson, John Fawks, of Columbia, Si Williams, of Augusta, Jacob Herrinton, of Montgomery, Ala, Lucius Gray of Nashville, Tenn, Bill Springs of Wilmington, N.C., and a thousand others, than we can compare with a nightingale. As for Si Williams, he could literally make his fiddle talk. He could ask the dancers by his fiddle 'to draw partners,' and then he could ask, 'if they were ready,' and finally, when they had danced sufficiently, he could say with his fiddle, 'you had better rest awhile.' Is there a Negro fiddler in the United States who can do it to-day? But why continue this comparison?" (*Voice of Missions*, reproduced in *Indianapolis Freeman*).

• ***August 29, 1895:*** "Notes from Puggsley Bros.," "We are in our third week at Shamokin, Pa., drawing big crowds. S. T. Whitney, our basso, is making hits every night in songs and doing his specialties. Master Erma's impersonations go well. W. H. Hunt, the baritone, has joined us for the Summer . . . We will produce 'Black South' this week, with Princess Josephine and S. T. Whitney in the leading roles" (*New York Clipper*).

Note: Under the guidance of Salem Tutt Whitney and his brother J. Homer Tutt, the Smart Set Company became one of the most successful black road shows of the 1910s. "Master Erma," a.k.a. "Ermie" Puggsley, young lion of the Puggsley family, is best remembered for his prowess at the piano. In 1916 he replaced the legendary Sam Davis as pianist and leader of the pioneering four-piece jazz band with Drake and Walker's Bombay Girls.

• ***August 30, 1895:*** "A Negro's Ballads," "Few of the many millions of people who have sung or otherwise enjoyed 'The Fatal Wedding,' 'The Light house by the Sea,' and 'The Maple on the Hill,' and numerous other popular songs are aware that Gussie L. Davis, the man who composed them, is a negro. Davis, who is still a very young man, spent his boyhood in Cincinnati, where he became acquainted with James K. Stewart, the author of 'Jenny, the Flower of Kildare' and other well known ballads. Davis had considerable talent for song writing..., and Stewart, before he died a drunkard in the Cincinnati work house, gave him a great many points concerning the business.

Davis' first song was 'Maple on the Hill'... and it was such a great success that he decided to make song writing his life work. With commendable pluck he procured work as a chore boy in a Chicago musical college and worked his way through the institution, devoting three years to hard study.

About this time he fell in love with a pretty octoroon girl of Cincinnati, Miss Lottie B. Stark, who gave him the inspiration for one of his most successful songs in prosaic manner. She sent him a pair of suspenders upon which was embroidered a good likeness of a lighthouse and a ship. Davis naturally admired the suspenders and looked at them so long and earnestly that he concluded to write a song about a lighthouse and a ship. The result was 'Lighthouse by the Sea,' a song that won wide popularity a few years ago and was played by street bands and hand organs from one end of the country to the other.

Davis married the pretty octoroon in 1885, and she has been of great assistance to him in his musical work. They live in New York, and Davis has already written about 500 songs" (*Kansas City American Citizen*).

• ***August 30, 1895 (Topeka, Kansas):*** "Dr. W. W. Watkins," "The well-known medicine company and show, Dr. W. W. Watkins' of Carthage, Mo., has begun giving nightly exhibitions at 4th and Quincy streets. They have with them the famous Pete and Lize, who were with this company two years ago, and Dr. Bruce, the renowned tooth extracter. See them" (*Kansas State Ledger*).

• ***September 13, 1895 (Topeka, Kansas):*** "The marriage of Mr. I. T. Owens and Dora Young took place at the family residence, 1226 Topeka Ave., last Friday evening...The Silver Leaf Quartette made merry the time with music

"DOWN ON THE SUWANEE RIVER."

"Down on the Suwanee River," the Afro-American, fantastical, farcical and musical extravaganza which will be presented at Crawford's Opera house tomorrow, Sunday night, is a great laugh-producer and was designed to be exclusively a fun show; the piece is divided into three acts. The first shows the Negro as a savage in Africa and presents him in all his natural environment on the burning sands of the Dark Continent. The background for this act is a gorgeous, tropical, spectacular scene, painted by John H. Young, the noted scenic artist of the Broadway Theater, New York. King Boom-de-Aye is disclosed in his royal village of Bakuba, beset by a world of trouble created by his fetichmen, his wives and myriad of mothers-in law, a white and a black missionary from America, a big gorilla who insists on pelting the king with cocoanuts, and the near proximity of a band of slave-hunters, who are intent on the capture of him and his entire village and their transportation to America as slaves. The king sentences the two missionaries to be boiled in a pot, and their efforts to escape their steaming liquid doom furnish a large part of the comedy in the first act. To capture the slave-hunters, the king pretends friendship and gives them an entertainment which serves to introduce several specialties in the way of war songs and dances. Instead of capturing the slave-hunters, they capture the king and his people and take them all to America, where they are sold as slaves to the orange-planters on the Suwanee river. All the costumes, weapons and musical instruments used in the first act are exact duplicates of originals brought from Matabeleland by a British traveler. The second act takes place on an orange plantation on the Suwanee river in Florida. This part is literally filled with most intensely interesting specialties in singing and dancing and original plantation diversions, showing the characteristic life of the slave in the South before the war. Two immensely great features of this act are a pie-eating match and a challenge dancing contest, in which fifteen solo dancers of great ability and the entire company appear. The finale of the second act is the emancipation of slaves by President Lincoln, which carries the Negro on to the third stage of his career. This act takes place in a social hall in Thompson street, New York, and displays the life of the Negro in a great city as he is today. This act, too, is filled with great specialties. The final feature of the entire performance is an old-fashioned Virginia cakewalk, more artistically presented than anything ever before seen, in which twenty ladies and gentlemen and a full brass band of sixteen colored instrumentalists appear. This piece has made a great hit in Detroit, where it was first presented five weeks ago, and in Chicago, St. Louis and Kansas City. The production will undoubtedly attract wide attention.

Extraordinary announcement: William McClain is the principal comedian with this show!

Leavenworth Herald, *September 14, 1895.*

2 ORIGINAL BLACK MASCOTS 2
Al and Mamie Anderson
WE ARE THE LEADERS IN OUR LINE.
ROUGH PLANTATION SKETCH TEAM
AND
Burlesque Buck Dancers.
HOTTEST GENUINE COLORED ACT IN AMERICA.
Couple of Warm Babies.
THIS WEEK, HOWARD ATHENÆUM, BOSTON, MASS.

New York Clipper, *September 21, 1895.*

suited for the occasion. The two distinguished young men of Watkins' Medicine Company were on hand, and everything was pleasantly carried out" (*[Topeka] Kansas State Ledger*).

• ***September 14, 1895:*** "Caldwell's Minstrel Notes," "(W)e opened with our Colored Operatic Minstrels at Silver City, Ia., on Aug. 31 . . . We carry sixteen people, including band and orchestra. Rob't Caldwell, proprietor, is managing the tour. The stage is under the direction of W. S. Levard, Jas. F. Wolfscale, S. J. Wright" (*New York Clipper*).

• ***September 14, 1895 (McKeesport, Pennsylvania):*** "Camp Meetings—Used To Make Money For Street Car Lines," "It is astonishing to what extent the almighty dollar will lead people. Two of our traction companies in different directions are running camp meetings Sunday to draw crowds over their respective lines. Each have a sort of a preacher employed, and one of them advertized for Sunday week that Rappanhanoc Somebody would prove that the world is flat, and for last Sunday that 'de sun do move.' Tis a pity that we have such characters calling themselves ministers of God, who will become a party to such questionable methods" (*Cleveland Gazette*).

• ***September 21, 1895:*** "I would like to make a reply to an article published in *The Freeman* on [August] 24th [1895] . . . I trust none of our noble and worthy, young 'school sent,' preachers will be discouraged by thinking they are not as eligible as the old ones . . .

We feel sorry for a person that would say there are no dancers, banjo pickers, etc. As to the dancing you may find a Negro anywhere that can dance every step as neat and pretty as you want to see, from the old 'back step' down to the 'Pas Malas,' the latest out. Besides this we have educated dancers. Why who would want to hear any better music, on banjos, guitars, fiddles or see any better steps performed than by the Nashville students? Now of course we know of no fiddlers who can make their instruments talk, but we know some that can make imitations of vocal sounds" (A. G. Lindsay, Neosho, Mo., *Indianapolis Freeman*).

• ***September 28, 1895 (Helena, Montana):*** "An Enterprising Citizen," "Prof. E. G. Cole has a second hand store which has been doing good business. He has everything for sale . . . Prof. Cole has his hands full. You can see him all over town buying furniture, collecting, taking contracts for painting, kalsomining, etc. He keeps from eight to ten men employed at the various jobs. Prof. Cole plays ten different instruments. He is director of the Cole's Colored Cornet Band" (*Indianapolis Freeman*).

• ***September 28, 1895:*** "Roster of S. B. Hyers' Colored Musical Comedy Co: Quegga (May C. Hyers), Nellie U. Small, Clara Johnson, Dora Peterson, Chas. U. Small, Billie Cook, Ed. Parker, E. L. Reynolds, Prof. J. C. S. Crooms, S. B. Hyers, promoter and manager, H. O. Wickham, business manager" (*New York Clipper*).

Note: Following the death of S. B. Hyers in 1896,[25] his company was taken over by L. Milt Boyer, who continued under the original banner of S. B. Hyers, with May C. Hyers as his principal star. In the *New York Clipper* of July, 25, 1896, Boyer announced "the opening of our twenty-second season... Harris' Pickaninny Band of fifteen pieces... joins at Muskegon, Mich." Between touring seasons in 1898 he reported, "May C. Hyer is singing better than ever. She is at present engaged, under my management, with the Kansas City Talking Machine Co.... Next season will see a revival of 'The Blackville Twins' and 'Out of Bondage' with a fine colored cast."[26] On September 15, 1899, "Boyer Bros. 'Uncle Tom's Cabin' Co." opened a new season at Gardner, Kansas, with "the Mobile Pickaninnies, Tennessee Jubilee Quartet, May C. Hyers," and others.[27] May C. Hyers remained active into the early 1900s, at least.

• ***October 12, 1895 (Dayton, Ohio):*** "W. C. Evans of Boston, was here representing a phonographic machine, with which he entertains hundreds of people" (*Cleveland Gazette*).

• ***October 19, 1895 (Chicago, Illinois):*** "The Globe Museum will have the Midway features, including dancing and oriental specialties. Coat's Colored Minstrels will present 'Way Down in Georgia" (*New York Clipper*).

• ***October 19, 1895 (Richmond, Virginia):*** "Mr. Theodore Drury, the eminent Afro-American Baritone, assisted by Richmond talent will give a grand Operatic Concert, Friday evening, October 25th at 8 P.M., at the Third St. A.M.E. Church... His songs embrace compositions by nearly all of the great masters from Wagner, Massenet, Gounod to Bizet, with springling [*sic*] of writers of higher music" (*Richmond Planet*).

• ***November 9, 1895 (Leavenworth, Kansas):*** "As THE HERALD has often said before, the stage is doing more to promote the interests of the colored people than any other profession of which we can at present speak. 'The Dazzler' of last year had colored performers; Cleveland's Minstrels had colored performers; 'The Derby Winner' carries colored performers; 'The Coon Hollow' company carries colored performers; Sam Jack's Extravaganza company has them; 'In Old Kentucky' has them; and a great many other shows, run by whites, have them. 'Down on the Suwanee River' and 'In Old Tennessee' are run by colored people, with a sprinkling of whites. Primrose and West's Minstrels, which showed here Thursday night, were no doubt the greatest aggregation of whites and blacks in point of number and talent seen in this city at any time. Primrose and West's minstrels have two colored bands—a Pickininny Band and a band composed of elderly gentlemen. They are both good and represent the colored contingent of the show admirably. We do not know whether or not it is because these shows can get a good many colored performers for the same price that they pay for a few whites, but we do know that the managers are opening an avenue which heretofore has been closed to colored performers; and we ought to feel thankful for that" (*Leavenworth Herald*).

• ***November 9, 1895:*** "Notes from Salter and Martin's 'U.T.C.' Co.," "We have just engaged the four pickaninnies who have been with Eddie Foy this season... We now have eight pickaninnies. Henry Higgins, one of the 'Georgia Shouters,' has rejoined after an absence of three weeks" (*New York Clipper*).

• ***November 16, 1895 (Hot Springs, Arkansas):*** "The Pickaninny Quartet is a coming quartet of the state" (*Indianapolis Freeman*).

• ***November 29, 1895:*** "The Slayton Jubilee Singers, a colored organization, were refused entertainment at the principal hotel at Hiawatha, Kan., and the manager threatens to bring suit

...JUBILEE SONGS...

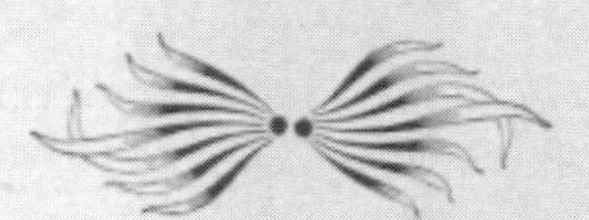

AS SUNG BY

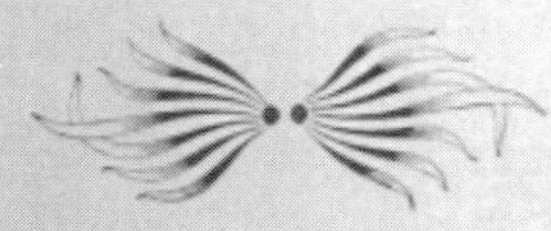

Slayton's Jubilee Singers

THE SLAYTON LYCEUM BUREAU,

PROPRIETORS AND MANAGERS.

CENTRAL MUSIC HALL. —— CHICAGO.

Cover of Slayton Jubilee Singers songbook, n.d. (courtesy Charles Horner) against the proprietor" (*Kansas City American Citizen*).

• ***November 30, 1895 (Westminster, Maryland):*** "A colored minstrel troupe has been organized in Westminster, known as the Frisby and Edwards Bros.' Refined Minstrels. It is one of the finest organized in this county. Among the troupe may be mentioned Wm. L. Edwards, stage manager; Frank S. Frisby, musical director; R. H. B. Edwards, foreman; Wm. Hill, tenor; Joseph Wilson, guitar soloist; Miss Gracella Blanch Edwards, the favorite soloist of Westminster" (*Baltimore Afro-American*).

• ***November 30, 1895 (New York City):*** "Proctor's Pleasure Palace," "Thanksgiving week found an interesting bill at this resort, and on the opening day, Nov. 25, the commodious house was well filled. The Black Patti (Siseretta [*sic*] Jones) made her first appearance since her return from Europe, and was received with tumultuous applause" (*New York Clipper*).

• ***December 7, 1895:*** "Ever since George Primrose popularized 'Standing On The Corner [Didn't Mean No Harm]' and May Irwin 'Mamie Come Kiss Your Honey Boy,' Negro songs are *the* thing, and those who sing them make big hits. Fanny Rice sang 'I Want You, My Honey, Yes I Do,' a Negro song, last Sunday night, and other good songs. Everybody knows that 'Little Alabama Coon' has grown to be a chestnut. 'I Don't Love Nobody' and 'Mama, Does You Love Your Honey?' which were sung in Primrose and West's Minstrels, are becoming popular with people who call themselves vocalists" (*Leavenworth Herald*).

• ***December 13, 1895 (Kansas City, Kansas):*** "The colored couple that refused to give up their seats at the Auditorium Saturday night were Mr. A. H. Jenkins head-waiter at the Contropolis and his wife" (*Kansas City American Citizen*).

• ***December 28, 1895:*** "Miss Ednorah Nahar has announced her intention of abandoning the field as a reader within a year, and will make a venture upon the legitimate stage. She believes that the outlook for the dramatic readers of the race is decidedly gloomy, and none but the best equipped can survive" (*Indianapolis Freeman*).

WANTED,
WHITE and BLACK
SPECIALTY PEOPLE
FOR THE
PICKANINNY MINSTRELS.

I want a good 60 or 70ft. Car; Pullman Combination preferred.
Can use an "A1" QUARTETTE who do Jubilee work, WHITE OR BLACK.
Keep your SALARY DOWN, as it is as SURE AS GOLD.
A good hustling ADVANCE MAN WANTED.
Nothing TOO GOOD for us.
I want PRICES on STAND WORK and other PRINTING.
Now send full particulars, and make your salary LOW.
No lushers wanted at ANY PRICE.
You must be clever or WE DONT WANT YOU.

We Want a Corking RED HOT AFTERPIECE.

No fares advanced unless we know you. All must be able to double in brass. Would like to hear from dealers in uniforms, with catalogue and lowest SPOT CASH PRICE, and DON'T FORGET we want a

"PICKANINNY BAND" AND ORCHESTRA AND PICKANINNIES

Who can do specialties. I almost forgot—must have a Leader who can double in brass and orchestra, and he must be GOOD. Address
HARRY J. RANDOLPH, Box 933, Lincoln, Ill.
Managers in the West and South with open time, write.

New York Clipper, *December 21, 1895.*

From the Criterion Quartet to "In Old Tennessee": The Rise of Ernest Hogan, 1889–1895

In 1909, the year of Ernest Hogan's death, theater critic Sylvester Russell asserted: "Mr. [Bert] Williams is looked upon today as the greatest stage Negro his race has produced, but the real honor of being the greatest comedy star actor belongs to Ernest Hogan, a fact which will go down in Negro history." A performer, writer, and producer of original musical comedies, Hogan relentlessly expanded the horizons of the African American stage and helped initiate a "golden age" of black theatrical touring companies. His lifetime body of work fueled the progressive movement toward a self-directed black cultural image.

Hogan was born in Bowling Green, Kentucky, April 17, 1865. This version of his family background and early life appeared in the *Freeman* of April 20, 1901:

> [Hogan's] grandfather was educated by a wealthy Southern family to go as a missionary to Africa, where the grandsire married a native African, the grandmother of the noted author and comedian. Being of unmixed blood he has been called "The Unbleached American." Mr. Hogan never attended school, but what he has accomplished in self education should inspire young boys who have an opportunity to educate, and never despair because of limited facilities. He began his theatrical career at the age of twelve years, when as a pickaninny he appeared with Robson & Crane in "Uncle Tom's Cabin." He next went to England with the Frohmans in a minstrel company.
>
> Returning to America he played "Topsy" in McFadden's "Uncle Tom." Next he was "starred" in Haliday's minstrels. Afterwards McCabe & Young found in him a remarkably clever addition to their famous minstrels. Our subject then entered vaudeville, heading the Criterion quartette assisted by Harry Eaton. The next season Hogan & Eaton's minstrels toured the country.
>
> About this time Mr. Hogan's fame as a songwriter began to attract the public. He wrote a drama called "In Old Tennessee" in which he introduced his famous song "Pas Ma La"—being the first "ragtime" song published. Then followed the world's famous hit, "All Coons Look Alike To Me."

Press reports of 1889–1895 plot Ernest Hogan's rise to stardom. In the spring of 1889, Hogan was mentioned in an advertisement for Eaton and Farrell's Original Georgia Minstrels, under the direction of Harry S. Eaton and Billy Farrell.

• ***June 22, 1889:*** "Eaton & Farrell's Georgia Minstrels closed for the season last week at Chicago, Ill. They reorganize at Milwaukee, Wis., Aug. 11, with a much larger and stronger company than last season" (*New York Clipper*).

Apparently, Harry S. Eaton, Ernest Hogan, and other members of Eaton and Farrell's Georgia Minstrels signed on for a summer tour with Peck and Jackson's Model Minstrels.

• ***August 17, 1889:*** "Harry S. Eaton writes that the Peck & Jackson Minstrels ceased their tour Aug. 6 at Fredonia, Kans. Too large a troupe, and the consequent non-payment of salaries, was the cause of the closing. Harry S. Eaton, Ernest Hogan and the Three Jones Brothers have contracted to play a ten weeks' tour over the Eden Musee circuit, commencing Sept. 2 at Omaha, Neb. They will be known as the Criterion Quintet" (*New York Clipper*).

LOOK, LOOK. A PHENOMENAL SUCCESS.

EATON & FARRELL'S ORIGINAL GEORGIA MINSTRELS.

25 TALENTED ARTISTS, 25, headed by the famous comedians, HARRY S. EATON AND BILLY FARRELL, the original STAR CALLIOPE QUARTET. BILLY JOHNSON, ERNEST HOGAN, BURRILL HAWKINS and BILLY ALLEN; also GEORGE BAILEY, the great Trombone Soloist; ALEX. MARSHALL, Basso Vocalist; PROF. JAMES LACEY'S CHALLENGE BRASS BAND. DAVE GILLIAMS' SUPERB ORCHESTRA; HENRY WHITE, the Greatest Street Drum Major in the World. We have nine weeks guaranteed. Managers North and East write at once. EATON & FARRELL, Proprietors and Managers, St. Joe. Mo. April 29 to May 5, Omaha 6 to 12, Lincoln 13 to 19. For open time address HARRY S. EATON.

P. S.—Would like to hear from performers who double in brass; also COATES AND WALKER.

Eaton & Farrell's Original Georgia Minstrels, with Ernest Hogan, New York Clipper, *April 27, 1889*

Note: The Jones Brothers were George, Will, and "Blutch." They originated the Criterion Quartette with Hogan in 1889, and ten years later they went to Australia with Hogan, as members of the M. B. Curtis Minstrels.

• ***September 28, 1889:*** "Eaton and Hogan's Criterion Quartet report good business in the west. They are traveling this way [east], and expect to sail for Europe in March next" (*New York Clipper*).

• ***February 15, 1890 (Chicago, Illinois):*** "Kohl & Middleton's Dime Museum," "South Side: The Pan Electric girls, with their frying pan overtures, and groups of singing dudines [i.e., female "dudes"], whistling girls and lady club swingers; Prof. Donar's mysteries in Theatre No. 1, and in No. 2 the Climax Quartet . . . West Side: Coko, the Esquimau; Wehrli, the elastic skin man . . . and Hogan and the three pickaninnies in 'Plantation Pastimes' " (*New York Clipper*).

• ***March 8, 1890:*** "Hogan and the three Jones brothers, who have been playing in the northwest, and who one week before last played at the Olympic Theatre Chicago, were booked for Slansbury's Theatre, Milwaukee, Wis., and according to contract were there after their rehearsal. Mr. Hogan received a note from Mr. Slansbury stating that he was subject of change. Mr. Hogan would not accept of the subjection as it would be breaking his contract. Mr. Slansbury was then forced and stated plain that no colored actors could play in his theatre, he would rather lose three or four hundred dollars in a law suit than to permit it. Hogan was compelled to cancel his engagement, and has entered suit against them for one hundred and thirty dollars and the case is in the hand of the eminent and well known Milwaukee lawyer, F. P. Hopkins, and there will be no compromise in it. Mr. Hogan says its an Afro-American care and half or all the damages shall go into the Afro-American League treasury. Mr. Hogan and the Jones Bros. will join the Gus Hill Specialty company at Cincinnati the 9th, and make the following cities as named: Cincinnati, Louisville, Pittsburg, Detroit and Washington" (*Indianapolis Freeman*).

Note: Throughout his career, Ernest Hogan repeatedly brought suit against parties who infringed on his civil rights. One famously successful episode took place April 11, 1900, while Hogan and company were returning from Australia. Enroute, Hogan's company played a four weeks' engagement at the Orpheum Theater in Honolulu, but when they prepared to board the steamer *Miowera,* from Honolulu to Vancouver, they were refused passage. The ship's captain and purser claimed they were not taken "as a result of their having been in countries where the plague was rampant";[28] the minstrels alleged the refusal was purely on account of racial prejudice. Hogan and company, through attorneys Kinney, Ballou, and McClanahan, filed twenty-nine separate lawsuits. According to reports in the *Cleveland Gazette* and the *Freeman*, a jury awarded damages totaling $15,000, including the sum of $2,250 to Ernest Hogan.[29]

• ***August 22, 1891:*** "The Criterion Quartet have had a successful fifty-seven weeks' tour of the West. They have fourteen weeks to play at Spokane, Butte and Ogden, after which they open at San Francisco for seventeen weeks. Lou D. Lewis, the tenor, is making a favorite impression singing 'The Lover's Quarrel' and 'The Lone Grave.' This colored quartet do not expect to return East for some time. They have received some very flattering offers from Eastern managers, which they have declined" (*New York Clipper*).

• ***November 1, 1891:*** "Stage Notes," "Earnest Hogan, late of Topeka, and the Jones trio, are making a big hit on the coast" (*Topeka Weekly Call*).

• ***November 14, 1891:*** "The Criterion Quartet are reaping a rich harvest on the Pacific Coast. After a very successful season at Butte City, Mon., they have been engaged for the season at Ned Foster's Bella Union Theatre, San Francisco. James Taylor has replaced Lon Lewis in the quartet, the latter having recently married a well to do non-professional, and retired from the profession" (*New York Clipper*).

• ***September 3, 1892:*** "The Criterion Quartet are reported to be meeting with success on the Pacific Coast. They are booked over the Northern and Sackett's Musee Circuits. They join one of Wm. Foote's colored attractions for the World's Fair. Jack Chew has joined them" (*New York Clipper*).

• ***February 24, 1893 (Spokane, Washington):*** "The Criterion Quartet, Mr. Ernest Logan [*sic*], manager, have been appearing at the Louvre Theatre for the past two weeks and have been meeting with ovations nightly. This wonderful aggregation of Afro-American talent and genius is one of the best known and most substantial organizations of the kind in the United States. Mr. Hogan has in his support four of the cleverest performers in their line extant, the gentlemen are Mr. W. C. Craft, 1st tenor and comedian; Mr. Willie Jones, 1st bass; Mr. Geo. Jones, 2nd tenor; Master Bluch, alto and juvenile; Mr. Hogan himself possessing a phenomenal tenor voice, as clear as a bell. These gentlemen began their present tour in San Francisco, Cal. and are billed full time up to June 2nd, when they open in Chicago, Ill. receiving the enormous salary of $672 while there. Mr. Hogan and Chas Hunn of minstrel fame will star jointly next season in a musical and farcical comedy that is being written for them by Mr. Carleton of New York. The libretto will be prepared by Mr. Charles Hoyt, of New York, the author of a 'Texas Steer,' 'Hole In The Ground,' and a 'Parlor Match.' These gentlemen will carry to the legitimate stage experience, versatility and well matured genius and talents of the higher order. The organization promises to be the first venture of the kind in the United States, and as Mr. Hogan is liberally supplied with capital and backed up with good judgement, success seems inevitable" (*Detroit Plaindealer*).

• ***February 25, 1893 (Spokane, Washington):*** "Mr. Earnest [*sic*] Hogan, an inimitable Afro-American comedian, . . . is sole proprietor and manager of the [Criterion] quartett . . . Mr. Hogan is a musical genius and the author of all acts his company presents. Among the many songs the gentleman has written, none enjoy more widespread fame and popularity, than 'Mar's Peter at the gate,' and 'the answer to Mar's Peter,' the 'Christmas Dinner,' etc., etc." (*Indianapolis Freeman*).

• ***April 15, 1893:*** "Ernest Hogan and the Criterion Quartet will return East next season, to join Harry Williams' Own Co. They have been on the Pacific Coast for the past two years" (*New York Clipper*).

• ***December 16, 1893:*** "[Charles] Hunn and [May] Bohee, comedy sketch performers, were presented Dec. 3 with two gold medals by manager Chas. Meyers, of the Wigwam Theatre, San Francisco. Ernst [*sic*] Hogan also presented them with two gold medals on the same date, the event being the closing of a successful seven months' engagement of this team" (*New York Clipper*).

• ***October 27, 1894:*** "Ernest Hogan writes that he is about to leave San Francisco, Cal., after a five years' sojourn there and come East. He speaks of his success on the Pacific Coast and reports having signed a five years' contract with Broder & Schlam, music publishers of San Francisco, to publish his songs" (*New York Clipper*).

• ***April 27, 1895:*** " 'In Old Tennessee,' a play in three acts, was acted for the first time in a revised form at the Gillis Opera House, Kansas

City, Mo., April 4. The play was originally written by Ernest Hogan [*sic*] and presented during the month of February of the current year at Butte, Mont., but the work was revised by Jas. E. Moore and presented as noted above. The scene of the play is located in the state of Tennessee, and tells a conventional story of the anti bellum [*sic*] days" (*New York Clipper*).

• ***May 18, 1895:*** "'In Old Tennessee' closes its season at Kansas City, Mo., May 25, and will reopen in Chicago, Ill., Sept. 6, under the management of Max Alexander and J. A. Tralle. The company will be headed by Earnest Hogan, and comprise thirty-eight people, including W. C. Craft, the Jones Bros., W. Tripp, Al. Williams, Jim Taylor, Nora Allen, Louise Although, Hattie Williams and Miss Ward" (*New York Clipper*).

• ***June 15, 1895:*** "'In Old Tennessee,' which closed its season in Kansas City, Mo., May 25, will open at Chicago, Ill., Sept. 8. The company will be, we are informed, stronger than last season, and headed by Ernest Hogan and Nora Allen. All new scenery and wardrobe will be prepared, and it is intended to make a feature of 'La Pas Mala'" (*New York Clipper*).

• ***July 6, 1895:*** "Prof. Payne's Colored Female Band, said to be the first and only organization of the kind in this country, will be seen with 'In Old Tennessee' next season, opening in Chicago, Ill., Sept. 8" (*New York Clipper*).

• ***July 13, 1895:*** "The 'In Old Tennessee' Co. will consist of thirty people, headed by Ernest Hogan and Nora Allen, and include, among others: E. I. Dalton, May Forrest, Burton Clarke, Jones Bros., C. A. Craft, Mattie Clarke, Prof. Levy Payne and band of twelve female pickaninnies" (*New York Clipper*).

• ***December 21, 1895:*** "Roster of the 'Old Tennessee' Co., which reports having a successful tour through New England: Ernest Hogan [and others, including] Eugene Speyer, musical director" (*New York Clipper*).

"I'M A GOOD THING WHEN I'VE GOT MONEY."
THE LATEST AND BEST SOUTHERN MUSICAL COMEDY,
OLD TENNESSEE.
A $10,000 PRODUCTION.
All our Own Scenery. New Special Paper. New Songs and Dances.
FEMALE PICKANINNY BAND. OUR OWN SPECIAL CAR.
ERNEST HOGAN, IN THE GREATEST OF ALL, **"LA PAS MALA."** SPLENDIDLY STAGED, GORGEOUSLY DRESSED, CHARMINGLY ENLIVENED.
Route Eastward through Canada and New England States. Time wanted in the Middle and Eastern States. First class houses only write for time.
ALEXANDER & TRALLE, 503 Walnut Street, Kansas City, Mo.

New York Clipper, *July 6, 1895.*

Ernest Hogan, Freeman, *April 20, 1901.*

During the 1889–1895 period, Hogan firmly established himself on the professional stage and was poised to ascend to the pinnacle of his profession on the billows of popular ragtime.

The Black Patti Troubadours and Madame C. C. Smith, "the Patti of Topeka"

The year 1895 marked the end of an era for America's great "Black Pattis" and "Colored Queens of Song." In 1896 Sissieretta Jones abandoned her quest for a rightful place on the mainstream opera stage and accepted an offer to reign as the principal star and figurehead of the Black Patti Troubadours. An early review of this major, white-owned African American minstrel-variety road show described it thus:

> "Black Patti" as the star of the operatic and singing forces and Tom McIntosh, the greatest of all ebony comedians as the leader of funmakers. The first part of the entertainment is devoted to the comedy forces which include Henry Wise, Bob Coles [*sic*], and Stella Wiley, delsartean dancers . . . May Bohee, the Creole nightingale and a chorus of thirty pretty girls with well trained voices. "At Jolly Coney Island" is the title of the opening skit which . . . is full of "hot stuff," song, story and dance . . . Incidental to the scenes, various character types are introduced, such as the "Bathing Girl," the "New Bicycle Woman," the "Coon Singer" and "buck dancer," the "Bunco Steerer," the "Con Man" with the glad hand, and the "Couchee Couchee" girl from the midway and many other peculiar creatures which Coney Island's Bowery is noted for.
>
> Following the skit comes the great Vaudeville Olio . . . Then comes the greatest feature of the performance which is called the Operatic Kaleidoscope in which the singing forces of the company led by "Black Patti" present reminiscences of "Faust," "Carmen," "Trovatore," "Grand Duchess," "Tar and Tar Tar [*sic*]," |"Daughter of the Regiment" "Bohemian Girl," "Maritana," "Rigoletto" and "Lucia."[30]

The opening skit, "At Jolly Coney Island," was more often referred to as "At Jolly *Coon-ey* Island." It seems to have been constructed as a parody on "At Gay Coney Island," a mainstream farce comedy production of the time.[31]

The Black Patti Troubadours ran the roads until 1915.[32] During the season of 1899–1900 their opening skit was "A Rag-time Frolic at Rasbury Park."[33] In 1906, on the occasion of their tenth anniversary, the Black Patti Troubadours presented "Scenes in the Southland," which included a serenade scene that "brought Madame Jones to a cabin window in the garden spot of Virginia. Here [she] sang 'My Dear Southern Home,' and for encores she gave 'Old Man Moon' . . . and 'Suwanee River,' at the conclusion of which two beds of flowers were passed over the footlights to her as an anniversary gift." The reviewer further noted that "more than two-thirds of the balcony was made up of colored people, which argues well for their patronage."[34]

The advent of the Black Patti Troubadours actually made Sissieretta Jones more accessible to the black community at large. Elements of her operatic vocal technique, her courtly deportment, and formal stage attire were emulated by the full array of black vernacular Queens of Song. By the time she retired in 1915, the first generation of "Blues Queens" had come forth in all their finery, to shape the classic style of blues singing that would be heard on early-1920s race recordings. In the realm of black religious music, the Queen of Song idea took even deeper hold. During the early 1900s, black newspaper critics such as Sylvester Russell and "Tom the Tattler" noted a surfeit of "church-house prima donnas";[35] in turn, the post–World War I years witnessed the primacy of the "refined gospel singer;" and the 1920s and 1930s brought forth the first "Gospel Queens." Palpable chains of historical continuity link the Black Patti to the entire range of blues, gospel, and soul music queens.

One early link in this chain was Madame Cecil Smith, "the Patti of Topeka," whose cultured soprano voice was often heard in the black neighborhood churches of Topeka, Kansas. In the mid-1890s she began to venture out in the commercial arena as a feature with P. T. Wright's Nashville Students and Ernest Hogan's original *In Old Tennessee* Company.

• ***April 21, 1894 (Topeka, Kansas):*** "Madame C. C. Smith the famous soprano singer of this city, will, in a few days make an extended professional tour throughout Kansas, Neb. and Iowa" (*Topeka Weekly Call*).

• ***June 9, 1894 (Topeka, Kansas):*** "The Progressive Musical Club gave a concert Wednesday evening, May 30th at the A.M.E. Church. Mrs. C. C. Smith, Mr. Chas. McNary, Mr. H. Jones and others singing was excellent and enjoyed by all. The concert was given for the benefit of Mrs. McNary's crazy quilt" (*Topeka Weekly Call*).

• ***July 21, 1894 (Topeka, Kansas):*** "Madame C. C. Smith, our colored prima donna . . . is known in the whole community to have the sweetest and most musical voice in the city. Madame Smith, with her lovely talent, is a credit to our city and race" (*Topeka Weekly Call*).

• ***July 27, 1894:*** "Mme C. C. Smith . . . goes Monday July 30th to join the jubilee singers of Nashville, Tenn., now at Kansas City and will travel all season with them. Her husband may go later to join the company also" (*Kansas State Ledger*).

• ***December 8, 1894 (Topeka, Kansas):*** "Mrs. C. C. Smith, famous prima donna of Topeka, who has been touring in Nebraska, Dakota, Iowa, Missouri and Kansas, with Wright's Concert Company, returned to the city last Sunday" (*Topeka Weekly Call*).

• ***December 22, 1894 (Topeka, Kansas):*** "Madame Cecil Smith will give a grand concert at the United Presbyterian church on Eighth and Topeka avenue next Wednesday evening. She will be assisted by her excellent jubilee club" (*Topeka Weekly Call*).

• ***April 27, 1895 (Topeka, Kansas):*** " 'In Old Tennessee' is said to have been a good show. Mrs. C. C. Smith, who is the Patti of Topeka, and Ernest Hogan, a Topeka comedian, were the stars and shared the honors of the three performances that were given in the city and at the Soldiers' Home" (*Leavenworth Herald*).

• ***May 17, 1895 (Topeka, Kansas):*** "The many friends of Mme. C. C. Smith, the famous songstress, who is now traveling in 'The Old Tennessee' company is expected home soon [*sic*]. Mme. Smith has never been stuck on traveling, since her husband, who takes lead as bass singer failed to secure employment with the company she was associated with" (*Kansas State Ledger*).

Madame Smith continued on the professional stage. In the spring of 1897 she closed a thirty-eight-week tour with the Georgia Graduates, in company with Ernest Hogan and rising comedian-producer Al F. Watts,[36] who became her new husband and professional stage partner. With Mahara's Minstrels in 1899, Al F. and Cecil Smith Watts were "prime favorites . . . Al in his funny sayings and queer antics, and Cecil, as a dainty soubrette, are all that could be desired."[37]

In 1900 they joined the Black Patti Troubadours; and by 1901 Al Watts was filling the position of stage manager, while Cecil Watts was leading the company chorus in support of Sissieretta Jones's "operatic kaleidoscope."[38] Critic Sylvester Russell noted in his 1901 "Review of the Stage" that "The Black Patti Troubadours seem to be the best singing organization of the season, the chorus being quite near perfection."[39]

While contributing to the Black Patti Troubadours' classical features, Madame Cecil Smith Watts also distinguished herself in other lines: "Mme Cecil as the dashing soubrette was awarded abundant applause for the way in which she presented the latest 'coon' songs."[40] She was one of the first in a long line of coon-shouting "dainty soubrettes" who were eventually recognized as pioneer female blues singers.

The Whitman Sisters

There are few who can appreciate the wonderful progress our group has made on the legitimate stage. Only those who have had something to do with pioneer work realize the task it has been to make it good. I wonder if we who have done the foundation work are not responsible for a greater day for the Negro stage artist?

—Mabel Whitman, 1924

One particular voice of the future to rise up from eastern Kansas in 1895 was the Whitman Family, headed by the well-known preacher and poet Rev. Albery A. Whitman with his wife, Caddie, and their three daughters, Mabel, Essie, and Alberta.

• ***August 8, 1891:*** "Albery A. Whitman—Poet," "Author of 'Rape of Florida,' " "The object of this sketch is to set forth the fact that the Negro race has produced a truly great poet. Among the rugged hills of Hart County, Ky., near the banks of Green river, May 30th 1851, in 'a poor log cabin,' one of the most remarkable characters of this century first saw the light. Albery A. Whitman was born in bondage . . . His life has been a struggle in common with all worthy persons who have been surrounded with such circumstances . . . In 1871 the poet married Caddie, the beautiful daughter of Rev. C. M. White. To them have been born one son and three daughters, completing one of the happiest of home circles.

He is just now entering the prime of his life, an active minister in the A.M.E. Church, and an enthusiastic advocate of his race. And shall it be said of him that 'he came to his own and his own received him not?' " (*Indianapolis Freeman*).

• ***January 8, 1892 (Lawrence, Kansas):*** "The Eureka Club," "On last Friday night the grandest banquet which has ever been given by colored people in Kansas took place in Lawrence. The upper ten people were all present. Every person present represented money, morals and mind . . . Mr. Lemuel King and his distinguished lady are entitled to a great credit for the success of this entertainment. The banquet was held in his large and airy dining room . . . There is no other colored man in Kansas who has a dining room large enough to accommodate at one time one hundred and fifty guests . . . He is . . . the owner and manager of a livery stable . . . All who were there will remember the services of the greatest lady reciter of the race in the state. She is a member of this club and resides with her four angel children at Mr. King's . . . The applause given her was tremendous. We need not call her name, for everybody who reads knows Mrs. Caddie Whitman, the wife of America's only Negro poet, A. A. Whitman . . . A very agreeable feature in the table service was the appearance of little boys and girls as waiters. These children before the invocation chanted the Lord's Prayer. They did not make a balk or a mistake in any particular. The ones deserving special mention [include] Misses May and Essie Whitman, daughters of Mrs. Caddie Whitman" (*Kansas City American Citizen*).

• ***November 24, 1893:*** "Dr. Alberry A. Whitman, poet laureate to the Afro-American race, lectured to the Woman's Missionary society at the Charlotte street Baptist church Tuesday evening. Dr. Whitman very strongly opposed the emigration of the American Negroes to Africa. At the close of the lecture he read several stanzas of that beautiful poem, 'The Freedman's Triumphant Song,' which he composed and read at the World's Fair September 22, 1893" (*Kansas City American Citizen*).

• ***September 14, 1895 (Topeka, Kansas):*** "Rev. Whitman, the poet and evangelist, occupied the pulpit at St. John's A.M.E. Church Sunday at 11 A.M. The Whitman choir favored the congregation with several appropriate selections and 'Little Essie,' Mr. Whitman's youngest daughter [*sic*], sang a very pathetic solo, which was appreciated by all. The Whitman company are holding camp meeting on Quincy St. with great success" (*Topeka Weekly Call*).

• ***September 20, 1895:*** "Topeka is a great town for amusements . . . Last week Whitman's serio-comic, semi-religious sacred concert camp meeting musical outfit held forth nightly to a mixed crowd of caucasian persons, although the outfit is colored" (*Kansas City American Citizen*).

• ***October 19, 1895 (Leavenworth, Kansas):*** "City Cullings," "Every night this week an excellent audience has greeted Rev. A. A. Whitman and his woman quartet, composed of his family of girls, assisted by Prof. Dorris and Misses Turner and Adams. Special mention must be made of the singing of the Misses Whitman, which has so highly pleased the audiences. Competent critics and musicians pronounced this concert company one of the best ever heard in the city" (*Leavenworth Herald*).

• ***October 26, 1895 (Leavenworth, Kansas):*** "City Cullings," "The Whitman woman quartet rendered a number of selections at the First Presbyterian Church last Sunday night to a large and appreciative audience. The solos, 'Flee As A Bird,' and 'Where Is My Wandering Boy Tonight,' by Miss Essie Whitman were very good" (*Leavenworth Herald*).

• ***April 25, 1896:*** "Essie Whitman, who will be remembered by a great many society young people in this city, and especially by the young men, is now starring in a comedy company which appeared in Pleasanton, Kas., last Monday night . . . She is supported by her sister, Mary [*sic*] . . . The *Dallas News* says of Miss Essie Whitman: 'Little Essie . . . sang a solo, "A Drama of Home," with effect. It is not commonly known what a singer this little girl is. At the recent Dallas Exposition she reached the grade of 95 out of a possible 100 in the contralto contest'" (*Leavenworth Herald*).

• ***May 2, 1896:*** "The Whitman Jubilee singers entertained our people the first four nights of this week in the Opera house. The troupe is composed of Dr. A. A. Whitman, his two daughters, Misses May and Essie, Ed. Anderson and wife, Miss White, Prof. Dardis and F. Mays . . . They are simply immense, and to use a common phrase, 'out of sight!' Miss Essie Whitman sings contralto, and her 'Shadow of the Pines' was the sweetest we ever heard . . . Ed. Anderson, the bass singer, eclipses anything ever heard in this city and his stump speech, 'The Watermillyun Spiling Down at Johnstown,' 'The Old Kentucky Home,' etc., are of themselves well worth double the price of admission. Miss May Whitman sings soprano . . . and her 'What Could the poor Girl Do,' 'Love Me Little, Love me Long,' etc., show great ability." (*Pleasanton Herald* of April 21, 1896, quoted in *Leavenworth Herald*).

In a 1918 interview, Mabel Whitman, alias "Miss May," recalled:

> I was born in the same town as George Walker [of Williams and Walker fame]—Lawrence Kan.—and with my sisters had taken a prominent part in church and concert work, our father being a minister. Mr. Walker . . . desired to be a sponsor for us on a trip to New York for the purpose of starting us on our professional career, but was met with parental objection. Myself, Essie and Alberta received our rudimentary education in our home town, and were then sent to Boston, Mass., where we attended the New England Conservatory of Music for five years, under the personal training of George M. Davis [*sic*, Dardis] . . .
>
> Our first professional engagement was as a "filler" for an open spot on the bill at the Orpheum

theater [in Kansas City] . . . we having arrived in Kansas City at the end of a short evangelical tour with our father . . . This was 1898–1899.[41]

By the spring of 1899, Reverend Whitman was pastoring Allen Temple A.M.E. Church in Atlanta, Georgia, which became the home base for his daughters' continuing adventures in popular entertainment. A note in the *Freeman* of May 6, 1899, informed, "The Whitman Sisters Comedy Company is still at Savannah, Ga., theatres showing to packed houses of both white and colored."

In 1901 Reverend Whitman died,[42] and the *Freeman* of July 27, 1901, made note that he had "left his family . . . a $10,000 life policy . . . God will bless the soul of Whitman . . . and his family will . . . sing his praises." By this time the Whitman Sisters were thoroughly engrossed in "the profession." They posted this notice in the *Freeman* of February 22, 1902:

> The Whitman Sisters Novelty Co. will open their mid winter tour at the Augusta Grand Opera house, Augusta, Ga., Feb. 24. From there they go to . . . all of the leading Southern houses. They feel highly honored, being the first colored ladies in the profession to play the Greenwall [mainstream theater] circuit, under the management of their mother. This being their third season, they feel that success is assured. Since the death of their father . . . they have been very quiet up to the present time . . . His last request was that his daughters continue in the profession and sing praises unto the Lord as he firmly believed that it was God given talent that enabled them to master the Southern world and secure the same courtesies as white young ladies in the profession. They carry a company of twelve but do the work of twice that number . . . They would like to hear from all good performers desirous of a sure salary and prominence in the profession.

Freeman, *December 23, 1916.*

The notice concluded with a quote from a "recent article" in what appears to have been a mainstream daily paper: "The *Birmingham News* . . . states as follows: 'These three bright, pretty, Mulatto girls . . . play banjos and sing coon songs with a smack of the original flavor.' "

An institution in African American entertainment for the next three and a half decades, the Whitman Sisters were intimately involved in the early development of blues and jazz. During the season of 1904–1905 their company featured the legendary New Orleans singer-pianist Tony Jackson.[43]

In 1921 Essie Whitman recorded blues songs for the Black Swan label, accompanied by Fletcher Henderson.[44] The musical director of the Whitman Sisters Company during the 1920s was jazz pianist Troy C. Snapp, whose band included clarinetist Ernest Michall, featured with Snapp on 1927 recordings by King Brady's Clarinet Band. Among the other twentieth-century jazz, blues, and rhythm recording artists who toured as members of the Whitman Sisters Company were "adopted Whitman sister" Mattie Dorsey,[45] Willie Too Sweet, Kid Brown, Ferman Tapp, and Willie Bryant.

"A Little 'Ragging' ": The Emergence of Ragtime in the Land of John Brown

The word "ragtime" wasn't in mainstream currency until 1897. Its derivation is somewhat mysterious. Since the dawn of ragtime's popularization, when Ben Harney's "Rag-Time Instructor" informed that the word "ragtime" could be literally translated as "Negro Dance Time,"[46] commentators have struggled to establish an etymological relationship between the word "ragtime" and nineteenth-century black vernacular dance.

In 1899 a professional writer named Rupert Hughes published a three-page essay that was cited in *They All Played Ragtime* and subsequently became one of the most often-quoted articles in the annals of ragtime scholarship:

> Negroes call their clog dancing "ragging" and the dance a "rag,". . . [T]he dance is largely shuffling.
>
> The dance is a sort of frenzy with frequent yelps of delight from the dancer and the spectators, and accompanied by the latter with banjo-strumming and clapping of hands and stamping of feet. The banjo-figuration is very noticeable in the rag-music and the division of one of the beats into two short notes is perhaps traceable to the hand-clapping.[47]

With titillating references to "shuffling," "hand clapping," and "banjo figuration," Hughes conjured a generalized picture of ragtime's origins that has since been accorded the weight of contemporaneous documentation. Although it has been used to defend diverging interpretations of the etymological relationship of ragtime to vernacular dance,[48] Hughes's essay was not intended as a scholarly report. The sentence which immediately follows the oft-quoted passage assures that "every American is familiar with the way the darkey pats his hands."

Articles and reports in the *Topeka Weekly Call*, the *Kansas City American Citizen*, and the *Leavenworth Herald* indicate that a "rag" was not just a particular sort of "shuffling dance," but a kind of grassroots social function, sometimes integrated, at which black string bands provided music for dancing. Before the word "rag" came into fashion, "breakdown" was most often used to describe similar dance affairs.[49] The words "rag" and "breakdown" both seem to have evolved into slang for a back-country hop, and also a *type* of dance music. It is quite common in the realm of American folk vernacular music and dance to find the same word used to indicate a dance occasion, a type of dance, and a musical style, or approach. These terminologies seem to link the traditional source with the latest cultural developments. In any case, dance was the medium through which the new music fashions were propelled.

The August 16, 1891, edition of the *Topeka Weekly Call* complained about the "rags" being held at Jordan Hall in Topeka's Tennesseetown community. The October 27, 1893, edition of the *Kansas City American Citizen* described a "shooting fracas" which occurred "at a 'rag' " held near Evansville, Indiana:

> A handsome colored woman was the cause of a general shooting fracas near Evansville, Ind., last week. A white man and colored man were killed and five colored men were seriously wounded. It was at a "rag" where this troublesome piece of femininity was prancing about serenely happy, unconscious, probably, of her dazzling beauty. If she happened to smile sweetly at one man without smiling at the whole batch of "Reubens" jealousy would creep into the hearts of those not favored, until at last it crept out by the Smith and Wesson route. Revolvers were flourished, reports were heard, and "after the cruel war was over," and the dead and wounded gathered together, it was found that the lovely queen of matchless beauty was still sniffing the ham-smoked atmosphere, looking the picture of pale health and sweeter even than when

the danger signal was first hoisted. When and wherever you find a handsome colored woman she is so exceedingly handsome that a white man is willing to be shot to death for her dear sake.

On December 29, 1893, the mainstream daily *Kansas City Star* added this frank observation: "Kansas Notes," "When an Atchison fiddler plays at a rag he always sits near the door so that he can get out when he hears the first fighting word."

A more sympathetic and detailed account of a rag appeared in the November 2, 1895, edition of the *Leavenworth Herald*:

> The old time "rag" dance is dying out. Nearly every thing which is done nowadays is called "Modern," which means that a thing is not near so good as it is when done in a way to designate that it is ancient. After all, a great many things that are called modern are really things that are ancient, polished over cunningly. People dance with a little more grace nowadays and wear finer clothes, and put on more airs, but they are probably less interesting than the old timers. It is alright to gaze upon a pretty woman, dressed becomingly, dancing with some gallant knight, or it may possibly look beautiful to see them executing the waltz, but it is much more interesting and amusing to see a coarser pair of individuals doing the Mobile buck, or the wide open shuffle, or the pigeon wing, or the break down. Before we die we want to attend a country "rag" dance and see the people "chasse," "balance all," etc. We want to hear the caller, we want to hear the patting of hands, and then we will die happy, because we will know that our last desire has been fulfilled.

A report in the *Leavenworth Herald* of December 28, 1895, documents what appears to have been a contemporary country rag dance, a "grand ball of the Buckskin Club," held in North Leavenworth, Kansas, on Christmas Eve: "After supper the round and square dances began. That ever favorite dance, the 'possum a la,' was introduced, and it seemed to carry the house by storm. The orchestra, which was composed of three pieces, a fiddle, bass fiddle and triangle, dispensed beautiful and melodious airs, which were fetching."

The "Possum a La," or "Pas Ma La," is generally considered to have been a "characteristic" African American folk dance. The title appears to be a phonetic corruption of a colloquial French term. Music historian Isaac Goldberg speculated in 1930 that it derived from "the French *pas mele*, or mixed step."[50] One 1895 sheet-music version is subtitled "'La Das [*sic*] Pas Malaise' (The Difficult Step)."[51]

The "Pas Ma La" may have been the dance pointed out by a correspondent from Louisville, Kentucky, in the April 1, 1893, edition of the *Freeman:* "Prof. J. T. Guillard, dancing master, lectured to young ladies and gentlemen about the dance called 'Possum.'" It is likely Guillard was admonishing his young pupils to refrain from indulging in this low-brow, up-from-under dance.[52]

Several months later, in 1894, Irving Jones introduced his sheet-music production of "Possumala Dance,"[53] which ragtime historians have cited for its "few measures of real ragtime scoring."[54] Irving Jones expressed his own opinion in a February 12, 1927, letter to the *Chicago Defender*, posted in response to a Dave Peyton article titled "The Birth of Jazz":

> Dear Editor: After reading your write-up regarding ragtime songs in last week's issue of the *Chicago Defender,* I want to say that I was the first to write syncopated music. My music was published in 1893, and the song was called "Pas Ma La Dance." I tried every first class orchestra leader in the East to have it taken down from my voice, but none of them knew anything about ragtime music, and could not understand the unusual syncopated style . . .
>
> —Irving Jones, 511 Lenox Ave., New York

Irving Jones's "Possumala Dance" appears to have been the first of a run of sheet-music renditions of "Pas Ma La." The second, and apparently the most popular, was Ernest Hogan's "La Pas Ma La," published in Kansas City in 1895.[55] Hogan featured "La Pas Ma La" in his original road-show drama, *In Old Tennessee*.[56] The September 1895 edition of the *Cadenza*, a mainstream Kansas City–based music journal, reported, "The latest vocal success, 'La Pas Ma La,' is being issued for mandolin, guitar and banjo by the publisher J. R. Bell, Kansas City, Mo. All the local bands and orchestras are playing it."

Marshall and Jean Stearns described Hogan's "La Pas Ma La" as a "transitional dance-song... one of the early efforts to combine folk steps with topical dances of the time" and move from the "*group* dance with improvising soloists" to the "*couple* dance with fixed steps in definite order":

> *Hand upon yo' head, let your mind roll far,*
> *Back, back, back and look at the stars,*
> *Stand up rightly, dance it brightly, That's the Pas Ma La.*[57]

Music historian Paul Oliver has demonstrated that Irving Jones's "Possumala" is "clearly linked" to country blues singer–guitarist Jim Jackson's 1928 recording, "I'm a Bad, Bad Man," and that another of Jackson's 1928 recordings, "Bye, Bye Policeman," is Ernest Hogan's "Pas Ma La":[58]

> *She puts her hand on her head*
> *And let her mind move on—*
> *Back way back. Look at this stop—*
> *Oh! She dances nicely and politely,*
> *This am the Pas-a-Ma-La.*[59]

As early as 1899, Ernest Hogan was actively promoting the notion that his version of "Pas Ma La" was the first published ragtime song. On the basis of an interview with Hogan that year, a reporter for the mainstream *Kansas City Star* pronounced him "the originator of rag-time music."[60] The mainstream daily St. Louis *Republic* of September 13, 1903, gave an anecdotal history of Hogan's "Pas Ma La" under the headline "Ernest Hogan, Father of Rag-Time." It told how Hogan had been eking out a living as a piano player at "dances... in a Negro locality in Kansas City, known as Bellvidere Hollow":

> The... idea for "Pas Ma La" was conveyed to Hogan... at one of... those widely advertised affairs for which Bellvidere was noted and the stellar attraction on this occasion was a negro man termed "The Swell Creole From New Orleans," who was to call the quadrilles.
>
> The negro had a peculiar dialect and he was made the more noticeable by a costume, which included a red shirt, while paste diamonds glared richly from his fingers.
>
> During the first quadrille the New Orleans darkey did fairly well until he... yelled out: "Pas!"
>
> "Pas, Pas," queried every negro in the room... [E]very one was asking what the caller meant by "Pas."... [T]hen, when the star caller yelled out, "Ma-La," the negroes, to use the Bellvidere term, were up a stump...
>
> "What you talkin' about?" asked several negroes...
>
> "'Pas-Ma-La,' 'Pas-Ma-La,' don't you know what dat means. It am the latest dance."...
>
> Soon after "Pas Ma-La" became the rage in the negro colony and Hogan saw in the strange term the foundation for a peculiar song and dance.
>
> As a piano player he used it at his own dances long before a piano copy had ever been written.
>
> Then when he put his play [*In Old Tennessee*] on the road, he had an orchestration made... His "Pas Ma-La" was the first ragtime piece ever written.[61]

Irving Jones's "Possumala Dance" and Ernest Hogan's "La Pas Ma La" are derived from folk tradition and vernacular fashion, no less than they are products of original inspiration. Both versions "stand way back" in the domain of the country rag dance and take one imaginative step forward into the realm of ragtime.

Ernest Hogan's "La Pas Ma La," 1895.

Closely following Hogan's "La Pas Ma La" into the marketplace was white minstrel comedian Harry Ward's "The Possum-a-la." Ward announced in the *New York Clipper* of July 13, 1895, that he intended to "feature the Pasmala next season . . . with Barlow Bros. Minstrels." On August 24, 1895, the *Clipper* correspondent for Barlow Bros. Minstrels informed that "The big song and dance feature of the show is the negro act arranged by Harry Ward, 'The Pas-ma-la,' which is a weird negro gliding dance. This is its first presentation by white performers in the United States."

Ward's sheet-music version of "The Possum-a-la" was advertised in the December 21, 1895, edition of the *Clipper:* "A red hot coon song, and now being introduced by Harry Ward, the author, Inman and Mulvey, Billy Williams and eight pickaninnies (with Harry Martell's 'South Before the War' Co.) and the America's Comedy Quartet (of Jas. J. Corbett's Co.)." Ward's generally deprecating lyrics harbor this one seemingly matter-of-fact pronouncement:

De coonjine am not in it, when
You dance De Possum-a-la![62]

In 1899, during the course of a ten-week stand at Madison Square Garden, Isham's Octoroons featured the "Alabama Possumala."[63] As late as 1929 the black fiddle and guitar duo Andrew and Jim Baxter recorded "Dance the Georgia Poss," in which they advise dancers to "get way back and 'poss' " (i.e., "pas"), thus perpetuating a provocative theme from the nineteenth-century black string-band dance heritage.[64]

Though legend has associated the birth of ragtime with events in Chicago and St. Louis, reports from black community newspapers of 1894 and 1895 point to eastern Kansas as a primordial breeding ground of ragtime. Kansas is remembered as "the land of John Brown," a hard-won "Free State" which African Americans recognized during the 1880s as a possible refuge from the post-Reconstruction backlash. It would appear that the onset of Jim Crow was somewhat delayed on this cultural frontier, allowing the necessary breathing space and integrative atmosphere in which ragtime first revealed itself. A remark in the February 26, 1892, edition of the *Kansas City American Citizen* suggests there was already something special about the black piano players in Kansas City: "It is said that certain ladies are again wearing hoops. If it's true it won't be long before the western ladies will begin to hoop'er up. The 'wild and wooly' will never consent to the effete east being in the lead for any considerable length of time. It is also said that back east elocutionists are quite 'the go.' Come out west and hear our 'peeaner thumpers!' "

While the *Kansas City American Citizen* refused, at first, to utter the word "ragtime," this cryptic report in its "Literary and Musical" column of November 11, 1893, seems to raise the specter of piano rags: "Now as to Kansas City's musical world we can say but little this week. However, something is to be done this season to maintain interest in this art, for which Kansas City has made herself somewhat noted. We have a number of real professional musicians here, who, so far as talent is concerned, would be creditable to Boston; but it appears that something has diverted the exercise of their powers into channels remote from society's path. Whether this is due to the proper amount of perseverance in a certain direction, or a lack of a proper appreciation of their power on our part, deponent saith not. *But so it is.*"

Eye-opening commentary on ragtime piano playing first appeared in the *Leavenworth Herald*, in the caustic observations of its young editor, B. K. Bruce Jr.

• ***May 5, 1894:*** "In Atchison a girl isn't considered thoroughly proficient in her musical studies until she has learned how to hammer away 'Forty Drops' on the piano" (*Leavenworth Herald*).

• ***August 18, 1894:*** "City Items," "It's a mighty poor colored family that hasn't got some kind of tin pan called piano nowadays" (*Leavenworth Herald*).

• ***November 24, 1894:*** "There are a great many Kansas City tramps called piano players in town" (*Leavenworth Herald*).

• ***December 8, 1894:*** "Kansas City girls can't play anything on pianos except 'rags,' and the worst kind of 'rags' at that. 'The Bully' and 'Forty Drops' are their favorites" (*Leavenworth Herald*).

Note: This is the earliest-known printed reference to the word "rags" to indicate a particular type of music.

"The Bully" (a.k.a. "Bully of the Town") has been popularly acknowledged as a seminal ragtime song, the origins of which have been loosely identified with roustabouts on the levee at St. Louis,[65] and with a legendary black St. Louis brothel singer named "Mama Lou."[66] "The Bully" was immortalized by May Irwin. A columnist wryly observed in the March 1896 edition of the mainstream journal *Cadenza* that "May Irwin's much vaunted 'Bully Song' is a pretty piece of rowdy writing—nigger rowdyism at that. Nice theme for a parlor gathering, the murderous refrain is so refined and elevating."

• ***December 22, 1894:*** "Kansas Matters," "A Kansas girl who attended a function in this town where they sang 'Answered' and 'Brown October Ale,' said it only needed 'O, Promise Me' and a little 'ragging' to make her feel entirely at home" (*Kansas City Star*, reproduced in *Leavenworth Herald*).

Note: "Brown October Ale" and "Oh! Promise Me" made their initial impact in the popular light opera production of 1890, *Robin Hood.* The fact that the *Leavenworth Herald* plucked this item from the December 11, 1894, edition of the mainstream daily *Kansas City Star* suggests that by the end of 1894 in eastern Kansas the notion of "a little 'ragging'" was familiar on both sides of the race line.

• ***December 29, 1894:*** "City Cullings," "In Kansas City, if a man can shoot craps and play 'Forty Drops' on a piano, he is called a 'society' man. In Leavenworth he must come highly recommended as a first class rascal. Leavenworth is the only real society town in the State . . . If you are a crapshooter and a 'piano pugilist' in Kansas City, it is a sign that you are a 'society man'" (*Leavenworth Herald*).

• ***January 12, 1895:*** "Kansas Matters," "Through the 'gas light dancing matinee' is the newfangled way the Newton [i.e., Newton, Kansas] heavy swells take their 'rags'" (*Leavenworth Herald*).

Note: This item also appeared first in the *Kansas City Star*, in the "Kansas Notes" column of December 28, 1894.

• ***April 13, 1895:*** "If the present 'rag' craze does not die out pretty soon, every young man in the city will be able to play some kind of a 'rag' and then call himself a piano player. At the present rate Leavenworth will soon be a close second to Kansas City as a manufacturer of piano pugilists" (*Leavenworth Herald*).

Editor Bruce's offhand references to "rags" and "piano pugilists" reveal the familiarity of a devotee, yet Bruce affected derisive condescension along class lines. His ambivalence characterizes the generally confounded response of the African American press to any new direction in popular music, particularly one that signaled a cultural movement "up from below."

Clearly, by 1894 in eastern Kansas, "rags" had become identified with music for piano, yet etymologically attached to the country string band "rag dance." Contemporaneous commentaries suggest other linkages between these two historically adjacent black secular music styles, the older country string band dance tunes and the piano rags of the early and mid-1890s.

Elements of the indigenous string band style and repertoire were adapted for piano and elaborated on by urban folk musicians. Eventually, the methods and particulars of this ripening grassroots music were submitted to a formalizing process which brought rags to the attention of young black and white composers in search of a new creative medium.

"40 Drops" appears to have been one of the first syncopated and otherwise up-to-date string band tunes, rag dance favorites submitted to piano rag adaptation. It is extraordinary, the extent to which "40 Drops" was contemporaneously associated with the appearance of this new popular piano music in eastern Kansas, particularly in view of the fact that it has completely escaped the probings of ragtime scholarship until this late date.

The only known sheet-music publication of "40 Drops" is dated 1898,[67] four years after *Leavenworth Herald* editor B. K. Bruce Jr. first identified it with the irrepressible hammerings of eastern Kansas' black society girl pianists. The published arrangement is not for piano, but for mandolin and guitar. No piano interpretations or representations of "40 Drops" appear to have been preserved in any medium. The tune most likely originated in the string band tradition *prior* to the 1894–1895 *Leavenworth Herald* commentaries. The 1898 sheet-music version credits its publishers with the *arrangement* only; the original composer is not indicated. This tends to confirm that "40 Drops" is a very early folk rag.

At least two commercial recordings of "40 Drops" were made during the 1920s and 1930s. In 1928 it was recorded by Andrew and Jim Baxter, a black fiddle and guitar duo. Andrew Baxter fiddles a roughed-out country interpretation of the essential theme, struggling through a muddy variation or two, while Jim Baxter posits a verbal elucidation of the song title: "Now this is the 'Forty Drops.' Forty drops of what? Forty drops of rye!... Who's gonna carry me home when the dance is over? 'Cause I'm getting about full of this rye."[68] The Baxters were separated from the source of "40 Drops" by more than a generation, so the accuracy of their explanation of the "forty drops of what?" is open to question. It more likely referred to morphine or laudanum, popular recreational drugs of the 1890s, typically dispensed in drops.[69]

"40 Drops" was also recorded by the Stripling Brothers, a white fiddle and guitar duo, in 1936.[70] In this version the initial theme is more distinctly articulated, but like the Baxters, the Striplings don't attempt to execute every movement of "40 Drops" as preserved in the 1898 published edition.

In its published form, "40 Drops" is a characteristic early rag. In places it resembles a standard country string band tune, but there is also an unmistakable something "oriental" or pseudo-Turkish, such as reverberated from the 1893 World's Columbian Exposition Midway. In 1996 a complete rendition of "40 Drops," as per the 1898 sheet-music publication, was recorded by Mentone, Alabama, fiddler James Bryan.[71]

One more testament to the significance of "40 Drops" and the socially integrative influence of ragtime music is contained in a *Leavenworth Herald* account of a racially mixed "rag" dance—"the third monthly ball of the Forty Drops club"—reported on May 25, 1895:

> While strolling around the town one night during the past week, THE HERALD reporter spied a crowd of young society leaders of both colors boarding a late Fifth avenue car, which aroused his curiosity, and upon joining the crowd, he learned that the young society leaders were going to the third monthly ball of the Forty Drops club, which was given at Taschetta's hall in West Leavenworth. With an eye for an item which would possibly interest the public, the reporter accompanied the boys and girls to the place in question. Arriving upon the scene he was highly amused at the apparent good nature of

The De Harport Bros.' arrangement of "40 Drops," 1898.
(courtesy Library of Congress)

> the guests, which was adverse to his expectations. The musicians were tuning their instruments and in a few minutes the ball opened. The usual grand march was omitted, as the Forty Drops club is strictly an up-to-date organization, and detests anything that savors of originality. Polkas, waltzes, etc., of the round dances were conspicuous by their absence, but quadrilles were certainly receiving the undivided and constant attention of those in attendance. The dancing was a revelation and was something no one would expect to see West of Chicago or any of the metropolitan cities of the east. There mingled, with no apparent difference, the society leader and the proverbial "rounder." And everything went on smoothly. Many of the young society leaders, both white and black, were present, and it seemed the time had been reached when social prejudice was a thing of the past. Everyone seemed to enjoy himself, and especially the reporter. None of the empty compliments, the deceptive and well-worn smiles, and the assumed indifference seen so often at grand balls could be found here, but, instead, everything was genuine and unfeigned. The 'possum a la seemed to be the favorite dance of the evening. It is certainly a treat to any pleasure seeker to attend one of the famous monthly balls given by the Forty Drops club.

Early rags were firmly associated with saloon culture. A Leavenworth Herald editorial of July 14, 1894, noted that Kansas saloons, "and there are thousands of them, have their doors so wide for our people that they select the better places." The integrated atmosphere of Kansas saloons provided a backdrop for the popularization of ragtime music. The Topeka Weekly Call of April 27, 1895, announced: "At the next meeting of the Leavenworth city council an ordinance prohibiting piano playing and other music in saloons is to be passed. The ordinance has been drafted by request of the police department. Music in Leavenworth saloons has become an almost indispensable feature. The penalty will be a fine of from $10 to $20."

By the end of 1894, when B. K. Bruce Jr. first acknowledged piano rags by name, they had invaded the parlor repertoire of black "society girls" in eastern Kansas. There are distinct aspects of parlor music in early ragtime. Knowledge of the piano was generally considered to be a sign of refinement. Piano recitals and piano teachers are mentioned regularly in the African American community press. It isn't difficult to imagine how rags could move from the saloon to the salon, and back again.

Despite their early appearance in black Kansas parlors, rags were initially judged to be outside the limits of socially respectable artistic endeavor. Perhaps even more significant than ragtime's enduring connection with "rowdy" saloons is the fact that rags plainly deviated from classical norms by asserting an *independent African American cultural sensibility*. To diehard defenders of the Western musical canon, including many educated black musicians and music lovers, this represented an unacceptable departure. The popular trend toward ragtime wasn't affected much by these conservative attitudes: popular taste soared inexorably.

When Ignace Paderewski, the world-famous Polish pianist, gave a concert in Kansas City in March 1896, the intrepid *Leavenworth Herald* editor remarked: "Paderewski will have a large audience of Kansas City piano players, if nothing more. But we want to say to Mr. Ignace Paderewski that if he doesn't pound the life out of 'Forty Drops' and 'The Sunny South,' he will not be appreciated in K.C. Kansas Cityans love classic music."

At the dawn of ragtime's commercial ascendancy, there was a coterie of male piano players whose broad-ranging skills had earned them popular recognition as "professors." Among the piano professors identified in African American press reports of 1894 were Prof. Ruby Shelton of Indianapolis and Prof. William Baynard of Philadelphia.

• ***January 27, 1894 (Indianapolis, Indiana):*** "City Happenings," "Don't fail to witness the

Piano Recital contest between Prof. R. B. Shelton and Prof. Wm. Baynard, of Philadelphia Pa." (*Indianapolis Freeman*).

• ***June 23, 1894 (Muncie, Indiana):*** "A Peculiar Effect of His Music," "Mr. Ruby Shelton of Indianapolis, formerly with the Ednah Nahar [*sic*] Concert Company, gave a piano recital at a Baptist church here this week, which was interrupted by some noisy boys in the rear. They were discussing whether the music was good or not. Razors were drawn, but no one was 'carved.' A policeman tried to stop the 'fuss' and was unmercifully beaten. Several arrests followed" (*Cleveland Gazette*).

The "piano recital contest" and the knife fight in the church suggest that Professors Shelton and Baynard were attempting to straddle the fence between legitimate musical society gatherings and the as yet uncharted commercial territories of ragtime.[72]

Literary societies were a popular activity among members of the African American bourgeoisie. At a typical literary society meeting, members and guests would give dramatic readings, recite poems, and deliver speeches. The meetings were commonly rounded out with presentations of vocal and instrumental music. In eastern Kansas, the end of each year was highlighted by the annual convention of the Inter-State Literary Association, which brought together representatives of various black literary societies from Kansas, Nebraska, and Missouri.[73]

News coverage of the Inter-State Literary Association conventions of 1894 and 1895 describes one of the first "legitimate" platforms for the public presentation of piano rags. It appears that the most accomplished ragtime pianists available were denizens of "joints" and other places of poor reputation. The inclusion of such cultural and social "outsiders" at the 1894 Inter-State Literary Association meeting created quite a stir in local black society. The January 4, 1895, edition of the *Kansas City American Citizen* ran two somewhat contradictory reviews of the meeting, side by side:

> 1. It is said that the late Literary convention opened with a ball on Thursday evening and ended with a ball on Friday evening. If this be true it certainly does not speak well for the institution. We believe that there is a time to "laugh and a time to dance," but we do not believe that at a literary convention is the time for a ball.
>
> 2. The singing of Mr. B. F. Perkins, Miss Lizzie Bell of St. Joseph, Miss LaFitte, of Atchison, Messrs. Rbt. Paterson and Tilford Davis, of Kansas City, Ks, and the instrumental music by Mrs. Cunningham, of Leavenworth, Misses Montgomery, Jackson and Orey of St. Joseph and Prof. Chas. Lee of Kansas City, Kas. formed the most charming and entertaining features of the Interstate Literary convention.

Note especially the participation of "Prof. Chas. Lee." Like Ruby Shelton and William Baynard, Lee was referred to as a professor. In some quarters, the vernacular use of the honorific "Professor" to denote a community-based music master was already considered derogatory. This comment appeared in the "Kansas Matters" column in the September 1, 1894, edition of the *Leavenworth Herald:* "There are some good men even in Atchison. A music teacher in that town gave up a money order rather than sign his name as 'professor.'" In August 1895 *Herald* editor B. K. Bruce Jr. employed the term to taunt his Kansas City neighbors: "In Kansas City, if a man can play one, two, three on the piano, they call him 'professor.'"

Bruce was so profligate with his use of the new slang that he was compelled, on December 21, 1895, to print an explanation:

> The article which appeared in *The Herald* recently about "professors" and piano players did not refer to the school teachers and school principals, who are *not professors*, but to the great crowd of piano thumpers and men whose title to "professor" does not admit of investigation . . .

> "Professor" these days means so much. To illustrate: A bootblack is a "professah;" a barber is a "professah;" a hashslinger is a "professah, sah;" the man who drums on the piano is a pastmaster-professor . . .
>
> The time has come when people who think pray for deliverance from the "professors."

The image conjured by editor Bruce brings to mind the 1936 Freddie Bartholomew film *Little Lord Fauntleroy,* set in Brooklyn in the 1890s, in which a sign above Mickey Rooney's new shoe-shine stand proclaims him a "professor." A more legitimate connection might be made between the barroom ragtime professors of this early period and their twentieth-century counterparts, in particular Professor Longhair (Henry Roeland Byrd), whose inventive syncopations and street-level imagery lend substance to the historical continuity from ragtime to blues and eventually to rock and roll.

Bruce's explanation of the term "professor" was the result of an editorial exchange regarding the impending Inter-State Literary Association convention of 1895. On November 30, 1895, with the convention date fast approaching, Bruce noted: "We hope that the Kansas City 'professors' and piano players will not be allowed to run the next meeting of the Interstate Literary association. If they are permitted to run things, the probabilities are that the convention of literary lights will end in a scrap. Kansas City society swells are never happy unless they are pounding some stranger or pounding some piano."

In the next week's *Leavenworth Herald,* Bruce further provoked: "The Interstate Literary societies will meet at Kansas City, Kas., this year. Elaborate preparations are being made to entertain visitors. The piano thumpers of the two Kansas Cities should be excluded from the programs."

On December 13, 1895, the *Kansas City American Citizen* editor responded: "Now Bro. Bruce we do not believe in slinging mud or ripping our contemporaries up the back; there are other things more important that demand our attention, but when you tramp on our feet we are sure to yell, because we know that they are large enough for all sensible people to see. We would respectfully inform you that if you are afraid 'Kansas City piano players' and 'professors' will run the Inter-State Literary Association you had best remain absent, being a professor yourself. Now as for a scrap, WE are scrapping people, and if there is anything started we will be 'in it.' "

Witness the tone of the *Leavenworth Herald*'s review of the 1896 Inter-State Literary Association convention, credited not to Bruce, but to "ONE WHO WAS THERE":

> Missouri and Wyandotte people have the temerity to place Charles Lee's piano playing on an equality with that of Mrs. Lulu Cunningham of this city, in view of the fact that Lee plays nothing but rags, "by ear!" It is said that Lee cannot distinguish the difference between a note and a Chinaman's wash ticket. Lee has the Missouri and Wyandotte people fooled, nevertheless; he plays rags with so many variations that the people's enthusiasm leads them to the belief that he is playing a "sonata," or a "symphony," or something or other. Mrs. Cunningham is truly a first-class musician; in comparison, Lee pales onto insignificance. And then, look who he is!
>
> —ONE WHO WAS THERE

Charles A. Lee may be the first visible luminary of Kansas' early community-based piano ragtime movement. By 1895 he appears to have already gained quite a following. A note in the September 20, 1890, edition of the *Indianapolis Freeman* mentioned, "Prof. Chas Lee, the pianist, passed through the city [Indianapolis] for his home, Kansas City, Kan., Sunday. Prof. Lee has accepted a position in Sacket's Musee at Lincoln, Neb., as piano player in the first hall." Lee was mentioned at least once more in the

African American press; the May 6, 1899, edition of the *Freeman* contains a report from Oliver Scott's Refined Negro Minstrels, telling how they had been tendered a banquet by the African American Pythian Lodge of Toledo, Ohio. Several local musicians were in attendance, including "Charles Lee, Toledo's famous piano soloist," who "played the piano in a manner that showed him to be a master of that instrument."

Throughout the Midwest, ragtime piano players began to gain local recognition. These barroom professors led the way through uncharted musical territories, but their fame was fleeting, and they were soon supplanted by more sophisticated musicians who were better equipped to exploit the new codes of commerce. Concerned that the names of the pioneers should not be lost to history, formidable African American vaudeville pioneer and journalist Salem Tutt Whitney left this article in the December 5, 1925, edition of the *Chicago Defender*, under the headline "Jazz Pioneers":

> Every country, every profession, every business, every science has its pioneers. So our music has had its pioneers and it is well and timely that we should call them to mind, not forgetting the debt we owe them. Wonder if Paul Whitman [*sic*], Leroy Smith, Will Marion Cook, Irvin Berlin [*sic*], Clarence Williams, Maceo Pinkard, Will Vodery, Perry Bradford and others who are riding on the jazz wave of popularity to success ever stop to think of our "ragtime" pioneers, the rag-time piano players, who played in honky-tonks and dives or for low-brow shindigs and dances and were happy to receive a dollar or two and their eats and drinks. Written music was as easy for them to read as Egyptian hieroglyphics or Jewish sanskrit. All the music they knew was in their souls and at their finger tips. And how those fellows could play. What bewildering, bewitching, animating, technique defying harmonies they could assemble. Then the onward march of progress overtook them. The schools began turning out musicians who could read music, who were familiar with technique and theory. These musicians put the pieces played by the pioneers upon paper; publishing houses began broadcasting this music so rapidly and the demand for this class of music became so great that only the musicians who could read were employed and the rag-time piano fakir was through.
>
> One night an old man, whose legs and arms were stiffened by rheumatism, dropped into Tom Smith's cabaret on Druid Hill Ave., Baltimore, Md. The music of the orchestra drew him like a magnet. Not a gesture of the musicians escaped him. He drank in the music of the band like a thirst-crazed "desert rat" prospector who suddenly stumbles upon the sweet spring waters of an oasis. It is intermission and the tired piano player goes in search of refreshments and a breath of pure air. The old man timidly seats himself at the piano. No one notices. The room is a bedlam of loud talk, hysterical laughter and noisy banter. He runs his fingers idly up and down the keyboard; the stiffness is leaving his joints; now he begins to play. As the weird and intricate harmonies speak from the piano board. There is a hush in the room. Now the crowd gravitates toward the piano. The old man does not heed the crowd, his soul is in the piano, and he plays—tunes that only a few had ever heard, and played as only he could play them. When he finished it took the storm of applause that followed to awaken him from his reminiscences.
>
> "Who is it," was the question asked simultaneously by a hundred persons. It was "Jack the Bear," once the rag-time king of the world. His real name is Jack Wilson. At one time he was a vaudeville partner with Lawrence Dean [*sic*, Deas]. He was nicknamed the bear because he was a bear at the piano. Jack won first prize in a rag-time piano playing contest at Madison Square Garden in New York and at the Academy of Music, Philadelphia. The pieces he played that won for him the coveted title of king of rag-time pianists were Sousa's "Stars and Stripes Forever" in rag-time and "The Lady's Dream." Jack is now mixing syrup in a syrup factory in Baltimore.
>
> There were others besides Jack who now have only the dreams of past glory to sustain them. I am indebted to Cuney Connor, our musical director for the names and much of the data contained in this article. Cuney came along at the tag end of the rag-timers. It was at Jack Broomfield and Bill

> Crutchfield's Midway hotel that he acquired the nickname of "Kid Music," because he was always plunking on the piano to the annoyance of the habitues. Later he won several prizes as a rag-time player.
>
> There were "Blue," famous about St. Paul, Minneapolis and Duluth; "Pig Ankle," popular about St. Louis and Chicago; and "Squirrel" of Toledo and Chicago; "Piano" Price, "Piano" Nelson, "Toadelo," "Dry Bread," "Plunker," "Ounie," "Snow," "Con-Con," and others who should be remembered as the forerunners, the pioneers of our popular jazz music.

While testifying that ragtime piano pioneers were generally confined to "honky-tonks and dives," Salem Tutt Whitney informed that the legendary Jack the Bear had also worked in vaudeville with Lawrence Deas. Another *Freeman* commentator remembered Deas and Wilson as "the first colored act to use a piano on the stage singing their own compositions."[74] According to a 1924 retrospective in the *Chicago Defender*, "Mr. Deas, a native of Toronto, Canada, first entered the show business in 1896, in partnership with Jack Wilson (Jack the Bear), and joined the 'Before the War' company. They left this show shortly and went to New York City."[75]

The *Freeman* of May 7, 1898, located Deas and Wilson with Eaton and Hammond's Colored Sports. Six months later they were with John W. Isham's Tenderloin Coon Company, "booming along through the eastern states... singing 'All I Want is my Chicken'" and "closing the olio good and strong."[76] A *Freeman* report on June 10, 1899, said, "Deas and Wilson, authors of 'All I Want is my Chicken,' has composed three new hits: 'I Just Naturally Love That Yellow Man,' 'I'm Wasting my Talent Fooling With You,' and 'I Thought You Said You Was a Friend of Mine.'" It seems Deas and Wilson parted ways some time before June 16, 1900, when the *Freeman* reported: "Charles H. Moore, the popular manager of the famous Douglass Club, 114 W. Thirty-first street, New York City, has opened another place at 144 W. Twenty-sixth street... and a bill of exceptional merit was presented. Jack Wilson presided at the piano. The new club will be known as the 'Little Douglass.'"

While Lawrence Deas went on to appear in *Shuffle Along* and other major race musicals of the 1920s, Jack "the Bear" Wilson remained in clubs and saloons. The legend of Jack the Bear survived into the modern era. Writing in 1964, Willie "the Lion" Smith recalled, "It was at Walter Herbert's joint on Thirty-seventh Street [New York] that I heard the famous Jack the Bear, whose real name was John Wilson. He... was a well-known dope addict who played piano when he felt like it."[77]

As late as 1976, Eubie Blake informed that, in order to appreciate ragtime piano development, "You have to know about the backrooms of bars..., the hook shops [i.e., whore houses], the beer and the sawdust all over the floor... these were the only places you could hear Jesse Pickett, Jack the Bear, Boots Butler."[78]

If pioneer ragtime piano players were most often heard in honky-tonks, dives, and hook shops, they also worked in vaudeville, toured with minstrel troupes and jubilee concert companies, and performed at literary society meetings and in dime museums, fraternal lodges, and churches. Ragtime was a multifacted musical phenomenon.

Preserving the Spiritual Legacy: The Last Days of Frederick J. Loudin

In June 1896 Frederick J. Loudin told an interviewer from the *Pittsburgh Wasp* that he felt "the prejudice throughout the South is as strong as it was twenty years ago."[79] He apparently found it impossible to live and work in the United States under existing conditions of racial oppression. Consequently, in August 1897 Loudin and his Fisk Jubilee Singers began another extended visit to Great Britain.

In Great Britain, unlike America, respect for the spiritual singing heritage and an empathetic feeling toward the formerly enslaved race that produced this music were still strong. The *Cambridge Independent Press* had these welcoming words for the Loudin troupe: "The entertainment had lost none of its novelty to English ears. To hear men and women of another race singing with intense piety and rare vocal power religious songs which had sprung spontaneously out of the heart of an oppressed people was like listening to the music of another sphere."[80]

If public sentiment in Great Britain had remained constant, Loudin found that other circumstances had changed during his eleven-year absence. In a letter dated October 25, 1897, paraphrased in the *Cleveland Gazette*, Loudin complained "that he had been in England just two months, and that during that time he had seen more Afro-Americans than during all the years he was over there before and that they do not 'help matters one bit.' 'They seem to be "left overs" from Uncle Tom's Cabin, minstrel, octoroon and snide jubilee companies and you know what sort of people as a rule they are and just about how they would "represent" us.' "

Even while negotiating the increasingly tricky requisites of professional jubilee singing, Loudin never abandoned his sense of historical identity and purpose. For two and a half decades, Loudin had lifted up his heavy voice in palaces, shrines, presidential chambers, prisons, hospitals, native villages; when he put music in the air, it was not necessarily intended only to entertain. Early in 1898, Loudin took his troupe to the city of Hull, England, where they made a pilgrimage to the birthplace of Britain's great emancipator, William Wilberforce. It was described in the *Hull Daily News:*

> Mutely for some moments these descendants of the south American slaves stood, and then without a sign their voices were raised in honor of Hull's great citizen, Wilberforce. First the sopranos, next the contraltos, followed by the tenors and baritones, and lastly the bass, the whole producing a great wave of melody, which filled the old building, thrilling all within earshot, and almost made one's hair stand on end. They poured forth their song to the tune of "John Brown's body lies mouldering in the grave," chanted by the victorious armies of the north during the war which decimated north and south America and eventuated the liberation of the slave. When they came to the lines—"Now has come the glorious jubilee, when all men are free"—the well trained voices rose to fortissimo. It was a shout of triumph; a veritable ring of victory flooded the sacred spot with enthralling and enrapturing music.[81]

After nearly twenty-five years as a professional jubilee singer, Loudin remained receptive to new trends in African American popular music style, while he continued to struggle free of the more corrupting influences of minstrelsy. Loudin's Fisk Jubilee Singers' enduring popularity reflects not only high artistic standards, but attention to entertainment value as well. The Fisk Jubilee Singers had always given a mixed presentation of sacred and secular music, and the mix hadn't changed significantly over the years. Nevertheless, in the face of an increasingly profane modern culture, religion-minded critics now repeatedly expressed the desire for a clearer distinction between the sacred and the mundane. In Great Britain, the "variety" in the Jubilee Singers' program apparently provoked a confused response from a portion of the audience. One newspaper critic described it thus:

> The performance was a varied one, and it had a singular incongruous effect upon the audience. It contained a laughing song and love songs as well as slave songs. In the course of a hymn or slave song,

when the heavy bass prayed vociferously to "God Almighty," some of the people thought it was the time to laugh.

The audience applauded the Lord's Prayer, and when the choir sang "Sinner, better get ready; the day will come when the sinner must die," the sentiment was greeted with loud applause. It appears to me that between musical services and concerts in churches the people are getting out of their reckoning.[82]

When Loudin's Fisk Jubilee Singers appeared in Belfast, Ireland, in April 1898, after an absence of many years, one unprogressive but observant newspaper critic wrote a long, irate diatribe in which he expressed his disappointment concerning certain "incredible innovations." His commentary suggests that Frederick Loudin had taken on some of the more demonstrative performance practices of his forward-looking American jubilee contemporaries. It also provides a rather clear indication that barbershop harmony had taken a hold with Loudin's troupe.

[T]hey set all the canons of Harmony and Form at defiance. We do not know whether it is in the harmony or in the artist, but the introduction of some of the dissonating notes, in the tenor and bass especially, was eminently absurd and incongruous. The reason for this incredible innovation may become clearer as we develop. However, they serve no useful purpose in point of expression or musical effect, and they are hateful to the ear. They jar and cross; still after all, the combined effect is, in the end, pleasing enough . . .

We do not care to make any invidious comparison between their former performances and their present ones . . . The most striking effect of the old singers was their simplicity, modesty, and absence of affectation of any sort or kind . . . Hence their great popularity. Their meekness and humility had everything to do with it.

They have been round the world, and all that is changed. All their hobnobbings with kings and princes and gilded potentates, have spoiled all that; and in fact the Jubilee Singers are as flippant and as extravagant as you make them . . .

And we do believe that Mr. Lane thinks that, when we are being sung to, we require to have our eyes attacked as well as our ears, in order to leave the proper mental effect. That is a sad and painful mistake on Mr. Lane's part. When we are assimilating the musical sounds we require rest for our eyes to enable us to proceed properly with the musical digestion. We do not want our attentions distracted there-from by a gymnastic display such as he gave us every night.

In the more riotous songs Mr. Loudin and Mr. Lane revelled in their extravagances and swayed their bodies backwards and forwards, and upwards and downwards, clutching downwards with their hands, as if they were dragging the substance of their parts out of their boots. This, too, while all the others were standing steadily and even demurely. And when Mr. Early, the basso, and Mr. Brooks, the tenor (both beautiful voices) got an inning, which was all too seldom, it was a positive relief from the riot and disorder created by the two rollicking colleagues.

Occasionally Mr. Lane would give a yell, a third, sometimes a fifth, above the true, harmonical note, that discovered an effort capable of lifting the roof off his head. He felt the absurd and unnecessary strain. So did the audience. And we feel sure the result was anything but pleasant to both. But Mr. Lane seemed to like it. It created an incredulous laugh. But however pleasant, if pleasant it was, to Mr. Lane when he let himself loose in this fashion, it detracted from what ought to be an artistic and circumspect performance. His howl was such as should shock a Quaker. And he adds to the absurd effect produced by these explosives by rolling his eyes in the approved Christy Minstrel style.

And if we take Mr. Loudin and Mr. Lane together we find that these extravagances of theirs prevent their voices from blending with the others. For example, in the "Unison" passages the ladies sang like one voice. That is what is meant in music by the word "unison." But by reason of the antics of Mr. Loudin and Mr. Lane, the male voices never blended either with their male colleagues or with the ladies. In fact, they refused to blend, and rendered the "Unison" impossible. A little care and circumspection would obliterate all this. A little more attention to their two able colleagues would go a long way to prevent it. For, if we mistake not, Mr. Brooks and Mr. Early, if they have not so big

> voices, have more musical voices, and blend and shade better with the voices of the ladies. Let us hope that our colored friends will not force us to think less of them than we have done, when all those years we have kept them on so elevated a pedestal.[83]

Beyond any attention to vernacular music fashion, Loudin's Fisk Jubilee Singers were devoted to the perpetuation of characteristic elements of the old Fisk vocal harmony arrangements in the spiritual choruses. This made Loudin's Fisk Jubilee Singers a fitting prototype for the ongoing effort to produce an original school of classical composition based on the Negro spiritual. A music critic from the *London Globe* affirmed: "In almost every number one hears snatches and sometimes even more than this, of melodies evidently heard by Dvorák, since they occur in his later compositions. Altogether, the Jubilee Singers' performance is most suggestive, and affords much food for thought."[84]

There is no known documented evidence that Dvorák ever heard Loudin's Fisk Jubilee Singers. On the other hand, the rising young "Anglo-Black" composer Samuel Coleridge-Taylor attended several of the concerts given by Loudin's Fisk Jubilee Singers in London and was deeply influenced by them. Coleridge-Taylor acknowledged that it was "the world renowned . . . Frederick J. Loudin, manager of the famous Jubilee Singers, through whom I first learned to appreciate the beautiful folk music of my race."[85]

A friendship developed between the aging jubilee maestro and the young composer, son of a native African father and white English mother. Coleridge-Taylor's accomplishments were a particular source of pride and pleasure to Loudin, and in 1901 he began to provide periodic reports on Coleridge-Taylor's progress. The reports were enthusiastically reprinted in the *Cleveland Gazette:* "Mr. Loudin is proud (as we all are) of Coleridge-Taylor's remarkable talent, success and wonderful career, and wants Afro-Americans generally to know of and appreciate them."[86] Coleridge-Taylor gratefully maintained, "[Loudin] more than anyone else, helped to make me known to our dear American people."[87]

In preparing the overture to his celebrated "Hiawatha Trilogy," a composition for choir and orchestra based on Longfellow's epic poem, Coleridge-Taylor used as a theme the jubilee hymn "Nobody Knows the Trouble I See." The work was successfully received. The efforts of Samuel Coleridge-Taylor to use folk-spiritual themes in the context of classical composition struck a responsive chord among the black "aspiring class" in America, where Coleridge-Taylor Choral Societies began to appear in several major cities. The most significant of these was the Coleridge-Taylor Choral Society of Washington, D.C. In London, Loudin had introduced Mrs. Mamie Hilyer to Coleridge-Taylor, and she went on to help organize the D.C. choral society.

Frederick Loudin's singing days came to a close in October 1902, when he was hospitalized at the Border Hydropathic sanitarium in Peebles, Scotland. His condition was described as "nervous prostration" or "rheumatism of the nerves."[88] Loudin's condition "became so alarming that an X-Ray examination was made which happily revealed no organic trouble. Electric treatment was then decided upon in addition to his medical treatment and the services of the best electrician in Scotland were obtained."[89]

Loudin's Fisk Jubilee Singers were forced to continue the tour without the aid of their director. Their season concluded on May 11, 1903, and the company was permanently disbanded. Before dispersing, the troupe paid a farewell visit to Professor Loudin at the Border Hydropathic and gave an informal concert for the residents. "Mr. Louden [*sic*] for once in a way, found himself compulsorily seated among the listeners—a change, no doubt, for he who possesses one of the finest bass voices man could wish to hear... Mr. Louden's acknowledgement ... was pregnant of meaning. 'My heart is too full to speak,' he said. But it was a 'memorable half-hour' for him... for all of us."[90]

With this private recital in a hospital in Scotland, the era of the Original Jubilee Singers came to a close. While they hadn't been connected to Fisk University since 1878, Loudin's Fisk Jubilee Singers nevertheless continued to represent the original Fisk musical *ideal*, the fundamental aesthetic vision; reverent, heroic, inviolable, it left a lasting imprint.

Loudin remained at Border Hydropathic until he was sufficiently recovered to return to America in October 1903. He spent his last days at "Otira," his Ravenna, Ohio, home, confined to a wheelchair and dependent on the aid of a nurse to wheel him out to his front porch or around town. Early on the morning of Thursday, November 3, 1904, Frederick J. Loudin died. He is reported to have spoken these last words to his wife: "God is calling me, God is calling me home."[91] Loudin was buried in Maple Grove Cemetery in Ravenna. Tributes and condolences came from many quarters. The *Cleveland Gazette* hardly exaggerated when it asserted, "We doubt that there lives today a member of the race who can number in many countries throughout the world anywhere near half the warm friends and admirers that the deceased has left."[92]

Samuel Coleridge-Taylor had been invited to visit America by the Washington, D.C., choral society which bore his name. By coincidence, he arrived on November 4, 1904, one day after F. J. Loudin's death. In expressing his condolences to Harriet Loudin, Coleridge-Taylor wrote of her late husband, "I have always thought of him as the best friend I ever had... He had accomplished a vast work and was known and loved the world over."[93] Later in his U.S. visit, Coleridge-Taylor paid a call on Harriet Loudin and her niece Leota Henson at "Otira."

Along with concerts conducted in Washington, D.C., Coleridge-Taylor concertized in Baltimore, Milwaukee, Boston, and Chicago. Harry T. Burleigh participated in the brilliant concert at Chicago Music Hall, which consisted of vocal and instrumental solos from Coleridge-Taylor's work, including piano solos played by the composer himself. Among the piano solos was a group of three "symphonically arranged" spirituals,[94] from a set of twenty-four such arrangements published the following year by Oliver Ditson Company, with a forward by Booker T. Washington. Dr. Washington wrote:

> It is especially gratifying that at this time... when the Negro song is in too many minds associated with "rag" music and the more reprehensible "coon" song, that the most cultivated musician of his race, a man of the highest aesthetic ideals should seek to give permanence to the folk-songs of his people by giving them a new interpretation and an added dignity...
>
> The question is often asked to what extent are these songs (spirituals) being sung by the colored people and to what extent are they being preserved. In the large city churches they are being used but little; but in the smaller towns, and in the country districts, where the colored people live in greater numbers, their use is quite general, and new ones appear from time to time—Several schools and colleges of the South make an effort to preserve these songs, and at Fisk, Hampton and Tuskegee, they are sung constantly. New students coming in from remote parts of the South occasionally bring in new ones. While some of the colored people do not encourage the singing of the songs because they bring up memories of the trying conditions which gave them rise, the race as a whole realizes ... [t]he Negro folk song is the only distinctively American music, and is taking pride in using and preserving it.[95]

A new preservationist movement had gained strength at historically black universities. Even

Loudin's Fisk Jubilee Singers, 1897. (courtesy Portage County Historical Society Museum)

though jubilee singing was no longer a profitable fund-raising enterprise, many black educational institutions maintained jubilee singing companies for public relations and student recruitment purposes; among them were the Claflin University Quintet, Curry College Concert Company, Eckstein-Norton University Singers, Seven Students Concert Company of Wilberforce University, Atlanta University Quartet, Hearne Academy Choral Union, Roger Williams University Glee Club, and Tuskegee Institute Quartet.

Nowhere was this revitalizing trend more pronounced than at "that old mother of the spirituals," Fisk. Under the inspired leadership of John W. Work II, a university-sponsored company of Fisk Jubilee Singers was re-established and sent out from Nashville on a fund-raising and public relations tour in September 1899.

By 1923, Professor Work was prepared to acknowledge ragtime as "our distinctive American national product;"[96] but at the turn of the century the overpowering appeal and disreputable associations attached to ragtime were obstacles to the success of his struggling jubilee singing enterprise. The blossoming of ragtime was a countercurrent to the movement to create a "serious class" of American music based on the slave spirituals. Eventually, initiatives to elevate the spiritual art form were forced to withdraw to cloistered academic environs.

The rise of "authentic Negro minstrelsy" provided a comfortable categorization for all African American performers. The public no longer cared to differentiate between jubilee singing and "authentic" African American minstrelsy, or between a spiritual hymn and a minstrel parody. By turning a blind eye to the prolonged torrent of civil rights atrocities in the South, the rest of the country had become complicit in "keeping the black man down." In that low spirit, the general public retained a taste for jubilee singing while emphatically rejecting its spiritual and cultural implications. Widespread corruption of the spiritual with derisive satire allowed white listeners to enjoy the music from an emotionally detached distance, without brotherly empathy.

By the latter half of the 1890s, African American creative energies were being redirected into more worldly musical expressions. With a sense of purpose, black stage performers of the ragtime era trended away from minstrelsy and the conventions of minstrelsy, toward vaudeville and musical comedy. The late-nineteenth-century assault on the dignity of the spiritual unwittingly built a fire under twentieth-century black popular music.

In the privacy of the black, rural southern church-centered community, where white folks had no influence, the unvarnished folk spiritual remained a staple liturgy and maintained its dignity and sacred essence. While they no longer bear the imprimatur of "the only distinctively American music," the slaves' spiritual songs have entered the twenty-first century with remarkable resilience and continuing popular resonance.

Appendixes

Appendix 1

Repertoire of the Tennessee Jubilee Singers, 1888–1889

Dozens of titles from the Tennessee Jubilee Singers' working repertoire of the 1888–1889 period are preserved in various West Indian newspaper reviews.

Jubilee songs, generally sung by the entire troupe, include "Mary and Martha," "Go Down Moses," "Steal Away," "Good News, The Chariot Is Coming," "Swing Low, Sweet Chariot," "Humble Yourself," "Talk about Your Moses," "Roll Jordan Roll," "The Gospel Train," "Gwine to Ride up in the Chariot," "John Brown's Body," "Rise and Shine," "Didn't Old Pharoah Git Lost," "Walk in Jerusalem," "Hard Trials," "Come Along Sinners," "Mr. Michael, Hand Me Down Your Robe" (quartet), "Old Time Religion," "My Lord Is Writing All the Time," "Peter, Ring Dem Bells," "Judgement Day," "Keep Me from Sinking Down," "The Rocks in the Mountains," "Old Ark Is A-Movering," "There's a Meeting Here Tonight," "I'se Gwine in de Valley," "Put on the Golden Crown," "I've Been Listening," "Which Road You Gwine to Take," "No More Auction Block for Me," "Turn Back Pharoah's Army," "Wide River," "Jesus Refuge of My Soul," "When Moses Smote the Waters," "Angel Gabriel," "Our Ship Is on the Ocean," "Angels Meet Me at the Crossroads," "The Foolish and the Wise."

Soprano solos performed by Matilda S. Jones include "The Night Birds Cooing," "Ship on Fire," "Magnetic Waltz Song," "Marguerite Farewell," "Home Sweet Home," "Ecstacy," "Huntsman's Horn," "Speak Love," "Love Comes like a Summer Sigh," "Life's Story," "In the Gloaming," "Stolen Glances," "Sweet Dreamland Faces," "The Spider and the Fly."

Bass solos performed by Louis L. Brown include "Only to See Her Face," "Anchored," "Hybrias the Creator," "The Old Sexton," "Wrecked and Saved," "Soldier and a Man," "Virginia Rose Bud," "Smuggler," "100 Fathoms Deep," "Thy Sentinel Am I," "Madeline," "Washed from the Wheel."

Tenor solos performed by Will H. Pierce include "Marguerite," "Sweet Heather Bells," "Veneta," "Lime Kiln Club," "The Maid of Dundee," "You'll Remember Me," "Let Me like a Soldier Fall," "Gentle Annie," "See Thee and Forget Thee Never."

Other songs include "God in Mercy" (duet, Mme Jones and Miss A. M. Smith), "Tell Me Ye Merry Birds" (duet, Mme Jones and Will Pierce), "Alice Where Art Thou" (duet, Mme Jones and Will Pierce), "Hope Beyond" (duet, Mme Jones and L. L. Brown), "Life's Dream Is O'er" (duet, Mme Jones and Will Pierce), "Old Oaken Bucket" (quartet), "Down by de Sunrise" (mixed voice quartet); "Swanee River" (mixed voice quartet), "Soldier's Farewell" (male quartet), "Basso Prophundo" (operatic quartet), "Moonlight on the Lake" (quartet), "Rock-a-Bye Baby" (quartet), "Farmer John" (quartet), "God Save the Queen" (chorus), "The Professor at Home" ("A dramatic musical conceit" by L. L. Brown, Mme Jones, Will Pierce, and K. Johnson), "Mary Had a Little Lamb," "Hail Hail," "Land Ahoy," and "The Last Chorus."

Appendix 2

Personnel Listings of Orpheus M. McAdoo's and M. B. Curtis's Troupes in Australia, 1899–1900

M. B. Curtis's Afro-American Minstrel Company included Ernest Hogan (director of amusements), Tom Logan (stage manager), Laurence Chenault (assistant stage manager), Amon Davis (call boy, Kentucky Four dancer), Chas. F. Alexander (musical director), N. Clark Smith (bandmaster), Madah A. Heyer (prima donna), Carl Dante (magician), Louis H. Saulsbury (cornet, tenor), Siren Navarro (skirt dancer and contortionist), Muriel Ringgold (Kentucky Four dancer), Master Livers [Aaron Taylor] (Kentucky Four dancer), Katie Carter (Kentucky Four dancer), Vincent Bradley, Percy Denton, Ladson B. "Kid" Alston, Palmer H. Locke, Turner Baskett, Harry St. Clair, George Jones, Will Jones, George Taylor, Needham Wright, Master Blutch Jones, Robert C. Logan, Marion Blake, Laura C. Moss, Carrie Carter,

Luella Price, H. S. Stafford, Harry Thompson, Irwin Jones, Ed W. Johnson, Jerry Chorn, F. E. Watts, Harry Thyus, Thomas Sterman, William Countee, Chas. A. Kennedy, Harry Hull, Frank Sanford, Oree Locke, and N. Clark Smith's Pickaninny Band.

Orpheus McAdoo's Georgia Minstrels and Genuine Alabama Cake Walkers included Orpheus McAdoo (manager), Henderson Smith (bandmaster), Billy McClain (stage manager), Flora Batson (prima donna), Madame Cordelia McClain (prima donna), Kate Milton and Hen Wise (song and dance team), William Ferry, a.k.a. Ferry the Frog (contortionist), Willis Gauze (female impersonator), Gerard Miller (concert baritone), Dave and Edith Barton (buck and wing dancers), Grace Turner (singer, cakewalker), Charles W. Walker (singer, cakewalker), Ida May Walker, Frank Poole, Jackson and Mabel Hearde (sketch artists), Leon P. Rooks, John Brewer and wife (sketch artists, buck and wing dancers, cakewalkers), Ed Tolliver, John Pamplin (juggler), George Henry, Turner Jones. The band consisted of Henderson Smith (leader, solo B cornet), Jessie E. Smith (solo B cornet), James P. Jones (solo clarionet), Oscar Lindsey (solo alto), John Brewer (1st alto), James Harris (1st trombone), Alonzo Edwards (2nd trombone), Pete Woods (baritone), Edward Tolliver (tuba), Turner Jones (bass drum), F. Poole (snare drums), J. H. Heard (cymbals), George Henry (drum major), John Pamplin (lightning gun driller).

O. M. McAdoo's Virginia Jubilee Singers, in March 1899, included Orpheus McAdoo (proprietor, bass), Eugene McAdoo (bass), W. H. Nott (first tenor), R. H. Collins (second tenor), Professor C. A. White (musical director, accompanist), Moses Hamilton Hodges (baritone), Susie Anderson (soprano soloist), Jalvan (juggler), Jerry Mills (acrobat), Mme. Mattie Allen McAdoo (lady tenor), Miss Marshall Webb, Miss Robinson, possibly also Belle Gibbons. Fred Dawson (advance agent). Miss Sadie Ganey joined McAdoo's Jubilee Company in June of 1899.

McAdoo's Virginia Jubilee Singers, in August 1900, included Eugene McAdoo (basso), Belle Gibbons (lady baritone), Mr. W. Nott (tenor), Miss Dazalia Underwood (soprano soloist), Miss D. Silva (contralto), R. H. Collins (baritone), Willis Gauze (male mezzo soprano); Professor C. A. White (musical director, piano accompanist).

Appendix 3

Repertoire of McAdoo's Virginia Concert Company and Jubilee Singers, 1892–1893

McAdoo's Virginia Concert Company and Jubilee Singers had a richly varied program and a large repertoire. The following titles are preserved in Australasian newspapers which covered the Singers' performances of 1892 and 1893.

Jubilee songs, generally sung by the entire troupe, include "The Lord's Prayer," "Get You Ready, There's a Meeting Here Tonight," "The Band of Gideon," "Ring Those Chiming Bells," "Good News, the Chariot's Coming," "Angels Roll the Stone Away," "Roll, Jordan, Roll," "There's a Great Camp Meeting," "Walking in the Light," "Hard Trials," "Swing Low" with "The Benediction," "Steal Away to Jesus," "When the General Roll Is Called," "Way Over Jordan," "Didn't My Lord Deliver Daniel," "Judgement Day Is Rolling 'Round," "Still, I'm Moverin' Along," "Come unto Me," "One More River to Cross," "My Way's Cloudy," "Keep a-Inching Along," "Look Away in Heaven," "We Shall Walk through the Valley," "Go Down Moses," "Religion Is a Fortune," "My Lord What a Morning," "I'm Rolling through an Unfriendly World," "The Gospel Train," "The Winter Will Soon Be Over," "Mother, Is Massa Going to Sell Me Tomorrow," "John Brown's Body," "They Crucified My Savior," and "Who Built the Ark."

Soprano solos performed by Madame J. Stewart Ball include "Palm Branches," "La Zingara," "Way Down on the Swanee River," "Our Last Ball," "Cinderella's Dream," "Tit for Tat," "Twickenham Ferry," "Caller Herrin," "Let Me Dream Again," and "Comes a Gallant Youth."

Soprano solos performed by Laura Carr include "Calvary," "Bird on the Wing," "Three Old Maids of Lee," "When the Swallows Come Again," "The Cows Are in the Corn," "We'd Better Bide a Wee," "Charlie Is My Darling," "Orange Blossoms," and "Flowers of the Alps" (Wekerlin).

Soprano solos performed by Belle Gibbons include "The Song That Reached My Heart," "Within a Mile o' Edinborough Town," "Comin' thro' the Rye," and Tosti's "Goodbye."

Bass solos performed by Orpheus McAdoo include "The Old Sexton," "Rocked in the Cradle of the Deep," "Darkies Gather Closer," "I'm King over Land and Sea," and "Old Black Joe."

Baritone solos performed by Hamilton Hodges include "Is Not His Word like a Fire" (Mendelssohn), "The Lost Chord," "The Erl King," "The Death of Nelson," "Scotch Lassie Jean," "Anchored," "Margarita" (Lohr), "Romany Lass," "Can It Be," "Only the Sound of a Voice," "A Roving Life Is the Life for Me," "The Patriot," "When the Kye Came Hame," "The Wooing o' It," "Nazareth," "Even Bravest Heart," and "The Maniac" (Russell).

Tenor solos performed by R. H. Collins include "Nobody's Darling but Mine" and "In the Morning by the Bright Light."

"Tenor" solos performed by Mattie Allen McAdoo include "The Castle Gate," "The Little Fishermaiden," "The

Dutchman's Leetle Dog" (Emmett), "The Maid of the Mill," "The Highland Man," "Robin Adair," "Only Once More," "The Old, Old, Words," and "We Met Too Late."

Secular choruses (glees) included "Come Where the Lillies Bloom," "Good Night, Beloved," "Medley of National Airs," "Jingle Bells," "Imitation of the [Christchurch] Garrison Band," and "Annie Laurie" (Buck).

Male quartettes performed "God Is Love" (Dow), "Farewell, My Own True Love," "They Kissed, I Saw Them Do It," "Bingo," "The Bulldog and the Bullfrog," "Who'll Smoke My Meerschaum Pipe?" "In the Silent Mead" (Emerson), "The Three Crows," "Old Folks at Home," "There Was a Scotchman Had Two Sons," and "Thuringian Volksleid."

Other songs included scenes from "Bohemian Girl," a scene from "Trovatore," "Hope Beyond" (duet by Collins and Eugene McAdoo), "Home to Our Mountains," "Hark! What Mean Those Holy Voices" (both duets by Mattie Allen and Belle Gibbons), and "Excelsior" (Balfe, duet by Mattie Allen and M. Hamilton Hodges).

Appendix 4

Roster of the Detroit City Band, 1891–1892

The Detroit City Band roster included John W. Johnson, director, cornet, trombone, clarinet, violin, bass vocal; John J. Griffin, 1st B-flat cornet, violin, piano, guitar, banjo, double bass; Thomas H. Moxley, solo B-flat cornet, violin, key bugle; Frank Smith, 2nd B-flat cornet, guitar; Branch Johnson, 3rd B-flat cornet; Monroe Wainer, solo alto, violin; Prof. Ed M. Rector, 2nd alto, guitar, banjo, mandolin, double bass, piano; Fred S. Stone, piano, euphonium, alto, trombone; William M. Stone, tuba, double bass, piano, trombone; Charles H. Stone, trombone; John Ward, slide trombone; William Pfeiffer, double bass, bass drum, tuba; James C. Moore, 1st alto; James Turner, snare drum; John M. Smallwood, clarinet; Ben Tannenholz, violin; Prof. Theodore Finney, violin. Other associates were E. Azalia Smith (Hackley), Kate O. Taliafero, Richard Harrison, and John Chew.

Notes

Introduction

1. See Ida B. Wells, *A Red Record: Tabulated Statistics and Alleged Causes of Lynchings in the United States, 1892–1894* (Chicago: Donohue & Henneberry, 1895); August Meier, *Negro Thought in America, 1880–1915* (Ann Arbor: University of Michigan, 1968); Leon F. Litwak, "Hellhounds," in James Allen, Hilton Als, Congressman John Lewis and Leon F. Litwak, *Without Sanctuary: Lynching Photography in America* (Twin Palms Publishers, 2000).
2. I. Garland Penn, *The Afro-American Press and Its Editors* (Springfield: Willey & Company, 1891).
3. For published inventories of what is known to have survived, see Georgietta Merritt Campbell, *Extant Collections of Early Black Newspapers: A Research Guide to the Black Press, 1880–1915* (Troy: The Whitston Publishing Company, 1981); and James Danky, *African American Newspapers: A National Bibliography* (Cambridge: Harvard University Press, 1999).
4. W. Allison Sweeney, "The Foremost Journalist, Of the Negro Race—Edward Elder Cooper, Editor and Proprietor of The Illustrated Freeman—A Practical Man, a Ready Man, a Business Man," *Freeman*, December 21, 1889.
5. "George Levy Knox," *Freeman*, January 5, 1889; "G. L. Knox's New Business Venture," *Freeman*, January 9, 1892; "Salutatory," *Freeman*, June 11, 1892.
6. "The Rope Was Got," *Freeman*, March 17, 1894.
7. "Editorial Perambulations," *Southwestern Christian Advocate*, January 27, 1887.
8. "Rev. A. E. P. Albert, D.D.," *Southwestern Christian Advocate*, June 6, 1889; "Editor A. E. P. Albert," *Cleveland Gazette*, June 29, 1889.
9. *Planet*, February 16, 1895.
10. Henry C. Bruce, *The New Man* (1895) (New York: Negro University Press, 1969).
11. *Who's Who in Colored America: A Biographical Dictionary of Notable Living Persons of Negro Descent in America* (New York: Who's Who in Colored America Corporation, 1927), p. 29.
12. John Edward Hasse notes in his article, "Ragtime: From the Top," in Hasse, ed., *Ragtime: Its History, Composers and Music* (New York: Schirmer Books, 1985), p. 7: "On August 3, [1896] Ernest Hogan's song *All Coons Look Alike to Me*, with an optional chorus labeled 'Negro "Rag" Accompaniment,' was copyrighted. Two days later a copyright was filed for Witmark's edition of Ben Harney's song *You've Been a Good Old Wagon But You've Done Broke Down*. The cover claimed that Harney was the 'Original Introducer to the Stage of the Now Popular "Rag Time" in Ethiopian Song.' "
13. See, for instance, Tony Thorne, *The Dictionary of Contemporary Slang* (New York: Pantheon, 1990) and Clarence Major, *Juba to Jive: A Dictionary of African-American Slang* (New York: Viking, 1994). The more venerable *Oxford English Dictionary* notes its appearance in 1893 in the Bowery slum vernacular portrayed in Stephen Crane's first novel, *Maggie: A Girl of the Streets*.

Chapter 1: 1889

1. Leota Henson Turner, "The Life of Frederick J. Loudin, by His Niece," n.d., prepared for the Portage County, Ohio Historical Society. Other sources give Loudin's year of birth as 1836 and 1847. The 1842 date is also given in Loudin's obituary in *Cleveland Gazette*.
2. Doug Seroff, "A Voice in the Wilderness," *Popular Music and Society*, (forthcoming).
3. See Doug Seroff, "The Fisk Jubilee Singers in Britain," in Rainer Lotz and Ian Pegg, eds., *Under the Imperial Carpet*, (Crawley: Rabbit Press, Limited, 1986), pp. 42–55.
4. Leota Henson Turner, quoted in Mary Folger, "Frederick Loudin: One of Ravenna's Most Illustrious Citizens," *[Ravenna, Ohio] Record Courier*, March 10, 1971.
5. "An Interview with Mr. Loudin," *[Melbourne] Daily Telegraph*, June 31, 1886.

6. *Argus*, August 7, 1886.
7. R. B. Williams's diary, quoted in Chris Bourke, "R. B. Williams—He Came, He Sang, He Stayed," *Music in New Zealand*, Autumn 1991, p. 49.
8. *L'Entre Act*, March 12, 1887.
9. *Newcastle Evening Call*, September 13, 1887.
10. H. P., "Coloured Evangels," *Dominion*, June 5, 1942.
11. These 1929 Columbia recordings were reissued in 1963, as "Maori Music, the Rotorua Maori Choir," World Record International (LP) LZ 7088, Auckland, New Zealand.
12. *Argus*, June 6, 1887. Thanks to Gary LeGallant.
13. J. J. Utting, "The Georgias in Slavery," *Saturday Advertiser*, July 21, 1877, p. 15.
14. Georgia Minstrels star Charles A. "Judge" Crusoe remained active into the late-1880s. *New York Clipper* of October 26, 1889, identified him as the business manager of Green's Colored Minstrels, in what may have been his final outing. *Freeman* of March 7, 1903 included this note:

    > The veteran Georgia Minstrel Judge, Charles A. Crusoe ("the man that speaks"), although a paralytic for seventeen years, is happy to announce that he is still in the land of the living and will at any time be greatly pleased to receive visits from any member of the profession in reminiscent moods inclined that will call on him for a chat at his home, No. 224 W. 17th street, New York City. Friends must necessarily realize that he is not a mendicant; in consequence will please leave their pocketbooks at home before calling.

15. Transcription of a story told by Mrs. Maggie Porter Cole to Mrs. James A. Myers, director of the Fisk Jubilee Singers from 1927 to 1947, in Louise Davis, *Steal Away* (unpublished manuscript, 1959), with permission of the late author.
16. *[Melbourne] Herald*, May 2, 1889.
17. "Mrs. Flora Batson Bergen at Her Old Home," *Providence Daily Dispatch*, October 12, 1888, reproduced in *New York Age*, October 20, 1888.
18. Tennessee Jubilee Singers Scrapbook, "Press Notices and Letters—Tennessee Jubilee Singers—J. R. Smith, manager—Book No. 5" (August 1888–January 1889), Special Collections, Fisk University Library.
19. *Colonial Standard*, August 13, 1888.
20. *Port-of-Spain Gazette*, December 5, 1888.
21. *Daily Chronicle*, December 15, 1888.
22. *Daily Gleaner*, c. August 16, 1888. A detailed list of the Tennessee Jubilee Singers's working repertoire during the 1888–89 tour appears in the Appendix.
23. *New York Age*, March 9, 1889.
24. *New York Clipper*, March 16, 1889.
25. *New York Age*, March 16, 1889.
26. Florence Williams, "The Ways of the World," *New York Age*, March 23, 1889.
27. *New York Age*, April 20, 1889; Florence Williams, "Music and Dramatic," *New York Age*, May 11, 1889.
28. *Freeman*, May 18, 1889.
29. Madam Selika appears to have taken her name from "Sélika," the title character-heroine of Meyerbeer's *L'Africaine*. Thanks to Wayne D. Shirley.
30. For an historical account of the New Orleans University Singers see Lynn Abbott, "'Do Thyself a' no Harm': The Only Original New Orleans University Singers," *American Music Research Journal*, vol. 6 (1996), pp. 1–47.
31. "City News," *Freeman*, September 15, 1888.
32. "The Stage," *Freeman*, October 9, 1897.
33. *Chicago Defender*, October 8, 1927.
34. Actually, it was in 1884. See "The New Editor," *Southwestern Christian Advocate*, June 5, 1884.
35. Actually, he had bought a home in Indianapolis, but when he died on September 11, 1887, Rev. Taylor was at his brother's home in Louisville, Kentucky. See "Marshall W. Taylor, D.D.," *Southwestern Christian Advocate*, September 22, 1887.
36. Newman I. White, *American Negro Folk Songs* (Cambridge: Harvard University Press, 1928), pp. 51–2.
37. See Dena J. Epstein, "A White Origin for the Black Spiritual? An Invalid Theory and How It Grew," *American Music* (Summer 1983), pp. 53–9.
38. George Pullen Jackson, *White and Negro Spirituals: Their Life Span and Kinship, Tracing 200 Years of Untrammeled Song Making and Singing Among Our Country Folk* (1943), pp. 142, 144, 147, 157, 177, 215, 217, 219.
39. Irene V. Jackson-Brown, "Afro-American Song in the Nineteenth Century: A Neglected Source," *Black Perspectives in Music* (Spring 1976), p. 22.
40. Robin Hough, "Choirs of Angels Armed for War: Reverend Marshall W. Taylor's *A Collection of Revival Hymns and Plantation Melodies*," in George R. Keck and Sherrill V. Martin, eds., *Feel the Spirit: Studies in Nineteenth Century Afro-American Music* (New York: Greenwood Press, 1988), pp. 17, 19.
41. "Sunday Bells in New Orleans," *Southwestern Christian Advocate*, October 16, 1884.
42. "Visit to Straight University and Breakfast with Col. James Lewis," *Southwestern Christian Advocate*, March 26, 1885.

43. Rev. W. H. Jackson, "Singing the Songs of Our Fathers," *Southwestern Christian Advocate*, October 22, 1885.
44. "Meridian, Mississippi," *Southwestern Christian Advocate*, February 25, 1886.
45. See Sam Rivers's bio in Eileen Southern, *Biographical Dictionary of Afro-American and African Musicians* (Westport: Greenwood Press, 1982), p. 321.
46. Sol Tibbs, "Mama, Mama Make Cinda Haive Herself" (New Orleans: Louis Grunewald Co., Ltd., 1901).
47. "Stage," *Freeman*, November 8, 1902. There is at least one reported precedent to Tibbs's "Goo Goo Eyes" parody of "Booker T. Washington's Reception by President Roosevelt." Correspondence from the Mascotte Theater, Tampa, Florida, in *Freeman* of January 11, 1902 notes: "James J. Helton opened Dec. 23 [1901] and made an instantaneous hit with his clever monologue and a parody on 'Goo Goo Eyes,' relative to the Roosevelt-Washington episode." Apparently, Sol Tibbs and James Helton were close to the original source of the outrageous topical song "Can You Blame the Colored Man (for Making Those Goo-Goo Eyes)," which was recorded in 1927 by black banjoist Gus Cannon, as "Banjo Joe" ("Can You Blame the Colored Man," Paramount 12571, 1927, reissued on Document DOCD-5032). According to Sheldon Harris, *Blues Who's Who* (1979) (New York: DaCapo Press, 1989), p. 106, Gus Cannon was born in 1885 and started touring with medicine shows around 1914.
48. "The Stage," *Freeman*, December 9, 1905.
49. See Geneva Handy Southall, *Blind Tom, the Black Pianist-Composer (1849–1908): Continually Enslaved* (Lanham: Scarecrow Press, 1999). Also, there is a noteworthy chapter on Blind Tom in James Monroe Trotter's pioneering work from 1878, *Music and Some Highly Musical People*.
50. See Charles Wolfe and Kip Lornell, *The Life and Legend of Leadbelly* (New York: Harper Collins, 1992), pp. 53–6.
51. See Judith Tick, "Old-folks concert," in *New Grove Dictionary of American Music*, vol. 3, p. 406. Thanks to Wayne D. Shirley.
52. Wayne D. Shirley letter to Lynn Abbott, October 11, 1992. Background information on William Batchelder Bradbury was also kindly provided by Wayne D. Shirley. See also Juanita Karpf, "Populism with Religious Restraint: William B. Bradbury's *Esther, the Beautiful Queen*," *Popular Music and Society*, vol. 23, no. 1 (Spring 1999), pp. 1–29.
53. "Stage," *Freeman*, March 26, 1898.
54. "Variety and Minstrelsy," *New York Clipper*, July 7, 1894.
55. "Stage," *Freeman*, May 11, 1901; June 1, 1901.
56. "The Contrabands of South Carolina," *National Anti-Slavery Standard*, November 23, 1861.
57. For historical background on pioneer black minstrel troupes see Robert C. Toll, *Blacking Up: The Minstrel Show in Nineteenth-Century America* (New York: Oxford University Press, 1974), pp. 195–213.
58. "Stage," *Freeman*, December 13, 1902.
59. J. J. Utting, "The Georgias in Slavery," *Saturday Advertiser*, July 14, 1877. This article continued through successive issues of July 21, 1877; July 28, 1877; and August 4, 1877.
60. Ibid.
61. Ibid.
62. A. D. Sawyer, Hicks's business partner since 1886, remained in the United States to field a domestic branch of the Hicks-Sawyer Minstrels.
63. *New York Clipper*, September 1, 1894; September 29, 1894; November 3, 1894; November 24, 1894.
64. "Chas. B. Hicks Reported Dead," *Freeman*, December 13, 1902.
65. *Everyone's*, May 14, 1924. Pope died in Melbourne in April 1928.
66. *Southwestern Christian Advocate*, May 20, 1886; W. C. Handy, *Father of the Blues* (1941) (New York: Da Capo Press, 1991), pp. 39–40.
67. Sylvester Russell, "Billy (Wisdom) Windom, Famous Minstrel Ballad Singer of the Past, Dies of Broken Heart—Was of Mulatto Birth," *Freeman*, September 20, 1913.
68. J. Ed Green, "Obsequies of Tom McIntosh," *Freeman*, March 12, 1904.
69. *Chicago Defender*, November 8, 1924.
70. "The Stage," *Freeman*, November 2, 1907; November 16, 1907.
71. Lester A. Walton, "Music and the Stage," *New York Age*, November 9, 1911. The song title—"The Upper Tens and the Lower Fives"—refers to the classes of black society. In *Freeman* of August 30, 1890, a columnist outlined "some clearly defined destructions" of 1890s black society: "The first-class is the aristocracy or the 'Upper Ten;' the second class is the 'high-toned commoners,' or 8's; the third class is the 'rank and file' or 6's; the fourth, the democracy, or 'lower five.' " The derivation of this terminology remains obscure. The "Upper Ten" is perhaps synonymous with the "Talented Tenth," the elevated class of formally educated, "acculturated" African Americans who were challenged by W. E. B. DuBois in 1903 to act as "missionaries of culture among their people."
72. "The Stage," *Freeman*, October 4, 1913; January 3, 1914; January 31, 1914.

Chapter 2: 1890

1. See Chris Bourke, "R. B. Williams: He Came, He Sang, He Stayed," *Music in New Zealand*, Autumn 1991.
2. "The Race Doings," *Cleveland Gazette*, May 3, 1890.
3. The Leota Henson Turner scrapbook is preserved in the Azalia Hackley Collection at the Detroit Public Library.
4. Frederick J. Loudin, "Supplement," in J. B. T. Marsh, *The Story of the Jubilee Singers* (Cleveland: The Cleveland Printing and Publishing Co., 1892), pp. 143–4.
5. *Indian Daily News*, November 18, 1889.
6. Marsh, p. 144.
7. Ibid, p. 145.
8. Ibid, pp. 146–7.
9. *Delhi Gazette*, December 1889, reproduced in *Fisk Herald*, April 1890.
10. Marsh, p. 144.
11. Ibid, p. 147.
12. *Daily Press*, February 26, 1890.
13. Marsh, p. 148.
14. Ibid, p. 150.
15. Ibid.
16. Ibid, p. 151.
17. Ibid, p. 152.
18. Ibid, p. 153.
19. *Cleveland Gazette*, December 3, 1892.
20. *Fisk Herald*, July 1890.
21. Paul Hutchison, *The Story of the Epworth League* (The Methodist Book Concern, 1927).
22. *Cleveland Gazette*, May 6, 1893.
23. It was explained in *Cleveland Gazette* of April 29, 1893, that the Loudin Key Locker and Loudin Window Locker prevented a window lock from being "picked" from the outside or pried up from the bottom.
24. Thanks to Rainer E. Lotz for sharing his research findings on African American musicians in Europe.
25. Thanks to Wayne D. Shirley for information on Ida Mae Yeokum.
26. "The Stage," *Freeman*, November 12, 1898; November 19, 1898; November 26, 1898.
27. Sunset Four, "Barnum's Steam Calliope," Paramount 12241, 1924, reissued on Document DOCD-5340; "Calliope Song," Seven Musical Magpies, Victor 19544, 1924, reissued on Document DOCD-5604; "The Steamboat," Birmingham Jubilee Singers, Columbia 14224, 1927, reissued on Document DOCD-5346.
28. Nan Bostick and Arthur LaBrew, "Harry P. Guy and the 'Ragtime Era' of Detroit, Michigan" *Rag-Time Ephemeralist* (no. 2), 1999, p. 111.
29. "Thibodaux Massacre," *Southwestern Christian Advocate*, November 24, 1887; Jeffrey Gould, "The Strike of 1887: Louisiana Sugar War," *Southern Exposure* (vol. 12, no. 6), November–December 1984, pp. 45–55.
30. For background information on Julia Yarrington and Abbie Wright Lyons, see Abbott, "Do Thyself a' no Harm."
31. See Ulysses "Jim" Walsh, "Favorite Pioneer Recording Artists: George Washington Johnson," *Hobbies*, September 1944, pp. 27–8; "Favorite Pioneer Recording Artists: In Justice to George Washington Johnson, Part I," *Hobbies*, January 1971, pp. 37–9, 50, 91; and "Favorite Pioneer Recording Artists: In Justice to George Washington Johnson, Part II," *Hobbies*, February 1971, pp. 37, 39–40, 50, 92.
32. *Freeman*, February 24, 1906.
33. *Daily Picayune*, September 28, 1887.
34. "The Stage," *Freeman*, October 24, 1896.
35. "The Stage," *Freeman*, December 31, 1898.
36. "The Stage," *Freeman*, April 8, 1899. For an historical account of the 400 Club and Scott Joplin's relationship to it, see Edward A. Berlin, *King of Ragtime: Scott Joplin and His Era* (New York: Oxford University Press, 1994), pp. 34–44.
37. *Freeman*, December 30, 1899. Ed Wyer, Jr. and his younger brother J. Paul Wyer were later associated with W. C. Handy's Memphis Blues Band.
38. "Stage," *Freeman*, January 26, 1901.
39. "Stage Gossip," *Freeman*, July 10, 1915.
40. *Freeman*, November 11, 1916.
41. Letter from Charles B. Hicks, June 17, 1902, in "Stage," *Freeman*, September 6, 1902.
42. "Gossip of the Stage," *Freeman*, February 8, 1913.
43. See Toll, *Blacking Up*, pp. 259–60.
44. The Singing Sentinels, "Old Aunt Jemima," Sonora 1137, included in 78rpm "Album Set" no. 483, "American Ballads," c. 1947.
45. James K. Kennard, Jr., "Who Are Our National Poets?" *Knickerbocker Magazine* (1845), reproduced in Eileen Southern, "Black Musicians and Early Ethiopian Minstrelsy," in Annemarie Bean, James V. Hatch, and Brooks McNamara, eds., *Inside the Minstrel Mask: Readings in Nineteenth-Century Blackface Minstrelsy* (Hanover: University Press of New England, 1996), pp. 43–63.
46. Toll cites Tally, *Negro Folk Rhymes*, 1922; and Scarborough, *On the Trail of Negro Folksongs*, 1925.
47. "Raise R-U-K-U-S Tonight," Norfolk Jazz Quartette, Paramount 12032, 1923, reissued on Document DOCD-5382; "Gonna Raise Rukus Tonight," Riley

Puckett, Columbia 15455, 1928; "Gonna Have Lasses in the Morning," Golden Melody Boys, Paramount 3087, 1928; "Raise a Rukus To-Night," Birmingham Jubilee Singers, Columbia 14263, 1927, reissued on Document DOCD-5346; "Poor Mourner," Four Dusty Travelers, Columbia 14477, 1929, reissued on Document DOCD-5538; "Come Along Little Children," Picaninny Jug Band, Champion 16654, 1932, reissued on RST BDCD-6002. In the latter three renditions the final line is given in variations of, "She got out of the notion of dying at all."

48. Columbia 14609-D, 1931, reissued on Document DOCD-5498. Also: Bryant's Jubilee Quartet, "Who Stole De Lock," Banner 32173, 1931, reissued on Document DOCD-5437; and The Blue Chips, "Oh! Monah," ARC 6–09–55, 1936, reissued on Document DOCD-5488.
49. "The Stage," *Freeman*, June 23, 1900.
50. For different explanations of the origin of the term see "The Stage," *Freeman*, January 4, 1908; and Henry T. Sampson, *The Ghost Walks* (Metuchen: The Scarecrow Press, 1988), pp. vii–viii.
51. "The Stage," *Freeman*, October 27, 1906.
52. "Stage Gossip," *Freeman*, July 10, 1915.
53. Salem Tutt Whitney, "Seen and Heard While Passing," *Freeman*, July 17, 1915.
54. "Our Billy Kersands, Pioneer in the Profession, Valued for His Long Record," *Freeman*, July 24, 1915.
55. Handy, *Father of the Blues*, p. 40.
56. "The Stage," *Freeman*, March 27, 1909.
57. Handy, *Father of the Blues*, p. 32.
58. "The Stage," *Freeman*, December 25, 1897.
59. *Freeman*, September 20, 1890.
60. Handy, *Father of the Blues*, p. 37.
61. "The Stage," *Freeman*, October 17, 1903.
62. "The Stage," *Freeman*, November 23, 1907.
63. George L. Moxley letter to W. C. Handy, quoted in *Father of the Blues*, pp. 38–9.
64. A review of 1870s editions of *New York Clipper*, conducted by researcher Rob Bird, uncovered references to dozens of jubilee singing companies professionally active during that period. Thanks to Rob Bird for sharing his *Clipper* research.
65. *Southern Workman*, February 1897, p. 24.
66. A photograph in Hampton Institute's Archives and Museum shows McAdoo as a member of a male quartet which also includes "Evans, Daggs, and [William H.] Hamilton." The photo is dated "1881–'83."
67. Orpheus M. McAdoo letter to General S. C. Armstrong, October 2, 1886, Sydney, N.S.W., Australia.
68. "Trage," "The Black Patti," *Freeman*, August 29, 1891.
69. In her *Negro Musicians and Their Music*, p. 225, Maud Cuney-Hare incorrectly states that Hodges left the U.S. to visit Australia in 1896. He left with McAdoo's Virginia Jubilee Singers, circa April 1890, and first visited Australia with McAdoo in early 1892. He remained with McAdoo's company until 1899–1900.
70. Orpheus M. McAdoo letter to General S. C. Armstrong, c. May 1890, London, England. This letter is housed at the Hampton Institute Archives.
71. "Jubilee Singers at Vaudeville," *[Cape Town, South Africa] Cape Argus*, July 1, 1890.
72. *[King Williamstown, South Africa] Imvo Zabantsundu*, October 16, 1890, reprinted in Josephine Wright, "Orpheus Myron McAdoo—Singer, Impressario," *Black Perspectives in Music*, Fall 1976, p. 323.
73. Orpheus M. McAdoo letter to General S. C. Armstrong, n.d., published in *Southern Workman*, November 1890, p. 120, reprinted in Wright, p. 322.
74. Veit Erlmann, *African Stars: Studies in Black South African Performance* (Chicago: University of Chicago Press, 1991), p. 41.
75. Eugene McAdoo letter, *Southern Workman*, no. 23 (January 1894), p. 15.
76. *Kaffrarian Watchman and Government Gazette*, reprinted in *Southern Workman*, January 1891, p. 134.
77. J. Semouse (English translation by N. Morie), *Leselinyana* (Morija, Lesotho), October 1, 1890. Thanks to Veit Erlmann for sharing this important reference.
78. For more details concerning the Native South African Choir see Erlmann, *African Stars*, and Veit Erlmann, *Music, Modernity, and the Global Imagination* (New York: Oxford University Press, 1999).
79. Good examples of African American spirituals commercially recorded in South Africa by black South African quartets and choirs include: "Oh Mary, Don't You Weep," Wilberforce Quartet of South Africa, Columbia GR7, 1930; "My Soul Is a Witness for My Lord," Wesley House Quartette of Fort Hare, Singer GE 180, c. 1937; "There's a Meeting Here Today," Kings Messengers Quartet, Number One LP9032, 1964; "Swing Low Sweet Chariot," Barosisi Ba Morena, RPM LP7042, 1979.
80. "A Phenomenal Vocalist," *Cleveland Gazette*, July 4, 1891.
81. "Mosquito," Livingstone College Male Quartet, Victor 20949, 1927, reissued on Document DOCD-5486.
82. "Bohunkus and Josephus," Birmingham Jubilee Singers, Columbia 14370-D, 1927, reissued on Document DOCD-5346; (Untitled), Old South Quartette, Broadway 5031, 1928, reissued on DOCD-5061.
83. See Appendix 3.

84. "The Jubilee Singers," *[Sydney, Australia] Daily Telegraph*, April 4, 1893. A similar, but more precise description appeared in *Sydney Morning Herald*, December 19, 1898: " 'Steal Away to Jesus,' marked by the sudden accelerations of time and the equally unexpected ritardandos—the 'Steal Away' in slow sustained chords of long-drawn harmony, the 'to Jesus' in a rapid staccato phrase."
85. *[Cape Town, South Africa] Cape Times*, June 28, 1897, reported in Erlmann, *African Stars*, p. 36.
86. *Freeman*, February 27, 1892.
87. *Chicago Defender*, August 24, 1929.
88. Thanks to Veit Erlmann for sharing this citation.
89. Erlmann, *African Stars*, p. 50.
90. *Sydney Morning Herald*, January 7, 1899.
91. *Freeman*, March 4, 1899.
92. "The Stage," *Indianapolis Freeman*, June 17, 1899.
93. Henderson Smith letter, May 16, 1899, published in *Freeman*, May 27, 1899.
94. "World of Players," *New York Clipper*, September 26, 1891; "Latest by Telegraph," *New York Clipper*, January 2, 1892; "M. B. Curtis's Trial," *New York Clipper*, February 27, 1892; "The World of Players," *New York Clipper*, March 5, 1892; "The World of Players," *New York Clipper*, June 4, 1892; "Latest by Telegraph," *New York Clipper*, August 26, 1893; and "World of Players," *New York Clipper*, September 2, 1893.
95. *New York Clipper*, November 17, 1894.
96. *Kansas City Star*, reproduced in Dennis Pash, "Ernest Hogan. 'The Originator of Rag Time Music,'" *Rag Time Ephemeralist*, vol. 1, no. 1 (1998), p. 38.
97. Henderson Smith letter, dated July 27, 1899, Ballarat, Victoria, published in *Freeman*, September 9, 1899.
98. *[Sydney] Referee*, July 12, 1899, reproduced in *Freeman*, August 26, 1899.
99. Henderson Smith letter, late-July 1899, posted from Goulburn, Australia, published in *Freeman*, September 2, 1899.
100. Henderson Smith letter, July 27, 1899, published in *Freeman*, September 9, 1899.
101. *Freeman*, September 23, 1899.
102. Letter from Billy McClain, posted from Melbourne, August 14, 1899, and paraphrased in *Freeman*, September 23, 1899.
103. Henderson Smith letter, August 15, 1899, Melbourne, published in *Freeman*, October 21, 1899.
104. *Freeman*, February 22, 1890.
105. Harry Rickards, born in Great Britain in 1841, was an important vaudeville pioneer. According to Richard Waterhouse, *Minstrel Show to Vaudeville: The Australian Popular Stage, 1788–1914* (Kensington: University of New South Wales, 1990), p. 116, "Beginning in 1892, Rickards enjoyed a virtual monopoly of the Australian stage," and Rickard's Tivoli Theater in Sydney "became the headquarters of a vaudeville business which eventually expanded to include all mainland [Australian state] capitals."
106. Henderson Smith letter published in *Freeman*, January 6, 1900.
107. *Freeman*, May 19, 1900.
108. Henderson Smith letter, August 15, 1899, Melbourne, published in *Freeman*, October 21, 1899.
109. Henderson Smith letter, August 27, 1899, Melbourne, published in *Freeman*, October 14, 1899.
110. *Referee*, January 10, 1900.
111. *Otago Witness*, January 18, 1900.
112. *[Wellington, New Zealand] Variety*, c. August 1899. Thanks to Tony Hale.
113. "The Afro-American Minstrels," *[Wellington, New Zealand] Evening Post*, September 1, 1899.
114. *Sydney Morning Herald*, September 4, 1900.
115. See especially C. Ware, " 'La Pas Ma La:' A Loose Assemblage of Observations," *Rag Time Ephemeralist*, vol. 1, no. 1 (1998), pp. 45–52.
116. *Sydney Morning World*, June 24, 1899.
117. Henderson Smith letter, August 27, 1899, Melbourne, published in *Freeman*, October 14, 1899.
118. James P. Jones (of McAdoo's party), quoted in *Freeman*, June 16, 1900.
119. Henderson Smith letter, Perth, Australia, published in *Freeman*, November 25, 1899.
120. Henderson Smith letter, published in *Freeman*, January 6, 1900.
121. Henderson Smith letter, Brisbane, Queensland, Australia, January 27, 1900, published in *Freeman*, March 17, 1900.
122. Henderson Smith letter, Melbourne, Victoria, August 15, 1899, published in *Freeman*, October 21, 1899.
123. "Four Column Card" written by Ernest Hogan, reproduced in *Otago Witness*, September 12, 1900.
124. *Freeman*, June 16, 1900. As recalled in *[Sydney] Daily Mirror*, January 14, 1987, an outbreak of bubonic plague in Sydney in the spring and summer of 1900 had spread to Queensland, and ultimately resulted in about 300 deaths.
125. *Sydney Morning Herald*, June 2, 1900.
126. *Table Talk*, October 11, 1900.
127. *Table Talk*, January 4, 1902; *Otago [New Zealand] Witness*, April 30, 1902; May 21, 1902; *Referee*, August 27, 1902; October 1, 1902. Thanks to Gary LeGallant.

128. "The Stage," *Freeman*, May 16, 1908.
129. *Otago Witness*, March 6, 1901. William Ferry, a.k.a. "Ferry the Frog," came back to Australia to perform in 1920. His wife, a New Zealand native, accompanied him on the long and successful return tour. *Theatre* of October 20, 1921, reported Ferry the Frog scoring heavily "with the 'Bluebeard' pantomime at the Grand Opera House, Sydney." Mr. and Mrs. Ferry were spotted in Brisbane in August 1922, and two years later were reported arriving back in New York City. Ferry, an enthusiastic world traveler, had expressed interest (*Everyone's*, n.d., c. 1922) in touring Manila, China, and Japan. Perhaps he did so before he returned to America.
130. According to *Daily Telegraph* of July 8, 1900, the operation was for appendicitis.
131. *Sydney Morning Herald*, July 18, 1900.
132. Registration of death, Orpheus Myron McAdoo, recorded at Sydney, N.S.W., retrieved by Gary LeGallant.
133. Willis F. Gauze letter, July 23, 1900, in *Freeman*, October 6, 1900.
134. *Sydney Morning Herald*, October 5, 1903.
135. *Otago Witness*, October 31, 1900.
136. *Table Talk*, October 20–7, 1904.
137. *Australian Variety and Show World*, September 13, 1916.
138. *Theatre*, June 2, 1919.
139. *Theatre*, September 2, 1918.
140. *Australian Variety and Show World*, May 16, 1919.
141. *Theatre*, December 2, 1918.
142. Gary LeGallant interview with Violet Palmer, 1985. See also *Table Talk*, December 23, 1920; and *Theatre*, April 1, 1920.
143. Advertising postcard in the A. Cabot theatrical scrapbook, Alexander Turnbull Library, Wellington, New Zealand. Thanks to Tony Hale.

Chapter 3: 1891

1. "Theatrical History," *Pittsburgh Courier*, July 9, 1932.
2. Handy, *Father of the Blues*, p. 33.
3. While *New York Clipper* consistently referred to Foote's company as "African-American," the black weeklies stuck to the more politically correct term of the 1890s, "Afro-American."
4. James Weldon Johnson, *Black Manhattan*, 1930 (New York: Da Capo Press, 1991), p. 95.
5. Sylvester Russell, "Chicago Weekly Review," *Freeman*, January 22, 1916.
6. *Black Manhattan*, p. 95.
7. "Florence Hines Dead," *Chicago Defender*, March 22, 1924.
8. Henry T. Sampson, *Blacks in Blackface: A Source Book on Early Black Musical Shows* (Metuchen: The Scarecrow Press), 1980, pp. 61–2.
9. "Mr. John W. Isham," *Freeman*, December 24, 1898.
10. "The Stage," *Freeman*, June 9, 1900.
11. See Paul Oliver, *Songsters & Saints: Vocal Traditions on Race Records* (Cambridge: Cambridge University Press, 1984), pp. 52–64.
12. Sylvester Russell, "Welcome Death! Slogan of Robert Cole," *Freeman*, August 12, 1911.
13. *Black Manhattan*, p. 102.
14. "Gossip of the Stage," *Freeman*, August 5, 1911.
15. "The Stage," *Freeman*, April 25, 1903.
16. The standard discography, *Blues and Gospel Records 1890–1943*, notes that a cylinder recording of "Dora Dean" was made in 1896 by the Unique Quartet, but an extant copy has yet to be found.
17. "Stage," *Freeman*, March 15, 1902.
18. See Tom Fletcher, *The Tom Fletcher Story—100 Years of the Negro in Show Business* (New York: Burdge & Company, 1954), p. 110.
19. "Mr. John W. Isham," *Freeman*, December 24, 1898.
20. "The Stage," *Freeman*, November 10, 1906.
21. George M. Davis, "The Mallory Brothers and Their Career," *Freeman*, December 23, 1911.
22. *Freeman*, December 30, 1899.
23. *[Fall River, Massachusetts] Daily Globe*, quoted in "Stage," *Freeman*, January 11, 1902.
24. "The Stage," *Freeman*, October 5, 1907.
25. "Gossip of the Stage," *Freeman*, September 20, 1913.
26. "Frank Mallory Laid to Rest," *Freeman*, June 2, 1917.
27. J. J. Sawyer, "Jubilee Songs and Plantation Melodies, Sung by the Original Nashville Students," 1884. Thanks to Rob Bird.
28. *Louisville Courier Journal*, March 21, 1886. "Rasper's Birthday Party" appears to have had its start as a song by Sam Lucas, published in 1884.
29. "World of Players," *New York Clipper*, March 30, 1889; "Illinois," *New York Clipper*, June 13, 1891.
30. "Hagerman's Success," *Cleveland Gazette*, October 29, 1892.
31. The October 29, 1893, edition of *Chicago Tribune*, Thearle's hometown daily paper, mentioned: "Harry B. Thearle will manage during the coming season the Remeny Grand Concert company, the Chicago Lady Quartet, the John Thomas company, and the Shipp Brothers, royal hand bell ringers. . . . He will also

manage George Francis Train and Ben King, and as usual Nye and Burbank."

32. *Freeman* of February 19, 1898, noted, "Thearle's Original Nashville Students played Montrose, Colo., last Saturday and Sunday night. . . . On Sunday night after the show the company was tendered a banquet by the colored people of Montrose. . . . Those present [included] J. Cox, manager Nashville Students."
33. *Freeman*, December 25, 1897.
34. *Chicago Defender*, January 20, 1923.
35. "The Stage," *Freeman*, September 3, 1898.
36. *Freeman*, April 2, 1898.
37. "The Stage," *Freeman*, June 17, 1899.
38. "Lash" Gideon continued to manage minstrel shows until his death in 1912. According to his obituary in *Freeman* of April 6, 1912, Gideon "first attracted attention as manager of a jubilee company and afterwards managed the Nashville Students . . ., and then consolidated the two forms of entertainment. The decline of jubilee in America had caused him to tour much in Canada.

    "His next venture was to convert the Nashville Students (not students in college) into minstrelsy and that was also successful."
39. P. G. Lowery letter to *Freeman*, November 10, 1900; "Stage," *Freeman*, December 1, 1900.
40. "The Stage," *Freeman*, September 8, 1906.
41. *Freeman*, July 31, 1897.
42. "The Stage," *Freeman*, May 11, 1907.
43. "Our Presiding Elders," *Southwestern Christian Advocate*, August 30, 1894; "Noble Sissle," *Freeman*, April 24, 1915; Robert Kimball and William Balcom, *Reminiscing with Sissle and Blake* (New York: Viking, 1973).
44. "Personal and General," *Southwestern Christian Advocate*, November 2, 1905; Kimball and Balcom, *Reminiscing with Sissle and Blake.*
45. "Bert A. Williams & Co. in 'Mr. Lode of Koal,'" *Freeman*, November 20, 1909.
46. "A Note or Two," *Chicago Defender*, May 12, 1917.
47. "Tom Brown Dead," *Chicago Defender*, June 28, 1919.
48. Luke Jordan, "Tom Brown Sits in His Prison Cell," Victor 23400, 1929, reissued on Document DOCD-5574.
49. Sylvester Russell, "George H. Primrose Retires," *Freeman*, May 16, 1903.
50. "Stage," *Freeman*, December 6, 1902; "Movie and Stage Department," *Chicago Defender*, June 18, 1927.
51. For a discussion of later African American fife and drum traditions, see David Evans, "Black Fife and Drum Music in Mississippi," *Mississippi Folklore Register*, vol. 6 (1972); and David Evans, "Traveling through the Jungle: Negro Fife and Drum Music from the Deep South," liner notes to Testament TCD-5017.
52. "A Note or Two," *Chicago Defender*, August 20, 1927; May 26, 1928.
53. The contradiction-riddled "Jeff Davis Monument" incident, Mrs. Albert's reaction to it, and Scott Joplin's part in it are more thoroughly explored in Berlin, *King of Ragtime.*
54. Bill Russell and Richard B. Allen interview with Edmond Hall, April 11, 1957 (Hogan Jazz Archive, Tulane University).
55. Thomas C. Cox, *Blacks in Topeka, Kansas, 1865–1915: A Social History* (Baton Rouge: Louisiana State University Press, 1982), pp. 31, 145.
56. E. C. Perrow, "Songs and Rhymes from the South," *Journal of American Folklore*, vol. xxvi, no. c (April–June, 1913), p. 124. The article goes on to say that this extraordinary race horse was "Evidently named for prominent Kentuckian Proctor Knott (died 1911)."
57. "Ragtime (Invented in St. Louis) Is Dead," *St. Louis Post-Dispatch*, April 4, 1909, quoted in John Edward Hasse, "Ragtime: From the Top," in John Edward Hasse, ed., *Ragtime: Its History, Composers and Music* (New York: Schirmer, 1985), p. 8.

Chapter 4: 1892

1. The origins of the cake walk remain mysterious. No contemporaneous references to cake walks have been unearthed from the literature of slavery days. For recent speculation on the origin and development of cake walks see C. Ware, "The 'Cake Walk,'" *Rag-Time Ephemeralist*, vol. 2 (1999), pp. 22–69.
2. "Stray Locals," *New York Age*, February 6, 1892.
3. "Emanuel Lodge Concert," *New York Age*, February 13, 1892.
4. "The Cake Walk," *New York Times*, February 18, 1892.
5. "Complimentary Words for Indianapolis Colored People," *Indianapolis News*, n.d., quoted in *Freeman*, March 19, 1892.
6. "Our Alternate at Large—Reflections," *Freeman*, March 19, 1892.
7. *Baltimore Afro-American*, n.d., reprinted in *Cleveland Gazette*, January 29, 1898.
8. It was announced in *Freeman* of January 25, 1902, that, "Luke Pulley will stage and direct the tenth annual championship cake walk and jubilee at Madison Square Garden, New York City on Feb. 5."
9. "Carnival Is King!" *Kansas City Star*, October 4, 1894.

10. "Some Things They Did," *Kansas City Star*, October 5, 1894.
11. "All the Town Made Merry," *Kansas City Star*, October 5, 1894.
12. "Some Things They Did."
13. For an excellent article on Doc Brown which incorporates several reports from *Kansas City Star*, see Dennis Pash, "'Doc' Brown: Champion Cake Walker of the West," *Rag-Time Ephemeralist*, vol. 2 (1999), pp. 70–7.
14. *National Anti-Slavery Standard*, October 18, 1862.
15. *National Anti-Slavery Standard*, February 28, 1863.
16. *National Anti-Slavery Standard*, March 11, 1865.
17. *National Anti-Slavery Standard*, April 15, 1865.
18. See Seroff, "A Voice in the Wilderness."
19. M. Marguerite Davenport, *Azalia: The Life of Madame E. Azalia Hackley* (Boston: Chapman & Grimes, 1947).
20. For more about B. F. Thomas's early life see Toni Passmore Anderson, *The Fisk Jubilee Singers: Performing Ambassadors for the Survival of an American Treasure, 1871–1878*, PhD. dissertation, Georgia State University, 1997.
21. James Monroe Trotter, *Music and Some Highly Musical People* (1878) (New York: Johnson Reprint Corporation, 1968), pp. 88–105.
22. "The Stage," *Freeman*, November 27, 1909.
23. It was reported in *Freeman* of December 3, 1910, that, "The Colored Vaudeville Benevolent Association held memorial services in memory of its departed members November 22nd. They [include] John W. Luca."
24. The usual phrase is "hay-foot, straw-foot," a command employed in training camps to help "rustic recruits" distinguish right from left while learning to march. *The Oxford English Dictionary* (second edition, vol. vii, p. 29) documents its use as early as 1851. Thanks to Wayne Shirley.
25. "Stage," *Freeman*, December 13, 1902.
26. "Hen Wise Dead," *Chicago Defender*, June 2, 1917.
27. "The Stage," *Freeman*, January 15, 1898; March 19, 1898; May 7, 1898.
28. "The Stage," *Freeman*, April 10, 1915.
29. "Shelton Busy," *Chicago Defender*, September 8, 1917.
30. Handy, *Father of the Blues*, p. 16; Abbe Niles, "Introduction: Sad Horns," in W. C. Handy, ed., *Blues: An Anthology* (New York: Albert & Charles Boni, 1926), p. 19.
31. James Weldon Johnson, "The Origin of the 'Barber Chord,'" *Mentor*, vol. 27, no. 1 (February 1929), p. 53.
32. *Cleveland Gazette*, October 6, 1894.
33. Exemplary black mandolinists whose 1920s and 1930s vintage recordings have been reissued on cd include Matthew Prater with Nap Hayes on the anthology "String Bands 1925–1929," Document DOCD-5167; James "Yank" Rachel, Document WBCD-007; Coley Jones with the Dallas String Band on the anthology "Texas: Black Country Dance Music 1927–1935," Document DOCD-5162; Charlie McCoy with various Mississippi string bands including the Mississippi Mud Steppers, RST BDCD-6013; and Vol Stevens with the Memphis Jug Band, Document DOCD-5021, DOCD-5022, and DOCD-5023.
34. "W. Philips Dabney," *Richmond Planet*, February 23, 1895.
35. Wendell P. Dabney, *Cincinnati's Colored Citizens*, 1926 (New York, Negro Universities Press, 1970), p. 177.
36. "The Stage," *Freeman*, February 2, 1907.
37. See Gail Estelle Berry, *Wendell Phillips Dabney, Leader of the Negro Protest* (unpublished dissertation, University of Cincinnati, 1965); Joseph T. Beaver, Jr., *I Want You to Know Wendell Phillips Dabney* (Mexico, 1958); and William David Smith, "Dabney, Wendell Phillips," in Rayford W. Logan and Michael R. Winston, eds., *Dictionary of American Negro Biography* (New York: W. W. Norton, 1982), pp. 154–5.
38. Handy, *Father of the Blues*, p. xiii.
39. Southern, *Biographical Dictionary*, p. 91.
40. C. S. Mattison, *Cadenza*, July–August 1896.
41. Doug Seroff correspondence with Doug Back and Peter Danner, 1997. Also, see Stanley Sadie, ed., *The New Grove Dictionary of Musical Instruments* (London: McMillan Press, 1984), vol. 2, p. 162.
42. "Reminiscences of the Colored Profession," *Freeman*, February 25, 1905.
43. Apparently, the Detroit City Band was not Ed Rector's only community outlet. A biographical sketch of Detroit-born minstrel comedian Harry Gillam in the *Freeman* "Stage" columns of January 15, 1898, notes that in 1885, when Gillam was thirteen years old, he "was the star of E. M. Rector's Juvenile Minstrels."
44. Evidence is given in Nan Bostick and Arthur LaBrew, "Harry P. Guy and the 'Ragtime' Era of Detroit, Michigan," *Rag-Time Ephemeralist* (no. 2), 1999, p. 112, which suggests that Johnson was with Richards & Pringle's Georgia Minstrels.
45. Ibid, p. 111.
46. Ibid, p. 114.
47. This date is given in Southern's *Biographical Dictionary*.
48. For additional biographical information see Anderson, p. 324.
49. *Fisk Herald*, December 1895.
50. *Cleveland Gazette*, December 11, 1897; December 18, 1897; December 25, 1897; January 22, 1898.

51. *Cleveland Gazette*, September 24, 1898.
52. According to Arthur LaBrew, *The Afro-American Music Legacy in Michigan: A Sesquicentennial Tribute* (self-published, 1987), p. 118, it was Fred Stone who recommended Shook to replace Finney on violin: "He had known of Shook's performance abilities during trips to Cleveland where the Finney and Johnson groups had performed."
53. *Cleveland Gazette*, June 10, 1899.
54. Bostick and LeBrew, p. 120.
55. See Lawrence Gushee, "A Preliminary Chronology of the Early Career of Ferd 'Jelly Roll' Morton," *American Music*, vol. 3, no. 4 (Winter 1985).
56. Dave Peyton, "The Musical Bunch," *Chicago Defender*, May 14, 1927.

Chapter 5: 1893

1. Note, for example, Rupert Hughes, *Famous American Composers: Being a Study of the Music of This Country, and of Its Future, with Biographies of the Leading Composers of the Present Time* (Boston: L. C. Page & Company, 1900), p. 22:

> The folk-music of the negro slaves is most frequently mentioned as the right foundation for a strictly American school. A somewhat misunderstood statement advanced by Dr. Antonin Dvorák, brought this idea into general prominence, though it had been discussed by American composers, and made use of in compositions of all grades long before he came here.
>
> The vital objection, however, to the general adoption of negro music as a base for an American school of composition is that it is in no sense a national expression. It is not even a sectional expression, for the white Southerners among whose slaves this music grew, as well as the people of the North, have always looked upon negro music as an exotic and curious thing. Familiar as it is to us, it is yet as foreign a music as any Tyrolean jodel or Hungarian czardas.

2. Rev. Theo. L. Cuyler letter to *New York Herald*, January 17, 1872, as quoted in G. D. Pike, pp. 117–19.
3. Josef Skvorecky, "How I Wrote 'Dvorák in Love,'" in John C. Tibbetts, ed., *Dvorák in America, 1892–1895* (Portland: Amadeus Press, 1993), p. 329.
4. Sylvester Russell, "The Great Dvorák Is Dead," *Freeman*, June 4, 1904.
5. Sylvester Russell, "Musical and Dramatic," *Freeman*, February 11, 1911.
6. "Dvorák Leads for the Fund," *New York Herald*, January 24, 1894, reproduced in *Dvorák in America*, p. 367. The event reportedly raised $1,047 for *New York Herald's* "Free Clothing Fund."
7. "Dvorák Leads for the Fund."
8. "Hear the 'Old Folks at Home,'" *New York Herald*, January 23, 1894, reproduced in *Dvorák in America*, p. 366.
9. Charles Hamm, "Dvorák, Stephen Foster, and American National Song," in *Dvorák in America*, p. 155.
10. Jean E. Snyder, "'A Great and Noble School of Music': Dvorák, Harry T. Burleigh, and the African American Spiritual," in *Dvorák in America*, p. 131.
11. Reid Badger, *The Great American Fair* (Chicago: Nelson Hall, 1979), p. 109.
12. "Music at the Fair," *Chicago Tribune*, August 11, 1893.
13. "The Musical Leak Stopped," *Chicago Tribune*, August 6, 1893.
14. "Craft of All Colors," *Chicago Herald*, August 23, 1893.
15. William S. McFeely, *Frederick Douglass* (New York: W. W. Norton, 1991), pp. 367–8.
16. Douglas Cole, *Captured Heritage* (Seattle: University of Washington Press, 1985), p. 128.
17. F. L. Barnett, "The Reason Why the Colored American Is Not in the World's Columbian Exposition," in Ida B. Wells ed., *World's Fair Pamphlet*, reproduced in Trudier Harris, ed., *Selected Works of Ida B. Wells-Barnett* (New York: Oxford Press, 1919), p. 52.
18. Alfreda M. Duster, ed., *Crusade for Justice: The Autobiography of Ida B. Wells* (Chicago: University of Chicago Press, 1970), pp. 115, 117.
19. McFeely, p. 370.
20. *Freeman*, August 12, 1893.
21. "Music in Cincinnati," *Detroit Plaindealer*, March 3, 1893.
22. This item was reproduced in Henry Henriksen, "Black Patti," *Record Research*, no. 167/168 (October 1979), p. 7.
23. "Honor to Their Race," *Chicago Inter-Ocean*, August 26, 1893.
24. "Appeal of Douglass," *Chicago Daily Tribune*, August 26, 1893.
25. Ida B. Wells, *Crusade for Justice—The Autobiography of Ida B. Wells*, p. 119.
26. "World's Fair Music," *Cleveland Gazette*, October 21, 1893.
27. "Colored Folks' Day," *Chicago Herald*, August 25, 1893.
28. "Appeal of Douglass."
29. "Douglass Is Bitter," *Chicago Herald*, August 26, 1893.
30. No trace of a manuscript of Cook's opera of "Uncle Tom's Cabin" survives. There is good reason to doubt that Cook ever actually completed the project.

31. "Honor to Their Race."
32. "Douglass Is Bitter."
33. "Music at the Fair," *Chicago Daily Tribune*, September 27, 1893; September 28, 1893.
34. Curtis M. Hinsley, "The World as Marketplace," in Ivan Karp and Steven D. Lavine, eds., *Exhibiting Cultures* (Washington: Smithsonian Press, 1991), pp. 351–2.
35. Badger, pp. 108–9.
36. Will Marion Cook, "Music of the Negro," *Illinois Record*, May 14, 1898, quoted in Lawrence Gushee, "The Nineteenth-Century Origins of Jazz," *Black Music Research Journal*, vol. 14, no. 1 (Spring 1994), p. 14.
37. Hinsley, p. 361. Hinsley continues: "It is an interesting consideration that dance played such a large part in the ethnographic exhibits, but the public evidence does not bear out Putnam's hopeful assertion." For a direct contradiction of Hinsley's unwarranted conclusion see Rudi Blesh and Harriet Janis, *They All Played Ragtime: The True Story of an American Music* (1950) (New York: Grove Press, 1959).
38. "Is Gone Dance Crazy," *Chicago Daily Tribune*, August 6, 1893.
39. "Appeal of Douglass." In his biography of Frederick Douglass (p. 368), William McFeely went so far out on a limb as to describe "the grass huts of the Dahomey village peopled with half-naked Americans in native skirts." Although such deceptions occurred at other fairs, notably the 1933 Century of Progress World's Fair in Chicago, the Dahomean Village inhabitants at the 1893 World's Columbian Exposition were entirely authentic.
40. Stanley Appelbaum, *The Chicago World's Fair of 1893* (New York: Dover, 1980), p. 97.
41. Eugene Levy, *James Weldon Johnson—Black Leader, Black Voice* (Chicago: University of Chicago Press, p. 39).
42. Benjamin C. Truman, *History of the World's Fair* (1893) (New York: Arno Press, 1976), n.p.
43. J. W. Buel, *The Magic City* (1894) (New York: Arno Press, 1974), n.p.
44. Ibid.
45. Hinsley, pp. 358–9.
46. George Brown Goode, quoted in Hinsley, p. 346.
47. Blesh and Janis, pp. 149–50.
48. Henry Edward Krehbiel, *Afro-American Folksongs* (1914) (New York: Frederick Ungar Publishing Co., 1975), pp. 60–5.
49. Blesh and Janis, p. 4.
50. Blesh and Janis, p. 150. An advertisement in the August 19, 1899, edition of *New York Clipper* described "There's No Coon That's One Half So Warm" as "the original Dahomey Village (World's Fair) song."
51. Ibid.
52. Julie [*sic*] Jones, "Show Shop," *Freeman*, August 22, 1908.
53. Edward A. Berlin, *Ragtime: A Musical and Cultural History* (Berkeley: University of California Press, 1980), p. 27. For a discussion of the inclination of music scholars to make the World's Columbian Exposition a particular starting place for ragtime, see Seroff and Abbott, "Black Music in the White City (African-Americans at the 1893 World's Columbian Exposition)," *78 Quarterly*, vol. 1, no. 9 (n.d), p. 49.
54. Contemporaneous documents specifically searched for World's Fair–related musical references include *Chicago Daily Tribune*, *Chicago Herald*, and *New Orleans Times Picayune*.
55. Blesh and Janis, p. 41.
56. Original source not known. Reproduced in Cunningham, *Paul Laurence Dunbar and His Song*, p. 104.
57. "Buffalo Bill's 'Wild West,'" *New York Clipper*, May 6, 1893.
58. "Illinois," *New York Clipper*, July 1, 1893.
59. "Illinois," *New York Clipper*, July 8, 1893.
60. It is not clear who Edith Pond was.
61. Cunningham, p. 101.
62. Levy, p. 37.
63. Roi Ottley, *The Lonely Warrior: The Life and Times of Robert S. Abbott* (Chicago: Henry Regenery Co., 1955).
64. Hinsley, pp. 362–3.
65. See Lynn Abbott and Doug Seroff, "'They Cert'ly Sound Good to Me': Sheet Music, Southern Vaudeville, and the Commercial Ascendancy of the Blues," *American Music*, vol. 14, no. 4 (Winter 1996), pp. 402–54.
66. Celia E. Davidson, "Freeman, Harry Lawrence," in Samuel A. Floyd, Jr., ed., *International Dictionary of Black Composers* (Chicago: Fitzroy Dearborn Publishers, 1999), p. 467. Davidson also states that "Freeman's second opera, *The Martyr*, was . . . performed by a group formed by the composer in October 1893 at the World's Columbian Exposition in Chicago."
67. For a scholarly discussion of the word "creole," see Gwendolyn Midlo Hall, "The Formation of Afro-Creole Culture," in Arnold R. Hirsch and Joseph Logsdon, eds., *Creole New Orleans: Race and Americanization* (Baton Rouge, Louisiana State University Press, 1992).
68. Carle Browne Cooke, "Letter from New York," *Freeman*, January 27, 1906.
69. Perry Bradford, *Born with the Blues* (New York: Oak Publications, 1965), pp. 163, 164.
70. James Weldon Johnson, *Black Manhattan* (1930) (New York: Da Capo, 1991), pp. 75–8.

71. "The Stage," *Freeman*, November 3, 1906; November 20, 1909.
72. Jim Towel, "I've Been Hoodooed"/"Buckwheat Cakes," Brunswick 7060, 1928, reissued on Document DBCD-6040.
73. See F. G. Rathbun, "The Negro Music of the South," *Southern Workman*, November 1893, p. 174.
74. "Proposal for Folk-Lore Research at Hampton, Va.," *Journal of American Folk-Lore*, vol. vi, no. xxiii (October–December, 1893). For much more on Alice Mabel Bacon and the history of the Hampton Folk-Lore Society, see Donald J. Waters, *Strange Ways and Sweet Dreams: Afro-American Folklore from the Hampton Institute* (Boston: G. K. Hall & Co., 1983).
75. Waters, p. 7; "Folk-Lore Meeting," *Southern Workman*, vol. 23, no. 1 (January 1894), pp. 15–16.
76. "Plea for Negro Folklore," *Freeman*, January 27, 1894.
77. The entire six years' worth of "Folk-Lore and Ethnology" columns is reproduced in Waters, *Strange Ways and Sweet Dreams*.
78. Vance Randolph and Nancy Clemens, "Ozark Mountain Party–Games," *Journal of American Folk-Lore*, vol. 49, no. 193 (July- September, 1936). Also, see Newman Ivey White, ed., *North Carolina Folklore, Volume One: Games and Rhymes, Beliefs and Customs, Riddles, Proverbs, Speech, Tales and Legends* (Durham: Duke University Press, 1952), pp. 59–60.
79. The Olympics, "(Baby) Hully Gully," Arvee 562, 1959, reissued on Ace cd 224, Great Britain, 1991. Composer credits for "(Baby) Hully Gully" belong to the pop songwriting team of Fred Smith and Cliff Goldsmith. Any and all history of the transition of "hully gully" from a gambling game to a dance song remains unknown.
80. Marshall and Jean Stearns, *Jazz Dance: The Story of American Vernacular Dance* (1968) (New York: Schirmer Books, 1979), pp. 4, 5.
81. Roark Bradford, *John Henry* (New York: Harper & Brothers, 1931).
82. Bradford, *John Henry*, p. 11.
83. See Roark Bradford, *John Henry: A Play with Music* (New York: Harper & Brothers, 1939), p. 12. Leonard de Paur directed the thirty-five voice de Paur Infantry Chorus assigned to Special Services during World War II. In the 1950s male choruses under de Paur recorded spirituals, work songs, Creole folk songs, and calypsos for Columbia and Mercury. Samuel A. Floyd sang bass with the Fisk Jubilee Quartet during the mid-1940s. He is the father of Samuel A. Floyd, Jr., of the Center for Black Music Research, Columbia College, Chicago.
84. Mary Wheeler, *Steamboatin' Days: Folk Songs of the River Packet Era* (Baton Rouge: Louisiana State University Press, 1944), p. ix.
85. Ibid, p. 6.
86. Ibid, p. 92. A similar observation, but without speculation about an etymological connection to Africa, was made in Lyle Saxon, Edward Dyer, and Robert Tallant, eds., *Gumbo Ya-Ya* (Cambridge: Houghton Mifflin, 1945), p. 382: "Early roustabouts were famed for their songs and their 'coonjines.' The 'coonjine' was a rhythmic shuffle affected to expedite loading and unloading; the songs were usually doleful, yet served to lighten their labors."
87. William Francis Allen, Charles Pickard Ware, and Lucy McKim Garrison, eds., *Slave Songs of the United States* (1867) (New York: Books For Libraries Press, 1971), p. 113.
88. George Washington Cable, "The Dance in Place Congo," *Century Magazine*, February 1886, reprinted in Bernard Katz, ed., *The Social Implications of Early Negro Music in the United States* (New York: Arno Press, 1969). One of Cable's examples includes a line transcribed as, "En bas hé en bas hé, Par en bas yé pé-lé-lé moin, yé pé-lé-lé, Counjaille a é-baut-ché," and translated as, "Way down yonder, way down yonder, Way down yonder they're calling me, they are calling, but Coonjye, has bewitched me."
89. For further speculation on the "Counjaille" to "Coonjine" connection, see Harold Courlander, *The Drum and the Hoe* (Berkeley: University of California Press, 1960), pp. 133–6, 352; and Lynne Fauley Emery, *Black Dance in the United States from 1619 to 1970* (Palo Alto: National Press Books, 1972), p. 146.
90. Blesh and Janis, pp. 38, 84.
91. Gushee, "The Nineteenth-Century Origins of Jazz," pp. 9, 13.
92. Edward Marble, "Can't-Yer-Koon-Jine" (New York: M. Witmark and Sons), 1893.
93. Spencer Williams, "Kune-Jine," 1919 (copyright deposit at Library of Congress, dated September 24, 1919).
94. Anton Lada's Louisiana Orchestra, "Kune Jine," Emerson 10580, 1922.
95. The Black Hillbillies, "Kunjine Baby," Vocalion 1450, 1929, reissued on Document DOCD-5075.
96. Newman I. White, *American Negro Folk-Songs* (Cambridge: Harvard University Press, 1928), p. 181.
97. For more on John Work III, Fort Valley College, etc., see Bruce Bastin, *Red River Blues* (Chicago: University of

Illinois Press, 1986), pp. 72–86; and Bruce Nemerov, "John Wesley Work III: Field Recordings of Southern Black Folk Music, 1935–1942," *Tennessee Folklore Society Bulletin*, vol. lii, no. 3 (1989).

98. Additional coonjine-related field recordings in the Library of Congress collection include "Coonjine" by E. Days, recorded in the "Darien area" of Georgia around 1926; "Coonjine" by Hettie Godfrey, recorded at Livingston, Alabama, in 1940; and "Coonjine, Roustabouts, Coonjine" by John "Big Nig" Bray, recorded at Morgan City, Louisiana, in 1934.
99. "The Stage," *Freeman*, May 25, 1901.
100. The 1900 U.S. Census, Jefferson County, Kentucky; Death Certificate, Robert. L. "Tobe" Brown. Thanks to Pen Bogert for sharing his research on African American musical activities in Louisville.
101. Carry B. Lewis *[sic]*, "Lodge Ready for Big Time," *Freeman*, August 24, 1907.
102. Thanks to Pen Bogert.
103. "The Eureka Dancing Class," *Nashville Globe*, April 10, 1908.
104. Lynn Abbott conversation with Adolphus "Doc" Cheatham, July 24, 1993.
105. Bill Russell interview with Willie Hightower, June 3, 1958 (Hogan Jazz Archive, Tulane University).
106. Hightower's Night Hawks, "Boar Hog Blues"/ "Squeeze Me," Black Patti 8045, 1927.
107. "Blind Musician Retires at End of Forty-Seven Years," *Pittsburgh Courier*, June 18, 1927.
108. "Blind Since Berth *[sic]*, Leaves a Fortune," *Pittsburgh Courier*, October 15, 1927.
109. For more on Boone's early life and career see Melissa Fuell, *Blind Boone: His Early Life and His Achievements* (Kansas City, 1915). For a more recent biography see Jack A. Batterson, *Blind Boone: Missouri's Ragtime Pioneer* (Columbia: University of Missouri Press, 1998).
110. "Blind Boone," *Kansas City American Citizen*, May 26, 1893.
111. See the "List of John William Boone Compositions and Transcriptions" in Batterson, pp. 101–5, and the "Music List" in Ann Sears, "Boone, John William ('Blind Boone')," in Floyd, ed., *International Dictionary of Black Composers*, p. 138. Sears points out (p. 141) that "When I Meet Dat Coon Tonight" (1892) "contains a section marked 'Dance,' which has a recurring syncopated pattern common in ragtime."
112. For a discussion of the "proto-blues anthem, 'I'm Alabama Bound,'" see Abbott and Seroff, "'They Cert'ly Sound Good to Me,'" pp. 406–8.

Chapter 6: 1894

1. Sylvester Russell, "George H. Primrose Retires," *Freeman*, May 16, 1903.
2. "Stage," *Freeman*, September 27, 1902.
3. "The Stage," *Freeman*, May 23, 1903.
4. "The Stage," *Freeman*, October 20, 1906.
5. Sylvester Russell, "Leroy Bland," *Freeman*, June 15, 1912.
6. "Double Show Liked," *Chicago Defender*, June 20, 1925.
7. *Pittsburgh Courier*, September 15, 1923.
8. "The Late Frank M. Hailstock, Jr.," *Freeman*, March 4, 1899.
9. "Stage," *Freeman*, October 6, 1900.
10. "The Stage," *Freeman*, July 11, 1903.
11. "Stage," *Freeman*, October 14, 1905; "The Stage," *Freeman*, June 30, 1906.
12. *[Pottsville, Pennsylvania] Miners Journal*, reprinted in "The Stage," *Freeman*, December 4, 1897.
13. Edward A. Berlin, "Ragtime Songs," in Hasse, ed., *Ragtime*, p. 72.
14. George Evans, "Standing on the Corner, Didn't Mean No Harm," (1894) (New York: Edward B. Marks Music Corporation, 1936).
15. Jimmie Rodgers, "Blue Yodel No. 9," Victor 23580, 1931, reissued on Rounder cd 1060.
16. Fred Lyons, "Swinging on de Golden Gate" (Providence: Callendar, McAuslan & Toup, 1882).
17. Fiddlin' John Carson, "Swinging on de Golden Gate," Okeh 45159, 1927, reissued on Document DOCD-8017.
18. *The McCravy Album of Fireside Songs* (New York: Southern Music Publishing Company, 1933).
19. The Wright Brothers Gospel Singers, "Wake Me, Shake Me, Don't Let Me Sleep Too Long," Bluebird 8755, 1941, reissued on Document DOCD-5496; National Independent Gospel Singers, "I Met My Elder This Morning," Savoy 4020, 1950.
20. The Coasters, "Wake Me, Shake Me," Atco 6168, 1960, reissued on Rhino R2 71090. The song is credited to Billy Guy, Trio Music Co., Inc./Unichappell Music, BMI.
21. Brother Joe May, "Wake Me and Shake Me," Nashboro 750, 1961.
22. Al Rose and Edmond Souchon, *New Orleans Jazz: A Family Album* (1967) (Baton Rouge: Louisiana State University Press, 1984), p. 95.
23. See, for instance, Samuel B. Charters, *Jazz New Orleans 1885–1963: An Index to the Negro Musicians of*

New Orleans (New York: Oak Publications, 1963), p. 7; or Martin Williams, *Jazz Masters of New Orleans* (1967) (New York: DaCapo Press, 1979), p. 226.

24. See Lynn Abbott, "Religious Recordings from Black New Orleans" (liner notes to 504 LP20), 1985.
25. "Mamma's Black Baby Boy," 1893, reissued on Document DOCD-5288; "Who Broke [the] Lock", c.1895, reissued on Document DOCD-5574.
26. "Stage," *Freeman*, December 27, 1902.
27. "About Our Performers," *Leavenworth Herald*, February 8, 1896.
28. "Vaudeville and Minstrel," *New York Clipper*, September 11, 1897.
29. Southern, *Biographical Dictionary*, p. 192.
30. W. H. Councill, "The Richmond Slave Pens," 1905.
31. W. H. Councill obituary, *Huntsville Democrat* (undated clipping, April 1909).
32. G. P. Keyes, "Educating the Negro," *Birmingham Age-Herald* (undated clipping, c. 1894).
33. *Detroit Plaindealer*, February 24, 1893.
34. "Normal, Alabama Notes," *Detroit Plaindealer*, April 14, 1893.
35. Handy, *Father of the Blues*, p. 60. Handy goes on to tell an anecdote about Prof. Councill's aversion to ragtime.
36. Handy, *Father of the Blues*, pp. 61–3.
37. A full account of the lynching of Louis Wright appeared in *Freeman* of March 15, 1902.
38. "The Stage," *Freeman*, December 26, 1903.
39. "The Stage," *Freeman*, September 15, 1906.
40. *Normal Index*, December 1912.
41. See Lynn Abbott, "'Play That Barber Shop Chord': A Case for the African-American Origin of Barbershop Harmony," *American Music*, vol. 10, no. 2 (Fall 1992).
42. William Francis Allen, Charles Pickard Ware, and Lucy McKim Garrison, eds., *Slave Songs of the United States* (1867) (New York: Books from Libraries Press, 1971), pp. v–vi.
43. W. C. Handy, "The Heart of the Blues," *Etude Music Magazine*, March 1940, reprinted in Eileen Southern, ed., *Readings in Black American Music* (New York: W. W. Norton, 1971), p. 204.
44. "Tom the Tattler," *Freeman*, December 8, 1900.
45. The "Kansas Notes" column in *Kansas City Star* and "Kansas Matters" column in *Leavenworth Herald* were both loose-leaf collections of abbreviated, "syndicated" news items, quips, and witticisms pertaining to various towns in Kansas. Race distinctions, normally clear-cut, are obscured when the same item appears in both newspapers.
46. See Abbott, "'Play That Barber Shop Chord,'" pp. 303–6.
47. Sigmund Spaeth, *Barber Shop Ballads* (New York: Simon & Schuster, 1925), p. 34.
48. James Bland, "In the Evening by the Moonlight," as recorded in 1927 by the Harmony Four, under the title, "You Can Hear Those Darkies Singing," Gennett 6285, reissued on Document DOCD-5605. The Harmony Four was a black quartet from Bessemer, Alabama, the same cultural community that produced the Birmingham Jubilee Singers and Famous Blue Jay Singers. Their version of "In the Evening by the Moonlight" survives as an outstanding recorded example of black barbershop harmonizing.
49. Edward Le Roy Rice, *Monarchs of Minstrelsy* (New York: Kenny Publishing Company, 1911), p. 51.
50. Robert Cogswell, "A Discography of Blackface Comedy Dialogues," *John Edwards Memorial Foundation Quarterly*, no. 15 (1979).
51. "Gossip of the Stage," *Freeman*, March 9, 1912.
52. "Gossip of the Stage," *Freeman*, February 24, 1912.
53. Thanks to Tim Brooks for sharing this product of his research.
54. For information on African American yodlers, see Lynn Abbott and Doug Seroff, "America's Blue Yodel," *Musical Traditions*, no. 11 (1993).
55. *New York Clipper*, June 10, 1893.
56. According to Rice, *Monarchs of Minstrelsy*, Williams's real name was Carmody. He was born in Baltimore in 1854 and died in 1910.
57. This is not the same Ben Harney who introduced ragtime piano playing in mainstream New York City vaudeville theaters in 1896. Reports in August–October 1898 editions of *New York Clipper* place the legendary ragtime pianist on tour, not with "South Before the War," but with Jermon's "Black Crook" Extravaganza Company. Claims made by Harney's widow, Jessie, that he actually originated "South Before the War," then sold it to Whalen and Martell, are contradicted by contemporaneous documents. For more on ragtime pianist Ben Harney's late-1890s career, see Lynn Abbott, "'A Worthy Copy of the Subject He Mimics': Ben Harney in Context, 1896–1898," *Rag Time Ephemeralist*, no. 3 (2002), pp. 42–7.
58. Carle Brown Cooke, "Letter from New York," *Freeman*, January 27, 1906.
59. The earliest Standard Quartette recording session listed in *Blues & Gospel Records 1890–1943* is from August 1891. It is not known what titles were recorded at that session.
60. The entry for the Standard Quartette in *Blues and Gospel Records 1890–1943*, pp. 859–60, lists two versions of

"Swing Low, Sweet Chariot;" "My Old Kentucky Home," two versions of "Way Down Yonder in the Cornfield" (one "with imitations"); "Steal Away to Jesus," "Keep Movin'," "Poor Mourner," "Who Broke the Lock on the Henhouse Door?" "Tapioca Medley," "Say Bo, Give Me Them Two Bits," two versions of "Every Day'll Be Sunday Bye and Bye;" "Annie Laurie," "Old Aunt Jemima," two versions of "The Old Oaken Bucket;" "Almost Persuaded," "Little Alabama Coon," "Genevieve Medley," "When the Mists Have Rolled Away," "Nationality Medley," "Widdy Wink," "You May Talk about Jeruselem Morning," "Rocked in the Cradle of the Deep," "Mississippi Steamboat Scene (with Descriptive Effects)," "Beautiful Star Medley (with banjo imitations)," "Good-bye Until We Meet Again," "Massa's in the Cold, Cold Ground Medley (with chorus of Alabama Coon)," "High Old Time," "Hail Jeruselem, Hail," and "Just Tell Them That You Saw Me."

61. "Keep Movin'," originally issued as an unnumbered Columbia cylinder, reissued on Document DOCD-5061; "Every Day'll Be Sunday Bye and Bye," originally issued as an unnumbered Columbia cylinder, reissued on Document DOCD-5288.
62. The final line may just as well say, "My left foot *slipped*" or "*stepped*" or "*stuck* in a hornet's nest."
63. *Freeman*, March 9, 1895.
64. See Doug Seroff, "Old-Time Black Gospel Quartet Contests," *Black Music Research Newsletter*, Spring 1980.
65. Here is an early commercial manifestation of the incipient ragtime dance-song, "Pas Ma La."
66. "The Stage," *Freeman*, November 26, 1898.
67. *Freeman*, October 27, 1900.
68. "The Stage," *Freeman*, April 1, 1911. There is no connection between this Golden Gate Quartette/Trio and the Golden Gate Jubilee Quartet that gained fame during the 1930s and thereafter.
69. "The Stage," *Freeman* September 26, 1903.
70. "Al Anderson Passes Away after Lingering Illness," *Chicago Defender*, December 19, 1925.
71. "Barnum Is Gone," *New York Clipper*, April 18, 1891.
72. Robert J. Loeffler, "An Appraisal of the Appearance of Jubilee Singers with the P. T. Barnum Circus of 1873," *White Tops*, vol. 73, no. 6 (November/December 2000).
73. "Under the White Tents," *New York Clipper*, October 19, 1889; January 25, 1890.
74. "Under the White Tents," *New York Clipper*, March 11, 1890.
75. "Under the White Tents," *New York Clipper*, May 17, 1890.
76. *Louisville Commercial*, March 28, 1880. Thanks to Pen Bogert for sharing this product of his research.
77. "The Stage," *Freeman*, October 23, 1897.
78. "The Stage," *Freeman*, October 2, 1897.
79. "P. G. Lowery, Originator," *Freeman*, July 9, 1910.
80. "Gossip of the Stage," *Freeman*, February 21, 1914; March 14, 1914; March 28, 1914.
81. "Stage Notes," *Freeman*, September 19, 1914; October 17, 1914.
82. *Chicago Defender*, October 29, 1921.
83. For background on the origin and development of dime museums, see Brooks McNamara, " 'A Congress of Wonders': The Rise and Fall of the Dime Museum," *ESQ*, vol. 20, no. 3 (third quarter 1974); and Andrea Stulman Dennett, *Weird and Wonderful: The Dime Museum in America* (New York: New York University Press, 1997).
84. Dennett, *Weird and Wonderful*, p. 8.
85. W. L. M. Chaise, "Gossip of the Stage," *New York Age*, June 6, 1891. For more on the Bohee Brothers, see Rainer E. Lotz, "The Bohee Brothers (1844–1897/1856–1926[?])," *78 Quarterly*, vol. 1, no. 7 (1992), pp. 97–111.
86. "I. McCorker," "Minstrels, Comedians and Singers," *Freeman*, March 22, 1902.
87. "The Stage," *Freeman*, July 31, 1897.
88. "I. McCorker," "Minstrels, Comedians and Singers," *Freeman*, March 22, 1902.
89. "The Stage," *Freeman*, April 19, 1902.
90. "The Stage," *Freeman*, July 7, 1900.
91. Sylvester Russell, "Smart Set in 'Enchantment,' " *Freeman*, November 1, 1902.
92. "The Stage," *Freeman*, August 29, 1908.
93. "Stage," *Freeman*, July 27, 1901.
94. *New York Clipper*, January 30, 1892; "The Stage," *Freeman*, April 1, 1899.
95. "The Stage," *Freeman*, September 18, 1897; Henry T. Sampson, *The Ghost Walks*, p. 219.

Chapter 7: 1895

1. Tom Fletcher, *100 Years of the Negro in Show Business* (New York: Burdge & Company, 1954), p. 94.
2. Ibid, pp. 91–7.
3. *New York Times*, May 26, 1895, quoted at greater length in Thomas Riis, *Just Before Jazz: Black Musical Theater in New York, 1890–1915* (Washington: Smithsonian Institution Press, 1989), pp. 23–4.
4. Fletcher, pp. 91–4.
5. "Andrea Razafkeriefo," *Pittsburgh Courier*, April 2, 1927; Allison Blakely, "Waller, John L[ouis]," in Rayford W Logan and Michael R. Winston, eds., *Dictionary of*

American Negro Biography (New York: W. W. Norton, 1982), p. 627.

6. "Wilber C. Sweatman," *Freeman*, January 29, 1910.
7. *Lionel Hampton's Swing Book*, Alice C. Browning, ed. (Chicago: Negro Story Press, 1946), p. 8.
8. Nathan W. Pearson, *Goin' to Kansas City* (Chicago: University of Illinois Press, 1987), p. 20.
9. For a synopsis of the plot of "In Old Kentucky," see *New York Clipper*, September 3, 1892.
10. "In Old Kentucky," *Freeman*, September 24, 1910.
11. Wayne D. Shirley letter to Lynn Abbott, October 11, 1992. Horace Clarence Boyer makes the same observation in his essay on Lucie Campbell in Bernice Johnson Reagon, ed., *We'll Understand It Better By and By: Pioneering African American Gospel Composers* (Washington, D.C.: Smithsonian Press, 1992), p. 81: "In 1893 Sherwood published a book in Petersburg, Virginia, called *Harp of Zion*, the first book to include gospel music by an African American composer." In the preface to *Harp of Zion*, Rev. Sherwood mentioned having already published a songbook titled *Soothing Songs* in 1891. However, there are no known extant copies of *Soothing Songs*.
12. Rev. Sherwood's introductory note to "Will You Go?" reveals: "This old time refrain is one of my earliest inspirations. When a boy, how many good old time Christians gathered in a log hut, sang and praised their God. My mother full 30 years ago, made it ring through my soul." Among the several allusions to Florida is this from the introductory note to Rev. Sherwood's own "Is Not This the Land of Beulah": "This sentiment was awakened in the author in 1878 as he was passing along a sparkling brook in a mellow scented region of Florida."
13. Rev. W. H. Sherwood, A.B., *Life of Charles B. W. Gordon, Pastor of the First Baptist Church* (Petersburg: John B. Ege, 1885). For more on Rev. Gordon's early work in Petersburg, see "Petersburg and Its Colored Citizens," *Lancet*, November 29, 1884; "The Young Divine," *Lancet*, May 30, 1885; "Our Thanks," *Lancet*, July 4, 1885; and "Dedication of the Harrison St. Baptist Church," *Lancet*, July 11, 1885.
14. Tabernacle Baptist Church remains active to this day. Although Rev. Sherwood's name was not recalled in the oral history of Tabernacle Baptist Church collected by Virginia State University archivist Lucius Edwards, it *was* recalled that, in addition to Tabernacle Baptist Church, Rev. Gordon had established an orphanage on his Halifax Street site, and the orphanage had sponsored a band. Thanks to Lucius Edwards for sharing this information from his oral history project.
15. It was registered for copyright on June 19, 1893.
16. Edward Boatner and Mrs. Willa A. Townsend, eds., *Spirituals Triumphant Old and New* (Nashville: Sunday School Publishing Board, National Baptist Convention U.S.A., 1927).
17. See John Chilton, *A Jazz Nursery (The Story of the Jenkins' Orphanage Band)* (London: Bloomsbury Book Shop, 1980).
18. See Thomas Hanchett, "The Shout Band Tradition in the United House of Prayer: Trombone Ensembles in an Urban African-American Denomination," 1991, reprinted in the liner notes to The Tigers Trombone Shout Band, "Dancing with Daddy G," Fire Ant CD 1004, 1993.
19. See the Charles Winter Wood bio in *Who's Who in Colored America: A Biographical Dictionary of Notable Living Persons of Negro Descent in America* (New York: Who's Who in Colored America Publishers, 1927).
20. Charles Winter Wood, "Honey You Sho Looks Bad" (Wood)/"When de Cornpone's Hot" (Dunbar), Black Swan 2123/Paramount 12108, 1923; and "High Culture"/"Getting up in the Morning," Paramount 12109, 1923.
21. Alexander MacKay, *The Western World*, 1849, quoted in Richard Wade, *Slavery in the Cities: The South, 1820–1860* (New York: Oxford University Press, 1964), p. 34.
22. See Reid Badger, *A Life in Ragtime: A Biography of James Reese Europe* (New York: Oxford University Press, 1985).
23. "The Stage," *Freeman*, March 5, 1898.
24. Sylvester Russell, "The Late Harry Eaton," *Freeman*, March 12, 1904. With regard to Eaton's age, a note in *New York Clipper* of February 1, 1890 said he "celebrated his twenty-sixth birthday at Minneapolis, Minn., Jan. 19." Eight months later, in *Clipper* of October 11, 1890, there was a note to the effect that Eaton "celebrated his thirty-ninth birthday last week."
25. *New York Clipper* of April 4, 1896, mentions the "recent death" of S. B. Hyers.
26. "Miscellaneous," *New York Clipper*, June 11, 1898.
27. "World of Players," *New York Clipper*, November 18, 1899.
28. *Cleveland Gazette*, June 2, 1900.
29. *Freeman*, June 6, 1900; *Cleveland Gazette*, September 15, 1900.
30. "Black Patti's Troubadours," *Freeman*, December 19, 1896.
31. *New York Clipper* of October 3, 1896, reported, "'At Gay Coney Island,' a farce comedy in three acts by Levin C. Tees, was given its first production on any stage at the

Lyric Theatre, Hoboken, N.J., August 29, by Matthews and Bulger and company."

32. A *Freeman* report of January 9,1915, said the Black Patti Troubadours had stranded in Memphis, Tennessee, the previous week. Sissieretta Jones returned to her home in Providence, Rhode Island. A subsequent *Freeman* item, February 20, 1915, added that she had "embraced religion . . . severed relations with the stage and its attractions."
33. "The Stage," *Freeman*, September 16, 1899.
34. Sylvester Russell, "Black Patti in New York," *Freeman*, June 30, 1906.
35. See, for example, "Tom the Tattler," *Freeman*, May 18, 1901.
36. "The Stage," *Freeman*, April 24, 1897.
37. "The Stage," *Freeman*, June 3, 1899.
38. "The Stage," *Freeman*, October 26, 1901.
39. Sylvester Russell, "Review of the Stage," *Freeman*, December 28, 1901.
40. "The Stage," *Freeman*, May 5, 1900.
41. "The Whitmans," *Chicago Defender*, January 26, 1918. For variations on these recollections, see "Have the Whitman Sisters Played Big Time?—An Answer That Will Suit," *Freeman*, February 10, 1917.
42. The July 7, 1901, edition of the mainstream daily *Atlanta Constitution* reported, through its occasional column of African American community news, "What the Negro Is Doing" by H. R. Butler, that "Rev. A. A. Whitman, D.D., one of the American negro poets, is dead, and was buried last Monday morning from Allen Temple, the church which he fostered so successfully for the past few years."
43. "The Stage," *Freeman*, July 23, 1904; March 25, 1905.
44. Essie Whitman and her Jazz Masters, Black Swan 2036, 1921, reissued on Document DOCD-5342.
45. For more on Mattie Dorsey, see Doug Seroff and Lynn Abbott, "Sweet Mattie Dorsey Been Here, But She's Gone," *78 Quarterly*, no. 8 (n.d.), pp. 103–12.
46. Ben Harney, "The Ragtime Instructor," 1897, as quoted in Isaac Goldberg, *Tin Pan Alley* (New York: John Day Co., 1930), p. 148.
47. Rupert Hughes, "A Eulogy of Ragtime," *Musical Record*, April 1, 1899, as quoted in *They All Played Ragtime*, pp. 103–4.
48. For two divergent etymological interpretations of the quote from Rupert Hughes, see Edward A. Berlin *Ragtime: A Musical and Cultural History*, (Berkeley, University of California Press, 1980), p. 13; and Samuel A. Floyd, Jr., and Marsha J. Reisser, "Social Dance Music of Black Composers in the Nineteenth Century and the Emergence of Classic Ragtime," *Black Perspective in Music*, vol. 8, no. 2 (Fall 1980), p. 171.
49. In present-day musical vocabulary, the term "breakdown" is most widely understood to describe a type of country fiddle tune. Hans Nathan points out in *Dan Emmett and the Rise of Early Negro Minstrelsy* (p. 92) that during the nineteenth century, "Any dance in Negro style was called a 'breakdown.' " Nathan reproduces this passage from Mark Twain's *Life on the Mississippi*, depicting a group of black keel-boatmen: "Next they got out an old fiddle and one played, and another patted juba, and the rest turned themselves loose on a regular old-fashioned keelboat breakdown."
50. Goldberg, *Tin Pan Alley*, quoted in *Jazz Dance*, p. 371.
51. Harry Ward, "The Possum-A-La" (New York: Spaulding & Gray), 1895.
52. Further news of Prof. Guillard came out in a "Louisville Ky. Special" to *Freeman* of April 5, 1902: "J. T. Guillard, probably one of the best known instructors on the mandolin, guitar, and violin in the South, is still doing an immense business in this line. His clientele is composed of the children of some of the most exclusive white families in Louisville. . . . Prof. Guillard graduates from the Louisville National Medical College some time in April."
53. Irving Jones, "Possumala Dance" (New York: Willis Woodward & Co.), 1894.
54. Blesh and Janis, p. 93.
55. Ernest Hogan, "La Pas Ma La" (Kansas City: J. R. Bell), 1895.
56. *New York Clipper*, June 15, 1895.
57. *Jazz Dance*, pp. 100–2.
58. Paul Oliver, *Songsters and Saints: Vocal Traditions on Race Records* (Cambridge: Cambridge University Press, 1984), pp. 53–4.
59. Jim Jackson, "Bye, Bye Policeman," Victor V38525, 1928, reissued on Document DOCD-5115, transcribed by David Evans.
60. See Pash, "Ernest Hogan," pp. 36–40.
61. This story was recycled under the headline, "Grand—Ernest Hogan, the Colored Comedian, Stager, and Dancer," in *Kansas City Star* of May 5, 1906, reproduced in Pash, "Ernest Hogan," p. 40. These two newspaper accounts are the only known sources for the notion that Ernest Hogan had played the piano for dances in Kansas City.
62. Harry Ward, "The Possum-A-La."
63. *Freeman*, July 8, 1899. Further evidence of the continued use of "Pas Ma La" by African American performers include a February 24, 1900, note from Stowe's

Double Mammoth Uncle Tom's Cabin Company: "O. C. Shelton and Miss Annie Dorsey are setting a pace for them all in our 'pas ma-la' cake walk." A Chicago news column of July 20, 1901, notes, "There is a comedian at Piper's whom nature has endowed with a good voice and lean, lank, long legs, and when he does 'The Rag Ma La'—well, you ought to see and hear him." And a September 5, 1908, report from the Blue Eagle Theater in Plant City, Florida adds, "Prof. Frank Jackson, better known as Punch, is now arranging a new rag on the piano, by the name of the 'Plant City Ragmala,' for next week's program."

64. Andrew and Jim Baxter, "Dance the Georgia Poss," Victor 38603, 1929, reissued on Document DOCD-5167. There is also at least one relevant field recording in the Library of Congress collection: "Possum-ala," as sung by Annie Brewer at Montgomery, Alabama in 1937.
65. Handy, *Father of the Blues*, pp. 118–19.
66. See David Ewen, *All the Years of American Popular Music* (London: Prentice-Hall, 1977), p. 118.
67. "40 Drops" (Denver: De Harport Bros.), 1898.
68. Andrew and Jim Baxter, "40 Drops," Victor 38002, 1928, reissued on Document DOCD-5167.
69. In James B. Jones, Jr., "Some Aspects of Drug Abuse in Nineteenth and Early Twentieth-Century Tennessee History," *West Tennessee Historical Society Papers*, vol. xlviii (December 1994), the author notes that the 1830 book *Gunn's Domestic Medicine, or Poor Man's Friend* defined "what may have been the proper medicinal dosage for opium as 2 to 5 grains, and laudanum 50 drops." Thanks to Dr. Robert Cogswell for bringing this article to the authors' attention.
70. Stripling Brothers, "40 Drops," Decca 5313, 1936, reissued on Document DOCD-8008.
71. James Bryan and Carl Jones, "Two Pictures," Martin MAR 2001, n.d., c. 1996.
72. Both Shelton and Baynard went on to distinguish themselves in vaudeville and minstrelsy. William A. Baynard emerged during the late-1890s as the pianist with Puggsley's Tennessee Warblers. In 1907, in company with Salem Tutt Whitney and Prof. Eph Williams, Baynard was instrumental in the creation of one of the most famous of all twentieth-century African American minstrel shows, "Silas Green from New Orleans." In *Freeman* of November 8, 1919, Salem Tutt Whitney reported that Baynard had retired from the "show game," and was living in Rocky Mount, North Carolina, working for "the Atlantic Coast line R.R. as Chief caller of crews and asst. to the train dispatcher."
73. *Kansas State Ledger*, November 23, 1894.
74. Harry Bradford, "Deas, Reed, and Deas," *Freeman*, October 6, 1909.
75. Allen C. White, "Lawrence Deas," *Chicago Defender*, January 5, 1924.
76. "Stage," *Freeman*, November 19, 1898.
77. Willie "The Lion" Smith, *Music on My Mind: The Memoirs of an American Pianist* (1964) (New York: Da Capo, 1978), p. 55.
78. Eubie Blake, forward to Terry Waldo, *This is Ragtime* (New York: Hawthorne, 1976), p. viii.
79. *Pittsburgh Wasp*, reprinted in *Freeman*, February 13, 1897.
80. *Cambridge Independent Press*, November 19, 1897.
81. *Hull Daily News*, January 24, 1898, reproduced in Seroff, "The Fisk Jubilee Singers in Britain," pp. 53–4.
82. Clipping from unidentified Bathgate, Scotland newspaper, n.d. (c. April 9, 1898) in Leota Henson scrapbook.
83. *Ulster News*, April 23, 1898.
84. *London Globe*, November 18, 1899, reprinted in *Cleveland Gazette*, January 6, 1900.
85. W. C. Berwick Sayers, *Samuel Coleridge-Taylor, Musician—His Life and Letters* (London: Caddel and Co., 1915), p. 258.
86. *Cleveland Gazette*, October 10, 1903.
87. Sayers, *Samuel Coleridge-Taylor*, p. 258.
88. "F. J. Loudin Dead," *Ravenna Republican*, November 3, 1904.
89. "Loudin Coming to His Home Here," *Ravenna Republican*, c. late September 1903.
90. A. S. Berwick, "A Memorable Half-Hour," *Berwick [Scotland] Journal*, May 14, 1903, reprinted in *Cleveland Gazette*, August 1, 1903.
91. "A Man of Strong Friendship," *Ravenna Republican*, November 10, 1904.
92. *Cleveland Gazette*, November 12, 1904.
93. Samuel Coleridge-Taylor letter to Harriet Loudin, published in *Cleveland Gazette*, December 24, 1904.
94. "Coleridge-Taylor in West," *Cleveland Gazette*, December 10, 1904.
95. Booker T. Washington, forward to S. Coleridge Taylor, *Twenty-Four Negro Melodies, for piano* (Boston: Oliver Ditson Co.), 1905.
96. John Work II, "Negro Folk Song," *Opportunity*, October 1923, p. 293.

Index

References to illustrations are in italics.